T0328217

WAKING THE ASIAN PACIFIC CO-OPERATIVE POTENTIAL

WAKING THE ASIAN PACIFIC CO-OPERATIVE POTENTIAL

Edited by

MORRIS ALTMAN
University of Dundee Business School, Dundee, United Kingdom

ANTHONY JENSEN
University of Newcastle, Callaghan, NSW, Australia

AKIRA KURIMOTO
Hosei University, Tokyo, Japan

ROBBY TULUS
Asia Pacific Co-operative Practitioner/Activist

YASHAVANTHA DONGRE
University of Mysore, Mysuru, India

SEUNGKWON JANG
Sungkonghoe University, Seoul, Republic of Korea

ELSEVIER

ACADEMIC PRESS
An imprint of Elsevier

Academic Press is an imprint of Elsevier
125 London Wall, London EC2Y 5AS, United Kingdom
525 B Street, Suite 1650, San Diego, CA 92101, United States
50 Hampshire Street, 5th Floor, Cambridge, MA 02139, United States
The Boulevard, Langford Lane, Kidlington, Oxford OX5 1GB, United Kingdom

Notices
Knowledge and best practice in this field are constantly changing. As new research and experience broaden our understanding, changes in research methods, professional practices, or medical treatment may become necessary.

Practitioners and researchers must always rely on their own experience and knowledge in evaluating and using any information, methods, compounds, or experiments described herein. In using such information or methods they should be mindful of their own safety and the safety of others, including parties for whom they have a professional responsibility.

To the fullest extent of the law, neither the Publisher nor the authors, contributors, or editors, assume any liability for any injury and/or damage to persons or property as a matter of products liability, negligence or otherwise, or from any use or operation of any methods, products, instructions, or ideas contained in the material herein.

British Library Cataloguing-in-Publication Data

A catalogue record for this book is available from the British Library

Library of Congress Cataloging-in-Publication Data
A catalog record for this book is available from the Library of Congress

ISBN: 978-0-12-816666-6

For Information on all Academic Press publications
visit our website at https://www.elsevier.com/books-and-journals

Publisher: Matthew Deans
Acquisitions Editor: Graham Nisbet
Editorial Project Manager: Devlin Person
Production Project Manager: Debasish Ghosh
Cover Designer: Christian J. Bilbow

Typeset by MPS Limited, Chennai, India

Working together
to grow libraries in
developing countries

www.elsevier.com • www.bookaid.org

For over 30 years the late Dr. Gary Lewis researched and wrote about the Australian co-operative movement. Co-operatives were his passion and a very significant part of his professional life. He was the doyen of Australian co-operative history with publications that included pathbreaking studies of consumer co-operatives, credit unions, and agricultural co-operatives. His research is crucial in terms of public policy and historical research. His submission and evidence before the Australian Senate inquiry into co-operatives and mutuals reminded the Committee of the historical contribution of co-operatives to Australia but argued that their full potential was yet to be realized.

Contents

Part 2
CASE STUDIES OF ASIAN CO-OPS, INCLUDING CROSS-COUNTRY COMPARISON

SECTION 1
AGRICULTURAL CO-OPS

Section 2
CONSUMER CO-OPS

22. Consumer cooperatives summary

AKIRA KURIMOTO

Section 3
CREDIT CO-OPS

23. Teachers Mutual Bank case study

PETER MASON

24. From resilience to unlimited opportunities: the First Community Credit Cooperative's (FICCO) experience

BIENVENIDO P. NITO, ISAGANI B. DABA AND ERNEST MARC V. CASTILLO

25. Existential challenges of cooperatives and credit unions in Indonesia

ROBBY TULUS AND MUNALDUS NERANG

26. The SANASA movement— Sri Lanka

ROBBY TULUS

27. Summary: credit union case studies

ROMULO M. VILLAMIN

Section 4
WORKER CO-OPS

28. The sociopolitical environment of worker cooperatives in the Philippines: basis for addressing the worker contractualization issue

LEO G. PARMA, MARIA ANTONETTE D. PASQUIN AND BIENVENIDO P. NITO

29. Collectivism as a strategy for success in Indian worker cooperatives: case study of Koppa Transport Cooperative Society
SURESHRAMANA MAYYA AND YASHAVANTHA DONGRE

30. Successful cooperatives across Asia: ULCCS—the icon of successful cooperatives in India
T.P. SETHUMADHAVAN

31. Worker cooperatives as a model for family business succession? The case of C-Mac Industries Co-operative Ltd in Australia
DR. ANTHONY JENSEN AND FRANK WEBB

32. Korea's worker cooperative and organizational transformation: the case of Happy Bridge Co-operative
JONGHO WON AND SEUNGKWON JANG

33. Workers' cooperatives as a solution to social exclusion in Japan
YURIE KUBO

34. Summary

ANTHONY JENSEN

Part 3

TOWARD AN ASIAN SCHOLARSHIP ON CO-OPS

35. Deconstructing cooperative success in the Asia Pacific region

YASHAVANTHA DONGRE, AKIRA KURIMOTO,
SEUNGKWON JANG, ROBBY TULUS, ROBBY ALTMAN
AND ANTHONY JENSEN

List of contributors

Morris Altman Dean & Chair Professor of Behavioural and Institutional Economics & Co-Operatives, School of Business, University of Dundee, Dundee, United Kingdom

Nabin Bhandari Nepal Multipurpose Cooperative Society Limited, Jhapa, Nepal

Ernest Marc V. Castillo Research Associate for the School of Economics, University of Asia and the Pacific, Philippines

Eunju Choi iCOOP Co-operative Institute, Seoul, Korea

Isagani B. Daba Former Chairman of First Community Credit Cooperative, Philippines

Emi Do Department of Agricultural Economics, Tokyo University of Agriculture, Setagaya, Tokyo, Japan

Yashavantha Dongre University of Mysore, Mysuru, Karnataka, India

Huong Ha School of Business, Singapore University of Social Sciences, Singapore

Balasubramanian Iyer International Cooperative Alliance Asia-Pacific, New Delhi, India

Seungkwon Jang Division of Business Administration and Department of Management of Co-operatives, Graduate School, Sungkonghoe University, Seoul, Korea

Anthony Jensen University of Newcastle, Callaghan, Australia; Business School, University of Newcastle, New South Wales, Australia

Anil Karanjkar Centre for Research and Publications, Vaikunth Mehta National Institute of Co-operative Management, Pune, India

Hwalshin Kim Department of Management of Co-operatives, Graduate School, Sungkonghoe University, Seoul, Korea

Sunhwa Kim Department of Management of Co-operatives, Graduate School, Sungkonghoe University, Seoul, Korea

Sudha Kornginnaya Department of Commerce, Mangalore University, Mangalore, Karnataka, India

Yurie Kubo School of Commerce, Meiji University, Tokyo, Japan

Akira Kurimoto Hosei University, Chiyoda City, Tokyo, Japan; Institute for Solidarity-based Society, Hosei University, Tokyo, Japan

Yena Lee Department of Management of Co-operatives, Graduate School, Sungkonghoe University, Seoul, Korea

Gary Lewis Byron Bay, NSW, Australia

Hui Shan Loh School of Business, Singapore University of Social Sciences, Singapore

Peter Mason Cufa Ltd, Sydney, Australia

Sureshramana Mayya Poornaprajna Institute of Management, Udupi, India

Munaldus Nerang Federation of People-Centered Co-operative Enterprises (INKUR), Indonesia

Bienvenido P. Nito Research Fellow, Center for Research and Communication, University of Asia and the Pacific, Pasig, Philippines; Senior Fellow of the Center for Research and Communication of the University of Asia and the Pacific, Philippines

Indira Pant National Cooperative Development Board, Pulchok, Lalitpur, Nepal

G. Parameshwari PES First Grade College, Mandya, Karnataka, India

T. Paranjothi Agricultural Co-operative Staff Training Institute, Thiruvananthapuram, India

Leo G. Parma Chairman, Kagawani Foundation, Inc., Founder and Former CEO and Chief Business Builder of Asiapro Multi-Purpose Cooperative, Social Entrepreneur and Advocate of Worker Cooperatives, Pasig, Philippines

Maria Antonette D. Pasquin Instructor, School of Law and Governance, University of Asia and the Pacific, Pasig, Philippines

Bui Hong Quy Faculty of Accounting and Business Management, Vietnam National University of Agriculture, Gia Lam, Vietnam

Punya Prasad Regmi Karnali Province Planning Commission, Surkhet, Nepal

T.P. Sethumadhavan Uralungal Labour Contract Cooperative Society, Madappallly, Kerala

Hyojin Shin Department of Management of Co-operatives, Graduate School, Sungkonghoe University, Seoul, Korea

Dang Thi Kim Hoa Faculty of Accounting and Business Management, Vietnam National University of Agriculture, Hanoi, Vietnam

Tran Thi Thu Huong Faculty of Accounting and Business Management, Vietnam National University of Agriculture, Gia Lam, Vietnam

Nguyen Anh Tru Faculty of Accounting and Business Management, Vietnam National University of Agriculture, Hanoi, Vietnam

Robby Tulus Regional Director (Emeritus) for Asia Pacific, International Co-operative Alliance (ICA). Founder and Chief Advisor, Federation of People-based Co-operative Enterprises (INKUR Federation), Indonesia, and Credit Union Central Organization (CUCO), Indonesia

Nguyen Trong Tuynh Faculty of Accounting and Business Management, Vietnam National University of Agriculture, Hanoi, Vietnam

Nguyen Van Phuong Faculty of Accounting and Business Management, Vietnam National University of Agriculture, Gia Lam, Vietnam

Romulo M. Villamin Institute of Cooperative Studies, MASS SPECC Cooperative Development Center, Tiano-Yacapin St., Cagayan de Oro, Philippines

Frank Webb Business Clarity, New South Wales, Australia

Jongho Won Department of Management of Co-operatives, Graduate School, Sungkonghoe University, Seoul, Korea

Bin Wu Hangzhou Dianzi University, Hangzhou, P.R. China

Preface

Cooperatives are enterprises capable of building a better world. The United Nations asserted this in 2012 by declaring it the International Year of Cooperatives. This has been ratified by organizations of the stature of the International Labour Organization (ILO) and the Food and Agriculture Organization of the United Nations (FAO), with which the International Cooperative Alliance (ICA) signed two memorandums of understanding.

Cooperatives are not just another type of company. They are enterprises with values and principles; generate wealth in their territories; distribute opportunities without leaving anyone out; and promote a world of solidarity, inclusion, and peace.

However, we are facing an increasingly complex global scenario, with rising inequalities that cause serious conflict within and outside national and regional borders; rapidly evolving technological revolution whose usefulness can be as positive as it may be harmful; and our common home—Mother Earth is warning us about the damages we are inflicting on the environment in the name of supposed indefinite progress of humanity.

In this context, the strength of the Asian region makes us all look toward its direction. Rapid growth with commensurate poverty reduction, rapid technological development, and the pace of innovation seems to have awakened a giant over the past few decades.

At the same time, millions of citizens remain excluded and social and environmental imbalances threaten the path of growth undertaken in many Asian countries. The increase of products at the hands of the profit economy is obviously not enough to end hunger and definitely not enough to reverse the poverty and inequality rates.

This is why the collective effort to *wake up the giant inside the giant* through this book is welcomed! Indeed, cooperativism in the Asia-Pacific region with its rich history, astute leadership, and on-the-ground experiences offer pathways that surpass the classic centralized or free-market models.

As president of the ICA and as a member of the ICA board, I have had the opportunity to visit several countries in this region. I have made direct contact with leaders of organizations, government officials, and members of cooperatives. I have seen, first-hand, the enormous work they are carrying out to meet the needs of increasingly large populations in a more demanding world. I can assure you that cooperativism is not asleep in the Asia-Pacific.

However, it still has a lot to do and a lot to show to the region and the world. The efforts made by the authors of this book are timely. In the pages that follow, we will read about the achievements of cooperatives in different contexts, without abandoning a critical look that makes us reflect on the mistakes and helps us find the best ways to continue serving our communities.

The central ingredient of this work is the 22 case studies that allow us to see first-hand how and why cooperativism can be the protagonist in sectors as diverse as agriculture, consumption, credit, and business. Moreover, in different sociopolitical contexts, with more or less favorable regulatory frameworks, with more or less consistent public policies, with more or less strong obstacles to overcome.

If the experiences alone do not tell us everything we need to know, the added value we find here are a series of chapters dedicated to strengthening our conceptual understanding of how and why cooperatives can model societies that are inclusive, fair, and peaceful. Indeed, the rigor with which the researchers handled their study gives account of concerns that go beyond the narrative of these 22 cases. These, after all, are triggers to encourage new projects and to challenge us to think and act in pursuit of the world that cooperativists long for.

The conceptual scaffolding that enriches these stories is combined with the historical journey of Asian cooperativism and touches upon the perspective raised around old and new challenges, such as gender equity, youth participation, and the 2030 Agenda for Sustainable Development.

Another virtue of this book is that it looks at issues from the lens of actual practice. It does not seek to be merely scholarly, but builds knowledge from the ground up. Nor is it foreign, because it starts from the local contexts to generate a collective knowledge of what works and serves the needs of people.

The economic, social, environmental, and demographic challenges that this region must face have, of course, varied responses. However, in the process one can generate value, distribute it proportionally to the needs of the populations, and develop actions for the well-being of all—one that puts people and the environment at the center and addresses growing economic needs. That alternative is there in cooperatives. It is a giant! And it is prepared to take on the challenges that Asia-Pacific societies face.

Despite the issues and obstacles that we often encounter as cooperative organizations,

I believe that the outlook is encouraging for the region. This book ratifies that hope. In contrast to the prevalent view that cooperatives are marginal players and subservient to other models, we see here the cooperative success, which is not a purely economic success. Cooperatives have their core in social capital, which makes us different. We have roots in each of the communities where we participate, that is, we are the cultural, economic, and social expression of the people that give us life.

We owe these to our people. That is why I welcome the brilliant initiative to carry out this research project which, from now on, will be a fundamental tool to consolidate the contribution of cooperatives toward sustainable development.

The 2030 Agenda proposes that the development of our societies has to be based on decent work, gender equity, and an ecosystem of care, among others. And it invites us, as cooperatives, to be part of the global alliance to address the 17 Sustainable Development Goals.

Among the conditions that make this compliance possible is knowledge. I add, not any knowledge if not shared knowledge, elaborated from collective experiences that have transformed the quality of life of people every day. If we add to that the contribution of researchers, thinkers, and scholars who give a theoretical framework to these trajectories, we are facing a very valuable contribution to think about our role in today's complex world.

This contribution will surely not end with this study. On the contrary, as the authors themselves propose, this is a first step toward the construction of genuine knowledge, developed from, by, and for cooperatives. A knowledge that helps to strengthen their virtues, to solve their weaknesses, to overcome threats, and to take advantage of the opportunities presented to them. It is also useful to those responsible for developing public policies, to look at cooperatives as strategic allies when it comes to improving the quality of life of people. Researchers can take this starting point to continue producing and sharing knowledge.

Finally, it provides the basis for leaders in cooperatives to advance the construction of a robust, dynamic, and integrated cooperative movement throughout the Asia-Pacific region.

Let's wake up the giant!

Ariel Guarco
President of the Internacional
Co-operative Alliance

1

Introduction

Morris Altman[1], Yashavantha Dongre[2], Akira Kurimoto[3], Anthony Jensen[4], Robby Tulus[5] and Seungkwon Jang[6]

[1]Dean & Chair Professor of Behavioural and Institutional Economics & Co-Operatives, School of Business, University of Dundee, Dundee, United Kingdom [2]University of Mysore, Mysore, India [3]Hosei University, Chiyoda City, Tokyo, Japan [4]Business School, University of Newcastle, New South Wales, Australia [5]Regional Director (Emeritus) for Asia Pacific, International Co-operative Alliance (ICA). Founder and Chief Advisor, Federation of People-based Co-operative Enterprises (INKUR Federation), Indonesia, and Credit Union Central Organization (CUCO), Indonesia [6]Division of Business Administration, Sungkonghoe University, Seoul, Korea

1.1 Cooperatives in the transforming Asian Pacific region

The cooperative movement has long been a collective response to individual and community disadvantage and exploitation. "Together we are stronger" has been followed by "Building a better world" and "Leave no one behind." These mantras continue to define the vision of one of the largest social movements in history. But for the collective response to be successful, there were considerable obstacles that had to be overcome. And these obstacles have differed over time and space. Understanding the evolution of cooperative or member-owned organizations needs to be placed in the context of where and when cooperatives evolved. Understanding the successes and failures of cooperatives is context dependent. Just because a cooperative succeeded in the United Kingdom, in a certain state in the United States, or in a certain state in India, it does not mean that the same type of cooperative adopting the same successful approach will succeed when applied to a particular region in the Philippines or in Vietnam.

It is clear that the context in which cooperatives emerge and succeed has and is changing rapidly. And this context differs across countries and regions across the globe. The Asian Century gathered pace and the moral and economic leadership of the Unites States waned. Free-market liberalism, with minimalist government involvement led by investor-owned firms focused solely on profits and short-term gain, is being questioned as the one true path to economic and social success and improved wellbeing. Much of this critical thinking was triggered by the global financial crisis, which was embedded in the extremes of free-market liberalism, and the serious economic and social challenges posed by climate change. Cooperatives are increasingly regarded has a means of achieving improvements in wellbeing globally whilst generating success in the economic domain. Cooperatives now need to be re-evaluated for their potential to provide a viable alternative for governments and policy makers.

The purpose of this book, which is the work of 34 academics in the Asian Pacific region, is to provide a timely review of how cooperatives across the region have overcome difficulties, succeeded, but also failed, and to point the way to the renaissance in cooperative research and analysis. This renaissance should impact on our understanding of cooperatives and member-owned organizations more generally in order to better inform cooperators, governments, and the general public. This renaissance in thinking about cooperatives is reflected and highlighted in an Asia Pacific compilation using 23 case studies across 11 countries and 4 cooperative sectors. Underpinning these empirical studies are contributions to the theory of cooperatives. The current theory, which remains dominant, maintains that cooperatives that are not economically sustainable tend to be rather marginal organizations, which from a developmental aspect are slow to get started and have problems scaling up. The theoretical contributions, which are part of the current renaissance on the theory of cooperatives, demonstrate that the cooperative model can equal or outperform rivals economically as well as generate superior social and environmental outcomes.

The cooperative movement has been tied to the cycles of capitalism for 200 years. Cooperatives have been an important riposte to mercantile, financial, and global capitalism and were introduced into the Asia Pacific by colonial powers as part of their developmental strategies or by local leaders who learned of successful experiences in the West. In the second half of the 20th century, many states promoted and supported cooperatives, which were often seen as engines for justice and economic development.

However, the emergence of stagflation in the 1970s led to the belief by many global scholars and leaders that a return to "free" market-driven economics and the further unleashing of the power of individualism would lead to an outcome with greater utility to society at large. Collectivism fell into disrepute in many countries and we saw the rise of what many have referred to as neo-liberal economics. In effect, this led to the gradual withdrawal of governments from leadership roles in the economy, less provision of social goods, less regulation, and the market economy being left to self-regulate. This transformed the world economy; it being driven by globalization on one hand, but coupled with serious ethical deterioration in business practices on the other.

This culminated in the global financial crisis, the heart of which was centered in the United States, one of the focal points of the call for unfettered, deregulated capitalism. This discredited, for many, the free market economic model. In this current period of extreme disruption, the calls for the transformation of capitalism and a rethinking of the "corporation" have reached a crescendo. Although capitalism and the freeing up of some markets from state control have coincided with a dramatic reduction of poverty in China and India, there is also more inequality and environmental damage. But the most successful Asian economies have introduced a mix of markets and governments and, in the West, amongst the most successful economies, this mix has been historic and is being maintained. Throughout these dramatic changes in the world economy cooperatives have remained a strong and vibrant force, demonstrating their resilience in the face of persistent economic and ideological challenges. In this period of disruption, when the intellectual and political underpinnings of the free market version of capitalism is being challenged, even among leaders in the West, the sustainable cooperative model again offers a credible and proven alternative to free market capitalism and state socialism.

This book offers a thoughtful and well-researched account on how the cooperative model works and what it can contribute to the sustainable development of the economy, society, and the environment. It makes known to the international community the extraordinarily successful cooperatives in Asia and the Pacific—many of which are not known in the West and, indeed, amongst many in the East. The targeted readers include cooperative leaders, researchers, policy makers, and development agencies in the Asian Pacific, while it can provide lessons and inspiration to those interested in the cooperative alternative and solution to the multifaceted socio-economic challenges in other regions around the world.

1.2 Waking the Asian Pacific cooperative potential

Before introducing the contents of this book, it is important that we explain the meaning of the title of this book. Asian Pacific cooperatives started under strong Western influence through colonialization, immigration, and knowledge transfer. They have evolved in specific patterns, often referred to as the "British-Indian Pattern of Cooperation." Today, they exhibit huge diversity in size, sector, and stage of development, reflecting the political and socio-economic diversity of the region. In fact, this is what one would expect and it parallels the diversity in the development of cooperatives in the West and, indeed, throughout the world. Asian Pacific cooperatives' membership has grown to such an extent that their membership is the largest in the International Cooperative Alliance (ICA); but their share of business remains much smaller than that of other regions, as documented in the World Cooperative Monitor.

Although there exist a great number of cooperatives, members, and employees, these are often regarded as sleeping giants since they are not thought to be innovative, dynamic, and easily responsive to ongoing and dramatic changes in their economic and political environments. But there remains the potential for Asian Pacific cooperatives to be dynamic engines of sustainable socio-economic and equitable development and growth. But we need to waken this potential and make more people aware of this viable cooperative alternative.

In this book, we wish to address several research questions to better understand the Asian Pacific cooperative potential, these include:

- How have Asian Pacific cooperatives evolved in diverse patterns (British/Indian, Japanese/Korean, and Australian/New Zealand)?
- What are unique Asian Pacific cooperative models? How have these been created/evolved?
- What challenges did Asian Pacific cooperatives overcome in order to succeed? What lessons were learned?
- What are the factors involved in their success?
- What is the future position of the Asian Pacific cooperatives of the world?
- What potential role could Asian Pacific cooperatives have in the Asian Pacific region in facilitating a more sustainable and equitable growth as compared to an overarching reliance on the state and investor-owned firms?
- How can the potential of Asian Pacific cooperatives be awakened?

1.3 Structure of this book

Section 1.1 is the synthesis of Asian and Pacific cooperatives from various perspectives including political economy, economics, historiography, and public policy, while debates on gender, youth, and the Sustainable Developing Goals (SDGs) are also addressed.

Akira Kurimoto has produced a definitive chapter entitled "Why Asian Pacific Cooperative Models," which includes how they evolved separately to the West. Morris Altman argues, in the chapter "The Theoretical Construct of Cooperative Comparative Advantage," that the application of cooperative principles enabled cooperatives to achieve sustained comparative advantages and can serve as engines of equitable growth and development. Akira Kurimoto, in "The Asia Pacific Cooperative History," presents a comprehensive history of the evolution of Asian Pacific cooperatives. Robby Tullus, a former director of the ICA, Asia Pacific, in "Cooperatives and Public Policy," produces a lucid account of how government policy on cooperatives in the Asia Pacific region has typically not been supportive of cooperative development. This deficit in government is an obstacle that Asian Pacific cooperatives must overcome to succeed. Balu Iyer director of the ICA, Asia Pacific, outlines how cooperatives can assist the United Nations to achieve its SDGs. Sudha Kornginnaya outlines, in "Gender and Cooperatives," the obstacles women face in achieving gender equity and how the cooperative movement has overcome these obstacles in many instances to assist women break through the glass ceiling. Yashavantha Dongre, in the chapter "Youth and Cooperatives," discusses the role and importance of youth in the cooperative movement and the development and sustenance of cooperatives. Anthony Jensen presents a theoretical model that could form the basis for gaining an understanding of why the presence of cooperatives varies so dramatically across the different countries in the Asia Pacific region and what the macro and micro factors are that tend to lead to success.

Section 1.2 presents an analysis of 22 successful cooperative case studies in the 4 core sectors of cooperative engagement, namely the agricultural sector, the consumer sector, the credit sector, and the worker-owned cooperative sector. Each sector-specific section is followed by a summary of what has been learned in relation to building sustainable cooperatives in each country.

The section on "Agricultural Cooperatives" provides trends based on six case studies from six economically, socially, and politically different countries. It would seem that states see agricultural cooperatives as important in political terms and agricultural cooperatives see state support as inevitable for them to remain competitive and sustainable amid a changing market structure. These cases represent primary cooperatives, secondary or regional level cooperatives, and sectoral cooperative apex organizations. Almondco from Australia is a primary agricultural cooperative, but has not been demutualized as is typical of the liberal market economy. Ruoheng Watermelon Cooperative from China is a primary cooperative, but has limited participative membership and, as is typical of the political and economic structure of the country, it has state supervision and patronage. Again, the Rajaram Bapu Cooperative in India is a primary cooperative, but has now grown into a cooperative conglomerate impacting on all aspects of members' lives. JA Hadano of Japan is a primary agricultural cooperative, but is part of the JA Group using a common logo. Van Duc Cooperative of Vietnam was initially a typically state-created and supervised cooperative that has now been converted into a membership-based cooperative based on the new cooperative legislation adopted in 2012. Unlike these examples, NACF from Korea is a federation of primary cooperatives that functions in close proximity with the state.

The consumer cooperative section covers four cases in Japan, Singapore, South Korea, and Vietnam, all of which have had extraordinary success. It had been given a lower priority compared with the agricultural sector; many governments have supported the sector when foreign retailers tried to penetrate this huge but unexplored market with mixed results. Singaporean and Vietnamese cooperatives have succeeded in becoming the largest retailers in their countries due to a variety of government support measures. In contrast, Japanese and South Korean cooperatives have developed as socially conscious entities from the bottom up without any government support. The macro and micro factors leading to success are analyzed.

Credit unions from humble beginnings parlayed peoples common desire to help themselves through collective action into ever growing membership and financial resources. They overcame adverse political and market conditions to create a space in their respective countries financial system for people who otherwise could have been excluded had they not pooled their resources and endeavored to institutionalize cooperation. The five credit unions featured in this section from Indonesia, Sri Lanka, Australia, the Philippines, and Nepal are success stories in their own right and a reflection of the historical, cultural, and socioeconomic circumstances in which they took root and prospered.

Worker cooperatives across Asia demonstrate the various ways workers can secure their jobs in democratic organizations that give them control over their destiny and liberate them from being precarious workers. This sector covers six case studies in five Asian states, namely Kerala and Karnataka in India, Korea, Japan, Australia, and the Philippines. Two extraordinary cooperatives have created thousands of jobs, demonstrating the power of collective action. These case studies illustrate the impact of the political economy on worker cooperative formation and the ability to stay true to its cooperative principles. The appropriate role of the state is examined, from communist-leaning Kerala to collectivist Japan while including the impact of civil society in the Philippines.

1.4 Creating the Asian Pacific scholarship on cooperative studies

Section 1.3 brings the book to a conclusion; this book is published as a first step toward further enriching and growing Asian Pacific scholarship on cooperative studies. Largely, much of cooperative scholarship is owed to the West. It is quite natural that the cooperative studies have been developed in Europe and North America since these regions have witnessed the emergence and evolution of cooperatives of various types since the 19th century. These studies and analyses have continuously involved multidisciplinary approaches and international perspectives. Cooperative ideas and practices had been spread from Europe to the Asia Pacific region, then followed by studies on Asian Pacific cooperatives. As we foresee the potential of Asia as the growth center of world, with China and India now playing increasingly important roles, we need to analyze the reality of cooperatives in the Asia Pacific region as the nations and subregions within the Asia Pacific face demographic, economic, social, and environmental challenges. Important ongoing questions include: To what extent have cooperatives dealt with these challenges and played a leadership role in addressing these challenges? How can cooperatives contribute to meeting SDG targets whilst contributing to improving the wellbeing of cooperative members and potential members as defined by cooperators and potential cooperators?

Further reading

Altman, M. (2014). Are cooperatives a viable business form? Lessons from behavioural economics. In S. Novkovic, & T. Webb (Eds.), *Co-operatives in a post-growth era: Towards co-operative economics*. London: ZED Books.

Birchall, J. (1997). *The international co-operative movement*. Manchester University Press.

Bowles, S., & Gintis, H. (2011). *A cooperative species: Human reciprocity and its evolution*. Princeton, NJ: Princeton University Press.

Cook, M. L., Chaddad, F., & Iliopoulos. (2004). Advances in cooperative theory since 1990: A review of agricultural economics literature. In G. W. J. Hendrikse (Ed.), *Restructuring agricultural cooperatives* (pp. 65–90). Haveka: Erasmus University Press, Haveka.

Münkner, H. (2013). Worldwide regulation of co-operative societies: An overview. *EURICSE Working Paper*, n. 53.

Novkovic, S., & Webb, T. (Eds.), (2014). *Co-operatives in a post-growth era: Towards co-operative economics*. London: ZED Books.

Nussbaum, M. (2003). Capabilities as fundamental entitlements: Sen and social justice. *Feminist Economics, 9*, 33–59.

Pencavel, J. (2013). In The International Library of Critical Writings in Economics (Ed.), *The economics of worker cooperatives*. Northampton, MA: Edward Elgar.

Witt, M., & Redding, G. (Eds.), (2014). *The oxford handbook of Asian business systems*. Oxford University Press.

PART 1

Analytical framework of Asian cooperative models

2

Why Asian Pacific cooperative models matter?

Akira Kurimoto

Institute for Solidarity-based Society, Hosei University, Tokyo, Japan

2.1 Introduction

Asian cooperatives started in the 19th century by importing European models. Consumer co-ops were set up to buy food at an affordable price following the Rochdale model, while credit cooperatives were created adopting the Raiffeisen model to combat usury. The Japanese Industrial Cooperative Act was enacted by bureaucrats in 1900 to regulate all types of cooperatives, while the Indian Credit Cooperative Societies Act was given by the British Empire in 1904 and became the prototype of the cooperative legislation in the developing world. In both cases, a government top-down approach was introduced in a wide area in incorporation, governance, and finance. Such an approach was applied by colonial powers, then succeeded by new independent states. Therefore cooperatives became parastatal entities under almighty cooperative ministers/registrars in many countries. In the Pacific region, immigrants started cooperatives applying the successful practices from their homeland that they had left behind.

Thus Asia Pacific cooperatives were created under strong Western influence brought about by colonialism, immigration, and learning from advanced models. They, however, evolved quite differently under the prevailing political and socio-economic circumstances. Largely protected from competition by licenses and trade restrictions and supported by subsidies and tax concessions, they had accepted stringent government control except for the British Dominions. Now they are in the process of transforming to become more independent and autonomous organizations to fulfill their objective of serving their member's needs, rather than the public good. In addition, there are a variety of self-help groups or pre-co-ops that may grow into more formal cooperatives. In many industrial sectors, national representative bodies are operating and are affiliated with the international co-operative alliance (ICA) Asia and Pacific.

Currently, Japanese agricultural cooperatives are ranked at high positions in the World Cooperative Monitor,[1] while consumer cooperatives had 71% of the membership and 27% of the turnover of the European counterpart in 2012. Asia Pacific cooperatives had a predominant share of membership, that is, 57% of the ICA affiliates in 1998, while their share in the number of larger co-ops in the World Cooperative Monitor was only 14.9% in 2010. However, given the growing population and the high growth rate in the past decades, and since it is forecast that the Asian economy will occupy 50% of the world's GDP in 2050, they have the potential to become the mainstream of the global cooperative movement, if they can grow in parallel with the whole economy.

This chapter starts with an overview of the vast diversity of the Asia Pacific region. Then it describes the emergence of the unique Asian Pacific cooperative models both at the organizational level and the inter-cooperation level. Finally, it calls for studies to identify the potential of Asian Pacific cooperatives.

2.2 Asia Pacific region's vast diversity

First, one may be impressed by the vast diversity of the Asia Pacific region compared with other regions. Its area extends from the Siberian tundra to New Zealand, from the Arabian desert to the Pacific islands. Asia has been the cradle of ancient civilizations and the birthplace of all the world religions. The political regimes range from capitalist to socialist political economies and the cold-war-type confrontation of divided nation states continues although it has ended in other regions. The

ethnic and religious divides often generate serious conflicts in many places. The level of economic development varies from poorly developed to highly developed, even though Asia has regained its share in the world's GDP after 200 years since the Great Divergence. The social construction is still immensely varied, reflecting dominant cultures, religions, and values, even the common trends transforming from traditional agrarian societies to postindustrial societies are widely observed.

"Asian values" were advocated as a political ideology of the 1990s, which defined elements of society, culture, and history common to the nations of Southeast and East Asia, aiming to use commonalities—for example, the principle of collectivism—to unify people for their economic and social good and to create a pan-Asian identity as contrasted with the perceived European ideals of the universal rights of man.[2] The popularity of the concept waned after the 1997 Asian financial crisis, when it became evident that Asia lacked any coherent regional institutional mechanism to deal with the crisis. Even now, the Asia Pacific region lacks clear prospect for regional integration such as the European Union.

The diversity in the Asia Pacific region can be explained by the perspective of Varieties of Capitalism (VoC). Hall and Soskice (2003) analyzed how firms coordinate through market or nonmarket relations and set out two distinct types of capitalist economies, namely Liberal Market Economies (LME) and Coordinated Market Economies (CME). The former is applied to the United States, the United Kingdom, Canada, Australia, New Zealand, and Ireland, while the latter includes Germany, Sweden, Austria, and Japan. But it is not strictly

---

[1] Zenkyoren was ranked No. 5, Zen-noh No. 11, and Norinchukin Bank No. 53 in the 2015 Global 300 ranking. Zen-noh was the largest and the Fonterra Group was No. 6 in the agricultural sector while Saitama Medical Co-op was ranked No. 9 in the health sector.

[2] The concept was advocated by Mahathir Mohamad (Prime Minister of Malaysia during 1981–2003) and by Lee Kuan Yew (Prime Minister of Singapore, 1959–90).

applicable to the Asian region due to historical and institutional differences. Witt and Redding (2014) suggested five types of Asian capitalism (postsocialist, advanced city-state, emerging Southeast Asian, advanced Northeast Asian, and Japanese), but it is mingling the typology of economies with geographic considerations. The author would like to suggest a classification of economies in the Asia Pacific region based on the institutional arrangements, that is, the role of state and freedom of association. Four types of market economies are identified in accordance with the extent of state intervention/involvement in the economic and social life of people.

1. Socialist market economies: China, Vietnam, etc.

   Rigid central planning economies have given way to "socialist market economies" under the slogan of "Reform and Opening-up" (China) or "Doi moi" (Vietnam) since the 1980s, but it is still characterized by a dominant public sector and strong government intervention into economic activities while it lacks a contestable election, an independent media, and freedom of association.

2. Developmentalist market economies: India, Singapore, Malaysia, Thailand, Philippines, etc.

   Colonial-style top-down management was inherited after independence. Nationalist governments pursued developmentalist policies and continue to dominate economic activities while free association and the media are often compromised. The plural political party system is taking over the "developmental dictatorship" in the Philippines, but authoritarian governments still dominate the political economy in Singapore and Malaysia.

3. State-coordinated market economies: Japan, Korea, and Taiwan

   This type escaped from being colonized by Western powers and developed into a unique system based on bureaucracy.

Japan had industrialized under government initiatives and maintains state control over industries (Aoki's "bureau-pluralism"). Korea and Taiwan followed Japan's pattern of development even after independence from it. A contestable election, an independent media, and freedom of association are ensured.

4. Liberal market economies: Australia and New Zealand

   This type follows the Anglo-Saxon pattern of LME characterized by the common law tradition, governments' laissez-faire economic policy, and unbridled market competition. But these countries have established a wide range of social security systems financed by tax to cope with market failure. A contestable election, an independent media, and freedom of association are ensured.

2.3 Emergence of Asian Pacific cooperative models

Asia and Pacific co-ops exhibit huge diversity, thus, reflecting the diversity of the region. The level of development varies from start-up groups to the most advanced enterprises. The industrial sectors in which cooperatives operate also range from agricultural supply and marketing, food retailing, banking, and insurance to industrial production and service provision. But the principal difference can be seen in a given state's policy and legislation on cooperatives. In many countries, cooperative ministers/registrars exercise overriding power on cooperatives, while in other countries, cooperatives are neglected or discouraged. In some countries, cooperatives are dominated by political parties or politicians, while the apex cooperative organizations often function as bureaucracy's agents. These elements have put cooperatives on quite different national

1. Analytical framework of Asian cooperative models

trajectories. Many cooperatives had been established from the top down to implement public
policies in priority areas, while some cooperatives had been created from the bottom up to
meet the unmet needs of people. They have the
common problems of lack of member commitment, entrepreneurial capacity, and capital.

Against such backdrops, we could witness
the emergence of successful cooperatives
grown from the grassroots. This book show-
cases some best practices and analyses the
micro and macro factors attributable to success.
The former includes organizational and business models, governance/management, human
resource processes, and adherence to the
Cooperative Principles, while the latter refers
to the enabling of state policy/legislation, the
market, and society at large.

Amongst these, some unique Asian Pacific
cooperative models have emerged. Asia Pacific
cooperatives were created under a strong
Western influence. This does not mean, however, that they are just copies of their European
forerunners; rather, they have evolved into
Asian entities adapting to the existing political
regimes, socio-economic structures, and traditional culture. The dominant shape is the hier-
archal structure under state-controlled or state-
sponsored apex organizations in many countries, although there are a wide variation reflecting the vast diversity of the region. However,
some successful Asia Pacific cooperative models
have emerged and need to be studied carefully.

In the agricultural sector, cooperatives were
expected to help small farmers to enjoy economy
of scale by jointly organizing sales of produce at
a better term and jointly procuring inputs at a
lower price. Amul dairy cooperatives in India
provided a model for the development of a program termed "white revolution" that began in
1965. Deeply rooted in communities, highly integrated at the village, district, and state levels,
and under members control, they have proved
the worth of the system, which offers every necessary service to small farmers breeding only

1–2 cows. This model has been emulated by several countries in Asia and Africa. On the other
hand, agricultural cooperatives in Australia and
New Zealand started producing meat and dairy
products for export. These export-driven co-ops
have grown as major exporters of dairy. The
Fonterra group has been at the forefront of global
expansion for over 50 years making up 25% of
New Zealand's exports.

In the consumer sector, cooperatives have
sought to provide safe and reliable products at
a lower price. In Japan, consumer co-ops developed a unique way of home delivery to
Han neighborhood groups (joint buying) and
have made a rapid expansion since the 1970s.
The active member participation in the governance and business operations of co-ops
has often been praised by ICA leaders and
researchers. Growing individualism has
caused a challenge to which co-ops are adapting
by shifting to home delivery to individuals.
University co-ops have developed a wide range
of businesses involving students as full-fledged
members, while health co-ops have grown as
user-owned co-ops with multistakeholder membership involving a minority of professionals.
Korean cooperatives have grown from grassroots taking a similar trajectory since the 1990s,
but iCOOP and Hansalim co-ops developed
multistakeholder co-ops involving both consumers and producers. Trade union-based con-
sumer/insurance co-ops are thriving in
Singapore, while Saigon Co-op has developed a
supermarket chain, strongly supported by the
government in Vietnam. There exist a great
number of co-ops at workplaces set up by
employees working in companies, government
offices, etc., that are often supported by trade
unions and employers.

In the financial sector, Grameen Bank in
Bangladesh was praised by the World Bank as
being a successful formula of micro credit
empowering poor women at the grassroots
level, and it was awarded the Nobel Peace
Prize in 2006. Its model is being diffused in

1. Analytical framework of Asian cooperative models

many parts of the third world, but credit unions have provided financial services in much greater magnitude in many countries. They have been created by farmers, workers, traders, and consumers based on the "common bond" in communities, work places, and religious organizations. They largely contribute to the reduction of poverty and empowerment of women. Credit unions in Korea, the Philippines, and Indonesia were created from the grassroots and extended to help establish other types of co-ops. The labor banks in Japan set up by trade unions and consumer co-ops to cater to workers/consumers also display a unique model of labor-oriented co-op.

In the worker sector, cooperatives are emerging to cope with widely spreading unemployment and deteriorating working conditions. Alpha Pro with 80,000 members is providing a solution to the contracting problem and precarious work in the Philippines. Also, the Uralungal Labour Contract Cooperative has 7000 worker members in south India, operating to secure jobs for unemployed workers. Workers cooperatives started to secure jobs for middle-age/elderly workers unions or to meet the unmet community needs of female members of consumer co-ops in Japan.

In addition to these traditional types of co-ops, there are specific co-ops in Asia. Medical/health co-ops have been organized by users (Japan, South Korea, the Philippines, and Singapore) or providers (India, Malaysia, Mongolia, and Sri Lanka) to provide medical services at hospitals and clinics. In many cases, these are run as multistakeholder co-ops involving both healthcare professionals and beneficiaries. They have proved to be effective providers of indispensable health services that were otherwise not accessible to ordinary people, thus, contributing to sustainable development. University/college co-ops have been organized mainly by faculty members to provide textbooks, food, appliances, and credit/insurance in more than 10

countries. Students are generally treated as customers, but they are encouraged to become full-fledged members in Japan and Korea where co-ops are run by multistakeholders to support campus communities. Women's co-ops have been formed exclusively by women in Malaysia, Indonesia, India, and Iran to encourage them to take leadership positions, which would often be difficult in mixed-gender co-ops due to the prevailing culture of discrimination against women.

We need to identify the factors that are attributable to successful co-op models. Institutional arrangements have played an important role in facilitating co-ops to develop business operations. Favorable conditions include the enabling legislation, tax relief, licensing of specific businesses, training/education of cadres, and so on. However, it should be noted the government support might have led to its having control over co-ops. In many countries, cooperative laws contain the provisions of strong supervising roles by cooperative ministers/registrars that might hamper the independence and autonomy of cooperatives.

A more important factor is cooperative leadership creating innovative business models responding to the unmet needs of producers, consumers, and workers. They play important roles in capturing opportunities and mobilizing resources of key stakeholders. They often built supporting structures such as federations and intermediary institutions.

We need to see the dynamics of cooperative development in the Asia Pacific region. Many traditional co-ops were built from the top down, while new co-ops are emerging from the bottom up in each sector. Cooperatives may thrive even under unfavorable conditions as some cooperative models have demonstrated. For example, Japan's consumer co-ops have developed their membership basis and business by persuading all customers to

1. Analytical framework of Asian cooperative models

become members and relying on their investment to outwit legal restrictions prohibiting nonmember trade and banking business.

2.4 Inter-cooperation as another Asia Pacific cooperative model

Asian Pacific cooperative models can be seen in the cooperation among cooperatives. There are two types of inter-cooperation, namely cooperation in communities and in the supply chain. The first model is what Dr. Laidlaw described, "building cooperative communities," as one of the priorities that the cooperative movement of the world should do for the future, illustrated by an example of Japanese rural multipurpose cooperatives.

The first model can be seen in the cooperative community in Wonju, a local town situated 140 km east of Seoul, which is widely seen as a typical cooperative community.[3] In 1972, when the local river flooded, the farming lands around Wonju were devastated, resulting in there being no harvest. Responding to the local bishop's call for international aid, the Caritas Internationalis and the West German government provided 2.91 million German marks in total. The locals created the Balgeum Credit Union with the purpose of promoting self-help and cooperatives, rather than directly distributing the aid to the poor. Soon this Credit Union established a mixed consumer/producer Hansalim cooperative and a medical cooperative. These cooperatives became the institutional basis for today's multiple cooperatives. The basic goals of the early cooperatives were a self-reliant local economy and a self-governing local community. They criticized the industrialization strategy, and brought in the "thoughts of life" concepts based on traditional Korean culture. They promoted community-based mutual cooperation between consumers and farmers as well as a self-reliant development model. To date, 29 cooperatives have been created in Wonju and have worked together as a part of the Wonju Network of Social Economy. In this network, multiple cooperatives have developed common goals/visions and jointly invested in the development of new cooperatives. This is acclaimed as an innovative network, contributing to the development of the social economy of Wonju.

Another cooperative community can be found in the small town of Maleny situated 100 km north of Brisbane, Australia.[4] The town has a high density of cooperative organizations, for which it is internationally known. Maleny has a long history of cooperative enterprises. The "pioneer" phase was marked by the Maleny Cooperative Dairy Association started by settlers in 1903. The second consolidation phase relates to the modernization and expansion of the dairy industry from the 1930s and into the early 1970s. Then came a "new wave" of cooperative community organizations from the 1970s to the 2000s. In this period, Maleny produced a number of social enterprises and seven incorporated cooperatives, beginning with the establishment of a consumer cooperative store in 1980. These have grown into a network of interdependent cooperatives as well as enterprises based on cooperative principles including a credit union, a cooperative club, a workers' co-op, a cashless trading co-op, a local exchange trading system, environmental cooperatives, and a

---

[3]   Sang-Il Han Moo-Kwon Chung Mun-su Park (2014) "Local stakeholder involvement and social innovation in Korean cooperatives: the cases of Wonju and Ansung cities", *Community Development Journal*, Volume 49, Issue 2, Oxford. The cooperative community can be found in Sonmisan moul in Seoul where community businesses have flourished ranging from a cooperative daycare to a school, a supermarket, a restaurant, collective houses, and a theater.

[4]   Ann El Khoury, "A Cooperative Town: Community Development in Maleny, Australia", Refereed Abstract.

business enterprise/incubation center that supports individual and group businesses. In the fourth phase from the 2010s, the "core" cooperatives are still going strong (the Maple Street Co-op and the Maleny Credit Union), while other cooperatives have suffered from the perennial problem of intergenerational succession. These issues are compounded by the changing demographic makeup of the town, which may also offer prospects for cooperative renewal by way of an elderly care cooperative. The contemporary history of Maleny is a key example of the benefits of cooperative approaches to community development.

The second model refers to the cooperation in the supply chain among producer and consumer cooperatives.[5] In the course of rapid industrialization and urbanization, the food supply chain has undergone drastic changes involving the many actors between the producers and consumers, namely collectors, processors, wholesalers, retailers, and food businesses, which have all contributed to the provision of value-added food products that offer both variety and convenience, thus, bringing higher consumer satisfaction. At the same time, the extended supply chain has increased the distance from farm to table, causing a number of problems associated with the asymmetric information; consumers have shown discontent with hazardous food additives, chemical residues, inadequate labeling, and the high price of products, while producers have often suffered from volatile prices, the dumping of surplus products, and a lack of knowledge about consumer preferences. To solve such problems, some initiatives have emerged among consumers and producers.[6] Consumer groups in Japan started collectively buying fresh milk directly from dairy farmers and some of these groups evolved into consumer co-ops during the 1960s and 1970s. Many of them expanded this form of direct transaction with farmers (Sanchoku) to ensure safety and reliability based on contracts that precisely defined the cultivating/feeding methods, the use of chemicals/drugs, and made record keeping obligatory. Sanchoku had the motto "buy produce with the producer's face on it," and the product range expanded to vegetables, fruits, rice, meat, and seafood. Consumers often visited farms to see the production sites firsthand and gain knowledge, while producers joined in Sanchoku Partner Groups to promote mutual learning and communication with consumers. Thus Sanchoku was established as a model of consumer–farmer partnership to reinstate trust and mutual understanding between them by bypassing conventional wholesale markets. During the 1990s, Sanchoku further evolved, partly in response to ever-increasing competition and the growing size of consumer co-ops. Its rationale and methods further diversified; institutionalized partnering with agricultural co-ops, networking with multiple production sites for the procurement of large volumes, emphasis on food safety and quality assurance, and concern for the

---

[5] Akira Kurimoto (2009) "Consumer-Producer Alliance in the Food Chain: Rationales and Evolution of Sanchoku," a paper presented at the ICA Research Conference in Oxford.

[6] Sanchoku is a consumer-led alliance, while farmers' markets that sell produce brought in by adjacent farmers fall under a producer-led alliance. The community-led alliance called Community Supported Agriculture (CSA) is the typical model consisting of a group of individuals who pledge support to a farm operation so that the farmland becomes the community's farm, with growers and consumers providing mutual support and sharing the risks and benefits of food production. This idea has taken took root in the United States since the 1980s, although its founders trace its roots to Europe's community agriculture and the Japanese *teikei* (alliance) in the 1960s.

1. Analytical framework of Asian cooperative models

community (i.e., *chisan chisho* or consume locally grown produce).[7] Sanchoku is also widely practiced in South Korea and Australia.

Another example is an industrial-logistic cluster in South Korea. The new complex involving food processors, a distribution center, and a food laboratory was built in Gurye, a small village in southwestern Korea, by the iCo-op group in 2014. It is composed of 17 food plants processing 360 items including noodles, bean curd, and so on that are bought by iCo-op and distributed throughout the country. It is a part of iCo-op's Gurye Natural Dream Park with conference rooms, restaurants and cafes, a cooking studio, a cinema, a fitness center, and lodging facilities located on 15 hectares of ground. It is intended to facilitate communication between consumers and producers and among co-op members and community residents.

2.5 Conclusion

This chapter starts with an overview of the vast diversity of the Asia Pacific region. Then it explains emerging Asia Pacific cooperative models both at the organizational and network levels. Cooperatives in the Asia Pacific region were born under strong influence from the West through colonization, immigrants, and knowledge transfer in the late 19th century, and they went through a unique evolution in the 20th century. The national trajectory was largely varied due to the different political regimes, socio-economic structures, and historical path dependency. The variety of capitalism is closely linked with the institutional framework that has been locked in the environment in which cooperative had to operate. The top-down culture of the colonial era was inherited and even intensified after independence, and persistently continues to date. Cooperative leaders and government officials have repeatedly pledged to make independent and autonomous organizations consistent with the ICA's Identity Statement, the corresponding United Nations Guidelines, and the ILO Recommendation, but the progress has been slow due to the organizational inertia and resistance of politicians/bureaucrats. It is not easy to answer to the question of whether Asia Pacific cooperative models continue to grow or converge with the dominant models in the West. We need to collect data, conduct case studies, and make comparisons within the region and with other regions aiming to enrich our understanding of cooperatives as a global phenomenon.

Certainly, there is huge potential for cooperative development to satisfy the unmet needs of millions of people and to make an effective contribution to attaining the Sustainable Development Goals. This book sets out to identify best practices and analyze factors attributable to success. There are multiple challenges to waking the Asian Pacific cooperative potential including to disseminate the findings of studies among cooperative leaders and government officers, to reform cooperative governance and federal structure, and to establish enabling legislation and policies for cooperative development.

References

Witt, M., & Redding, G. (Eds.), (2014). *The oxford handbook of Asian business systems*. Oxford University Press.
Hall, P. A., & Soskice, D. W. (2001). *Variety of capitalism*. Oxford University Press.

Further reading

Alagappa, M. (Ed.), (2004). *Civil society and political change in Asia*. Stanford: Stanford University Press.

---

[7] This notion is popular in Korean agricultural and consumer co-ops. It is also resonant with "Buy Local" campaigns in the United States and Germany and the "Slow Food" movement in Italy.

Birchall, J. (1997). *The international co-operative movement.* Manchester University Press.

Hasan, S., & Lyons, M. (Eds.), (2004). *Social capital in Asian sustainable development management.* New York: Nova Science Publishers, Inc.

Kurimoto, A. (2007). *Social economy in communities: An Asian view.* A paper presented at the 1st CIRIEC Conference on Social Economy, Victoria.

Kurimoto, A. (2013). *Mainstreaming the Asian co-operative studies?* A key-note lecture at the ICA AP Research Conference in Mysore.

Lyons, M. (2001). *Third sector.* Cows Nest: Allen & Unwin.

Madane, M. V. (1990). *Agricultural co-operatives in Japan.* ICA ROAP.

Muenkner, H. (Ed.), (2005). *100 years: Co-operative credit societies act, India 1904.* ICA AP.

Prabhu, P. V. (2004). *Third critical studies on co-operative legislation and policy reforms.* New Delhi: ICA ROAP.

Prestowitz, C. (2005). *Three billion new capitalist: The great shift of wealth and power to the east.* Basic Books.

Rhodes, R. (2012). *Empire and co-operation: How the British Empire used co-operatives in its development strategies 1900-1970.* Edinburgh: West Newington House.

Schak, D. C., & Hudson, W. (Eds.), (2003). *Civil society in Asia.* Hampshire: Ashgate.

Schwarz, F. J., & Pharr, S. J. (Eds.), (2003). *The state of civil society in Japan.* Cambridge: Cambridge University Press.

Taimuni, K. K. (2001). *Cooperatives in Asia.* Geneva: ILO.

3

Are there core cooperative principles required for cooperative economic success and sustainability?

Morris Altman

Dean & Chair Professor of Behavioural and Institutional Economics & Co-Operatives, School of Business, University of Dundee, Dundee, United Kingdom

3.1 Introduction

Are the ICA's (International Co-operative Alliance) principles and values (P&V) and those of the Rochdale cooperative little more than a matter of ideology? Or, do they signify practices that are necessary (representing necessary conditions) for cooperatives to be economically sustainable? It is important to note that the ICA is the peak organization amongst cooperatives internationally. And the Rochdale cooperative, a consumer cooperative, is considered to be representative of the modern cooperative movement, founded in 1844 in Rochdale, Lancashire, England. It is argued here that, overall, the ICA's P&V represent core P&V for the success of cooperative organizations, wherein a cooperative is a member-owned and democratic organization as opposed to an investor-owned and undemocratic hierarchical organization.

If the application of ICA P&V are necessary for the economic (and social) success of cooperatives, then a critical question is:

What degree of freedom do cooperatives have in shaping themselves differentially in terms of culture and history? It can be hypothesized that such degrees of freedom must lie outside of the domain of core P&V. It can also be hypothesized that there is some flexibility in the implementation of core P&V. But this flexibility can't negatively affect the effective implementation of core cooperative P&V, without which the edifice of the cooperative organizational form can be expected to collapse. Developing differentiation outside of the core can potentially enhance the cooperative advantage to the extent that this differentiation is consistent with the core P&V.

One requires both theory and evidence to examine how core and differentiating P&V affect the socio-economic viability of cooperatives.

19

Evidence-based modeling and principles are important. This chapter focuses on the modeling of the necessary conditions for cooperative success in terms of a given cooperative organization's economic sustainability in the context of the ICA's core cooperative P&V, and to examine the extent to which cooperative organizations can remain cooperatives whilst differentiating themselves in terms of local conditions with regards to operationalizing the cooperative. This raises the question of what is an Asian-style and Asian Pacific-style cooperative wherein the Asian Pacific region itself is highly differentiated in terms of local conditions. No one Asian Pacific country is the same and within each country there can be tremendous differentiation in local conditions.

A critical argument of this chapter is that there is a universality of P&V necessary for the success of cooperative organizations, be this cooperative in different parts of India and China, for example, or any other country or region in the world. Very much central to universal core cooperative P&V is member ownership and control and democratic governance.

3.2 Cooperative principles and values in context

It is important to note that the discussion of the relationship between cooperative P&V and cooperative success is empirically framed in the relative success of cooperatives internationally. For example (Altman, 2017a, 2017b; International Cooperative Alliance, 2019a; World Cooperative Monitor, 2019):

- Currently, there are about 3 million cooperatives and mutuals in the world.
- About 12% of the planet's population are members of a cooperative or mutual.
- Cooperatives and mutuals contribute 10% to global employment.

- Proper value-added estimates on the contribution of cooperatives and mutuals to gross domestic product are not available apart from Australia, Canada, and New Zealand, where they contribute about 8%, 4%, and 8% respectively (Altman, 2017a, 2017b; Karaphillis, Duguid, & Lake, 2015).

3.3 Cooperative principles and values: international cooperative alliance

A useful starting point for this chapter is a critical reflection of the ICA cooperative P&V (International Cooperative Alliance, 2019b). These are P&V that member organizations are supposed to adhere to both in theory and practice. Our modeling narrative links these P&V with cooperative success. Linking cooperative P&V to the operationalization of cooperatives is a weak point in cooperative organization literature. But the cooperative organizational form or business model is critiqued in mainstream economics literature, which tends to inform policy, as being fundamentally flawed and economically unsustainable because of the assumed cooperative P&V. An important point made in this chapter is that, on the contrary, it is the core P&V of the cooperative organizational form that provide cooperatives with a cooperative advantage including in the realm of economic efficiency, consumer loyalty, and equity. Indeed, as pointed out previously, cooperatives have been highly successful economic entities internationally, competing with the much more celebrated investor-owned firms. Investor-owned firms have no embedded commitment to their workers, consumers, clients, or communities. Apart from the idiosyncratic preferences of owners, the first order commitments are to profits, often irrespective of how these profits are realized. The below is derived from the ICA cooperative P&V (International Cooperative Alliance, 2019b).

3.4 What is a cooperative?

"A co-operative is an autonomous association of persons united voluntarily to meet their common economic, social, and cultural needs and aspirations through a jointly-owned and democratically-controlled enterprise."

Key to the definition of a cooperative is its voluntary, autonomous, and democratic nature. This clearly distinguishes it from the traditional investor-owned and state-owned enterprise. Therefore for example, an organization referring to itself as cooperative, but that is coercive and undemocratic can't be a cooperative.

3.5 Values

"Co-operatives are based on the values of **self-help**, **self-responsibility**, **democracy**, **equality**, **equity,** and **solidarity** [author's emphasis]. In the tradition of their founders, co-operative members believe in the ethical values of honesty, openness, social responsibility, and caring for others." [author's emphasis].

These values inform the ICA definition of what a cooperative is. It is argued (and modeled) here that there can't be a cooperative organization that does not fulfill the *basic conditions of democratic governance and voluntary solidarity*. Deviating from these conditions generates an organizational form that is *different substantively from a cooperative*. The more that a cooperative deviates from *democratic governance and voluntary solidarity*, the more the cooperative melds into an investor-type firm organization. It can be argued that this would also *undermine the competitive or, at least, the productivity advantage* of such a noncooperative organizational form. It would also undermine the potential cooperative on the market with regards to consumer preferences for products sold or produced by a cooperative. [author's emphasis].

3.6 Democracy

Democratic control by members refers to one person, one vote, active membership participation, and elected officials responsible to membership. This incorporates a certain degree of hierarchical leadership, but members have the last say on key decisions and are well informed of elected or appointed leadership decisions (transparency). Larger cooperatives and even smaller ones will have managers and boards of directors, for example, but the key to democratic governance is member control over who is elected, the electoral process, and members' ultimate control over the key decisions of their cooperative.

Democratic control of capital should be based on member contributions to a cooperative's capital (could be an equitable contribution). Ultimate control over the raising and allocation of capital rests with members of the cooperative.

The principle of democratic control by members is vital for members to have a voice, which yields solidarity, loyalty, a sense of fairness, and ownership of the decision-making process. These principles, when properly executed, can also translate into accountability and transparency in the decision-making process— decisions can't be hidden from members. This also limits moral hazard as well as overconfidence bias and loss aversion in decision-making. This relates also to how a given cooperative's decision-makers are incentivized.

As discussed below, member control of capital does not and need not translate into cooperatives not being able to raise capital outside of the cooperative organization.

Capital can be raised by borrowing from banks or by issuing financial paper on the market, but where the latter does not have any voting rights to nonmembers attached. This is an organizational possibility consistent with cooperative P&V.

3.7 Surpluses

Surplus can be used for a variety of purposes as determined by cooperative members. Only part of the surplus is usually distributed to members. Surpluses can be used to build up reserves or to invest in the cooperative and in the larger community. There is nothing stipulated in the rules pertinent to cooperative governance that states that surpluses can't be entirely invested to further develop or grow a given cooperative. Cooperatives, if successful, can generate surpluses, which can be reinvested in the cooperative organization. Such reinvestment of surpluses is consistent with cooperative principles. This reality is often denied by economic modelers of cooperatives, arguing that cooperatives end up dispersing surpluses to members, hence, being short of necessary surpluses to maintain or strengthen the cooperative organization.

Cooperatives can also sell shares and other financial paper on the market as long as these shares have no voting rights, hence, increasing the capacity of the cooperative to raise funds for investment purposes without reducing members' control of the cooperative.

3.8 Autonomy and independence

To maintain cooperatives as autonomous self-help organizations ultimately controlled by members, the terms by which cooperatives enter into agreements with other organizations, inclusive, private, or public organizations, or raise capital externally (as opposed to from members or surpluses) must ensure continued democratic control by members. Once again, we have the overriding significance of member control and, relatedly, democracy to the cooperative organizational form. This, in turn, contributes, to the cooperative advantage. The hypothesis here is that autonomy and independence by contributing to solidarity and fairness incentivizes increases in productivity, contributing to the cooperative advantage.

3.9 Education

Cooperative members, elected representatives, managers, and employees are supposed to be educated and trained so that they can contribute to the development of their cooperatives. Without cooperative education, members and members of the executive may not be aware of cooperative P&V and how these can be operationalized in a cooperative. In these cases, the cooperative might be run along the lines of an investor-owned firm. This would undermine the cooperative advantage.

Education also requires cooperators to understand how to run a sustainable cooperative business (which is different from a profit maximizing enterprise). What is often neglected in discussions about education, is the need to create a cadre of professional cooperative managers, consultants, analysts, and leaders. Hiring generic managers and board members will undermine the cooperative advantage and can even generate a leadership team that perceives cooperatives as being inherently inefficient, thereby incentivizing such leadership to attempt to demutualize the cooperative. Also being educated on what a cooperative is, is not sufficient to develop competitive and sustainable cooperatives. Political cronyism, for example, yielding the hiring of "good" cooperators over good managers can be the death knell of a cooperative.

Related to this, technical education is also critically important. One needs experts who not only understand the nuisances of cooperative P&V, but who also understand the rules of accounting as they pertain to cooperatives, legal parameters, the ins and outs of supply chain management, how to improve crop yields, and how to improve the quality of output in a cost-effective manner, for example.

There is significant overlap between the ICA P&V and those of the Rochdale cooperative, upon which the ICA has drawn heavily upon. Critical are the principles of member ownership and control and, relatedly, democratic governance (Rochdale Pioneers Museum, 2019).

3.10 Noncore differentiating attributes and the cooperative advantage

If the assumption that the ICA/Rochdale core P&V are key to cooperative success and their advantage is valid, then other attributes of a cooperative, which would differentiate it from other cooperatives, must be consistent and compatible with the core P&V. These differentiating factors might have historical, cultural, and religious roots, for example. It can be argued that the interventions listed here, for example, would serve to undermine the cooperative advantage as they violate member control and democratic governance:

- Reducing the democratic base
- Reducing voice
- Reducing member control over the co-op
- Increasing state control over the governance of the cooperative
- Reducing accountability
- Reducing transparency
- Disconnecting from community
- Sexism
- Racism

One might argue that any of these might be consistent with the history, culture, and social context of a particular country. Certain of these interventions might distinguish a non-Western country from a Western country, for example. But one should note that the term "Western" country is highly misleading as all Western countries differ from each other quite significantly and there are considerable social, cultural, and institutional differences even within western countries just as there are within non-Western countries (where the term non-Western is, for the same reason, a highly misleading generalization). One should also note that the absence of democratic governance,

limited voice, and limited organizational control by workers, consumers, or suppliers as well as gender inequity, for example, were all part of the cultural history of so-called Western countries (Crick, 2002; Nussbaum, 2000; Sen, 2000). The P&V of cooperative governance have evolved over time and were a product of social agitation and change. What some would label as western values are not "naturally" or inherently western. But what has evolved into the ICA/Rochdale P&V (very much related to democratic governance and member control), play a critical role in providing cooperatives with their cooperative advantage. There is, in other words, an opportunity cost in terms of income and wellbeing to cooperators and society when deviating from core cooperative values and principles, even if many of these might be embodied by western values (albeit these have been relatively recently evolved). On the significance of culture positively and negatively impacting economic development and economic sustainability see: Altman, 2001, 2003; Harrison, 1992; Jones, 2006; Nussbaum, 2000; Sen, 2000.

This point is illustrated in Diagram 3.1. All other things remaining the same, adhering to cooperative principles yields maximum productivity, given by a. All other things remaining the same, this minimizes unit production costs. The latter equals input costs divided by productivity. As productivity increases, unit costs fall. To the extent that deviating from core cooperative P&V reduce productivity, given by ab, this would have the effect of increasing unit costs. This also reduces the size of the economic pie produced by the cooperative. After point b, decreases in productivity are assumed to stabilize at a relatively low level. An argument can be made that if one wishes to operate a cooperative outside of the frame of cooperative P&V, productivity might be higher in a more transparent and honest investor-owned firm. But if the objective is to be a cooperative, productivity is enhanced by

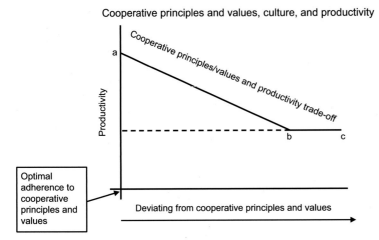

DIAGRAM 3.1   Cooperative principles and values, culture, and productivity.

moving up the ba trajectory through a greater adherence to cooperative P&V.

Other interventions, however, can contribute to social cohesion and solidarity amongst cooperative members. This, in turn, can contribute to enhancing a cooperative's economic efficiency and to the cooperative advantage on both the supply and demand side of the market. For example, countries and even states or provinces within regions can have different sets of laws to which a cooperative must adapt to if it is to be established and to become sustainable. Different countries face different challenges, which translates into different types of cooperatives and mutuals being relatively more dominant in different countries. In these cases, one size does not fit all. One might also have cooperatives that derive their inspiration from the cultural specificity of their country, region, or even neighborhood. A cooperative might even be dominated by individuals from the same religion or ethnic background. This can contribute to a sense of solidarity and trust within such cooperatives, even if they might appear to be exclusionary with regards to individuals from other backgrounds. But within such a cooperative, the cooperative can still adhere to the principles of member control and democratic governance.

It is useful to speak briefly about the role of gender issues and cooperatives. Equality across gender is a principle of cooperative organization. But different cultures treat women differently and, in many countries, after years of agitation and struggle, the extent of gender discrimination has dramatically diminished. It can be argued that gender discrimination not only violates an important ICA principle, but it also can be expected to have a negative effect on productivity, reducing the overall wellbeing of cooperative members and their communities. This point can be simply illustrated in the hypothetical case given here:

Let's assume that a cooperative prefers to hire men over females as a matter of principle. Other cooperatives might prefer not to employ women at all, and they are relegated to household work. Assume that the productivity of potential employees is normally distributed, and it is the same for men and women. This is illustrated in the bell shape curve in Diagram 3.2. This should be the case, on average, if men and women have similar access to education and training opportunities; if not, this can be corrected through policy. At the extreme right, one has the most productive workers and the on extreme left, the least productive. A nonsexist firm will employ the most productive

Sexism and productivity: a footnote

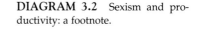

DIAGRAM 3.2 Sexism and productivity: a footnote.

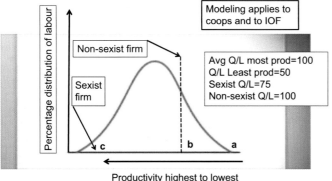

workers first, females and males alike. If the laboring population is split 50/50, then females and males will be hired 50/50 across the productivity spectrum. But a sexist firm will employ as many men as possible before hiring any women, even if the women are more productive. Hence, a sexist cooperative will be employing more of the relatively less productive individuals than a nonsexist cooperative. This would yield higher average productivity for the nonsexist firm, possibly also yielding lower unit costs and possibly higher levels of material wellbeing for members of a non-sexist cooperative. From a cooperative perspective, being nonsexist also has the advantage of building solidarity and trust that can further contribute to increases in productivity.

3.11 The cooperative advantage

3.11.1 Supply side

Given good governance in a cooperative or mutual, research suggests that one can expect a higher quality and quantity of effort inputs,

less turnover, smarter management, less free-riding, and greater incentives for applied technical change (Altman, 2002, 2006, 2009a, 2015; Ben-Ner & Jones, 1995; Bonin, Jones, & Putterman, 1993; Davis, 2004; Doucouliagos, 1995; Gordon, 1998; Lampel, Bhalla, & Jha, 2010; Sexton & Iskow, 1993). When members are in control of their organization and have a meaningful and effective voice, this creates the incentive to make decisions and behave in a manner that would positively affect productivity and negatively impact on costs. This is assumed away in the conventional economic model. The latter assumes that productivity is typically unaffected by the overall incentive environment. In particular, the quantity and quality of effort put into the production process is assumed to be fixed. In a behavioral economics framework, rooted in x-efficiency theory, effort is a function of the incentive environment. Therefore to the extent that cooperatives provide an improved incentive environment to member-owners and other stakeholders, one would expect that the quality and quantity of effort put into the production process will increase.

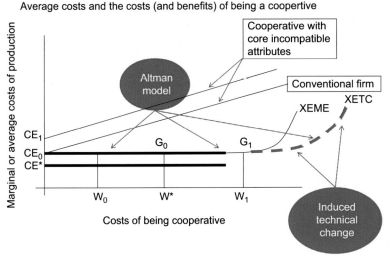

DIAGRAM 3.3   Average costs and the costs (and benefits) of being a coopertive.

In a simple model (this narrative and Diagram 3.3, is adopted from Altman, 2002, 2005, 2009b, 2012, 2015), from which one can generalize to more complex scenarios, average or unit cost is determined by the unit costs such as the wage rate and productivity, as per the equation:

$$AC = \frac{w}{\frac{Q}{L}}$$

Where average cost is given by AC, unit cost by w, and productivity by Q/L, where Q is real output and L is labor unit per unit of time. The cooperative advantage serves to incentivize increases in productivity and reduce cost (AC). One would expect that in an investor-owned firm or cooperatives that do not abide by cooperative principles, Q/L would be lower and, therefore, average cost would be higher, unless neutralized by a lower unit cost. The cooperative incentive environment can, at a minimum, offset (neutralize) the costs of being cooperative such as improved benefits to members and improved working conditions. Turnover could also be reduced, which would also have the effect of increasing productivity or reducing the unit cost. Basically, this means that even if cooperatives are more expensive to run, these

costs are offset by the increasing productivity through the cooperative advantage. The cooperative advantage could also serve to generate greater surpluses that could be used for investment purposes, when productivity increases are large enough. Overall, the total output can be expected to increase in a cooperative that abides by cooperative P&V. This can contribute to increasing surpluses to the cooperative. Additionally, the pressure to remain competitive as a cooperative whilst increasing member wellbeing, maintaining or improving product quality, and improving community wellbeing, incentivizes cooperators into being more innovative and engaging in more technological chances as compared to an investor-owned firm, all other things remaining the same.

Some of these arguments are illustrated in Diagram 3.3. From the perspective of the conventional economic model or narrative, a cooperative firm generates higher costs as per line segment CE_0. But given the more realistic assumptions underlying the behavioral model, there is no reason to expect unit costs to increase within a cooperative organizational framework as per line segment CE_0G_1, as increasing productivity offsets the possible increased costs of being cooperative. It might also be the case that the cooperative advantage would yield even lower average costs. This is reflected in line segment CE*. Eventually such increased costs can no longer be neutralized by increasing productivity as the cooperative hits the brick wall of eventual diminishing returns.

However, by being more innovative, a cooperative remains competitive even as it seeks to improve on member and community wellbeing. In this instance, as costs increase, so does productivity, this is the case even as a cooperative no longer has any flexibility to further increase the quantity of effort input. This is illustrated by the shift in the behavioral cost curve from XEME to XETC. But this would be the case only if the cooperative abides by cooperative P&V. Otherwise the cooperative's costs would be reflected in increasing average costs, just like the conventional economic model predicts, as per line segment CE_0. Indeed, it would be quite possible that a dysfunctional cooperative's average costs would be even higher, reflected in line segment CE_1.

3.11.2 Demand side

My research (and others) suggests that many consumers prefer to purchase from a cooperative, especially if the quality and price point of the cooperative product is at least the same as what is sold by an investor-owned firm (Altman, 2016). Research also suggests that many individuals are willing to pay a premium for cooperative products. Hence, the demand for cooperative products is less price sensitive (elastic) than for the products of investor-owned firms, at least on average.

This cooperative advantage is based on the perception that cooperatives or member-owned organizations are somehow better organizations worthy of consumer patronage and preferential treatment by consumers. An example of this would be paying a higher price for cooperative products because cooperatives are deemed to provide cooperative members and even nonmembers with higher levels of socioeconomic wellbeing. Also, for cooperative members such as in consumer cooperatives and mutuals the cooperative product is regarded to be a better match for the needs of its members since the cooperative, if adhering to cooperative P&V are driven by meeting member preferences and doing so in a cost-effective manner.

Borrowing from Paul Sweezy's (1939) early work on oligopolistic competition, one can illustrate some of these points using "kinky" demand curves (Diagram 3.4). In this case, any increase in price results in a lesser decrease in demand for co-op output compared to the demand for products produced by investor-owned firms. Any decrease in price leads to a greater increase in demand for co-op output compared to the demand for products produced by investor-owned firms. This is given by the kinky *co-op demand curve* in Diagram 3.4. The *IOF demand curve* is the demand curve for an investor-owned firm. Being identified as a cooperative protects a cooperative when charging higher prices, even when its products are identical to those produced by Investor owned firms (IOFs). This is given by the pivot of the cooperative demand curve from ab to ac— one has a more inelastic upper portion of the demand curve. Additionally, cooperatives have an advantage over IOFs when lowering their price for identical products. This advantage is increased if the cooperative output is better in terms of the consumers' preferred characteristics. This is given by the pivot of the cooperative demand curve from ad to ae—one has a more elastic lower portion of the demand curve.

This demand-side cooperative advantage is contingent upon the administrators and members of a cooperative believing that being a member-owned organization is actually beneficial from a marketing perspective and believing that consumers (including members) believe that purchasing from cooperatives

The cooperative advantage: demand side

DIAGRAM 3.4 The cooperative advantage: demand side.

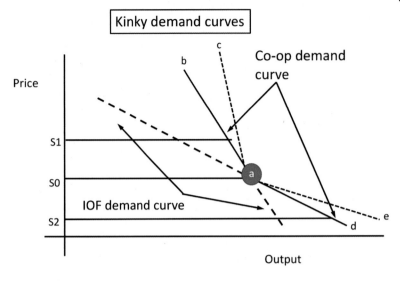

provides them with an increased sense of well-being (what some economists refer to as a warm glow) and/or a better product. If this set of beliefs is present and cooperatives market their cooperativeness, that is, that they are member-owned and what exactly this implies for potential consumers, then the demand-side cooperative advantage can be realized.

3.12 The long and the short run

A central differentiating characteristic of cooperatives or member-owned organizations, by their very nature, given their focus on membership value, broadly speaking, is their long-term orientation, as opposed to the short-term focus of many investor-owned firms. This is especially the case when such firms are listed on the stock market and where the decision-makers benefit from maximizing short run returns as a basis for their compensation packages.

Focusing on member benefits orients a cooperative to concentrating on the long-term sustainability of the organization and also, for this reason, mitigating risks and, therefore, paying attention to potential downsides of risky investments that might be characterized by high returns in the short run and by severe losses in the long run. This is especially the case when members are aware of the investment strategies and related risks proposed by decision-makers. The latter is most secure when a cooperative abides by the principles of transparency and meaningful consultation with members where members typically have a vested interested in maintaining the economic viability of their organization.

3.13 Incompatible attributes revisited

It can be hypothesized that cooperatives that violate the cooperative norms of accountability, transparency, and member control, which build upon the norms of democracy, will fail to be competitive, even if this appears to be compatible with local customs and social norms. One should note that when initially established, cooperatives were custom and norm breakers. The investor-owned firm organizational form was and remains the norm. Democracy in the workplace and member ownership of an organization remains an exception, albeit an important exception, to the rule.

More research is required in this area, but here is a vignette on the problems experienced by cooperatives in India to illustrate the importance of cooperative P&V for the sustainable performance of a member-owned organization.

3.14 Indian cooperatives

India should be no different than "Western countries" in terms of how a particular aspect of cooperative success is evaluated. One Indian scholar writes (Ghosh, 2007):

> The success of a cooperative should be judged in terms of the efficiency of its services and profitability of its operations as well as in terms of the degree of its achievement in promoting the social and economic well-being of its members including the weaker sections of society.

Fundamentally, if a cooperative is an economic failure, it survives at the cost of the larger society. Moreover, if it is an economic failure or relatively inefficient, it is highly unlikely that it can support and assist the communities within which it is embedded—it simply will not have the resources to do so. And, such support could be related to its customary and normative obligations to the wider community. Hence, inefficient and ineffective cooperatives can also result in failure in the cultural, ethnic, and normative spaces.

With regards to the success of specific Indian cooperatives, Ghosh (2007) finds:

> Cooperative sugar factories in Maharashtra and dairy cooperatives in Gujarat have achieved this success due to a dynamic interplay of a various

combination of factors. One of the factors which may be attributed to this success is the dynamic leadership of its members. The success of cooperatives also depends on the local initiative and spirit of cooperation, the leadership pattern and minimum intervention of the state.

The importance of quality leadership to the success of Indian cooperatives and the minimization of government interference (government policy that contravenes that expresses preference of cooperative members) is a point reiterated by other experts analyzing problems with Indian cooperatives (Das, Palai, & Das, 2006; Ghosh, 2007). But these factors would be identified as being of importance to successful investment-owned firms as well. However, cooperatives adhering to cooperative P&V are expected to increase the probability of good governance. But government policy, which can be affected by the relative power of cooperatives and more specifically peak cooperative organization, determines the extent to which government interferes with cooperative governance introducing top-down (from government to cooperative) decision-making.

Factors that are understood to have negatively impacted the development of cooperatives in India include (Das et al., 2006; Ghosh, 2007):

- Government intervention to the extent that a given cooperative becomes a quasi-state organization. This, in effect, limits the extent of member control over the cooperative.
- Inadequate information given to cooperative members, which limits the extent to which members can influence and control the decision-making process and reinforces top-down decision-making.
- Inadequate education, which limits the extent to which members can exercise effective voice within the cooperative, hence, limiting bottom-up decision-making and, thereby, member control.
- Poor management as a consequence of inadequate training of those responsible for

Cooperative principles

DIAGRAM   3.5   Cooperative principles.

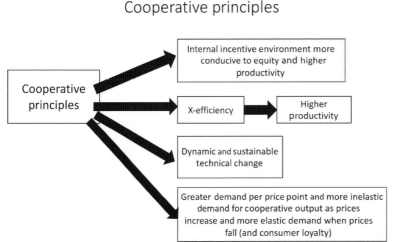

the day-to-day operations of the cooperative. This speaks to inadequate education, where properly educating cooperative personnel is one of the imperatives of cooperative P&V.

All of these factors speak to the importance of democratic governance in the economic (and social) sustainability of cooperatives.

The dynamic relationship that I argue for between core cooperative P&V and the supply and demand cooperative advantage is illustrated in Diagram 3.5. Given the assumptions made, abiding by these P&V serves to create an incentive environment conducive to higher productivity, which can translate into lower costs and/or improved benefits to cooperative members and their communities. An increasing productivity can take the form of increased x-efficiency or technological change (it can also take the form of product development). On the demand side, one has greater consumer loyalty, which provides cooperatives with significant advantages over investment-owned firms.

Diagram 3.6 further illustrates some of the points made with regards to the relationship between cooperative success, at least in terms of productivity, and core cooperative P&V.

And, what stands out as vital cooperative P&V are informed democratic governance and member control. It can be argued that cooperative performance is at its best when the cooperative adheres to cooperative P&V. This is given by the cooperative principles production possibility frontier (maximum output given the inputs). This performance is enhanced by the introduction of noncore attributes that are consistent with core P&V. This is given by the core compatible attributes curve, which lies above the cooperative production possibility frontier. This improved performance could be, for example, grounded in the domain of culture, which can increase solidarity and trust amongst cooperative members. This could also incorporate increasing solidarity and trust between general membership and the cooperative decision-makers, who might also be members. Both of these production possibility frontiers lie above that which represents the investor-owned firm. But if the cooperative breaks with core cooperative P&V, this shifts the production possibility frontier inward. And, it is possible that the cooperative would, in this case, be less productive than an efficiently managed investor-owned firm.

Noncore attributes and the production possibility frontier

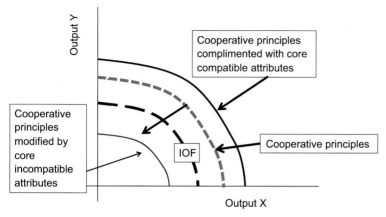

DIAGRAM 3.6 Noncore attributes and the production possibility frontier.

3.15 Conclusion

It is important to identify what core cooperative P&V are. These can be modeled in terms of their potential impact on productivity. Unlike with the conventional modeling of a firm, given reasonable assumptions, core P&V, but only if effectively implemented, can yield higher productivity and lower immediate costs on the supply side than investor-owned firms. This provides cooperatives with a competitive advantage on the supply side. Cooperative P&V impact the incentive environment of member-owned organizations, increasing efficiency and incentivizing technological change. They also incentivize and nudge decision-makers to focus on the long run interest of members as opposed to shorter run objectives, which are all too often the focus of investor-owned firms.

On the demand side, cooperative P&V also generate a competitive advantage yielding a lower price elasticity (sensitivity) of demand on the up side and high elasticity on the down side and a preference for cooperative products at a competitive price and quality. But this demand side cooperative advantage can only materialize if consumers are aware of which products are produced or sold by cooperative organizations. Moreover, cooperative decision-makers must understand that there is an

advantage in identifying their cooperative as a cooperative.

Deviating from core P&V can generate higher costs (or, at least, lower productivity) than in investor-owned firms . It can also generate a price elasticity of demand similar to that of investor-owned firms and a preference for non-co-op products. Choosing P&V that are specific to a culture, ethnicity, or religion, for example, that clash or contravene with cooperative P&V can be predicted to undermine the cooperative advantage. However, building upon cooperative P&V or supplementing these with cultural, ethnic, or religious attributes, for example, that are consistent with cooperative P&V can have positive supply and demand side effects on the cooperative. Upon this platform one can build approaches to being cooperative that can be enriched by national, regional, urban, village, cultural, and religious spaces within which a cooperative is being established and developed. But this enrichment need be of a bottom-up origin recognizing the multifaceted diversity and richness across these spaces.

References

Altman, M. (2001). Culture, human agency, and economic theory: Culture as a determinant of material welfare. *Journal of Socio-Economics, 30*, 379–391.

Altman, M. (2002). Economic theory, public policy and the challenge of innovative work practices. *Economic and Industrial Democracy: An International Journal*, 23, 271–290.

Altman, M. (2003). A review of 'The record of global economic development', by Eric L. Jones. *EH. NET BOOK REVIEW*, March.

Altman, M. (2005). Behavioral economics, rational inefficiencies, fuzzy sets, and public policy. *Journal of Economic Issues*, 34, 683–706.

Altman, M. (2006). Workers co-operatives as an alternative competitive organizational form. *Advances in the Economic Analysis of Participatory and Labor-Managed Firms*, 9, 213–235.

Altman, M. (2009a). History and theory of co-operatives. In H. Anheier, & S. Toepler (Eds.), *International encyclopedia of civil society*. New York: Springer.

Altman, M. (2009b). A behavioural-institutional model of endogenous growth and induced technical change. *Journal of Economic Issues*, 63, 685–713.

Altman, M. (2012). *Behavioural economics for dummies*. New York: Wiley.

Altman, M. (2015). Cooperative Organizations as an engine of equitable rural economic development. *Journal of Co-operative Organization and Management*, 3, 14–23.

Altman, M. (2016). Is there a co-operative advantage? Experimental evidence on the economic and non-economic determinants of demand. *Journal of Co-operative Organization and Management*, 4, 66–75.

Altman, M. (2017a). The importance of co-operatives to the New Zealand economy: constructing a cooperative economy. *International Journal of Social Economics*, 44, 2086–2096.

Altman, M. (2017b). *The size of Australia's co-operative and mutual sector*. Report commissioned by the Business Council of Co-operatives and Mutual, Australia. Available at: <https://bccm.coop/wp/wp-content/uploads/2017/11/5095-Newcastle-Brch.pdf>.

Ben-Ner, A., & Jones, D. (1995). Employee participation, ownership, and productivity: A theoretical framework. *Industrial Relations*, 34, 532–554.

Bonin, J. P., Jones, D. C., & Putterman, L. (1993). Theoretical and empirical studies of producer co-operatives: Will ever the Twain meet? *Journal of Economic Literature*, 31, 1290–1320.

Crick, B. (2002). *Democracy: A very short introduction*. Oxford/New York: Oxford University Press.

Das, B., Palai, N. K., & Das, K. (2006). *Problems and prospects of the cooperative movement in India under the globalization regime*. XIV International Economic History Congress, Helsinki, Session 72. Available at: <http://www.helsinki.fi/iehc2006/papers2/Das72.pdf>.

Davis, P. (2004). *Human resource management in co-operatives. Theory, process, and practice*. Geneva: ILO Cooperative Branch.

Doucouliagos, C. (1995). Worker participation and productivity in labor-managed and participatory capitalist firms: A meta-analysis. *Industrial & Labor Relations Review*, 49, 58–77.

Ghosh, A. K. (2007). Cooperative movement and rural development in India. *Social Change*, 37, 14–32.

Gordon, D. M. (1998). Conflict and cooperation: An empirical glimpse of the imperatives of efficiency and redistribution. In E. O. Wright (Ed.), *Recasting egalitarianism: New rules for communities, states and markets* (pp. 181–207). London/New York: Verso.

Harrison, L. E. (1992). *Who prospers? How cultural values shape economic and political success*. New York: Basic Books.

International Cooperative Alliance. (2019a). *Cooperatives: Facts and figures*. Available at: <https://www.ica.coop/en/cooperatives/facts-and-figures?_ga = 2.227061661.1627807247.1544099999-1292705627.1498045955>.

International Cooperative Alliance. (2019b). *Cooperative identity, values and principles*. Available at: <https://www.ica.coop/en/cooperatives/cooperative-identity>.

Jones, E. L. (2006). *Cultures merging: A historical and economic critique of culture*. Princeton, NJ: Princeton University Press.

Karaphillis, G., Duguid,, F., & Lake,, A. (2015). *The economic impact of co-operatives in Canada*. Measuring the Co-operative Difference Network. Available at: http://ec.msvu.ca:8080/xmlui/bitstream/handle/10587/1677/Infographic%20-%20%20Economic%20Impact%20ENG.pdf?sequence = 1&isAllowed = y.

Lampel, J., Bhalla, A., & Jha, P. (2010). *Model growth: Do employee-owned businesses deliver sustainable performance?* Employee Ownership Association. http://www.employeeownership.co.uk/publications/model-growth-do-employee-owned-businesses-deliver-sustainable-performance/. Accessed 15.03.14.

Nussbaum, M. (2000). *Women and human development: The capabilities approach*. New York: Cambridge University Press.

Rochdale Pioneers Museum. (2019). *Rochdale principles*. Available at: <http://www.rochdalepioneersmuseum.coop/about-us/the-rochdale-principles/>.

Sen, A. (2000). *Development as freedom*. New York: Anchor Books.

Sexton, R. J., & Iskow, J. (1993). What do we know about the economic efficiency of co-operatives: An evaluative survey. *Journal of Agricultural Cooperation*, 8, 15–27.

Sweezy, P. (1939). Demand under conditions of oligopoly. *Journal of Economic Theory*, 47, 568–573.

World Cooperative Monitor: Exploring the Cooperative Economy, Report 2018. (2019). Available at: <https://monitor.coop/sites/default/files/publication-files/wcm2018-web-803416144.pdf>.

Further reading

Global300 an ICA Initiative. (2011). *Global300 report 2010: The world's major co-operatives and mutual businesses.* International Co-operative Alliance. <http://ica.coop/ sites/default/files/attachments/Global300%20Report%202011.pdf> Accessed 15.03.14.

International Co-operative Alliance. (2008). *What is a co-operative?* Available at: <http://www.ica.coop/coop/index.html#difference>.

Leibenstein, H. (1966). Allocative efficiency vs. 'x-efficiency. *American Economic Review, 56*, 392–415.

Pérotin, V., & Robinson, A. (Eds.), (2004). *Employee participation, firm performance and survival, advances in the economic analysis of participatory and labor-managed firms* (Vol. 8). Amsterdam: Elsevier-North Holland.

4

Emerging Asian Pacific cooperative models from a global history perspective

Akira Kurimoto[1] *and Yashavantha Dongre*[2]
[1]Hosei University, Tokyo, Japan [2]University of Mysore, Mysore, India

4.1 Introduction

This chapter discusses how Asia Pacific cooperatives have evolved based on imported Western models and how some unique models have been created from a global history perspective. A large part of the Asian region has been colonized by Western powers since the 17th century. The British Empire dominated the Indian subcontinent, Malay Peninsula, and Hong Kong, while the French colonized Indochina and the Dutch ruled island-studded Indonesia. Spain, Portugal, and even the United States ran colonies in Asia. Sidney had been built as a colony of convicts from the late 18th century and Australia became one of the British Empire's dominions in 1901, while New Zealand became a dominion in 1907. As such, the Asia Pacific region was under the strong impact of Western colonialism in building political, economic, and social institutions and cooperatives could not escape from such an overriding influence, although they maintained cultural and religious traditions.

Asia Pacific cooperatives were created and evolved under a strong Western influence. They received strong impacts from founders of cooperative ideas; for example, Rochdale pioneers for consumer cooperatives, Danish/German farmers for agricultural cooperatives, and Raiffeisen, Schurze-Delitzsch, and Desjardin for credit cooperatives. They had evolved to the typical state-sponsored cooperative model even after independence, but some cooperatives created unique cooperative models by their own efforts and learning from other cooperatives.

This chapter will shed light on the origin and evolution of Asia Pacific cooperatives from what is called a global history perspective. It is a new trend of historiography that has been developed since the 1980s partly reflecting the globalized political economy, society, and culture. It is challenging the orthodoxy of methodological nationalism and Eurocentrism, seeking a holistic interpretation of histories while taking international connectedness through colonialization, migration, trade, and exchange of ideas/experiences into consideration. It is especially relevant when Asia is resurging in the "Great Convergence" by which Richard Baldwin described the impact of the IT-led globalization of the 1990s after the "Great Divergence" by which Kenneth Pomeranz explained the European supremacy over Asia since the 1820s.

35

Here the dynamics of the integration, differences, conversion, and diversion of cooperative models is discussed. The research question is "How have Asia Pacific cooperatives evolved from imported Western models to create the unique Asia Pacific models?"

4.2 Origin of Asia Pacific cooperatives in the late 19th and early 20th century

We can trace many examples of indigenous cooperation that existed before the industrial revolution. Münkner called them "autochthonous forms of self-help organizations" based on local value systems and norms of behavior without planned influence from outside, the most common forms of which are rotating savings and credit associations and communal work groups (Münkner, 1994). For example, in Japan, *Koh* as a rotating credit society was organized to finance new businesses or insure against risks, while *Yui* as communal work groups on occasions of crop sowing/harvesting or thatching were an indispensable institution in the rural economy. However, modern cooperation was introduced from western Europe through immigrants, national governments, or colonial powers.

In Australia and New Zealand, Robert Owen's utopian methods were tried among emancipated convicts as early as the 1820s, and a variety of production and retail cooperatives was set up by the 1830s when free immigrants began to arrive. Then, friendly societies took root to provide mutual insurance, while building societies also flourished to help home ownership. By the 1890s agricultural co-ops began to develop and became major businesses in the export-led economy, although they were inhibited by a growing involvement of the state during the interwar period (Birchall, 1997, pp. 162–163). As such, cooperatives were founded to follow the model of the home country in the British dominions.

In most parts of Asia colonized by Western powers, cooperatives were transplanted under colonial rule. In India, colonial officials identified farmer's indebtedness as the main problem holding back rural development and cooperatives were introduced to check this enslavement to moneylenders. In the 1890s, Sir Frederick Nicholson was seconded to study the Raiffeisen system in Europe and his report of 1897 led to the enactment of the Cooperative Credit Societies Act of 1904 supporting Raiffeisen-style agricultural credit co-ops. It was very much a top-down approach based on an imported theoretical concept without practical experience with this form of organization. Because there was no indigenous support for the cooperative idea, it had to be promoted by a specialized government agency headed by a registrar with supreme power. In 1912 a second act extended to all types of co-ops, introducing limited liability and allowing for the formation of federations. Urban credit societies began to grow, attracting salaried public servants and small traders, while consumer co-ops began to make some progress in the towns, but were weakened by too much credit being given. Because of resistance from established buyers, agricultural marketing co-ops could not easily become established except for new areas of sugar refining and milk products. The classic "British-Indian Pattern of Co-operation" (BIPC) spread throughout the British colonies and became the prototype of cooperative legislation in developing countries (Pakistan, Bangladesh, and Myanmar in 1904, Sri Lanka in 1911, and Malaysia in 1920). The BIPC served as the basis of the Co-operative Model Law of 1946, recommended by the British Colonial Office to all governments of British dependencies. It is still applied in many former British dependencies in Asia, Africa, and Pacific and Caribbean island states (Münkner, 2013).

Japan escaped from colonization due to a number of contingencies in the late 19th century when it was forced to abandon the closed-door policy after 300 years, but started creating a modern nation state through introducing Western ideas and technologies. The marketing societies of silk and tea as major export items of the time had been operating since the late 1870s, while the first consumer co-ops were founded modeling the Rochdale Pioneers Society in 1879. Industrialization began at the end of the century with state promotion of heavy industry, while worker societies began to open cooperative stores. Because Japan had built its legal system based on imperial sovereignty after Prussian legislation, the German legal advisors to the government such as Paul Mayet and Udo Eggert suggested creating Raiffeisen-style cooperatives. In 1891 Yajiro Shinagawa, the then Interior Minister, and Tosuke Hirata, the then Legislation Bureau officer, who had both visited Germany to study the legal system, submitted the draft of the Credit Society Law, but it was not enacted due to political reasons. They finally succeeded in getting the Industrial Co-operative Act passed in 1900 influenced by the German Industrial and Economic Societies Act of 1889. This Act had paternalistic elements, reflecting the bureaucrat's top-down approach. Cooperatives had been placed under strong government control. The governor could give permission for the establishment of cooperatives, order reporting at any time, make inspections, reverse the resolutions of general assemblies, order the re-election of office bearers, and even suspend or dissolve them. Therefore the Act had many common features with the Indian Cooperative Credit Societies Act of 1904, although it did not provide for the direct injection of share capital and management by the state. The Act regulated all types of cooperatives for credit, marketing, supply, and production (later replaced by service) (Kurimoto, 2017, pp. 671–672).

4.3 Evolution of Asia Pacific cooperative models after the Second World War

4.3.1 Inheriting colonial patterns of cooperatives after independence

The highly authoritarian approach by cooperative registrars or ministers was inherited by the newly independent governments, which promoted cooperatives as engines for national economic development. Since most Asian countries' economy had been based on agriculture before they took off with industrialization, agricultural co-ops were promoted as a way of modernizing rural economies. Birchall distinguished two phases in development (Birchall, 1997). The first, lasting until around 1960, was characterized by a top-down, "blue-print" based approach, with a new cooperative sector being organized by the state. In China, multipurpose village co-ops achieved considerable success in the early 1950s, until they were turned into People's Communes by the decree, which led to a catastrophic famine. In India, Prime Minister Nehru urged co-ops to act as engines for economic development proving a tremendous boost after independence in 1947; governments decided to promote all forms of cooperatives, contributing share capital, dispatching government officers as CEOs, and setting up powerful development agencies. In Malaysia, agricultural, nonagricultural, and fishery co-ops were sponsored and controlled by different authorities. In Iran, multipurpose agricultural co-ops were set up and supervised by a central body with direct assistance from the government. The second phase from the 1960s onward was accompanied by a change of emphasis. Against a background of economic growth and rapid urbanization in some countries, cooperatives were expected to become a major tool of rural development. To enable them to fulfill this ambitious role, widespread amalgamations between co-ops were brought about by government decree and/or state subsidies. In India, there were voluntary amalgamations and mergers of primary co-ops, helped by state subsidies, while in Sri Lanka, Indonesia, and Bangladesh, mergers were brought about by government decree. There was a gradual emergence of integrated cooperative structures; notably in the dairy (Amul) and sugar sectors in India. Supply co-ops also started the business of manufacturing/marketing fertilizers, which led to the Indian Farmers Fertiliser Cooperative Limited (IFFCO).

Even though cooperatives evolved in almost all Asian countries due to European influence, a lot of local factors, local leaders, and even local ideologies have contributed to shaping their development. Interestingly, leaders of different political backgrounds have shaped cooperatives in Asian countries at different points in time. While colonial rulers promoted cooperatives as a measure of mitigating poverty and releasing rural households from the clutches of moneylenders, there was also a feeling among a lot of local leaders that cooperatives in the form and manner of their establishment were pro-colonial and, hence, indigenous. Therefore they tried to promote different forms of cooperatives. "The cooperative movement was frequently divided into factions by colonialism and nationalism" (Yamao, 1993). For instance, nationalist leaders like Gandhi and his guru Gokale were more in favor of a self-reliant cooperative movement. After independence, the socialist ideals of Jawaharlal Nehru, who wanted to shape the Indian economy through centralized planning motivated by the Soviet Union model, continued to promote state sponsored and supported cooperatives. This was in stark opposition to the Gram Swaraj (self-reliant village) model advocated by Gandhi who spearheaded the freedom movement. For Gandhi, cooperatives were important as a tool of self-sufficiency and self-reliance for farmers. But the sudden death of Gandhi, in 1948, pushed his ideas to the backseat and the Nehruvian idea came to the fore. Nehru "had visualized certain postulates on the basis of which cooperatives were to be organized and their functioning to be carried out" with state support and direction. After 1965, when cooperation was formally declared as an activity under state list and every state came out with its own cooperative enactment, cooperatives became a political instrument in the hands of the ruling parties. Thus started a process of states nominating members to the boards and indirectly controlling the day-to-

day operations of cooperatives. Cooperatives became a battleground for political parties. Every time there was a change in the party that came to power at the state level, there would be a reversal of some policies and an introduction of new ones. This finally compelled the national government to initiate the process of the Constitutional Amendment in 2012 to virtually impose an element of uniformity in the cooperative model based on independence and autonomy throughout the country, but its implementation has been hampered by legislators in some states.

Similarly, in Indonesia, a nationalist party also expanded its own setup of cooperatives, opposing the cooperatives regulated by the Dutch colonial authority (Yamao, 1993). After the great depression around 1932, Thailand witnessed a revolution, and the reform era started. This was also the time that the cooperative movement picked up momentum. Even though the first cooperative in Thailand was started in 1915 during the period of monarchy, the actual spread of cooperatives of all forms started after the revolution. It is held that "during the height of the Great Depression, the Siamese Revolution of 1932 came; it abolished the system of absolute monarchy. Shortly after, a young revolutionary leader—Pridi Banomyong—had an idea: He was to restructure the entire governmental apparatus and turned it into a loose network of co-ops throughout the country" (CODI, 2013). But beginning from the 1950s, the Thai cooperative movement also became a state directed movement with large focus on agricultural and credit cooperatives. Not just democratic governments, but even dictatorial regimes have encouraged as well as influenced the modeling of cooperatives in some Asian countries.

The top-down patterns of development have persisted in many places. In the Philippines, the military government of President Marcos launched an agrarian reform program in which pre-cooperatives (samahang nayons—barrio associations) should have played a major role in 1973, but it finally failed because of top-down planning without the participation of the target groups. In Indonesia, a village development program was launched by government including a cooperative type village enterprise—Koperasi Unit Desai (KUD)—in each village from 1973, but this program also largely failed. In South Korea, President Park initiated the Saemaul (New village) movement in 1970 aimed at modernizing rural life through diligence, self-help, and cooperation, which led to the creation of Saemaul Bank. In many Asian countries, federal bodies were created with their leaders being nominated by governments. In this process emerged some powerful apex organizations that have often functioned as government agencies embracing all types of cooperatives.

4.3.2 Changing environment affecting Asia Pacific cooperatives

4.3.2.1 Economic change: From backward agrarian economy to growth center

A large part of Asia had been colonized by Western powers from the 19th century through to the mid-20th century. The latter's "divide and rule" policy had lasting impacts on the formation of nation states and economic development. Asia has been split by competing ideologies, which brought about both Cold and Hot Wars after the Second World War. Thus it was not realistic to talk about regional integration until recently.

As a matter of fact, the Asian economy had been based on primary industries where farmers were doomed to live with low productivities in populous areas compared with limited farmland. First, Japan accomplished the industrial revolution in the late 19th century and rose to challenge Western powers. Although heavily damaged during World War II, it was revived to become a major economic power

through export-driven industrialization under strong government guidance. The Four Dragons (later labeled NIES) followed Japan's lead in the 1960s. Then ASEAN member countries took-off, transforming battlefields into markets and shifting from import-substitution to export-driven industrialization. Since the 1990s, we have witnessed hyper-economic expansion in China, India, and Vietnam. Such successful development was often described as a flying geese pattern. It should be noted, however, that most of these "economic miracles" have taken place under authoritarian governments, which have played pivotal developmental roles.

In 1997—98 many Asian economies faced the serious contagion of financial crisis starting from the crash of the Thai Baht, which resulted in 3- to 10-fold unemployment in those affected countries. The ensuing economic crisis led to an upheaval that brought about the fall of the Suharto government and forced Thailand, South Korea, and Indonesia to turn to the IMF. But those countries recovered in a few years after implementing emergency relief programs and ruthless austerity policies, while Malaysia rehabilitated its economy without swallowing the IMF's prescriptions.

Asia is now seen to be the most vibrant growth center of the 21st century. Further expansion will no doubt face several bottlenecks including limited resources and energy, environmental degradation, uncertain political stability, and expanding gaps in people's incomes, but the region seems to have enormous potential as an engine of the world's economy. Ex-Reagan administration trade official Prestowitz forecasts that China and India will become economic superpowers in 10—20 years focusing on trade and industrial policies, while the United States will face economic decline under globalization with crushing trade and budget deficits, a zero savings rate, failing schools, dwindling investments in scientific training and research, a collapsing dollar, and a debt-dependent economy (Prestowitz, 2005). But such a power shift to the East will pose a challenge to the whole world if the global imbalance is not solved.

4.3.2.2 Political change: from authoritarian rule to more democratic governance

In Asia, populous farmers have been ruled by a few elites composed of royal families, bureaucrats, or military generals. But economic growth resulted in the emergence and expansion of the working and middle classes. They expressed dissent to the "developmental dictatorship" often associated with military intervention in politics and urged a shift to more democratic governance. They pursued political reforms through parliaments in some countries or mobilized demonstrations in the streets in others and succeeded in changing the political leaders in the late 1980s. For instance, the Peoples Power revolution ousted the dictator Marcos from the Philippines. The persistent protest movement of workers and students led to the democratization of South Korea where the ex-presidents were deprived of power and even imprisoned. In these processes, traditional and new social movements played important roles. Therefore newly elected political leaders portrayed themselves as coming from the people's movement.

The reality, however, cannot support the assumption that economic growth and the growing middle class will automatically lead to democratic governance. There exist gaps among new and old movements, competing sectionalism, and paternalism within organizations as witnessed in Thailand. Popular movements have not been organized nor coordinated to promote more comprehensive political reforms and the democratization of the society at large). Another problem is the tradition of state corporatism; administrations have pursued the destruction or exclusion of the independent labor movements while they supported pro-government trade unions. Such a shift from exclusion to inclusion can be observed in Taiwan, Singapore, and other nations where states allowed partnering unions to enjoy a variety of privileges including social insurance systems for workers, while they often deny the freedom of associations and human rights.

Politically, the end of the Cold War and globalization seem to be depriving the legitimacy of authoritarian rule, but there still exists stringent control over popular movements in China, while planned economies are giving way to a kind of market economy, which would invalidate all-inclusive protection and regulation of social and economic life. The emerging civic organizations at the grassroots level are not without conflicts with the state apparatus, but authorities are reluctantly encouraging the media to support their anticorruption campaigns and they are admitting that there is a slow transformation of hitherto party-controlled mass organizations into relatively independent ones (Hasan & Lyons, 2004, pp. 1−2).

Therefore it is premature to envision a clear-cut linear perspective toward liberal democracy in Asia. We are still facing a mixed situation; there have been backlashes by military coups, setbacks by political disputes, and takeovers by fundamentalists.

4.3.2.3 Societal change: from traditional society to emerging civil society

The most visible dimension of social changes caused by rapid industrialization has been the unprecedented demographic shift from rural areas to large cities, resulting in a concentration of population and economic activities. This has often been accompanied by the formation of large-scale slums at the outskirt of capitals, while a large part of the depopulating rural areas is deprived of infrastructure to support basic human needs. Therefore there is a growing gap in the provision of social services, especially in deprived areas and abandoned villages. Through this process, the historic extended family has been giving way to the nuclear family, which makes the domestic care of weaker members (infant, handicapped, or elderly) more difficult. Hence communities and families are weakening their traditional ties, while government social safety nets are yet to be installed.

Another dimension of the social changes taking place is the growing capacity and role of women. In traditional societies, women have been subordinating to men in every aspect of life. They had no access to education, training, or property. They were assigned specific roles within families and not allowed to make decisions about their own destiny. Such traditions were socially embedded and often justified as conforming to Confucian or other traditional norms. However, the growing middle class families have allowed more girls to have higher education pursuing careers. Now, female workers are becoming indispensable in the workforce in more and more branches of industry. Many women wish to continue working, but often clash with the traditional way of thinking based on the gender division of labor urging women to stay at home to take care of their families while depending on their husbands' earnings. We are witnessing an increasing number of female leaders in newly created organizations, but the established ones are still dominated by male leaders and managers.

So-called "Asian values" are also being challenged. This was a concept that came into vogue in the 1990s, often advocated by politicians, predicated on the belief in the existence of a unique set of institutions and political ideologies, which reflected the region's culture and history. They typically encompass some flavor of Confucianism, in particular, loyalty toward the family, corporation, and nation, the forgoing of personal freedom for the sake of society's stability and prosperity, and a work ethic and thrift. Their proponents, who tend to support Asian-style authoritarian governments, claim they are more appropriate for the region than the democratic values and institutions of the West.

This concept began to lose currency after the Asian financial crisis; it was criticized as contributing to crony capitalism. With the major social and cultural transformation underway in the past few decades, there is a growing consensus that there should be a universally accepted values system.

Socio-economic globalization and the Internet have accelerated these changes. The middle class, equipped with information beyond boundaries, have recognized problems, which were hitherto not addressed, and started using their voices to change these situations. We have witnessed the proliferation of civic initiatives in many parts of Asia.

Policy makers, at the same time, are affected by the discourse on restructuring welfare states as in Western societies. The governments in many Asian countries are generally reluctant to increase public expenditures for social security and tend to resort to private service provisions. This is the reason why governments in Singapore and Hong Kong are encouraging voluntary organizations and a viable third sector to deliver social services while cautioning not to slip into welfare states (Osawa, 2004).

Australia also witnessed a change from white Australia policy to multiculturalism since 1973 when the United Kingdom joined the European Community. Economic and political ties with Asian nations have been deepened in the framework of the Asia Pacific Economic Cooperation (APEC) since 1989, although a remnant of white nationalism still exists. New Zealand is a multiethnic nation with rapidly growing Asian immigrants (12%), while Caucasians and Maori occupy 74% and 15% respectively.

4.3.3 Asia Pacific cooperatives responding to the impact of globalization

Globalization has had unprecedented impacts on agricultural co-ops since the late 1980s. They have been placed under pressure from lowering trade barriers and increased competition from foreign food imports. They have been exposed to competition in domestic markets as well and lost their monopoly or dominant positions through a series of deregulation measures. They have faced structural adjustment policies urging the withdrawal of public subsidies and preferential treatment, although governments did not necessarily give up control of co-ops. Multipurpose co-ops operating supply/marketing and financial businesses had been the dominant form of agricultural co-ops in Japan, South Korea, and Taiwan. They were praised as being cooperative communities that have provided a wide range of services to help the economy and daily lives of farmers (Laidlaw, 1980), while they are experiencing the impact of globalization and deregulation. The financial and supply/marketing functions were separated into holding companies in South Korea, while Japan Agriculture Co-ops (JAs) are urged to increase competitiveness in the marketing/supply function while streamlining their financial function. However, some JAs succeeded in bringing about innovations mobilizing member's patronage.

Consumer co-ops were also affected by globalization. This sector has been characterized by small size, weak member participation, shortage of capital, lack of managerial capacity, and ineffective federative system. The shift from a heavily regulated market to a competitive market has brought both threats and opportunities; Indian consumer co-ops have faced stiff competition after losing their monopoly in trading basic commodities, while some co-ops could thrive attracting wider consumer support. In some ASEAN countries, powerful consumer co-ops in capital cities are lost in domestic and foreign competition, while co-ops have survived or even grown in the competitive market in some countries (Japan, South Korea, Singapore, and Vietnam). Japanese consumer co-ops have evolved from housewives' buying clubs for buying safe milk in the 1960s to growing into the largest co-ops in the world in the 1990s.

Consumer co-ops have also grown, mobilizing housewives since the 1990s in South Korea. In these cases, they have made bottom-up development despite an adversarial legal environment. On the other hand, FairPrice Co-op established itself as the dominant retailer in Singapore during the past few decades and has helped Saigon Co-op to develop a major supermarket chain since 2000. In these cases, they could enjoy favorable treatment by governments. In the financial sector, cooperative banks and credit unions in many countries provide financial services to members ranging from micro credit at the grassroots level to full-fledged banking services through regional and national networks. In particular, credit unions and saving co-ops provide invaluable services to those who are excluded from finance. Workers' co-ops are quite new, but they are taking root to create jobs and incomes in some counties.

To cope with such situations and to facilitate the necessary changes in the cooperative legislation and public policy, the ICA Asia and Pacific has convened the biennial Asia Pacific Cooperative Ministers Conferences (APCMC) since 1990, while the ICA's Statement of Co-operative Identity introduced a new 4th Principle of Autonomy and Independence in 1995. In tandem with the ICA Statement, the UN's Co-operative Guidelines in 2001 and ILO's Recommendation 193 on the Promotion of Co-operatives in 2002 set out guidelines for government policies to promote cooperative autonomy and forge equal partnerships between governments and cooperatives. But state withdrawal from control is occurring at different speeds in different places. The ICA's critical studies on cooperative legislation and policy reforms revealed that the progress in implementing the APCMC resolutions was rather slow and needed to gather momentum in many countries, while governments' control over co-ops is still prevalent in some countries, placing them in a disadvantageous position in comparison with the private sector (Prabhu, 2004).

1. Analytical framework of Asian cooperative models

4.4 Changing mode of exchange: from unilateral assistance to mutual learning

Asia and Pacific cooperatives have been given the development assistance by the UN agencies and the Western donors after the Second World War. The ILO has provided training manuals and seminars to promote cooperative development. The Food and Agriculture Organization (FAO) has organized seminars and training courses for rural development, while United Nations Educational, Scientific and Cultural Organization (UNESCO) has given opportunities to cooperative leaders to learn from advanced countries. Cooperative development agencies in Western countries have also provided development assistance to transfer their experience and knowledge. The Swedish Co-operative Center (SCC) played a pivotal role in setting up the ICA Regional Office and Education Center for South-East Asia in 1960 in New Delhi (renamed the ICA Asia Pacific or ICA-AP in 1990). The Canadian Co-operative Association (CCA) and the Development International Desjardins (DID) have also provided assistance to cooperatives in Anglophone and Francophone countries since the 1970s. Today these UN agencies and donor organizations concentrate on the least developed countries in Africa, realizing that cooperatives in the Asia Pacific region have got the capacities to extend development cooperation.

Cooperatives in some advanced Asian countries also extended development cooperation to their Asian counterparts using the Official Development Assistance (ODA) money and their own resources. The Institute for the Development of Agricultural Cooperation in Asia (IDACA) was founded in 1963 by the Central Union of Agricultural Co-operatives (JA Zenchu), with funds raised among Japanese agricultural cooperatives and with the support of the Government (JICA, etc.). It has trained more than 6000 overseas agricultural cooperators and government officers in half a century as part of its international cooperation projects. On the other hand, the Japanese Consumer Co-operative Union (JCCU) started development cooperation using its own funds in 1987, and conducted regional and bilateral projects to promote consumer co-ops and gender sensitization programs. The National Federation of University Co-operative Associations (NFUCA) and the Japanese Health and Welfare Co-operative Union (HeW Co-op Japan) also carried out development cooperation to promote university co-ops and health co-ops. Zenrosai (Japan) and the NTUC Income (Singapore) collaborated in a project to promote union-based insurance co-ops in the 1980s. The National Agricultural Co-operative Federation (NACF, South Korea) and the Indian Farmers Fertilizer Co-operative Limited (IFFCO) started development cooperation in 2000.

These endeavors represent development cooperation based on peer-to-peer collaboration rather than technical assistance for development. They have promoted the mutual learning of advanced experiences among Asian cooperatives. Since cooperatives in the region are operating in quite different contexts, there is no "one size fits all" solution, but they can pick up elements that they think may be relevant to them. For instance, the multipurpose agricultural co-op model has been adopted in some Asian co-ops, while *Han* groups in Japanese co-ops are emulated in South Korea and India. FairPrice Co-op's expertise in running supermarkets was closely studied by Saigon Co-op. In such a way, cooperatives in the Asia Pacific region could develop their own cooperative businesses through mutual learning.

4.5 Conclusion

This chapter begins with a description of how Asia and Pacific cooperatives started under the influence of Western countries through immigration, colonization, and importing ideas.

1. Analytical framework of Asian cooperative models

They had been evolving under stringent state control in most parts of the region, characterized as BIPCs. Such a top-down approach was inherited and even fortified after independence since national leaders have seen cooperatives as an engine of economic development. However, globalization urged the state to change roles from controlling cooperative development to facilitating it. Therefore the APCMC has been held every other year since 1990, but the progress is slow. The top-down pattern is still dominant in many parts of the region, while the emergence of bottom-up cooperatives can be observed in some places to be further explained in this volume. Now, it is important to identify successful Asian and Pacific co-op models and analyze them from a multidisciplinary perspective.

Are the Asian and Pacific co-op models converging with or diverging from the dominant Western models? This question has been discussed comparing Japanese consumer co-ops with their European counterparts (Kurimoto, 2005). The new economy characterized by globalization and IT urges all organizations to concentrate on core businesses, accomplish the economy of scale, and cope with governance and management problems on the resultant large scale. These requirements also apply to both European and Japanese co-ops operating in a highly competitive environment. On the other hand, member relations, employee's roles, community involvement, and social dimensions are areas where both models seem to be diverging. The changing institutional framework may drive Japanese co-ops into convergence in some areas such as governance and structure, but they are likely to maintain their distinctiveness while adapting their business to meet changing needs. This tentative conclusion will be just as valid for Asian Pacific cooperative models.

What is the implication of Asian and Pacific co-op models in this and other regions? First,

these cases can be emulated by cooperatives in the region adapting to the local environment. It is important for cooperative leaders and government officers to understand why they need to radically change their way of thinking so that cooperatives can develop on their own. Second, successful Asia and Pacific cases can be studied and carefully emulated in other regions, for instance, in Africa. Some elements can be learnt from Western cooperatives as happened in Canada where manuals were made to learn about the Japanese *Han* as neighborhood member groups.

The promotion of cooperatives by governments became a common feature in most Asian and Pacific countries. Barring Australia and New Zealand, every other country of notable size, both colonized and noncolonized countries have experienced this trend. The most visible trend is the interest of governments in agricultural cooperatives. Irrespective of the status (underdeveloped, developing, or developed) and dominant ideology (centrally planned, free market, or mixed) of a country, governments have supported and controlled agricultural cooperatives. Certain subsegments of the cooperative sector such as cooperative banks and consumer and workers' cooperatives remain relatively independent in most countries including even countries like India where cooperatives are generally seen to be a government department. When we look at the contemporary scenario it appears that the status of the economy and the nature of the market has started impacting on the cooperative sector in the region. As the economy becomes stronger and the market opens up, there is both scope for cooperatives to become independent and a compulsion from the government to let cooperatives have a larger autonomous space. So, the Asian cooperative sector is slowly but clearly moving away from the clutches of state control and emerging as autonomous entities. But this depends on the changing attitudes of both the state and the sector in waking the potential of cooperatives.

References

Birchall, J. (1997). *The international co-operative movement.* Manchester University Press.

CODI, *From Co-ops to CODI: A Glimpse of Thailand's Hidden Legacy.* The Community Organizations Development Institute, Bangkok, 2013.

Hasan, S., & Lyons, M. (Eds.), (2004). *Social capital in Asian sustainable development management.* New York: Nova Science Publishers, Inc.

Kurimoto, A. (2005). *The institutional change and consumer co-operation: Japanese vs European models. Consumerism versus capitalism?* Amsab-Institute of Social History.

Kurimoto, A. (2017). *Building consumer democracy: The trajectory of consumer co-operation in Japan. A global history of consumer co-operation since 1850.* Brill.

Laidlaw, A. F. (1980). *Co-operatives in the year 2000.* London: The International Co-operative Alliance.

Münkner, H. (1994). *Pre-co-operative forms of cooperation. International Handbook of Co-operative Organizations.* Vanderhoeck & Roprecht.

Münkner, H. (2013). Worldwide regulation of co-operative societies: An overview. *EURICSE Working Paper* 53/2013.

Osawa, M. (Ed.), (2004). *Ajia Shokoku no Fukushi Senryaku (Welfare strategies in Asian nations).* Minerva Shobo.

Prabhu, P. V. (2004). *Third critical studies on co-operative legislation and policy reforms.* ICA ROAP.

Prestowitz, C. (2005). *Three billion new capitalist: The great shift of wealth and power to the East.* Basic Books.

Yamao, M. (1993). Political economy of agricultural co-operatives in South East Asia. *South Pacific Study, 14*(1).

Further reading

Conrad, S. (2016). *What is global history?* Princeton University Press.

Kurimoto, A. (2018). Japanese co-operative legislation: Its characteristics and recent legal reform's impact. *International Journal of Co-operative Law, 1.*

Münkner, H. ed. (2005). *100 years Co-operative Credit Society Act, India 1904.* ICA A-P.

Rhodes, R. (2012). *Empire and co-operation.* Edinburgh: West Newington House.

Zamagni, V. (2017). *A worldwide historical perspective on co-operatives and their evolution. The oxford handbook of mutual, co-operative and co-owned business.* Oxford University Press.

Asian cooperatives and public policy
Approach, process, and prospect

Robby Tulus

Regional Director (Emeritus) for Asia Pacific, International Co-operative Alliance (ICA). Founder and Chief Advisor, Federation of People-based Co-operative Enterprises (INKUR Federation), Indonesia, and Credit Union Central Organization (CUCO), Indonesia

5.1 Introduction

This chapter[1] seeks to examine the challenges encountered by Asian cooperatives in the realm of public policy approaches, processes, and prospects. In the first place, public policy approaches cannot be oversimplified owing to the fact that the Asia region is so widespread and diverse. The cooperative movements in the region are, as a consequence, widespread and vastly heterogenous as well,[2] therefore approaches in public policy must remain relevant to each specific movement. Therefore public policy must be approached in a well-diversified and coherent fashion. Also, in terms of the public policy process itself, the long drawn-out colonial legacy in the region has made it quite arduous and complex for newly independent governments to navigate

the progression in a proper and prudent manner. Despite all these challenges, however, the prospect of public policy making has seen gradual improvements thanks to the lessons learned from, and concerted efforts made by, the ICA over the past 30 years.

The defining characteristic of a healthy public policy is active participation of people and representative governments, in a democratic space, that is aimed at achieving fairness and equality. Therefore active participation becomes an important ingredient for the success of any development process, making opportunities more widely shared in order to achieve more equitable growth and development. The same requirement applies to public policy on cooperative development. In order to frame an effective cooperative legislative agenda, governments must engage cooperative representatives to

---

[1] By chapter is meant Chapter 5, Asian co-operatives and public policy of this book of "Waking the Asian Pacific Cooperative Potential."

[2] The extent to which cooperatives in Asia are widespread and varied are discussed in many other chapters of this book, especially in the preceding chapter on Asia Pacific History by Akira Kurimoto.

DOI: https://doi.org/10.1016/B978-0-12-816666-6.00005-7

participate actively during all its proceedings so in the final analysis it will be the cooperative members that will obtain fair and equal benefits from the social and economic gains of the cooperative.

Historical evidence has shown that public policy making in the Asian cooperative context is essentially quite distant from being healthy. Control of the state had remained dominant even after countries became independent, curbing any form of proper public policy participation and debates of cooperative representatives in the process. During the preindependence period of most colonized countries in Asia, cooperative laws were designed by colonial masters without any involvement of the native cooperative representatives themselves. The main consideration of framing cooperative laws at that time had been "what is good considered by the rulers and not by cooperative members or the people" (Sharma, 1997). Subsequent amendments of the cooperative laws by postindependent governments also failed to incorporate Asian cultural values and the local wisdom of the people, therefore the gist of most cooperative laws was more attuned to the political expediencies of those governments.

This chapter is, thus an endeavor to illustrate how state control over the cooperative movement was dominant, which prompted the leadership of the ICA to initiate a good public policy discussion forum. The public policy endeavor was primarily focused on reviewing and improving the regulatory framework for cooperatives in the Asia Pacific region. The program methodology utilized by the ICA Regional Office for Asia and the Pacific (ICA ROAP)[3] was to conduct biennial regional consultations followed by Asia Pacific Cooperative Ministers Conferences (APCMC).[4] The very first APCMC was held in Sydney, Australia, in 1990, and the most recent one (at the writing of this paper) was the 10th APCMC held in Hanoi, Vietnam, in 2017. This bold and thoughtful initiative of the ICA AP was relevant as well as prospective as evidenced by the results of four successive critical studies[5] that preceded the APCMC proper. This chapter tries to encapsulate common public policy issues faced by countries in South and Southeast Asia,[6] involving three case studies in Bangladesh, Indonesia, and the Philippines. Although top-down approaches vary among different countries in Asia they are not necessarily as pervasive as depicted by the three case studies, the phenomena seem quite omnipresent in the region on account of the feudalistic and patriarchal values inherent in Asian culture.[7] This chapter also focuses more on countries in the Asia, rather than the Pacific, region, without any disregard to the latter, in

---

[3] ICA ROAP stands for International Co-operative Alliance, Regional Office for Asia and the Pacific, which was the popular abbreviation used before it changed into ICA AP (Asia Pacific) more recently, rightly putting more emphasis on the region than the office.

[4] The term APCMC is used throughout this chapter to depict the successive Asia Pacific Co-operative Ministers Conferences being conducted by the ICA AP over all these years.

[5] The first critical study was undertaken in 1996 to furnish the fourth APCMC held in Chiangmai, Thailand, with indepth analysis of the failures of government-led co-operatives in Indonesia and the Philippines.

[6] Three developing countries in South and Southeast Asia were selected for the case studies pertaining to a "top-down" approach in cooperative development as they were quite comparable as postindependent developing countries and where the agricultural sector was dominant.

[7] The pervasiveness of Asian values in the public policy context was emphasized in a paper by Robby Tulus on "Co-operative Legislation," *Legislative and Regulatory trends—with special reference to co-operatives in Asia and the Pacific*, a presentation at the National Congress of the Canadian Co-operative Association, Winnipeg, Manitoba, June 23—26, 1998.

as much as existing studies on public policy were more obtainable in Asian countries.

5.2 Colonial legacy and cooperative legislation in Asia

Cooperative laws and regulations in postcolonial countries in Asia were by and large created by their foregoing rulers. Despite the richness of cultures and traditions in Asia, which ought to be taken into consideration when drafting and enacting cooperative laws and regulations, most postcolonial governments simply adopted the cooperative laws left behind by their colonizers. The first cooperative law in India was enacted in 1904 based on the model of the United Kingdom, and in the Philippines, while ruled by the United States, the initial cooperative legislation was based on the corporation law of 1906, patterned after the legislative frameworks of European countries (Sharma, 1997).

In India, cooperative societies were established based on the Raiffeisen model in 1892 to supply rural credit,[8] and thereafter, the 1901 Famine Commission under British rule recommended that farm credit should be continued to improve agriculture and to prevent famine. By 1904, the Co-operative Society Act was passed. Pakistan was part of India until 1947. Cooperatives in Pakistan originally applied the Bombay/Sindh Co-operative Societies Act of India in 1925. Cooperatives in Bangladesh were subjected to the cooperative legislation of Pakistan until it became independent from Pakistan in 1972, but were originally subjected to the provincial Co-operative Societies Act of

1912 of India as it was then the Indian State of Bengal. The first cooperative law in Sri Lanka was enacted in 1911, meant primarily for credit cooperatives, and modeled after the Indian Co-operative Law of 1904. These examples of cooperative legislation in South Asia signify the influence and intensity of foreign rulers in framing the initial cooperative legislation in the region.

Colonial legacy applies to the early cooperative legal frameworks in Southeast Asia as well. In Indonesia, the first cooperative legislation was enacted by the Dutch government in 1915 based on the Dutch Law (Staatsblad) on Cooperatives of 1876. In Malaysia, the first Co-operative Societies Act was enacted in 1922 and patterned after the Indian Co-operative Societies Act of 1912. In Burma (now called Myanmar), the primary credit societies were regulated by the (Burma) Provincial Registrar of Co-operative Societies under the Indian Co-operative Societies Act 1904, and amended in 1912 and 1927, to fight the "Chettiars" or moneylender communities (Turnell, 2013). Thailand, being a country that has never been colonized, developed its first cooperative law called the "Amended Associations Act" in 1916, focused on farm-based cooperatives to provide loans to rice growers, but patterned after the Indian and Burmese cooperative laws.[9]

The European colonial powers have left a lasting impact on the social economic landscape in Asia. India, Sri Lanka, and Malaysia were under British rule, Indonesia was under Dutch rule, the Philippines was under Spanish rule, East Timor was under Portuguese rule, and Vietnam was under French colonial domination. The British, Spanish, Portuguese, and

---

[8] The Raiffeisen model was linked to rural indebtedness as a product of the land revenue system enforced by colonial powers to gain revenues from the Indian peasants without regard for the repayment capacity of these poor farmers. The model was introduced half-heartedly because the democratic aspect was omitted for fear of bolstering independent movements.

[9] Summarized and excerpted from country presentations and background papers from the first to the third APCMC (1990–94).

Dutch colonial powers had different approaches and objectives for colonization. The Dutch and French were interested in accumulating wealth as well as ensuring hegemony.

Apart from wealth accumulation, the Spanish and Portuguese were also interested in spiritual conversion. The English imperial power, by contrast, was interested exclusively in the wealth of the colonies. The latter had a more flexible and noninterventionalist approach and, thus outlasted all other colonial powers (Samiul Hasan, 2008). It may help to explain why the Indian Co-operative Law of 1904—drafted by British rulers—continued to render a formidable influence and impact on many other cooperative laws in Asia. The creation of cooperative laws in many Asian countries, wherein European model laws were embedded at the outset, was further enforced by the establishment of institutions that had colonial underpinnings. The institution of the registrar was established as the sole authority to guide, develop, and preserve the cooperative enterprise with unmitigated absence of members' participation in any decision-making process. This was rationalized by the notion that peasant farmers, who were not well-educated enough to understand and to form a cooperative enterprise in the rural areas, were in need of an authority—called a registrar—that would be recruited and selected by the colonial masters themselves. Such control over cooperative enterprise also meant that colonial governments could maintain their domination over the massive rural jurisdiction under the guise of well-developed cooperative legal frameworks.

Upon independence, at the beginning of the second half of the 20th century, the residual legal framework of colonial powers continued to prevail in Asian countries, prompting governments in Asia to practice top-down domination of cooperatives for political expediencies.

Cooperatives became mere handmaidens of the government to serve their prevailing policies

without much space for self-governance and autonomy. Governments maintained full authority by enacting legal and policy frameworks for cooperatives that suited their political needs. The "registrar" syndrome predominated, leaving little space for public policy debates to ensue. Residues of the European cooperative development model remained uninterrupted, whereas opportunities to enshrine Asian values that are based on religion and tradition were missed. These top-down policies led to the failure of cooperatives in many Asian countries in the 1960s to the 1980s, as will be described in the subsequent chapter.

5.3 Failed government top-down approaches in cooperative development: three case studies

Postcolonial governments in Asia were quite inflexible, allowing cooperatives to self-govern in the postindependence period up until the 1980s. The preponderance of the agricultural sector to meet food sufficiency in many Asian countries has led governments to set up cooperatives that will increase agriculture and food production, and simultaneously raise farmers' income. This well-intentioned yet controversial approach continued to preserve state control over cooperatives, leaving cooperative members to become objects rather than subjects of their own development. Government intervention and assistance had been highly noticeable in rural areas where agricultural cooperatives were vigorously created within the realm of existing national development policies.

In Indonesia, the government approach to cooperative development during the early 1970s was the promotion of the village unit cooperatives, popularly known as Koperasi Unit Desa (KUD). The legal basis for these government-initiated KUDs was a series of Presidential Instructions, starting from PI 4/1973, to which the Ministry of Co-operatives and Small and Medium Enterprises became the implementing agency. KUD is essentially a multipurpose agricultural-based cooperative that provided multiple services to member farmers such as agricultural credit via the Peoples' Bank of Indonesia (BRI), field extension services, supply of agricultural inputs, and the processing and marketing of agricultural products. Under PI 4/1973, the idea was to have KUDs promote agricultural productivity, especially in the food subsector, increase small farmers' incomes, sustain the growth of agriculture, and attain self-sufficiency in staple products for food security (Soedjono/Cordero, 1997). However, subsequent Presidential Instructions such as PI 4/1984 transformed the KUD into an expanded multisectoral cooperative to play a dominant role in all other economic activities at the subdistrict (Kecamatan) level, be they agricultural or nonagricultural-based activities. The KUD concept was further bolstered by the launching of the KUD Mandiri (Self-Reliant KUD) Program in 1989, which allowed membership of KUD to include non-farmers at the subdistrict level (Soedjono/ Cordero, 1997). The dominance of these KUDs was further demonstrated by business tie-ups with the private sector to the extent that KUDs owned a monopoly on the procurement of cloves as a lucrative agricultural product at that time. In addition, to the KUDs, the government promoted cooperatives in urban areas among professional workers, the military, and police.

The establishment of these professional and employment-based cooperatives was considered a form of political intervention by the government over these professional and agricultural entities, causing the downward drift of cooperatives in both the rural and urban areas in Indonesia (Baswir, 2000).

In Bangladesh, the Comilla Model precedes the KUD model of Indonesia, with the same visionary concept of a rural development program, founded by Akhter Hameed Khan. The Comilla Model was Khan's reply to the failure of the Village Agricultural and Industrial Development (V-AID) program, launched in 1953 in East and West Pakistan with technical assistance from the US government (Yousaf, 2003). The technical assistance was a governmental level attempt to promote citizens' participation in rural development. Khan argued that for Comilla to develop rapidly, the farmers in its villages must be able to rapidly expand their production and sales, and local infrastructure must be built. However, even if the government had the resources to build this infrastructure, Khan argued, the problem would not be solved. Once constructed, infrastructure must be regularly maintained. In Khan's view, it was essential to develop "vigorous local institutions" capable of performing this type of local maintenance and management of infrastructure. After the independence of Bangladesh, while the First Five Year Plan gave general endorsement, both theoretical criticisms and practical difficulties became more severe.

There are similarities between the Comilla Model and the KUD model since both were researched and initiated by academicians; in Bangladesh by Akhter Hameed Khan, who was the founder of the Bangladesh Academy for Rural Development, and in Indonesia by Mubyarto, who was a well-known researcher and lecturer on agricultural and village economics at the Gajah Mada University in Indonesia. Both academicians started with pilot projects on rural development based on two goals; first, to provide a real-life learning situation for rural development, and second, to devise pilot programs with a basic institutional framework (precooperatives), which could serve as models capable of replication. The basic institutional framework was called Badan Usaha Unit Desa (BUUD) in Indonesia, a precursor to KUD. However, both these well-intentioned initiatives were usurped by the government, and replications of the Comilla and BUUD programs suffered from distortion, mismanagement, corruption, and subversion (Quddus, 1993).

In the Philippines, during the same period in the 1970s, a similar top-down approach of cooperative development could be witnessed. Philippines was under martial law, and a Presidential Decree (PD), No. 175, was issued with the aim of strengthening the cooperative movement. Moreover, PD No. 175[10] was tied to the Marcos land-reform program (PD No. 27), which made it compulsory for tenant farmers to join a cooperative called Samahang Nayon, which is a precooperative farmers' organization. The Samahang Nayons were encouraged to form area marketing cooperatives on a municipality-wide basis, and also to form cooperative rural banks on a province-wide basis. Farmers' benefits would include the right to borrow funds from government banks through cooperative rural banks (CRBs) or local rural banks, with the assurance of being supplied with farm inputs such as seed, fertilizers, pesticides, etc.

However, since the formation of Samahang Nayons was haphazard, the resulting AMCs and CRBs formed were few and weak. The Samahang Nayons peaked at 200,000 involving at least 3 million farmers. Only 3% survived. The 14-year program reportedly utilized billions of dollars in loans and grants from the World Bank and other international financial institutions, which were wasted by the government for quick fixes through weak and haphazardly created cooperative institutions.

All three cases—the KUD in Indonesia, the Comilla in Bangladesh, and the Samahang Nayon in the Philippines—bore evidence of the fact that government-initiated cooperatives from the top-down are doomed to fail. From a public policy point of view, there seem to be inadequate legislative processes to seek a balance between government's desire to initiate and control cooperatives for the public good on the one hand, and the desire of cooperative institutions themselves to have the flexibility to respond to challenges in the marketplace and, hence, adjust their strategies based on their members' needs. The failure of these top-down approaches is attributed to a misconception of the basic identity of cooperatives. Instead of promoting self-help, self-governance, and self-responsibility of cooperatives for long-term transformation, governments were instead using cooperatives as means for political expediencies, for quick and technical fixes that were mired with fraud and corruption in the process.

Several case studies mentioned previously focused primarily on postcolonial countries in South and Southeast Asia where excessive state control predominated, and which caught the attention of the ICA as will be described in the following chapter.

Whereas case studies on public policy issues are quite palpable in the foregoing three countries, this chapter is by no means trying to neglect policy anomalies, which also exist in other more developed countries in East Asia such as Japan, Korea, and China including Singapore in Southeast Asia. Other case studies written in this book bring to light the extent to which governments in more developed countries also continued to carry the day.

The revelation of government control over cooperatives in the preceding case studies could be the subject of further in-depth studies in the public policy domain insofar as cooperative laws are concerned. Cooperative laws corresponding to the three case studies were omnibus laws, which encompassed all cooperative types and sectors. The omnibus law seems prevalent in most Asian countries, and

---

[10] Presidential Decree No. 175, April 14, 1973, "Strengthening the Cooperative Movement". PD 175 repealed all past cooperative law. Portions or parts of any other laws inconsistent with PD 175 are likewise repealed. This Presidential Decree, thus, overruled laws enacted by the congress as the legislative arm in the Philippines.

presumably drafted, for the most part, by governments that could well perpetuate their own interests to exercise ongoing control over cooperatives. Two countries in Asia, namely, Japan and South Korea, are the only ones adopting sectoral cooperative laws, to the extent that there exist different laws for different cooperative sectors, and these are regulated by different ministries as well. The presumption that cooperatives could be better supervised and be more autonomous and independent to foster growth under sectoral laws, is subject to another study. While vertically well-regulated and well-supervised, one could argue that horizontal coordination among so many ministries involved in cooperative regulation and supervision is conducive for the overall growth, development, and independence of cooperatives.

The choice of one omnibus cooperative law vis-à-vis sectoral laws has an *effect on the legislative procedure, for example on the designation of the lead ministry in charge of the formulation of the law or the amendments to the law. Worldwide one finds any thinkable combination, from many laws to no law. The trend is towards having one single general law covering all types of cooperatives.*[11]

5.4 Public policy initiatives of the International Co-operative Alliance

The disproportionate roles and relationship between the government and the cooperative movement in a number of ICA member countries in Asia have caught the attention of the ICA, notably its ROAP. This challenging reality led the ICA ROAP (currently called ICA AP) to initiate a consultation in Singapore in 1987 to bring together permanent secretaries and top cooperative leaders from Asian countries to begin an honest dialogue. Prof. Hans-H Münkner, an advocate of this dialogue, stated

that *Co-operatives must be allowed to play their role as self-help organizations, representing and defending the interests of their members and to work according to their own fundamental ethic ideals expressed in the co-operative principles.* The consultative process in Singapore produced a relationship-promoting element as it did raise the awareness among regulators and cooperative leaders regarding current impediments obstructing cooperative growth, chiefly among ICA members in developing countries at that time. On account of this awareness, the initial public policy dialogue began in earnest.

Following the Singapore dialogue, and with support of head-office, ICA AP formulated a public policy forum by instituting two successive events; first, a dialogue between the cooperative movement and high-ranking officials in charge of cooperatives to assess current cooperative policies and legislation, and second, a policy endorsement by a ministerial level delegation. These events were more popularly known as the Asia Pacific "Regional Consultation" and the APCMC, organized mostly on a biennial basis from 1990 until 2012, and conducted more sparingly of late.

This well-received public policy initiative set forth fresh debates about the role of the state and how such a role should be transformed from a predominantly top-down mechanism into that of a partnership approach. Until 2018, 10 consecutive APCMCs had been successfully organized in Sydney (1990), Jakarta (1992), Colombo (1994), Chiangmai (1997), Beijing (1999), Nepal (2002), India (2004), Kuala Lumpur (2007), Bangkok (2012), and Hanoi (2017). While applauding the successful organizational labors of the ICA AP in staging all ten APCMCs, the ICA AP was determined to put more emphasis on substantiating the results of the APCMCs, particularly the impact on government policies to create a more enabling

---

[11] An extensive assessment of one versus several cooperative laws or no cooperative law whatsoever was revealed in the Third Revised Edition of the "Guidelines for Co-operative Legislation" by Hagen (Henrÿ, 2012).

environment for cooperatives to self-regulate and, thus achieve self-reliant growth and development. A significant instrument used by the ICA AP was a series of in-depth critical studies, enriched with field investigations, which had been conducted since 1996 prior to the Co-op Ministers Conference in Chiangmai, Thailand, in 1997.

Reflecting on all 10 APCMCs, it is safe to conclude that governments and cooperative movements are becoming more aware of the imperatives of good policies and legislation that are predisposed to enhancing the competitive strength of cooperatives in an ever-changing environment. It also enabled the ICA AP and its members to embark on relevant public policy issues pertaining to cooperatives, all aimed at cooperative development and the wellbeing of its members. One big challenge was to defeat the stigma within the public sector at large in that cooperatives were by and large government-led and, hence, destined to fail. The combination of Regional Consultations, Critical Studies, and subsequent discussions at all nine APCMCs constituted tangible settings to debate about the right prerequisites for developing genuine cooperatives. The prevalence of genuine cooperatives would be the only means to defeat the lingering stigma. Thus it would be incumbent on the part of governments to create an enabling policy and legal environment that are conducive to the development of genuine cooperatives. The arduous process of policy debates toward building a consensus on what constitutes a genuine cooperative was buoyed up with the promulgation of International Labour Organization (ILO) Recommendation 193 in 2002,[12] stating that

Governments should provide a supportive policy and legal framework consistent with the nature and function of cooperatives and guided by the cooperative values and principles. The ILO Recommendation 193, which applies to all types and forms of cooperatives, reenforces some of the key and contextual declarations of all preceding APCMCs.

Critical lessons drawn from the initial five APCMCs can be summarized as[13]:

1. The need to maintain regional—national—local links to ensure that inputs at the Regional Conference reflect the needs and concerns of members at the primary level. Legislative issues must first be addressed at the grassroots level, and subsequently at the national and regional levels by linking local responses with different higher-level stakeholders including governments, universities, and civil society organizations.

2. Current sponsorship of the APCMCs could be defined as equal funding from ICA sponsors (Swedish Co-operative Center, SCC; Canadian Co-operative Association, CCA; Développement International Desjardins, DID, as well as ICA Members) for the preparation of the "content" on the one hand, and from host governments for the preparations and implementation of the actual execution of the conference itself on the other. The ICA must acquire the skill to craft a strategy that increases member financing, matched by cooperative sponsors and government funds so as to avoid shifting the ownership of the Conference from members (i.e., ICA ROAP) to that of external agencies.

---

[12] ILO Recommendation 193, Recommendation concerning Promotion of Cooperatives, Adoption: Geneva, 90th ILC session (June 20, 2002), the full text could be seen in the NORMLEX website; NORMLEX is a new information system that brings together information on International Labor Standards www.ilo.org/dyn/normlex/en/f?p = NORMLEXPUB:1

[13] These lessons learned are quoted from a paper "The ICA Asia Pacific Co-operative Ministers' Conferences and Regional Consultations: A Technical Paper on Lessons Learned," by Robby Tulus, p. 26.

3. There is a significant time gap between the execution of the Regional Consultation and the actual APCMC itself. Such a gap tends to diminish the momentum created by the Consultation that needs to be picked up and confirmed by the high-level Ministers' Meeting. It seems plausible to link the Regional Meetings of cooperative Chief Executives and government bureaucracy directly to a high-level conference among cooperative ministers and elected cooperative leaders in quick succession. Such a mechanism will not only keep the momentum active, but also the overall cost down.

4. Most governments and members of the ICA AP have become used to making statements at the APCMC, which are frequently unrelated to the issues being addressed by the respective APCMCs. Member countries of the ICA AP should be motivated to take greater interests and self-initiatives in legislative reforms. Through this experience, cooperatives could document processes that show how an independent enterprise is critical to making "self-regulation" work by encouraging healthy movement, and, at the same time, public accountability of state institutions. Statements reflecting these experiences would be relevant and useful for others.

5.5 Sustaining the momentum of public policy debates on cooperatives

The initiative of the ICA AP to launch policy debates by means of Regional Consultations and the APCMCs is worth sustaining in view of the varying degrees of government dictates that are still in existence across the growing cooperative movements in Asian countries.

There continued to be changes in the political landscapes that prompted cooperative ministers or corresponding ministries to be subjected to unavoidable sociopolitical and structural changes. The predicament is the changed outlook of cooperative ministers operating under such new political settings, which is often different from their predecessors, and worst still when positive outlooks are being annulled for their political conveniences.

With the realization that the cooperative ministry, or the ministry in charge of cooperatives, is only a subcategory of the government system, reforms in cooperative legislation and policies could take some time to materialize. Critical Studies and Regional Consultations would be inclined to reprocess old themes to keep new cooperative ministers/officials abreast with fundamental issues that were still unresolved. In other words, tools and standards were missing that would allow both old and new players to undertake a joint assessment in a consistent manner. The only constant is the dedicated pursuit of the ICA AP to convene APCMCs so as to keep the wheels of government—cooperative relations running smoothly (Shankar/Cronan, 2001).

A new milestone arose following the UN International Year of Co-operatives in 2012 when governments, international development actors, and UN agencies credibly recognized the significant contribution of cooperatives in achieving a socially just, economically equitable, and culturally inclusive society. This augurs well with the newly promulgated SDGs by the UN, to which the ICA has pledged its contribution by way of concrete actions of its members, and in close partnership with the government and its stakeholders as well as within the context of its "Blueprint for a Co-operative Decade."[14]

---

[14] "Blueprint for a Co-operative Decade," a paper written under the guidance of the Planning Work Group of the ICA by Cliff Mills and Will Davies, the Center for Mutual and Employee-Owned Business, and the University of Oxford, originally published in January, 2013.

Realizing that limitations still exist where APCMCs are concerned, the ICA AP took a progressive step in 2016 to include and engage parliamentarians during its Regional Consultation in Nepal. This allowed members of the legislative body who are knowledgeable about cooperatives to take part in the policy debates in addition, to government officials and ministers in charge of cooperatives.

And in addition, to addressing and concentrating on legal issues like in the past, the Consultation was a first attempt to address other specific issues affecting cooperative development in the region. This new initiative was a breakthrough in terms of getting ICA AP member cooperatives to deliberate on issues including (1) food sovereignty (and security); (2) new cooperative approaches (innovation); (3) cooperatives and the transition from the informal into the formal economy; (4) regional and global engagement of cooperatives; and (5) enabling environment (legislative and regulatory frameworks)[15] both at the Regional Consultation and at the APCMC agendas. Such a holistic discussion within the 10th APCMC framework has allowed the ICA AP not only to keep, but to sustain, the momentum of its public policy advocacy so much so that it will (1) enrich the partnership of the cooperative movement and their respective governments as well as key stakeholders to bring about sustained economic democracy; (2) comprehend the substantive progress made by the cooperative movement in Asia Pacific; (3) capture and outline well-defined key elements of the SDGs, which cooperatives could contribute to the attainment of the SDGs of the UN.[16]

5.6 Conclusion

The far-reaching influence of European colonial powers, which has left an enduring imprint on cooperative development in Asian countries, cannot be undermined. Asian norms and values, driven by rich cultural traditions and religion are critical elements to enhance the workings of cooperatives in most Asian countries.

They were historically ignored for the sake of satisfying the political interests of postcolonial political leaders. The preponderance of government control over cooperatives after independence only helped to create a lingering dependency on government support. Cooperative leaders, instead of promoting the cooperative values and creating benefits for members, opted to please the government for their rent-seeking purposes. The examples of the KUD in Indonesia, Samahang Nayon in the Philippines, and Comilla in Bangladesh, all served to show that cooperatives were by and large run by the government rather than by the people. Cooperatives were stigmatized as being government organs, and, as a result, the public lost interest in joining cooperatives in most developing nations in Asia over the post-independence period. Evidence-based data has shown that the credit union movement in Asia[17] seems to be the only perceptible cooperative sector that is an independent and member-driven one that is not government controlled.

The unhealthy environment for cooperative development in the Asia region up until the late 1980s had urged the ICA, notably its

---

[15] Concept Note, 10th APCMC, April 18–21, 2017, Hanoi, Vietnam

[16] Excerpt from the HANOI 10th APCMC Resolution on Multi-Stakeholder Partnerships in Realizing the SDGs, April 2017, and from a Critical Appraisal of "Strengthening Co-operative Multi-stakeholders' Partnerships in Asia Pacific" by Robby Tulus.

[17] Data on Credit Union Network Strength 2017 in Asia published in the Annual Report 2017–18 of the Asian Confederation of Credit Unions, p. 5.

leadership in Asia and the Pacific, to initiate a public policy forum to overcome the stigma attached to cooperatives. In the late 1980s and the early 1990s, the ICA AP began to open up a set of policy debates to rebuild the image of cooperatives as being genuinely people-centered and member-based. The historical milestone of the ICA Centennial Congress in 1995[18] afforded cooperators all over the world a keen understanding of the Co-operative Identity Statement, thus creating a new space to empower the ICA AP to advocate the cooperative identity in various public policy domains, most notably during the Asia Pacific Regional Consultations and the APCMC.

Slow as the case may be, governments begun to see cooperatives more as a partner for creating welfare for people, rather than viewing them as mere instruments to expedite their national policy agendas, or worst still, to cater to their narrow political needs and interests. The ILO Recommendation 193 provided a parallel empowerment tool to advocate and create autonomous and self-reliant cooperatives in many developing as well as developed countries due to the realization of a more enabling environment that is favorable for cooperative development.

The adoption of the Blueprint for a Co-operative Decade by the ICA in 2012 was another milestone that has showcased a dramatic improvement of the visibility and understanding of the cooperative model. The Blueprint came as the UN declared its International Year of Co-operatives; so its adoption is a repositioning of cooperatives as a democratic enterprise where members have a voice and must actively take part in bringing about socioeconomic as well as environmental sustainability. This is a far cry from when governments tended to dictate cooperatives from the top-down in the past toward a more favorable conduct as partners that work together with cooperatives in meeting the SDGs of the UN. The fact that the UN recognized cooperatives in its core documents as playing a central role in meeting the SDGs certainly helped in obliterating the old stigma of cooperatives being mere handmaidens of governments.

It became apparent that the potential of cooperative development in Asia has now been awakened and must, therefore be sustained, and doing so by integrating inherent Asian values, by responding to members' start-ups among young entrepreneurs, and by incorporating the wisdom and strength of women members.

References

Baswir, R. (2000). *Co-operatives and the new order authority.* Jakarta, Kompas Newspaper.

Comparative Third Sector Governance in Asia. (2008). *Structure, process, and political economy*, Edited by Samiul Hasan and Jenny Onyx. UAE & Sydney. Springer.

Henrÿ, H. (2012). *Guidelines for co-operative legislation* (3rd revised ed.). Geneva: International Labour Office.

Quddus, M. A. (1993). *Rural development in Bangladesh: Strategies and experiences.* Book/Working Paper, Bangladesh Academy for Rural Development.

Shankar, R., & Cronan, G. (2001). *2nd critical study on cooperative policy and legislation.* International Co-operative Alliance.

Sharma, G. K. (1997). *Co-operative Laws in Asia and the Pacific.* New Delhi, India: Bonow Memorial Trust, The COOP Times.

Soedjono, I., & Cordero, M. (1997). *Critical study on co-operative legislation and competitive strength.* India: Document Press. International Co-operative Alliance, Regional Office for Asia and the Pacific.

[18] The ICA Centennial Congress held in Manchester in September 1995 adopted new Co-operative Principles that are to be contained within a "Statement on the Co-operative Identity," which also crafted an official definition of a cooperative as well as identified the basic cooperative values of self-help, democracy, equality, equity, and solidarity.

Turnell, S. (2013). *History of Burma's financial system.* Australia: The Nordic Institute of Asian Studies Press.

Yousaf, N. (2003). *Allama Mashriqi & Dr. Akhtar Hameed Khan: Two Legends of Pakistan.* New York. Allama Mashriqi is one of the founding fathers of Pakistan and Akhtar Hameed Khan, a world-renowned social scientist.

Further reading

Münkner, H.H., (1989). *Cooperative ideas, principles and practices.* Marburg/Lahn.

Tulus, R. (2017). *Strengthening co-operative multi-stakeholders' partnerships in Asia Pacific.* A critical appraisal of past, present and future APCMCs. Presentation at the 10th Asia Pacific Co-operative Ministers' Conference, Hanoi, Vietnam.

6

Cooperatives and the sustainable development goals

Balasubramanian Iyer

International Cooperative Alliance Asia-Pacific, New Delhi, India

6.1 Introduction

In September 2015, the United Nations Member States adopted the 2030 Agenda for Sustainable Development, which takes forward the work begun in 2000 by the Millennium Development Goals (MDGs). The Transforming our world Agenda sets a course to eradicate poverty, protect the planet, and ensure prosperity for all by 2030. Cooperatives are recognized as important partners to achieve the SDGs, because they promote democracy, enhance income, foster social inclusion, and care for the environment, all while having a significant economic impact on the world economy. The International Cooperative Alliance (ICA), as the representative body of cooperatives worldwide, is playing a lead role in promoting and highlighting the role of cooperatives in the implementation of the SDGs. Cooperatives across the Asia Pacific region are actively involved in the implementation of the SDGs and gaining recognition for the work they are doing. The commitment by cooperatives to the SDGs cuts across all sectors of the economy— agriculture, banking and credit, consumer, health, and work. However, there are issues relating to monitoring targets and indicators for cooperatives, systematic data collection and reporting, increasing awareness about the SDGs, and building linkages across the spectrum of stakeholders.

6.2 Sustainable development

Sustainable development as defined in Our Common Future, also known as the Brundtland Report is, "development that meets the needs of the present without compromising the ability of future generations to meet their own needs." The report was prompted by the negative environmental consequences of economic growth and globalization and issued a call to find solutions to the problems caused by population growth, industrialization, and unhindered consumption.

The concept of sustainable development includes economic, social, and environmental sustainability. Economic sustainability includes equal economic growth that generates wealth for all by minimizing waste and maximizing resources and without harming the environment. At the social level, sustainability is the development of people, communities, and cultures to help achieve a reasonable quality of life, healthcare, and education. Environmental sustainability includes protection of the environment and preventing nature from being used as an indefinite source of resources.

6.3 Background to the Sustainable Development Goals

The MDGs was a global effort started in 2000 with a 15 years agenda to tackle development priorities of extreme poverty and hunger, the prevention of deadly diseases, and the expansion of primary education to all children. The key achievements of the MDGs were:

- one billion people lifted out of extreme poverty since 1990;
- a drop in child mortality by more than half since 1990;
- a drop in the number of out of school children by more than half since 1990; and
- a fall in HIV/AIDS infections by almost 40% since 2000.

However, there was still work to be done to get people out of poverty, end hunger, achieve gender parity, improve health services, and get every child into school.

The SDGs were born at the United Nations Conference on Sustainable Development in Rio de Janeiro in 2012. The objective was to produce a set of broad goals to meet the economic, environmental, political, and social challenges facing the world. The 17 SDGs are a clarion call to tackle the pressing challenges facing the world today with each goal being interconnected, so that success in one has a cascading effect on others. SDG 12 (Responsible consumption and production), SDG 10 (Reduced inequalities), SDG 1 (No poverty), and SDG 8 (Decent work and economic growth) have links with 10 other goals or more, while the rest are linked to at least two or more (Blanc, 2015).

The SDGs are unique in that they address issues that affect us all and reaffirm the international communities' commitment to end poverty, everywhere. They are ambitious in making sure no one is left behind.

The SDGs also coincided with two other landmark frameworks in 2015. These were the Sendai Framework for Disaster Risk Reduction and COP21—the Paris Agreement on Climate Change. These frameworks and agreements set out goals and targets to address disaster, sustainable development, and the climate challenges of today. Cooperatives and mutuals have been involved in all of these and in the process have not only been recognized, but, more importantly, called upon to implement.

6.4 Cooperatives and sustainable development

Cooperative Principle 7: Concern for Community enshrines the role of cooperatives in sustainable development. It states, "Cooperatives work for the sustainable development of their communities through policies approved by their members." The 7th Principle combines two elements of the Co-operative Values in the ICA's Statement on the Cooperative Identity, namely, those of "self-help and self-responsibility" and "the ethical values of honesty, openness, social responsibility and caring for others." The combination of these two elements arises because cooperatives emerge from and are rooted in the communities in which they conduct their business operations. Their success is based on their ability to support those communities to develop in a sustainable way (ICA, 2015).

Sustainable development, at the core of cooperative enterprises as the business model, is based on ethical values and principles whose goal is to provide for the needs and aspirations of its members. Self-help and empowerment, enhancing local resources and capacities, and reinvesting surpluses guide cooperatives to respond to local community needs and objectives. Instead of looking at the short-term goal of maximizing profits, cooperatives have a long-term aim of sustainable economic growth, social development, and environmental responsibility. Therefore cooperative enterprises support and promote a vision of sustainable development based on a triple bottom line approach, namely, economic, social, and environmental.

The global financial crisis of 2008, which bought with it painful consequences in relation to financial and economic losses; unemployment, particularly youth unemployment; and increases in poverty and social exclusion, showed that investor-owned business models suffer from the crisis of unsustainability, in economic, social, and environmental terms. The financial crisis has been an epic example of the perils of valuing short-term gain over longer-term viability. The dominant model of capitalism of the past three decades has also been accompanied by increased levels of inequality, translating into lower levels of "social capital" and wellbeing (Wilkinson & Pickett, 2010).

The CECOP-CICOPA report, *The Resilience of the Cooperative Model*, details, with concrete examples, the resilience of worker cooperatives, social cooperatives, and other worker-owned enterprises. At the "micro" (enterprise) level, a number of short-term measures aimed at facing the immediate effects of the crisis (in particular, aimed at temporarily reducing costs) were taken rapidly and with a high level of legitimacy by cooperative members thanks to the regime of democratic control that characterizes these enterprises. In particular, cooperative groups have proven to maintain and even, in a number of cases, to increase the number of jobs and the turnover, and, thus to show a particularly strong resilience (Roelants et al., 2012).

In declaring 2012 as the International Year of Cooperatives, former UN Secretary-General Ban Ki-moon said, "Through their distinctive focus on values, cooperatives have proven themselves a resilient and viable business model that can prosper even during difficult times. This success has helped prevent many families and communities from sliding into poverty."

It is no surprise that the UN Transforming our world: the 2030 Agenda for Sustainable Development explicitly recognizes cooperative enterprises as important players within the private sector to achieve the SDGs. The outcome document, which is available in all UN official languages, has these references to cooperatives:

> *We acknowledge the role of the diverse private sector, ranging from micro-enterprises to cooperatives to multinationals, and that of civil society organizations and philanthropic organizations in the implementation of the new Agenda. Point 41*
> *We acknowledge the diversity of the private sector, ranging from micro-enterprises to cooperatives to multinationals. We call on all businesses to apply their creativity and innovation to solving sustainable development challenges. Point 67*

It is unprecedented that the UN has recognized cooperatives as an important player to achieve inclusive economic growth and job creation within the SDGs (Means of Implementation of the Global Partnership). The cooperative sector is seen as an important player in the SDGs, especially in relevant areas such as poverty, hunger, quality education, decent work, responsible consumption and production (food security), gender equality, and in building strong institutions.

The international community also recognizes the role cooperatives have to play in sustainable development. The European Union Consensus on Development, the framework for a common approach to development policy that guides their actions in their cooperation with all partner countries, acknowledges cooperatives as a sustainable business model;

recognizes the role that cooperatives play in driving poverty eradication and ensuring food security; and the need for a diversity of actors, cooperatives among them (Points 49, 55, and 72). The International Labor Organization in its meeting in Geneva in June 2016, while discussing the revision of 1944 recommendation on employment and decent work for peace and resilience in the chapter on "Employment and income-generation opportunities" the creation or restoration of an enabling environment for sustainable enterprises including the promotion of small and medium-sized enterprises as well as of cooperatives and other social economy initiatives, with particular emphasis on initiatives to facilitate access to finance (Points 49, 51, and 52). The B20, focusing on the sustainability of small and medium enterprises, said the cooperative structure would allow businesses to maintain their independence while allowing greater collaboration to, among other things, negotiate better market conditions (p. 15). The SDGS provide an opportunity for cooperatives to position themselves as partners with global, national, regional, and local institutions to achieve sustainable development.

6.5 International Cooperative Alliance and the Sustainable Development Goals

The SDGs mirror many of the objectives laid out in the ICA Blueprint for a Cooperative Decade, a global strategy for and by cooperatives to become the acknowledged leaders in economic, social, and environmental sustainability, the model preferred by people, and the fastest growing form of enterprise. The blueprint outlines a strategic agenda for the cooperative sector with a five-point plan that aims to:

1. Elevate participation within membership and governance to a new level.
2. Position cooperatives as builders of sustainability.
3. Build the cooperative message and secure the cooperative identity.
4. Ensure supportive legal frameworks for cooperative growth.
5. Secure reliable cooperative capital while guaranteeing member control.

The ICA as the global voice of the movement is committed to educating cooperatives about the SDGs, helping cooperative enterprises respond to the UN's call to action, and collecting information about cooperative contributions to the 2030 Agenda in order to better position cooperatives as partners throughout the implementation process. With one in every six people on the planet as cooperators and through its membership of 1.2 billion people from any of the 2.94 million cooperatives worldwide, the ICA wants to show that cooperatives play a triple role:

- As economic actors they create opportunities for jobs, livelihoods, and income generation.
- As people-centered enterprises with social goals they contribute to social equity and justice.
- As democratic institutions they are controlled by their members, playing a leading role in society and local communities.

The ICA:

- Educates members about the SDGs and how cooperatives are well-suited to achieve them.
- Sets ambitious targets to contribute to the SDGs and shares their progress with the world.
- Meets with local and national government officials to discuss how cooperatives are drivers of sustainable development and what they need in order to grow.
- Hosts events celebrating the International Day of Cooperatives (IDC) to educate community members about the benefits of cooperation.

6.5.1 International Day of Cooperatives

The theme of the IDC from 2016 has focused on the contribution of cooperatives to the SDGs. The Committee for the Promotion and Advancement of Cooperatives (COPAC) of which the ICA selects the theme and slogan in the first quarter of each.

The theme of the 2016 IDC was, "Cooperatives: The power to act for a sustainable future" to emphasize cooperatives' contribution to the SDGs. The theme was chosen to convey to governments, international bodies, and civil society that cooperatives are important partners to achieve the SDGs because they foster democracy, practice social inclusion, and operate with concern for the environment all while having a significant economic impact on the world economy. The theme for the 2017 IDC was, "Cooperatives: Ensure no one is Left Behind" was to show that globalization should be done through a set of values such as those of the cooperative movement; otherwise, it creates more inequality and excesses that render it unsustainable. The theme of the 2018 IDC focused on SDG 12 with the theme of sustainable consumption and production and the slogan, "Sustainable societies through cooperation" to show that efficient management of natural resources, reduction of waste, and sustainable patterns of consumption can help with food security and help the shift toward a resource-efficient economy. The theme for 2018 will focus on SDG 8, Decent Work and Economic Growth to show that cooperatives are people-centered enterprises characterized by democratic control that prioritize human development and social justice within the workplace.

6.5.2 Coops for 2030

"Coops for 2030" (www.coopsfor2030.coop) was created as an online platform for cooperatives to learn about the SDGs, make pledges to help achieve them, and track their progress. The language of the SDGs can be difficult for grassroots cooperators to translate into everyday business terms, so the ICA regrouped the SDGs into four key action areas where cooperatives can be most impactful, namely, eradicating poverty, improving access to basic goods and services, protecting the environment, and building a more sustainable food system. Coops for 2030 was launched on July 2, 2016, the IDC, and, since the launch, 80 cooperatives in 31 countries have made 167 pledges. These pledges cover all of the SDGs and touch all regions of the world. Some pledges come from large enterprises who are leaders in their sectors, and others come from small community groups who touch the lives of those most in need of a helping hand. Members from Australia, Bhutan, India, Indonesia, Japan, Korea, Maldives, Nepal, Pakistan, Palestine, Philippines, Sri Lanka, Thailand, and Timor-Leste have pledged their commitment on the platform.

6.5.3 World Cooperative Monitor

The World Cooperative Monitor (WCM), is a joint project between the ICA and the European Research Institute on Cooperative and Social Enterprises (Euricse) to collect data (economic, organizational, and social) about cooperatives, mutual organizations, and noncooperative enterprises controlled by cooperatives worldwide. Starting in 2018 the WCM will provide information about the top 300 cooperative enterprises and mutuals (based on turnover) in the world based on the sustainability reports from the United Nations Global Compact project and/or the Global Reporting Initiative. The 2018 report shows that the top 300 organizations are working to ensure sustainable consumption and production patterns (Goal 12). They are also combating climate change and its impacts (Goal 13); ensuring healthy lives and promoting wellbeing for people of all ages (Goal 3); and promoting sustained, inclusive, and sustainable economic growth and full and productive employment and decent work for all (Goal 8) (WCM, 2018).

6.5.4 Cooperatives and the Sustainable Development Goals

Table 6.1, from the ICA's *Co-operatives for 2030: Cooperative Initiative to Achieve a Sustainable Future for All* shows that cooperatives from all sectors are making key contributions to many of the SDGs:

6.6 Asia Pacific cooperatives implementing the Sustainable Development Goals

In the Asia Pacific region many cooperatives are actively involved in the implementation of the SDGs.

The Japanese Consumers' Cooperative Union has taken a wholistic approach and created a "Co-op Action Plan" for implementing all the SDGs (Table 6.2). The aim is to "dedicate themselves to the realization of a more human lifestyle and sustainable society" under the ideal of Japanese Consumer Co-ops Movement for the 21st century. This was adopted at the JCCU Annual General Assembly in 2017.

JCCU received the Japan SDG Award in 2018 in recognition of its work on the development and supply of CO·OP Brand Products by adopting the concept of ethical consumption and as a national federation for supporting its member coops nationwide in their initiatives for achieving the SDGs.

Goal 2 is focused on ending hunger, achieving food security, and improving nutrition and promoting sustainable agriculture. Indian Farmer Fertilizers Cooperatives Limited (IFFCO) in India, as one of the largest cooperatives, not only in India, but in the world, is playing an important role in enabling farmers to prosper through timely supply of reliable, high quality agricultural inputs

and services in an environment sustainable manner. IFFCO's Vision-2020 emphasizes sustainable development through integrated resource management, financial inclusion, and advanced agriculture practices to empower farmers and rural India. A detailed list of IFFCO's commitments can be found at http://www.coopsfor2030.coop/en/the-pledges#.

In Australia, the National Health Co-operative (NHC) is focused on Goal 3 and Goal 12. NHC was formed in 2011 by patients in Canberra's West Belconnen region as a response to market failure; in this case, the lack of bulk billing clinics in the region. Now, NHC has 42,000 members in the Australian Capital Territory and New South Wales. NHC's patient-centered approach has led to holistic healthcare design to meet the needs of the various communities its members are drawn from including people living with mental illness, chronic disease, and refugee trauma. NHC has undertaken research that demonstrates that bulk billing rates have increased in Canberra beyond its own clinics. NHC pledges its commitment to the SDGs in its annual report (BCCM, 2017).

In Singapore, cooperatives contribute to the provision of healthcare and also support members in financing healthcare and in the process to address Goal 3, Goal 10, and Goal 11. NTUC Health provides an integrated suite of services to meet the growing needs of families and their dependents. In addition, to dental clinics and a family medicine clinic, NTUC Health also has one of the most comprehensive ranges of eldercare services in Singapore. These include facilities such as senior daycare centers, nursing homes, and senior activity and wellness centers as well as a sheltered/senior group home. TCC Credit Co-operative Limited (TCC), AUPE Credit Co-operative Limited (AUPE), Singapore Government Staff Credit Co-operative Society Limited (SGS), and Customs Credit Co-operative Society Limited (Customs Credit) offer members hospitalization benefits (SNCF, 2018).

TABLE 6.1 Contribution of cooperatives from cooperatives for 2030: cooperative initiative to achieve a sustainable future for all.

COOPERATIVES /for 2030

ANNEX

SDG	Type of cooperative	Some key contributions
1 **No poverty**	All	10% of world employment
	Credit	Micro-credit to the poor
	Insurance	Micro-insurance to the poor
	Social	Employment for disadvantaged people
2 **Zero hunger and food security**	Agricultural	Estimated 32% of food products market share;
	Fishery	providing food security; enhancing diversified agricultural production
	Consumer	Providing quality foodstuff at lower prices
3 **Good health and wellbeing**	Health	Health services including HIV/AIDS to over 100 million patients
4 **Quality education and lifelong learning**	All	Education as one of founding principles
	Student	Providing practical training on how to run a cooperative for children and teenagers
	Worker / social	Imparting education (in particular through around 2700 cooperatives)
	Credit	Providing educational micro-lending and financial education
	Consumers	Providing consumer education
5 **Gender equality**	All	High ratio of women's inclusion in membership and elected positions as shown in several studies
	Worker / producers'	Important cooperative networks are exclusively dedicated to women
6 **Clean water and sanitation**	Water	Safe water filtration and distribution
7 **Affordable and clean energy**	Energy	Energy channelled to rural and remote areas; generation of renewable energy
8 **Decent work and economic growth (including sustainable tourism)**	All	10% of world employment; decent, stable and resilient work, market access; more value in hands of members
	Social	Providing employment to disadvantaged people
	Worker / social	Sustainable tourism, cultural heritage
	Producers' / freelancers	Providing shared services and social protection
9 **Industry, innovation and infrastructure**	Worker / social Agricultural (agro-industries)	Virtually all industrial activities, maintaining enterprises in their communities
	New types (multi-stakeholder, community, platform etc.)	Innovating in new business forms and democratizing online platforms
	Water, energy & telephone supply	Promoting energy, water and internet infrastructure in remote areas
10 **Reduced inequalities**	All	Redistribution of surplus to members, reinvesting in communities, lower wage gap than average
	Credit	Financial inclusion
11 **Sustainable cities and communities**	Housing	Upgrading slums and providing affordable housing for a significant part of the population in a number of countries, either through ownership or rental
	All	Resilience to disaster and contribution to after-disaster measures
12 **Responsible consumption and production**	Agricultural Consumer New food coops	Networks between agricultural and consumer cooperatives increasingly promote responsible consumption, including organic food, food chain and fair trade products, limiting food waste, promoting circular economy

11

COOPERATIVES /for 2030

ANNEX

SDG	Type of cooperative	Some key contributions
13 **Climate action,** 14 **Life below water and** 15 **Life on land**	Worker / social Fishery Agricultural	Green jobs, protecting natural spaces, dealing with waste recycling
16 **Peace, justice and strong institutions**	All	Key role after several armed conflicts, participation in reconciliation processes
	Social / worker	Increasing involvement in welcoming refugees and addressing their plights
17 **partnerships**	All	International development cooperation developing within the cooperative movement and with other actors, including South to South cooperation

+ Cooperatives' role after disasters

1. Analytical framework of asian cooperative models

TABLE 6.2   Presentation made at the Asia Pacific development conference in Mongolia, 2017.

The Rah-e-Roshd Cooperative in Iran is focusing on Goal 4—quality education. In 1985 seven mothers in Tehran founded the kindergarten Rah-e-Roshd, hoping to provide a better education for their children despite the ongoing war with Iraq. The small school blossomed from its beginnings in a family house to five schools across Tehran, and by 1996 it had grown into a cooperative primary school. Today it provides all levels of primary, middle, and high school education for both boys and girls. Rah-e-Roshd has over 600 personnel and 162 shareholders, with 75% thereof being its employees. In 2017 it was enlisted as a Nationally Selected Cooperative thanks to its two outstanding characteristics, that is an educational field of activity—a rare cooperative field—and a decent social endeavor in promoting cooperative values.

The Nepal Agriculture Cooperative Central Federation Limited (NACCFL) is focusing on Goal 5 to enhance the representation of women at all levels of their cooperative. They have developed a database system that helps them place volunteers, identify potential women members for training, and organize various programs. NACCFL has also been working toward translating the targets given under Goal 5 to cater to the needs of their members. For target 5.1—end all forms of discrimination against all women and girls everywhere—NACCFL's strategy is to include at least 50% participation of women in trainings. They believe this will have a cascading effect and result in a decrease in domestic violence, enhance the entrepreneurship skills of women members, and give them easy access to loans. NACCFL hopes to increase women led institutions by 75%, make it compulsory to have at least 50% women participate in training programs, and have at least 50% of their staff being women.

In New Zealand, six of the largest cooperatives are involved in the production and/or retail distribution of food—Fonterra, Foodstuffs North Island, Foodstuffs South Island, Silver Fern Farms, Alliance, and Zespri—between them currently turning over more than $NZ 30 billion per annum and around 14% of New Zealand's GDP. Foodstuffs cooperatives, in terms of their commitment to Goal 12, have a strong focus toward supporting New Zealand's environment, local communities, and those in need. Among the targets they have set for themselves are for 100% of all retail and private label packaging to be either reusable, recyclable, or compostable by 2025; waste minimization programs in all stores, involving a 90% diversion of all waste away from landfills; banning of single-use plastic bags at the checkout from all New World, PAK'nSAVE, and Four Square stores by the end of 2018; supporting the development of a circular economy for plastic by moving to specify recycled content in more of its packaging, along with working with industry partners to develop domestic markets for recovered plastics; and working in partnership with Sea Cleaners to help clean up waterways and oceans around New Zealand. (Presland, 2018).

In Pune, India, the trade union Kagad Kach Patra Kashtakari Panchayat (KKPKP) unites more than 9000 waste pickers, waste buyers, waste collectors, and informal recyclers, 80% of whom are women from socially disadvantaged groups. The union founded the worker-owned cooperative SWaCH to comply with new laws and rules that required the segregation of waste, door to door collection, and waste processing rather than dumping. Through SWaCH, more than 3000 waste pickers in the informal economy were able to improve their working conditions (i.e., improved occupational safety and health, ID cards, etc.), benefit from training, and participate in democratic decision-making. In addition, to improving workers' livelihoods directly, the cooperative's members also advocate for sustainable waste management and better labor practices.

SANASA Federation Ltd. (Federation of Thrift and Credit Cooperative Societies Ltd.), in Sri Lanka, is implementing the "Lassana Lanka" (Beautiful Sri Lanka) program as part of the "Sri Lanka NEXT Blue-Green Economy," and contributing to Goal 14 and Goal 15. SANASA is a national partner of the Ministry of Mahaweli Development and Environment to achieve the SDGs. The short-term target is to rollout sustainability programs in 100 villages, with the long-term aspiration of delivering programs in 10,000 villages.

In the Philippines, the Cooperative Development Authority is working on Goal 16—peace, justice, and strong institutions by launching the "Marawi Rehabilitation through Cooperativism" program The region of Marawi, the Islamic city in the southern Philippines, was rendered into rubble after a siege on May 23, 2017, by the Islamic State of Iraq and the Levant (ISIS) affiliated Maute and Abu Sayyaf terror groups. In the five-month war, more than 353,000 people were displaced and have been seeking refuge in different areas of Mindanao. Included in the displaced were 73 active cooperatives with some 8000 members. The project, through cooperativism, is to rehabilitate Marawi city holistically and establish a sustainable and resilient society.

6.7 Issues and challenges for cooperatives

There are a few challenges when it comes to cooperatives and the implementation of the SDGs. These could be classified in terms of awareness, targets and indicators, consistent data, and engagement.

6.7.1 Awareness

The voice of cooperatives is not adequately heard and reflected in the SDGs space.

While cooperatives are working on all the SDGs, they neither reflect nor incorporate the SDG language. For example, while a majority of agriculture cooperatives contribute to zero hunger, they rarely mention SDG 2 and any of the associated indicators. Also, many members of cooperatives are unaware of the goals and whether they are contributing to any of them. Cooperatives need to incorporate the goals in their messaging, record their contributions, communicate the same, and engage with stakeholders.

6.7.2 Targets and indicators

The 17 SDGs have 169 targets and 232 indicators. When we look at the targets and accompanying indicators there are none specifically related to cooperatives. In order for cooperatives to be able to monitor, track, and report, there is need to ensure they are recognized in national plans and included in monitoring mechanisms. An example is from the Status and Roadmap 2016−30 prepared by the National Planning Commission, Government of Nepal. Table 6.3 from the Status and Roadmap shows two targets where cooperatives are mentioned. While there could be more specific indicators added, it is gratifying to see indicators relating to cooperatives. The cooperative movement in Nepal needs to see how they interact with the National Statistical Agency and have mechanisms to monitor, track, and report to be able to specifically signal their contribution.

TABLE 6.3 The sustainable development goals—status and roadmap 2016−30 by the National Planning Commission, Government of Nepal.

Target 5.5 Ensure women's full and effective participation and equal opportunities for leadership at all levels of decision-making in political, economic and public life					
5.5.1	Proportion of seats held by women in (a) national parliaments and (b) local governments				
1	(a) national parliament (%)	29.5[a]	33	34.4	36.5	40
	(b) provincial parliament (%)		33	34.4	36.5	40
	(c) local government bodies (%)		40.5	41	41.5	42
5.5.2	Proportion of women in managerial positions				
1	Women's participation in decision making level in the private sector (%)	25[f]	30.3	34.3	38.3	45
2	Women's participation in cooperative sector (%)	50[g]	50	50	50	50
3	Women in public service decision making positions (% of total employees)	11[d]	17	21.3	25.7	33
4	Ratio of women to men in professional and technical workers (%)	24[a]	28	31	35	40

Target 8.3 Promote development-oriented policies that support productive activities, decent job creation, entrepreneurship, creativity and innovation, and encourage the formalization and growth of micro-, small- and medium-sized enterprises, including through access to financial services					
8.3.1	Proportion of informal employment in non-agriculture employment, by sex	70[b]	54	42	30	10
1	Contribution of Micro-,Small-, and Medium-scale enterprises in GDP (%)					
2	Access to Financial Services					
3	Access to Cooperatives (% of households within 30 min walk)	54[e]	60.9	66.1	71.3	80

6.7.3 Data or lack

A larger challenge for cooperatives is that they are not monitored by national statistical agencies. Further, the line departments responsible for cooperatives are neither clued up on the SDGs nor do they respond in a timely fashion. There are efforts underway to remedy the situation. The ILO Department of Statistics and the Cooperatives Unit of the Enterprises Department with the COPAC Technical Working Group on Cooperative Statistics are working to redress this situation by coming up with a conceptual framework to develop international standards, concepts, definitions, and methodologies on the statistics of cooperatives.

6.7.4 Engage with stakeholders

The success of the SDGs will depend on effective implementation and monitoring, especially at national levels where actions will be taken and progress and impacts measured. This calls for multistakeholder partnerships to support the implementation of the SDGs at different levels. Cooperatives are networks of individuals and organizations that encompass members, government agencies, development agencies, business partners, and others. The relationships among stakeholders' matter and there is need to bring synergy between and among all in the network to create an "ecosystem" for cooperatives to sustain themselves and to be sustainable. There is need for an enabling environment in terms of legal frameworks, policies, and programs, and to have mechanisms in place to promote the work of cooperatives. In order for this to happen there needs to be active engagement from cooperatives with the different stakeholders in order to give voice and visibility to cooperatives in the implementation of the SDGs.

6.8 Conclusion

Even though cooperative enterprises contribute every day and in almost every sector of the economy toward the achievement of the SDGs, there are still several obstacles that prevent them from fully exploring their potential. Development is not entirely on-the-ground work at a community level. There needs to be recognition of the contributions that cooperative enterprises are making toward the SDGs. This requires promotion and advocacy of the cooperative model. Toward this end, there is need to educate members and engage with stakeholders; ensure inclusion of specific targets and indicators related to the promotion and development of cooperatives; access to specific implementation measures and programs including funding, which are adapted to the specific characteristics of cooperatives and respect their specific business model; and need on the part of cooperatives to participate in discussions and decision-making processes regarding the SDGs.

References

Business Council of Co-operatives and Mututals (BCCM), Australia. (2017). *Co-operatives and the UN Sustainable Development Goals: Submission to the Senate Standing Committee on Foreign Affairs Defence and Trade.* <https://bccm.coop/wp/wp-content/uploads/2018/05/BCCM-Submission-Senate-Economics-References-Committee.pdf>.

Department of Economic & Social Affairs, David Le Blanc. (2015). *Towards integration at last? The sustainable development goals as a network of targets.* <http://www.un.org/esa/desa/papers/2015/wp141_2015.pdf>.

International Cooperative Alliance. (2015). *Guidance notes to the cooperative principles.* <https://www.ica.coop/sites/default/files/basic-page-attachments/guidance-notes-en-221700169.pdf>.

Presland, C. (2018). *Environmental sustainability and the role of co-operatives.* <https://nz.coop/environmental-sustainability-and-the-role-of-co-operatives/>.

Roelants, B., Dovgan, D., Eum, H., & Terras, E. (2012). *The resilience of the cooperative model: How worker cooperatives, social cooperatives and other worker-owned enterprises respond to the crisis and its consequences.* <http://www.cecop.coop/IMG/pdf/report_cecop_2012_en_web.pdf>.

Singapore National Cooperative Federation (SNCF). (2018). *Singapore co-ops help contribute SDGS.* <https://www.sncf.coop/publications/87-2018-cooperator/june-2018/590-singapore-co-ops-help-contribute-sdgs>.

Wilkinson, R. and Pickett, K. (2010), The Spirit Level: Why Equality is Better for Everyone, London: Penguin.

2018 World Cooperative Monitor. (2018). *Exploring the cooperative economy.* <https://www.ica.coop/sites/default/files/publication-files/wcm2018-web-1542524747.pdf>.

Further reading

CDA Celebrates International Day of Co-operative through the launching of 'Marawi Rehabilitation through Cooperativism' Program. (2018). Retrieved from <http://www.cda.gov.ph/resources/updates/news/905-cda-celebrates-international-day-of-cooperatives-through-the-launching-of-marawi-rehabilitation-through-cooperativism-program>.

Committee for the Promotion and Advancement of Cooperatives. (2017). *Conceptual framework on measurement of cooperatives and its operationalization.* Report discussed at the COPAC Technical Working Group on Cooperative Statistics Meeting Geneva.

B20 Cross-Thematic Group Small and Medium Enterprises Policy Paper. (2017). *Think big for small small and medium enterprises as pillar for future-oriented, sustainable growth.* <https://www.b20germany.org/fileadmin/user_upload/documents/B20/B20_CTG_SMES_Final_Policy_Paper_2017-04-11.pdf>.

European Union. (2015). *The new European consensus on development 'our world, our dignity, our future.* <https://ec.europa.eu/europeaid/sites/devco/files/european-consensus-on-development-final-20170626_en.pdf>.

International Cooperative Alliance. (2013). *Blueprint for a cooperative decade.* <https://www.ica.coop/sites/default/files/media_items/ICA%20Blueprint%20-%20Final%20version%20issued%207%20Feb%2013.pdf>.

International Cooperative Alliance. (2018). *Co-operatives for 2030 — Cooperative initiatives to achieve a more sustainable future for all.* Retrieved from <https://www.ica.coop/sites/default/files/basic-page-attachments/1663-doc-subv-coop-12-p-ven-vok-84046514.pdf>.

International Cooperative Alliance. (2019). *Co-operatives for 2030. Cooperative initiative to achieve a sustainable future for all.* <https://www.ica.coop/sites/default/files/basic-page-attachments/1663-doc-subv-coop-12-p-ven-vok-84046514.pdf>.

International Labor Organization. (2016). *Employment and decent work for peace and resilience.* Revision of the Employment (Transition from War to Peace) Recommendation, 1944 (No. 71) <https://www.ioe-emp.org/index.php?eID = dumpFile&t = f&f = 125334&token = 2c41992ce941e83ca1259864e63b5a85b1657930>.

Japanese Consumer Cooperative Union. (2019). *JCCU received the 2nd Japan SDGs Award.* Retrieved from <https://jccu.coop/eng/news/2019/01/jccu-received-the-2nd-japan-sdgs-award.html>.

National Planning Commission, Government of Nepal. (2016). *The sustainable development goals — Status and roadmap 2016—2030.* <https://www.npc.gov.np/images/category/1__SDG_Report_final_version.pdf>.

Sri Lankan President launches national program to develop 10,000 Green Smart Villages. (2016). Retrieved from <http://www.colombopage.com/archive_16B/Jul01_1467389754CH.php>.

United Nations. *About the sustainable development goals.* Retrieved from <https://www.un.org/sustainabledevelopment/sustainable-development-goals/>.

United Nations. *Millennium development goals.* Retrieved from <http://www.un.org/millenniumgoals/poverty.shtml>.

United Nations. (2000). *Report of the world commission on environment and development: Our common future.* Retrieved from <http://www.un-documents.net/our-common-future.pdf>.

United Nations. (2012). *International year of cooperatives.* Retrieved from <http://www.un.org/en/events/coopsyear/>.

United Nations. (2015). *Transforming our world: The 2030 agenda for sustainable development.* Retrieved from <http://www.un.org/ga/search/view_doc.asp?symbol = A/RES/70/1&Lang = E>.

7

Asian cooperatives and gender equality

Sudha Kornginnaya

Department of Commerce, Mangalore University, Mangalore, Karnataka, India

7.1 Introduction

In Asia, growth accompanied by structural transformation, poverty reduction, and considerable progress in gender equality, particularly in education and healthcare, have led to transformative development in the past two decades (World Bank, 2011b). In the cooperative sector in the region, due to prioritized focus and the persistent policy interventions and programs of international organizations, considerable advancement in the status of women is being made, more so than ever before. The adoption of the historic Beijing Declaration and Platform for Action (Beijing Platform for Action) at the Fourth World Conference on women in 1995 gave further impetus to various gender specific programs in the region (ICA-AP, 2015, 2017a). Financial and social inclusion, women entrepreneurship, and self-help group initiatives at the grassroots level have contributed immensely toward women empowerment, providing momentum to gender parity in the cooperative landscape. The success stories of many gender responsive cooperatives in Asia such as the Mann Deshi Mahila Sahakari Bank in India, Koperasi Kopi Wanita Gayo in Indonesia, and gender-fair cooperatives in the Philippines testify how cooperatives are the preferred choice for collective organizing among many women across diverse sectors who were once marginalized. With the adoption of the Sustainable Development Goals (SDGs) to be achieved by 2030, commitment to reduce the gender gaps and enhance member participation has become a critical mandate and vital to the trajectory of cooperatives.

Despite the good strides in cooperatives, gender imbalance persists, reflecting the low level of participation among women and their underrepresentation in leadership and decision making (ILOCOOP, 2014). Persistent sociocultural, legal, economic, and political barriers have impaired women's access to opportunities that are enjoyed by their male compatriots, constraining women's progress (Wanyama, 2014). In view of this, this chapter is organized as described here. The second section explains the rationale for gender equality to successfully leverage gender potential in cooperatives. The third section highlights the key challenges to the advancement of gender equality in Asian cooperatives. The fourth section delineates the contribution made by cooperatives toward gender integration in the Asia region. The chapter concludes with the policy implications.

7.2 Rationale for gender equality in the cooperatives

The historical legacy of gender equality (GE) in cooperatives can be traced back to the Rochdale Pioneers founded in 1844. Eliza Brierley, the first woman member of the society who joined in 1846 enjoyed equal and full rights as those of her male counterparts in a rigid patriarchal society where women were excluded from equal participation in society (Barker, 2012). The Co-operative Women's Guild in the United Kingdom also promoted women in cooperative structures, their health, and peace issues. Gender parity has been a fundamental right since the first half of the 19th century where women were accepted as members (Green, 2012). Historically, the cooperative movement in Asia was more seen as "cooperation of the poor" for their alleviation of poverty irrespective of gender, class, and caste.

According to the International Co-operative Alliance's (ICA) definition of a cooperative, values and principles are the essence of cooperative identity and gender equality. Membership and leadership in cooperatives affirm nondiscrimination, assert the right to freedom of association, accord equal rights to control and power in cooperative affairs, and bestow equal opportunities to participate, avail services, and equitably gain benefits. Primacy of member centrality over capital has intrinsic significance and instrumental relevance only when gender equality is upheld to realize the common goal of economic and human development (ICA-AP, 2015; ILO, 2005). So, gender equality is a common thread weaving the fabric of cooperative democracy. Cooperatives driven by the precept of "all for each and each for all" and with the triple symbiotic roles as "democratically-controlled, social, and economic enterprises" are an apt instrument for espousing the cause of gender integration and women empowerment unlike

their corporate counterparts (Kornginnaya, 2014; Nippierd, 2002).

If a cooperative is to be called a "cooperative" that is built on a foundation of mutuality and the tenets of cooperation, then gender development is crucial for retaining the true character of the movement. It is only then that members will realize that it is their own, they are the owners and their wellbeing is solely dependent on their constructive participation. The self-awareness of the true meaning of cooperation will definitely ensure gender equality and preserve member identity. This makes the movement successful and this will continue no matter how the economy changes in its phase, structure, policies, and thinking (Sudha, 2005).

Gender-responsive cooperatives have been able to meet the needs of their members, take advantage of market opportunities, and to explore new markets and transform potential customers into satisfied and active members. Instances abound in which such cooperatives have survived challenges and have been the fittest and fastest in ruling the market.

In South Asia, most countries lag behind in terms of income, human and ecological poverty, and human and gender development indices (Acharya & Ghimire, 2005). Gender equality is central for the reduction of poverty and sustainable development as it drives balanced development faster and with no one being left behind. Cooperatives have been promoting human and social capital through human resource development interventions and financial and social inclusion. Cooperatives knowing the pulse of the community are a fitting institutional option that can fill the social and gender void that is unaddressed by the public and private sectors. They have sheltered millions of needy women who have faced multiple deprivations and helped them shape their own lives to achieve self-reliance, thus contributing to the development of their communities and countries (World Bank, 2016).

7.3 Challenges to the advancement of gender equality in cooperatives in Asia

The Beijing Declaration and Platform for Action 1995, the SDGs of the United Nations (UN) 2015, UN Women, the initiatives of the International Labor Organization (ILO), the International Co-operative Alliance (ICA), and the International Co-operative Alliance Asia Pacific (ICA AP) have advanced gender equality in cooperatives in Asia in myriad ways, keeping women at the center of advances. Though the committed efforts toward gender diversity are compelling, progress toward parity remains sluggish. Alongside improvements, inequalities persist due to various key challenges mentioned here.

7.3.1 Sociocultural and legal factors

The traditional cultural norms deeply entrenched in society that are manifested in societal customs, patriarchal ideology, and structural and legal constraints have restricted stereotyped gender roles to women and men, accentuating gender disparity in cooperative functions and operations (ILOCOOP, 2015). Cooperatives that exist in society mirror the same patriarchal mindset, influencing their objectives, roles, and operation (Laidlaw, 1980).

A report by Esim and Omeira (2009) on rural women in conflict settings in Arab states reveals that women experience a lack of formal protection and restricted physical mobility. Women-only cooperatives are controlled by their families or community members, while mixed cooperatives function as men-led cooperatives.

In South Asia, large numbers of people are poor and suffer concomitant ills. Two-thirds of rural women in the region are from low-income households, working in a paid and unpaid informal economy without food security, skills, social safety nets, and the protection of labor laws (World Bank, 2011b). These women workers know the least about the potential of cooperatives and would benefit the most through their collective action. Cooperatives being inclusive organizations need to include the excluded and refute the fact that gender disparity is more pronounced for the poor and marginalized.

Women are further burdened with triple roles of unpaid housework including water and fuel wood collection, child and geriatric care, and agriculture production (ADB & FAO, 2013; ILO, 2000). Time constraints have disadvantaged women discharging their cooperative duties and responsibilities.

Women face legal barriers, though cooperative laws are gender neutral or proactive, that underscore the representation of women in decision-making bodies (ILO, 2002). The laws of each country are a reflection of the sociocultural norms that disadvantage women. In some countries, women are barred from conducting business independently. Though women's legal rights are stipulated in law, they are neither implemented nor complied by customary law (Nippierd, 2002). Some Asian countries lack state and cooperative laws for gender parity and have discriminatory judicial practices that do not concede women's rights concerning work force participation (ILO, 2002, 2015b; World Bank, 2011b). Informal women workers are often excluded in labor laws and barred from forming trade unions in the majority of Arab countries (Majurin, 2008).

7.3.2 Economic factors

In Asia, women represent, on an average, only 10% of all agricultural landholders. Barring Bhutan, the inheritance laws and land registration practices of most of these countries are discriminatory, which hamper property ownership for women and condition their voluntary membership. Women lack control over assets, income, and production inputs, and face unequal access to technology and infrastructural facilities (FAO, 2017; World Bank, 2011a). This has impeded their participatory and investment potential, and limited new livelihood opportunities, compelling them to work in nonlucrative informal sectors (ICA, 2016). It is more prevalent in South Asian countries such as Bangladesh, Pakistan, and Nepal (FAO, 2011). Assetless women and men lacking collateral securities are hindered in availing credit to fulfill basic financial needs and help diversify livelihoods. Besides, it also curtails women's economic participation and access to market and weakens their bargaining power (ICA-AP, 2017a; ILO, 2013). Resource-poor members are underrepresented in cooperative affairs with a power and voice deficit rendering democracy at peril.

Women's contribution to entrepreneurship often goes unnoticed, underappreciated, and unrecognized as they function in the informal economy. Most often economic compulsion forces women, more so than men, to pursue entrepreneurship. Women's cooperatives are often discriminated against due to a lack of experience, managerial knowledge, and a lack of access to the financial, technical and physical resources, and marketing support required for growth in the long run. Women's cooperatives have not yet formed a federation in the region, which hinders their active representation in regional and global bodies (Datta & Gailey, 2012; ILO, 2015b).

Capacity challenges for men and women in terms of low business and managerial acumen and marketing skills reflect in low economic productivity and competitiveness. Gender disparity persists in the access to capacity building interventions in terms of numbers, attendance, exposure, and the types of trainings organized for members, executives, and nonexecutives. Cooperative education and training, qualitative gender awareness, and sensitization programs in terms of quantity, quality, and investment for

the purpose are inadequate at all levels in the cooperative movement in the region. Rural women hardly get access to agricultural extension as compared to men. Concerning capacity building of officers and staff, men dominate more so than women in leadership training as the numbers of the latter are low in managerial and administrative positions in cooperatives across Asia, except in Korea and the Philippines (ICA-AP, 2017a).

7.3.3 Organizational factors

Women are underrepresented in leadership and decision-making bodies as compared to men across all sectors and nations. Although women have proven abilities in governance and political participation, the gender and power relations in hierarchies limit their active participation and upward mobility in all spheres in cooperatives. The ICA AP (2017a) report reveals that, with the exception of South Korea and the Philippines, at the apex level, female representation was abysmally low with women as chairpersons (10%), as vice chairpersons (18%), at the cooperatives' level as board members (23%) and as chief executive officers (CEO) (18%). Men dominated in terms of representation in committees, the boardroom, and executive positions as compared to women in the whole of Asia. The sectors represented were agriculture, consumer, credit and savings, fishery, fertilizers, finance and banking, and service. Singapore, China, and Thailand also reported the presence of vice chairpersons and CEOs. The number of women as board members was below 10% in Myanmar, Pakistan, and India. If the presence of women in annual general meetings (AGMs) was observed as 50% in South Korea and the Philippines, it was only 5% in Pakistan. Researched literature reports the dismal representation of women in board meetings and AGMs in banking and finance, housing, manufacturing, fishery, and agricultural sectors, with an exception in women's cooperatives. Adoption of female quotas mandating more female representation in the Board was found bereft of equal representation of women proving ineffective to influence the decision making leading to the governance deficit (ICA, 2005; Lodhia, 2009).

In Asia, leadership is considered a prerogative right and skill of men, conditioning women to become members and not leaders. The lack of exposure of members and leaders to education and training and gender investment in cooperatives undermines the capability potential of those who would otherwise excel in leadership positions (ICA-AP, 2015; ICA, 2016; ILOCOOP, 2014). Political activism by women is often derided or tabooed by cultural hegemony in cooperatives.

Women's participation shows a rising trend in terms of membership and their economic and democratic engagement, while capacity building interventions are minimal in the agriculture, financial, consumer, service, and marketing sectors. A dearth of economic opportunities and by extension exposure, favoring men for membership and service facilities over resource-poor women, tokenistic participation of women for benefitting their spouses, gender bias and general apathy, lack of voice space for women, and time constraints have stalled the perpetual engagement of women. Most often women's involvement is limited only to trading terms or self-help group (SHG) activities, hampering the spirit of empowerment (ICA, 2016; Sudha, 2008).

In the agriculture sector, women's membership remains scant as compared to their numbers in the work force across Asia. In Northern China, men dominated in presence in cooperative meetings and decision making, although women were doing most of the farming work (Garnevska, Liu, & Shadbolt, 2011). Women are discriminated against in availing services and benefits in terms of health insurance, loans, technical input for farming, except for maternity leave and micro credit. Excluding Mongolia, paternity services were the lowest availed services in the region. A Body of Literature documented that engendering database in cooperatives in the region is weak across different levels, sectors, and countries impairing the visibility of gender equality in a real perspective. The majority of cooperatives are unaware of the ICA's gender strategy (68%) and denied the receipt of the ICA AP Women Committee's newsletters (74%) (ICA-AP, 2017a).

7.4 Contribution of Asian cooperatives to gender equality

Alongside identified challenges, countries across Asia have reported achievements in gender equality due to the decades-long, unremitting, collaborative role of international development entities, the legislative and operational commitment of respective governments, and the synergetic support, strategies, and committed involvement of the cooperative movement.

In a follow up of the Beijing Platform for Action, the Governments of most Asian countries have embarked on policies, legislation, normative frameworks, institutional mechanisms, gender committees, plans of action, gender-responsive budgeting and strategies along with the accession to international covenants such as the UN's SDGs (SDG 5), 2015; the Millennium Development Goals, 2000; ILO recommendation No.193 (7.3), 2002; the Convention on the Elimination of All Forms of Discrimination Against Women (CEDAW), 1979 (ica.coop, 2017; UNESCAP, 2015). These measures have set pathways for cooperatives to achieve the goals and targets laid out in the 2030 Agenda for Sustainable Development.

UN agencies such as UN Food and Agricultural Organization (FAO), the International Labor Organization (ILO), and the UN Development Programme (UNDP) and international development organizations such as the Canadian Cooperative Association (CCA), WE Effect, the European Union (EU) Delegation, and Asian Women in Cooperative Development Forum (AWCF), have all played key roles in creating and funding cooperatives, the advocacy and formulation of policies, and development projects for furthering gender diversity and inclusion in the cooperative movement in Asia (ICA-AP, 2017a).

7.4.1 International Cooperative Alliance (ICA Asia Pacific)

Extant literature in the cooperative galaxy provides headway for the ICA AP toward women empowerment and gender advancement across sectors and countries in Asia. The ICA AP's initiatives toward gender integration started with a special women's program during the UN Women's Decade (1975–85) that created a conducive environment for enhancing women's participation in cooperatives. The need for a women's capacity building program was felt in 1990 by the ICA's Human Resources Development Project, leading to a study on the situation analysis of 14 different countries followed by a Gender Planning Conference in Tokyo in 1993. The ICA ROAP was able to establish a specific gender program unit. In 1995 the adoption of the ICA's Identity Statement emphasizing the significance of gender, led to the organizing of several regional consultations/conferences and the formation of the ICA Regional Women's Committee for Asia and Pacific in 1997. The Women's Forum is organized under the aegis of the ICA AP Committee on Women and it has been conducting various conferences on gender integration themes. The Women's Committee works to promote gender integration in cooperatives and encourages the participation of women at all levels in cooperatives, especially at the leadership and decision making levels (ILO, 2005).

The ICA, with the AWCF, held a first regional conference in Tagaytay, Philippines in May 1997 on "Women in Decision-Making in Co-operatives" focusing on building women's capacities for equal participation in cooperative functioning, leadership, and decision making and for gender integration at all levels of cooperatives in the region (ILO, 2005). The conference culminated in the "Declaration and Platform for Action for the Enhancement of Women's Participation in Leadership and Decision-Making in Co-operatives."

The ICA AP Committee on Women has organized a number of programs to train, build capacity, and sensitize cooperative members and leaders. Some key programs include: Training of Trainers for Leadership Development of Women in Cooperatives; Development of Resource Guide on Advance Training of Cooperatives for Entrepreneurship Development and Women; ICA Blueprint for a Co-operative Decade—20/20 Vision; Collection and Analysis of Sex-disaggregated Data in 2005 and 2015; Institutionalizing the Gender Disaggregated Data (GDD) System in Cooperatives; Exposure and Networking Programme for Empowerment of Women and Cooperative Development; Institutionalization of Gender Integration in Cooperatives of at least 33%–50% of women in all levels, particularly in decision making of the Board of Directors; Inclusion of Youth as Future Leaders in Cooperatives; Regional Conference for Gender Integration in Co-operatives; Establishing a Fund for the Empowerment of Women in Co-operatives generated from within the cooperative movement as well as from other institutions; and Gender Mainstreaming with the support of International Organizations (ICA-AP, 2017b; ica-ap.coop, 2019).

7.4.2 Cooperative federations

Several web reports of the activities of the federations of countries in East and Northeast

Asia, Southeast Asia, and South and Southwest Asia confirm that their committed initiatives are in tandem with the National Gender Policy and the laws of their countries at varying levels (ICA-AP, 2017b). This includes initiating gender-sensitive cooperative laws and bylaws through advocacy; fulfilling quotas at all levels of management (one-third of total seats) for representation in leadership; capacity building programs for leaders and members; facilitating access to finance and market through SHGs and micro credit and business and technical training; livelihood activities for the deprived, ensuring women's rights in the areas of health, child care, and labor; enhancing women labor force participation; fostering national and international linkages; the creation of websites to disseminate useful information to both men and women and popularizing success stories of women cooperatives.

Delineations of the ICA AP Report (2017a) authored by Nandini Azad on a 10-year sex disaggregated database from 28 countries reaffirm the status of women advancement in the Asia Pacific region, which are outlined here:

19 out of 26 countries with 28 apex federations in the Asia Pacific region across the agriculture, consumer, credit and savings, informal, fishery, fertilizers, finance and banking, land and land settlement, and service-related sectors were represented in the survey. Though women's leadership at the top echelons were found to be low, women's presence in governance structures showed an increasing trend as compared to 2005. The comparative gender disaggregated data collected on two different periods (2005 and 2015) demonstrated that the number of women chairpersons increased from 7% to 10%; vice chairpersons from nil to 18%, representing apex federations in Korea, Singapore, China, Thailand, and the Philippines; board representation from 18% to 23%; and women development committees in apexes reached 75%. Gender segregated participation at executive and nonexecutive levels in cooperatives also showed a favorable picture.

Women executives increased from 2.4% to 32%. At the nonexecutive level, the disparity between men and women employees was almost bridged with 43% female employees and 57% male employees. Men and women's participation in annual general body meetings (AGBM) also consistently increased as compared to board meetings. Most apex organizations accorded high priority for women's capacity building and, accordingly, the participation of board members in trainings also increased. Excluding China, iCOOP in Korea and VICTO in the Philippines outperformed other apex bodies in terms of women's presence in board, attendance in board meetings and AGBMs, and participation in committees. Apex cooperatives in Bhutan, the Philippines, India, and Malaysia were found to be proactive in organizing capacity building programs for women members. If the participation of women officers and staff outnumbered men in technical skills training in basic computer, work ethics, and gender awareness, their counterparts outpaced women in training in credit awareness and business principles.

The aforesaid findings of the Report is indicative of the integration of gender perspectives in direction and diffusion process of GE by federations.

The federations of most countries, either having representation in national mechanisms or through their collaboration with national machineries for GE, played key roles in realizing GE in critical areas of Beijing Platform for Action.

Concerning women in power structures, the quota of women board members has increased (for instance, 30%−50% in Japanese Consumer Cooperative Union (JCCU) in Japan and 33% in National Cooperative Union of India (NCUI) in India), reflecting in the increased number of women in membership and leadership. For instance, The National Confederation of Cooperatives (NATCCO) had 66% women and 48% men in membership and 52% women and 48% men at board level in 2016 as compared to 65% men and 35% women in board representation in 1998 (AWCF, 1999; ICA-AP, 2017a). This trend is also documented in the National Cooperative Federation Ltd (VICTO) in the Philippines, Singapore National Co-operative Federation (SNCF), National Cooperative Federation of Nepal, All China Federation of Supply and Marketing Cooperatives (ACFSMC), and iCOOP in Korea (ICA-AP, 2017a). This is mainly attributed to the mandate of the mainstreaming of gender and development (GAD) to realize GE in all its dimensions.

In the area of the education and training of women, apex federations of all the countries in Asia have institutional mechanisms and infrastructures in place to enhance the capability of all the human resources at different levels in their structures. They provide technical, financial, and human resource support downward to fortify the employable and entrepreneurial skills of their members. In JCCU in Japan, women account for 95% of cooperative users and 70% of the cooperative working force. A platform of GE is created and gender programs have been designed and implemented (jccu.coop, 2010). Members of JCCU and iCOOP, actively participate in all the theme-based activities ranging from food safety, gender, and business development activities to disaster recovery and peace movements. VICTO organized several "Men talking to Men about Manhood" (M3) trainings and modules for men, women, and older persons to sensitize men, specifically on gender roles. iCOOP in Korea also conducts political courses for members to enlighten them of participatory democracy, an advanced course for activists in iCOOP college, and university education for professionals in the Department of Management of Cooperatives in Sungkonghoe University (ICA-AP, 2017a).

The NCUI has been organizing a wide range of education and training programs exclusively for women, youth, and deprived sections encompassing labor, fishery, handloom, and tribal cooperatives and leadership development programs. In addition, cooperative education field projects including exclusive women projects, underdeveloped North Eastern projects and socioeconomic development programs are undertaken for the promotion of SHGs and women ensuring employment and income generation for the target groups (NCUI, 2018).

Most federations from Japan, the Philippines, Korea, Thailand, Malaysia, Singapore, Vietnam, India, Nepal and Cambodia have been organizing various gender-related workshops, seminars, and projects in partnership with AWCF, ICA AP, and CCA to build the capacity and skills of women.

Concerning women and the environment, as a part of social agenda, more gender-sensitive programs are being implemented by apex federations addressing issues related to climate change, the environment, and disaster risk reduction in Japan, China, and Korea in Northeast Asia; Indonesia, the Philippines, Malaysia, Thailand, and Vietnam in Southeast Asia; and Sri Lanka, Nepal, Bangladesh, India, and Afghanistan in South and Southwest Asia to strengthen the awareness, response capabilities, and disaster preparedness of member organizations and individual members (jccu.coop, 2010).

Across the region, federations played a vital role in increasing women's access to economic opportunities, furthering their participation in the economy. Their contribution in capacity building, employment generation, and the reduction of poverty is immense. They have engendered leadership opportunities at the grassroots level in rural areas through microfinance and SHG models and entrepreneurship in the green economy in Central, Northeast, South, and Southeast Asian countries. The exposure to training, entrepreneurial activities, and social protection, easing the formation of women's cooperatives, and decent jobs have contributed to the increased work force participation of women in the economy. ACFSMC in

China, through a network of specialized cooperatives and village level comprehensive service agencies, created immense job opportunities in diverse areas for rural and urban women. It provides financial support and credit guarantee services for small loans to women-exclusive cooperatives in rural areas. The increasing scale and number of rural women specialized cooperatives in China speaks volumes of the entrepreneurial enthusiasm and public participation capacity of rural women leading to rural economic growth. iCOOP in Korea is an exemplary model of a cooperative federation where both consumers and employees want to work together and female employees outnumber their male counterparts (UNESCAP, 2007). In SNCF in Singapore, 71.6% of staff working in local cooperatives and 51.1% of management are women (ICA-AP, 2017b). JCCU in Japan has created a satisfactory working environment for their women employees with a favorable work—life balance for women after marriage and child birth, motivational awards for cooperatives offering best practices, child care leave for male employees, and giving the "Kurumin" certification mark to cooperatives satisfying certain gender equality standards (jccu.coop, 2010). Apex federations in Sri Lanka, Malaysia, Nepal, India, Thailand, Indonesia, and Myanmar have fostered an enabling ecosystem for catalyzing gender work force participation, livelihood opportunities, and poverty reduction.

7.4.3 Initiatives of cooperatives and members

Research evidences have identified the contribution of cooperatives at the base level with the collective efforts of the members in four key areas of gender advancement in East and Northeast Asia, Southeast Asia, Southwest Asia, and some countries of Central Asia. Key areas are interrelated and interdependent in nature converging into a single goal of advancement of women and are outlined here.

7.4.3.1 Inclusive participation in membership and governance

Cooperatives provide a place for all their members for inclusive and meaningful participation in their functions and governance. This is key to ensuring gender justice and a means for addressing gender biased social mores. Researched reports show a general rise in the participation of women in the consumer, worker, financial, and agriculture inclusive of the dairy and fishery sectors across Asia.

In Japan, women's active presence and participation is evident at all levels of cooperative institutions, particularly in the agriculture, credit, consumer, and producer sectors (ILO, 2015a). Both men and women have enhanced their membership and customer base. There are around 600 consumer cooperatives with 27 million members where women constitute more than 80% of those members. Cooperatives provide a wide range of services from daycare for children to homecare for the elderly with women's active participation. Women members participate in the management of these cooperatives with their viewpoints of daily living (COPAC, 2015; jccu.coop, 2010). 120 consumer cooperatives provide healthcare for around 3 million members, who regularly meet in small Han groups to discuss preventive health issues (Marathe, 2017; SCCCU, 2004). Congruent results are also reported in web resources in artisan and handicraft cooperatives in Indonesia; savings and credit cooperatives in Bangladesh and Nepal; tea cooperatives in Sri Lanka; financial, agricultural, industrial, and multipurpose cooperatives in the Philippines; thrift societies in Malaysia; dairy and women worker cooperatives in India; and in women specific multipurpose cooperatives all over Asia.

Although gender stereotypes and structural inequities pose leadership challenges in Asia, when compared to their corporate and public sector counterparts, due to the presence of GE integration mechanisms such as a quota system, women's pronounced visibility in governance positions at the primary levels is documented in research reports in the Philippines, Japan, India, Indonesia, Singapore, Sri Lanka, Thailand, Korea, Nepal, and Malaysia. A lack of gender disaggregated data also gives an incomplete picture of women's and men's positions in cooperatives in Asia. Considering the number of women's cooperatives operating across different sectors and the proliferating number of women's dairy units at the grassroot level, women's participation concurrently shows an increasing trend in Asia. Women are well represented in management structures in financial, consumer, dairy, and workers cooperatives. In Japan, regional cooperatives have higher percentages of women chairpersons, deputy directors, and board members. Ninety five percent of the governance positions in cooperatives are occupied by women (Wanyama, 2014). In Korea, in 2002 61% of the members at the decision-making level of community-based consumer cooperatives were women and have been providing equal opportunities for income generation and job creation (Park, 2004; Warman & Kennedy, 1998). In the Philippines, GAD initiatives have increased female membership and representation in the board composition with 54% and 40% respectively (Cooperative Development Authority, 2018). Evidences showed that women's meaningful participation in the provision of services, management, and decision making have helped in redressing exclusionary discrimination and overcoming gendered structural and sociocultural limitations (COPAC, 2000; ICA, 2005).

7.4.3.2 Entrepreneurship development

Cooperatives have trailblazed social entrepreneurship among rural and deprived women and metamorphosed their gender roles from unpaid familial domestic care to the work economy. The growth of women cooperatives in number and scale in Japan, Korea, India, Sri Lanka, Nepal, Malaysia, Vietnam, China, Arab states, Bangladesh, and Kyrgyz Republic across different sectors speaks volumes of their entrepreneurial involvement and the realization of women's rights (COPAC, 2015; ILOCOOP, 2015).

Womenlink, a leading women's green consumers' cooperative in the Republic of Korea, pioneered in promoting green entrepreneurship in organic agriculture. It has strengthened its business linkages with green producers' cooperatives at the community level in rural areas and with other women's green cooperatives in Japan and Taiwan province of China. Being unbiased in terms of gender and class, it redresses situations that are prejudiced against women. With technical, marketing, and managerial support and active participation in need-tailored committees, women are professed in green business ventures. Womenlink started with only 220 households and has grown into 12,000 multicommunity-based membership and increased sales volume 24 times between 1990 and 2005 (UNESCAP, 2007).

WEAN Multipurpose Cooperative Ltd—a women producers' marketing cooperative in Nepal—has been marketing handicraft and food products locally as well as exporting to Japan, New Zealand, Australia, Germany, the Netherlands, the United Kingdom, and the United States. The cooperative has created a group of producers called "Women Power," which helps its members to become competitive in the market (WEAN, 2013).

Indian Cooperative Network for Women (ICNW) is the first women cooperative in South India with an innovative bottom-up structure for, by, and of poor women. It has sheltered 589,724 women entrepreneurs involved in 276 occupations and enterprises from 6449 slums and villages in 14 cooperative branches in three Southern States of India federated by a multistate cooperative.

ICNW has become a beacon for all the historically discriminated, economically exploited, and socially oppressed poor women. It facilitates access to credit, insurance products, technology, skill building, and secured employment. The diverse training and field exposure offered by the cooperative have facilitated women to participate at all levels of the organization and local government bodies. By organizing poor women as shareholders in credit cooperatives, it has transformed women from a state of indebtedness and oppression to successful micro entrepreneurs and empowerment. Women are bolstered to counter gender discrimination fraught by class exploitation, caste inferiority, male dominance, and societal isolation. The installation of digitalization and automated software for credit operations has also generated employment and enhanced the technological skills of fisher and daily wage worker women (icnw.in, 2019).

Coastal Electrification and Women's Development Cooperative, which started by manufacturing solar lamps in 1999 has transformed women in the southern part of Bangladesh. It trained women in assembly line and encouraged them to set up small businesses, on the side, turning them into entrepreneurs in renewable energy, tailoring, poultry, and a myriad other areas, addressing the entrenched historical gender disparity (Bergman, 2017).

Progressive women's cooperative microenterprises are also visible in the Kyrgyz Republic, the Republic of Tajikistan, and Kazakhstan in Central Asia, where agriculture is a prime occupation and laden with cultural bias. The initiatives of the state and external agencies have driven women to engage in handicraft, agricultural processing, household articles, and in pasture and livestock cooperatives. Technical training, financial, and organizational support and Fair Trade Gender Leadership School have helped women to integrate into agriculture value chains and pursue producer cooperatives in Central Asia (ADB, 2012; wecf.org, 2019). Cooperative entrepreneurship has accorded multiple benefits to members in terms of work—life balance,

flexible hours, ease of entry, micro capital, and control over collective resources.

Publications discuss cooperative entrepreneurship led by SHGs among disadvantaged groups at the grassroots level across Asia in agricultural, financial, and worker cooperatives (Bhatt, 1994; Bibby & Shaw, 2005; FAO, 2012; Kornginnaya, 2015a; Rao, 1996). They showcase how SHGs' progress and their access to micro credit, insurance, financial literacy, and group lending have perpetuated their members' entrepreneurial engagement, reflected in the rise of microenterprises in Asia. Women are venturing into market themselves, negotiate and leverage market potentials. The increased savings and asset creation of members lifted them out of poverty traps, bolstered their economic resilience, and catalyzed their upward and social mobility, unshackling women from the glass ceiling. It has enhanced their financial decision-making power both in the household and outside of it, transforming them from a state of utter illiteracy to being functional literates, from dependence on spouses to interdependence on the group, family members, and cooperatives. Women are able to contribute to the welfare, health, and education of their children and families and live a life they value (UNDP, 2010).

7.4.3.3 Women empowerment

Women empowerment in cooperatives means the ability of women to exercise their choice of organizing themselves into cooperatives to fulfill their common socioeconomic and cultural needs, to assert collective rights and control resources and decisions for the greatest good of a large number of members through their enlightened participation in all the social, economic, cultural, and political activities of cooperatives, leading to their self-reliance and the elimination of their subordination (Kornginnaya, 2015a). In the literature, examples abound of socioeconomic and political empowerment of women in cooperatives across Asia (ILO, 2018; Jhabvala, 1994). In some countries in South Asia, South East Asia, Central and Middle East Asia,progress of gender advancement albeit slow, the efforts are on foot due to pressing gender mandate.

Self-Employed Women's Association (SEWA) and Anand Milk Union Limited (AMUL) in India have epitomized women empowerment and formalized the informal economy through the cooperative model and are worthy of national and international replication. SEWA, being a convergence of three movements—labor, cooperative, and women's movement—was formed in 1972 as a union of poor women workers without socioeconomic protection. It has organized over 2 million self-employed women representing 17 states in India under member-based organizations including 130 cooperatives in diverse fields. By adopting a joint strategy of economic organizing of women in unions and cooperatives, it has enhanced members' identity and increased their collective voice and bargaining power in the market place, with the public authorities, and in society. All the members have been able to achieve full employment and self-reliance in terms of work, income, and food and social security through the strategy of struggle and development. Members leveraged their equitable roles in the decision-making process whilst maintaining full control as owners and leaders. Women have dismantled the economic and societal barriers that have relegated them and made their contribution visible to policy makers (Bhatt, 1991; ILO, 2018; SEWA, 2019).

The AMUL model in India, being the largest milk producer in the world, has sheltered more than 15 million milk producers who pour their milk into 144,500 dairy cooperatives, ensuring a better life for millions through regular livelihood, food and nutrition, livestock, and biogas. The value chain of dairy cooperatives from procurement to marketing managed by women farmer members is a testimony for women empowerment, leading to the success of the White Revolution, the world's biggest dairy development program. Besides making the country self-sufficient in milk, leadership development training and employment programs targeting asset-less urban and rural poor women have transformed their lives from dependence to self-dependence and from drudgery to sustainable development (AMUL, 2018).

7.4.3.4 Access to resources and opportunities

Despite the disparities, many all-women cooperatives in the region have provided access to resources, rights, economic opportunities, and a whole range of services to members, which were otherwise denied and discriminated, reflecting in gender inclusion in real perspectives. A large body of evidences have uncovered the efficacy of accessing resources on multiple fronts. Resources are central to rectify development imbalances, to acquire other assets, diversify livelihoods, sustain enterprises, augment economic choices, build capabilities to obtain opportunities, ignite women's agency, enhance their social acceptance, and remove oppressive traditions (UNDP, 2010).

Evidences show that opportunities in terms of capacity building interventions, the provision of services, simple registration procedures, networking, and advocacy have addressed the participatory inertia among women in cooperatives. Examples include the institutionalizing of GAD initiatives in the Tagum Financial Cooperative and the Lamac Multi-Purpose Cooperative in Cebu in the Philippines (CDA, 2018); leadership development programs in women's dairy cooperatives in India and youth cooperatives in Japan (UN, 2009); financial services in women's cooperatives in Sri Lanka and Nepal; micro credit facilities in saving and credit cooperatives across Asia; the provision of jobs in "associated work" workers' cooperatives in Japan and advocacy and networking by SEWA in India; diversified livelihood and a peer education program in Usha Multipurpose

Cooperative Society by sex workers in West Bengal in India; the emergence of new cooperatives alongside the formal cooperative sector such as credit cooperatives in Indonesia; and mutually aided cooperatives in Andhra Pradesh in India (Nippierd, 2002). All the aforesaid cooperatives have enlisted increased participation of women in cooperatives.

Literature indicates that member engagement in nonfarm activities accounts for 32% of income of rural households in Asia. The equal access to training, productive inputs, and opportunities for secured livelihood and markets have led to the productivity enhancement of over 3 million fishers from over 18,000 fishery cooperatives in India (ILO, 2014).

The Women's Worker Cooperative in Japan, having a membership of 12,000 worker members, provide suitable employment opportunities, contributing significantly to the new middle-class lifestyle. Besides, cooperatives fulfill the twin goals of enabling housewives to work part-time and equally help women to take up familial caring responsibilities (Marshall, 2006; Sager, 2017).

Agriculture, dairy, and fishery cooperatives in rural areas have been an important model of enterprise and a crucial economic source for many rural women who form a large share of the agricultural labor force as contributing family workers in the region. Cooperatives have helped women organize and have access to land, market, information, technology, financial and social services, and training in marketing skills leading to their socioeconomic progress (FAO, 2011; ILO & ADB, 2011).

The Indian Farmers Fertilizer Co-operative Limited (IFFCO), Indian Farm Forestry Development Cooperative Limited (IFFDC), and SHG structures promoted by IFFCO have provided innumerable opportunities for women empowerment and gender integration. These include a 5% reservation for women in the Representative General Body in IFFCO; indigenous and SHG women's involvement in afforestation and microenterprises in bee keeping, poultry, tailoring, sanitary napkin making, incense stick and wick making, embroidery, and fruit and vegetable preservation; the provision of solar-based, safe drinking water and the construction of smokeless stoves and toilets ensuring women health, safety, and sanitation programs; initiating drudgery reduction activities to save the time and labor of women and the utilization of the same on women development activities (IFFCO, 2017–2018).

Cooperatives across all sectors and in engendered community structures formed by SHGs in the region have provided their members an equality of opportunities to assume leadership and governance roles propelling the growth of themselves and their organizations. The equal access of women to human and capital endowment begets human and social capital, enhancing the cultural affinity and social solidarity among them.

7.4.3.5 Cultural advancement

Gender equality in society is paramount to achieving the full potential of women as it is the role of society that limits women's freedom and rights of participation. Cooperatives have enabled women to break the glass ceiling conditioned by the societal cultural norms helping them to enjoy freedom in expression, mobility, socializing, public life, and pursuing vocation (Jhabvala, 2013).

For Iranian women, who are under the glass ceiling and the actualization of gender equality at an individual level is difficult, cooperatives made their tangible visibility through women's enhanced participation reflecting in exponential business growth. For instance, as Kabeer (1999) advocated, Rah-e-Roshd Educational Cooperative has helped its members to realize their agency in terms of achieving their individual goals and career growth through the provision of access to resources and power leading to their empowerment. Women are given equal access to leadership positions and opportunities in stock trading, to participate in collaborative decision making, negotiating, voting, and in the job market (Pazir & Shah, 2016).

The potential of cooperatives in empowering rural women in conflict settings in areas such as Arab states, which include Lebanon, Iraq, and West Bank and the Gaza Strip (WBGS) is discerned by the disadvantaged rural women producers of that region. Cooperatives strengthened their power of resilience against poverty and powerlessness who braced the high risks and challenges of forced displacement, deficits in all forms of security, shrinkage in employment opportunities, deplorable working conditions, and social infrastructure. Cooperatives in this region, although functioning with the support of political and donor initiatives, have repositioned themselves to promote entrepreneurship, helping women to mobilize themselves to share risks, pool resources, accumulate savings, and access credit (Esim & Omeira, 2009).

In summary, the literature indicates that the gender concerns of many women entrepreneurs and leaders in cooperatives enabled them to consolidate their voice against market exclusion, systemic discrimination, policy paralysis, societal aberration, democratic deficit, and patriarchal rigidities that subjugated and exploited them in the world of work and the cooperative domain. Thus through the efforts of cooperatives women have been the catalysts of the socioeconomic change of themselves and the locale (Jhabvala, 2013; Korginnaya, 2015b). Their equal economic partnership in their families reflects in the equal sharing of domestic responsibility by men, testifying to the essence of gender equality in cooperation and the community. The increased participation in diverse economic options has helped them to contribute to the welfare, health, and education of their children and families. Women are emboldened to counter discrimination and social exclusion,

leading to their physical mobility and political participation (ICA, 1991; Jhabvala, 1994; Kabeer, 2005). Examples include Small Farmers Cooperative limited (SFCL) in Nepal and savings and credit cooperatives in Bangladesh, Nepal, India, and Sri Lanka.

Many cooperatives in the region have discerned that instilling gender equality in their cooperative affairs in letter and in spirit will strengthen their democratic nature, fostering the meaningful participation of their members. It has promoted the collective agency transforming the lives of men and women, in particular, and society in general. Besides enhancing the use of endowments and economic opportunities for members, gender equality has fostered the formation of physical, human, social, and financial capital, reducing the social norms that constrained their individual agency (World Bank, 2011a). Instilling gender equality in cooperative fundamentals adds sense, sensitivity, and sensibility to their enshrined cooperative values, principles, and cooperative identity.

7.5 Conclusion

This chapter explains the rationale for gender equality and the challenges and barriers preventing the realization of this ideal. The barriers were identified as sociocultural, legal, economic, and organizational. However, in many instances these have been overcome. The contribution of Asian cooperatives in overcoming these barriers has been immense due to the ICA, cooperative federations, cooperatives, and members themselves through inclusive participation in membership and governance, entrepreneurial development, women empowerment, access to resources and opportunities, and cultural advancement. There is still much do be done.

The policy implications include an imperative need for gender responsive national cooperative laws within the entire government approach, regulatory frameworks, structural reorganization, policy mandates, advocacy, gender investment, and strategies and action plans for institutionalizing gender equality in the cooperative movement in Asia. Supportive legal and administrative reforms are vital to ensure gender equal rights, access to resources, particularly land and credit, and socioeconomic opportunities to both men and women. This is paramount to closing historic legal, sociocultural, and structural gender gaps that have impaired women's participation. Strengthening collaboration between international agencies, women's organizations, cooperatives at all levels, and civil society is crucial to accelerating the implementation of gender equality.

Gender sensitive bylaws and policy should be instituted in every cooperative ensuring increased women membership and their participation in leadership positions. An enabling environment with a level playing field is imperative for promoting women cooperatives, women entrepreneurship and labor force participation with flexible hours, social security, and legal entitlements and endowments. Gender integration committees akin to the SHG model at the primary level, awareness raising, and gender-sensitive programs at all levels in governments and cooperatives are essential for transforming the patriarchal mindset of institutional human resources and society at large. The inclusion of the youth and the transgender community is imperative to leverage the demographic dividend catalyzing social change in cooperatives. Gender statistics and disaggregation of data collection and utilization systems should be promoted for timely mapping of gender progress and gaps and for reviewing and renewing gender policies in cooperatives. Gender learning materials, resources, and tools and gender analysis and evaluation mechanisms should be in place and tailor made to the learning needs of women members.

Capacity building of both cooperatives and women members is integral to enhancing their active participation in cooperative management. Governments and cooperative departments and federations should provide support in terms of finance, human resources, infrastructure, and technology to resource-poor primary cooperatives for the effective implementation of programs. Initiatives such as member education on cooperative basics, training in leadership development, governance practices, vocational and computer skills, business and entrepreneurship development, awareness on legal and women's rights, and health and the environment should be organized as a bottom-up approach at regular intervals without discrimination. This is critical for perpetuating member engagement, securing their life-long allegiance, and for building women's capacity for leadership and decision-making in cooperatives. Internalizing cooperative principles and commitment to gender diversity endeavors is key for building a better world without poverty where men and women live lives with equal power, voices, rights, freedom, social justice, and democracy.

References

Acharya, M., & Ghimire, P. (2005). Gender indicators of equality, inclusion and poverty reduction: Measuring programme/project effectiveness. *Economic and Political Weekly*, 40(44/45), 4719–4728. (October 29–November 4, 2005), Retrieved from https://www.jstor.org/stable/4417358.

AMUL. (2018). *Gujarat cooperative milk marketing federation Ltd (GCMMF)*. About us- The AMUL Model. Retrieved from <http://www.amul.com/m/about-us>.

Asian Development Bank (ADB). (2012). *A story within a story: ADB helps rural women in the Kyrgyz Republic become entrepreneurs*. Retrieved from <https://www.adb.org/sites/default/files/publication/29716/story-kgz-women-entrepreneurs.pdf>.

Asian Development Bank (ADB) and Food and Agriculture Organization of the United Nations (FAO). (2013). *Gender equality and food security. Women's empowerment as a tool against hunger*. Philippines: ADB. Retrieved from http://www.fao.org/wairdocs/ar259e/ar259e.pdf.

Asian Women in Cooperative Development Forum (AWCF). (1999). *The hidden half: Women co-op leaders and decision-makers*. Monograph 1. Quezon City, Philippines: AWCF.

Barker, E. (2012). *Where are all the women? Looking back on the Rochdale Pioneers*. Retrieved from <https://www.thenews.coop/39259/topic/history/where-are-all-women-looking-back-rochdale-pioneers/>.

Bergman, D. (2017). *Women power in Bangladesh*. Retrieved from <https://www.wartsila.com/twentyfour7/environment/women-power-in-bangladesh>.

Bhatt, E. R. (1991). Women cooperatives. *Cooperative Perspective*, 26(2), 121–123.

Bhatt, E. R. (1994). Empowerment of women: Are cooperative appropriate instruments. In Bhatia, et al. (Eds.), *Cooperatives and human resource development: Tapping manpower resources. Encyclopaedia of cooperative management* (5, pp. 111–121). New Delhi: Deep & Deep Publications.

Bibby, A., & Shaw, L. (2005). *Making a difference: Cooperative solutions to global poverty*. Manchester: Cooperative College.

Committee for Promotion and Advancement of Cooperatives (COPAC). (2000). *Decent work: Can cooperatives make a difference?* Retrieved from <http://www.copac.coop/decent-work-can-cooperatives-make-a-difference/>.

Committee for Promotion and Advancement of Cooperatives (COPAC). (2015). *Cooperatives, women & gender equality*. Retrieved from <http://www.copac.coop/wp-content/uploads/2015/07/COPAC_PolicyBrief_CoopsWomen.pdf>.

Cooperative Development Authority (CDA). (2018). *GAD-transforms women, men, and co-ops socially and economically*. A report on the 2nd National GAD Summit. Retrieved from <http://www.cda.gov.ph/resources/updates/news/653-gad-transforms-women-men-and-co-ops-socially-and-economically-a-report-on-the-2nd-national-gad-summit>.

Datta, P. B., & Gailey, R. (2012). Empowering women through social entrepreneurship: Case study of a women's cooperative in India. *Entrepreneurship: Theory and Practice*, 36(3), 569–587. Available from https://doi.org/10.1111/j.1540-6520.2012.00505.

Esim, S., & Omeira, M. (2009). Rural women producers and co-operatives in conflicts settings in the Arab States. In *Pathways out of poverty*. Workshop on Gaps, Trends and Current Research in Gender Dimensions of Agriculture and Rural Employment: Differentiated Pathways out of Poverty. Rome, Italy: FAO, IFAD, ILO, p. 28. Retrieved from <http://www.google.com/url?sa = t&rct = j&q = &esrc = s&source = web&cd = 1&cad = rja&uact = 8&ved = 0CB4>.

Food and Agriculture Organization of the United Nations (FAO). (2011). *The role of women in agriculture*. ESA Working Paper No. 11-02. Rome. Retrieved from <http://www.fao.org/3/am307e/am307e00.pdf>.

Food and Agriculture Organization of the United Nations (FAO). (2012). *Agricultural cooperatives and gender equality*. International Year of Cooperatives Issue Brief Series. Retrieved from <http://www.fao.orgdocrep/017ap669e/ap669e.pdf>.

Food and Agriculture Organization of the United Nations (FAO). (2017). *Regional gender strategy and action plan 2017–2019 for Asia and the Pacific*. Regional Office for Asia and the Pacific. Food and Agriculture Organization of the United Nations, Bangkok. Retrieved from <http://www.fao.org/3/a-i6755e.pdf>.

Garnevska, E., Liu, G., & Shadbolt, N. (2011). Farmers for successful development of farmer cooperatives in Northwest China. *International Food and Agribusiness Management Review*, 14(4). Retrieved from http://ageconsearch.umn.edu/bitstream/117603/2/20110028_Formatted.pdf.

Green, D. P. (2012). *Co-operatives are building a better world for women*. Retrieved from <https://www.thenews.coop/37434/topic/equality/co-operatives-are-building-better-world-women/>.

ICA-AP. (2015). *Resource guide for advanced training of co-operatives on entrepreneurship development of women and gender equality*. Retrieved from <https://www.ica.coop/sites/default/files/publication-files/ica-asia-pacific-resource-guide-2051395662.pdf>.

ICA-AP. (2017a). *Gender is more than a statistic – Status of women in the cooperatives of the Asia Pacific region*. Ten Year Gender Disaggregated Database. Retrieved from <http://www.ica-ap.coop/sites/ica-ap.coop/files/Data%20Study%20Report.PDF>.

ICA-AP. (2017b). *ICA-Asia Pacific committee on women, 2017 report & gender equality strategy 2017–2020*. Retrieved from <https://www.ica.coop/sites/default/files/publication-files/icaap-on-women-2017-report>.

ica-ap.coop. (2019). *Constitution of the ica regional women's committee for Asia and the Pacific*. Retrieved from <http://ica-ap.coop/Structure/constitution-ica-regional-women%E2%80%99s-committee-asia-and-pacific>.

ica.coop. (2017). *Gender affirmatives – Why women in cooperatives-power point presentation by Nandini Azad at International Cooperative Alliance: Global conference and general assembly, Kaula Lumpur, Malaysia*. Retrieved from <https://www.ica.coop/sites/default/files/publication-files/integrating-gender-equality-into-your-cooperative-icnw-15-november-536658489.pdf>.

icnw.in. (2019). *Indian cooperative network for women Ltd.* Retrieved from <http:/www.icnw.in/home/>.

ILO. (2002). *Legal constraints to women's participation in cooperatives, compilation of 11 Country Studies in Asia, Africa and Latin America.* Cooperative Branch: ILO.

ILO. (2005). *Leadership training manual for women leaders of cooperatives.* Retrieved from <https://www.ilo.org/wcmsp5/groups/public/---asia/>.

ILO. (2013). *Helping women to help themselves escape poverty in Myanmar.* ILO Newsroom. Retrieved from <http://www.ilo.org/global/about-the-ilo/newsroom/features/WCMS_215298/lang--en/index.htm>.

ILO. (2014). *The role of cooperatives in achieving the sustainable development goals — The Economic dimension — A contribution to the UN DESA expert group meeting and workshop on cooperatives.* The Role of Cooperatives in Sustainable Development for All: Contributions, Challenges and Strategies, December 8–10, 2014, Nairobi, Kenya, Jürgen Schwettmann, PARDEV. Retrieved from <https://www.un.org/esa/socdev/documents/2014/coopsegm/Schwettmann.pdf>.

ILO. (2015a). *Progress on gender equality at work remains inadequate.* International Women's Day 2015. Retrieved from <https://www.ilo.org/global/about-the-ilo/newsroom/news/WCMS_348035/lang--en/index.htm>.

ILO. (2015b). *Cooperating out of isolation: The case of migrant domestic workers in Kuwait, Lebanon, & Jordan.* International Labour Organization. Retrieved from <http://www.ilo.org/beirut/WCMS_344646/lang--en/index.htm>.

ILO. (2018). *Advancing cooperation among women workers in the informal economy: The SEWA way.* Retrieved from <https://www.ilo.org/wcmsp5/groups/public/---ed_emp/---emp_ent/---coop/documents/publication/wcms_633752.pdf>.

ILO & ADB. (2011). *Women and labour markets in Asia: Rebalancing for gender equality in labour markets in Asia.* Retrieved from <https://www.ilo.org/wcmsp5/groups/public/---asia/---ro-bangk>.

ILOCOOP. (2014). *Leveraging the cooperative advantage for women's empowerment and gender equality, cooperatives and the world of work.* International Labour Organization, Geneva, Switzerland. Retrieved from <http://www.ilo.org/empent/Publications/WCMS_307217/lang--en/index.htm>.

ILOCOOP. (2015). *Advancing gender equality: The co-operative way.* Geneva, Switzerland: International Labour Organization. Retrieved from <http://www.ilo.org/wcmsp5/groups/public/---ed_emp/---emp_ent/---coop/documents/publication/wcms_379095.pdf>.

Indian Farmers Fertiliser Cooperative Ltd. (IFFCO). (2017–2018). *Annual report.* Retrieved from <http://www.iffco.in/assets/download/IFFCO_Annual_Report_2017-18_web.pdf>.

International Cooperative Alliance (ICA). (1991). *Gender integration in cooperatives.* Report of Country Surveys. New Delhi: ICA.

International Cooperative Alliance (ICA). (2005). *Statistics on cooperatives.* Retrieved from <www.ica.coop/gender/statistics.htlm>.

International Cooperative Alliance (ICA). (2016). *Gender equality and women's empowerment in co-operatives- A literature review.* Retrieved from <https://www.ica.coop/sites/default/files/publication-files/womencoops-literature-review-1641374184.pdf>.

International Labor Organisation (ILO). (2000). *ABC of women worker's rights and gender equality* (p. 48). Geneva: ILO. Retrieved from <http://womenwatch/osagi/pdf/factsheet1.pdf>.

jccu.coop. (2010). *JCCU NEWS-coop monthly news Letter.* Retrieved from <https://jccu.coop/eng/jccunews/pdf/201011_jccunews.pdf>.

Jhabvala, R. (1994). Economic development through women cooperatives. *Cooperative Catalogue, 3*(1), 15–20.

Jhabvala, R. (2013). Informal workers and the economy. *Indian Journal of Industrial Relations, 48*(3), 373–386. Special Issue on Unorganized Workers (January), Retrieved from https://www.jstor.org/stable/23510784.

Kabeer, N. (1999). Resources, agency, achievements: Reflections on the measurement of women's empowerment. *Development and Change, 30*(3), 435–464, Institute of Social Studies, Oxford, UK: Blackwell Publishers Ltd.

Kabeer, N. (2005). Gender equality and women's empowerment: A critical analysis of the third millennium development goal. *Gender and Development, 13*(1), 13–24. Retrieved from https://doi.org/10.1080/13552070512331332273.

Kornginnaya, S. (2014). *Inclusive participation of members in primary co-operatives in India — A study.* A paper presented in the 9th ICA Asia Pacific Regional Research Conference on ICA Blueprint for a Co-operative Decade, Bali, Indonesia, 16th September.

Kornginnaya, S. (2015a). *Women empowerment through participatory strategies in India — A study.* A paper presented in ICA-ILO International Research Conference on Cooperatives and the World of Work, Antalya, Turkey, 10–11 November.

Kornginnaya, S. (2015b). *Women in leadership for effective governance- issues and challenges.* Paper presented at the 10th ICA- Asia-Pacific Regional Research Conference on Governance of Co-operatives: Issues and Challenges, November 05–06. Pune, India: VAMNICOM.

Laidlaw, A. F. (1980). *Co-operatives in the Year 2000.* London: ICA.

Lodhia, S. (2009). *Gender inequality in decision making in co-operatives: A cross national study of Asia and Pacific countries.* Social Science Research Network, March 31, Retrieved from <http://ssrn.com/abstract = 1370967>.

Majurin, E. (2008). *Business group formation empowering women and men in developing communities.* Bangkok, Thailand: ILO Subregional Office for East Asia, Bangkok. Retrieved from <http://www.ilo.org/wcmsp5/groups/public/---ed_emp/---emp_ent/documents/publication/wcms_116164.pdf>.

Marathe, S. (2017). *Cooperatives for inclusive growth.* Text of speech delivered at the technical session held at Vigyan Bhavan, New Delhi on 21st September as apart of Sahakar Sammelan. Retrieved from <https://sahakarbharti.org/index.php/co-ops-inclusive-growth/>.

Marshall, B. (2006). Japan's worker co-operative movement into the 21st century. *Asia-Pacific Journal: Japan Focus, 4*(3), 1−18.

National Cooperative Union of India (NCUI). (2018). *Annual report-2017−2018.* Retrieved from <https://ncui.coop/wp-content/uploads/2019/01>.

Nippierd, A. -B. (2002). *Gender issues in cooperatives.* Geneva: ILO Cooperative Branch. Retrieved from <www.ilo.org/images/empent/static/coop/gender/genderissues.pdf>.

Park, S. (2004). *Current situiations and challenges of green cooperatives.* Retrieved from <www.coop.or.kr/data/coopdata.htm?selmode = view&gotopage/wh = coopdata&selkey>.

Pazir, A. E., & Shah, S. (2016). *Mechanisms of women empowerment through educational cooperative.* A Case Study of Rah-e-Roshd Cooperative School. Retrieved from <www.ica-ap.coop/sites/ica-ap.coop/files/Anahita%20Estahpazir%2C%20Iran.pdf>.

Rao, V. M. (1996). *Warana milk co-operatives and women producers.* Paper presented at the national seminar on women dairy co-operatives, July 18−21. Pune: VAMNICOM.

Sager, M. (2017). *Cooperatives in Japan (Articles Series): Part 4/4- Overview of the Japanese Cooperative Sector.* Retrieved from <https://mathias-sager.com/2017/10/22/cooperatives-in-japan-article-series-part-44-overview-of-the-japanese-cooperative-sector/>.

Seikatsu Club Consumers' Co-operative Union (SCCCU). (2004). *Seikatsu club group introduction.* Retrieved from <www.seikatsuclub.coop/english/index.html>.

SEWA. (2019). *Self employed women's association.* Retrieved from <http://www.sewa.org/About_Us.asp>.

Sudha, K. (2005). Micro initiatives: An effective member relationship management strategy in Indian cooperatives. *Review of International Co-operation,* Geneva: ICA, 98(1), 90−98.

Sudha, K. (2008). *Leadership development for women in cooperatives − A study with reference to primary cooperatives in Dakshina Kannada District in Karnataka State.* A minor research project report submitted to the University Grants Commission.

United Nations (UN). (2009). *2009 world survey on the role of women in development women's control over economic resources and access to financial resources, including microfinance.* Retrieved from <https://www.un.org/womenwatch/daw/public/WorldSurvey2009>.

United Nations Development Programme (UNDP). (2010). *Power, voice and rights. A turning point for gender equality in Asia and the Pacific.* Asia-Pacific human development report. UNDP, Colombo: Macmillan Publishers India Ltd. Retrieved from <http://www.undp.org/content/dam/india/docs/power_voice_and_rights_turning_-point_for_gender_equality_in_asia_and_pacific.pdf>.

United Nations Economic and Social Commission for Asia and the Pacific (UNESCAP). (2007). *Developing women's entrepreneurship and e-business in green cooperatives in the Asian and Pacific Region.* Guidebook on developing women's entrepreneurship in green cooperatives in the Asian and Pacific region. Retrieved from <http://www.uwcc.wisc.edu/info/women/escap2468.pdf>.

United Nations Economic and Social Commission for Asia and the Pacific (UNESCAP). (2015). *Gender equality and women's empowerment in Asia and Pacific.* Perspectives of governments on 20 years of implementation of the Beijing declaration and platform for action. Retrieved from <www.unescap.org/sites/default/.../B20%20Gender%20Equality%20Report%20v10-3-E.p...>.

Wanyama, F. O. (2014). *Cooperatives and the sustainable development goals: A contribution to the post-2015 development debate.* A Policy Brief. International Cooperative Alliance, International Labour Organization, Geneva, Switzerland. Retrieved from <http://www.ilo.org/wcmsp5/groups/public/---ed_emp/documents/publication/wcms_240640.pdf>.

Warman, M., & Kennedy, T. L. (1998). *Understanding cooperatives: Agricultural marketing cooperatives, USDA, rural business cooperatives service.* Retrieved from <http://www.rurdev.usda.gov/RBS/pub/cir4515.pdf>.

WEAN. (2013). *WEAN multi − Purpose cooperative.* Retrieved from <https://www.weancop.org.np/>.

wecf.org. (2019). *Women engage for a common future.* Retrieved from <https://www.wecf.org/category/country/kyrgyzstan/>.

World Bank. (2011a). *Promoting women's agency − World bank group.* Retrieved from <http://siteresources.worldbank.org/INTWDR2012/Resources/7778105-1299699968583/7786210-1315936222006/chapter-4.pdf>.

World Bank. (2011b). *World development report 2012: Gender equality and development.* World bank. Washington, DC: World Bank. Retrieved from <https://openknowledge.worldbank.org/handle/10986/4391> License: CC BY 3.0.

World Bank. (2016). *World bank group gender strategy (FY16-23): Gender equality, poverty reduction and inclusive growth.* Retrieved from <http://documents.worldbank.org/curated/en/820851467992505410/pdf/102114-REVISED-PUBLIC-WBG-Gender-Strategy.pdf>.

8

Cooperatives and youth in Asia

Yashavantha Dongre[1], T. Paranjothi[2] and G. Parameshwari[3]

[1]University of Mysore, Mysuru, Karnataka, India [2]Agricultural Cooperative Training Institute, Thiruvananthapuram, Kerala, India [3]PES First Grade College, Mandya, Karnataka, India

8.1 Introduction

Young people are key resources for the present and the future and yet their potential is far from being fully exploited. Their lack of access to education, challenges in terms of health, and their deteriorating working conditions, represent a serious challenge, not only for their future, but also for the future and the sustainability of the social welfare system. The share of youth in the population (15–34 years) as estimated by the United Nations Population Division shows an increase in Africa and a decrease in Asia, Europe, and Northern America, and not much change is observed at a global level. However, there is variation within the region, especially in Asian countries, with big demographic dividend for countries like India, Indonesia, and the Philippines, but a falling youth population is creating tensions in countries like Japan, Korea, and China.

Young people are an important asset for cooperatives, not only because they ensure the generational renewal of membership and will be cooperatives' future leaders, but also because they have a greater capacity for innovation and entrepreneurship and, therefore are more inclined to work with new technologies and generally have higher levels of education than older cooperative members. In fact, youth had shown a great deal of enthusiasm and actively participated in the cooperative movement in its early stages. Cooperatives coming to the center stage in Europe had a lot to do with youth participation as members and the willingness of young people to work for cooperatives. In the Asian region too, there are evidences to show that a fair share of youth took active interest in cooperatives. It was observed that "in developing countries young people are the section of the population most actively and willingly involved in the cooperative movement" (Maslennikov, 1990, p. 27). In Japan, the consumer cooperative movement was built around university cooperatives in which young students took an active part. In India, from the early stages, cooperatives in educational institutions were among the most successful consumer cooperatives (Bhatnagar, 1927).

But today the situation seems to have changed totally, so much so, that the cooperative movement is coming to be known as a movement of the aged. Asia Pacific region houses the largest chunk of youth in the world, but the youth participation in cooperatives is not up to the desired level. We, therefore need to understand the demographic features of the region so as to be able to facilitate youth integration in cooperatives.

8.2 Profile of youth population in Asia Pacific region

Asia and Pacific region are the most youthful region both in terms of the number of young people as well as the rate at which their population is growing. South Asia in particular accounts for the largest share of youth population of the globe even with a broader parameter of defining youth as those aged between 15 and 35 (Paranjothi & Dongre, 2006). However, the spread of youth population within the region is very uneven. In East Asia the share of youth population is said to be around 17%, while it is around 18% in South East Asia and the Pacific. The South Asian region houses the world's largest pool of youth accounting for about 26% of world's youth population (UNECA, 2010).

India has more than 50% of its population below the age of 25 and more than 65% below the age of 35. Vietnam is a young nation with those aged 21−34 making up around 24% of the population. The Philippines has a young growing population with 50% below 23 years of age. In contrast Japan, China, South Korea, and Singapore have an ageing population. In these countries, one-quarter of the population fall under the bracket of being aged and the share of those above 35 years of age is around 70%. There is a trend in these countries of increased welfare expenses to care of the aged and universities not getting adequate domestic students and businesses not getting enough workforce.

8.3 Challenges faced by youth

On an overall basis, the youth segment in the region is enjoying various benefits accrued through faster economic growth. However, in comparative terms with developed countries, the majority of Asian countries still have various challenges for young people. Some important areas of such challenges are:

1. Education: Significant achievements have been made in the region in terms of enrollment in secondary education. At 64.1%, the enrollment rate is actually higher than the world average of 62.5% (UNESCAP, 2015). However, barriers also remain in accessing education due to persistent rural−urban disparities, rising socioeconomic inequality, and continuing exclusion of children with disabilities, etc. In Indonesia and the Philippines, for example, around 25% of youth are "not in education, employment or training" (UNESCAP, 2015).

2. Employment: In terms of economic development the Asia Pacific region is in the forefront, so much so that the 21st century is often referred to as the Asian century. The avenues of employment are increasing as compared to the preglobalization days. Nonetheless, at the global level, there is a youth employment crisis. Young people can be as much as three-times more likely than adults to be unemployed, and the ILO estimates that more than 73.6 million young people are looking for work (ILO, 2015). With employment being the most critical element that determines quality of life, this issue needs a great deal of attention in the Asian region.

3. Health: Health is another important area that poses several challenges to young people in the Asian Pacific region. Here again, as a spillover effect of an increased rate of growth and increasing GDP in many countries of the region, access to health has generally increased. However, the issues of malnutrition, female access to health, infant mortality, early marriage and the consequent health problems of women, increasing rate of HIV infection among the

youth, and the increasing cost of medical services leading to reduced access, etc., continue to trouble the youth of the region.

4. Civic Engagement: Over the past two decades, youth civic engagement has acquired some prominence in research, policy, and practice in many parts of the world. At the international level, the World Bank has identified the exercise of active citizenship as one of the most important activities for a healthy transition to adulthood for both the youth of today and the next generation. The focus on youth civic engagement is driven in part by the assumption that young people, if involved in and connected to society, are less likely to engage in risky behavior and violence and are likely to stay engaged as they grow older. The region doesn't seem to have proper policy in place and has not used the institutional infrastructure to the full extent to facilitate the civic engagement of youth.

5. Migration: Young people may choose to move within their home countries as internal migrants or beyond their national borders as international migrants. The majority of migrants stay in their own countries as internal migrants. Estimates place the number of migrants at approximately 740 million. The reasons for youth migration may vary from person to person and region to region. Often, a combination of several major factors leads to the decision to migrate. It is observed that migrant youth often find it difficult to find proper jobs and get lesser chances of getting into the mainstream population.

8.4 Why cooperatives are ideal platforms for youth

How far can cooperatives be the institutional choice the youth in the region would embrace?

If cooperatives can be of help in addressing the mentioned challenges, they would certainly be an important choice for young people. There are ample evidences and grounded arguments to demonstrate that cooperatives can effectively address the varied needs of the youth. Cooperatives, being principle-based organizations, exhibit a sense of social commitment and, hence, their member communities can always hope to get their needs fulfilled.

With unemployment being the most critical challenge faced by youth, cooperatives can be an important source to look for. It is estimated that cooperatives around the world can create around 100 million jobs (ILO, 2012). It is also well argued that cooperatives could be an important mode of entrepreneurship and young people can take the cooperative way for establishing new start-ups and run their own businesses. It is said that if one is looking to establish one's own venture working with others to gain scale and share risks or if one wishes to work with others in a business that all would own or if one has an idea for a community owned business then the cooperative model offers an innovative solution (McDonnell, McKnight, & Donnelly, 2012).

Cooperatives are seen to be an ideal option for providing better and affordable healthcare facilities. As has been well demonstrated in the case of Bangladesh, "cooperative societies act as a risk management strategy for members, working on the basic principle of risk pooling during illness" (Sarker, Sulthana, & Mahumud, 2016). There have been studies that demonstrated the ability of cooperatives to help youth access their health needs as well as providing youth the space to serve people in need of healthcare (Matthew, 2017).

Cooperatives are seen to be supporting educational services in a variety of ways. University cooperatives in Japan are an outstanding example for providing student support services and contributing to studying and learning apart from providing part time jobs to the youth. There are examples of cooperative educational institutions that provide educational services to youth with a focus on access, equity, and quality.

It is, therefore evident that cooperatives can empower the youth in many ways. They not only provide a participatory opportunity to young people and thereby enhance their skills in leadership, financial as well as business management, but also meet their varied needs. Therefore cooperatives can be a humane, democratic, and trustworthy institutional choice for the youth of the region to address their varied challenges.

8.5 Why cooperatives need youth participation

Any socioeconomic movement needs infusion of young blood to keep up the momentum and facilitate continuity. Cooperatives across the world are looking for and striving to integrate youth both as members and as a human resource. Young people are forward looking, dynamic, tech savvy, and tend to be more democratic. All these qualities are very much required for cooperatives to be sustained in the emerging competitive marketplace.

Cooperatives need a succession plan for their leadership and the availability of young members make it that much easier to identify potential leaders and nurture them. There are instances of many successful cooperatives failing after some time, mainly due to the vacuum created by the exit of a leader. It is, therefore important for cooperatives to keep the second and third line of succession plans ready to ensure long term sustainability.

Cooperatives also need youth as a workforce. Because of the presence of a sound network of university cooperatives in Japan, Japanese consumer cooperatives get a sustained flow of young staff, who, with a background of being active members of campus cooperatives, choose to work for cooperatives. Not many countries in the Asian Pacific region has this advantage.

Young people bring contemporary skills and values into an organization in whatever capacity they participate. Cooperatives need to exploit this potential of youth to the fullest extent in order to remain relevant to the times. An organization where the average age of the staff is below 50, is said to be a healthy organization. Such an organization is more likely to see a smooth transition by adapting quickly to changes.

It is, therefore evident that there is a lot of give and take between youth and cooperatives. Young people need cooperatives in order to realize their potential and get their needs fulfilled. Cooperatives need youth to ensure that they remain dynamic entities keeping with the times and responding to their clientele at all times.

8.6 Campus cooperatives: the Asian model of youth integration

The presence of cooperatives within the campuses of schools, colleges, and universities is a unique feature of the Asia Pacific region. Cooperatives of students/youth do exist in Europe and Northern America, but these are mostly single service cooperatives offering either housing services or bookstore facilities. Also, these are cooperatives having only one constituency, that is, students as members. But what we find in the Asia Pacific region is the presence of multiservice cooperatives within the campuses of educational institutions with students, teachers, and staff as members. These cooperatives have a long history and in countries like Japan and India they are contemporaries of the earliest cooperatives in the country. It would be appropriate to illustrate the Asian Pacific model of youth integration in cooperatives through the example of some select types of campus cooperatives.

8.6.1 School cooperatives in Malaysia

Cooperatives in schools, consisting of students, teachers, and staff as members exist in many countries of the Asia Pacific region. India, Sri Lanka, and Malaysia are the main countries to have such cooperatives. At present, the Malaysian case is a good example to illustrate how young students get involved in cooperative activities.

School cooperative societies have been established in some secondary schools in Malaysia for decades. They were started as small book and stationery shops within school premises to provide much-needed retail services to students. Currently, it is not uncommon to observe a hive of activity (the cash register ringing, chatter from transactions, and students in their uniforms busily replenishing products on the shelves) at retail outlets before and after school hours as well as during recess time.

Cooperatives in schools were started with the primary objective of establishing habits of thrift and independence among students, creating an atmosphere of practical training in the application of management and commercial techniques taught in the classroom., inculcating democratic values among students, encouraging the attitude of self-help and mutuality, and nurturing leadership skills among the younger generation.

Since their inception in 1972 some of the current school cooperatives have been highly innovative in diversifying their activities. Besides selling stationery and books, some provide binding, laminating, and photocopying facilities, while others engage in tourism activities for students and staff. The aim of the tourism activity is to train students to operate small local tour agencies to promote local attractions in their states. Cooperatives that are established in residential schools even provide telecommunications, laundry, and hair salon services (Ong and Angeline, 2011). Students who are members and shareholders of their school cooperatives receive annual dividends for their investments.

School cooperatives in Malaysia are generally well supported by the schools themselves, the government, apex organizations of the cooperative movement, and the local community. They are unique and have the potential to groom a new batch of Generation Z entrepreneurs and employees who are trustworthy, accountable, and generous. The Ministry of Education, some agencies under the Ministry of Domestic Trade, cooperatives, and Consumer Affairs (e.g., the Co-operative College of Malaysia or CCM), the apex organization of the cooperative movement (ANGKASA), and school principals and teachers, have all been supportive of school cooperatives.

The CCM and ANGKASA, for example, provide relevant courses to assist young board members to manage their cooperatives professionally. Among others, they provide accounting, auditing, retail management, leadership, and team-building courses. Similar courses and relevant seminars are also organized by the CCM and ANGKASA to equip school principals and teachers, who act as advisors and mentors respectively, with the relevant knowledge and skills to enable them to lead school cooperatives successfully.

At the microlevel, among the benefits that students obtain from being members and serving their school cooperatives actively are the achievement of invaluable hard and soft human capital skills. These include having hands-on experience in running a small business, a better understanding of working and serving as a team, and appreciating the need to be responsible, accountable, transparent, and committed. Besides learning how to lead well and to be creative and confident in making good business and financial decisions, they also learn how to communicate effectively.

At a more macrolevel, successful school cooperatives have been known to use the profits that they earn to help improve the infrastructure of their schools and to help needy students to purchase books, school uniforms, and to pay for their school fees. One can only imagine how proud the students who are active members of their school cooperatives would feel when they are able to make a difference in the lives of others.

8.6.2 University cooperatives in Japan

University cooperatives are campus cooperatives formed with the membership of all constituents of the campus community, that is, students, faculty members, and the non-teaching staff. In the case of Japan, these are registered as consumer cooperatives, under Consumer Co-operative Law. Though there is a long history of university cooperatives in Japan, a large number were started after the Second World War. During 1945, after the war, when students and teachers returned to the campus of the University of Tokyo to pursue their academic endeavors, they faced an acute shortage of academic infrastructure including books, stationery, food, and other support services. It is at this juncture that the students, teachers, and staff joined together and started the University of Tokyo Co-operative. Taking their lead from this, many other universities started similar cooperatives over the years. At present, the National Federation of University Co-operative Associations (NFUCA), the umbrella organization of such cooperatives in Japan, has 215 university cooperatives as affiliated members with a total individual membership of 1.5 million, a large majority being student members. As of 2017, these cooperatives had a paid-up share capital of more than 967 million Yen (with their national federation—the NFUCA) and an annual turnover of 182 billion Yen (NFUCA, 2013). Most importantly, university

cooperatives in Japan provide a range of services to campus communities and the universities themselves including a supply of stationery, books, running canteens and other food services, providing travel services, managing hostels, parking facilities, etc., arranging for driving licenses, ICT-related training, career guidance, etc., and most importantly, offering services such as credit facility (through credit cards), student housing, and mutual insurance services. University cooperatives have created regional business consortiums, undertake joint buying activities, provide services based on feedback from students, conduct annual nationwide surveys of student life related issues, and also undertake the publication of various study materials. Since they are essentially organizations driven by student members, university cooperatives conduct a host of cocurricular activities such as activities related to global peace, international solidarity, the environment and global warming, health education, etc. By becoming a member of a university cooperative, a student can virtually be eligible to access a wide range of support services at a highly affordable price.

Currently, university cooperatives in Japan have a strong democratic base and have made significant contributions to the consumer cooperative movement. The degree of student participation is high since most cooperatives have a separate student committee that reports to the board, while students unions have almost disappeared after their heyday in the 1970s. Students are involved in gathering member feedback on cooperative activities, in bringing out cooperative magazines and reports, and in promoting their cooperatives among the new students entering their university. "It is a regular feature for cooperative student members to take part in the development of new menu for the cafeteria, oversee the management in the cafeteria, participate in the activities related to Peace, Fair Trade and

Environment" (Kuriki & Rie, 2008, p. 30). It is also well recognized in Japan that university cooperatives contribute not only to the betterment of campus life, but have been making significant contributions toward strengthening the cooperative movement in general and consumer cooperatives in particular (Shoji, 2012; Tanaka, 2005). It is common to find a good deal of cooperative staff and cooperative leaders in Japan citing their experience when they were students with university cooperatives as a motivating factor to get into the cooperative movement.

8.6.3 Youth/student cooperatives in Indonesia

In Indonesia, there exist youth cooperatives both within university campuses as well as outside. These cooperatives are generally called student cooperatives when they are formed by university students. The main feature of these cooperatives is that the members are students only and the entire operations of these cooperatives are also managed by student board members.

There are also youth cooperatives outside the campuses, and, in this case, only those below the age of 40 are members of these cooperatives. The majority of youth/student cooperatives are involved in retailing services. There is also a separate federation of these cooperatives, Indonesian Youth Cooperative, which does both promotional activities and business activities.

These examples show that the Asia Pacific region has built-in cooperative structures that provide hands-on experience to the youth with direct participation in the capacity of members, board of directors, and even business managers. The potential for youth integration in cooperatives is, therefore, immense. However, with the exception of Japan, other countries in the region do not seem to have utilized the

potential of campus cooperatives to the fullest extent and translated that into youth getting into regular cooperatives as members and staff. Keeping this in mind, the ICA AP has initiated many promotional measures.

8.7 Role of ICA Asia Pacific

Even though youth in the Asia Pacific region have had the rare benefit of direct participation in cooperatives right from their school days, there are evidences to show that youth participation in cooperatives both in the capacity of members and elected leaders was rather low. At the same time, the need to integrate youth into the cooperative movement was well recognized in many countries in the Asia region. Thanks to the concerted efforts of the Japanese Consumer Co-operative Federation (JCCU), the NFUCA of Japan, and the ICA AP, many initiatives have been taken beginning from the late 1980s.

The ICA AP established the University Co-operative Sub-Committee as part of the Consumer Co-operative Committee in the early 1990s to create better awareness and strengthen the campus cooperatives that were already found in many Asian and Pacific countries. The experience of university cooperatives in Japan contributing in terms of better human resource both as staff and leaders of consumer cooperatives was seen to be an important lesson for the need for youth to participate in cooperatives. The Sub-Committee of the ICA AP became a full sectoral committee in 2008 and has since been organizing regional and global events to encourage youth to take active part in cooperatives.

Another significant initiative of the ICA AP is the establishment, in 2006 of the Youth Committee. This is established as a thematic committee, similar to a women's committee, to focus on youth development and bringing more youth into the fold of the cooperative movement. The Youth Committee has been organizing regional youth forums and youth summits apart from joint activities with the committee on cooperatives in educational institutions. Young cooperators as well as cooperative leaders are provided with opportunities for the exchange of ideas, exposure visits, and even training opportunities in different countries of the region. These initiatives have greatly benefitted youth in the region to know more about the cooperative movement and also made the governments of many countries of the region address the issue of youth integration in cooperatives with greater vigor.

8.8 Conclusion

Youth constitute the most significant part of the population in the Asia Pacific region. There is, of course, a situation in different countries of the region, where we see both the youth population being the largest as well as the youth population declining. However, the challenges faced by young people and the need to harness the power of the youth remain the same for all countries of the region. The cooperative sector has the potential to help youth in meeting their contemporary challenges and the youth have the energy to make the cooperative movement a strong and vibrant movement. It is, therefore necessary that the region needs to put in place a policy mechanism to facilitate such youth integration. It may be observed from this analysis that even though the cooperative movement in the Asia Pacific region has come up with strong foreign/western influence, the movement has built up its own unique grassroots level cooperative institutional infrastructure in the form of campus cooperatives. It is unfortunate that barring exception to a couple of countries like Japan and Korea, the rest have not fully used the potential of such cooperatives. In many countries, youth/students do not get involved in campus cooperative activities either because of legal hurdles or because their curricular activities do not provide adequate space for such participation or simply because there is not adequate awareness about the importance of participating in campus cooperatives. These issues need to be addressed, both by governments and apex cooperative organizations. If these cooperatives are allowed to evolve as autonomous, multipurpose, and multistakeholder organizations, the cooperative movement in general has a lot to gain.

References

Bhatnagar, B. G. (1927). *The cooperative organization in British India*. Allahabad: Ram Narain Lal — Publisher and Bookseller.

ILO. (2012). *A better future for young people: What cooperatives can offer, Cooperative Branch*. Geneva: International Labour Office.

ILO. (2015). *Rediscovering co-operatives: Young people finding work the co-operative way, co-operatives and the World of Work No. 4*. Geneva: International Labour Office.

Kuriki, T., & Rie. (2008). Student participation in the management of Campus/University Cooperatives, — in — ICA-AP (2008). In *Report of the ICA Global Workshop on University/Campus Cooperatives* (pp. 29—30): New Delhi: International Cooperative Alliance-Asia Pacific.

Maslennikov, V. (1990). *The co-operative movement in Asia and Africa: Problems and prospects*. Moscow, USSR: Progress Publishers.

Matthew, L. (2017). *Providing care through co-operatives — 2: Literature review and case studies*. Geneva: ILO.

McDonnell, D., McKnight, E., & Donnelly, H. (2012). *Cooperative entrepreneurship: Co-operate for growth*. <http://aura.abdn.ac.uk/bitstream/handle/2164/7699/Co_operative_Entrepreneurship_Co_operate_for_growth.pdf;jsessionid = D6492990FBD90F678A6419748F827681?sequence = 1>.

NFUCA. (2013). *Annual report — 2012*. Tokyo: National Federation of University Cooperative Associations.

Ong Lin Dar, Angeline Tay (2011). *School cooperative societies in Malaysia: The inconspicuous and unique retail format with promising potential*. <http://eprints.um.edu.my/12817/1/53-OngLinDar.pdf>.

Paranjothi, T., & Dongre, Y. (2006). *Youth and co-operatives in India*. Bengaluru: Regional Institute of Co-operative Management.

Sarker, A. R., Sulthana, M., & Mahumud, R. A. (2016). Cooperative societies: A sustainable platform for promoting universal health coverage in Bangladesh. *BMJ Globe Health., 1*(3), e000052.

Shoji, K. (2012). *University cooperatives in nurturing 21st century citizens: For the International Year of Cooperatives.* Bulletin of SEISEN University Research Institute for Cultural Science, No. 33, March 2012, pp. 47–70.

Tanaka, M. (2005). *University co-ops: Development and excellent leaders: Toward contemporary co-operative studies: Perspectives from Japan's Consumer Co-ops.* Tokyo: Consumer Co-operative Institute of Japan.

UNECA. (2010). *Dialogue and mutual understanding – Fact sheet developed as part of the International Year of Youth.* Washington: UNO.

UNESCAP. (2015). *Regional overview: Youth in Asia Pacific.* Fact sheet prepared by UNESCAP.

The theoretical model of Asian capitalism and the varieties of cooperation

Anthony Jensen

Business School, University of Newcastle, New South Wales, Australia

9.1 Introduction

Using a biological metaphor one can plant cooperatives in different soils across Asia and the co-operative will grow differently due to institutional failure, public policy, historical and cultural factors.

Cronan (2017)

Different cooperative forms are unevenly spread across the Asia Pacific region and range from outstanding economic and social success in Japan and Singapore to underperformance in India and Indonesia. This is a major conundrum for policy makers endeavoring to develop regional policy to solve social and economic problems as, on the one hand, cooperatives are advocated at the highest level by the United Nations to assist in achieving their Sustainable Development Goals, but on the other hand, for the past 20 years have been ignored by Association of South East Asian Nations ministers. Cronan (2017) comments:

The Co-operative Ministers Conference has existed for twenty years and has wrestled with the issue of the development of co-operatives from a public policy setting addressing the enabling factors of institutional and legislative initiatives all the while endeavoring to answer — Which countries? What sectors? Why [is it] embraced in some countries. Why [has it] not resonated in others?

This chapter's objective is to promote discussion on what the factors determining cooperative presence in different Asian Pacific nations are, and as a result achieve an understanding of national differences as a prelude to good policy development. We do this by using a comparative research methodology incorporating 11 countries and 22 case studies of successful cooperatives. The focus of this research is on identifying the obstacles that cooperatives face in starting up, how they overcome those obstacles, and the factors involved in success within the context of national cultures. This theoretical chapter will serve as a lens through which to view the studies presented in later chapters, a lens that brings into focus and sharpens the strengths and individualities of Asian cooperative models.

We feel this search for a common perspective can best be done through the use of a theoretical model to develop a uniquely Asian scholarship on cooperatives and use a model that helps explain emergence, success, decline, and renewal in the Asia Pacific region. Here we aim to include social indices such as solidarity, mutuality, leadership, and trust. Financial shortcomings can be eclipsed by increased social and human capital. This model needs to assist us understand the nature of degeneration and the tensions that play out between cooperatives as a transforming initiative or cooperatives as an incorporating movement. This chapter will make the case that Asia Pacific scholarship on cooperatives needs to reflect the particular cultural and business influences in which these cooperatives emerge and succeed.

Witt and Redding (2013) have set a framework for this research. They argue that "Asian business systems cannot be understood through categories identified in the West" and state that the VoC dichotomy is not applicable to Asia and that "none of the existing major frameworks capture all types of capitalism" (Hall & Soskice, 2003, p. 265).

Tullus (2017) describes the challenge of understanding the cooperative model in Asia and providing a common perspective on which researchers can agree:

> The challenge for cooperatives will be to genuinely share and prove the power of the co-operative model, so that co-implementation among partners towards the pursuit of a common agenda, namely, the UN Sustainable Development Goals, could be realized.

It is within this statement that other assets of cooperatives have space to shine. Essential to a case study approach is the necessity to contextualize the study in a historical review of the emergence, success, and decline over the past 120 years. It helps us locate the ongoing dialectic between economics and social values. The historical analysis provided here highlights the ebb and flow of cooperative formation, degeneration, where it can be financial, but also in terms of mission drift, decline of participative democracy reduction in membership, and bureaucratization However, we also see renewal, where this renewal is concluded to point to an emerging praxis in cooperative advancement.

9.2 Toward a theoretical model for Asia Pacific

The cultural and historical differences between Asia and Europe have had an impact on business ethos and procedures, the type of institutions, and the nature of business systems that have emerged. Asia displays very distinct clusters of characteristics along collective cultural dimensions, namely, acceptance of hierarchy, risk avoidance, and long- and short-term perspective. Cronan (2017) comments:

> Asian countries play the 'long game' contingent on building trust and long-term relationships. Some would see deference to and respect of authority in the Asian hierarchy.
> *Cronan (2017)*

The difficulty in providing a single perspective through which to view the Asian Pacific cooperative community is the diversity that lies within. Cronan (2017) questions:

> "Why are there only agricultural co-operatives in China?" Why did Australian co-operatives demutualise while [co-operatives did] not in New Zealand? Why are co-operatives in some national constitutions and not in others? Is the success in Korea and Japan because they have strong corporate families and conglomerates? It is important to understand this unevenness, not what they have in common.

It is helpful to adopt the approach of Witt and Redding (2013) as a starting point to answer these questions. They used eight institutional dimensions to group the countries of Asia into clusters accounting for four new major types of capitalism giving order and structure to this research. The clusters are, namely, (post) socialist, advanced city, emerging Southeast Asian, advanced Northeast Asian, and Japanese in a continuum from post socialist (China and India) on one extreme to a coordinated market economy (Japan) at the other end. This extended our understanding from that of Hall and Soskice (2003), who developed the varieties of capitalism approach with two types of capitalism—the liberal market economy and the coordinated market economy.

Asian countries are grouped by Witt and Redding (2013) into four clusters highlighting their different business systems. They included Japan as a Western style coordinated market economy and we have included Australia as a liberal market economy; an interesting spectrum of groupings for comparative research using 22 case studies.

- Post socialism—China, Vietnam, Laos, and India—central planning and state control are still strong; here Sri Lanka can be added
- Advanced city—Hong Kong and Singapore
- Emerging Southeast Asian—Indonesia, Philippines, Thailand, and Malaysia
- Advanced Northeast Asian—Korea and Taiwan
- Coordinated market economy—Japan
- Liberal market economy—Australia

The question now is whether this grouping will help us understand why cooperative formation is highly uneven and then what can be done to rectify this problem. This format provides a framework to the research so we can explore the type of a given cooperative, how it emerges, and the factors at play in its success, which we hypothesize will vary from cluster to cluster. The

TABLE 9.1 The theoretical model.

Jensen (2013) Macro factors	Witt and Redding (2013) Macro factors
Role of state	Role of state
Civil society	Employment relations
	Multiplexity
Market	Interfirm relations/family groupings
Micro factors	**Micro factors**
Legal structure	Informality and formality
Governance	Corporate governance
	Access to finance
Human relations	Access to skills and competencies
Life cycle	Social capital/trust

complexity of the methodology behind these eight factors is far beyond the scope of this chapter. However, to bring a richness to our understanding of Asian cooperation, we combined Witt and Redding's (2013) eight institutional dimensions plus three factors into Jensen's (2013) theoretical model of seven factors. See Table 9.1.

Witt and Redding (2013), unlike Hall and Soskice (2003), did not see their factors as problems to be overcome, but rather as factors to distinguish different types of capitalism. We argue that we can use this modeling of Jensen (2013) and Witt and Redding (2013) to assist us to understand the differences in cooperative type and formation across the Asia Pacific region.

Kurimoto (2018), one of the key researchers on cooperatives in Asia, reinforces this conclusion and sums up the position of the VoC from the perspective of an Asian researcher.

I think this chapter on the Varieties of Capitalism approach is very important to show the context under which Asia/Pacific co-ops operate. But the VoC approach was primarily developed on the basis of the Western countries and needs to be modified when applying to the East (Asia/Pacific). For example, Singapore with highest GDP per capita is still under the authoritarian/corporatist regime while Japan is largely controlled by bureaucracy under the LDP rule. China is under the one-party control while India is progressing to the democracy although it has suffered from the caste system. Most of Asian countries are under the authoritarian/developmentalist regime while they are running market economies of diverse shapes. So we need the solid basis of macro factors to analyze the micro factors leading to co-op's success.

This case study research of successful cooperatives in the four sectors that is provided in the coming chapters, namely, credit, agricultural, consumer, and worker cooperatives, will illuminate how these obstacles to cooperative emergence and success can be overcome. First, we need to build a theoretical model applicable to the Asia Pacific region.

9.2.1 Building the model

9.2.1.1 Culture

Culture was not one of the main factors used by Witt and Redding (2013) in their modeling, but it was one factor that they considered needed further research and should be included. However, we consider it an important fundamental factor as it enables us to explore the implications on cooperatives in the "relatively strong hierarchical values in Asia" and "the institutional configurations" that emerge. Also, as there is a "prevalence of top down decision making" with managers "rarely seeking input from subordinates before reaching a decision" where "power is a measure of hierarchy." These present significant challenges regarding cooperative degeneration, participation, and governance in Asian Pacific cooperatives (Witt & Redding, 2013, pp. 291–292). These cultural traits pose issues for cooperatives due to the possible formation of male autocratic elites. Mason (2017) states: "This is critical, cultural elites at a high level and certainly local elites all play a significant role in management and

direction of the cooperative and can influence its success."

Redding (2005) states: "It is normal in the wider business systems literature to observe the description of four trajectories, each seen in terms of complex antecedent conditions (i.e., contexts) and present-day responses in the form of stable structures. The four fields are as follows: (1) the sourcing of capital; (2) the stabilising of labor markets, skill systems, and employment patterns; (3) the norms of ownership; and (4) the stabilising of production systems."

Therefore we can conclude that by altering these four factors, we can create a different political economy and that is what the cooperative movement does, and in so doing, delivers a different outcome to capitalism.

Poole also talks about latent power and values "shaped by economic factors, technological factors and government action" as key to the basic explanatory framework of cooperative emergence.

9.2.1.2 Macro factors

Three macro factors are chosen to bring an expression of the potential of agency, the potential of communities or groups to act to take matters into their own hands and form a cooperative to service a particular need or solve a social or economic problem such as taking over a failed business to preserve their jobs. At the macro level, Jensen (2013) identifies three factors that impact on the emergence of a cooperative and enable or disable its emergence, nanely the state, civil society institutions, and the market. The understanding of these in Asia has been enriched by the work of Witt and Redding (2013).

The role of state

The state, as has been shown, has been a prime influence on the emergence and promotion of cooperatives across the Asia Pacific region as part of a nation's initial struggle for independence after colonization; for instance,

Vietnam, in its postindependence vision for a just and egalitarian society. But what is important is the correct role of the state, "the right type of government support," where Isaac and Williams (2017, p. 294) argue that a top-down state is detrimental to cooperative sustainability. Getting the balance right is difficult as illustrated by the comment from Villamin (2017) "India has too much state involvement – the Phillipines has too little.

Most states across Asia Pacific have played the role of a "pseudo co-operative entrepreneur" in taking a leading role in setting cooperatives' legal and regulatory structures and sometimes providing finance and resources. The state played a key role in assisting cooperatives overcome the early obstacles, but remained with too much control.

We now explore five models of the state that result in different cooperative movements taking note that many states are hybrids, namely, developmental state, regulatory state, predatory state (Witt & Redding, 2013), and revolutionary/postrevolutionary state (Greenberg, 1983). We now turn to Witt and Redding (2013).

Developmental state: the state is a partner with the private sector in national industrial transformation, but preserves sufficient distance for the renegotiation of goals and policies when capital interests are inconsistent with national development and the values embedded in society. For example, Japan, Korea, Singapore, and Taiwan.

Regulatory state: the pluralist model sees the state aiming to achieve balance in society through regulatory networks enabling free and fair competition. For instance, Hong Kong and Singapore.

Predatory state: policy is formed through the competition of elite groups that exert pressure on the state. Families use the state to enrich themselves resulting in lower levels of output and popular welfare. For example, China, Vietnam, Indonesia, Laos, the Philippines, and India.

Revolutionary state: (Giles, 1989, p. 142) delivers a radical critique of capitalism where the state's "bias in favor of the dominant classes" is "swept away in a revolutionary context ushering in the transformation of production relations." For example, China, Vietnam, and Laos. In addition, the state of Kerala in India, which regularly elects a communist government that is a supporter of the autonomous Labor Co-operative Construction Societies. Here the role of the state works best when it creates an enabling environment conducive to the cooperative model emerging from a bottom-up process (Isaac & Williams, 2017, p. 292).

In Vietnam, cooperatives are the fifth pillar of the economy where the role of the state is to assist cooperatives overcome financial and operational obstacles and it subsequently plays a key role in these cooperatives, which are seen as an instrument of state policy such as the Saigon cooperative. Some would argue that members do not get a vote. Alternatively, this could be seen as a dialectal process that may well evolve into autonomous cooperatives through an externalization process similar to the privatization of state-run enterprises in the West.

Multiplexity Multiplexity reflects "multiple business systems within the same economies" (Witt & Redding, 2013, p. 293) as in Hong Kong within China, for instance—a two systems, one country ethos. In Europe, we see the Italian experience where the cooperative movement has become a "state within a state" based on being endorsed by the Italian Constitution and underpinned by a sound legal structure. The potential to reproduce this in Asia is associated with high multiplexity in the region. This coexistence in the same institutionalized space is related to high institutionalized trust and informality of institutions, which can lead to institutional convergence (Witt & Redding, 2013, p. 294). The SANASA credit/thrift cooperative movement in Sri Lanka is a prime example.

Role of civil institutions

A number of writers argue there is a requirement for latent power and values to act as precursors to cooperative emergence, "there is a need for social cooperation within the community before the creation of a co-operative enterprise can take place" in Mazzarol et al., page 4.

- Trade unions:

  Trade unions are one of the most important civil institutions and their position varies across the region from being embraced to being persecuted.

  A corporatist approach to development is evident in Korea where the government created a tripartite commission. In Singapore, the trade unions are a de facto partner in government with union leaders receiving cabinet posts. This arrangement is an enabling mechanism for cooperative formation and for the practice of solidarity and mutuality. For example, the trade union supporting the formation of the Fair Price grocery chain. Conversely in China, the trade union is an arm of the state (Witt & Redding, 2013, p. 278) and does not venture into corporatist projects.

- Religious movements:

  In more predatory states like Indonesia, China, and the Philippines, the Catholic Church, especially the Jesuit Order, has been instrumental in the founding and support of cooperatives and credit unions. In India, the Hindu religion requires successful citizens to give back to society and many cooperatives are started by religious social entrepreneurs. In Sri Lanka, Buddhist values underpin the credit thrift and co-operative credit societies movement.

Role of the market

Markets are associated with risk, but Asian societies are risk-averse, according to Hofstede and Hofstede (2005). In addition, Asians play the long game, eschewing short-term gain and

entrepreneurial activity by untrained potential cooperators. The role of the market, its structure, and cycles have a bearing on cooperative emergence and survival. It is argued that cooperative formation takes hold in a counter cyclical manner of formation in market down swings and degeneration in upswings.

- Interfirm relations:

  "The presence of business groupings is a key feature across all Asian nations" (Witt & Redding, 2013, p. 279). Interfirm relationships are channeled through networks of conglomerates, state-owned enterprises, and cultural groups such as the Hongs in Hong Kong and Keiretsu and Hungs in Japan. A fundamental principle of the cooperative movement is building networks by cooperating with other cooperatives—this seems to be a natural fit with Asia. However, they can give rise to political elites dominating cooperatives and family-centered cooperatives as in India.

9.2.1.3 *Micro factors*

Organizational/legal structure

Informality is a characteristic of Asian business. This refers to the reliance on uncodified institutions that are preferred to state-initiated legal models. In other words, the law defines the rules, but there are different ways by which business is conducted, for example, a village makes pots and ovens for 1000 years then in 2010 institutionalizes as a worker cooperative. In Asia, the degree of informality is inversely related to the degree of institutionalized trust. This is a manifestation of culture where informality is easier to control within a group-based society (Witt & Redding, 2013).

Governance

- Ownership and corporate governance:

  It is typical of Asian economies that control rests predominantly with families or in socialist countries, the state. Corporate governance rules to protect minority shareholders are weak. The lack of institutionalized trust discourages delegation and hinders the separation of ownership from control, which is crucial in the modern firm (Witt & Redding, 2013). Cooperatives can become vehicles for state welfare in a predatory state where there is both political interference in governance and corruption. This became a feature of many Indian agricultural cooperatives.

- Internal structures:

  Decision making in Asian firms is predominantly hierarchical and top down, except for in Japan, which has a participatory mode of decision making. This model could lead to the abrogation of responsibility in cooperatives and lack of participation at governance level, especially at annual general meetings. Decisions at the top level are sometimes based on family relationships. However, we could also ask whether there is a lack of participation or conversely a respect for hierarchy.

- Financial structure:

  Financial structure and finance raising are related to corporate governance. As with control, finance is raised from banks owned by business groups on preferential terms. Major banks are state controlled and are involved in policy-driven directed lending. In a developmental state, certain sectors are targeted (Witt & Redding, 2013). Some economists argue that member-based organizations increase corporate risk, and subsequently, the ability to borrow is reduced and the cost of borrowing increases. However, local finance systems have played a key role. In India, there is a traditional microfinance system, Panam Payattu, a money gathering game that informally supported cooperatives such as uralungal labour contract co-operative society to get through the start-up phase (Isaac & Williams, 2017, p. 91).

Human relations management

- Social capital:

  "Asian countries are rich in interpersonal trust expressed in networks of reciprocal relationships between individuals both inside and outside the firm," but they are low in institutional trust (Witt & Redding, 2013, p. 281). Trust can be both interpersonal (knowledge of another's honesty) or institutionalized (sanctions required to prevent dishonesty). In this regard, endeavoring to encourage communities to invest in mutual institutions such as credit unions may be difficult and problematic. Institutionalized trust is low in the Philippines, Laos, and Indonesia and high in Hong Kong and Singapore (Witt & Redding, 2013, p. 282), which are important clues to cooperative formation.

- Education and skills development:

  In Asia, universal education has not yet been achieved ranging from 61% in India to 100% in Japan (Witt & Redding, 2013, p. 270). This may well result in a lack of skill levels at committee level and management in cooperatives in some countries.

  In summary, Gordon states that, "Society needs to be highly cohesive before cooperativeness can become widely enacted. This entails a strong sense of identity beyond that with the core family unit. This in turn is somehow connected with the releasing of power into the society, so is usually absent in autocracies, and in any case only works to provide people with confidence in the system's reliability (as to protecting them) if a strong civil order has evolved with their participation. This works in Japan and Singapore, partially in South Korea and Taiwan, but only weakly elsewhere in Asia, and is clearly associated with democracy/modernization, hence also partially in India. The Confucian premodern societies and Indonesia, Malaysia, are all still in a condition of powerful identity with core extended family and specific reciprocally bonded outsiders, but civicness as such is low, as also in most developing countries such as Africa and South America."

9.3 Conclusion

We grapple with the issue of Asia having the highest number of cooperative members regionally, but not large cooperatives as rated on the Global 300 list. However, this examination of the 11 factors of Witt and Redding (2013) enrich the understanding of Jensen's (2013) theoretical model of 3 explanatory macro and 4 micro factors, which are used in most of the case studies. Jensen (2013) and Bin address cooperatives from a political economy perspective where a cooperative is either a foreign body in a market system or an organization capable of creating an alternative system to capitalism in the presence of enabling factors and embark on a journey to multiplexity.

Jensen (2013) sees the cooperative as a hybrid that has to deal with the tension, on one hand, of being a transformative organization, resisting degeneration, and maintaining its cooperative principles and values of solidarity, equality, and democracy. On the other hand, it can be an organization incorporated into the capitalist system with its values of individualism, self-interest, and acquisitiveness.

Asia, it has been argued, is composed of collectivist hierarchical cultures with family ownership connected by business groups, finance obtained from banks dependent on personal contact, and social capital as a feature of noninstitutionalized trust. The Asian states do not offer an inclusive participatory model, but an elitist model that tends to revert to predatory practices (Witt & Redding, 2013).

We conclude from this analysis that cooperative formation and scaling up in Asia, based on implementing the Seven International Principles of Cooperation, is difficult as citizens face severe obstacles in the lack of financial and managerial planning skills, are risk-averse when it comes to institutional trust, and exhibit high power distance and lack access to finance.

However, successful cooperatives that have scaled up and avoided degeneration are a feature of the Asian cooperative landscape due, in some instances, to the state's role as an enabler and, in other situations, due to the impact of the role of exceptional social entrepreneurs both individual and collective. We now need to explore the case studies to enable us to come to conclusions about what is needed to awaken the potential of cooperatives in the Asia Pacific region.

References

Cronan, G. (2017). *Unstructured interview.*

Giles, A. (1989). In Jack Barbash, & Kate Barbash (Eds.), *Industrial relations theory, the state and politics in theories and concepts in comparative industrial telations* (pp. 123–154). Columbia, SC: University of South Carolina Press.

Greenberg, E. S. (1983). Context and co-operation: Systematic variation in the political effects of workplace democracy. *Economic and Industrial Democracy SAGE London, 4,* 191–223.

Hall, P. A., & Soskice, D. (2003). *Varieties of capitalism.* Oxford: The Institutional Foundations of Comparative Advantage Oxford University Press.

Hofstede, G., & Hofstede, G. J. (2005). *Cultures and organisational software of the mind.* London: Mc Graw Hill.

Isaac, T., & Williams, M. (2017). *Building alternatives. The story of India's oldest construction worker co-operative.* New Delhi, India: Left World Books.

Jensen, A. (2013). The labour managed firm — A theoretical model explaining emergence and behavior. In Kruse D. (Ed.), *Sharing ownership profits, and decision making in the 21st century. Advances in the economic analysis of participatory and labor managed firm* (vol. 14). Somerville, MA: Emerald.

Kurimoto, A. (2018). *Personal correspondence.*

Mason, P. (2017). *Unstructured interview.*

Redding, G. (2005). The thick description and comparison of societal systems of capitalism. *Journal of International Business Studies, 36*, 123–155.

Tullus, R. (2017). *Personal correspondence.*

Villamin, R. (2017). *Unstructured discussion.*

Witt, M. A., & Redding, G. (2013). Asian business systems: Institutional comparison, clusters and implications for varieties of capitalism and business systems theory. *Socio Economic Review, 11*, 265–300.

Further reading

Altman, M. (2020). The theoretical construct of comparative co-operative advantage. In M. Altman, Y. Dongre, S. Jang, A. Jensen, A. Kurimoto, & R. Tullus (Eds.), *Waking the Asian Pacific C-operative Potential.* London: Elsevier.

Bratton, J., & Gold, J. (2012). *Human resource management – Theory and practice.* London: Palgrave M Macmillan.

Holyoake, G. J. (1906). *The cooperative movement today.* London: Methuen.

Kalmi, P. (2007). The disappearance of co-operatives from economics textbooks. *Cambridge Journal of Economics, 31* (4), 625–647.

Mazzarol, T. (2011) *Simmons R and Mamoumi Limnios E. A conceptual framework for research into cooperative enterprise.* CEMI Discussion Paper Series DP 1102 Centre for Entrepreneurial Management and Innovation.

Poole, M. (1986). *Industrial relations. Origins and patterns of national diversity.* London: Routledge and Kegan Paul.

Rhodes, R. (2012). *How the British Empire used cooperation in its development strategies.* Edinburgh: John Donald.

Shambaugh, D. (2013). *China goes global: The partial power.* Oxford: Oxford University Press.

Thornley, J. (1981). *Jobs and dreams.* London: Heinemann.

Welzel, C., & Delhey, J. (2015). Generalizing trust: The benign force of emancipation. *Journal of Cross-Cultural Psychology, 46*(7), 875–896.

PART 2

Case studies of Asian co-ops, including cross-country comparison

Agricultural co-ops

How small farmers enter the big market? A case study of agricultural cooperatives in China

Bin Wu

Hangzhou Dianzi University, Hangzhou, P.R. China

10.1 Introduction

The agricultural products market in developing countries today is undergoing structural and management changes, which are not only an important factor for the sustainable development of the rural economy and the reduction of poverty, but also affect the role of agriculture in overall economic development. The large-scale production and circulation of small-scale farmers in some countries is a huge "bottleneck" for agricultural trade liberalization and circulation globalization (Tan & Zhu, 2004). At present, the agricultural product supply chain system in China exhibits a variety of forms of characteristics including small farmers, retailers, processing enterprises, wholesalers, retail vendors, and other traditional production and supply systems formed by the connection of production areas and wholesale markets (Huang & Liu, 2005). There is also a modern supply chain that is formed by new retail formats such as supermarket chains, which is based on new marketing terminals,

constrained by technology and standards, and characterized by organizational cooperation and value-added circulation. The scattered small farmers are far from enough to cope with the ever-changing agricultural product market, and there are various dilemmas of "small farmers facing the big market," mainly including:

First, due to the imperfect distribution mechanism and the unbalanced risk sharing mechanism of the agricultural product supply chain, small farmers bear the dual risks of nature and the market, and their benefits are obviously not corresponding to their risks and labor. Farmers in a weak position tend to receive only a small portion of the value-added portion of the production chain, while the vast majority of agricultural products are held by other entities in the supply chain. The addition and rapid development of new agricultural product supply chain entities such as supermarkets have brought about various changes in the agricultural product supply chain system (Liu, 2004). Farmers must get rid of poverty and get rich from the traditional rural market to the new

113

urban market. This "new market" is full of various new supply chain entities. The various chain supermarkets, fresh supermarkets, and fruit supermarkets that have developed rapidly since the 1990s and the various private standards they have set, set the threshold for farmers to approach or enter the market. Farmers must meet a range of standards and trading characteristics required by the new market including not only product standards such as appearance, quality, taste, packaging, and safety, but also characteristics and requirements such as transaction volume and trading time. Obviously, scattered small farmers cannot meet these needs.

The continuous development of the modern logistics industry and the establishment of agricultural product distribution centers have reduced the transportation cost and transaction cost of agricultural products, and also provided the space and possibility of price reductions for agricultural products. It is obviously difficult for scattered small farmers to join the circulation chain of agricultural products. Of course, they cannot enjoy the reduction of transaction costs, but they may face pressure from price reductions. Under the background of the rise of new agricultural product supply chain entities such as supermarkets, logistics distribution centers, and the globalization of agricultural products circulation, agricultural production organizations are constantly innovating to adapt to changes and improvements in the supply chain and market. Farmer cooperatives are one of the new industrial organizations that have been affirmed by theory and practice. To a certain extent, cooperatives have alleviated or eliminated the dilemma of small farmers participating in the market, and organized scattered small farmers into agricultural

product supply chains to cope with the various product standards and transaction characteristics required by the modern market. Through a case study analysis, this chapter analyzes the significance and development reasons behind cooperatives in China, and has obtained some inspirations.

10.2 Case study

10.2.1 Brief profile of Yulin watermelon cooperative[1]

Yulin watermelon cooperative located in Ruoheng Town of Taizhou City in Zhejiang Province, which is in Southeast China and next to the East China Sea. The emergence of the Yulin watermelon cooperative reflected the characteristics of the era. Since the late 1990s, local farmers have switched from food crops to watermelon cultivation. However, due to the lack of effective technical services, many farmers have poor quality and low yield. Most watermelons can only be used locally. Cheap sales cannot achieve economic benefits. On the other hand, it is difficult for melon farmers to effectively connect to the market, watermelons are difficult to sell, and quite a few farmers suffer major economic losses. Faced with various contradictions and dilemmas, there is an urgent need for an industrial organization that can provide technical services to farmers, establish uniform production standards, and rely on quality and brand to connect with the market.

In July 2001 Yulin watermelon cooperative was founded under the leadership of 29 large watermelon growers led by Youda Peng with the help and support of the local government.[2] The initial capital subscription by members

---

[1] In fact, since 2010, the cooperative's products have expanded to other fruits (such as grapes, sugar cane), vegetables, and rice, but watermelon is still the most important product.

[2] Youda Peng, male, born in 1961. He is a member of the Communist Party of China and served as a representative of the Zhejiang Provincial People's Congress. Mr. Peng is the founder of the cooperative and serves as the chairman and the president until now.

was 52,200 yuan[3] and it changed to 5 million yuan in 2007.[4] In the capital subscription, the chairman Peng contributed 1 million yuan (20%), and the whole board of directors contributed 3.25 million yuan (65%). By the end of 2017, the cooperative had 826 members (only watermelon growers) and now has sales outlets in more than 70 fruit wholesale markets in 25 provinces and cities nationwide. The cooperative has 9 full-time directors, 3 full-time supervisors, and has hired 35 full-time employees including 5 professional managers, 2 auditors, 15 sales representatives, 10 technicians, and 3 college-graduate village officials. The cooperative is a well-known national brand "Yulin Watermelon." Besides, the cooperative has 26 planting bases in Hainan province, Guangdong province, Jiangsu province, Jiangxi province, and overseas (such as Australia and Myanmar), with a total planting area of 36,500 mu[5]. Each base is managed by 5–10 cooperative members, while a certain number of local farmers are employed as part-time workers. In 2017 the total sales revenue reached 437 million yuan, the profit reached 96.1 million yuan, and the surplus was 56.8 million yuan, which was returned to the members. It can be considered that Yulin watermelon cooperative is the most well-known cooperative in China and was selected as one of the top 100 farmer cooperatives in China.[6]

10.2.2 The operating mechanism of Yulin watermelon cooperative

10.2.2.1 Members' rights and obligations

The rights of the members include: (1) The right to participate in membership meetings and the right to make decisions, vote, and be elected. (2) To enjoy the priority trading rights of various services and products provided by the cooperative. (3) The right to distribute surplus according to the number of shares and the amount of transactions. (4) The right to democratic management and democratic supervision, and the right to question, criticize, and suggest the work of the cooperative. (5) The right to suggest that the cooperative hold a membership meeting. (6) The right to refuse the unlawful burden of the cooperative. (7) The right to apply for withdrawal from the cooperative. (8) The right to distribute the remaining property after the termination of the cooperative.

The obligations of the members include: (1) To comply with the cooperative's bylaws and various systems, to implement the decisions of the members' assembly and the board of directors, and support the board of directors and the board of supervisors in performing their duties. (2) To subscribe for shares in accordance with the provisions of the cooperative, and assume the corresponding responsibilities. (3) To strictly perform various agreements or contracts signed with the cooperative, and to organize the production and supply of products according to the specified production quality standards and requirements. (4) To actively participate in activities such as study and training organized by the cooperative, and actively report the situation to the cooperative and provide information. (5) According to the division of work, carry forward the spirit of mutual assistance and cooperation, and actively carry out production, operation, and service activities. (6) Maintain the interests of the cooperative, protect cooperative property,

---

[3] 1 Chinese Yuan equaled to around 0.65 dollars in 2017.

[4] In July 2007, the Farmers Specialized Co-operative Act of P.R. China was promulgated and then the Yulin watermelon cooperative changed the registration informations in the local market administration bureau.

[5] 1 Chinese mu is roughly equal to 0.16 acres.

[6] See: www.zgnmhzs.cn/yw/201812/t20181226_6311850.htm (in Chinese).

and protect cooperative facilities. (7) Undertake other responsibilities that the cooperative believes the member needs to bear.

10.2.2.2 Accession conditions

(1) Engage in the watermelon industry, the watermelon business scale is more than 10 mu and the watermelon is planted for more than 3 years, and basically mastering the production technology of the "Yulin" brand watermelon. (2) Recognize and abide by the cooperative's bylaws, have the capacity for civil conduct, and voluntarily submit a written application for admission. (3) Subscription for a certain number of cooperative shares.

10.2.2.3 Shares arrangement

The cooperative determines the operating area and subscription shares of its members according to the ratio of the production and management capacity of the members and their contribution performance. The value of each share is 1000 yuan, and the shares held by one member cannot exceed 20% of the total shares.[7] The cooperative is divided into registered share capital and production share funds. The registered share capital is composed of the contribution of members at the time of registration of the cooperative; while the funds for the production of shares are composed of the funds invested by members of the production base in accordance with the agreed upon area base, which is the source of production funds and the basis for the distribution of surplus.

10.2.2.4 System of organization

The cooperative set up three management bodies, namely, the member assembly, the board of directors, and the board of supervisors. The member assembly is composed of all members and is the highest authority of the coopera-

tive. The board of directors is the executive agency of the cooperative, responsible for daily work and responsible for the member assembly. The board of directors consists of nine members. The board of supervisors is the supervisory body of the cooperative. It supervises and inspects the work of the board of directors on behalf of all members and is responsible to the members' assembly. The board of supervisors consists of three supervisors.

Cooperative operating agencies include: (1) An office as the functional department responsible for handling the daily affairs of the cooperative. (2) A production base department as the functional department of the cooperative that is responsible for base expansion, production management, technical guidance, technology development, business training, and demonstration and promotion. (3) A marketing department as the functional department of the cooperative that is responsible for market development, product sales, and information feedback. (4) A finance department as the functional department of the cooperative responsible for finance and internal audit.

10.2.2.5 Decision-making

The cooperative is based on the transaction amount and the number of shares combined with the "one-person relative multi-vote system" method for democratic decision-making. The members who contribute to the cooperative can have voting rights of no more than 20% of the total votes, and play a role as core members, while preventing "one big share" to protect the democratic decision-making power of ordinary members.

10.2.2.6 Profit distribution

The cooperative uses the production base as an independent accounting unit to carry out

---

[7] So, as the largest shareholder, chairman Peng contributed 1 million yuan, just 20% of the total shares.

secondary interest distribution.[8] The first benefit distribution is the wage income obtained by members participating in labor management and included in the cooperative operating costs. The second benefit distribution is the cooperative surplus distribution. After deducting the cost and various expenses and after extracting certain surplus reserves and risk protection funds, it is 100% allocated according to the proportion of members invested in production.

10.2.3 Related cost and benefit analysis

The survey respondents were the president, some members of the cooperative, and five nonmember farmers. The cost, benefit data, and other relevant information required for the research were obtained through a more detailed interview survey with them. The following sections (10.2.3.1 and 10.2.3.2) will describe the costs and benefits to cooperative members and nonmember farmers, and compare the two to show whether the existence of the cooperative has produced benefits.

10.2.3.1 Some explanations and assumptions

Before describing the data, several points and assumptions need to be made: (1) The production and sales process of watermelon roughly includes soaking seeds and raising seedlings in November, moving seedlings in Daejeon in early December, and harvesting head-shaped melons in May of the following year. Sales time can last until November. In other words, a complete cycle of watermelon from production to sales is just a year. (2) The basic salary paid by the cooperative to its members is 3000 yuan/month, and each

member is responsible for planting 5 mu of watermelon on average, so that the monthly salary per mu is 600 yuan, calculated in 12 months, and the salary of each member in the year is 7200 yuan (per mu of watermelon). In this study, assume the labor cost (or employment salary) of nonmember farmers is also calculated at 3000 yuan/month. In addition, the labor costs of nonmember farmers and the wage income of members will be listed as farmers' income. (3) In the investigation, the control of the survey site and the respondents excluded the differences in the natural conditions such as the area, soil, and temperature of the cooperative and nonmember farmers on the watermelon base. (4) In the cost data of the cooperative and nonmember farmers, the cost of some reusable production materials should be apportioned over several years such as plastic film, bamboo, etc. In order to simplify the calculation, all these costs are included in the current cost. Therefore the net income of the cooperative and nonmember farmers is small, but the net income of the two is still comparable. (5) When surveying 5 nonmember farmers, farmers with more than 3 years of experience in planting melons were chosen. They have a clear understanding of watermelon planting techniques and cost benefits. It is worth mentioning that the data on the cost and benefit of the survey of a farmer are consistent, which indicates that the data are typical and credible. (6) According to the survey, in the whole watermelon production cycle, non-member farmers need to hire 0.9 labor per mu per year. And the average daily wage of each worker is 150 yuan, so the annual labor cost per mu is 135 yuan and it will accounting into the production cost of watermelon.

---

[8] When conducting certain accounting calculations, it is necessary to set up separate accounts for each member to be accounted for separately. Therefore according to the Farmers Specialized Cooperatives Act, the independent member account mainly includes three items, namely (1) to record the member's capital subscription, (2) to record the transaction between the member and the cooperative, and (3) to record the change of the member's capital reverse.

TABLE 10.1 Costs and revenues of watermelon planting (Unit: Chinese Yuan).

Items	1. Members of the cooperative	2. Nonmember farmers	Difference (1−2)
Total cost per mu	6415	4625	1790
• Seeds	95	80	15
• Fertilizers and pesticides	1300	1300	0
• Plastic film	1200	1200	0
• Bamboo	850	470	380
• Agricultural machinery service	520	410	110
• Packaging fee	1500	−	1500
• Dropper	−	80	−80
• Hiring labor	−	135	−135
• Land rent	950	950	0
Total revenue per mu	9450	4160	5290
• Average price of watermelon per kilogram	3.5	1.6	1.9
• Average yield per mu (kilogram)	2700	2600	100
Net income per mu	3035	−465	3500

10.2.3.2 Description of costs and revenues of cooperative members and nonmember farmers

The 2017 costs and revenues of cooperative members and nonmember farmers are shown in Table 10.1.[9]

In the production cost of watermelon, the cooperative members and nonmember farmers were 5645 yuan/mu and 3744 yuan/mu respectively, and the cooperative members had more expenses. The biggest source of the gap is the cooperative's maintenance costs of watermelons for the initial processing of watermelons, that is, labels, net bags, and cartons used in packaging, which resulted in a cost difference of 1500 yuan. Other production materials such as bamboo chips and machinery costs are also sources of the difference. The costs of the different seeds and fertilizers, plastic greenhouses, etc., are almost the same. Although the cooperative invested more than 1790 yuan, it directly brought about a significant difference in the price of the watermelon. The price of watermelon for nonmember farmers was 1.6 yuan, while the watermelon of the cooperative reached 3.5 yuan/kg, which is 2.2-times higher. The price gap is obviously not accidental, but the high return on the appearance, packaging, quality, taste, and safety of the cooperative's standardized production and higher investment and its brand effect. Under the combined effect of the acre yield and price, the incomes per mu of the cooperative and nonmember

[9] The author acknowledges that due to market fluctuation, using only one year of cross-sectional data may be biased. Therefore the author asked the respondents to provide stable and relevant data as much as possible in the survey.

farmers have produced significant differences, which are 9450 yuan and 4160 yuan respectively. Finally, the difference in net income per mu between cooperative members and nonmember farmers is 3500 yuan.

10.3 Further thinking

10.3.1 The reasons for the successful operation of the cooperative

In addition, to the local government's support and guidance to the cooperative, the achievements and good development model of the Yulin watermelon cooperative has a systematic structure and operation mode suitable for its own development. On the basis of the members, some typical principles of the new generation cooperatives were adopted, and appropriate innovations were made to better suit their development model. The continuous improvement of the technical level and good brand image of the cooperative also injected vitality into its development.

10.3.1.1 Appropriate use and innovation of the principles of cooperatives

In the traditional "Rochdale principles," including the freedom of admission, freedom of resignation, democratic control, one person one vote, fair trade, return of profits, etc., the new generation of cooperatives are no longer strictly adhering to those traditional principles. The principles have been revised and innovated to make them more suitable for the development of the market economy and to achieve the goal of increasing farmers' incomes. The proper use of the principles of cooperatives by the Yulin watermelon cooperative is the basic guarantee for its good development. It can be argued that the Yulin watermelon cooperative is a hybrid organization between traditional marketing cooperatives and the new generation of cooperatives.

1. Quasimembership (membership is not open). The assessment conditions for the cooperative to absorb members include experience of more than 3 years of growing melons, basically mastering the production technology of the "Yulin" brand of watermelon, and having the ability to lead farmers to organize production. Before becoming a full member of the cooperative, farmers must undergo an internship and probationary assessment before they can become a full member. The watermelon cooperative adopts a quasimembership system when recruiting members, and it is not open to all farmers. This does not change the purpose of the cooperative to serve the people, but it plans to rationally absorb farmers. On the one hand, the quasimembership system enhances the effect of the cooperative in the technical training and services of farmers. On the other hand, the number of cooperative members and the production base (area) are simultaneously expanded in scale, avoiding the "trap" of inefficiency and ensuring the original members' interests are met.

2. One person one vote system. When a cooperative makes a major decision or election, it usually adopts the one-person, one-vote format for all shareholders (members). The difference between one-person, one-vote and one-lot is also the choice between fairness and efficiency. As an economic entity, the cooperative participates in market competition, pursues profits, and internally serves the purpose of service, not for profit, for all its members. All are equal, and the one-person, one-vote system is implemented to ensure the democratic nature of decision-making and to avoid the joint manipulation of cooperatives by minority shareholders.

3. The clarity of the member's property and the internality of the stock. In the

cooperative, all the shares are owned by the members, but each member has a certain number of shares to avoid the minority holdings, thus violating the nature of the services of the cooperative. The respective shares and property owned by each member are clear and are "visible and tangible." Members have the right to freely withdraw shares, but the shares cannot be transferred to ensure the internality of the shares. For farmers with low levels of knowledge, risk awareness, and relatively low risk resistance, it is obviously important to ensure the clarity and transparency of their property.

4. Double rebate according to the share and transaction amount. The principle of a double rebate based on shares and transaction volume is also an important guarantee for the development and good operation of the cooperative. More capital and labor input bring direct benefits, which not only encourages members' investment, but also enhances members' production enthusiasm. It avoids the inefficiency caused by the "free rider" mentality and greatly saves the incentive costs and supervision costs of the cooperative members.

10.3.1.2 Continuous improvement of production technology and good brand image

For any company, continuous improvement and innovation in production technology is a necessary condition for ensuring vitality and sustainable development. Cooperatives are not only an institutional innovation, but also promote technological advancement through "knowledge spillover effects" (Jin & Guan, 2005). The village where the cooperative is located and its neighboring villages have even expanded to Wenling City, and the proportion of watermelon growers is quite high, forming a "community" in which people are closely connected, information is highly shared, and a large number of people gather together. Technical talents, technological innovation, or information acquisition can be quickly promoted and exchanged almost without cost. The knowledge utilization efficiency is high, and the promotion of new technologies is rapid. Especially within the cooperative, relying on human and financial investment in research and development, the continuous updating and improvement of watermelon production materials, and the continuous improvement of production technology have been realized. Just like Bingen, Serrano, and Howard (2003) mentioned, programs that focused on developing community-level management skills and human capacity could increase the opportunities for small farmers to benefit from market participation.

Brand is an important reason for enterprise development and product upgrading. A family cannot make a good brand, and agricultural cooperatives can overcome the weakness of farmer families in this respect. The cooperative is aware of the importance of the brand. They are striving to create the "Yulin" brand, and under the premise of unified production and packaging, have established standards for appearance, quality, taste, and safety for "Yulin" watermelons. The brand has greatly increased the sales price and popularity of their watermelons. The cooperative was established and developed on the basis of "one village with one brand." This brand is not only the brand image of the cooperative, but has also become a regional brand. Compared with the brand of a single company, the regional brand has a more direct image and a broader and continuous brand effect. It is an intangible asset that all farmers in a certain area can share. This regional brand has attracted a large number of wholesalers and consumers. While promoting the sales of watermelons in the company, it also provided trading information for nonmembers of scattered farmers, established sales channels, and reduced trans-action costs. This is the collateral effect of regional brands, which are powerful and extensive.

10.3.2 The effectiveness and resistance of the expansion of the cooperative

10.3.2.1 The effectiveness of the expansion of the cooperative's scale

The cooperative continued to open up new production bases and expand its scale. The marketing network continued to expand and the market share was further increased, which led to a reduction in transaction costs. However, the expansion of scale must have certain limits. This size limit depends on the relative increase in benefits brought by coop-eratives and the relative size of institutional innovation and maintenance costs. When the difference between the former and the latter reaches the maximum, the optimal economies of scale are realized.

Based on the characteristics of the seasonal production of watermelons, continuous crop-ping, and small sales radius, the cooperative implements the "going out" strategy on the basis of stable development in the local area, establishes a watermelon production base out-side the province, conducts off-site develop-ment and dislocation development, and strives to expand. The development space not only lengthens the sales season of "Yulin" brand watermelons, but also realizes the annual sup-ply of "Yulin" watermelons, expands the sales radius, and greatly reduces operating expenses and increases economies of scale.

10.3.2.2 Resistance encountered in scale expansion of the cooperative

As far as the watermelon cooperative is con-cerned, the biggest obstacle to scale expansion is not funds, but the shortage of technical talents, the inability to manage, and the scarcity of land. Having good production technology is key to the development of watermelon production and cooperatives. When the scale of cooperatives is expanded to a certain extent, it is already difficult to continue to absorb talents who have experi-ence of farming with the requirements needed in cooperatives. The training and pos-itive innovation of farmers on the basis of solid technology are necessary conditions for a cooperative to develop continuously.

The ever-expanding scale of cooperatives poses a challenge to the management of coop-eratives. When cooperatives are in a small and strong community, their management and internal trading order are mainly guaranteed by the prestige of cadres or leaders, the homo-geneity of culture, skills, and expectations with community members, and the traditional rules and practices. Compliance also facilitates the management and trading of all kinds of man-agement, and the required management level and cost are relatively low. With the expansion of the scale of the cooperative, the management targets have been extended to farmers outside the province (even abroad), the allocation and balance of funds between the various bases, the completely different natural conditions between different bases, and the corresponding different production technologies have greatly increased the complexity and difficulty of man-agement. This poses a huge challenge for farm-ers and entrepreneurs with relatively low levels of education and relatively weak knowl-edge systems.

The limited land has also hindered the fur-ther expansion of the scale of the cooperative. In this case, because watermelon cultivation has the special nature that it cannot be rotated, the land that has been planted with waterme-lons must at least be rotated other crops for more than three years to restore the soil needed to continue planting watermelons. Therefore the cooperative must constantly be looking for new land for the next year's watermelon production. Watermelon planting has certain requirements for the pH, temperature, and humidity of the soil. These are the needs for the cooperative to continue to expand and continue to develop.

10.4 Conclusion

1. Farmer cooperatives play a central role in providing information and technology to dispersed smallholders and placing small farmers in the market. This not only enhances farmers' sense of security and risk resistance, but also enhances farmers' bargaining power and status through large-scale production, quality assurance of agricultural products, and the brand effects of products, so that farmers gain a greater share of the agricultural product value chain. Farmers are no longer simply price acceptors. Farmer cooperatives reduce the high transaction costs of small farmers in the market, and retain the economic surplus formed by transaction cost savings in agriculture to enhance the accumulation and development capacity of agriculture itself, and increase the income of farmers and the development of agriculture as a whole. This cannot be ignored.

2. Establishing farmer cooperatives on the basis of "one village with one brand" is a better development model. Compared with the development status of all kinds of agricultural products, albeit on a small scale, the development model of "one village with one major agricultural product brand," which is a concentrated product of thousands of households, is more conducive to improving the quality of agricultural products and making it easier to enter the market. If a cooperative can be established on the basis of "one village with one brand," it will greatly save its institutional innovation costs and transaction costs.

In addition, in the area with the characteristics of "one village and one brand," the production technology of this product often becomes mature and stable. Through the establishment of a cooperative, a unified production technology or a brand is established for the product, and there is no development relative to one. The basic product will be much easier.

3. Achieving a continuous and batch supply of products should be a goal of cooperative development. After supermarkets entered the agricultural product supply chain as one of the main subjects, it brought a series of changes. Supermarkets guide the production of agricultural products through feedback from consumer information and the implementation of various private standards. Whether it is the demand transmitted by consumers or the private standards of supermarkets, in addition, to the requirements for the quality and packaging of the products themselves, the requirements for the continuous and large-volume supply of agricultural products are put forward. If necessary, cooperatives should establish the required storage facilities to ensure a rapid response to the needs of the wholesaler and to ensure the continued supply of the agricultural products.

4. The education and training of farmers can promote the development of cooperatives. The development of farmers' cooperatives in China is subject to the concept level and cultural quality of farmers to a considerable extent. One of the prerequisites for the promotion and healthy development of a cooperative lies in the recognition and acceptance of cooperatives by farmers. The local government carries out some education and training for farmers, raises their awareness of the market, enhances their understanding of cooperatives, and provides them with the technical guidance and assistance to guide and promote the

development of cooperatives. Only by letting farmers change their own ideas and rationally compare the benefits and costs will they have the willingness to form or join cooperatives spontaneously and will truly promote the healthy development of cooperatives.

5. Consider the appropriate size of cooperatives. Unrestricted absorption of members does not violate the purpose of cooperative services to the people, but many cooperatives are committed to absorbing as many farmers as possible though they have not established the corresponding management and operational mechanisms, and, thus have not placed farmers to enter the market for trading, but have just formed the organization of production, which is actually a low-level "industrial agglomeration," and has no substantial income-increasing benefits for farmers. Such a form of cooperation will not bring the efficiency of cooperation. Therefore in the operation and management of cooperatives at this stage, the excessive absorption of members should be avoided, and scale expansion and the absorption of members should be carried out within the scope of the cooperative's management capabilities, so that farmers can gradually become rich in batches, and eagerness for seeking will hinder the function of cooperatives.

6. March and Simon (1958, p. 119) pointed out that due to the influence of technological development, our current living environment is no longer a simple market economy, but more accurately it should be an organizational economy. Therefore as an economic organization deeply embedded in the social and political structure, an important task of cooperatives must be to obtain (external) legal status in order to obtain official attention, permission, and strive for resource input. Thence, from the very beginning, cooperatives rely heavily on government agencies, and cooperatives allow the government agencies to act as a "quasi-cooperative entrepreneur" under the shortage of real cooperative entrepreneurs (Xu, 2005, p. 133; Yuan, 2001). However, the first rule of the cooperative principles stipulated by the International Co-operative Alliance is autonomy. That means cooperatives must be as independent as possible from the government or other private companies. Thus the government should not interfere too much with the daily management of cooperatives. The leaders of cooperatives are often technical talents, village cadres, or local township cadres. The establishment and management of cooperatives with the prestige of cadres is beneficial to the management of cooperatives. However, some cadres confuse the management of cooperatives with government work, often using the government's power to intervene too much and even control the operation of the cooperative, which will violate the democratic management principles of the cooperative, and ultimately the farmers. Therefore local governments should not be too involved in the daily management of cooperatives, but should support, encourage, and properly guide cooperatives, which will be beneficial to the healthy development of cooperatives.

7. Furthermore, in general, the Chinese government's expectation of the functions of cooperatives has generally gone through the sequence: (1) Farmer cooperatives as the mainstay of the market economy, on the basis of rural household contract management, unified procurement, unified sales, and unified services, leading scattered small farmers into the big market. (2) To cooperate with the scale operation of agriculture and the transfer of agricultural land, establish land share cooperatives. These cooperatives are regarded as the

main body of the large-scale production and management of modern agriculture. (3) Cooperatives breaking through the boundaries of self-services, and they expands and exerts the functions of agricultural socialization services. A large number of social service cooperatives such as agricultural machinery cooperatives and plant protection cooperatives have emerged. (4) The cooperative forms are no longer confined to the traditional agricultural field, but are widely applied to the areas of large-scale agriculture, agricultural business, and the integration of the development of the first, second, and third industries; various forms of cooperatives such as tourism cooperatives, labor cooperatives, and property cooperatives have emerged. (5) Applying the form of cooperatives to the reform of rural collective property rights systems, making it an effective form of reform of rural collective property rights systems. It is not difficult to see that during this period, cooperatives are considered a perfect tool or platform by the government

Acknowledgment

This study was funded by the Philosophy and Social Science Foundation of Zhejiang Province Project (No. 20NDQN288YB).

References

Bingen, J., Serrano, A., & Howard, J. (2003). Linking farmers to markets: Ddifferent approaches to human capital development. *Food Policy, 28*(4), 405–419.

Huang, Z., & Liu, D. (2005). Analysis of the construction of Agricultural product logistics system in China. *Issues of Agricultural Economics* (4), 49–53. (in Chinese).

Jin, B., & Guan, H. (2005). Analysis of the formation mechanism of industrial agglomeration. *Social Sciences Journal of Colleges of Shanxi* (3), 53–55. (in Chinese).

Liu, C. (2004). Reconstruction of agricultural products circulation organization: Based on the supply chain. *Chinese Cooperative Economy* (5), 53–66. (in Chinese).

March, J. G., & Simon, H. A. (1958). *Organizations*. New York: John Wiley & Sons.

Tan, T., & Zhu, Y. (2004). Research on the organization mode of agricultural products supply chain. *Discussion on Modern Economy* (5), 24–27. (in Chinese).

Xu, X. (2005). *Institutional analysis of Chinese farmer cooperatives*. Beijing: Economic Science Press. (in Chinese).

Yuan, P. (2001). Research on farmer cooperative organization in the process of China's rural marketization. *Chinese Social Science* (6), 63–73. (in Chinese).

Successful agricultural cooperative model in Vietnam. A case study: Van Duc Co-operative

Nguyen Van Phuong, Tran Thi Thu Huong and Bui Hong Quy

Faculty of Accounting and Business Management, Vietnam National University of Agriculture, Gia Lam, Vietnam

11.1 Overview

Agricultural production is one of the earliest and most important human activities as it creates food and substance for human life. This sector, however, always suffers from the external environment like weather, from the market, and from competition (FAO, 2016). Farmers are accordingly easily vulnerable. To be stronger, farmers tend to cooperate or be part of either associations or organizations. There are many forms of linkages between farmers. Literature has shown that agricultural cooperatives are the most viable form of linkage among farmers (Vinh, 2015). Despite a long history of development, agricultural cooperatives also reveal their successes and failures both in developed and developing countries.

Vietnam's agricultural cooperatives have a long history of establishment and development from the 1950s. Agricultural cooperatives have developed fast and contributed significantly to

the process of Vietnam's economic development. The agricultural cooperatives movement experienced a rise and fall in the period between 1958 and 1986 when they operated under conditions of a centrally-planned economy along with the aftermath of war (Nghiem, 2006). For example, 4723 agricultural cooperatives were established by 1958. The number of agricultural cooperatives sharply increased to 41,446, which accounted for 85.8% of farm households and 76.5% of the agricultural land of the whole country in 1960.

It has showed that there have been many successful agricultural cooperative models over the past years in Vietnam. The Van Duc Cooperative located east of the Hanoi capital is considered to be a successful model specializing in vegetables and providing services for production to the local people. In this chapter, a part from an analysis of the macro and micro factors affecting cooperatives in Vietnam, we examine particular factors leading to success

Waking the Asian Pacific Cooperative Potential
DOI: https://doi.org/10.1016/B978-0-12-816666-6.00011-2

and challenges faced by the Van Duc Co-operative, and shed light on the impact of the Van Duc Co-operative on the community.

11.2 Macro factors affecting cooperatives in Vietnam

11.2.1 Political and legal framework

In Vietnam, agricultural cooperatives represent a business model that enjoys a lot of supportive policies from the central government. These policies have considerably contributed to the production and business of cooperatives. The most recent policy favoring cooperatives, for example, is the Cooperative Law 2012. Accordingly, cooperative management boards and their members would be provided with formal training to enhance their professional and technical capacity and given financial support from the central government. In addition, cooperatives would get advantages from relevant policies regarding trade promotion, market expansion, sciences and technologies application, and capital access for further development of cooperatives. These changes led to Vietnam's cooperatives changing their operation and organizational structures.

11.2.2 Socioeconomic and cultural context

In the past few years, Vietnam has been rising as a leading agricultural exporter and has attracted many international investors. The main agricultural products of Vietnam for exporting include rice, cashew nuts, black pepper, coffee, tea, rubber, and fishery products. Manufacturing, information technology, and high-tech industries also constitute a fast-growing part of the national economy. On average, the incomes of Vietnamese people have increased more than 3 times over 10 years, from USD835/capita in 2007 to USD2385/capita in 2017. An annual growth rate of 6%−7% will be a great motivation for the development of production and trading of goods, especially the business activities of cooperatives (GSO, 2018).

Vietnam is ranked as the 14th most populous country in the world. Vietnam represents a huge pool of both potential customers and employees for many investors given its over 92 million people and median age of 30 (VCCI, 2017). Fig. 11.1 shows the changes in the population of Vietnam from 1990 to 2017. It shows that Vietnam's population has increased fast over the past years. The rural population accounts for 65% of the total population, yet it is facing a downward trend. That urbanization in Vietnam has accelerated in the past 30 years has led to a significant increase in the population in cities and towns throughout the country. As a consequence, the labor structure in the agriculture sector has been changed (MARD, 2018). The less people living in rural area in has reduced human resource for Vietnam's agricultural cooperatives over the past years.

In practice, agricultural cooperatives have complemented efforts of the state to improve the livelihood of the local people. Specifically, much employment has been created and poverty has been alleviated. The agricultural cooperatives are reflecting well their key role in attracting internal efforts from the local people to solve their own problems.

11.2.3 Global climate change

For agricultural production, the effect of increased temperature will depend on the agricultural production's optimal temperature for growth and reproduction. In some sectors, warming could benefit the kind of production that typically is produced there or climate change may increase diseases that affect plants or livestock. Warming may lead to an increased number of pest insects and bacteria, harming yields of production. Vietnam's cooperatives have been changing their crop

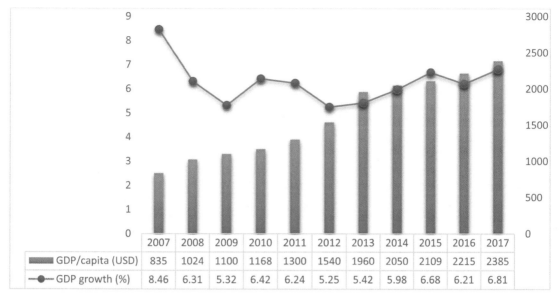

	2007	2008	2009	2010	2011	2012	2013	2014	2015	2016	2017
▬ GDP/capita (USD)	835	1024	1100	1168	1300	1540	1960	2050	2109	2215	2385
━●━ GDP growth (%)	8.46	6.31	5.32	6.42	6.24	5.25	5.42	5.98	6.68	6.21	6.81

FIGURE 11.1   GDP growth and GDP/capita over period 2007-2017. Source: *GSO, 2018.*

structures and production methods to adapt to the global climate changing.

11.3 Micro factors affecting cooperatives in Vietnam

11.3.1 Business model

Vietnam's transition economy has experienced privatization, the launch of new private firms, and fundamental legal changes. Vietnam has also experienced changes that have improved the overall business environment including the legal framework for agricultural cooperatives (Anne & Le, 2014). The model of cooperatives that is organized in accordance with the Cooperative Law 2012 has been much improved compared to the previous one established before 2012. There are currently two types of cooperative models operating in Vietnam, namely transformed cooperatives, which were established before 2012 and transformed in accordance with the new Cooperative Law 2012, and newly-establishment cooperatives,

which are found to present from 2012. The only difference between these types of cooperatives is the capital contributed by cooperative members. In the latter model, a contribution of a prescribed amount of money is a must for all members, while household members may decide whether they would contribute capital to the cooperative in the former model. Accordingly, those who have contributed no capital, called informal members, would not share from a given cooperative's profit at the end of the year. Meanwhile, those who contributed to the cooperative's capital, called formal members, receive a shared-profit from the cooperative's business.

11.3.2 Cooperative principles

Article 7 of the Cooperative Law 2012, specifies seven principles for the organization and operation of cooperatives. Mobilization of members and employees is also adopted from the International Co-operative Alliance's Co-operative Principles (Prakash, 2003) including:

1. Individuals, households, and legal entities establish, join, or leave cooperatives voluntarily.
2. Cooperatives shall widely admit members.
3. Members have equality and equal vote regardless of contributed capital in determining the organization, management, and operation of cooperatives and are provided information completely, promptly, and accurately on production activities, sales, finance, income distribution, and other contents as prescribed by the charter.
4. Cooperatives shall control and take responsibility for their activities before the law by themselves.
5. Members and cooperatives have responsibilities to carry out their commitment under service contract as prescribed by the charter. The income of cooperatives shall be distributed by the level of use of products or services of the members or by members' contributed labor for job creation.
6. Cooperatives shall pay their interest in education, training, and retraining for their members and affiliated cooperatives, managers, employees of cooperatives and give information about the nature and benefits of cooperatives.
7. Cooperatives shall care for the sustainable development of their member communities and work together to develop the cooperative movement on a local, regional, national, and international scale.

11.4 Characteristics of the Van Duc Co-operative

11.4.1 History of the Van Duc Co-operative

The Van Duc Co-operative was established in 1977 and originally named Trung Chu Son Co-operative. Since then, the cooperative has experienced remarkable changes as a consequence of the Co-operative Law 1996; the Revised Co-operative Law 2003; and the newest Cooperative Law 2012. In 1998 it was transformed into a membership-oriented service cooperative and renamed the Van Duc Agricultural Service Co-operative. The cooperative was restructured in accordance with the Cooperative Law 2012, and renamed again as the Van Duc Agricultural Production Business-Services Co-operative in 2016 (hereafter Van Duc Co-operative).

11.4.2 Organizational structure of Van Duc Co-operative

The organizational structure of the Van Duc Co-operative is illustrated in Fig. 11.2.

As of June 30, 2018, there are 29 staff members in the Van Duc Co-operative and they are grouped into 4 managing units, namely general management board, control unit, accounting unit, and team supplying services. The number of staff in each unit is decided in the Co-operative Congress, which is organized once every five years.

At the moment, the Van Duc Co-operative has 168 formal members and 708 informal members. Formal members have the rights of cooperative members according to the Cooperative Law 2012. They share the annual profit based on their contributed capital. Moreover, they are also prioritized to sell produce through the cooperative's marketing channel. The number of formal members increased from 150 in 2016 to 168 members in 2018 as people became aware of the benefits of being formal members of the cooperative.

Van Duc Co-operative provides diversified services to its members including field protection, irrigation, inputs supplying (i.e., fertilizers, pesticides, and seedlings), agricultural extension, and marketing.

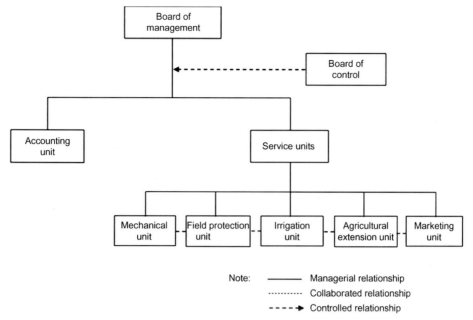

FIGURE 11.2   Organizational structure of Van Duc Co-operative.

11.5 Challenges faced by Van Duc Co-operative

Urbanization led to rural to urban migration flow and increases in the nonfarmer population in rural areas. These decreased the proportion of the population working in agriculture. Agricultural land is used for building roads with the purpose of serving the new suburban population. This leads to reduced farming land.

Due to Vietnam's Co-operative Law, the awareness of the cooperative's staff members as well as most of members about changes of the Vietnam's cooperative law is limited. The cooperative managers still have limitations in terms of qualifications, management capacity, and professional skills. Therefore the implementation of cooperative law still takes a long time. Van Duc Co-operative needs to intensify the propagation of the new cooperative law.

In the past few years, food safety issues have been raised by Vietnam's consumers as well as Van Duc Co-operative members. The Vietnamese people are more aware of health risks and higher demand for food safety (Dungz, 2015). However, domestic consumption of safe food in Vietnam is still considered low (Sahota, 2009). This may be caused by a lack of food safety in the market and consumer confidence in domestic producers. Therefore they tend to switch to imported food from a trusted food source. This presents challenges to domestic food production in Vietnam, especially to smallholders. Van Duc Co-operative should pay more attention to building consumers' trust.

Apart from competition, weather plays an important role in the vegetable production of Van Duc Co-operative. Recently, weather has been changing more extremely and these changes have had a great impact on local people's vegetable production. For example, the variation in temperature by season might lead to the ability to increase the number of vegetable crops cultivated in a year. While, heavy rainfall and storms from May to September may cause low productivity of vegetable production for the cooperative. To reduce the negative impacts from such unfavorable conditions, the cooperative is planning to build net houses for vegetable cultivation.

11.5.1 Challenges from the internal environment

In fact, access training courses provide new methods to increase the productivity and quality of their products. However, many of the cooperative's members did not participate fully in training course that were organized by Van Duc Co-operative. Training and development of cooperative members increase the productivity and quality of their products. So, the benefits of training courses need to communicate widely to all members. Most cooperative members follow safety or VietGAP requirements. However, there are still households that violate these requirements. Van Duc Co-operative should enhance their member's awareness.

Farm product processing and marketing, internal credit, clean water supply, and waste collection are considered new services that have been organized by cooperatives (Nghiem, 2006). Currently, services supplied by the Van Duc Co-operative are mostly input-oriented. The most recent service developed is the marketing of vegetables, however, the cooperative markets only 10% of the total vegetables produced.

Similar to the general characteristics of agricultural land in Vietnam, vegetable production in Van Duc Co-operative is facing land fragmentation. On average, there are 7−8 plots of agricultural land per household. Land fragmentation is the major reason for the limited labor productivity in Vietnam compared to other regional countries (CAP, 2013), and it has a negative impact on crop productivity and other expenses (Hung, MacAulay, & Marsh, 2007). To solve land fragmentation, land consolidation has been encouraged by the Van Duc Co-operative. However, the percentage of agricultural households that have completed land consolidation is still small (less than 30%). Therefore managers should continue to promote and intensify the propagation of the benefits of land consolidation.

11.6 Factors contributing to success

Factors contributing to success of Van Duc co-op including both internal and external ones. Experiences and awareness of farmer, and the governance of Van Duc co-op are internal factors while natural conditions, public investment in infrastructure, and policies support for land consolidation are composed of external elements.

11.6.1 Experience and awareness of farmers in agricultural production and vegetable growing

Historically, the main occupation in the Van Duc commune is agriculture, specializing in corn and vegetable cultivation, and in cattle and poultry raising. Unlike many other villages and communes in the Red River Delta of Vietnam focusing on rice production and rice culture, Van Duc is known to be traditionally specializing in vegetables. In 1997 the Van Duc commune management board, aiming to improve the efficiency of agricultural production, piloted two hectares of vegetables in accordance with safety procedures issued by the Hanoi Plant Protection Unit. The output, amounting to 30 tons, was immediately accepted by consumers. Since then, safe vegetables are produced throughout the commune.

As a result, infrastructure for vegetables production has been invested in including bringing electricity to the fields, digging ditches, and planting flooded areas with vegetables. In addition, dozens of training courses are held annually on updated techniques for safe vegetables production. Farmers are aware of benefits from participating in such training courses, and the role of vegetable production in their livelihood. These advantages have strongly helped Van Duc Co-operative managers in implementing vegetable-related programs or activities.

11.6.2 Governance process

According to Chris Cornforth (2004, cited in Co-operatives UK, 2011) governance is *"The systems and processes concerned with ensuring the overall direction, supervision and accountability of an organization."* The key distinction to be made is between the governance of an organization and the day-to-day running of it. Governance is used as a term to describe all the internal processes within an organization that relate to accountability to any stakeholder both within and outside the organization (Co-operatives UK, 2011). Cooperatives, not like many other organization, face additional challenges in that the internal processes and decision making need to involve a larger number of members.

Governance concerns the way cooperatives are directed and controlled, and is, therefore, central to the work of the board. According to Co-operative Governance Expert Reference Panel (cited in Harvey, 2017), the key areas of governance are an effective board, operations and processes, performance and roles, and members and participation.

In this section, the Van Duc Co-operative's governance is, therefore, reflected through its effective board; operations and performance (including production strategy, input quality control, providing updated technical training courses, and production process management); and its members and their participation.

11.6.2.1 Active and effective management board

In agriculture, the greatest concern of farmers is always where and how to sell their produce. Today, Van Duc Co-operative's safe vegetables have a foothold in the market, which is firstly due to skilled managers. The cooperative management board has done well marketing and in product promotion. Annually, 10% of the total vegetables (i.e., 3500 tons) produced by both formal and informal household members can be marketed through Van Duc Co-operative, of which 55% (i.e., 1925 tons) is sold in wholesale markets like Long Bien, Ha Dong, Nha Xanh, and Mai Dong, another 35% (i.e., 1225 tons) is bought by supermarkets such as Aeon Mall Long Bien, Vin Mart, Metro Thang Long, Metro Ha Dong, and Metro Hoang Mai. The remaining 10%, mainly Chinese cabbage, is exported to Taiwan, Japan, and Korea. Both formal and informal cooperative household members can benefit from selling their produce at a 10% higher price through the cooperative's marketing channels in comparison with the market price.

Before 2011, safe vegetable producers in the Van Duc Co-operative sold their products with difficultly because the selling price was always higher and consumers could not distinguish their safe vegetables from normal ones in the market. Since 2011, vegetables produced by the Van Duc Co-operative have been labeled with the technical support of the Hanoi Plant Protection Unit. Identification consists of a label stating the production address and date of harvest, and seals. With the label, vegetables produced by the Van Duc Co-operative are more easily marketed. Marketing by packaging and labeling vegetables is the most efficient way to introduce the safe vegetables of the Van Duc Co-operative to consumers.

11.6.2.2 Van Duc Co-operative's operation and performance

Production strategy

Van Duc Co-operative's production strategy is to produce diverse types of vegetables and to balance their corresponding cultivated area. Cooperative household members are accordingly able to produce more than 30 varieties of vegetable during the proper seasons. Diversification of the vegetables produced, on the one hand, is considered as the cooperative's advantage in order to meet increasing consumer demand for a wide variety of products. On the other hand, it has contributed to alleviate selling price fluctuation as a huge volume of the same type of vegetable would suffer from a low selling price if all farmers did not grow different types of vegetables.

In practice, during the last months of the year, in the central region of Vietnam, vegetable production is challenging due to heavy rain. Meanwhile, in the north of the country, the weather in winter favors cold-loving vegetables such as cauliflower, kohlrabi, and cabbage (Table 11.1). As a consequence, a certain area of Van Duc Co-operative has been deserved for growing such kinds of vegetable. This opened an opportunity for expanding the market of Van Duc Co-operative's vegetables in provinces in the central region of Vietnam.

Input quality control

Van Duc Co-operative household members, regardless their level of capital contributed, are serviced high quality inputs, but a cheaper selling price compared to other private stores nearby. There are currently nine stores operated by Van Duc Co-operative household members selling seedlings, fertilizers, and pesticides in the Van Duc commune. The owners of these stores are asked to buy inputs from reputable companies such as Vietnam National Seed Joint Stock Company.

On the one hand, farmers financially benefit from buying cheaper and controlled-origin inputs for their production. On the other hand, it saves Van Duc Co-operative managers time to monitor the farmers' usage of fertilizers and pesticides if they have to buy inputs at a competitive selling price from any stores.

Providing updated technical training courses

Despite the awareness and experience of farmers in safe vegetables cultivation, Van Duc Co-operative managers organize dozens of training courses annually on updated techniques of vegetables production, and on integrated pest management. In addition, the cooperative management board connects to other agricultural cooperatives specializing in vegetables like Le Chi, Dang Xa, and Yen Vien

TABLE 11.1 Main types of vegetables produced by season in Van Duc Co-operative.

Winter−spring season	Summer−autumn season
• Kohlrabi • Cabbages: head cabbage, Chinese cabbage, field cabbage • Cauliflower, broccoli • Spices: herb, mint, lemon grass, dill, basil	• Water morning glory, amaranth, see qua • Spinach, Ceylon spinach, cucumber • Thai eggplant, round eggplant • Bitter melon, pumpkin, squash • Okra, string bean • Chili

Van Duc Co-operative (2018).

TABLE 11.2   Training courses organized in 2017 by the Van Duc Co-Operative.

Topic	Quantity (Course)	Participants
Identification of pesticides in the list of permitted uses	2	Van Duc Co-operative members
Method to make vegetable byproducts into compost	3	
Modeling off-season vegetables	3	

Authors' interview, 2018.

for technical exchange and support in order to expand raw material areas. Table 11.2 shows the training courses organized by the Van Duc Co-operative in 2017.

Through participating in training courses, farmers' knowledge is improved, for example, they know well the list of pesticides and fertilizers permitted or which pesticides and fertilizers are best for a specific type of vegetable. In addition, farmers know how to compost the leaves and roots of vegetables after harvest. These techniques have gradually strengthened the knowledge of experienced vegetable-growers in Van Duc Co-operative.

Production process management

The production philosophy of Van Duc Co-operative is *"Three NOs—No factory, No highway, and No hospital."* Van Duc Co-operative is known to cover one of the biggest areas in Hanoi producing safe vegetables. Van Duc Co-operative supplies approximately 100 tons a day, on average, of diverse types of vegetables including leaf-, root-, and spice-vegetables.

The Van Duc Co-operative currently manages 285 ha of agricultural production of which 250 ha, accounting for 87.7% of the total area for agriculture, is certified by the Hanoi Department of Agriculture and Rural Development to produce vegetables in accordance with safety requirements. In 2016 the cooperative designated 15 ha to start producing vegetables that meet the VietGAP standards, which requires higher investment and more regulations. The cooperative's management

board is, however, planning to expand the area in the near future due to its advantage of having a higher selling price. Farmers are aware of the benefits of selling safe vegetables without pesticides and growth stimulants.

Safe vegetable production is managed by group. A total of 876 members are classified into 20 groups and 5 intergroups. Each group includes 25—30 farm households growing vegetables. One group leader is selected to be in charge of monitoring and management to ensure that vegetables produced comply with safety requirements. Fields are mapped and numbered by group and by area to be easily managed. Following the VietGAP standards, each household is provided with daily field-diary writing activities including the type of vegetable grown, respective area, date of fertilizing, seeding, and name of pesticides, etc. This document is daily shown to group leaders to identify households violating either safety or VietGAP requirements and to make timely adjustments. In addition, households and groups are cross-checked. If any households or groups violate the requirements, they will immediately be criticized on the loudspeaker system of the commune. In addition, toward effective management, vegetables are specialized by areas, for example, fields of chili, fields of cabbage and kohlrabi, and fields of premature/early corn.

11.6.2.3 *Nature of co-op member participation*

Before the Cooperative Law 2012, one factor among many factors that caused the poor performance and failure of agricultural cooperatives (i.e., the so-called *old model of agricultural cooperatives*) was their almost compulsory and not voluntary membership (Wolz, 2000). Such membership resulted in a vague perception among members regarding the purpose and principles of cooperatives, cooperatives' values and identities, and especially their rights and obligations (Duong, 2012). The decision-making powers of members and management were almost nonexistent as cooperatives had to follow the instructions of central plans, and cooperative membership was usually determined by place of birth (Fforde, 1987, p. 198, cited in Wolz, 2000).

Today, the Van Duc Co-operative, which operates under the Cooperative Law 2012, basically comprises individuals who voluntarily join social groups. In addition, the Van Duc Co-operative performs as a business unit that has to be registered to participate in economic life. On the one hand, a member is a shareholder and, therefore, a co-owner of the cooperative. On the other hand, a member is a client of the cooperative to take advantage of its offered services. It follows that members are integrated as holders, clients, and decision-makers, simultaneously (Wolfle, 1996, p. 26, cited in Wolz, 2000). These aspects are important and they reflect well the autonomy of the Van Duc Co-operative.

11.6.3 External support

11.6.3.1 Natural condition

The Van Duc commune is located nearby the Red river. Agricultural land in the commune is, therefore, considerably suitable for annual crop cultivation, especially vegetables. The natural characteristics of the area favor vegetable production in the Van Duc Co-operative. According to the chairman of Van Duc commune, temperature in 2009–2017 for example, was around 22°C on average, which suits diversified vegetables. In addition, the rainfall and humidity present also favor vegetable production, which is confirmed by the local people.

11.6.3.2 Infrastructure

At present, the Van Duc Co-operative has a preliminary processing area of $4000\,\mathrm{m}^2$ for vegetable category, classification, packaging, and labeling. The cooperative owns four pumping stations to drain water from the Red river for irrigation in the Van Duc commune. Apart from self-investment, the Van Duc Co-operative also receives support from outside. In 2015 for example, the central government spent 180 billion Vietnamese Dong to build an in-field canal system in the Van Duc commune.

11.6.3.3 Supportive policy environment

Fragmentation is one of the highlighted characteristics of agricultural production in Vietnam. Recently, the central government of Vietnam encouraged provinces to merge land consolidation and plot-exchange movement. As of December 31, 2017, approximately 30% of total households in the Van Duc commune have completed plot-exchange movement. As a result, the average number of agricultural plots per household declined from 7.5 to 3.5 plots after movement. This result has facilitated farmer's investment in building up vegetable-specialized areas.

11.7 Impacts

The Van Duc Co-operative benefits the local people and the community in many ways, namely the cooperative's brand of safe vegetables has been creating pride amongst the local people; changing local peoples' minds toward safe products production; improving economic efficiency; and improving the environment.

The Van Duc Co-operative's safe vegetables have been creating pride amongst the local people for owning a well-known brand. Today, the Van Duc Co-operative covers the biggest area producing safe vegetables in Hanoi. The Van Duc Co-operative was selected by the Vietnam Ministry of Agriculture and Rural Development to be a standard model of chain management from production to marketing. According to the Department of Agriculture and Rural Development of the Gia Lam district, the Van Duc Co-operative model will be multiplied throughout the whole district so as to meet the demand for safe vegetables of consumers in Hanoi, nearby provinces, and for export. That safe vegetables produced by the Van Duc Co-operative were originated shows Van Duc vegetable growers' commitment to the health of consumers. In other words, consumers can be completely comfortable to eat vegetables labeled Van Duc Co-operative. And the fact that Van Duc Co-operative vegetables can be marketed in Taiwan, Japan, and Korea has strengthened the trust of consumers.

The way local people are thinking is changing. Farmers in the Van Duc Co-operative have completely changed their minds on production toward safe products to meet the market demand. This has been proved by their participation in technical training courses on vegetables cultivation, writing field-dairies, and the volume of vegetables that is sold and exported.

Economic efficiency is improved. While many other areas producing vegetables are challenged in finding stable markets for their products, vegetables grown by the Van Duc Co-operative are completely sold out. On average, the gross output generated per hectare of vegetable per year was 180—200 million Vietnamese Dong in 2013. This figure increased to 400 million Vietnamese Dong, of which 30% was production costs, in 2017. The local people have confirmed that the latter figure is much higher than that in other crops cultivation.

The environment is also improved. That farmers strictly follow the regulations of safe vegetable production and the VietGAP standards has considerably contributed to a fresh environment. This in turn benefits the lives of the local people and their production as well.

11.8 Conclusion

This chapter examines the Van Duc Co-operative as a successful agricultural cooperative. Van Duc is a transformed cooperative that has 168 formal members and 708 informal members. The number of formal members shows an upward trend. The results reveal that the Van Duc Co-operative is attractive to local households. The results also demonstrate that many factors have contributed to the success of the Van Duc Co-operative. These are result of change operation of co-operative to adapt new situations and meet market demand. The cooperative has taken the initiative to change their operation and find a new market including the domestic and international markets. The achievements of the Van Duc Co-operative are empirical evidences that could be multiplied in other cooperatives in agriculture in other regions with similar conditions.

References

Anne, N. V., & Le, V. (2014). *Governmental influences on the evolution of agricultural co-operatives in Vietnam: An institutional perspective with case studies.* Faculty of Business — Papers, University of Wollongong, Australia.

CAP. (2013). *Land consolidation for poor people in Vietnam.* Report Summary. Report Summary. <https://data.opendevelopmentmekong.net/dataset/e0fd00de-a0d8-4f35-ae9b-4b983b8ebe64/resource/f2474a15-0426-4e93-a9cd-93d1090feebd/download/02-pro-poor-land-consolidation-summary-report-eng.doc>.

Cooperative Law. (2012). Pursuant to the Constitution of the Socialist Republic of Vietnam 1992 amended, amending and supplemented by a number of articles under Resolution No.51/2001/QH10.

Co-operatives UK. (2011). *Simply Governance A comprehensive guide to understanding the systems and processes concerned with the running of a sustainable community enterprise.* Manchester, UK: Co-operatives UK Limited.

Dungz, L. T. (2015). *Comsumer behavior of organic agriculture products in Vietnam.* International Conference on Emerging Challenges: Managing to Success.

Duong, P. B., 2012. *Một số vấn đề lý luận và thực tiễn về phát triển các hợp tác xã kiểu mới trong nông nghiệp. Nghiên cứu Kinh tế số 415, tháng 12/2012.*

FAO. (2016). The State of Food and Agriculture 2016, ISBN 978-92-5-109374-0.

Fforde, A. (1987). Socio-economic differentiation in a mature collectivised agriculture: North vietnam. *Sociologia ruralis, 27*, 197–215.

GSO. (2018). *Different databases.* Accessed March 2018.

Harvey, R. (2017). *A guide to governance: How do we steer the co-operative ship?* <https://www.thenews.coop/118280/sector/regional-organisations/guide-governance-steer-co-operative-ship/> Accessed 16.12.18.

Hung, P. V., MacAulay, T. G., & Marsh, S. P. (2007). The economics of land fragmentation in the north of Vietnam. *The Australian Journal of Agricultural and Resource Economics, 51*, 195–211.

MARD. (2018). *Different databases.* Accessed March 2018.

Nghiem, N. V. (2006). *Agricultural Cooperatives in Vietnam: Innovations and Opportunities.* 2006 FFTC-NACF International Seminar on Agricultural Cooperatives in Asia: Innovations and Opportunities in the 21st Century, Seoul, Korea, 11–15 September 2006.

Prakash, D. (2003). *The principles of cooperation a Look at the ICA Cooperative Identity Statement.* International Cooperative Alliance [World Headquarters] 15 Route des Morillons, CH-1218 Grand Saconnex, Geneva. Switzerland.

Sahota, A. (2009). The global market for organic food & drink. In H. Willer, & L. Klicher (Eds.), *The World of Organic Agriculture: Statistics and emerging trends 2009* (pp. 59–64). Bonn, Geneva: IFOAM, FiBL, ITC, cited in.

VCCI. (2017). *Doing Business in Viet Nam 2017*, 6th Edition, July 2017.

Vinh, P. Q. (2015). *Mô hình kinh tế hợp tác đầu tiên ở Việt Nam có từ bao giờ?* <http://thoibaokinhdoanh.vn>.

Wolz, A. (2000). *The Development of Agricultural Co-operatives in Vietnam since Transformation.* Issue 72 of Discussion Paper. Heidelberg, Germany, 2000.

Wolfle, A. (1996). Cooperative GmbH and cooperative KG - suitability and importance for typical medium-sized cooperative organizational forms - In German: Genossenschaftliche GmbH und genossenschaftliche KG - Eignung und Bedeutung fuer mittelstandstypische genossenschaftliche Organisationsformen. Berliner Schriften zum Genossenschaftswesen, Bd. 8, Goettingen, Vandenhoeck & Ruprecht Van Duc Co-operative, 2018. *Annual report of Van Duc cooperative 2018.*

Further reading

Anh, D. T. (2017). *A Vietnamese Agricultural Cooperative's Involvement in the Food Safety Value Chain: Perspective and Policy.* <http://ap.fftc.agnet.org/ap_db.php?id = 788&print = 1>.

Anh, H. (2018). *Phát triển kinh tế hợp tác, HTX: Nhu cầu cần thiết của hộ cá thể.* Link: <http://www.nhandan.com.vn/kinhte/thoi_su/item/35336902-phat-trien-kinh-te-hop-tac-htx-nhu-cau-can-thiet-cua-ho-ca-the.html>.

Campbell, K., Lucas-Martínez, G., Martín-Ugedo, J. F., & Mínguez-Vera, A. (2016). *The governance of Agricultural Cooperatives: Evidence from Spain.* <http://www.aeca1.org/pub/on_line/comunicaciones_xviiicongresoaeca/cd/177i.pdf>.

Co-operatives UK. (2013). *Corporate governance code for agricultural co-operatives.* Manchester: Co-operatives UK Limited.

Huong, P. T. T., Everaarts, A. P., Neeteson, J. J., & Struik, P. C. (2013). Vegetable production in the Red River Delta of Vietnam. I. Opportunities and constraints. *NJAS – Wageningen Journal of Life Sciences, 67*, 27–36.

ICA (International Cooperative Alliance). (2005). [Online] <http://www.ica.coop/> Accessed 18.07.07.

VCA. (2018). *History of formation and development of cooperative movement in Vietnam- Lịch sử hình thành và phát triển phong trào HTX ở Việt Nam.* <http://www.vca.org.vn/tin-vca/diem-tin/18193-lich-su-hinh-thanh-va-phat-trien-phong-trao-htx-o-viet-nam.html>.

VCI. (2018). *Thống kê HTX trong cả nước theo lĩnh vực hoạt động năm 2017.* <http://www.vca.org.vn/thong-ke/bao-cao-tong-hop/17909-thong-ke-htx-trong-ca-nuoc-theo-linh-vuc-hoat-dong-nam-2017.html>.

12

Cooperatives: a panacea for rural population

A case study with reference to Rajarambapu Patil Sahkari Sakhar Karkhana Ltd in Maharashtra

T. Paranjothi[1] and Anil Karanjkar[2]

[1]Agricultural Co-operative Staff Training Institute, Thiruvananthapuram, India [2]Centre for Research and Publications, Vaikunth Mehta National Institute of Co-operative Management, Pune, India

12.1 Introduction

India is predominantly an agricultural country and 61.5% of the Indian population is rural and dependent on agriculture. However, the contribution of agriculture to the economy is just 15.87%. The government, at the state and central levels, is continuously taking initiatives by introducing various programs for agricultural and rural development. Cooperatives are chosen as organizations to implement these programs. In the cooperative agriculture sector, there are primary agricultural credit societies, primary cooperative agricultural and rural development banks, processing cooperatives like dairy cooperative, sugar cooperatives, fisheries and so on. The purpose of this chapter is to showcase the functioning of Rajarambapu Patil Sahakari Sakhar Karkhana Ltd, hereafter referred to as RSSK Ltd; which is a unique model where the entire economy revolves

around the cooperatives. This chapter attempts to demonstrate that the government and society working together can bring about a social and economic revolution and transform a poor area through agricultural cooperatives. Agricultural cooperatives in India have a long history of 115 years and have witnessed ups and downs in their performance. Most of them carry out a single function, while some have diversified their business activities. Generally, cooperatives carry out their operations after carry out their operations' singularly and independently. However, we rarely come across cooperatives that have been able to bring the entire local population into the fold of cooperatives.

RSSK is one among few cooperatives in India that has been able to bring the population in that area into the fold of cooperatives. It is in this context a case study of RSSK Ltd is undertaken. This chapter is divided into three sections. The first section explains how the cooperatives were introduced legally by the government in India, unlike in England and Germany where the movement started out of the need of the people. It further discusses the various types of agricultural cooperatives in India. The second section brings out in detail the functioning and contribution of the Rajarambapu Co-operative Sugar Factory. The third section summarizes the factors contributing to the success of the cooperatives in that area and the impact created.

12.2 Section I

12.2.1 Cooperative legislation

In India, the cooperative movement was initiated by the government through the Co-operative Credit Societies Act of 1904. The Act was known for its simplicity and had just 29 sections.

The shortcomings of the Act of 1904 were:

- it provided for the formation of *agricultural credit societies only* and societies for production, distribution, purchase, and sale, etc., could not be formed under it;
- it classified societies into (1) urban and (2) rural, which was artificial;
- it did not provide for the formation of federal institutions;
- it did not provide for the distribution of profits by rural societies;
- registration was not conclusive under the provisions of this Act; and
- dealings with nonmembers at least in certain types of cooperative societies were not permissible.

With the expansion of cooperative societies, coupled with demand for organizing other types of cooperative institutions and generally to provide for the all-round development and progress of the cooperative movement, the Cooperative Societies Act II of 1912 was passed. The Act of 1912 is the basis of cooperative legislation in India, though Act X of 1904 was the earlier legislation. The two salient features of the Act are *simplicity and elasticity*. It conferred special privileges on and gave facilities to cooperative societies with a view of promoting their development. It has provided safeguards in respect of the property and funds of such societies. The Act of 1912 is an amalgam of many basic principles carefully chosen from different sources and to remove the shortcomings of Act X of 1904 such as the organization of noncredit societies and federal societies. In 1919 the subject of cooperation was transferred to provincial governments. Bombay province was the first state to pass the Co-operative Societies Act of 1925 followed by Madras in 1932. Even today cooperation is a state subject and each State regulates cooperatives through this Act. The legislation was evolved to organize cooperatives and to break the hold of money lenders over Indian farmers. Primary Agricultural Credit Societies (PACS) were an outcome of the legislation, which provided a comprehensive financial system that was raised independently of the government and that could reduce the hold of money lenders and other noninstitutional agencies.

12.2.2 Primary agricultural cooperative credit societies

The agricultural credit structure comprises two separate structures for short-term credit dealing with production credit and long-term credit dealing with investment credit. The PACS form the foundation on which the entire edifice of the cooperative credit structure is based. A PACS is generally for one village. The minimum initial membership is 10 and ultimately the membership of the credit society expected to reach full coverage of the village. The liability of members is limited in absolute terms. The management of society lies in the hands of the general body of members who elect the board and the secretary looks after the day to day work. PACS provide short-term and medium-term loans for agricultural purposes. These societies raise funds through share capital, entrance fees, reserves, deposits, loans, and income from investment and loans, etc. In short, the broad functions of primary cooperative societies are the assessment of credit needs, disbursement of credit to members, recovery of credit, and the promotion of the economic interests of members. PACS cover 644,458 villages, that is, 90.8% of the villages in the country (NCUI, 2018).

The long-term credit structure is based on a two-tier structure. At the apex level in each State, there is a central land development bank, while at the bottom there are primary land development banks. The apex bank operates through the primary unit. Normally, the area of operation of the primary unit is a taluka. In some state where the primary units have not developed, the central land development bank operates either through its own branches or through district central cooperative banks. The short-term loans issued by these cooperatives were Rs.131,880 crores, while the medium-/long-term loans issued were Rs.10,878 crores during 2016–17.

12.2.3 Dairy cooperatives

In India, there are 185,903 primary milk producers' cooperative societies with a membership of 16.6 million farmers, 198 district milk unions, and 21 state-level federations as of March 31, 2018. It is worth mentioning here that the present trend is that there is new generation cooperatives (NGC) being formed as cooperative producer companies under the Indian Companies Act in various sectors. There are 9900 milk producer industries and 245,000 producers are members. Further, there are 41 lakh women members in dairy cooperatives.

12.2.4 Sugar cooperatives

Sugar is the second largest industry in India, the first being the textiles industry. Prior to 1932, there were hardly any sugar factories in this country. By 1931–32, there were 31 sugar factories in India, all of which were in the private sector. The total production of sugar at that time was only about 1.5 lakh tons, whereas the consumption was about 12 lakh tons. To meet the domestic demand of sugar, India had to import sugar mainly from Java (Indonesia). In 1930 the Tariff Board appointed by the Government of India decided to recommend a grant of protection to the Indian sugar industry by way of imposing a customs duty of 7.25% plus surcharge of 25% on the sugar imported into India. Accordingly, the Government of India promulgated, in 1932, the Indian Sugar Industry Protection Act for a period of 15 years, thereby enabling the Indian sugar industry to develop, stabilize, and compete with imported sugar. As a result of this protection granted to the Indian sugar industry, there was a spurt in the establishment of sugar factories and by 1933–34, there were 111 sugar factories producing 4.6 lakh tons of sugar. But the development was mainly in the private sector and in the subtropical belt, comprising the states of Uttar Pradesh, Bihar, Punjab, and Haryana. By 1940–41, the number of sugar factories had increased to 148 and production was around 11 lakh tons. After 1940–41, there was no expansion in the Indian sugar industry for some time and India continued to depend heavily upon imported sugar. Further, as all the factories were established by private capitalists, the sugarcane farmers were exploited and the government had to take various measures and pass laws relating to the price of sugarcane and its payment to protect sugarcane growers.

The Cooperative Societies Act of 1904 enacted in India had a limited objective to provide cheap credit to farmers and save them from the exploitation of money lenders. It was only in the early 1930s that the cooperative movement penetrated into the sugar sector. However, the real growth of the cooperative sugar sector started after India's independence, when the government decided to industrialize the country by expanding the cooperative sector. The Government of India passed the Industrial Policy Resolution on April 6, 1948, followed by the Industrial Act, 1956, wherein the principle of cooperation was assigned an important role for the country's economic development, particularly for industries based on agricultural produce such as sugarcane. Under this policy, the Government of India started giving preference to the licensing of new sugar factories in the cooperative sector. As a result of the preferential policy adopted by the government in the matter of licensing, there was a spurt in the establishment of sugar factories, especially in the cooperative sector of Maharashtra. The evolution of the cooperative sugar industry in Maharashtra has been a trend setter for all cooperatives in India. After independence, India adopted a five year plan system, called as "Panchvarshik Yojana", starting from year 1950. The Second Five-Year Plan (1956–61) set a target of establishing 35 cooperative sugar factories. During the Third Five-Year Plan (1961–66) about 25 cooperative sugar factories were to be organized. The Fifth Five-Year Plan (1974–79) noted that considerable success had been achieved in the establishment of sugar factories in the cooperative sector. It envisaged the setting up of 30 sugar factories and 20 sugar byproduct units. The Sixth Five-Year Plan (1980–85) proposed to set up 185 sugar factories. The Eighth Five-Year Plan proposed to organize 49 new cooperative sugar factories. Thus we find that until the Eighth Five-Year Plan, the government encouraged the formation of sugar cooperatives. The establishment of sugar factories in areas that did not have any irrigation facilities and that were almost barren, that is, Pravara, Sanjivani, and Sangamner represented a category of considerable significance, not only because of the

success they achieved as agro-industrial units concerned with the production of an important commodity like sugar, but also in terms of the distribution of socioeconomic benefits to all their members spread over the entire sugarcane belt in the country.

Ahmednagar district has the highest number of sugar factories in Maharashtra. Asia's first cooperative sugar factory was established at Pravaranagar in the Ahmednagar district of the then Bombay state in 1950 by Vithalrao Vikhe Patil and Economist Dhananjayrao Gadgil. Sugar production is the primary business among farmers of Maharashtra, especially in the western region.

During 2017–18, India had 525 operative sugar mills those consisting of 252 mills from the cooperative sector and 134 mills from the private sector and there are 173 operating cooperative sugar factories in Maharashtra. The presence of this industry has led to the development of rural places from which the sugarcane is drawn to factories including an improved road network, transportation facilities, medical facilities, education facilities, and banking.

12.3 Section II

12.3.1 Rajarambapu Patil Co-operative Sugar Factory

Rajarambapu Patil Co-operative Sugar Factory is one of the nonpareil companies of India, which was instituted in 1969 and its operations commenced in 1970, named the Walwa Taluka Sahakari Sakhar Karkhana Ltd by Rajarambapu Patil. It was started with a motive to create employment opportunities for the people of Walwa block. It was started with 1 plant at Sakharale crushing 1250 tons per day in 1970, and since then it had expanded with 3 more plants at Wategaon in 2003, Karandwadi in 2008, and Tippehalli in 2013, with a conglomerate crushing capacity over 7000 tons per day.

Rajarambapu Patil Co-operative Sugar Factory has the biggest liquor manufacturers in the cooperative sector of Maharashtra state with a total sales turnover of INR 35 crores (US$5 million). The unit is ISO 9001-2008 certified, adhering to a quality management system and quality control. The unit has two modern liquor units, country liquor and Indian-made foreign liquor using cane molasses to produce alcohol with the staff of more than 60 employees.

The overview presented in Table 12.1 gives the initiatives taken during the period between 1970 and 2018. It is observed that the first crushing season started in 1970 with 1250 metric tons and expanded to 2000 metric tons in 1977. The sugar factory covered 111 villages and had a membership of 12,598. It is worth noting that during the subsequent years a biogas plant, bioearth (compost) organic manure, an acetone plant, and a microbiological laboratory were established.

The gross working days refers to the total number of days between the starting date of the crushing season and closing date of the crushing season, while the net crushing days refers to the actual time crushing started and the actual time crushing closed, that is, the number of hours minus the number of stoppages divided by 22. It is observed from Table 12.2 that the net working days were either equal or higher in most of the years; it is less only in 2006−07 and 2009−11 and that too is meager. In ordinary parlance the gross should be more than the net, but in the case of RSSK, the term gross refers to the number of working days and net refers to the working hours. Hence, we can infer that Rajarambapu Patil Sahkari Sakhar Karkhana Ltd has utilized its capacity fully.

The area of sugarcane under cultivation in Islampur Taluk shows a mixed trend ranging between 8123 hectares and 12,351 hectares. The average yield of sugarcane was above 90 metric tons after 2009−10. It was 68 metric tons in 2003−04. The production of sugar from 2002−03 to 2011−15 also shows a mixed trend.

TABLE 12.1   Overview of Rajarambapu Cooperative Sugar Mill.

Details	Capacity	Year of commencement
First crushing season	1250 metric ton	1970
First expansion	1250−2000 metric ton	1977
Number of villages covered	111	
Number of members	12,598	
Distallation capacity	90,000 L/day	2018
Country liquor production capacity	50,000 cases/month	1976
Foreign liquor production capacity	50,000 cases/month	
Extra neutral alcohol plant capacity	20,000 L/day	1985
Biogas gas plant	28,000 m^3/day	1995
Bioearth (compost)	25,000 metric ton	1997
Vermicompost	4000 metric ton/day	2002
Organic manure	80,000 metric ton/day	2003
Acetone plant	15 metric ton plant	1984
Microbiological laboratory	150 metric ton/annum	2004

TABLE 12.2 Work performance.

Year	Gross working days	Net number of hours
2000–2001	178	192
2001–2002	160	186
2002–2003	165	166
2003–2004	98	101
2004–2005	121	125
2005–2006	145	151
2006–2007	149	148
2007–2008	152	152
2008–2009	147	147
2009–2010	146	142
2010–2011	171	172
2011–2012	167	164
2012–2013	156	159
2013–2014	132	140
2014–2015	170	178

A decrease is witnessed in 2003, 2004, 2008, and 2014. The recovery percentage of sugar from sugarcane has been ranging from 11% to 12% showing a minor variation. It was the highest in 2013–14 and lowest in 2003–04 (Table 12.3).

The rate for sugarcane per ton provided to the farmers by the factory steadily increased from Rs 910 in 2002–03 to Rs 2580 in 2013–14 and thereafter a decline is observed. Thus the factory has been able to support sugarcane growers by giving a fair and remunerative price. The total sugar sales show wide fluctuation during the entire period ranging from 867,176 quintal to 2,659,085 quintal. The table also presents the average price per quintal received by society. The average price per quintal has been increasing over the period with some minor variations (Table 12.4).

The net profit shows wide variation. It was high in 2006–07, 2009–10, and 2012–13. The

RSSK sustained a heavy loss during 2014–15, that is, Rs 78.18 crores. The heavy loss is due to the fact that RSSK Ltd took over another sugar factory and also diversified its operation. Rajarambapu Patil Co-operative Sugar Factory produces two grades of sugar, namely M-30 and S-3.(Table 12.5).

A cogeneration plant was introduced at Wategaon in 2006. The factory installed bagasse optimum cogeneration plants with a total installed capacity of about 40 MW from 2 plants, under a scheme on bagasse cogeneration to generate electricity and export. The plant generates 28 MW of electricity from which 11 MW is used in households; the surplus energy of 17 MW is exported to the Government of Maharashtra (MERC). Wategaon plant's 12 MW is used in households for sugar production with a turnover of more than INR 13 crores (US$2 million). Its per day liquor production capacity is 6200 cases, consisting of 3500 cases of country liquor with a sales turnover of INR 32 crores (US$4.8 million) and 2700 cases of Indian-made foreign liquor with a sales turnover of INR 3 crores (US$0.46 million).

12.3.2 Management of RSSK

The board of management consists of 21 members, elected from sugarcane producers, women members, members of economically backward class, socially backward class, and B class member co-ops. State government and district co-operative central bank nominate one director each on the board. The board is normally elected by consensus and there is no election. Generally, we find that elections are fought on political lines in most of cooperatives in India, resulting in the elimination of good cooperators getting elected. The managing director is appointed by the board from amongst a panel approved by the Commissioner of Sugar. He works as per the

TABLE 12.3 Cultivation, production, and yield in Islampur Taluk.

Year	The area under cultivation (hact)	Total production of sugar (Qtl)	Average yield of sugarcane (MT hact)	Recovery (%)
2000–2001	10,493	1,137,125	92	12.31
2001–2002	10,732	1,139,570	86	12.7
2002–2003	9192	1,038,285	90	12.35
2003–2004	11,927	638,500	68	11.6
2004–2005	12,351	718,375	78	11.75
2005–2006	9405	967,650	81	12.94
2006–2007	11,059	1,002,821	77	12.36
2007–2008	10,855	1,053,100	80	12.95
2008–2009	8694	877,620	83	12.35
2009–2010	8123	893,450	94	12.13
2010–2011	10,670	1,169,450	92	11.92
2011–2012	10,334	1,140,550	92	12.2
2012–2013	9294	1,121,340	97	12.66
2013–2014	8908	1,034,210	92	13.08
2014–2015	10,873	1,299,100	96	12.84

TABLE 12.4 Rate, sales, and average price.

Year	The rate of sugarcane (per ton)	Total sugar sale in QTL	Average price Rs/Qtl
2000–2001	953	1,041,884	1211
2001–2002	850	1,082,452	1222
2002–2003	910	3,947,109	1086
2003–2004	948	867,176	1126
2004–2005	1394	1,123,100	1396
2005–2006	1525	1,089,177	1633
2006–2007	1140	1,749,698	1532
2007–2008	1085	1,773,785	1089
2008–2009	1855	1,417,640	1560
2009–2010	2677	2,153,103	2458
2010–2011	2270	2,035,619	2380
2011–2012	2420	2,029,575	2583
2012–2013	2645	2,086,248	2873
2013–2014	2580	2,659,085	2667
2014–2015	2050	2,533,147	3000

TABLE 12.5 Net profit/loss.

Year	Net profit/loss (rupees in lakhs)
2003–2004	368,302
2004–2005	1,698,882
2005–2006	7,745,799
2006–2007	26,198,165
2007–2008	2,122,970
2008–2009	18,320,733
2009–2010	56,300,689
2010–2011	9,717,824
2011–2012	24,022,601
2012–2013	58,373,385
2013–2014	5,324,922
2014–2015	−781,874,631

policy decisions are taken by the board. However, the board does not interfere in the day to day working of the factory. There are five subcommittees that guide the managing director, namely Executive, Audit, Civil, Irrigation, and Construction.

12.3.3 Rajarambapu Patil: A visionary leader

Rajarambapu Patil was born on August 1, 1920 in Kasegaon, a small village in Thaluka Walva Sangli district in Maharashtra. After schooling he joined the Sykes Law College at Kolhapur and in 1945 obtained an LLB degree. As he was the first to obtain an LLB, not only in Kasegaon, but in the surrounding Taluka area, he was honored and praised everywhere with great admiration. During his law education at Kolhapur the freedom movement was at its peak.

Rajaram, a well-built wrestler and a patriot since childhood could not keep himself away from the nation-wide freedom movement. He was already a member of "The Seva Dal" and "The Young Movement." He frequently began to meet the revolutionary freedom fighters who

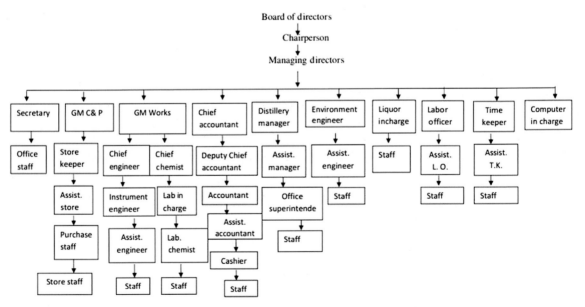

Organization Chart of Rajarambapu Patil Co-operative Sugar Factory.

visited Kasegaon and discussed and planned with them.

Consequently, in 1945, he founded "Kasegaon Education Society" in Kasegaon and began pioneering educational work in Walva Taluka. At the outset, Rajarambapu started a high school in Kasegaon in 1945 and named it "Azad Vidyalaya" as a token of the freedom movement. Rajarambapu himself began to work as a teacher without any expectation of monetary gain. He met many, rich and poor and requested them to donate generously for the cause. He arranged a sort of lodging and boarding in an adjacent small temple for poor students coming from other villages. He wished them to have free education. In a few days, in 1946, Rajarambapu established a small hostel for poor boys and encouraged them to learn. Encouraged by the success of the first attempt, Rajarambapu now decided to enlarge the field of his activities. Kasegaon Education Society now established "Wateshwar High School" in Wategaon (1959), "New English School," in Peth Naka (1957), "Yashwant High School" in Islampur (1961), "Jawahar Vidyalaya" (1960) in Kapuskhed, "Maharashtra High School" in Ashta, Taluka Walva (1965) and made provisions for higher education for all the boys and girls who had completed their high school education. This was a significant step in the educational activities of Shri. Rajarambapu Patil.

In 1962 he was elected as a member of Vidhan Sabha (MLA or Member of Legislative Assembly) and the Walva constituency. He became the deputy minister and was given the portfolio of revenue and forest. In 1965 he became the cabinet minister and was entrusted with the portfolio of revenue. It is a matter of pride that Rajarambapu was continuously elected from then by the same constituency for 22 years. He did not only represent the constituency in the House, but he labored for its all-round development. He followed ideology of Pandit Jawaharlal Nehru and followed his path of social service. Rajarambapu observed and studied the needs of the people and spent all his energy to bring about necessary reforms on all fronts. First of all, he took a lead in the establishment and spread of cooperative business and industries. It must be accepted that the network of various organizations that we find today in Walva Taluka is the outcome only of Rajarambapu's long penance. His name and contribution can never be forgotten so long as Walva Co-operative Doodha Sangh, Walva Co-operative Bank, Walva Co-operative Sugar Mill Walva Grahak Bhandar, and Walva Spinning Mills have been continuously at work in the area.

He was a rare personality; Rajarambapu could win the 1967 election easily. This time he was given the important portfolios of business and industry and electricity in the Ministry of Maharashtra. In 1972 Rajarambapu was once again elected for the Assembly with tremendous majority. The poll confirmed that Rajarambapu was perhaps the only alert and active leader of the ruling party who could put forward people's problems in the Assembly fearlessly and fight for them. He was the Minister for 10 years from 1962 to 1972 in the Ministry.

In 1982 Rajarambapu arranged another Padayatra or walking tour to study the problems of famine area from October 2 to October 11, 1982, covering a distance of 250 km from Sangli to Umadi. The areas of Talukas Jata and Kawathemahankal are yet not free from want and scarcity. The land is still barren in many places. Rajarambapu wished to bring about industrial and agricultural development like that in Walva Taluka. He intended to work on the same line for the removal of poverty and unemployment with the help and cooperation of the local people. Rajarambapu started Shri Mahakali Co-operative Sugar Mills Ltd in 1982 at Kavathemahankal. Since the death of Rajarambapu in 1984, the area is now recognized as Rajarambapu Nagar.

Rajarambapu's Walva Co-operative Sugar Mills Ltd had proved to be an ideal organization. A number of subsidiary industries and small businesses were also started to aid the agro-industrial revolution brought about for the welfare of the people. Now with the intention that they should not remain deprived of knowledge and learning, Rajarambapu laid the foundation for an engineering college and a polytechnic at Sakharale and, thus, provided the common people with facilities of higher technical education.

The sugar industry flourished in Maharashtra on a large scale only because of the specific industrial policy of the state government. The sugar industry in the state is chiefly spread on a cooperative basis. The state government encouraged and supported the cooperative movement for rapid industrial progress in the state. Rajarambapu, therefore, could issue licenses then to 15 cooperative sugar factories in Marathwada that could have an ample supply of sugarcane growing on Godavari River. He also encouraged the establishment of some subsidiary industries such as paper mills, alcohol and liquor production, among others, which could get raw material from sugar factories at minimum cost. The sugar factories and their subsidiaries could, thus, provide employment for the jobless and financial support to farmers; Rajarambapu always thought of the welfare of farmers. He took lead in the establishment of factories of fertilizers so that farmers could avail themselves of manure for better crops. Almost all these factories were also working on a cooperative basis.

By 1967 there were only 20 sugar mills in Maharashtra. Rajarambapu, who was in favor of still more development of the sugar industry in the state, recommended for 20 more sugar factories in Maharashtra. He encouraged not only the establishment of a number of sugar factories, but also for the establishment of spinning mills, oil mills, and others to bring about the all-round development of the state. As the raw material for any industry is mainly produced by farmers, the Government of Maharashtra gave all possible help to the farmers for the improvement of farming and also to

facilitated the industries in the private or public sectors run on a cooperative basis with an adequate supply of water and electricity. The policy of the state government had also been liberal in issuing permission to open new industries in the state. All these factors contributed to the rapid growth of industries in Maharashtra. Thus we see that Rajarambapu had a holistic view of development and contributed toward its development. He breathed his last on January 17, 1984 at the age of 64.

12.3.4 Contribution of Cooperative Water Supply Schemes in the Area of RSSK Ltd

There was a need to bring down the dry land farming into irrigated area and Rajarambapu Patil took the initiative and got government approval for perennial/12 months of water supply clearance from the Krishna and Warana Rivers to provide irrigation water to the dry land of Walwa Talukas.

The great leader Rajarambapu dreamed of bringing water to the dry land in the village of Walawa Taluka, as the taluka received water permits for 50,000 acres from the Maharashtra Irrigation Department. In 1983 during the Bhumipujan program of the Vaibhav Cooperative Water Supply Institute Ltd, Borgaon in Borgaon, he decided to spend his remaining life providing irrigation to the all dry land of Walwa Taluka and to make it prosperous. However, his dream remained incomplete due to his sudden death on January 17, 1984.

After the sudden death of Honorable Rajarambapu, Jayant Patil came to the social life in the village of Walwa Taluka due to the solicitation of the people and took over the chairmanship of Rajarambapu Patil Cooperative Sugar Factory. After accepting the chairmanship of this cooperative sugar factory in the public domain, Honorable Jayant Patil resolved to fulfill Honorable Rajarambapu's dream to bring the entire land under irrigation in Walwa Taluka. Undertaking steps to propagate and promote the scheme, Jayant Patil undertook an extensive "padayatra" (walking tour), he traveled extensively throughout the Taluka, visited every town and village in the factory area, and met and interacted with them; and they have done great work to ensure the importance of water. The RSSK Ltd came to the rescue by mortgaging its land and availing a loan. With the help of Nabard subsidy, Buvikas bank (land development bank) and nationalized banks,the factory raised a loan of Rs. 500 crores to help the water schemes. A water supply system has been completed in a timely manner and the shortfall of Rs 16 crores was met with a contribution by the sugar factory's own fund. In the 46 villages, 37 water societies were set up out of funds from Rajarambapu Patil Sahakari Sugar Factory and, thus, as many as 50,000 acres of land was brought under irrigation; Jayant Patil's efforts fulfilled the dream of Rajarambapu in the Walawa Taluka.

These 37 water supply organizations raised the standard of living of 16,600 families. For these 37 water supply institutions, 27,878 hp is being used at different points; 412 cusecs are lifted from the Krishna and Warna Rivers. This water supply facility assured 12,000 acres area under sugarcane cultivation and supply, per year to the factory. Before the implementation of these water supply organizations, approximately 3000 acres of area for sugarcane cultivation depended on wells, rivers, and bore holes. There was a shortage of the availability of sugarcane, and people had to go outside the area of the sugar factories for crushing.

As the water supply agencies were set up, the availability of sugarcane increased in the factory area, and this resulted in the fact that the original 1250 metric ton per day crushing capacity was transformed into 7200 metric tons per day. Apart from this, there was a need to start at 4000 metric tons per day capacity for a branch unit of Vategoan Surul.

Farmers who were previously unorganized in the field have strictly implemented the guidelines of the Irrigation Department, and

the result is that all these water supply agencies are free from the debt of the bank and factory and today the institution has fixed deposits of Rs 21 crores. Some of these institutes are well equipped with state of the art buildings. These water supply organizations have created a social and economic revolution in the villages. The impact of this is visibly seen with Kutcha houses being replaced by reinforced cement concrete buildings. Bicycle and bullock carts have been replaced by motorcycles, Jeeps, tractors, and cars. Farmers of Taluka that adopted dry drip irrigation, agricultural mechanization polyhouse greenhouses, and others have witnessed a huge increase in agricultural yields and production of cash crops like turmeric, banana, etc. Due to the economic revolution caused by irrigation, children are getting higher education and they are becoming technicians, engineers, doctors, and professors, and knowledge of the Ganga has started in Taluka.

The RSSK has used their waste and byproducts to earn more revenue and become environment-friendly. The Quality Policy and the Environment Policy are presented here.

12.3.5. Quality policy

The RSSK Ltd is committed to contributing to the socioeconomic growth of farmers and society. The commitments of the sugar factory are met through.

- Satisfying applicable requirements by ensuring that customer and applicable statutory and regulatory requirements are determined, understood, and consistently met.
- Effective management process.
- Continually improving performance through the adaption of new technology, quality management systems, and the involvement of employees
- Efficient manufacturing of quality sugar and byproducts, thus, satisfying customer requirements.

- Providing supports to cane growers and external service providers.
- Maintaining the environment.

12.3.6. Environment policy

The RSSK Ltd is committed to monitoring and controlling the significant environmental aspect of the manufacturing processes of their sugar and byproducts as well as to the prevention of pollution to achieve an improvement in their environmental performance in line with their social responsibility toward global initiatives to save the environment.

We shall—

As part of its environment policy, the sugar factory ensures that it.

- Complies with all applicable legal and other requirements by maintaining pollutant parameters to achieve pollution control board norms.
- Intensifies efforts for conserving key resources, water, and energy with the aim of totally recycling water and the optimum use of steam and electricity.
- Mitigates environmental impacts arising out of their activities.
- Uses effective management practices for the handling, treatment, and reuse and safe disposal of liquid and solid wastes.
- Employs skilled manpower and educates and motivates people regarding their contribution in the implementation of policy.
- Makes necessary financial arrangements, renders all the necessary assistance, and provides guidance and support to achieve their objectives.

12.4 Section III

It is generally found that cooperatives do not succeed if they are not able to provide a variety of services to their members. Members, after availing a particular service, become passive as other services are not provided. We find that only in few places do cooperatives play a major role in the economy of the area.

The Rajaram group of cooperative institutions, which started as a sugar factory, has organized other cooperatives such as an urban cooperative bank, dairy cooperatives, and a spinning mill. The urban cooperative bank has a deposit base of Rs 1174.81 crores with a membership of 35,636 and total business of Rs 1963.04 crores, 46 branches, and is fully computerized. The unique feature is that the non-performing asset (NPA) has been nil during the past 4 years. The Rajarambapu Patil Sahakari Dudh Sangh Ltd, established in 1975, has 175 primary dairy cooperatives with an individual membership of 5089 handling a milk collection of 3 lakh liters per day and dealing with a number of value-added products. The Shetakari Vinakari Sahakari Soot Girni Ltd was established in 2003. The Rajarambapu Group of Textiles is a unique, vertically integrated setup practicing value addition in textile manufacturing processes right from cotton yarn (raw) to garment (readymade) "Raw To Readymade."

12.4.1 Salient features Rajarambapu Patil Sahakari Sakhar Karkhana Ltd

RSSK Ltd had a strong focus on quality initiatives to deliver better products to their customers. Their strategies and operational efficiencies have allowed them to consistently pay a higher cane return to their farmers than any other adjoining factories.

12.4.2 Social activities of the sugar factory

RSSK Ltd, Rajaramnagar, is involved in various social activities for the development of rural people and of society. They undertake various welfare programs including.

1. In order to increase the yield of cane production per hector, many activities were undertaken by the RSSK Ltd like the supply of clean and uninfected sugarcane seeds provided to cane farmers as well as the supply of chemical and biofertilizers.
2. Training and development programs regarding cane development to cane growers at Vasantdata Sugar Institute, Pune. Enabling the farmers in the application of modern methods of agriculture and sugar cultivation.
3. They undertake projects that relate to educational, medical, agricultural, and charitable purposes.
4. Help in creating, establishing, and running hospitals, medical charities, and welfare.
5. Educational aid for Montessori education, schools, colleges, and research. The RSSK Ltd helps to run institutions for grant aid for the care of orphans, handicapped, retarded children, old and disabled people, and similarly weak, poor, and needy persons.
6. Granting aid for research on high yielding varieties of seeds, manures, fertilizers, insecticides, etc.
7. It encourages young people by providing social services and gives scholarships and prizes to students achieving excellence. They also support coaching classes for making students better equipped to face competitive examinations.
8. It provides grants to run public libraries, sport complexes, etc.
9. Arranging fair shops for agricultural equipment, chasing, and modern methods of agriculture as well as activities for the general upliftment of the rural and agricultural community.
10. Provide training and guidance to run cottage industries. They also make efforts toward the preservation of cultural heritage and traditional arts and crafts.
11. It undertakes and carries out irrigation projects.
12. Organizes surveys for minerals and natural resources in the region as well as surveys for manpower in the region.
13. Provides guidelines regarding dairy and poultry farming and animal husbandry by arranging expert lecturers.
14. One of the biggest and most challenging developmental activities the RSSK Ltd has carried out in this area is the development of lift irrigation schemes that now provide much-needed water to farmers. This has ensured a steady and guaranteed supply of sugarcane to RSSK Ltd.

Due to these developments, today a backward area, once with no infrastructure and development, has become developed with many facilities and cooperatives have taken care of the rural population by enrolling them as members and providing them with opportunities to earn their own livelihoods and RSSK Ltd is being recognized as one of the leading cooperatives in the country on social education and financial matters. RSSK Ltd is proud to mention that this is possible only due to the visionary creative leadership of Jaywantrao Patil MLA.

The unique feature of this sugar factory is the quality and environmental policy followed, which is absent in many other cooperative organizations. The motto of the cooperative is to strive for enhancing effective production on quality in sugar and byproduct units and to provide better functions to cane suppliers.

The motto adopted by the sugar factory was to strive for enriching effective production and quality in sugar and byproducts and to provide better facilities to cane suppliers.

The main challenge for the sugar factory is the mismatch between raw material cost and sugar prices and the availability of labor for harvesting and transportation. The factory has no control over the sugarcane prices nor the sugar prices. The only area where it can try is to cut down the cost is operational cost. The laborers need to be paid in advance and sometimes they do not come and work in the field. Thus the problem lies with the policy of the government and as such the problem is not with the cooperative sugar factory, but the industry itself. This drives home the point that profitable functioning depends not only on the governance and leadership, but on the overall sugar industry, which is regulated by the government. It may not be out of place to mention that most private sugar factories (IOF) that entered the market thinking of making big money are failing miserably today and collapsing.

12.4.3 Salient features of Rajarambapu Co-operative Bank

The bank is rendering various services to members of the bank and to needy people in the area of operation. But the bank has concentrated basically on financing small farmers, artisans, traders, transport operators, self-employed persons, and small-scale industries in rural areas, in particular for creating job opportunities in rural areas and improving the standard of living of the rural population. Some of the salient features of the Rajarambapu Co-operative Bank Ltd include.

- The Rajarambapu Cooperative Bank has 45 branches, is fully computerized, and uses the latest electronic and mechanical technologies in its daily transactions to provide prompt and timely services to its customers.
- All branches are connected by core banking system and working 7 days a week with extended business hours.
- The bank has an "A" audit classification since establishment.
- The bank has its own training center to provide training to staff. Now, it has trained staff in computer operation.
- The bank always tries to provide financial aid to members, employees, and their

families for medical, educational, and other extracurricular activities.
- The Rajarambapu Co-operative Bank always aims for maximum disbursement of loans to priority and weaker sectors.

12.4.4 Socioeconomic activities of Rajarambapu Co-operative Bank

The Rajarambapu Co-operative Bank Ltd is involved in various social activities for the development of rural people and society. They undertake various welfare programmes of various natures including.

1. Providing scholarships and prizes to students achieving excellence. They also support coaching classes for making students better equipped to face competitive examinations.
2. Through "Vikas Nidhi," the bank provides funding to different hospitals in various corners of the state for operating on heart, kidney, and cancer patients.
3. The bank is an active participant in the Jayant Poverty Eradication Campaign, which is a well-chalked out and need-based initiative meant to help poor families in the Walwa block in the Sangli district.
4. They promote capacity building and human investment through employee training and education programs in various topics of interest to employees.

12.4.5 Salient features of Rajarambapu Patil Sahakari Dudh Sangh Ltd

Rajarambapu Patil Sahakari Dudh Sangh Ltd has been awarded an ISO 9001, hazard analysis and critical control point certification by det norske veritas, Netherlands, and has a unique management systems in place that was raad voot accreditatie certified in February 2004. Their ISO 9001 certification provides advantages such as minimizing mistakes, improving reporting, and ensuring better quality and services, reliable production scheduling, delivery, and maintenance of standards through annual assessments. The milk union is completely computerized with enterprise resource planning solutions.

Rajarambapu Patil Sahakari Dudh Sangh Ltd covers other relevant parameters related to assisting primary milk cooperative societies such as.

1. A veterinary service including year-round 24-hour mobile clinics.
2. Artificial insemination mobile routes.
3. A dairy herd improvement program action (DIPA).
4. Implementation of artificial insemination with Indigent Ltd, Hyderabad.
5. Vaccination and deworming programs of the cattle feed.
6. Programs of fodder seed development.
7. Rajarambapu Gram Abhiyan for education and training at milk producer level.
8. Providing women development and cooperative leadership programs.
9. Implementation of clean milk production programs.
10. Bulk milk cooler (BMC) foundation.

12.4.6 Salient features of Shetakari Vinakari Sahakari Soot Girni Ltd

1. Shetakari Vinakari Sahakari Soot Girni Ltd is engaged in the manufacturing of 100% gray combed cotton yarn; only the highest standard is acceptable as ensured by their striving for excellence in all areas.
2. It has accepted a policy to deliver to the consumer only products and services that meet or exceed the buyers' requirements.
3. The company uses world class technology and machinery.
4. It provides an excellent and consistent quality of yarn.
5. Shetakari Vinakari Sahakari Soot Girni Ltd is always looking toward the value addition and vertical integration of their products.

The Shetakari Vinakari Sahakari Soot Girni Ltd decided to integrate all textile manufacturing activities under the umbrella of the Rajaram Group. Textile cooperatives for manufacturing activities in the textile industry like yarn, yarn dyeing, weaving, knitting, and processing of fabrics and manufacture of garments, among others, are established. The group is dedicated to production, quality, and versatility in textile manufacturing. The Rajaram Group have all the necessary facilities on one premise including.

1. Jay Maharashtra Co-operative Industries Ltd.
2. Jayant Textile Co-operative Industries Ltd.
3. Indraprastha Knitting and Garments Co-operative Industries Ltd.
4. Prerna Magaswargiya Co-operative Industries Ltd.
5. Parivartan Magaswargiya Co-operative Industries Ltd.
6. Pratibimb Magaswargiya Co-operative Industries Ltd.

There are similar cooperatives in Gujarat. Tushaar Shah studied the cooperatives in Gujarat. The quote provided here is reproduced from his research work of 1995 from his book "Making Farmers' Cooperative Work:"

The sum total of my experience in Surat suggested the powerful influence of local culture on the way Surat's Cooperatives functioned; correspondingly, the necessity of a robust design seemed obviated somewhat by a strongly supportive culture. At the end of my field work, I continued to feel that what I saw and learnt in Surat was more of an exception from which we can learn more than what we can from analyzing the common place.

Most of these co-operatives seemed to be doing well; they ran in profit; but more importantly, they were patronage central (that is, they commanded a large share of their respective businesses); member central (that is, they controlled their members' economies); and domain central (that is, there were important relative to the entire economy of their domain). In Kudsat village where I camped, for example, the Sion sugar factory accounted for over 80 percent of the cane area which in turn was 70–80 percent of the total cultivable area of the village. The factory pumped into the village Rs 3.00 to 3.5 crore per year. The village's 400 Patel families represented the wealthiest rural communities one could find anywhere in the country. The dairy cooperative, in addition, pumped Rs 20–25 lakh as milk payments. Together, these accounted for no less than 60–70 percent of the domain's economy. Few cooperatives seemed to have failed here. Even fewer failed because of poor management or incompetent/dishonest leadership.

This discussion brings out the power of sugar cooperatives in providing better prices supported by other services and encompassing the entire life of a farmer by making him realize the existence of the cooperative. Apart from the sugar cooperative, the urban cooperative bank, dairy cooperative, and spinning mills have played an important role by providing banking services, promoting dairy activities as a subsidiary occupation, and the cooperative spinning mills and its units by providing employment opportunities to the local people. All this has been possible due to visionary leadership combined with a professional approach, which is required by cooperatives, especially agricultural cooperatives, to help member farmers carry out agricultural operations in a sustained manner. This can be replicated only when we have visionary leadership supported by a favorable environment through government policy.

References

NCUI. (2018). *Indian Co-operative Movement: A Statistical Profile – 2012*. New Delhi: National Co-operative Union of India.

Further reading

Adams, C. A., Muir, S., & Hoque, Z. (2014). Measurement of sustainability performance in the public sector. *Sustainability Accounting, Management and Policy Journal, 5*(1), 46–67.

Annual Reports of organizations of Rajarambapu Group 2013–14 and 2015–16.

Bolden, R., et al. (2000). *A review of leadership theory and competency frameworks*. Edited Version of a Report for Chase Consulting and the Management Standards Centre for Leadership Studies University of Exeter Crossmead, United Kingdom.

Bosselmann, K., et al. (2008). *Governance for sustainability: Issues, challenges, successes*. IUCN Environmental Policy and Law Paper No. 70.

Calvert, H. (1959). *The law and principles of cooperation*. Calcutta: Thacker Spink & Co. (1933) Private Ltd.

Government of India. (1904). The Cooperative Credit Societies Act, 1904 (India Act X of 1904) (Passed on 25th March 1904), Government of India.

Government of India. (2018). *Agricultural Statistics at a Glance 2017*. Ministry of Agriculture and Farmers welfare Department of Agriculture, Co-operation and Farmers Welfare, New Delhi.

Government of India (Press Information Bureau). *Evolution of co-operatives in India*. <http://pib.nic.in/feature/fe0299/f1202992.html>.

Government of India Various Five Year Plan Documents Planning Commission (now NITI Ayog) New Delhi.

Jakhar, B. R., & Dwivedi, R. C. (2012). *Cooperative Development in Independent India (December 1947–May 2012)*. New Delhi: Centre for Promotion of Cooperativism.

Javed, B. R. (1988). *Problems and prospects of co-operative sugar factories in Maharashtra with special reference to centralized leadership as determinant to authority structure, power structure and power differentiation*. University of Pune. Department of Economics.

Rao, I. (2009). *Implications of Global Crisis: Integrate Sustainability with Organizational Culture*. Working Paper No. 2009-10-03, Indian Institute Of Management Ahmedabad.

Taborga, J. (2012). *Leadership stage development and its effect on transformational change*. Articles from Integral Leadership Review.

Vidwans, M. D. (1969). *Cooperative Law in India, Committee for Cooperative Training*. New Delhi: NCUI.

Wakle, B. G. (2005). *Politics of cooperative sugar industries in Marathwada: A study of development problems*. Dr Babasaheb Ambedkar Marathwada University, Department of Political Science.

Websites of Rajarambapu Group.

Korea's multipurpose agricultural cooperatives and the developmental state: the case of the National Agricultural Cooperative Federation (NACF)*

Eunju Choi[1], Hwalshin Kim[2] and Seungkwon Jang[3]

[1]iCOOP Co-operative Institute, Seoul, Korea [2]Department of Management of Co-operatives, Graduate School, Sungkonghoe University, Seoul, Korea [3]Division of Business Administration and Department of Management of Co-operatives, Graduate School, Sungkonghoe University, Seoul, Korea

13.1 Introduction

The National Agricultural Co-operative Federation[1] (hereafter, NACF) and its primary agricultural cooperatives have the longest history and the biggest scale in Korea. Other farmers' (or fisheries') associations began to be organized to use their common utilities and to have a partnership for shipment, processing, and export from the 1990s. The NACF is the apex organization of 1122 primary cooperatives representing more than 2.15 million farmer-members among a total of 2.42 million farmers in Korea as of 2018 (NACF homepage). In addition, to agri-business, the NACF as a multipurpose cooperative runs a financial business delivering services to nonfarmer members as well as farmer members. NACF's asset was about US$113.6 billion, and the equity was US$15.5 billion in 2017.[2] While the financial

---

* An earlier version of the paper was presented at the 10th ICA Asia Pacific Regional Research Conference held at VAMNICOM, Pune, India, November 05–06, 2015.

[1] NACF (National Agricultural Co-operative Federation) is the Federation of primary agricultural cooperatives in Korea, which was formed based on the 1961 Agricultural Co-operative Act. This article mainly focuses on NACF rather than other agricultural co-ops that existed before and after NACF.

[2] 1 US$ = 1071.4₩ (Korean currency) (December 29, 2017).

business holding company (NH financial group), which was split, reported that its asset was US$19.6 billion and the equity was US$15.9 billion, the asset of the agribusiness holding company was US$10.4 billion and its equity was US$5.0 billion at the end of the year in 2017 (NH financial group homepage; NH agribusiness homepage) (Table 13.1).

Since its establishment in 1961, the NACF has been enlarging its scale and its farmer members came to 88.8% of all farmers at the end of 2018. This chapter aims to explain the evolution of the NACF and to discuss the factors that had a significant influence on the development of the NACF. Following Jensen (2013), who shows macro and micro factors causing the Labor-Managed Firm (LMF) to emerge, the research questions are: What effects have the nature of the state had on the characteristics of the NACF since the 1960s? How did market changes and the farmers' movement affect the development of the

NACF? A brief history of the NACF will be introduced before the factors are discussed.

13.2 The early stage of National Agricultural Co-operative Federation from 1961 to 1980

There were three important turning points in the history of the NACF. The first one was in 1961, when the Agricultural Co-operative Act was legislated to create the NACF. The second one was in 1989, when members won the direct voting right of chairpersons for primary cooperatives as well as the president of their apex organization. The third one was in 2012, when the government bill reforming the NACF was eventually passed. Fig. 13.1 shows the major structural changes of the NACF.

13.2.1 Birth of National Agricultural Co-operative Federation in 1961

Although there had been relentless attempts to establish agricultural cooperatives during the Japanese occupation from 1910 to 1945, all of them didn't get a successful result. After liberalization, there were diverse debates among relevant stakeholders about any kind of agricultural cooperatives to be had. The government intended to improve the rural economy through reorganizing cooperatives. At first,

TABLE 13.1   Current state of NACF.[a]

Year	Number of primary cooperatives	Number of farmer-members
2018	1122	2,146,585

[a]*In Korea, NACF and its member cooperatives are called NONG-HYUP, which means "agricultural co-operatives." NH NONG-HYUP is NACF's communication brand name. (www.nonghyup.com/eng/main/main.aspx).*

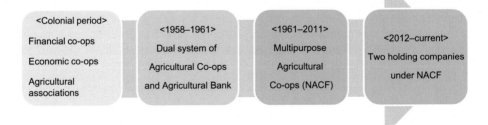

FIGURE 13.1   Major structural changes of NACF.

agricultural cooperatives and agricultural banks were made separately for their own needs. But the agribusiness of the cooperatives was considered to be sluggish because of them not being financed appropriately by the agricultural banks (Lim, 2014). At last, primary agricultural cooperatives were established through a merger of the agricultural cooperatives and the agricultural banks based on the Agricultural Co-operative Act legislated in 1961. They were made multipurpose cooperatives having financial services for farmer members as well as agribusiness as the economic business of agricultural cooperatives was expected to be financially supported by agricultural banks. The NACF was organized as an association of primary agricultural cooperatives.

13.2.2 Growth

Multipurpose agricultural cooperatives were considered appropriate for the situation, where most farmers were self-sufficient and small landowners cultivated very diverse items. The NACF and its primary cooperatives gave important services to their farmer members. A supply of agricultural materials and daily commodities was important enough to farmers for it to expand rapidly. For the production, processing, marketing, and distribution of agricultural products, collaborative shipment facilities were built up. In the situation that most farmers had been troubled in loans at a high rate, the NACF and its primary cooperatives operated a mutual credit business. Owing to the active participation of farmer members, the mutual credit business accumulated funds and lent it to members at a lower rate (Park, 2016).

After multipurpose agricultural cooperatives launched, the number of primary cooperatives incremented, and the members amounted to over 90% of all farmers at the end of 1962 (Nyeo-Rm, 2011; Park, 2016). Primary cooperatives had increased their size through the merger between themselves to obtain the economy of scale. The number of primary cooperatives was reduced from 21,239 in 1963 to 1545 in 1973, whereas the membership of each cooperative grew from 139 in 1968 to 1300 in 1973 (Lim, 2014).

13.3 Challenges to National Agricultural Co-operative Federation

13.3.1 The state: support and control

13.3.1.1 Characteristics of the state from 1960 to 1980

Park Chunghee's military regime seized power in 1961. It wielded authoritarian control over the whole society including the economy. The state made long-term economic development plans and drove forward forcefully. The policy direction was export-centered industrialization. Control of capital, acquisition of aid and loans from foreign countries, advanced technology from Japan, and exports to the US market were available (Ji, 2011). The nature of the state was a military dictatorship, and people were not allowed to participate in planning and practicing the state's destiny. Democracy, as well as the quality of life, had to make way for state-led economic growth throughout the 1960s to the 1980s. Agriculture and cooperatives were no exception.

13.3.1.2 Control and support of the state

It was an important task for the state to support poor farmers that were a large majority of people after liberalization. Even though there were highly diverse debates and efforts to establish agricultural cooperatives, the state actively intervened in establishing the NACF. To use the NACF as an instrument to implement their agricultural policies, the state wanted to control the selection of executives in the NACF and its primary cooperatives. The 1961 Agricultural Co-operative Act originally stipulated that presidents of primary cooperatives should be elected mutually among directors and that auditors should be elected by members at the general assembly. However, the state enacted a Temporary Measures Act allowing the chairman of the NACF to be appointed by the president and the vice chair and directors appointed by the chair after getting a stamp of approval from the government. The chair of the NACF should appoint the presidents of primary cooperatives under the approval of the government.

The management of cooperatives was also controlled by the state. The new foundation of primary cooperatives and the enactment of cooperative articles had to be approved by the Minister of Agriculture and Forestry. Primary cooperatives were aligned with the local administration system to execute the agricultural policies. The Minister of Agriculture and Forestry, the Minister of Finance, and the Governor of the Bank of Korea joined the operating committee of the NACF. It even had to submit the annual report and the financial statement to the government.

The developmental state speeded up the rebuilding of the country to promote economic development. Since the establishment of the NACF, it pushed the policy task to enhance food production and then sustain low-wage urban dwellers. It consigned the NACF and the primary cooperatives to supply farmer members with agricultural inputs including fertilizers and pesticides. It also distributed the policy fund to farmers through the NACF (Park, 2016). It distributed the policy fund to support the NACF's financial business. The cooperatives improved plant breeding and educated farmer members on farming technology. Due to the support of the state, the NACF's operating performance has been growing fast since its establishment and the agricultural production has greatly increased.

13.3.2 Farmers' movements for the development of National Agricultural Co-operative Federation

Although farmers' movements to own the agricultural land and to improve productivity had been active after liberalization, it was oppressed by the Unites States military government and weakened through the Korean War. In the 1960s, farmers' capacities were not strong and farmers were not organized enough to resist against the oppression of the state. Farmers did not affect the establishment of the NACF and its primary cooperatives. Campaigns for enlightening rural communities and for agricultural improvement, which were held by diverse participators including college students, spread. Farmers were interested in cooperative farming as a way of solving the problems of rural areas, and meetings to study how to farm cooperatively were held. This played the role of enlightening farmers, of building a base for organizing farmers' groups, and of highlighting rural problems (Jang, 2010).

Some voluntary groups tried to organize farmers into groups to resist the authoritarian regime and to protect farmers' rights from autocratic agricultural cooperatives in the 1970's. One of the resisting movements was aimed to reform the NACF and primary agricultural cooperatives. Some farmers struggled against the corruption of some agricultural cooperatives, refused a compulsory contribution to a cooperative, or requested compensation of farmers' loss caused by a cooperative (Lee, 2010; Lo, 1989). Farmer members urged the democratization of the NACF and primary cooperatives by means of voluntary and autonomous cooperatives, the direct election for chairpersons of primary cooperatives and the NACF, and the establishment of agricultural cooperatives and associations by item or type of business.

In the 1990s, farmers' movements occurred a lot as market liberalization had been expanding. These focused on blocking the UR

(Uruguay Round) negotiation and resisting the liberalization. The movement led to demands relating to the reform of agricultural cooperatives. Farmer-members organized a committee for reforming the NACF and announced some proposals for democracy in agricultural cooperatives (Nyeo-Rm, 2011). The proposals promoted debates on how to reorganize the NACF, of which the core issue was about the division of financial business and agribusiness.

Meanwhile, the farmers' movement addressed another issue about the NACF. NACF's financial business and agribusiness achieved high growth rates in the 1960s and the 1970s, but through the 1980s, the financial business surpassed the agribusiness (Park, 2016). While the NACF focused on the financial business, the agribusiness went into the red. The NACF faced strong criticism about the abnormal business structure that put too much priority on the financial business (Park, 2004). It was suggested that restructuring of the NACF in 2012 was considered as evidence for the failure of the agribusiness (Park, 2014). The NACF was criticized because it could not keep up with farmers' needs in the changing agricultural environment and has even competed with some primary cooperatives in the same business areas (Park et al., 2015). Farmers demanded that the NACF should more positively make policies to help farmer members with farming, shipping, and the supply of farming utilities. They also insisted farmers should be allowed to form freely any types of cooperatives and associations in any areas.

13.3.3 Market liberalization

Because of the protection by the developmental state and the aid of overproduced agri-foods from the United States, the domestic market had been blocked from growing enough as it needed to at that time (Kim, 1992). The state protected agriculture through the regulation of imports

and a two-tier grain price system (Hwang, 2011; Park, 1993). The agricultural productivity had been gradually increasing and at last, the staple grain, rice, got self-sufficient in 1975 (Hwang, 2011). However, the protective policy had limits in making the agricultural economy fundamentally independent. It didn't intend to change the main agricultural structure in which most farmers were smallholders (Lim, 1997). And the farming industry achieved a growth rate lower than the overall economy did.

Since the 1980s, the domestic market had to be opened to the global market due to the economic liberalization policy and the forceful request by the United States (Kim, Jang, & Granovetter, 2005). The agricultural sector was faced with difficulties without state protection (Park, 1993). Imports of agricultural products increased to US$3.7 billion in 1990. Agriculture gradually declined as a proportion of gross domestic product from 29.2% in 1970 to 7.65% in 2005. The rate of grain self-sufficiency continuously came down to 29.1% in 2005. The agricultural growth rate became far lower from the 1990s, and real agricultural production per a farming family was getting lower. As the farm household economy became worse, farm household debts grew bigger, and the income gap between urban and rural areas expanded (Park, 2007).

The NACF was expected to activate the agribusiness by farmer members drove into a corner due to the globalization since the 1990s, but it was not easy to respond to the changing situation.

13.4 Responses for the betterment of National Agricultural Co-operative Federation

13.4.1 Democratization and expansion of National Agricultural Co-operative Federation since 1987

There had been a call by farmer members for the democratic governance of the NACF and its primary cooperatives, but it was not realized until the overall society changed. Affected by the 1987 democratization movement, the identity of the NACF and its primary cooperatives was sharply improved (Nyeo-Rm, 2011). The act prescribed some ways for members to participate in democratic governance. Presidents of the primary cooperatives came to be elected and dismissed by members at the general assembly or a board of representatives. The chair and auditors of the NACF would be elected by the presidents of the primary cooperatives at their annual general meetings.[3] Members got the right to read the minutes of the board of directors and financial documents. The control and vigilance of cooperatives by the state, for example, prior approval of an annual business program and the revision of a given cooperative's article, was relieved and members' autonomy seemed somewhat strengthened.

According to the revision of the Agricultural Cooperative Act in 1988, NACF's business scope was expanded. The details were farmland brokerage, commodity cooperatives dealing with the financial business, equity investment in related companies, relaxation of restriction against NACF's fund management, and so on (Lim, 2014). These actions were the result of farmer members' long efforts to demand fundamental reform of agricultural cooperatives (Nyeo-Rm, 2011). As the federations for livestock and ginseng cooperatives, which separated from the NACF in 1981, faced a crisis of management, they were integrated into the NACF in July 2000 (Lim, 2014). It introduced the CEO system for each division; agricultural, livestock, and financial businesses. However, the reforms were not innovative enough to meet the farmers' needs to strengthen and efficiently manage the agribusiness. Further, to respond to the pressure of

market liberalization, the NACF and the primary cooperatives had to innovate their organizational structures.

13.4.2 Two holding companies of National Agricultural Co-operative Federation in 2012

The openness of the domestic agricultural market and free trade promoted the debate to improve business performance by reforming the NACF (Park, 2016). The debate began with the recognition that more than 80% of employees and assets were allotted to the financial business and less than 10% was given to the agribusiness and support unit respectively. The original mission of the NACF's financial business was supposed to supply rural areas with surplus capital from cities. However, rural areas became able to supply enough funds by themselves and then the financial business was considered to lose its validity. The financial business justified itself as a profit center to assist the agribusiness through the profits of the financial business. Eventually, the disparity between the two business parts became an issue that needed to be resolved.

Diverse ways to reform were proposed by stakeholders. First, farmers wanted to strengthen the capacity of the agribusiness to support members' economic activities by separating the financial business and the agribusiness from the NACF. An important thing was that both businesses should be under the control of farmer members through the NACF. But the NACF opposed this opinion claiming that multipurpose agricultural cooperatives are more fitted to the condition of Korean agriculture and the capital for the separation is insufficient. Second, the government proposed to separate the financial business and the

---

[3]   Later the appointment and dismissal of the NACF chairperson again became subject to the decision of a board of representatives from the primary cooperatives.

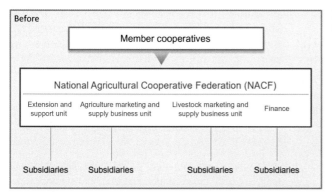

FIGURE 13.2 Transformation of NACF after restructuring.

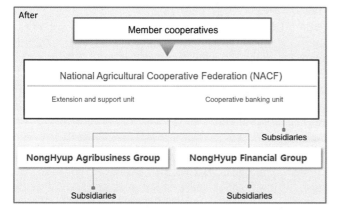

agribusiness from the NACF and then to confine the role and capacity of the NACF to education and support for member cooperatives. Afterward, the government bill was revised into them splitting into financial and agribusiness holding companies under the control of the NACF. The bill faced opposition from farmers because farmers were concerned about the conflict of interests between the companies and the primary cooperatives. Also, it would be difficult for farmer members to democratically control subsidiaries owned by these holding companies (Kim, 2013). In this viewpoint, the foundation of a financial holding company would not be an authentic separation because the NACF would still control the financial business as the largest shareholder (Yoon & Jang, 2015).

Despite controversy, the government bill eventually passed the National Assembly in March 2011 (Park et al., 2015). In 2012 NongHyup Agribusiness Group Inc. and NongHyup Financial Group Inc. launched their business. The former takes charge of the sales, distribution, and processing of agrifoods, and supplying agri-inputs and machines. The latter is responsible for the financial businesses, for example, banking, insurance, investment, asset management, and so on (Lim, 2014). The two-tier organizational structure of the primary cooperatives and the NACF survived. The NACF assumes responsibility for the education and support of farmers and primary cooperatives and owns shares of the holding companies and controls them (Fig. 13.2).

13.5 Conclusion

This chapter described the early history of the NACF and its primary cooperatives; the stakeholder's needs erupted, and a reform was executed to respond to their needs. In the evolution process, the state, farmers, and the market have been affecting the characteristics of the NACF.

The state took the initiative in setting up the NACF and intervened in the management for quite a long time. It supported the NACF through various policies. The NACF was not managed autonomously by farmer-members and the voluntary establishment of primary agricultural cooperatives and associations was limited. The NACF, as a multipurpose agricultural cooperative, put too much weight on the financial business for nonfarmer-members and the scale of the financial business grew far bigger than the agribusiness. Farmer members had an important role in the NACF's reform. They proposed innovation plans for the democratization of the NACF. Confronted with the pressure of market liberalization farmer members demanded that the NACF strengthen the agribusiness efficiently. There were debates about the reform of the organizational design in favor of farmer-members. The NACF decided to establish two holding companies in 2012.

The NACF is said to be one of the most successful agricultural cooperatives in the world. The NACF grew so fast due to the supportive intervention of the developmental state and the characteristics of a multipurpose agricultural cooperative. The democratic control of farmer members on the NACF and the primary cooperatives has been enhanced. But it still has tasks to be solved.

The reform of the NACF is still underway. For about 60 years since the establishment of the NACF, it has evolved in different organizational designs, and a lot of ideas have been proposed by various stakeholders to make the NACF more democratic and more efficient. The NACF's current experiment could write a new history in the future.

References

Hwang, B. (2011). Changes of the agriculture production process through Saemaeul Movement and winning farmers over (in Korean). *Society and History, 90*, 5–48.

Jang, S. (2010). Liberalization and War, and farmers' movement after the War (in Korean). *The Rural Society, 20*(1), 7–46.

Jensen, A. (2013). The labor managed firm-a theoretical model explaining emergence and behavior. In D. Kruse (Ed.), *Sharing ownership, profit, and decision-making in the 21st century* (pp. 295–325). Emerald.

Ji, J. (2011). *Origins and formations of Korean Neoliberalism (in Korean)*. Book World.

Kim, E., Jang, D., & Granovetter, M. (2005). *Sociology under an economic crisis: Transition from the Developmental State and a network among corporate groups (in Korean)*. Seoul National University Press.

Kim, S. (1992). *A theory of the Korean Industrialization State (in Korean)*. Paju: Nanam.

Kim, Y. (2013). Problems and solutions of NACF and the NH financial holding company (in Korean). *Argument for Law, 44*, 239–270.

Lee, H. (2010). *The history of farmers' movement in the 1960s to the 1980s, Korean History (in Korean)*. Seoul: Hangilsa.

Lim, S. (1997). A political economic review of the small-scale farmers system in Park Chunghee era: egalitarianism, capitalism, and authoritarianism. *Journal of the Korea Political Science Association, 31*(4), 109–130.

Lim, Y. (2014). *Theory and reality of Co-operatives (in Korean)*. Seoul: Korea Institute of Co-operatives.

Lo, K. (1989). *Revision of the Agricultural Co-operative Act and its Democracy (in Korean)*. Working paper.

NACF Homepage: http://www.nonghyup.com.

NH agribusiness Homepage: http://www.nhabgroup.com.

NH financial group Homepage: http://www.nhfngroup.com.

Nyeo-Rm. (2011). *The goal and direction of agriculture reforms (in Korean)*. Seoul: Nyeo-Rm Agriculture and Farmers Policy Institute.

Park, H. (1993). Uruguay round, a long-term measure needed (in Korean). *People Looking for a Way, 93*(1), 96–99.

Park, J. (2004). *A critical review on a revision proposal of the Agricultural Co-operative Act: focusing on the reforms of NACF and spin-off of the financial business and agribusiness* (in Korean). Working paper for the Conference at the Korean Society for Co-operative Studies.

Park, J. (2007). Opening of the agricultural market and aggravation of problems of agriculture and rural areas. *Korean Association for Political Economy, 29*(1), 1−37.

Park, J., et al. (2015). *Agricultural co-operatives in crisis, finding a way; five Goals, fifteen tasks for making good agricultural co-operatives (in Korean).* Seoul: Hankyoreh.

Park, S. (2014). *The role and performance of NongHyup (in Korean).* Working paper.

Park, S. (2016). The changes and perspective of Korean agricultural cooperatives since Liberalization of 1945. *Agricultural Economics Research (in Korean), 57*(1), 53−82.

Yoon, J., & Jang, S. (2015). Narratives of organizational identities: The constructive process of organizational identities in national agricultural cooperative federation (NACF) (in Korean). *Korean Journal of Management, 23* (4), 125−157.

Further reading

NACF. (2017). *NACF Annual Report* (in Korean). Retrieved from <http://www.nonghyup.com/eng/IR/InformationList/AnnualReport.aspx>.

co-ops, including cross-country comparisonNepal Multipurpose Cooperative Society Limited

Punya Prasad Regmi[1], Indira Pant[2] and Nabin Bhandari[3]

[1]Karnali Province Planning Commission, Surkhet, Nepal [2]National Cooperative Development Board, Pulchok, Lalitpur, Nepal [3]Nepal Multipurpose Cooperative Society Limited, Jhapa, Nepal

14.1 Brief history of cooperatives in Nepal

The history of traditional cooperatives in Nepal goes back to time immemorial since there is no record of when Guthi, Dharmabhakari, Parma, and Dhikuti were exactly started. However, the modern history of cooperatives began in 1954, when the Department of Cooperatives was established within the Ministry of Agriculture. Being an agricultural country, most cooperatives are directly or indirectly related to the promotion of agricultural development. Therefore the history of cooperatives in Nepal has been characterized by government initiatives linking with development programs. The first cooperatives were cooperative credit societies established in Chitwan district in the name of flood relief and resettlement programs. These cooperatives were legally recognized after the first Cooperative Societies Act of 1959 was

enacted. Cooperatives have been considered as important vehicles for socioeconomic development since the First Five-Year Plan (1956/57 to 1960/61) till the ongoing Fourteenth Three-Year Plan (2015/16 to 2018/19). During the First Five-Year Plan, the Nepal government had an ambitious program to organize 4500 agricultural multipurpose cooperatives; however, only 378 cooperatives were organized. In fact, the restoration of democracy in 1990 helped the cooperative movement in Nepal to flourish in a rapid and sustained manner. The Cooperative Act of 1992 provided the legal base to register and function based on cooperative principles.

Nepal has a four-tiered cooperative system, namely primary, secondary, tertiary, and national. In the due course of the cooperative movement in Nepal, the government provided a legal base for cooperative societies, unions, federal unions, and federations. Realizing the growing importance of cooperatives, the

Nepal government established the Ministry of Cooperatives and Poverty Alleviation in 2012. It was merged with other ministries in 2017 and called as the Ministry of Agriculture, Land, and Cooperatives. The Department of Cooperatives is functioning under this Ministry and responsible for supporting and monitoring the 34,512 cooperatives as of today in Nepal.

14.2 Nepal Multipurpose Cooperative Society Limited

NMC-COOP is one of the most successful cooperatives in Nepal. Located in the far eastern part of the country, it is helping people in the border area save their earnings in a safe manner despite sending them to India's network businesses and saving institutions. In the beginning it was not thought by any one regarding the current level of success of NMC-COOP. It was established by a group of 26 local people with a share capital of US$2486.

Members attached to this cooperative society are of different genders, casts, religions, cultures, follow different festivals, and have different occupations. They have their own lifestyles and habits. Irrespective of all the different kinds, NMC-COOP heartily welcomes every individual for membership. The membership is open to all local people who are residents of the specified geographical area covered by NMC-COOP. Members of NMC-COOP seem satisfied as their voices are heard. They enjoy several rights and services provided by the organization. In gist, NMC-COOP renders services like accepting deposits from shareholders, providing remittance payment and collection facilities, providing loans to entrepreneur members, conducting various awareness programs in villages, and other functions. The major focus of the cooperative has been the economically backward section of society to uplift their livelihood and social recognition.

14.3 Nepal Multipurpose Cooperative Society Limited: a successful cooperative

Though the meaning of success can be defined in different ways, we must consider some of the achievements gained against its plans and targets to measure the degree of success of NMC-COOP. The most important part of its success is its goal succession. For example, the Mission 2018 was declared in 2007 and achieved before 2015. Based on this success, Vision 2023 has already been set and aggressive plans are being made and implemented. In addition, aggressive financial projection, active participation of members in financial and nonfinancial (social) activities, enhancing management abilities, and the development of the business skills and habits of entrepreneurs are in place. In this way, the cooperative is clearly making pathways to success by meeting its vision, missions, goals, and objectives.

From both the financial and social perspectives, NMC-COOP has been found to be successful. Rapidly increasing balance sheet figures with US$60 million (NRs. 6 billion) is a sign of its success. This balance sheet amount has increased six-times compared to the amount of US$10 million (NRs.1 billion) 6 years ago. The regular employees 400 plus have been a great success too. Business diversification and the multibusiness concept adopted by the organization has created more employment opportunities to the society. The changed saving patterns of members is another success initiated by NMC-COOP. The creation of funds and their proper utilization can only be done with financially aware members. "NMC Time" is the successful implementation of NMC-COOP. People wonder to see that all the programs run by the cooperative are always started at the accurate time. Complete financial solutions for the members are another important aspect of their success. NMC-COOP considers members from their birth to death. Celebrating all the moments of members' lives and participating in the sorrow of members along with their financial facilities have added value in becoming the most successful cooperative.

14.4 Macro factors contributing to the emergence of cooperatives

Cooperatives are considered as the third pillar of the Nepalese economy. Cooperative societies in Nepal are registered as separate legal entities and they have their own rights of electing the board of directors, preparing plans and policies, and implementing them. Cooperative societies are governed by government and encouraged to meet their economic and social needs. The Co-operative Act of 2017 has been in place, which has clearly defined the scope and requirements of cooperatives. Cooperative societies are nonpolitical organizations and no political influence should work in its operation. NMC-COOP has adopted the rule and it has been key to its success. Cooperative societies in Nepal are bound to pay tax. They pay 20% income tax on net profits.

14.5 Market functioning and capitalism

Nepal is following a mixed marketing system; however, the current trend is more toward a free market economy and capitalism. Private and public sectors are running in parallel in most businesses. People are free to start any legal business in any part of the country. It has helped entrepreneurship to emerge among the people. Being a developing country, large numbers of poor people are wishing to do small businesses. The informal economy is still prominent. Street businesses and vehicle businesses are popular in rural areas. These small businesses are the focus of NMC-COOP since they need capital and business environments.

14.6 Social movements and cooperatives

Social movements in Nepal are focused on changes in political and social beliefs rather than economic growth. Superstitions are deeply rooted. Gender discrimination and blind political support are major problems. Industrial policies do not favor cooperative societies starting new businesses. Cooperative societies are facing trouble with businesses with high profession. A substantial percentage of the urban population is homeless; however, most of the housing projects started by cooperative societies have failed. Agriculture is subsistence in nature and therefore majority of the farmers is poor in Nepal. Having seen this, new generations have little motivation in involving agriculture for their livelihood. NMC-COOP has been successful in motivating people in agricultural enterprises, not only through providing capital, but also technical support with business environments. This has changed the living standard of poor and small farmers.

14.7 Internal factors leading to success

There are numerous internal factors contributing to the success of NMC-COOP. The most important factor is the committed team of the Board of Directors, which developed clear guidelines and 42 policies and procedures. Required Subject Committees were formed, and employees have been highly motivated. Strong organizational structures and networks to communicate to every member were established and society-based programs were launched with the active participation of members. Geographical coverage was ensured by applying a unit concept (ranging from 50 to 500 members in a unit). One of the keys of the success of NMC-COOP is doing everything within the specified time. NMC-COOP always follow the time schedule which is termed as

"NMC Time". Clarity and honesty in financial transactions and effective implementation of all the decisions with an efficient internal control system have also contributed to the successful results of NMC-COOP. The NMC Member Tag distribution to member families, regular and quality products and services, following the rule of laws, and maintaining high quality loans have been found equally important to NMC-COOP's success.

14.8 Business model and development strategy

Since NMC-COOP is a multipurpose cooperative society, it has a plan for business diversification and multibusiness strategies. Primarily, its saving and credit business has been operating; however, their dairy business has been started in the past 3 years. Promoting milk production and supplying quality dairy products to the local markets is the prime motto of the NMC-COOP dairy industry. Their Model Farming Project has just been initiated this year. Members engaged in farming will be trained there and the production of organic agricultural products is encouraged. Marketing of such products will be initiated by NMC-COOP through its own Marketing Department.

There is provision for a separate Research and Development Department in NMC-COOP. Product development as per the requirement of members and society are initiated with the best practices in the market. Beyond the existing business, as per Vision 2023, other possible businesses will be initiated in future after detailed study of the market and possibility studies of the projects. There is a 15-member Board of Directors that is responsible for good governance, policy formulation, regular communication, and analysis of financial and nonfinancial achievements. Authorities are delegated to other 15 Office Committees and 15 Subject Committees to operate the office smoothly and

organize programs in an independent way. There is the provision of committee policy, which is mandatory for all to obey. Self-regulation for directors and committee members is strictly applied.

14.9 Human resource management

One of the key factors of the success of NMC-COOP is that it has a well-formulated human resource management policy and its effective implementation. Electronic attendance and their electronic employee inventory are maintained by the Human Resource Department. Advanced software is in operation for the efficient utilization of NMC-COOP's human resources. Around 400 employees are working with high morale resulting in the generation of a high level of productivity. Efficiency measures are declared and adopted as per international standards. Employees are well paid in comparison to local organizations. The recruitment system of employees is fair through the NMC Service Commission and regular training has been enhancing their capacity. Member satisfaction is key for the success of NMC-COOP and, therefore, all employees try their best to satisfy clients.

14.10 Cooperative members and financial structure

As of July 2018, there are altogether 53,000 NMC members constituted by 27,364 females (52%), 24,962 males (47%), and 674 institutional members (1%). Recently, 2600 school-going children have started operating child saving accounts. All local caste and ethnic groups have been involved in NMC-COOP. Even differently abled people are also engaged in NMC-Coop with high priority services. More than 99% of the shareholders are of low and middle class people whose share capital ranges from Nepali Rupees 1000 to 50,000. NMC-COOP's financial structure is dominated by members' share capital (49%) followed by reserve and surplus (33%) and the remaining 18% is borrowed in loans. In total, NRs. 520 million share capital is collected from 53,000 members. The contribution of individual members in the share capital ranges from NRs. 1000 to 1 million. The plan of NMC-COOP is to make members' share capital at least 10% of total assets by the end of the coming fiscal year, which is nearly 9% at present.

In a broader sense, NMC-COOP is currently engaged in two types of business, namely banking business focusing on their saving and credit program for 53,000 members who are actively participating in their own business, and the NMC dairy industry. This dairy industry is a dream project of NMC-COOP, which is currently running 15,000 L per day. Another dream project is NMC Model Agro Farming starting from 2018/19.

14.11 Challenges and overcoming measures

Until the establishment of NMC-COOP near the Eastern Nepal border, money and business were controlled by Indian traders. Nepali people were cheated and victimized most of the time. So, NMC-COOP was established to overcome these challenges. NMC implemented "NMC Time" and it was hard to apply. It had become a hurdle even for the directors. Other challenges include tax burdens, labor disputes, security threats, manual work reduction, electricity load shedding, hiring employees through free competition, calculating and paying the correct amount of tax, the establishment of a network in between offices at different locations, and loan management.

In the beginning stages of the establishment of NMC-COOP, people were standing in long queues at teller counters where one or two employees were paying cash and verifying instruments. Other employees were in the market searching for people who had faith in NMC-COOP and were ready to deposit. All the people trying to withdraw money got the amount they were seeking and they trusted NMC-COOP.

The dairy business is risky since milk has a short lifespan especially in high temperature environments. It is difficult and risky to preserve milk for a long time. Increasing the production by farmers in order to meet the demand of the dairy industry was extremely difficult. NMC-COOP developed a business scheme, and based on which, advanced loans for dairy farming with an insurance package. Dairy farmers got interest, started their dairy farming, and marketed their product through separate outlets in different locations for the NMC dairy industry.

NMC-COOP was not actually affected by the Nepal Rastra Bank withdrawing its Limited Banking Certificate. A few innocent members did not understand the implications of this. They even came and withdrew their deposits. Later, when they knew that nothing bad was happening with the Nepal Rastra Bank withdrawing of its Limited Banking Certificate people regained good faith in NMC-COOP.

In different forms, NMC-COOP is paying a huge amount of tax to the government of Nepal such as income tax, tax on interest on members' deposits, dividend tax, employee remuneration tax, house rent tax, service tax, allowance tax, and social security tax. Despite several efforts made by cooperatives, this double taxation is ongoing.

Labor disputes took place many times, and were resolved through collective bargaining and discussions. Office materials, fixed assets, and cash were of prime importance from a security perspective. These threats were overcome by using CC TV Cameras, an effective highweight vault, and the provision of 24-hour security.

All the work was performed manually for a long time from the establishment of NMC-COOP; however, later, accounting tasks were replaced by Core Banking Solution Software. Collection sheets were replaced by a collection tab and a mobile collector application. The human resource inventory was recorded in HR Software replacing employee's huge and heavy personal files. Minute books were replaced by electronic minutes. Filings of documents are managed in an E-filing system in Google drives and on hard drives despite having hard copies. Member surveys are being done through mobile application in spite of many paged forms.

Regular power supply remained a problem for a long time due to load shedding, and this was solved by the installation of inverters in offices. Later, online uninterruptible power supply systems were used. Currently, solar systems are used for small offices and electric generators are installed in many-storied buildings. NMC-COOP has its central server at its corporate office. It is connected to all other offices. It had its own intranet connected through network towers and devices previously. Now they are connected by a wired ISP network (LAN).

Tax evasion is common all over Nepal; however, NMC-COOP obeys true and fair tax determination procedures and has received awards three times from the Inland Revenue Office, Jhapa, for being the highest income tax payer of the year.

14.12 Factors contributing to cooperative failure

The history of cooperative business in Nepal is relatively new. Cooperatives have to struggle hard to become successful by fulfilling the cooperative principles and objectives. Most cooperatives failed in their business during the initial stages. Especially those cooperatives that were started without knowledge of the fundamental principles or those established with high expectations have failed. Many cases of failure have been found to be because of management failure. The role of the board of directors (BODs) remains crucial and any problem with the BODs always leads to failure. Even if the BODs is sincere and has good willpower, if they have no management capacity, it again leads to cooperative failure. Overambitious people sometimes establish cooperatives to fulfill their dreams, but these cannot be successful. Misunderstanding the principles and objectives of cooperatives leads to goal displacement. This disqualifies the ability of the cooperative and failure occurs. Defective financial management leads to failure. Financial discipline and efficiency in financial management with innovations lead to success. Providing a high interest rate on deposits, collecting heavy deposits, and the inability to invest properly also lead to failures. Assets appropriation or cash embezzlement leads to failure. If the properties of a given cooperative are used for personal purposes or businesses, then a shortfall in funds occurs and ultimately the cooperative fails.

14.13 Factors contributing to cooperative success

The key to success includes good governance and management, a cohesive culture, full advisory support, motivation of members, market, information symmetry, and access to capital. NMC-COOP has a strong and efficient management team with an able and visionary BODs. At the same time, it has a strong and able Account Committee, highly committed employees, and good governance in all respects. Core values adopted by NMC-COOP that have led to success are:

- Members are considered as the base of the cooperative
- Member-oriented financial transactions with quality service for sustainable business

- Accountability, transparency, honesty, and good governance following the rules and policies
- Unity and integrity, organizational clarity, and no discrimination
- Enhancing the local economy and livelihood
- Confidential financial transactions
- Maintaining punctuality by strictly following "NMC Time"

14.14 Impacts on members and local community

The fundamental principle of any cooperative is to strengthen its members in social and economic terms. NMC-COOP has been operating several programs for the members and the local community. The main programs described here have a direct impact on both members and local communities, for instance:

- *My One Rupee in Social Contribution*: There are several local Unit Committees responsible for collecting one Rupee at least from 50 members for this campaign. All members contribute 1 Nepali Rupee per day and that becomes 365 Nepali Rupees a year. NMC-COOP adds the same amount to the sum of all members and this fund can be utilized in any social development works in the local community. This innovative idea has cultured saving habits as well as helped people and community development works.
- *Student Saving Club*: In order to provide financial education to school students, NMC-COOP started student saving clubs and let students save a certain amount on a regular basis. They can organize programs for themselves with the interest earned. After the completion of their school education, members can withdraw and use a principle amount for higher education.
- *Environment and Sanitation Campaign*: The idea behind this is that our places should be kept clean by us. This campaign has taught people to keep their surroundings clean and it is supervised by supervisory committees formed by themselves.
- *Lemon Plantation Campaign*: All members are requested to plant at least two lemon tree plants in their kitchen garden. This is going to make the district self-sufficient in the production and consumption of lemons.
- *Member Relief Distribution*: NMC-COOP contributes financial support and relief materials to members affected by fatal diseases (cancer, brain tumors, etc.,), natural disasters (floods, earthquakes, storms), and other accidents (like fire, robbery, etc.). Beyond that, it provides funeral expenses to the family members of a deceased member.
- *Presence in Sorrow of Member*: The NMC-COOP group participates in the funerals of deceased members and their family members with a letter of condolence and funeral expenses as well.
- *Sharing Maternity Happiness and Infant Account*: NMC-COOP participates in maternity cases by providing 1 kg of ghee for mothers and an account is opened in the name of the infant.
- *Happy Birthday*: NMC-COOP celebrates the birthdays of children and saving accounts are opened in the cooperative while meeting them.
- *Respect to Senior Citizens*: NMC provides respect to senior citizens and rewards them with NRs 2000 for festival expenses at times of festivals.

NMC-COOP has formed different subject committees responsible for effectively organizing related programs that have a direct impact on members and society. The subject committees are:

- Education and Training Committee
- Agriculture Committee
- Women Committee

- Environment and Sanitation Committee
- Extra Activities Committee
- Youth Concern Committee
- Sports Committee
- Health Committee

Every year, an NMC member survey is done to discern the impact of NMC-COOP on its members and the community. This also helps in formulating future plans and programs of the cooperative and bringing improvements in areas facing problems.

14.15 Conclusion

Among the more than 34,000 cooperatives in Nepal, NMC-COOP has been popularly known as one of the most successful cooperatives. It is in the Jhapa district, Province number 1, in eastern Nepal. The total population of Jhapa district is approximately 900,000 and NMC-COOP has 53,000 members. This is about 6% of the total population. NMC-COOP has a balance sheet of US$6 million by now. This is the biggest balance sheet in comparison with other cooperatives having the same geographical area of coverage. The most recent of the product diversification efforts of NMC-COOP is their dairy industry, which is utilizing 15,000 L of milk produced by members. The total milk production per day in Jhapa district is about 100,000 L, which means that 15% of the total milk production is covered by NMC-Dairy.

The regular and encouraging guidance of their highly experienced advisory committee is considered to be key to the success of NMC-COOP. Members' feedback plays a crucial role.

There are several members engaged in social programs that always remain sources of inspiration through their feedback to NMC-COOP. It has encouraged the BODs to go further, achieving extra mileage. NMC-COOP has a large market in terms of population (900,000), area (1606 km^2), activities, and opportunities in local resources. Business centers and fertile agricultural lands have added value to the opportunities that NMC-COOP is harnessing. Directors in the BODs represent all the working areas and they have enormous local knowledge. NMC-COOP has strong networks between its Official Committees and Unit Committees, which are playing vital roles in making NMC-COOP the most successful cooperative. NMC-COOP is putting a lot of effort in achieving the target share capital of 10% of the total assets. The good practices of NMC-COOP in terms of good governance, transparency, accountability, financial discipline, team spirit of employees, punctuality through NMC Time, and the involvement of people of all ages in financial and social programs have made NMC-COOP most successful.

Further reading

Badal, K. (2004). *Cooperative* (in Nepali). Kathmandu: Nebula Printers.

Bharadwaj, B. (2012). Roles of cooperatives in poverty reduction: a case of Nepal. *Administration and Management Review*, 24(1), 120–139, January, 2012.

Shimkhada, N. R. (2013). Problems and prospects of the cooperative sector in Nepal for promoting financial inclusion. *Enterprise Development and Microfinance*, 24(2), 146–159, June 2013.

Upreti, R. (2018). *Cooperative roadmap* (in Nepali). Kathmandu: Manjari Publication.

15

Japan: cooperatively facilitating membership engagement—employee-led initiatives at JA Hadano

Emi Do

Department of Agricultural Economics, Tokyo University of Agriculture, Setagaya, Tokyo, Japan

15.1 Introduction

The complex group of primary agricultural cooperatives and federations that comprise the Japan Agriculture Co-operative Group (JA Group) is said to be one of the largest agricultural cooperative groups in the world. This dominance is exemplified by the ubiquity of its sleek JA logo in villages, towns, and cities across Japan. JA Hadano is one of the more than 650-member primary agriculture cooperatives in the JA group. Like the majority of primary agricultural cooperatives in Japan, it is both a multistakeholder (farmer and nonfarmer members) and multipurpose (offering a diverse array of services) cooperative. Its organizational structure has enabled the cooperative to continue to thrive despite the decline in agricultural production and increasing urbanization in the region it serves. This chapter examines JA Hadano's various strategies, with a focus on membership education as a means of maintaining membership engagement and accountability, thereby leading to increased membership engagement in the cooperative.

15.1 Emergence

Though the roots of JA cooperatives can be traced back to the traditional cooperative movement during the Tokugawa period (1603–1868), its true birth came from the Farmers Association Law in 1899 and the Industrial Co-operative Law enacted in 1900 by the Meiji government following the Meiji restoration (the abolishment of feudal rule in 1868). The Farmers Association Law was compulsory in all villages to channel government subsidies into agricultural technologies aimed for increasing productivity and self-sufficiency. The Industrial Co-operative Law, based on the Raiffeisen cooperative model, encompassed credit, marketing, purchasing, and production associations. Two big surges in the number of cooperatives occurred between 1900 and 1918, once after the Russia—Japan war (1904—05) and the other during World War I (1914—18), and the cooperative law was revised numerous times to suit the needs of the time. By the 1930's, co-operatives were used as the agency for implementing the government's agricultural policy resulting in compulsory membership for any farmer wanting to access government resources. Notable from this period is the struggle in membership alignment: landlord and tenant farmers had often competing interests and there were often conflicts between them. In 1943 the Agricultural Organizations Law was passed that integrated industrial co-ops, farmer associations, and other miscellaneous farmer organizations. The passage of this law ensured compulsory membership of all farmers and it became the mechanism through which farmers were mobilized during wartime.

With the end of World War II, legislation affecting agricultural cooperatives was introduced by the General Headquarters (GHQ) of the American Occupation Army between 1945 and 1951 along with other measures in an attempt to transform Japan into a democratic state in accordance with the Postdam Declaration of 1945. In 1946 agricultural land was redistributed, breaking up large estates into small farms, alleviating previous conflicting interests between landholding farmers and tenant farmers. To ensure that agricultural land remained in the hands of working farmers, the Agricultural Land Law was enacted in 1952, placing restrictions on the transfer of land to nonfarmers, the prohibition of absentee landowners, and the prohibition of corporations from purchasing agricultural land. The passage of the Anti-Monopoly Law in 1947 exempted cooperatives from its application under the conditions that those cooperatives met four requirements: (1) aimed at mutual benefits among small producers or consumers; (2) voluntary and open membership; (3) equal voting rights for each member; and (4) limited

compensation when distributing surplus. Perhaps most significant among the measures implemented by the GHQ was the adoption of the Agricultural Co-operative Law in 1947. Although vast in scope, one provision that continues to affect operations of JA to this day is the stipulation that at multipurpose cooperatives there should be a differentiation between the membership classes, that is farmer members and associate members, of which only the former are able to have voting rights. Through the Agricultural Co-operative Law, 17,000 agricultural organizations transitioned into more than 22,000 agricultural cooperatives and 400 federations (Kurimoto, 2004).

There are currently more than 650 primary agricultural cooperatives (JA) operating 9000 branch offices, employing over 200,000 workers who serve over 10.3 million cooperative members (Zen-noh, 2017). The group is comprised of cooperatives and federations that operate at the regional (primary), prefectural, and national levels. At the primary level are JAs, multipurpose cooperatives that offer banking, insurance, marketing, aggregated purchasing, and agricultural extension services. Each of these services offered at JAs have a corresponding federation in the JA group that operates at the prefectural and national levels. One such federation, Zenkyoren (the National Mutual Insurance Federation of the JA group), has assets whose value is rated alongside Japan's largest banks and insurance companies.

As previously mentioned, in addition to being multipurpose, JAs are also multistakeholder cooperatives, having farmer and nonfarmer (associate) members, with only the former being privy to voting rights. Currently the overall number of associate members exceeds that of farmer members. The associate to farmer member ratio is particularly skewed in urban and periurban JAs where urbanization has impacted regional agricultural production, with the number of associate members sometimes tripling the number of farmer members.

The change in membership numbers is a reflection of a greater shift that has occurred in the agricultural sector in Japan. After WWII, Japan entered a rapid industrialization phase resulting in increased urbanization that led to a decline in the number of agricultural workers. This rural to urban trend continues to this day, with the majority of those who continue to farm doing so on a part-time basis. In addition to this shift in membership demographics, JAs have also had to contend with larger membership numbers. As the decline in agriculture continued to plague many rural communities, regional JAs began to amalgamate. This not only increased the territory over which one JA had jurisdiction, it has also led to average membership numbers ballooning from 3000 in 1992 to 13,800 in 2012 (Masuda, Senda, & Nishii, 2015). These changes in the composition of the membership at JAs, namely the dramatic increase of nonvoting associate members, requires re-evaluation of governance processes to ensure that the co-operatives are still reflecting the principles of member-ownership and member-control.

In an urban environment, the resilience of a food system is often measured by how it is able to maintain availability and stability of food post disaster. How is the city able to feed itself if distribution arteries are cut off? However, equally important is how an urban food system can withstand longer shocks such as an economic downturn or political instability. How do these factors play into food security and food sovereignty of the urban food system? The issues of food security and food sovereignty are exacerbated in urban environments, so much so that urban historian Arnold Toynbee defines a city as "a human settlement whose inhabitants cannot produce, within the city limits, all of the food that they need for keeping them alive" (Pothukuchi & Kaufman, 1999). In this context the food consumed by residents of cities has to be imported, creating a physical barrier between producers and consumers with both groups being dependent on intermediaries. Urban and periurban agriculture is defined by the FAO as "an industry located within (intraurban) or on the fringe (periurban) of a town, city, or metropolis, which grows and raises, processes and distributes a diversity of agricultural products, using largely human, land and water resources, products and services found in or around that urban area" (Warren, Hawkesworth, & Knai, 2015). In this way, urban and periurban agriculture provide a source of food for urban and periurban residents that can be accessed on terms negotiated without intermediaries. With consumers and producers having opportunities to communicate and interact directly, urban and periurban agriculture facilitates the humanization of food, imbuing it with the human and environmental forces required to produce it. This type of connection, or humanization of food production, is especially important when examining food systems from a food sovereignty perspective which aspires to achieve "food production, distribution, and consumption based on environmental, social, and economic sustainability" (Patel, 2009).

The JA group has sought to adapt to the changing agricultural landscape by reorienting its mission to that of regional cooperatives supporting agriculture rather than an agricultural cooperative that promotes the growth of the agricultural sector. The JA group has long engaged in nonagricultural activities, such as providing insurance services, supermarkets, gasoline/LP gas stands, and funeral services in rural areas. As the population ages, and after the passage of the Long-Term Care Insurance Act in 2000, JAs have also begun to operate retirement homes and offer elderly nursing care services. This shift in services reflects the changing needs of the communities within which JAs are situated, however, it means their ties to agriculture have become more tenuous. Additionally, these issues are further exacerbated in urban and periurban areas where there are plentiful service providers for these nonagricultural services. Here, the multi-stakeholder nature of JA, that its membership is comprised of primary producers and consumers, and provides a unique opportunity to bring all parties of the food system to the table. Though hindered by the legal constraints of the Agricultural Co-operative Law, JAs must foster an effective governance system in order to be able to effectively facilitate the democratization of the food system, particularly in rapidly urbanizing regions.

15.2 Governance

The formal governance mechanism for JAs consist of a General Representative Members Council (GRMC) who elect a board of directors. Representative members who serve on the GRMC are elected at the community or hamlet level, though this can vary from JA to JA. At an average-sized JA of 13,800 members, around 500 representatives will be selected to the GRMC. As stated previously, the Agricultural Co-operative Law prohibits associate members from being able to participate in voting for representatives to serve on the GRMC, which also precludes them from being elected to serve on the GRMC. Thus the formal governance process excludes associate members' voices.

Though this lack of inclusion of an entire membership class from the formal governance process is not ideal, there is an implicit understanding among those familiar with the operations of JAs and rural Japanese culture in general, that organizational feedback occurs in more informal settings than that of the GRMC or the general assembly. In fact, although hamstrung by the legal constraints, many JAs have implemented different strategies to elicit membership feedback into cooperative management. In 2016 Fukuda categorized these

nontraditional governance efforts into three categories: (1) structured, (2) unstructured—activity based, and (3) semistructured—employee driven. Structured approaches to informal governance include committee meetings or assemblies that are convened at the community or branch level prior to the general assembly where associate and farmer members are encouraged to share their opinions about the business direction of the JA. Although there are no official voting rights awarded to those who attend these meetings or assemblies, staff members are on hand to answer questions and to take feedback back to the cooperative's management. Unstructured, activity-based approaches to governance can be observed at most primary JAs. Often activities are organized by branch-level committees such as Nouka-kumiai (farmer and farmland owners' association), Seisounen-bu (young farmers' association), Josei-bu (women's association), Fresh-Miz (young women's association), Nenkin Tomonokai (pensioner friendship association). These activities can range from excursions, cooking classes, sports tournaments, and community festivals. Through engagement in these types of associations and event organization committees, members build social capital and become more familiar with the cooperative staff, leading to greater opportunities for them to learn about, and give feedback on, the business management of the cooperative. Semistructured, employee driven initiatives in informal governance are prevalent among leading primary JAs. These initiatives can include the publication of monthly newsletters, membership education courses aimed at enhancing membership awareness of cooperative values and monthly engagement days where staff solicit feedback from members by going door to door. Therefore it can be said that JAs are active in their attempts to solicit membership feedback using a variety of methods outside of the traditional governance means.

JA Hadano is particularly exemplary among primary cooperatives in their commitment to membership engagement and employ all three forms of informal governance approaches. The remainder of this chapter describes the challenges, strategies, and outcome of these initiatives at JA Hadano.

15.3 Case study: JA Hadano

Hadano is a suburb located 60 km outside of central Tokyo, with a population of 168,204 (JA Hadano, 2013). Though Hadano has a long history of agriculture, the number of farms in the municipality are diminishing as urbanization has led to a doubling of the municipality's population, causing the area of arable farmland to decrease by two-thirds since 1970. JA Hadano, the local agricultural cooperative, was established in 1963 through a merger with five other cooperatives in the area, and merging with an additional two cooperatives in 1966. Reflecting the national trend, the number of members at JA Hadano increased dramatically from 2560 in 1966 to 14,084 in 2014, with the recruitment of new associate members accounting for 93% of the total increase in members (Fig. 15.1).

In many ways, JA Hadano is a reflection of the greater trends among primary JAs: the increasing heterogeneity in its membership from one based primary on farmers to one that predominantly has associate members, as well as encroaching urbanization leading to a decrease in agricultural production in the region. In 2016 the net profit of services rendered at JA Hadano was 21,703,437.66 USD (2016 exchange rate 1USD = 116.94 JPY). We can see this shift away from primary agricultural services in JA Hadano's profit and loss statement from 2016. Whereas sales and marketing of agricultural products accounts for 11% of the gross revenue and 3% of net profit, both credit and insurance services accounted for 32% and 12% of gross revenue and 59% and 27% of net profit, respectively (JA Hadano, 2017).

Unlike most other primary JAs in rapidly urbanizing regions, JA Hadano has not undergone any additional amalgamations or mergers since 1966, indicating stability in the organizational structure. This is important as stability has been said to reduce the risk of free-riding or failing to reciprocate which tends to occur as membership accountability decreases with anonymity (Nowak, Sigmund, & Leibowitz, 2000). From the perspective of organizational social capital, the longevity of JA Hadano after its mergers in 1966 can provide a buffering effect to the increase in scale of the cooperative. Organizational social capital has been tied to economic performance of cooperatives in several studies (Liang et al, 2015; Nilsson, Svendsen, & Svendsen, 2012). This inherent social capital, together with the employee-led initiatives to foster organizational social capital are what make JA Hadano an interesting case study to examine how one cooperative is tackling challenges in

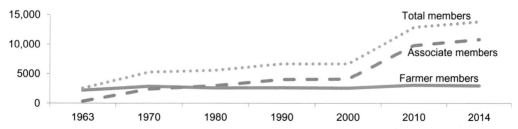

FIGURE 15.1 JA Hadano membership numbers from 1963 to 2014. Source: Data from *Hadano, J. A, (2015).* 2015 overview of JA Hadano: For creation of a century of symbiosis. *(In Japanese).*

2. Case studies of Asian co-ops, including cross-country comparison

membership heterogeneity and changes in the national agricultural sector.

15.4 Governance at JA Hadano

At JA Hadano the board of directors consists of 36 board members who are elected by farmer members through an election. Unlike a majority of primary cooperatives, JA Hadano does not use the GRMC system; all members, including associate members, are encouraged to attend the annual general assembly. In 2014 over 1500 members attended the AGM, slightly less than half were associate members despite their lack of voting privileges. Farmer members who are not able to attend the AGM are permitted to send in their paper ballot prior to the assembly. Prior to the AGM, all members are invited to convene in smaller community-level groups to discuss issues, relay concerns, and ask questions regarding cooperative operation. In 2014 there were 84 roundtable discussions held prior to the AGM. This structured approach to including associate members, from the desegregated approach to the AGM to the equal opportunity to participate in pre-AGM branch-level meetings is an example of JA Hadano's commitment to cultivating a nonhierarchical dynamic between the different member classes.

15.5 Employee-driven membership engagement initiatives

JA Hadano is unique in its employee-driven membership engagement initiatives. Like most JAs, JA Hadano publishes a monthly newsletter outlining community and cooperative events, cooperative news, features on the membership, recipes, and other pertinent information. However, JA Hadano uses the monthly publication as an opportunity for membership engagement by having staff personally deliver the newsletter door to door to all members. This occurs on the 26th and 27th of every month, ensuring that the days fall on different days of the week each month, enabling staff the opportunity to engage with members despite varying weekly schedules. On average, staff are able to engage with 60%−70% of all members every month. Furthermore, staff are encouraged to solicit feedback from members regarding cooperative services that are reported back to management following these membership engagement days. Not only does this process enable the cooperative to ensure that they are meeting the needs of their cooperative members, it provides a reliable and regular opportunity for members to have their voices heard by management on a monthly basis. Additionally, JA Hadano strives to treat all members equally whether they are associate or farmer members. This is demonstrated in their commitment to visit farmer and associate members when delivering the monthly newsletter and to having both farmer and associate members attend their AGM. Lastly, JA Hadano has offered their members access to educational courses aimed at fostering a deeper understanding of cooperative values. More information pertaining to the membership education courses will be explored later in Section 15.7.

15.6 Jibasanzu

In 2008 JA Hadano decided to eliminate aggregated sales and distribution of its agricultural products, instead focusing on the operation of a storefront, Jibasanzu, that acts as a point-of-sale for farmers and residents in the region. This storefront enables farmers and associate members who grow food in their backyards or community gardens to sell as much, or as little, as they are able to produce at whatever cost the farmer deems appropriate, and at whatever time during the season that they are able to produce it. For small scale,

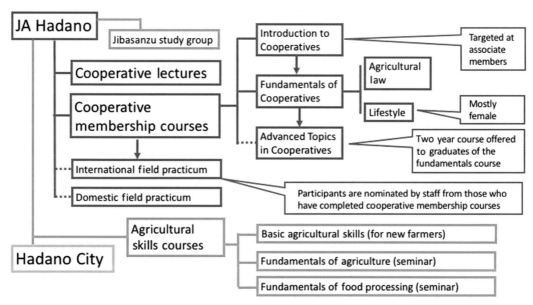

FIGURE 15.2 Education courses offered to members at JA Hadano (membership education courses are in blue) (JA Hadano, 2015).

part-time, or inexperienced farmers this flexibility reduces the pressure of having to be responsible for committing to a production plan that aggregate sales schemes necessitate. To support its larger-scale farmers, the cooperative facilitates direct marketing opportunities for farmers to sell to local supermarkets, restaurants, and at their own farm stands. Though this strategy is growing in popularity among urban and periurban JAs, the success and scale that JA Hadano has been able to achieve with this strategy has been celebrated in the greater JA community. This decision can be seen as a reflection to meet the growing heterogeneity of their membership, from one centered around primary producers to that of a growing number of part-time or hobby farmers.

15.7 Membership education

Another key initiative at JA Hadano is the membership education courses. There are two main categories of education courses on offer at JA Hadano: one addresses the development of technical skills through hands-on practical education (highlighted in green in Fig. 15.2), while the other is more knowledge-based and offered in a more traditional lecture format (in blue in Fig. 15.2). Of these numerous education courses, of particular interest are the membership education courses that have the objective "to return to the foundation of cooperatives and promote co-operative renewal through training members to become leaders with a broad perspective of the co-operative philosophy, to deepen the understanding of the co-operative spirit among associate members and to encourage participation in co-operative activities" (JA Hadano, 2015). Table 15.1 is an overview of the course content of the membership education courses offered at JA Hadano.

A 2016 study examining factors predicting organizational social capital at JA Hadano found that participation in membership education courses was statistically significant in

TABLE 15.1 Summary of curricula of membership education courses at JA Hadano.

	Membership education courses			
Introductory course	Fundamental (agricultural law)	Fundamental (lifestyle)	Advanced topics	
Curriculum JA as a regional cooperative association that fosters community development				The heart and structure behind cooperativism
JA Hadano as a source of support for the lifestyle of the local community	JA Hadano's three objectives concerning symbiosis and virtue		JA's business activities and future efforts	Efforts to provide "safe, secure, and delicious agricultural products"
Learning from Ninomiya Sontoku "The spirit of virtuous living"	Field visit: Nerima, JA Tokyo Aoba	Learning about the Hadano Clean Center	The latest in agricultural technology development	Striving for a better city
Celebrating local traditional culture	Examining agricultural policy	Agricultural leaders of the Edo period	Advancing "Ending Note"	Awareness of the different facets of dementia
Cultural Lecture: How our lifestyle affects the global environment				Cultural Lecture
The importance of the "eat local" campaign	Inheritance and Donation Tax	Disaster Management ∼ Being Prepared ∼	Deliciously Reducing Salt Consumption	Promoting urban agriculture in Kanagawa
Learning from farmers: field visit and hands-on learning harvesting at a farm	Overview of Food Product Labeling and JAS labeling laws	Striving for health and longevity	Possibilities for agriculture and social welfare	Parliamentary visit with Agriculture, Forestry and Fisheries cabinet
Role of women in agriculture and JA	Farm Inheritance basics	The enjoyment of food culture and lifestyle	Farm Inheritance basics	Exchanging ideas with House of Representatives
Strengthening "co-operative strength" to realize our "dreams"			n/a	Advanced topics in Farm Inheritance

JA Hadano course materials, 2015.

predicting higher social capital scores on a questionnaire designed to probe three aspects of organizational social capital: structural, relational, and cognitive social capital.[1] Through factor analysis, three major factors were identified from the pattern of responses.

[1] Organizational social capital: Organizational social capital is a growing area of research in management science, which examines the effect of social capital within an organization. Studies have shown that there are strategies that can be adopted by an organization to foster the development of organizational social capital (Bolino, Turnley, & Bloodgood, 2002; Cohen & Prusak, 2001). Organizational social capital transposes the concepts of social capital into the organizational framework, theorizing that the increased social capital within an organization can lead to greater organizational advantage (Andrews, 2010). Social capital within an organization can be analyzed using three dimensions: structural (connections among actors), relational (trust between actors), and cognitive (shared goals and values among actors) (Nahapiet & Ghoshal, 1998).

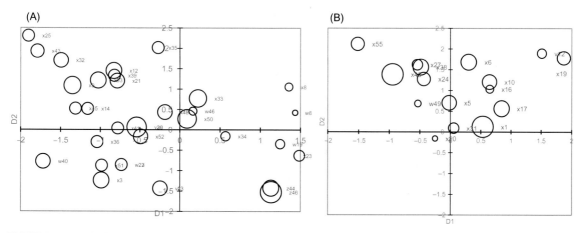

FIGURE 15.3 (A) Scatterplot (F1 × F2 × F3) Jibasanzu users, education course nonparticipants. (B) Scatterplot (F1 × F2 × F3) Jibasanzu users, education course participants.

By drawing on the similarities between the statements associated with each factor, the first factor can be grouped as "communication-based forms of governance," the second factor as "structured or defined forms governance," and the third as "cooperative use." Fig. 15.3A and B are scatterplots using the factor scores after varimax rotation of all of the participants (Fig. 15.3A) versus the participants of the education program (Fig. 15.3B). We can see that participating in the education program shifts the points on the graph further toward the upper-right quadrant, indicating greater value in governance and participation. It was clear then that there was a positive correlation between participating in the membership education course and higher values of social capital.

To better understand the relationship between the membership education program and membership participation and governance, follow-up interviews were conducted with cooperative members who had participated in at least one membership education course. JA Hadano staff in the membership education department were also interviewed. Interviews were semistructured and conducted either at farms or in a conference room at JA Hadano headquarters. Interviews were recorded, transcribed, and then coded using thematic codes deduced by observational techniques as outlined by Ryan and Bernard (2003). The themes derived for the study include sense of responsibility (with a subtheme of participation, governance, self-criticism, initiative), empathy, satisfaction, acceptance, confusion, and explanation.

When asked directly, all members said their behavior before participating in the course, and after completing the course had not changed. All, however, claimed to have gained a greater sense of community and sense of belonging within the cooperative after learning more about the services being offered by the cooperative. Each interviewee used the word "kaomishiri" whose literal translation means recognition by face, however, culturally it refers to a sense of familiarity with other cooperative members and staff. The majority interviewees said they felt more comfortable greeting other members when they encountered them at JA facilities. For those new to the co-op, becoming more familiar with the services offered by the cooperative (interest clubs, activities) along with feeling more comfortable with other members led to an increased likelihood and confidence in trying new things at the cooperative.

All interviewees stated satisfaction in the content of the course and indicated interest in participating in other courses offered by the cooperative. However, several members felt they were missing a fundamental part of the debate about cooperative reform that is currently quite topical and prevalent in national media. Members expressed that they felt the course only covered the strengths of the agricultural cooperative system, but they lacked an understanding as to the critical arguments against the cooperative. Thus they felt that they hadn't grasped the entirety of the controversy and felt no better informed or able to form their own opinions or suggestions for how the cooperative could be reformed. Fairbairn (2003) concludes that "how members see their co-operative and its activity is the question of transparency (which is facilitated by) not only by good communication, but by structures and operations that members can see are designed around their own needs." Though graduates of the membership education course still felt there were areas wherein they are unclear, by fostering awareness of the role of members within the governance process of the cooperative, JA Hadano is demonstrating a commitment to creating the structures and operations that facilitate greater transparency.

15.8 Conclusion

The outcome of this study indicates that creating opportunities for members to gather, share, and feel like they are members of a community and ownership over the cooperative increases actions indicative of greater participation in governance. Though graduates of the membership course did not feel their behavior or actions had changed as a result of having participated in these education courses, those same graduates stated that they shared a greater sense of community, greater familiarity with other members, staff, and services of the cooperative, and experienced greater empowerment when it came to utilizing the cooperative due to their participation in the education program.

Agricultural cooperatives are integral in sustaining the survival of small-scale farms being left behind in the increasingly globalized food system. These farms, dismissed as being resistant to development, play an important role in the food sovereignty of vulnerable and rapidly urbanizing regions. This role in maintaining food sovereignty is contingent in the autonomy and independence of these individual farms. Japanese agricultural communities are undergoing changes due to population shifts, increasing urbanization, and political pressure. Particularly in urbanizing areas, where farms are typically managed on a part-time basis or for self-sufficiency purposes, there is a risk of losing food production completely, thereby diminishing the food sovereignty of these communities. One of the greatest strengths of a cooperative lies in its ability to uphold the autonomy of the individual members. It is through its adherence to user-ownership, user-control, and user-benefit that differentiates a cooperative from an investor owned firm(IOF) and embeds it within one of the models through which democracy within Japan's economic system can be expressed. However, having the structure to support democracy is not the same as members demonstrating their autonomy by exercising their democratic rights to governance over their cooperative. A cooperative's ability of being successful in this role is dependent on it being truly governed by its membership, which in the case of JA is comprised of farmers and consumers. JA Hadano, with its membership education programs, is demonstrating alignment and investment in this vision.

References

Andrews, R. (2010). Organizational social capital, structure and performance. *Human relations*, 63(5), 583—608.

Bolino, M. C., Turnley, W. H., & Bloodgood, J. M. (2002). Citizenship behavior and the creation of social capital in organizations. *Academy of Management Review, 27*(4), 505–522.

Cohen, D., & Prusak, L. (2001). *In good company: How social capital makes organizations work.* Harvard Business Press.

Fairbairn, B. (2003). *Three strategic concepts for the guidance of co-operatives: Linkage, transparency, and cognition* (No. 1754-2016-141533).

Fukuda, J. (2016). *Agricultural Cooperative (JA) Organization Reform Consideration.* 20th Conference of Progressive Economics (In Japanese).

Hadano, J. A. (2015). *2015 overview of JA Hadano: For creation of a century of symbiosis.* (In Japanese).

Hadano, J. A. (2013). *Second local agricultural promotion plan.* (In Japanese).

Hadano, J. A. (2017). *2017 disclosure.* JA Hadano.

Kurimoto, A. (2004). Agricultural cooperatives in Japan: An institutional approach. *Journal of Rural Cooperation, 32* (2), 111–128.

Liang, Q., et al. (2015). Social capital, member participation and cooperative performance: Evidence from China's Zhejiang. *International Food and Agribusiness Management Review, 18*(1), 49–78.

Masuda, Y., Senda, T., & Nishii, K. (2015). Creating competitive advantage in agricultural co-operatives through improving governance systems and enhancing member and community engagement. In *Co-operative governance fit to build resilience in the face of complexity* (Chapter 4, pp. 45–59). International Co-operative Alliance.

Nahapiet, J., & Ghoshal, S. (1998). Social capital, intellectual capital and the organizational advantage. *Academy of Management Review, 23*(2), 242–266.

Nilsson, J., Svendsen, G., & Svendsen, G. (2012). Are large and complex agricultural cooperatives losing their social capital? *Agribusiness, 28*(2), 187–204.

Nowak, M. A., Sigmund, K., & Leibowitz, M. L. (2000). Cooperation versus competition. *Financial Analysts Journal, 56*(4), 13–22.

Patel, R. (2009). Food sovereignty. *The Journal of Peasant Studies, 36*(3), 663–706.

Pothukuchi, K., & Kaufman, J. L. (1999). Placing the food system on the urban agenda: The role of municipal institutions in food systems planning. *Agriculture and human values, 16*(2), 213–224.

Ryan, G., & Bernard, H. R. (2010). *Finding themes in analyzing qualitative data* (pp. 53–105). Thousand Oaks, CA: Sage Publications.

Warren, E., Hawkesworth, S., & Knai, C. (2015). Investigating the association between urban agriculture and food security, dietary diversity, and nutritional status: A systematic literature review. *Food Policy, 53,* 54–66.

Zen-noh, J. A. (2017). *Zen-noh Report 2017.* National Federation of Agricultural Cooperative Associations.

Further reading

Masuda, Y. (2013). Structure and Challenges of JA Governance. In *To whom does JA belong? JA Governance in an era of diversification* (Chapter 1, pp. 12–38). Ienohikari Association. (In Japanese).

Yokoyama, S., & Sakurai, S. (2009). Social capital and the local food movement in Japan: The Case of the Chiba Prefecture. *Asian Journal of Agriculture and Development, 6*(1), 29–48.

16

Almondco: an Australian cooperative success story

Gary Lewis[†]

Byron Bay, NSW, Australia

16.1 Introduction

Co-operative Almond Producers Limited (CAP) was formed in 1944 to rid the fledgling South Australian almond industry of exploitative "middle men." Later restructured as "Almondco," this highly successful cooperative company became the processor of choice for the majority of almond growers in Australia, without succumbing to the forces of business degeneration.[1]

In its first decade, the cooperative struggled with opportunistic members opting in and out as it suited them, while foreign almonds flooded the market. Then issues with water availability and rising land prices in the 1970s saw the industry begin to relocate north from near Adelaide to the River Murray, near the Victorian border.

By the early 1980s, CAP was handling all of the almonds produced in Australia. With almond production increasing,[2] however, the cooperative was required to expand or leave new fields to competitors. Ditching the cooperative business model was considered, but members were opposed to the idea of external investors, which risked grower-ownership and control, something that was precious to them. Instead, the cooperative was restructured as an unlisted public company, retaining its status as a cooperative under the Income Tax Assessment Act.

Utilizing government loans, Almondco expanded rapidly thereafter, and by its 70th birthday represented 85% of all Australian almond producers, processing and marketing approximately one-third of estimated national production.

---

[1] Anthony Jensen A.E. (2013) *The Labour Managed Firm: A Theoretical Model Explaining Emergence and Behaviour* in Advances in the Economic Analysis of Participatory and Labour Managed Firms (14: 297) 'Sharing Ownership, Profits and Decision-Making in the 21st Century', D. Kruse (Ed), Group Publishing.

[†] Deceased

[2] Explanatory Memorandum on the proposed changes to the Rules of Almondco Co-operative Limited and on the Proposed Transfer of the Undertaking of Almondco Co-operative Limited to Almondco Australia Limited (a company to be incorporated pursuant to the Corporations Law) p. 6.

16.2 Historical overview

The vast island-continent of Australia has been inhabited for at least 60,000 years, barely 230 of them by nonindigenes.

In that brief moment, the driest inhabited continent on Earth grew from a scatter of primitive British penal colonies and the free-settler colony of South Australia into a federation of parochial states characterized by a strong element of state intervention, protectionism, and centralized industrial relations, and was transformed in the post–World War II period into a wealthy, multicultural, laissez-faire, liberal-market, capitalist economy marked by growing gaps in wealth distribution.

In the 1860s and 1870s, cooperatives started forming in free-settler South Australia, a colony characterized by nonconformist religious beliefs and, by the interwar period, that state, where this discussion is focused, at one stage, boasted more cooperatives per capita than any other in the Australian federation.[3]

16.3 A cooperative success: Almondco

South Australian settlers started planting almond trees in the mid-1830s, and by the early 20th century, a commercial industry had emerged around Willunga, approximately 50 km south of Adelaide, and near Marion, a suburb close to the city. Seeking to rid the industry of "middle men," who were manipulating prices to growers' disadvantage and, inspired by a Rochdale Centenary Congress held in Adelaide in 1944, farmers formed CAP.[4]

Attention now turns to the several phases through which Almondco passed in achieving a remarkable success, logically dealing with commercial realities through the application of a democratic cooperative decision-making process.

16.3.1 Phase 1: favorable conditions and government support

Purchasing a building in Edwardstown in suburban Adelaide, CAP's pioneer cooperators installed sorting and bagging facilities and employed a secretary/manager, a warehouse manager, and kernel sorters. Operating initially as a bulk-processor, the producers sold bags of kernels to food processing companies such as Cadburys, Sanitarium, and a few smaller buyers.

Fewer than 3000 tons of almonds were produced in the whole of Australia at this time. However, while CAP processed more than half of this, volumes were insufficient to generate economies of scale, meaning that the cooperative could not afford to employ skilled people or install a more efficient plant and equipment. With opportunistic members simply opting in and out as it suited them and private traders and merchants offering higher ad hoc prices, the resulting inefficiencies diminished returns even further; a vicious cycle persisting throughout the cooperative's first developmental phase to the late 1950s.

Then, following a bumper crop in Italy and with imported almonds flooding the Australian market, CAP applied to the Commonwealth Government for a tariff and was successful. Stabilized by this, the cooperative installed a blanching facility and began exporting almonds to Japan, the beginning of what grew into a thriving export trade.

16.3.2 Phase 2: relocation

The next phase in the cooperative's development involved nothing less than a relocation of the industry's geographic location. With the city of Adelaide expanding, most almond trees around Marion were pulled, while production intensified near Willunga, where about 300 growers cultivated 4000 acres on mostly small

---

3   Gary Lewis *The Democracy Principle: Farmer Co-operatives in Twentieth Century Australia*, 2006 p. 72.

4   Gary Lewis *The Democracy Principle*, op cit p. 74.

blocks. By the late 1970s, however, there were issues with water availability and quality, and rising land prices saw many leave to take up larger parcels of cheaper land to the north in the Riverland District along the River Murray, near Renmark and Loxton, and across the river in Victoria and New South Wales. There, with broad acres and abundant supplies of irrigation water available in excellent climatic conditions, the industry flourished. By the early 1980s, CAP was handling nearly all the almonds produced in Australia.

As the supply of locally grown almonds to the Adelaide factory in Edwardstown dwindled, CAP members sold it, and had the almonds sorted under a contract arrangement at Berri. Hulling and shelling were done at Laragon in the Riverland, near Lindsay Point and at a facility at Lyrup. However, Willunga members still supplied CAP and it subsidized transport and insurance costs, a serious consideration with Australia's vast distances. Moreover, with more farmers moving away from grapes and citrus on the Murray attracted by better-yielding almond crops and the higher prices available and with production tipped to increase by 70%,[5] CAP's problem was now not one of undersupply, but of incapacity to process the supply that existed, leaving a gap for competitors. This was particularly true as large plantings in the Sunraysia region of Victoria were coming on stream and some growers there were reluctant to use a South Australian processing plant.

16.3.3 Phase 3: resisting demutualization and scaling up

Meanwhile, the commercial environment was also changing as deregulation,

privatization, and competition policy gathered momentum. Many long-established agricultural cooperatives considered demutualization. CAP was not immune to this debate where self-interest vied with the broader good for ascendancy, and the cooperative passed through a highly unstable third phase.

Communication gaps appeared in the leadership, serious differences of opinion arose concerning direction and management styles, and there were personality clashes, and, were it not for the sterling efforts of a few board members committed to the idea of farmer cooperation, the cooperative would likely have been taken over or simply collapsed.

A committee of CAP growers formed to consider possibly changing the cooperative business model. The rationale seemed straightforward enough; already almonds from the Unites States accounted for 30% of the Australian market[6] and, with Spain poised to enter European markets,[7] that share could only grow, especially as domestic tariffs were progressively reduced. The cooperative needed to position itself strategically and promptly to handle members' increased tonnage and attract major suppliers away from competitors, who were improving in efficiency, scale, and capacity. The cooperative needed to achieve greater economies of scale and efficiency; the argument went, produce better quality products, find ways of funding acquisitions, expansion and diversification, and build a world-class processing facility and heighten its marketing presence. At least AUD$2.3 million would be required to fund this ambitious plan and the need for capital would be ongoing. The cooperative business model was unsuited, some argued, as the need for finance to stay abreast of the market exceeded members' ability to

---

[5] Explanatory Memorandum op cit p. 6.

[6] Explanatory Memorandum op cit p. 6.

[7] Explanatory Memorandum op cit p. 6.

provide this through the retention of earnings or levies. Moreover, the introduction by the Commonwealth of dividend imputation and a decline in the availability of limited partnership agreement (LPA), a type funding,[8] had largely removed the taxation advantage that cooperatives once possessed. There was talk of issuing shares to attract capital so shareholders could access real value as the business appreciated and not simply redeem them at par value upon exit of the then current situation.

But CAP's predominantly small-scale producers, true to their cooperative vision and principles, vigorously opposed the idea of courting external investors and "dry shareholders" (nonsuppliers), which risked them forfeiting something they valued highly, that is, democratic ownership and control of their *own* business. Instead, they proposed restructuring the cooperative in such a way as to appeal to new growers *and* corporate entities who were interested in *jointly* processing and marketing almonds along cooperative lines,[9] thereby improving returns and services for *all* growers, large *and* small.

The restructuring of CAP proceeded, leading to the formation of Almondco Australia Limited (AAL, hereafter "Almondco"). Structured as an unlisted public company registered under South Australian corporations' law, Almondco retained its status as a cooperative under S117 of the Income Tax Assessment Act in respect *inter alia* of rebates, bonuses distributed, and payment of interest and principal on government loans. To qualify as a cooperative for taxation purposes, the cooperative company was required to limit the number of shares that could be held by, or on behalf of, any one shareholder; desist from quoting shares for sale on a stock exchange; include in its objects the provision of services to primary producers; and to source at least 90% of supply from members, while ensuring that more than 90% of its members supplied the cooperative company with product—the mutuality principle.[10]

Shares at par were issued broadly proportionate to the volume of supply,[11] meaning in effect about 10 producers held approximately 80% of them. Fortunately, each shareholder was strongly committed to the cooperative idea and the broader interests of growers (notwithstanding the potential for them to receive only a pittance for shares when exiting the industry), a point not lost on smaller suppliers who loyally rallied behind them.

Recalling limitations to the voluntary principle from an earlier phase when members simply delivered or withdrew product as it suited them, growers also agreed to binding contractual supply arrangements.

16.3.4 Phase 4: commercial reality versus cooperative vision

So it was that in February 1994, a fourth phase in the cooperative's development began. No longer a "pure" cooperative, insofar as the democracy and voluntary principles were pragmatically adjusted to match prevailing commercial realities, growers nevertheless clung tenaciously to the central cooperative idea, that is, democratic ownership and control of a business that they had formed by *themselves* for the purpose of serving *their* interests.

---

[8] Explanatory Memorandum op cit p. 8.

[9] Explanatory Memorandum op cit p. 6.

[10] Sections 117–120 of the Income Tax Assessment Act, 1936.

[11] Explanatory Memorandum op cit p. 4.

Almondco quickly began work on a state of the art secondary processing plant with in-shell capacity on 10 acres near Renmark, which, upon completion, would finally give the cooperative company control over grading, value-adding, and marketing. Meanwhile, and helpfully, the privately-owned Lyrup and Lindsay Point primary-processing plants continued to hull and shell local growers' product and maintained a close association with the company with regard to product quality, and Lyrup also provided storage facilities.

The new plant was a resounding success. With a capacity to process approximately 20,000–30,000 tons of almonds including poorer quality nuts, significant improvements in the speed and efficiency of sorting and processing were realized as concerted efforts continued to constrain costs, improve end-product quality, and value-add.

16.3.5 Phase 5: rapid development

Building a reputation for high-quality product, reliability, and good returns, and attracting many new suppliers, Almondco entered a fifth and dynamic developmental phase in the late 1990s. In 1998 for instance, 4750 tons of almonds were supplied to Almondco, 55% up on the previous year.[12]

However, early in the new century a large corporate supplier suddenly withdrew following what appears to have been a personality clash. A new buyer or buyers needed to be found quickly or a slew of shares could fall into the hands of "dry shareholders." Rallying to the cause, albeit with considerable personal inconvenience and expense, growers hurriedly raised sufficient money for a share buy-back, thus, stabilizing the situation, but exacerbating the question of disproportionate representation in the membership.

In this context, the commercial climate again changed, quite literally this time, as protracted droughts hit California (where about 85% of world almond supply was sourced from). With high-quality Australian product attracting a premium on world markets, the advantage of southern-hemisphere counter-seasonality, and with yields and quality amongst the best in the world, the Australian almond industry now entered a period of even more rapid development, quickly becoming one the fastest growing and most valuable horticultural industries in the world (though fundamentally still a price-taker).

Riding this star along with the rest of the industry, Almondco members planted even larger orchards, encouraged more growers to join the industry, and forged strategic partnerships with Australian food manufacturers, repackagers, wholesalers, food servicers, and confectioners. After forecasts in 2005 that the supply of almonds available would double between that period and December 2010,[13] the reenergized cooperative company purchased and installed a state of the art pasteurization plant, a first for the industry, bought the privately-owned almond hulling, processing, and storage plant at Lyrup funded by a South Australian Department of Primary Industry loan and guaranteed by Bank SA, the company's banker, and constructed a processing plant in New South Wales, Riverina, funded through a New South Wales Treasury loan, again supported by a Bank SA guarantee.

16.4 A mature democratic business emerges

Almondco then embarked upon a sixth phase of development and consolidation reaching to

---

[12] Joint Chairman's and Managing Director's Report in Almondco Ltd. *Annual Report* 1997–98 p. 3.

[13] The Chairman's Report in Almondco Ltd *Annual Report* 2005–06 p. 5.

the present. Owned and controlled by 143 grower-shareholders, by its 70th birthday in 2014,[14] Almondco represented 85% of all Australian almond producers processing and marketing approximately one-third of the estimated national production and operating on an annual turnover reaching as high as AUD$200 million. Membership subsequently expanded to include suppliers in Western Australia, Victoria, and New South Wales, ranging in size from large corporations to small family farms. With such broad representation, dispersed plants and equipment, and a capacity to direct product to plants as need dictated, Almondco operated as a fully vertically-integrated business, effectively "bookending" the industry.

16.5 Overcoming obstacles to success

In achieving this remarkable success Almondco was required to overcome many obstacles including the predations of "middle men;" "free rider" opportunists; dumping; land and water pressures; the geographic relocation of orchards, plants, and equipment; structural changes in the economy; "white knights" eroding confidence in the idea of cooperation; and the sudden departure of a major supplier, to name a few. That each challenge was successfully dealt with in turn suggests strongly that, historically speaking, Almondco's members and leaders, committed to a democratic cooperative decision-making methodology, viewed obstacles more as *incentives* to action than *barriers* to progress.

Our attention now turns to other macro and micro factors that also contributed to the success of Almondco.[15]

16.6 Macro factors

16.6.1 The role of the state

No business achieves success on its own and Almondco was no exception, benefitting from governmental, institutional, legal, and tax-payer subsidized supports. For instance, the South Australian Parliament and Registrar of Industrial and Provident Societies provided suitable legislative, regulatory, and administrative frameworks to make the cooperative possible. Government loans enabled growth. Government settlement schemes and public and private irrigation schemes helped the almond industry to become a reality. Sympathetic taxation consideration in recognition of the company's dual economic and social objectives, assisted. A Commonwealth Government tariff saved the cooperative from extinction in the 1970s. And at a time of rampant deregulation, the Almond Board of Australia (ABA) was formed in 2002, a statutory body designed to represent growers' interests. Without proper certification, quarantine, and food-safety safeguards, the industry could never have flourished. The contributions of agriculture departments and agronomic research centers and general educational and training institutions need also be considered when accounting for the success of Almondco.

16.6.2 The role of economic, social, and cultural contexts

For decades, Almondco members successfully navigated their tiny vessel of "self-help" cooperation true to the star of democratic ownership and control. However, to describe or explain how Almondco was molded by

---

[14] The Chairman's Report in Almondco Ltd. *Annual Report* 2013–14.

[15] Discussion drawn from conversations and correspondence with Almondco Ltd. Members and Board, 2014–18.

changes in the economic, political, social, and cultural contexts spanning seven decades would be far too rash an undertaking for this chapter. Suffice it to say, nothing stood still long enough in the period for the cooperative company to develop the symptoms of degenerative complacency, as reference to a summary of key social and economic world events given below will indicate.

Nuclear warfare desecrated the Earth for the first and, hopefully, the last time the year after the cooperative was formed. In the postwar reconstruction boom that followed, when cooperative idealism, protectionism, regulated markets, and centralized industrial relations prevailed, the cooperative struggled but survived, buffeted thereafter by the combined impacts of the Cold War, wars in Korea and Vietnam, Organization of the Petroleum Exporting Countries oil-price hikes, globalization, deregulation, privatization, the waning of trade unionism, the rise of China, the collapse of the Soviet Union, the triumph of neoliberalism and the emergence of consumer society, perennial regional warfare, mass migration, population displacement, transformative and disruptive technology, growing wealth disparities within and between nations, and a global financial crisis, all occurring in the potentially suffocating context of climate change. That the cooperative should not only *survive* but *prosper* in this turbulent ocean of change stands as testament to the dedication of members, the quality of their leadership, and the conservative resilience of the cooperative idea.

16.7 Micro factors

16.7.1 Changes in the business model

It may seem surprising, then, given this volatile background how little the company's business model actually *changed* over the decades. But as farmers are wont to say, "Why fix what ain't broke?"

Similarly, Almondco's financial structure remained remarkably stable, consistently placing a higher priority on grower-returns than on shareholder dividends. Rather than issuing new shares, growth generally was funded through debt and, in particular, tax-effective guaranteed government loans available to cooperatives.

One change, however, was momentous, that is, adapting the one-person one-vote principle to reflect shares broadly proportionate to the volume of supply whilst maintaining democratic ownership and control. The longer-term implications of this remain to be seen as the cooperative company develops new policies suited to generational change and succession planning. Nevertheless, it is fair to say that the company's business model, adapting across decades to fluid and challenging commercial contexts through a process of democratic member participation, remained remarkably stable.

16.7.2 Organizational, governance, and cultural factors contributing to success

Ultimately, however, Almondco's success is attributable to the commitment of members, the quality of their products, the skills and dedication of management and employees, and the governance, management, and developmental strategies adopted by the board. Almondco's primary *purpose* has always been to provide members with the services they need while delivering the best returns achievable and retaining ownership and control in growers' hands. In this mission, the cooperative company has been demonstrably successful. Time and time again the membership sent forward quality leadership (and more recently external directors with specialist knowledge) to drive growth through a skilled grower-centered board, which, at time of writing, consists of four grower directors, two independent directors, and a managing director. The other important change was in 1996 to allow an independent director to be appointed chairman. This allowed skilled people to be chairmen without the need to be a grower, and avoided some of the difficulties of the dual grower/chairman role. With few exceptions, highly-motivated directors served selflessly in the best interests of growers as a whole, whether large or small, supported by a competent and dedicated management team convening monthly to deal with arising business and identify emerging issues.

Almondco boards have traditionally encouraged member participation and remained responsive to members' business savvy, achievable only through the lived experience of farmers. Guided by such practical "grass-roots" advice, boards have stayed focused on core business and have avoided treating growers and shareholders as separate and competing stakeholders—simply because members would not permit them to; cooperative producers know what's best for them and make sure their company does too.

In Almondco's cooperative business culture, everyone shares a sense of obligation in advancing the best interests of growers, many of whom are *known personally* by directors, management, and employees. This, in turn, creates a high level of trust both *within* the company and *between* it and the people with whom it does business, thus, improving productivity and competitiveness. This has been no more evident than in the bold decisions taken by the board to install a modern plant and equipment, not simply to stay *abreast* of the competition, but to actually set the industry *benchmark*.

16.8 Degeneration or staying true to cooperative principles?

Cooperatives, like all other businesses, are susceptible to degeneration and Almondco was at all times required to tread carefully in managing its way through this tendency. Did it stay true to cooperative principles in the

process? And do its resilience and durability demonstrate that business degeneration is *not* inevitable in a market capitalist system?

The answer to both questions would seem to be in the affirmative. Reference to the International Co-operative Alliance (ICA) Statement of Co-operative Identity suggests Almondco *did* stay true to core cooperative principles and was at all stages a self-help organization controlled by members; dedicated to autonomy and independence; offering voluntary, open membership to anyone able to use its services; and enabling the direct economic participation of producers, who retained control of their investments. Whilst the principles of democratic member-control and voluntary and open membership were adapted to suit the prevailing business realities, this large, multifaceted cooperative company consistently conducted its affairs democratically and fairly in the interests of *all* members, never losing sight of *why* it existed or what it *excelled* at, namely receiving, pooling, and processing quality almonds on behalf of owner-suppliers with no external shareholders, unknown investors, or stock exchanges taking a share on the way.

Observance of principle alone, however, does not adequately explain Almondco's success in negotiating the business degeneration problem and nonfinancial factors have been at least as important, for example, consistently producing the best returns per kilogram of product supplied relative to competitors; providing quality services reliably; and supplying markets with quality products, engendering, in turn, that most valuable of all intangible assets—supplier and customer *trust*.

A long-term study of cooperative history suggests that members will continue to support a cooperative so long as it can be trusted to fulfill its *dual* economic *and* social needs. Heeding this, Almondco never once defined success solely in economic terms. Growers chose to join and stay with the company, not simply because of the generally better returns available, important as these were, but because the business was *run* cooperatively, meaning in a practical sense that it treated them fairly, consistently, and respectfully with no special treatment for anyone including major suppliers. They chose to join and support their cooperative because they knew how it empowered them, enabling them to give expression to personal and practical experience, their own ethical standards, and social objectives in the conduct of their business affairs, thereby satisfying economic *and* social aspirations; Almondco was a business members trusted and felt *good* about.

16.9 Cooperative principles

16.9.1 Education and training

At time of writing, Almondco employs approximately 140 people in its South Australian Riverland plants and up to 8 at the Riverina plant. Widely seen as an employer of choice, the cooperative company encourages all senior employees to undertake training in areas relevant to their position, for example, courses for cooperative businesses conducted by the Business Council of Co-operatives and Mutuals (BCCM), which includes a module on ICA principles, along with other relevant programs run by the Institute of Company Directors.

In light of the scientific proof of their health benefits and as demand for almonds and almond products grew, Almondco was required to install ever more sophisticated plants and equipment. Doing so safely and efficiently required training personnel in high-level technical skills, improved production methods, and preventative maintenance, always with an eye to occupational health and safety, especially in the seasonal rush when management, staff, skilled workers, and machines were required to work longer and even more efficiently than usual to turn out quality products on time.

16.9.2 Cooperating with other cooperatives

The ICA principles encourage cooperatives to cooperate with each other in educating the public about cooperation. The extent to which Almondco applies this principle is not clear from sources, but the cooperative company's affiliation with the BCCM, generally seen as Australia's peak cooperative and mutual-business industry body and that includes strong educational and advocacy elements in its services, suggests it understands the importance of the concept.

16.9.3 Concern for members and community

Almondco's focus has always been its members, but, in addition, the sense of mutual obligation and trust traditionally permeating the company's *internal* operations has extended to a feeling of *responsibility* for the communities in which it operates. This is because growers understand and take pride in the fact that surpluses (less costs and provision for growth) are *returned* to local communities, not siphoned off by remote investors, meaning more wealth is retained in the local area, which, through the multiplier effect, creates more prosperous and harmonious regional economies—the cooperative way.

16.10 Future challenges

To meet future challenges Almondco will need to demonstrate a continued ability to:

- fund necessary and suitable expansion;
- preserve existing plants and equipment;
- consistently and reliably meet customer demands;
- retain key staff living in the local area;
- manage generational change;

- resolve the question of disproportionate representation;
- match and meet investor-funded competition;
- function as a socially and environmentally responsible citizen;
- sustain the case for retaining its cooperative structure.

Traditionally Almondco's suppliers have been predominantly family-owned farming businesses, but, more recently, super and pension funds, managed investment, and tax-driven schemes have seen a number of large Australian and overseas corporate growers take membership. Satisfying the demands of these large entities brings challenges of its own and the board must stay constantly on the alert for a possible preemptive move detrimental to small-scale producers. This requires something of an intuitive "sixth" sense capable of detecting emerging problems and taking timely steps to resolve these while discovering paths to the common good. With 4 suppliers controlling approximately 60% of shares and 10 controlling approximately 80%, this is not always straightforward, but so long as democratic ownership *and* control remain important to growers, Almondco's resilient history suggests it is manageable.

16.11 Lessons to be learned

CAP was formed by farmers in 1944 as a democratically owned and controlled business to eliminate exploitative "middle-men" and improve returns.

Growing from humble origins and initially highly unstable, CAP's successful direct descendent, Almondco, provides important lessons for managing tensions *within* a cooperative and *between* a cooperative and the economic, social, and cultural contexts in which it functions; possibly of value to national and international cooperative movements seeking to make cooperation and cooperatives better known.[16]

Almondco has shown how success devolves upon member commitment to cooperation, the quality of their products, and the practical governance, management, and development strategies they adopt.

The cooperative company's success demonstrates the importance of remaining responsive and adaptive to fluid changes in economic, social, and cultural contexts in managing the degenerative–regenerative business-cycle.

It shows how producers who value the principles of democratic ownership and control are well equipped to withstand forces that might otherwise impel them toward integration with conventional for-profit business models in which they have less or no control.

The Almondco experience confirms that a business simultaneously fulfilling members' economic *and* social aspirations is likely to retain a cooperative identity and that where the alternative is forfeiting democratic ownership and control, the adaptation of "pure" cooperative principles in response to prevailing business realities may be necessary.

Almondco's success demonstrates that, whether in a conservative or bold, expansive disposition, boards must stay focused on members' needs and the core business with producer returns *always* the priority and *not* shareholder dividends.

---

[16] See Charles Gould in Co-op News, February 9, 2013: International Co-operative Alliance (ICA) *Blueprint for a Cooperative Decade: the 2020 Vision*. The ICA, based in Brussels, Belgium, is an independent nongovernmental organization formed in 1895, which unites, represents, and serves cooperative organizations of which there are more than three million around the world comprising over one billion memberships. The blueprint is designed to make the cooperative form of business the acknowledged leader in economic, social, and environmental sustainability; a business model preferred by people and the world's fastest growing form of enterprise.

It demonstrates how care must be taken in growing membership to not dilute the original bond of association that members have little or nothing in common. Communication gaps, differences of opinion, and personality clashes are inevitable in a business, but manageable and potentially beneficial in a democratically-controlled association where the nature and potential of cooperation is fully understood and valued.

Finally, and a corollary of the challenges mentioned, the Almondco "hands on" experience in participatory democratic management demonstrates how member education in cooperative philosophy, whether achieved formally or informally, is as important to an enterprise's well-being as simply training in cooperative business principles.[17]

16.12 Conclusion

Almondco's impressive historical record demonstrates how a large agricultural cooperative company can grow from small beginnings by successfully managing tensions between the contesting imperatives of commercial viability and democratic ownership and control and by maintaining a sensible balance between grower expectations and fluctuating market conditions.

Today, after nearly 75 years of solid achievement and overcoming many obstacles, Almondco stands as a bastion against a world ultimately controlled by megacorporations, where individuals are mere servants of powerful vested interests with no scope for independence and individual initiative.

[17]   Hans Munkner: *The Four Threats to Co-operative Identity* in Report: New South Wales Registry of Co-operative Societies, Key Issues Conference, Sydney, October 19−20, 1995.

Agricultural cooperatives in Asia: state, market, governance, and sustainability

Yashavantha Dongre

University of Mysore, Mysore, India

17.1 Introduction

Cooperatives are inward looking economic organizations catering primarily to the needs of their members. As differentiated from state-owned and investor-owned organizations, they are driven by members for their own benefits. In this sense, cooperatives will have a captive clientele, develop need-based businesses, and provide for member centrality, networking, and collective decision-making and, therefore are stable and resilient organizations (Johnson, Boarda Rodrigues, Shaw, & Vicari, 2016). However, in reality, a lot of cooperatives face both structural and market-related challenges. When they confine to their membership, they may not be able to achieve the advantages of economies of scale and when they look beyond membership for their business interest, they will have to face stiff competition from private enterprises as well as state-owned organizations (Nakkiran, 2006). At the same time, cooperatives are seen to be a part of civil society and, hence, are expected to set benchmarks for better governance and ethical practices of business. Added to this, governments in many countries treat cooperatives as windows to

channel state programs to the needy. It is even opined that "agricultural cooperatives are related to the state as an interest group with the purpose of furthering their own economic interests" (Fregidou-Malama, 2000). This is especially true of agricultural cooperatives since they are in a highly sensitive domain of the economy. All this makes the ground realities for cooperatives rather complicated.

Agricultural cooperatives were the first type of cooperatives to emerge in most Asian countries. Obviously at the time of genesis of the cooperative movement in these countries, agriculture was the main economic activity and the people and economies were largely dependent on the agricultural sector. By around the 1890s, agricultural cooperatives were functioning both in Asian countries like India and Pacific countries like Australia and New Zealand (Birchall, 1997). Western influence and the direct involvement of state in promoting cooperatives are visible features of cooperatives in general and agricultural cooperatives in particular in most Asian countries.

Based on the nature of enterprises, both cooperative and other forms, different interpretations of organizational features are made. The most notable one in the Asian context comes from Witt and Redding (2014). They have classified Asian economies into (post) socialist economies, advanced city economies, emerging Southeast Asian economies, advanced Northeast Asian economies, and Japan. The analysis further suggests that with the exception of Japan, which bears features of a developed welfare state, others are either predatory or developmental or a mix of both with some being more developmental and others leaning more toward being predatory. It is also held that the nature of enterprises in the economy has a lot of bearing on the state of the economy at a given point of time, essentially pointing out that there are varieties of capitalism that are the result of the political and economic status of the country.

Another important work that helps us build the context for analyzing the situation of cooperatives is that of Kurimoto (2017). He classifies Asian economies as socialist market economies (P.R. China and Vietnam), developmental market economies (India, Singapore, Malaysia, and the Philippines), state coordinated market economies (Japan, Korea, and Taiwan), and liberal market economies (Australia and New Zealand). Kurimoto's work is of greater importance to us here since he provides a comprehensive background of Asian economies and posits cooperatives in the specific socioeconomic context.

None the less, both these works underline the fact that the Asia Pacific region is highly diverse and the "one size fits all" approach does not suit while understanding and analyzing these economies. The case examples discussed in previous chapters well illustrate these features.

17.2 Case studies

The case studies presented in the preceding chapters represent a diverse domain in terms of their size, legal status as well as the activities

they are involved in. Almandco in Australia is a primary cooperative owned and controlled by 143 almond growers. It is a producer's cooperative focusing primarily on a single crop. Similarly, JA Hadano of Japan is also a primary cooperative, but unlike Almandco, it is a multistakeholder and multipurpose cooperative. The Rajarambapu group of cooperatives from India, is a conglomerate of primary cooperatives. Here one agricultural cooperative created many other cooperatives to respond to the needs of farmer members. Van Duc Cooperative of Vietnam is also a primary cooperative, but has both formal members with share in profit and informal members who make use of the services of the cooperative with no share in profits. This is primarily an agricultural marketing cooperative. Ruoheng Watermelon Cooperative in China is again a primary cooperative, but it has the unique feature of having members and quasi members and operates through a set of hybrid principles that combine the idea of cooperatives and corporates. The national agricultural cooperative federation (NACF) in Korea, on the other hand, is a federated organization functioning at the national level with primary agricultural cooperatives as members.

Diverse they are in terms of their size, organizational structure, functions, and legal status, but there are a host of commonalities as well. That all of them have their activities built around agriculture and for the common good of agriculturists is one thing, but the more pronounced is that they have all faced similar challenges in the pursuit of their goals. All five cases presented represent successful cooperatives in their respective countries. They have all been in existence for a long time, have evolved over changing political and economic contexts, and established themselves firmly in the market through struggles and innovative strategies. It is, therefore pertinent to put them in comparative perspective.

17.3 Legal regime

Interestingly, the legal regimes governing cooperatives in the countries that the case studies have come from, have a long history, but in all of them the legislations have been under review until recently. Japan has had a stable legal environment with cooperative laws being put in place on sectoral lines. However, the laws are still in the making in the case of some sectors like workers cooperatives (Okayasu, 2006). Legislation related to agricultural cooperatives were amended during 2015 (Akeda, 2015) with a focus on delinking agricultural cooperatives from state support/patronage. There are major legal changes in the two centrally planned economies in Asia, with China promulgating a new legislation in 2006 to facilitate the establishment of farmers specialized cooperatives and Vietnam putting in place its first national level cooperative legislation in 2012. Korea, which is clearly an economically advanced liberal democratic nation (developmental state), has enacted a comprehensive cooperative legislation recently. In India too, there has been a major shift in policy and legal domains. With the 97th Constitutional Amendment approved in parliament in 2012 greater functional autonomy has been provided to cooperatives. These changes in the legal regime have brought greater legitimacy and functional autonomy to agricultural cooperatives. It is important to note that the legal regimes are undergoing changes driven primarily by changes in the market structures and consequent changes in political priorities. It is observed that the "majority of the developing countries in Africa, Asia and Latin America have been confronted since the mid-1980s with the effects of economic liberalization, globalization and structural adjustment. In addition, many of them have introduced internal democratic reforms and decentralized their national administrative structures and decision-making

processes. These developments have had a considerable impact on the cooperative movements of the developing world, especially in those countries where cooperatives were considered part of the government structure or an arm of the ruling party. As a result, the cooperative legislation of many developing countries has been subject to profound reform" (ILO, 2001). Be it Japan, economically the most advanced Asian nation, Korea, considered to be a developed country by far, India, one of the fastest growing economies with a long legacy of liberal democracy, or China and Vietnam, with state-controlled economies slowly integrating into the globalized market system, all have felt the need for or come under pressure to make changes in the legal regimes governing cooperatives. Obviously, the landscape for agricultural cooperatives will change faster in the years to come.

17.4 Role of state

As demonstrated in the case study of Almondco, the state in Australia and other major countries of the Pacific region have largely accorded greater freedom and autonomy to cooperatives. However, in the Asian region, where the agricultural sector is important in terms of its contribution to GDP and/or in terms of the share of population depending on agriculture for their livelihood, the perception of the state that the sector that contributes more in terms of income and employment needs both state support and regulation has clearly influenced the operations and governance of agricultural cooperatives. However, even in countries where agriculture has long ceased to be an important sector in terms of income and employment (Japan and Korea), we can see governments' reluctance to give up their control on agricultural cooperatives. It could be because agriculture still remains a politically sensitive sector, if not important in economic terms.

In all postsocialist states of Asia—Indonesia, the Philippines, and India—government activism in terms of promoting agricultural cooperatives, providing patronage to them, monitoring and controlling them as well as using them to push through some state sponsored programs to people are witnessed. Interestingly, even in a development state like Korea agricultural cooperatives were highly state directed until recently as evidenced through the case study of the NACF.

The role of the state in relation to cooperatives is a highly debated and contested issue in the Asian region. While government support systems certainly helped agricultural cooperatives to sustain, they also lead to dual problems of inefficiency and political interference. Overcoming these challenges seem to be the most difficult phase faced by many agricultural cooperatives. It emerges from the case studies that agricultural cooperatives have always had close proximity to government and cooperatives were struggling to become more independent. But "as a result of the changing environment in the developing countries and transition economies the roles of the State and cooperative apex organizations in cooperative development have altered. While some countries have taken radical measures to extricate the State and Party from the cooperative movement, ... others have developed 'planned transition' alternatives for a 'softer' reorganization of the State to enable it to provide the necessary support services and the cooperative movement to shift from state-sponsorship to autonomy" (ILO, 2001).

17.5 Social capital

The role of social capital in the sustainable development of institutions and economies has been well articulated (Hasan & Lyons, 2004). The much-acclaimed work on Asian business systems of Witt and Redding (2014), has brought home some interesting features in Asian countries in relation to social capital. Interpersonal trust is high in all countries, whereas institutional trust is low and negative in most countries. Institutions like cooperatives, especially agricultural cooperatives that are mostly institutions for and by rural people with lesser education and professional skills, find this situation both positive and negative. Cooperatives as member-driven organizations need a high degree of mutual trust, which seems to be available. This means both organizing a cooperative and operating at a certain level of efficiency are possible. In fact, the success stories of many agricultural cooperatives in India are related primarily to the mutuality and trust among the member community. The case study on Rajarambapu Cooperative quite well evidences the fact that farmer members have full faith in the members of the board and, in turn, the leadership believes that the members are always available when support is needed. In the case of JA Hadano, the author has observed that "inherent social capital, paired with the employee led initiatives to foster organizational social capital are what make JA Hadano an interesting case study." The cases of Almondco, Ruoheng Watermelon Cooperative, and Van Duc also reveal that social capital has played a large part in overcoming challenges and savoring success.

However, there is a dichotomy when we look at institutional trust. The reason for people having a lower level of institutional trust could be because institutions like states and businesses care more for themselves than for the common man. The case studies reveal such a tendency among cooperatives too. This is evidenced by the case of the NACF in Korea. It is largely true of a lot of well-performing agricultural cooperatives in India as well. Institutional interest becomes central and members' interests take second fiddle. This could be the reason for low institutional trust. Balancing member interest with institutional interest is probably the greatest challenge that agricultural cooperatives in Asia need to overcome.

Maybe a better strategy to overcome this challenge is to not make the cooperative too big of an organization. It is reported through many European experiences that when agricultural cooperatives became too big, member participation and member interest were neglected in the eagerness to strengthen the cooperative institution and, therefore there were "bee hiving effects," with groups of members moving away from the cooperative and starting their own cooperative. In this background, the case of Rajarambapu Cooperative group may be said to be following a better strategy. Instead of creating one big cooperative with different functional divisions, they created different cooperatives with optimal sizes for each functional area. This may be is similar to the Mondragon group, where there are a large number of smaller cooperatives.

17.6 Addressing the challenges

Each of the cooperatives under study had faced periodic challenges on their way to success. These challenges were related to both the external environment and the internal environment. Some of the common challenges faced and strategies followed are discussed here.

The State: As already discussed, in almost all countries the state has been closely associated with the promotion and regulation of agricultural cooperatives. The majority of cooperatives, the cases of which are presented here, had to deal with a dominant state at one point or another. They did benefit through state patronage, but also had to forego part of their autonomy. It is good that state withdrawal became inevitable, though not due to the efforts of cooperatives, but to changes in market dynamics, and these cooperatives got the space to operate with greater freedom. There is reluctance on the part of the state to withdraw in some countries (India and Vietnam), but the extent and intensity of state intervention has certainly decreased.

The Market: Globalization and the consequent changes in market dynamics has been a common problem for almost all cooperatives under study. The dominance of private players in the market, the entry of global players into the local market, and the unstable agricultural price situation, among others, are identified as major challenges. Cooperatives have tried to address these issues through a series of strategies such as diversification of activities, adoption of technology, brand building, maintaining closer ties with member/clientele groups, etc. It is important to note that these market issues were addressed through a professional approach, but without compromising on cooperative identity.

The Governance: Cooperatives being peoples' organizations need to set benchmarks of good governance for other organizations. Of course, good governance, that of ensuring transparency, accountability, democracy, and rule of law in the day to day operations, is a prerequisite for long-term sustenance as well. All the cooperatives in the present study have tried to ensure this. Cooperatives being multistakeholder organizations, all constituencies were brought on board through member interaction strategies. Representative general assemblies were put in place where cooperatives had a large number of members. New businesses were developed with due regard to the changing needs of members. Optimally sized organization structures were created to do away with cost escalations. It is such multipronged strategies that have helped these cooperatives to achieve sustainable growth and position themselves on par with the best of the organizations in their sector.

17.7 Conclusion

Are the challenges faced by agricultural cooperatives different in different countries depending on their political and economic status? The political system—whether the country is a liberal democracy or a conservative regime—does not seem to make notable difference. There are democratic regimes that are not so inclined to provide a conducive environment for agricultural cooperatives, but treat them as an arm of the state, however, at the same time, there have been more conservative regimes that have promoted cooperatives on a large scale. However, the status of the economy and changes in the market dynamics correlate much better and provide a better context to explain the performance of agricultural cooperatives. As the economies move from agrarian to manufacturing/service-oriented economies, as the overall growth of the economy picks up and they move from a state of underdevelopment to developmental economies, and as liberal market policies are pursued, the nature of the working of cooperatives seems to change from state control to greater autonomy and from single service to multipurpose orientation.

References

Akeda, T. (2015). *A study of the latest amendments to the agricultural co-operatives act of Japan.* Papers & Reports, Norinchukin Research Institute Co. Ltd., Tokyo. <https://www.nochuri.co.jp/english/pdf/rpt_20161026.pdf>.

Birchall, J. (1997). *The international co-operative movement* (p. 280) Manchester University Press (Paperback).

Fregidou-Malama, M. (2000). The relationship between agricultural co-operatives and the State in Sweden: The legislative process. *Annals of Public and Co-operative Economics, 71*(1), 79–103.

Hasan, S., & Lyons, M. (Eds.), (2004). *Social capital in Asian sustainable development management.* New York: Nova Science Publishers, Inc.

ILO. (2001). *Report V(I) — Promotion of co-operatives.* International Labour Office, Geneva. <http://www.ilo.org/public/english/standards/relm/ilc/ilc89/rep-v-1.htm#3.2>. The status of cooperative legislation.

Johnson, H., Boarda Rodrigues, A., Shaw, L., & Vicari, S. (2016). What makes rural co-operatives resilient in developing countries. *Journal of International Development, 28*(1), 89–111.

Kurimoto, A. (2017). *Current state of co-operative research in Asia.* Paper presented at the ICA-AP Research Conference, New Delhi.

Nakkiran, S. (2006). *Co-operative management: Principles and techniques.* New Delhi: Deep & Deep.

Okayasu, K. (2006). *Worker co-operatives in Japan.* Unpublished paper presented at Expert Group Meeting on Co-operatives and Employment, Shanghai, China, 15–19 May 2006. <http://okayasu.tokyo/_files2.pdf/Japan_Worker_Coops.pdf>.

Witt, M. A., & Redding, G. (Eds.), (2014). *The oxford handbook of Asian business systems.* Oxford University Press.

Consumer co-ops

The success of the Saigon Co-op in the retail sector of Vietnam

Nguyen Anh Tru, Dang Thi Kim Hoa and Nguyen Trong Tuynh

Faculty of Accounting and Business Management, Vietnam National University of Agriculture, Hanoi, Vietnam

18.1 Introduction

According to International Co-operative Alliance (ICA) cooperatives are the largest social movements in history. Citing data from 145 countries across the world, it is estimated that there are over one billion people who are members of cooperatives and globally they have generated US$2.98 trillion in annual revenue in 2014. Cooperatives make up a significant part of national economies—for instance, in France there are 147 million cooperative clients and members in a country with a population of 65 million people. The cooperative economy accounts for more than 10% of the gross domestic product (GDP) of four countries, including New Zealand (20%), The Netherlands (18%), France (18%), and Finland (14%) (United Nations, 2014). The Asian cooperative sector is the largest.

The consumer cooperative enterprise has become an increasingly noteworthy business form. Currently cooperatives that rely on customer ownership can be found in various sectors of the economy, including banking, insurance, and retail, where they account for about a trillion US dollars in annual revenue (Talonen, Jussila, Saarijärvi, & Rintamäki, 2016). A consumer cooperative, or consumer-managed firm, can be defined as being managed by elected representatives of at least some of its retail customers, the latter constituting its membership (Carson, 1977). The role of consumer cooperatives has increased because of their success in improving management efficiency and developing a financial basis (Hall & Hall, 1982).

Consumer cooperatives emerged along with industrial capitalism and the exploitation of lower-income social classes. The Rochdae Pioneers in England founded the cooperative movement when they opened their first shop in 1844 to bring quality, well-priced food to the working class. Currently studies in Denmark have identified that there are complex motivating factors of the emergence of consumer cooperatives, namely, cooperative ideology, survival of local shops, and nutrition (Bager, 1988).

Cooperative theorists argue that consumer cooperatives are the best possible representatives

203

for consumers in the marketplace (Nilsson, 1985). According to the Rochdale principles, the most successful and enduring working-class influence of cooperatives is to articulate and maintain alternatives to joint-stock (neo)liberal capitalism. Operations of Scottish consumer cooperatives should be implemented in a different manner compared to the Rochdale principles through redistributing economic value and convincing and reassuring members that their behaviors make a significant contribution. In addition, alternative models constructed by voluntary means that displace the dominant political-economic paradigm are unlikely to succeed (Watts, 2017). In the context of decreasing return to scale, consumer cooperatives contribute more to social welfare when operating on behalf of all their consumers (Marini, Polidori, Teobaldelli, & Zevi, 2015). In The Netherlands risks related to cost sharing and expected benefits are key factors determining the participation of consumers in cooperatives (Sadowski, 2017).

The issues related to the theory of the development of consumer cooperatives in Asia and the Asia-Pacific have been discussed by scholars over recent years, providing a greater understanding of consumer cooperatives. In Japan the amount of equity that a consumer cooperative can raise by issuing membership shares is greater than what a capitalist firm can raise by issuing shares (Mikami, 2015). In the Republic of Korea, profitability and cooperative size have a significantly negative effect on leverage of consumer cooperatives, but tangibility and growth have a significantly positive effect on coops due to different characteristics in governance, costs of bankruptcy, agency, informational asymmetry, and securities issuance (Seo & Choi, 2016). Expansion of members participating in consumer cooperatives in Malaysia is fostered when members are also shareholders, stakeholders, and owners of the cooperative as depicted by the principles (Hasbullah, Mahajar, & Salleh, 2014). Study

results of Nigeria show that there is a significant correlation between consumers' cooperatives and household food security, and among educational status, income, and food security. However, family size negatively affects food security in that the greater the family size, the greater the level of food insecurity (Adebo & Oladebe, 2010).

18.2 The socialist republic of Vietnam and its cooperatives

Historically cooperatives have made tremendous contributions to the socioeconomic development of Vietnam, such as generating employment, reducing poverty, improving the livelihood of members, as well as producing and providing products and services to the society. The cooperative economy is considered to be one of five economic components in Vietnam and the government has shown great interest in furthering the development of the cooperative sector.

After the unification of Vietnam in 1975 the development of cooperatives expanded rapidly in provinces and cities. Cooperatives contributed significantly to the process of economic development in Vietnam. For example, by 1975, there were 17,000 agricultural cooperatives in Northern Vietnam covering 96% of farm households. In 1986 there were 79,000 cooperatives in several sectors. In 1986, consumer cooperatives had accounted for about 20% of total domestic retail turnover and procured about 60% of the agricultural products in the whole country (ICA, n.d.).

However, in the late 1980s, Vietnam implemented the Reform (DOI MOI) of the economic management mechanism. Specifically, the centrally planned economy has been eradicated and substituted by international economic liberalization, and establishing a market-oriented economy. Therefore cooperatives in Vietnam moved into a crisis period due to the adverse impacts of the new competitive economy, inconsistent management, and inappropriate structures. Consequently cooperatives faced hardships and many had to be dissolved. For example, by December 1996, the number of cooperatives declined to 17,462, equivalent to 22.1% of the 1986 total.

By 2013 there was a slight rise in numbers to 19,800 cooperatives in Vietnam that accounted for 13.5 million members, equivalent to 25.4% of the labor force, and contributed 5% to the GDP. In 2014 the annual average profit of a cooperative accounted for VND246 million (US $11,000) (ICA, n.d.). However, the number of cooperatives began to decline again because Vietnam implemented the Cooperative Law in 2012 and a number of cooperatives dissolved due to inefficient operations, inconsistent business strategies, and weak competitive capacities (General Statistics Office of Vietnam, 2017).

This chapter aims to provide an overview of cooperatives in Vietnam though a study of Saigon Co-op (SC) the largest retailer in Vietnam with 17,000 employees and the winner of the best supermarket in Asia award on a number of occasions. SC demonstrated how an internationally competitive cooperative can be brought into existence by overcoming a number of obstacles with appropriate support. This chapter explores the nature of these obstacles, how they were overcome, and what factors contributed to SC's success.

This chapter is organized as follows. The foundation of SC is provided in Section 18.3. Section 18.4, presents the organizational structure, management, and business outcomes of SC. Factors affecting cooperative emergence in Vietnam are analyzed in Section 18.5. Section 18.6, examines factors contributing to the success of SC. Section 18.7, investigates current challenges faced by SC. The impacts of SC on the Vietnamese society are discussed in Section 18.8, and the Conclusion is presented in Section 18.9.

18.3 The foundation of Saigon Co-op

SC has been successful due to the creation of a new hybrid cooperative model by forming a partnership with other successful national cooperatives, thereby demonstrating how the consumer cooperative model can be scaled up.

The first supermarket (Co.opmart) was established on February 9, 1996, in 189 C Cong Quynh, District 1, Ho Chi Minh City with the collaboration and assistance of cooperatives from Japan, Singapore, and Sweden. Co. opmart emerged as a new type of retail outlet and this is pertinent to the development strategy of Ho Chi Minh City Committee.

However, one year later, due to inefficient operations of SC, the managerial board decided to reconsider the operation of the cooperative in which 100% of working capital came from the contribution of the Ho Chi Minh City People's Committee.

In 2002 the first Co.opmart supermarket was founded in Can Tho province (Mekong River Delta Region, Vietnam) and then a number of Co.opmarts were established in provinces and cities in the southern and central regions of the country.

In 2010 a Co.opmart supermarket was opened in the capital, Ha Noi, the first SC supermarket in Northern Vietnam. By 2010 the total number of Co.opmart supermarkets in country had reached 50.

On May 3, 2013, SC opened a Co.opXtraplus hypermarket in the Thu Duc district, Ho Chi Minh City. The Co.opXtra and Co.opXtraplus are two hypermarket chains and are a joint venture between SC and Singapore National Trade Union Congress (NTUC) FairPrice Co-operative (FairPrice). The joint venture operated with an initial investment of US$6 million, in which 64% was contributed by SC and the rest (36%) by FairPrice. The purpose of this venture was to expand the two hypermarket chains throughout the country. Target customers of the Co.opXtra include individuals and households, while Co.

opXtraPlus focuses on enterprises, organizations, schools, hotels, and restaurants.

SC opened their first SenseCity shopping Centre in Ninh Kieu district, Can Tho city in 2014. The SenseCity shopping Centre was established by SC Investment Development Company (SCID), which is a member of SC. Operations of the SenseCity shopping center include fashion and beauty business, entertainments, and food courts. The target customers of the SenseCity shopping center are middle-income clients.

By April 2016 there were 82 Co.opmart supermarkets operating in Vietnam, of which 32 supermarkets were in Ho Chi Minh City and 50 in other provinces and cities.

18.4 Organizational structure, management, and business outcomes of Saigon Co-op

SC has been an economic and social success on the regional scale. The business activities of SC comprise retailing, producing consumer goods, importing and exporting, and distributing goods. The functions of SCID include scouting for appropriate land on which to develop Co. opmart supermarkets, attracting investment in Co.opmart supermarkets, and trading real estate for commercial purposes. Co.opmart supermarket is headed by a general manager. Under the general manager, there are four managers of the Co.opmart supermarket in Ho Chi Minh City, southern, central, and northern regions, respectively. These managers are in charge of managing the Co.opmart supermarkets in their areas (Fig. 18.1).

The Xtra hypermarket focuses on retailing consumer goods and providing restaurant and entertainment services to individual customers, households, and organizations. The Co.opmart is a supermarket chain managed by SC and sells consumer goods. Co.op Food is a food store chain owned by SC. Co-ops are members of SC that operate as convenience stores (Fig. 18.1).

Currently in Vietnam, SC stores have appeared in more than 40 provinces and cities, and SC owns more than 500 stores and supermarkets in the country, including more than 90 Co.opmart supermarkets, three hypermarkets, Co-op Food, Coops, commercial centers, and a

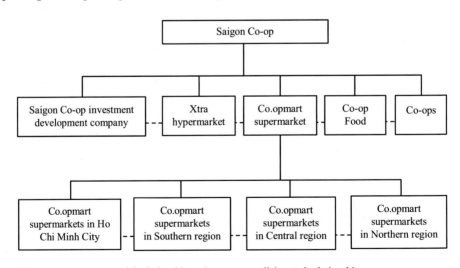

Notes: ———— : managerial relationship and - - - - - : collaborated relationship

FIGURE 18.1   Members of Saigon Co-op.

retail channel on the Ho Chi Minh Television Co.op (HTV Co.op). HTV Co.op is an online purchasing channel, which is a result of cooperation between SC and Ho Chi Minh City Television. On October 1, 2011, the first program of HTV Co.op was broadcasted.

According to Do Quoc Huy, the director of SC, by 2017 the total revenue of SC reached VND30,000 billion (or US$1.3 billion), which is an increase of 7% compared to that in 2016 in which the revenue of Co.opExtra rose by 35%, followed by Co.op Food (20%) and Co.opmart supermarket (10%−12%) (Ha, 2018). The total amount of capital owned by SC accounts for 5000 billion VND and total revenue reaches VND300 billion annually. In 2017 the growth of SC exports increased by about 30% and labor productivity and the average income of employees increased. By 2017 a total of 130 stores were opened across the country and storage capacity of warehouses increased by 30%. By 2017 the total authorized capital of SC reached VND3200 billion (or US$138 million).

From 2016 onward, SC attempted to overcome its difficulties and has achieved remarkable outcomes, such as: (1) retaining the title of Vietnam's leading retailer and to be included in top the 500 leading retailers in Asia and Asia-Pacific; (2) increasing sales by 11% compared to the same period of the previous year; (3) opening 42 new outlets (Co.opmart, Food Coop, and Smile Coop); (4) upgrading 186 stores by adjusting sale patterns and services; (5) contributing to stabilization of consumer goods markets in Ho Chi Minh City and Southeast region of Vietnam; (6) facilitating the movement of labor; (7) contributing to community activities by donating more than VND6 billion (or US$257 thousand) to the country's GDP; and (8) increasing employee income by 8.2% (PWKD, 2017).

The SC is a trade union of cooperatives and therefore its members voluntarily join by contributing capital and being approved by the SC board of members. The operation of SC is organized based on the Cooperative Law of Vietnam.

SC is working on how consumers can become members. The board of members has the highest right in making decisions. Cooperative members can elect representatives to attend the board of members to discuss and decide on SC matters; stand for election to the board of directors, board of controllers and other positions in SC; vote to select and grant authority to the board of directors, board of controllers, and other positions in SC; vote to select and grant authority to the board of directors, board of controllers, and other positions in SC; and submit opinions, questions, and require explanations from the board of directors and board of controllers concerning the activities of SC. The board of controllers are in charge of examining operations of the board of directors and other units of SC (SCID; Xtra hypermarket; Co.opmart supermarkets; Co-op Food, and Coops) (Fig. 18.2). Currently, SC has more than 17,000 employees. In SC there are nine members on the management board, while the control board has three members.

18.5 Factors affecting the emergence of cooperatives in Vietnam

The emergence of a cooperative and its subsequent success is dependent on a number of macro and micro factors. The macro factors include the state, civil society, and the market—these factors were all favorable for the successful start-up of SC.

18.5.1 The state

Across Asia the state has played a key role in spreading cooperatives; however, this function of the state is not always the most appropriate role. Cooperatives in Vietnam continue to evolve in a dialectical enabling encouraging

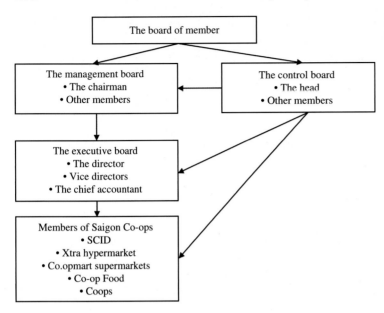

FIGURE 18.2 Organizational structure of Saigon Co-op.

relationship between the state and the cooperative movement with international cooperative principles enshrined in law. In Vietnam, cooperatives are still considered as the second-most important economic sector after stated-owned enterprises from the point of view of the government. SC has obtained support from the state in numerous ways, such as providing new technology, human resource investment, and trading activities. In particular there has been a resolution that provides cooperatives with a 50% reduction of rental fee for state-owned land. Besides this, SC operates as a cooperative and therefore it benefits from the market stimulus program and some noninterest loans from the government over the short term. The following demonstrates the importance of how the state views cooperatives:

- Cooperatives in Vietnam are encouraged under regulations and legal documentations such as the Cooperative Law, Decision 62, Decree 107, and Circular 44.
- The Cooperative Law was approved by the National Assembly on November 20,

2012. This law includes 9 chapters (64 articles) that regulate the establishment, organization, and operation of cooperatives in various sectors. This law is an important legal platform to supervise and adjust the operations of cooperatives.
- Decision 62 of the Prime Minister, issued on December 10, 2013, comprises 10 articles. The aim of this decision is to enhance cooperation and coordination in production, processing, and marketing of agricultural products.
- Decree 107 of the Government, issued on September 15, 2017, supervises the implementation of articles of the Cooperative Law.
- Circular 44 of the Ministry of Finance, issued on April 26, 1999, offers tax incentives for cooperatives.

A number of policies have been implemented in order to support cooperatives in Vietnam. That means cooperatives have to pay lower income taxes and registration fees than those of other firm types, such as limited liability company and joint stock company. According to Article 24 of Decree 193/ND-CP in 2013 issued by the government, cooperatives are supported by the state in terms of training managerial boards and members; participating in exhibitions and trade fairs; developing brands and electronic commerce transactions for cooperatives; adopting scientific and technological advances in production; accessing credit; and raising the cooperative's development fund.

18.5.2 Civil society

On May 12, 1989, the Ho Chi Minh City People's Committee (local party government) decided to transform a retail cooperative into the Saigon Trading Co-operatives (SC). SC carries out two missions, business and development of the cooperative. SC has operated as a cooperative based on collective ownership, independency, and self-responsibility with the consultancy of Sweden. The long-term objective of transforming the cooperative is to develop SC to become a modern retailer in the domestic market.

18.5.3 The market

SC was formed during the rising state of consumer spending. The value of retail sales in Vietnam rose sharply by VND0.48 trillion from VND2.18 trillion in 2014 to VND2.66 trillion in 2016. The growth of retail sales opened opportunities for domestic and foreign retailers. Historically the retail market of Vietnam has been dominated by local markets. However, the growth in the number of supermarkets and commercial centers reflects the change in structure of the retail sector in Vietnam as it transformed from traditional retailers to modern retailers, and this pattern also implies a change in the purchasing habits of consumers in this country. Satisfaction of consumers in the domestic market is an important factor contributing to success of SC. In reality, SC is contributing to change purchasing habits of consumers from traditional purchasing in wet markets to modern retail systems in Vietnam such as hypermarkets, supermarkets, and convenience stores.

18.6 Factors contributing to the success of Saigon Co-op

18.6.1 Operational strategy

The achievement of SC is a result of having state-of-the-art operational strategies in place that assisted SC to transform itself from an inefficient cooperative to a modern cooperative in Vietnam by identifying and overcoming obstacles. Operation as a cooperative along with the investment from the Ho Chi Minh City People's Committee by contributing 100% of its working capital has afforded SC more advantages than other cooperatives in the domestic market. For instance, SC is supported by local people's committees in finding land on which to build stores in convenient sites in Ho Chi Minh City and other provinces. Moreover, SC has obtained support and incentives from the central government in terms of credit and reducing income taxes.

18.6.2 Finance, skills, and technology

Working people starting a cooperative in a competitive market face a number of obstacles relating to access to finance, technology, and skills. SC resolved this by being a member of the global cooperative movement generally and as a member of ICA–Asia Pacific (ICA-AP). Thus SC was able to gain significant support from other cooperatives in the world such as Kraton Formosa Polymers Corporation (KFPC) of Sweden, Japanese Consumers' Co-operative Union (JCCU) of Japan, and NTUC

FairPrice of Singapore. These cooperatives supported SC in terms of sharing experience in cooperative management and retail activities.

For example, to set up the first supermarket in 1996 SC contacted KFPC in Sweden and regularly went to Europe to learn about supermarkets at the basic level. Every year SC sends a number of delegates to attend workshops or management training programs in Singapore, the Republic of Korea, and Japan hosted by ICA-AP, JCCU, and other cooperatives. The most successful case is the cooperation between SC and NTUC FairPrice, Singapore, which has been established as a joint venture company to set up a new brand, that is hypermarket Co-opXtra, and bringing the convenience store Cheers from Singapore to Vietnam.

18.6.3 Systems

Business targets and strategies of members of SC are planned every year. Managerial methods of SC include revenue contracts, inputs provision, and product codes control. Every year, revenue for the next year of Co.opmart supermarkets is contracted between SC and Co.opmart supermarkets. If Co.opmart supermarkets overcome contracted revenue, the surplus will be calculated as gains and losses, the rest is distributed to Co.opmarts, and then these supermarkets will give incentives to employees based on the regulation of SC. SC is in charge of providing products to all its hypermarkets, supermarkets, and convenience stores. If a product is sold slowly in a supermarket, this will be delivered and sold in another supermarket that has a stronger demand. To ensure adequate and sufficient commodities for the whole system, SC has made contracts with producers and suppliers such as enterprises, other cooperatives, and importers. Codes of products are managed strictly to avoid low-quality products from entering supermarkets.

18.6.4 Human resources

The total number of employees working for SC is for more than 17,000 people, of which the majority have worked in commercial centers and supermarkets. There are 45 employees working in the head office of SC in Ho Chi Minh City. The average salary of an employee who has worked as a vender and cleaner in a supermarket is about VND5−6 million a month and the salaries for managerial staff ranges from VND8 million to VND15 million a month. In addition, employees obtain further incentives (equivalent to the salary of 2−4 months) annually. Besides salary and incentives, health insurance, social insurance, and unemployment insurance for employees are covered by SC. Moreover, according to policy of SC, all employees are given annual health checks in order to enhance the social welfare for employees.

Employees are recruited from external or internal sources based on the procedure of SC. The procedure of recruitment includes receiving applications, reviewing these, interviewing, training, assessing after trainings, and signing contracts. A center for training employees has been established and is operated frequently with the help of 20 trainers. The role of this center is training managers and employees in skills and customer communication. An employee is often given a job based on their capacity and expectations and, as a result, employees for SC are enthusiastic and active in serving customers and many have worked for SC for more than a decade.

18.6.5 Marketing

The business philosophy of SC is to engage and to share in serving customers and this reflects the commitment of SC to customers in terms of creating values for its customers. This cooperative is attempting to become the leading retailer in Vietnam and to expand to the

Asia-Pacific market to create and offer the best benefits to customers and communities.

Various marketing programs have been designed and implemented over recent years such as buy one take one, premium prices during holidays, and mobile selling in local stores or venues. Mobile selling means consumer goods of SC are transported and sold to consumers in local stores or venues in order to meet demand of consumers. Promotions and discounts are announced widely to customers through panos, slogans, and announcements in public media. Customer cards are used to maintain loyal customers, including the super very important person (VIP) card (for customers who purchase commodities with the value from VND50 million or above for two months), VIP card (for customers who buy goods with the value from VND15 million a month), and casual member card (for customers who purchase commodities with the value under VND15 million a month).

18.6.6 Procurement

Based on local advertisements, SC sends requirements in quantity, categories, quality, and prices of products to suppliers and producers such as enterprises and cooperatives. Next, staff of from the department of materials will come to examine production zones and if production zones meet criteria, a contract will be signed between the two parties. After receiving products, samples are randomly tested to check the quality. All commodities sold in hypermarkets, supermarkets, Co-op Food, and Co-ops in the whole system are only supplied by SC. Moreover, product codes are imposed and provided to SC members and product codes are strictly controlled to ensure that no external goods enter supermarkets without being checked.

SC is also one of the first retailers to participate in producing and marketing farm products based on Vietnam Good Agricultural Practices. Therefore they have established a network for providing materials to the whole country. From 2012 to the present, SC has implemented contracts with 100 suppliers in the southern region of Vietnam with revenue accounting for more than VND925 billion (US $53 million).

18.6.7 Finance

During the late 1980s and early 1990s, after its official establishment, SC was following the traditional method of retail distribution as a family business in the subsidy period. In Vietnam, the subsidy period occurred prior to 1986 when enterprises and cooperatives operated under the decision and support of the state and this led to low-business efficiency and a weak distribution system of goods and service. However, the leaders of the organization embarked on a new concept of retail, the supermarket. The supermarket was a very new notion for the country, especially for a cooperative organization. Nobody had experience in setting up and operating a big supermarket. The top managers with the support of Vietnam Cooperative Alliance, contacted cooperatives in Sweden (KFPC), Japan (JCCU), and Singapore (NTUC FairPrice) for experience sharing. These organizations were willing to help SC without conditions to develop a modern retail. Currently SC still sends a number of delegates to attend workshops or management training programs in Singapore, Korea, and Japan that are hosted by ICA-AP, JCCU and other cooperatives.

Currently the competitiveness in modern retail in Vietnam is considered to be the toughest ever experienced. Most of the players are from developed countries such as Europe, Japan, and the Republic of Korea with a strong background in finance, experience, and technology. Therefore SC has had to compete with them in the domestic market. Network development thus became a prioritized strategy and requires a significantly strong financial background. According to the Cooperative Law, the main source of capital in a cooperative can be raised from the members. The majority of SC's members are small cooperatives and therefore the amount of capital injection is limited. To overcome this issue, SC decided to borrow capital from commercial banks in addition to cooperate with partners such as NTUC FairPrice and MapleTree to establish joint venture companies that can invest in new projects.

18.7 Identifying and overcoming current challenges faced by Saigon Co-op

18.7.1 Salary policies

Currently the wage systems of Co.opmart are ineffective due to a number of reasons. First, salaries are mainly calculated based on the governmental system and the level of experience of the staff and, as a result, working motivation of staff have not been encouraged. In addition, wage is dependent on the business performance of each supermarket in the different locations and therefore does not facilitate the creativity of staff who work for Co.opmart supermarkets.

18.7.2 Technology, warehouses, and logistics

Due to small and short counters in addition to lack of conveyor belt, customers do not have enough spaces to leave goods. In Vietnam, Co.opmart has become the first supermarket which applied the International Standardization for Organization 9001-2000 and Hazard Analysis and Critical Control Point System. Furthermore, software packages are used to control sales, revenue, and inventories for each commodity and this assists to make decisions on time.

Moreover, every supermarket has warehouses to store commodities. In 2009 with the assistance of SCID, warehouse systems of Co.opmart has been extended to up to 25,000 m^2, and a distribution center and grocery warehouse were established in Mekong River Delta and Ho Chi Minh City. However, the average area of each Co.opmart accounts for 200 m^2 and this leads to challenges in storing commodities as well as managing logistics.

18.7.3 Competitive pressures from rivals in the market

SC has had to face a strong competition from domestic and foreign retailers in recent years. According to the General Statistics Office of Vietnam, by 2017 the turnover of the retail sector of this country accounted for VND2.9 trillion (or US$130 billion), an increase by 10.6% compared to the previous year, and reached the highest record in the history. The growth of retail sector in Vietnam is a result of the expansion in spending of the middle-class in the urban area. By 2020 about one third of the Vietnamese middle-class citizens is projected to live in Ha Noi and Ho Chi Minh City. A number of foreign retailers, such as H&M, Zara, Seven Eleven, and Uniqlo have entered the Vietnam market. In addition, Vingroup—a domestic brand—has opened more than 1000 convenience stores in some of the country's big cities.

18.7.4 Food safety

Unsafe food is an issue faced by not only SC, but also by several other retailers in Vietnam because of ineffective management in food safety and degradation of ethic of producers. For instance, food safety is managed by three organizations, including the Ministry of Health, the Ministry of Industry and Trade, and the Ministry of Agriculture and Rural

Development. Moreover, overwhelming use of chemicals of producers in agricultural production has negative impacts on food product quality and consumers' health. To overcome these problems, staff in the department of production have been to local stores to examine production zones. If production zones meet criteria required by SC, contracts in providing materials will be signed with suppliers such as enterprises and cooperatives. After procuring products, samples of products are randomly tested to check the quality of products.

18.8 The impact of Saigon Co-op on vietnam

With the revenue and profit account for thousand billion VND and hundred billion VND annually, SC presents a tremendous contribution to economic growth and income of provinces and cities, especially in Ho Chi Minh City. After a quarter of a century of foundation and development, 100,000 jobs have been generated awarding employees with stable incomes and this contributes to improve the livelihood of laborers. By 2009, a campaign "Vietnamese people purchase and use Vietnamese commodities" was launched by the Vietnamese Government, and SC participated in this campaign with specific programs. For instance, the SC managerial board decided to substitute imported products with domestic goods in their supermarkets and, as a consequence, currently the rate of domestic products accounts for more than 90% in Co. opmart supermarkets. From 2012 to present, SC has made contracts with more than 100 suppliers in Ho Chi Minh City and provinces in southwest region with the revenue of more than VND925 billion (or US$40 million). The first Co.opmart supermarket in Cong Quynh, Ho Chi Minh City in 1996 that sold about 5000 items and served 1000 customers accounted for VND80 million (or US$3500)

revenue. Currently, SC has expanded its retail chains in the country and sells more than four million items, serves 300,000 clients, and supplies 250 tons of goods for price stabilization. From 2009 to 2014, the total revenue of SC more than tripled, with an average annual growth reaching nearly 30%, while total capital increased more than 65 times.

SC also contributes to establishing and developing purchasing habits of consumers in modern retail systems in Vietnam such as hypermarkets, supermarkets, and convenience stores. The growth of SC also positively impacts domestic production, particularly in agricultural products. Last, consumers always believe that SC is a true destination in terms of selling safe food.

18.9 Conclusion

In the context of a market-orientated socialist state, SC can be seen as a successful unique hybrid cooperative model in partnership with other international cooperatives, that overcame the obstacles to contribute significant economic and social benefits to Vietnamese society. This chapter discusses the role of cooperatives in Vietnam and assesses factors leading to the success of SC in particular. In this regard, SC presents an innovative hybrid model for other countries to emulate relating to how cooperative formation can be accelerated.

Due to the transformation of the economic mechanism from a central-planned economy to a market-oriented economy, in addition to competitive pressure from rivals in the retail market, many cooperatives have had to either stop working or dissolve. However, SC has overcome these difficulties to achieve its business targets and become the leading domestic retailer in Vietnam. Although SC must deal with issues relating to salary policies, technology, warehousing, logistics, competitive pressures, and food safety, the success of SC can be seen as specific evidence that consumer cooperatives in Vietnam are able to overcome challenges in the domestic market to achieve business targets in the retail industry.

Clearly the achievement of SC in recent years is the result of different strategies in system development, human resources, marketing, procurement, and operation. In the context of international economic integration, support from the state and consumers are crucial factors that contribute to the development of a domestic, cooperative retailer like SC.

References

Adebo, G. M., & Oladele, C. A. (2010). Consumer cooperatives, food security and the sustainability of civil servants in urban cities of Ondo State, Nigeria. *Journal of Food, Agriculture & Environment*, 8(3&4), 202–206.

Bager, T. (1988). Identity problems of Danish consumer cooperatives. *Journal of Consumer Policy*, 11(2), 223–233.

Carson, R. (1977). A theory of co-operatives. *The Canadian Journal of Economics*, 10(4), 565–589.

General Statistics Office of Vietnam. (2017). *Statistical yearbook of Vietnam 2016*. Ha Noi: Statistical Publishing House.

Ha, T. (2018). Saigon Co.op thu 30.000 ty ð—ng trong 2017. Retrieved May 26, 2018, from <https://kinhdoanh.vnexpress.net/tin-tuc/doanh-nghiep/saigon-co-op-thu-30-000-ty-dong-trong-2017-3700082.html> (Vietnamese).

Hall, B. F., & Hall, L. L. (1982). The potential for growth of consumer cooperatives: A comparison with producer cooperatives. *Journal of Consumer Affairs*, 16(1), 23–45.

Hasbullah, N., Mahajar, A. J., & Salleh, M. I. (2014). The conceptual framework for predicting loyalty intention in the consumer cooperatives using modified theory of planned behavior. *International Journal of Business and Social Science*, 5(11), 209–214.

ICA. (n.d.). *Vietnam: Highlights of consumer co-ops*. Committee on Consumer Cooperation for Asia and the Pacific. International Co-operative Alliance.

Marini, M. A., Polidori, P., Teobaldelli, D., & Zevi, A. (2015). Welfare enhancing coordination in consumer cooperatives under mixed oligopoly. *Annals of Public and Cooperative Economics*, 86(3), 505–527.

Mikami, K. (2015). Raising capital by issuing transferable membership in a consumer cooperative. *International Journal of Social Economics*, 42(2), 132–142.

Nilsson, J. (1985). Consumer cooperatives as consumer welfare organizations. *Journal of Consumer Policy*, 8(3), 287–301.

PWKD. (2017). *Vietnam: Saigon Co-op 2017 new business models*. Retrieved October 31, 2017, from <http://petrol-world.com>.

Sadowski, B. M. (2017). Consumer cooperatives as an alternative form of governance: The case of the broadband industry. *Economic Systems*, 41(1), 86–97.

Seo, J., & Choi, W. (2016). What determinants affect the capital structure of consumer co-operatives? The case of Icoop Korea. *Annals of Public and Cooperative Economics*, 87(1), 117–135.

Talonen, A., Jussila, I., Saarijärvi, H., & Rintamäki, T. (2016). Consumer cooperatives: Uncovering the value potential of customer ownership. *AMS Review*, 6(3–4), 142–156.

United Nations. (2014). *Measuring the size and scope of the cooperative economy: Results of the 2014 global census on cooperatives*. Division for Social Policy and Development. Department of Economic and Social Affairs. The United Nations, April 2014.

Watts, D. C. H. (2017). Building an alternative economic network? Consumer cooperation in Scotland from the 1870s to the 1960s. *The Economic History Review*, 70(1), 143–170.

19

NTUC FairPrice supermarket and cooperatives in Singapore

Huong Ha and Hui Shan Loh

School of Business, Singapore University of Social Sciences, Singapore

19.1 Introduction

Singapore is a successful corporatist city state that has blended economic development and the social mission of looking after its citizens through an innovative tripartnership of employees, employers, and trade unions. This has resulted in innovative institutions such as NTUC FairPrice, which was launched in 1973 in Singapore. As a consumer cooperative, the mission of NTUC FairPrice supermarket chain is different from other commercial or for-profit business entities. It has focused on serving the community, meeting the needs of its members as well as improving their lives. From having one outlet at the time of establishment, NTUC FairPrice is now one of the largest supermarket chains in Singapore. In addition, it has dealt with one of the most pressing issues for older workers, namely employment. NTUC FairPrice has made much effort to provide employment opportunities for older workers in order for them to remain in the labor market. This chapter aims to first introduce NTUC FairPrice cooperative and second to discuss the critical factors leading to its success and overcoming of difficulties using a SWOT (strengths, weaknesses, opportunities, and threats) analysis framework.

19.1.1 History, socioeconomic background, and institutional framework of consumer co-ops

Consumer co-ops are an early form of consumer activism to protect working-class citizens against expensive low-quality goods (Mansvelt, 2011). The main objective of consumer co-ops was to enable cooperation between businesses and consumers to bring about mutual benefits in the market. However, consumer co-ops begin to decline when market competition allows accessibility to better goods, lower prices, and more choices in the market. Owing to a pluralistic market, co-ops today are enterprises conducted in a cooperative manner and are no longer linked to a particular group of consumers with specific socioeconomic traits (Fici, 2013).

The co-op concept was introduced in Singapore with the passing of the Straits Settlement Co-operative Societies Ordinance on November 3, 1924 (National Library Board, 2013) by the British colonial administration (REASON). In 1925 the Singapore Government Servants' Co-operative Thrift and Loan Society was established and became the first co-op in Singapore (Singapore National Co-operative Federation, 2018). This co-op provided a platform for workers to offer mutual financial aids (Prakash & Tan, 2014). Given the lack of financial institutions at that time, more than 43 thrift and loan societies were set up from 1925 to 1940 to meet the financial needs of various groups of employees (e.g., teachers, farmers, civil servants, etc.) in both the public and private sectors (Singapore National Co-operative Federation, 2014). One of the most well-known co-ops, the Singapore Urban Co-operative Union Ltd (now known as the Singapore Amalgamated Services Co-operative Organisation Ltd), was registered in 1933. Its main function is to coordinate the thrift and loan societies in Singapore (National Library Board, 2013).

Governments usually enact laws that permit the formation of co-ops. Cooperatives such as agricultural co-ops in the United States enjoy immunities. The reason for their exemption from certain anticompetition laws is that co-ops are seen as nonprofit organizations in some cases. In addition, co-ops also enjoy different tax treatments to other types of businesses as they are distinguished from other for-profit capitalistic businesses. However, it has to be noted that such different tax regimes are not seen as a preferential treatment as long as they are consistent with the nature of co-ops. In particular, certain types of co-ops such as social co-ops might receive promotional tax treatment due to their effects on general interest (Fici, 2013). With regard to institutional frameworks, co-ops worldwide are represented by the International Co-operative Alliance (ICA). The principles set out by the ICA can be found in many national

co-op laws. Many jurisdictions impose regulations on different types of co-ops, instead of a generic regulation for all co-ops. By 1960, the number of co-ops had increased to 105 (National Library Board, 2013).

A turning point in cooperative development in Singapore was in 1969 when the National Trades Union Congress (NTUC) proposed to set up trade union co-ops that promote cooperation (not confrontation) among the involved parties, that is, employees and employers. How did this occur? About 10 years later, 13 co-ops were established based on this motto, and some of them have sustained and grown to be Singapore's largest and best-known co-ops such as Comfort (Co-operative Commonwealth for Transport Ltd in 1970) (now known as ComfortDelGro); Income (Insurance Co-operative Commonwealth Enterprise Ltd in 1970); and Welcome (now known as NTUC FairPrice in 1972) (National Library Board, 2013). Such co-ops have built trust with their members, and their reputation has been leveraged over the years due to their approaches and credentials.

Last but not least, the Singapore National Co-operative Federation Ltd (SNCF) was established in September 1980 to address social welfare issues (National Library Board, 2013). This co-op will be further discussed in Section 19.2.2.

19.1.2 Principles and nature of co-ops in Singapore

Co-op societies or co-ops are associations of like-minded people who come together to achieve common socioeconomic and/or cultural objectives. They usually do so by establishing a jointly-owned and jointly-controlled business entity (The Registry of Co-Operative Societies, Ministry of Culture, Community, & Youth, 2016). In Singapore, the Registry of Co-operative Societies ("the Registry"), under the Co-operatives Societies Act (Chapter 62) and

Co-operative Societies Rules 2009, regulates the registration and operations of all co-ops (Ministry of Culture, Community, & Youth, n.d.). All registered co-ops are required to hold an annual general meeting (AGM) and submit their annual report (AR) and audited financial statement (AFS) to the Registry within 6 months after the end of the financial year (The Registry of Co-Operative Societies Ministry of Culture, Community, & Youth, 2016).

Traditionally, the main principles of co-ops are self-reliance, self-help, and reciprocal support for one another in order to achieve their social mission. Their main task is to generate benefits for various groups of recipients in society including the poor, the disadvantaged, the mentally and physically handicapped, the elderly, exinmates, women, and children, etc. (Prakash & Tan, 2014). According to the ICA, the importance of co-ops is reflected in (1) their creation and maintenance of jobs, (2) contribution to economic growth, and (3) ability to gather a significant number of members.

Given the political, sociocultural, and economic development model of the political economy in Singapore, the nature and principles of co-ops and their way of overcoming obstacles to start up and succeed have also evolved in a unique way. As mentioned previously, the main approach adopted by co-ops is cooperation. This is a tripartism that has been introduced to be guide posts of action for key cooperatives such as NTUC FairPrice and SNCF. A tripartism is a collaboration between unions, employers, and the government to help promote a harmonious working relationship between the different parties. Australia had a similar arrangement when it became independent in 1901, but veered away from cooperatives to concentrate on incorporating trade unions through collective bargaining.

According to the spectrum or categorization provided by Prakash and Tan (2014), there are three types of organizations, namely traditional charity organizations (the main driver is to provide social value), social enterprises (the main drivers are to gain financial returns and, at the same time, to achieve social impacts), and traditional businesses (the main driver is to gain financial returns) as shown in Fig. 19.1. Traditional charity organizations are usually nonprofit in nature; whereas traditional businesses are for-profit. Social enterprises can include both nonprofit and for-profit activities.

If we analyze co-ops along this line, co-ops can be classified as social enterprises since they operate in the market to earn financial returns, which, in turn, can be used to create social value through hosting activities to help various groups of stakeholders and/or to enhance the lives of their members and others (Voinea, 2016). For example, Fonterra Co-operative Group Ltd in New Zealand is a big dairy cooperative co-owned by thousands of farmers. It uses part of their profits to subsidize farmers. Another co-op in Japan provides healthy meals to people (Voinea, 2016). The Singapore Police Co-operative Society Ltd (2015) (SPCS) and NTUC FairPrice are also considered as social enterprises that are owned by their respective

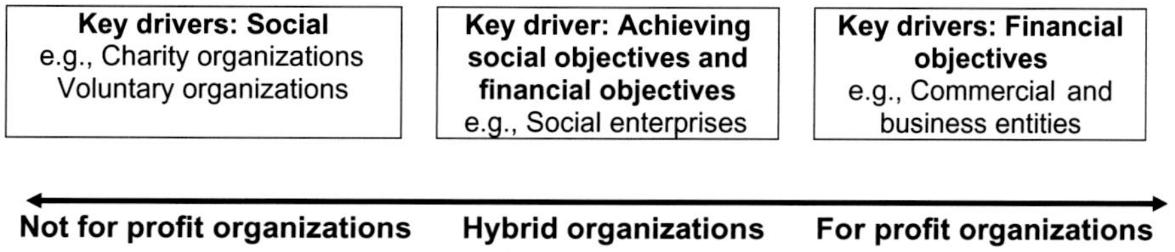

Key drivers: Social e.g., Charity organizations Voluntary organizations	Key driver: Achieving social objectives and financial objectives e.g., Social enterprises	Key drivers: Financial objectives e.g., Commercial and business entities

Not for profit organizations   Hybrid organizations   For profit organizations

FIGURE 19.1 Spectrum of organizations. Source: *Adapted from Prakash, R., & Tan, P. (2014). Landscape of social enterprises in Singapore (p. 10). Singapore: Asia Centre for Social Entrepreneurship & Philanthropy (ACSEP), NUS.*

members and serve their members, for example, NTUC FairPrice was established to provide food and groceries at competitive prices in a market that was becoming expensive.

19.1.3 Types of co-ops in Singapore

There are various types of co-ops around the world including worker co-ops, producer co-ops, consumer co-ops, credit unions, retail co-ops, housing co-ops, and social co-ops operating in both the for-profit and nonprofit spheres (Cultivate.Coop, 2016). In Singapore, four main types of co-ops exist and have been adopted by different organizations to address market failure and comply with government self-help preferences.

Credit Co-ops: These co-ops include loan societies that contribute to economic development by providing schemes and programs for their members. The aim of such programs is to prevent long-term indebtedness and to educate members about financial aspects, for example, encouraging savings, thrifting, and reducing monetary waste (Singapore National Co-operative Federation, 2016).

Consumer and Service Co-ops: These co-ops "provide a wide range of services to their members, from aged care, environmental services, food retailing and catering, maritime, security, trading, travel, and welfare" (Singapore National Co-operative Federation, 2016).

School or Campus Co-ops: These are societies and associations established by educational institutions such as alumni associations of universities. Such co-ops aim to offer members opportunities and expertise in managing and running a co-op (Singapore National Co-operative Federation, 2016).

NTUC Co-ops: This is a unique type of co-op in Singapore including nine co-ops that were established by Singapore's NTUC. The mission of these co-ops is to support members and Singaporeans by providing affordable and high-quality products and services. The NTUC co-ops have a total 10,000 employees and a revenue of S$4 billion (Singapore National Co-operative Federation, 2016).

19.2 Key cooperatives in Singapore

In 2016 there were 82 co-ops and 1,461,460 members in Singapore. There was a slight increase in the number of co-ops in 2016 as compared to the 80 co-ops existing in 2015. These 82 co-ops have a total asset of $8729 million (The Registry of Co-Operative Societies Ministry of Culture, Community, & Youth, 2016). The distribution of the number of the co-ops, their members, and total assets are presented in Table 19.1. Out of Singapore's population of 5.61 million, there are 1.47 million members in their 84 co-ops as of March 2017. Co-ops have 26.2% of the market (Ministry of Culture, Community, & Youth, 2017).

The following section introduces examples of the range of some of the main cooperatives in Singapore.

TABLE 19.1 Facts and figures of cooperatives in Singapore (2016).

Types of cooperative	Number	Members	Total assets (S$)
Credit co-ops	25	141,000	959 million
Consumer and service co-ops	53	1,329,000	7769 million
School co-ops	4	460	0.8 million

Source: *Data from The Registry of Co-Operative Societies Ministry of Culture, Community, & Youth. (2016) Annual report on the co-operative societies in Singapore 2016. Singapore: Ministry of Culture, Community and Youth.*

19.2.1 Singapore National Co-operative Federation

SNCF has been Singapore's collective representation of the cooperative movement since 1980, representing about 99% of all co-ops in Singapore. It has a huge membership of more than 1 million members, and contributes significantly to the economy of Singapore. SNCF adopts a business model that is similar to that of a social enterprise, that is, to help its members meet their needs and to serve the wider community. SNCF has supported start-up co-ops and their stakeholders to build capabilities and capacities in order to sustain their operations. It has also leveraged the reputation and principles of co-ops via corporate social responsibility efforts (Singapore National Co-operative Federation, 2016).

19.2.2 Singapore Police Co-operative Society Ltd

In 1926 SPCS as a credit union was formed as "the first co-operative for uniformed personnel in the Singapore Government Service" (Singapore Police Co-operative Society Ltd, 2015, para. 1). It aims to provide support and financial assistance to its members who are uniform and nonuniform civil servants.

19.3 Case study: NTUC FairPrice Co-Operative Ltd

NTUC FairPrice was first established as NTUC Welcome Supermarket by the National Trades Union Congress (NTUC) in 1973 amidst a global oil crisis. The then Prime Minister, Mr. Lee Kuan Yew, officiated the launch. In 1983 it merged with another co-op, Singapore Employees Co-operative (SEC), to form the enlarged co-op known as NTUC FairPrice Co-operative Ltd (Pradhan, 2009). Most of the existing employees (over 10,000 employees) are

nonexecutive females and almost half of all employees are nonexecutives above 50 years old (NTUC FairPrice Co-operative Limited, 2016).

The NTUC FairPrice board comprises 11 nonexecutive members, 2 of whom are women. As a co-op, NTUC FairPrice is regulated by the Registry of Co-operative Societies in Singapore. The Co-operative Societies Act requires NTUC FairPrice to contribute to the Central Co-operative Fund and Singapore Labour Foundation. The group's net profit stood at S\$271.3 million in 2016 (NTUC FairPrice Co-operative Limited, 2016). The personal members of FairPrice collectively held about S\$123 million worth of shares, patronage rebates were nearly S\$60 million, and S\$17 million of dividends were paid out in 2016 (NTUC FairPrice Co-operative Limited, 2016). Altogether, the patronage rebates and dividends distributed were about 85% of net retail profits.

Future investments will be on data analytics, enhancing both store features and online services as well as expansion of fresh food distribution centers in order to address business challenges. The social mission of NTUC FairPrice is to moderate the costs of living in Singapore. To serve the varied needs of the community, FairPrice adopts multiple retail formats that include FairPrice Supermarkets, FairPrice Xtra, FairPrice Finest, Cheers, FairPrice Xpress, FairPrice Online, Warehouse Club, and FairPrice Shop. Table 19.2 compares the characteristics of the different retail formats.

After four decades, NTUC FairPrice is now a leading chain of supermarkets with a network of more than 230 outlets in Singapore. It has been well developed to become a must-know and home-grown business entity with a social mission, that is, providing affordable and quality products to its members and customers (Singapore National Co-operative Federation, 2014).

TABLE 19.2 Characteristics of FairPrice's different retail formats.

Retail formats	Number of outlets	Focus
FairPrice Supermarkets	108	Conventional supermarket selling goods such as fresh products to household products
FairPrice Xtra	7	Extensive range of products and services including electronics and clothing
FairPrice Finest	23	Upmarket products
Cheers	134	24-hour convenience store
FairPrice Xpress	26	Petrol mart with 24-hour shopping convenience
FairPrice Online	na	Virtual supermarket for e-consumers
Warehouse Club	1	Bulk shopping and wholesale buying
FairPrice Shop	7	Budget-conscious shoppers
Unity	68	Provide healthcare related product

Source: *Data from FairPrice. (2018). Annual and Sustainability Report 2018 (p. 40). NTUC FariPrice. From <https://s3-ap-southeast-1.amazonaws.com/www8.fairprice.com.sg/fpol/media/pdf/corpcomms/AnnualReport/1905/AR201905.pdf> Accessed 19.02.20.*

19.3.1 Discussion of success factors and the overcoming of barriers

19.3.1.1 Building on strengths

NTUC FairPrice has developed a successful business model with a wide distribution network (Yeo, 2013). It has adopted a hybrid for-profit and nonprofit business model to run its business. This business model has proved to be successful in terms of financial returns and creating significant social impact that benefits both members and nonmembers. For example, it was the first supermarket in Singapore that had its own central warehousing and distribution company (Yeo, 2013).

Also, is its ability to build trust with customers. Apart from the co-op business strategies, it has gone beyond what is required by economic and legal obligations, that is, it has carried out several corporate social responsibility activities to give back to the community as well as improve its reputation and brand name. NTUC FairPrice has also exercised its corporate social responsibility to launch several schemes to assist the needy such as "FairPrice Food

Voucher Scheme" and "Share-a-Textbook Project" (Singapore Police Co-operative Society Ltd, 2015, p. 5). These are NTUC FairPrice's initiatives to practice their corporate social responsibility to assist low-income people by giving food vouchers to them, and to help needy students by organizing book donation drives.

Finally, it has invested in training and technology that aims to improve productivity and reduce the reliance on manpower. For example, NTUC FairPrice launched new Joo Koon headquarters where a training institute is located (Yong, 2015). The training institute was equipped with a state of the art automated distribution center that can increase productivity twofold. Its warehouse also uses robots to manage, store, and transport goods (Yong, 2015).

19.3.1.2 Seizing market opportunities

NTUC FairPrice's popular brand name in Singapore may facilitate its venture to new overseas markets. With the aging population in Singapore and the mission to serve its members, NTUC FairPrice can focus on offering products and services that can meet the demand of the aging population and the need for healthy products. For instance, NTUC FairPrice has sold healthy rice products at discounted prices to encourage customers to stay healthy in response to a call by government for a healthy lifestyle (Toh, 2017). This may enhance NTUC FairPrice's position in the market as a responsible entity.

19.3.1.3 Overcoming weaknesses in the market

Singapore is a small market, and, thus, the market share of supermarkets is limited. This may weaken NTUC FairPrice's potential in market development. However, NTUC FairPrice has extended its reach to overseas markets such as Vietnam. According to Lim (2013), NTUC FairPrice has a 36% share in Co.opXtra Plus, a joint venture with the Saigon Union of Trading Co-operatives Limited (Saigon Co-op).

Another weakness is the insecure nature of the online platform on which customers may be scammed. For example, there was a phishing scam that "promises to give away $500 in vouchers to consumers who fill in an online survey" (Chew, 2016, para. 1). Also, it was perceived that ordering items from NTUC FairPrice online was frustrating given the immature technology used (Ting, 2015).

Last, NTUC FairPrice has been associated with a brand of cheap/discounted products. Products sold at its supermarkets were perceived as not of a high quality. This will make it difficult for NTUC FairPrice to sell high-end products in future from a business strategy view point.

19.3.1.4 Identifying emerging threats

The emergence of online shops such as RedMart online grocery store, Fishwives, and Tangy Tangerines, has posed threats to NTUC FairPrice and other supermarkets in Singapore. Although NTUC FairPrice does offer e-store services where customers can order from, the level of competition is high. Thus this requires NTUC FairPrice to continuously create a new competitive advantage.

19.3.2 Critical success factors of NTUC FairPrice

NTUC FairPrice's success lies with government support and the co-op business model. Throughout the years, NTUC FairPrice has aimed to deliver social good to the Singapore community. Today, it is Singapore's leading grocery retailer with an annual revenue of about $3.4 billion, employs more than 10,000 employees and serves over 600,000 customers a day (Seah, 2016). FairPrice's success can be attributed to its collaborative working relationship with the government, business formats, distribution operations, commitment to its social mission through the core operations and by taking a holistic view in its corporate social responsibility efforts that resonate well with the community.

Singapore's labor relations are built on tripartism, which refers to a collaboration among the government, unions, and employers. NTUC is a national confederation of trade unions in Singapore, representing unionized workers. It works closely with the Ministry of Manpower and The Singapore National Employers Federation (SNEF). Through a collaborative working relationship, the tripartism is able to address issues in job recreation, wage systems, employment practices, and retirement age (Ministry of Manpower, 2016). Such joint efforts between the three parties raises awareness of the issues faced by the Singapore community. For example, FairPrice penetrates Singapore's social strata with its different retail formats serving the diverse needs of the residents.

NTUC FairPrice's multiple retail format enables it to remain competitive in the market that sees changing consumer lifestyles, needs, and behavior. In particular, it has been successful in moderating the cost of living for the average Singaporean in the largely price-driven sector. It has done so through precautionary measures to stabilize grocery prices and to prevent profiteering by other retailers as well as a series of initiatives such as "Everyday Low Price" and "Pioneers OK!" (Seah, 2016). These are promotional campaigns to offer products at a discounted price to the elderly and the public on certain days of the week. These initiatives are customized to different categories of consumers such that each group receives the benefits most relevant to them.

Furthermore, NTUC FairPrice uses technology and effective risk management in its supply chain management to overcome the manpower and land constraints it faces in Singapore. Its self-checkout counters, Click & Collect service, and partnership with grocery concierge reduce reliance on its frontline employees. To mitigate price fluctuations, NTUC FairPrice adopts forward buying and has a diverse food source to hedge risks (Seah, 2016). To boost productivity and reduce reliance on manpower, NTUC FairPrice uses centralization and automation at its distribution centers (Yeo, 2013).

NTUC FairPrice seeks to achieve its social mission not only through its retail business, but also takes on a broader view of its social mission through philanthropic activities that may or may not be related to its business. For instance, the Share-a-Textbook initiative has been running for more than 30 years, bringing together more than 150 partners and 400 volunteers (Lee, 2016; Seah, 2016). Another initiative is the NTUC FairPrice volunteer program, which welcomes members of the public to join its staff in its volunteering events (Tan, 2016). Such initiatives enhance NTUC FairPrice's brand identity, and by involving the public, it creates a sense of unity and community. The formation of the FairPrice Foundation, which is a registered charity, also creates a more pronounced concept of NTUC FairPrice's alignment to its social mission in a sustainable manner.

In addition, NTUC FairPrice provides a conducive workplace through creating opportunities for older employees, designing staff development plans that are aligned with its objectives, and offering an inclusive workplace for people with special needs (Seah, 2016).

While cooperatives have a social approach, they should be distinguished from nonprofit organizations. Most of the time, cooperatives generate profits that they distribute as dividends to their members. Though members may enjoy dividends out of profits generated by both members and nonmembers, they pay membership fees regularly to get other benefits such as access to legal aid and member rates when they sign up for trainings. The way the profits are distributed by co-ops should be decided by their members. The fact that nonunion members cannot become co-op members ensures that the members are people who benefit from the business. These are in line with the essential principles found in cooperative practice, which include open and voluntary membership, democracy, limited interest on capital, equitable return of surpluses to members, provision of education, and cooperation between cooperatives (Birchall, 2011).

19.4 Conclusion

This chapter has briefly introduced the co-op movement in Singapore and discussed how co-ops in Singapore have evolved over time using NTUC FairPrice as a case study. NTUC FairPrice's success lies with government support and the co-op business model. NTUC FairPrice has been able to build a trusted brand and has acquired a large membership through its business strategies, mission, and vision of being a home-grown brand with corporate socially responsible behavior.

NTUC FairPrice and other co-ops in Singapore have played an important role in the national economy. Not only being active at the national level, they have also been involved in the global cooperative movement. For example, SNCF (2017) has been a member of the ICA

(1985), Association for Asia Confederation Credit Union (2009), and World Council of Credit Unions (2010). They have also extended their reach to assist the needs of other countries. For instance, NTUC FairPrice has raised funds and provided essential food and necessities to the victims of the China Earthquake (2008), the Pakistan Earthquake (2005), the Asian Tsunami (2004), the Avian Flu (2004), the SARS (2003), and many others (Singapore National Co-operative Federation , 2014).

In short, the cooperative sector in Singapore has been considered as an advanced hybrid economic stakeholder model involving the state, trade unions, and customers, which contributes significantly to the national economy and enhances the welfare of the people. Given the current economic turbulence, any new or modified economic and business models that can help countries navigate through the crisis should be further explored, and, hence, the future of the cooperative sector is promising. The NTUC FairPrice case illustrates the benefits that can be achieved by cooperatives when the barriers to start up and success are overcome with state support.

References

Birchall, J. (2011). A 'member-owned business' approach to the classification of co-operatives and mutuals. *Journal of Co-operative Studies, 44*(2), 4–15.

Chew, H. M. (2016). Online survey promising $500 in supermarket vouchers a scam: NTUC FairPrice. *The Straits Times*, July 13, 2016. From <http://www.straits times.com/singapore/online-survey-promising-500-in-supermarket-vouchers-a-scam-ntuc-fairprice> Accessed 27.10.17.

Cultivate.Coop. (2016). *Types of cooperatives*. Cultivate. Coop (Online). From <http://cultivate.coop/wiki/Types_of_Cooperatives> Accessed 17.08.17.

FairPrice. (2018). *Our Stores*. NTUC FariPrice. From <https://www.fairprice.com.sg/wps/portal/fp/ourretailformats> Accessed 15.09.18.

Fici, A. (2013). An introduction to cooperative law. In D. Cracogna, A. Fici, & H. Henrÿ (Eds.), *International handbook of cooperative law*. Springer-Verlag Berlin Heidelberg.

Lee, J. (2016). Donating old textbooks to the needy. *The New Paper*. From <http://www.tnp.sg/news/singapore/donating-old-textbooks-needy> Accessed 5.10.17.

Lim, J. (2013). NTUC FairPrice opens joint venture store in Vietnam. *The Straits Times*, May 15, 2013. From <http://www.straitstimes.com/singapore/ntuc-fair-price-opens-joint-venture-store-in-vietnam> Accessed 27.10.17.

Mansvelt, J. (2011). Consumer activism. In P. Robbins (Ed.), *Green consumerism: An A-to-Z guide*. Thousand Oaks: SAGE Publications Inc.

Ministry of Culture, Community and Youth. (n.d.). *Co-operative societies*. Singapore: Ministry of Culture, Community and Youth.

Ministry of Culture, Community and Youth. (2017). *Annual report on the co-operative societies in Singapore*. Singapore: Ministry of Culture, Community and Youth.

Ministry of Manpower (2016). *What is tripartism*. From <http://www.mom.gov.sg/employment-practices/tripartism-in-singapore/what-is-tripartism> Accessed 5.11.17.

National Library Board. (2013). *Co-operative societies ordinance is passed, 3 Nov 1924*. Singapore: National Library Board.

NTUC Fairprice Co-operative Limited. (2016). FairPrice annual and sustainability report 2016. Singapore.

Pradhan, S. (2009). The internationalisation of retail. In R. Jagantahan (Ed.), *Retailing management: Text and cases*. India: Mcgraw Hill Education (India) Private Limited.

Prakash, R., & Tan, P. (2014). *Landscape of social enterprises in Singapore* (p. 10). Singapore: Asia Centre for Social Entrepreneurship & Philanthropy (ACSEP), NUS.

Seah, F. P. (2016). *Here to make lives better*. Presented at Singapore Healthcare Management 2016, Singapore.

Singapore National Co-operative Federation. (2018). *What are Co-Ops?* Singapore: Singapore National Co-operative Federation. From <https://sncf.coop/about-co-ops/what-are-co-ops>.

Singapore National Co-operative Federation. (2014). *NTUC FairPrice co-operative*. Singapore: Singapore National Co-operative Federation.

Singapore National Co-operative Federation. (2016). *Co-op Stories (local)*. Singapore: Singapore National Co-operative Federation (SNCF). From <http://www.sncf.coop/about-co-ops/co-operative-stories/local-co-ops#-read-more-of-the-sgscc-story> Accessed 11.08.17.

Singapore National Co-operative Federation. (2017). *About global co-operative bodies*. Singapore: Singapore National Co-operative Federation.

Singapore Police Co-operative Society Ltd (SPCS). (2015). *The history of police co-op*. Singapore: Singapore Police Co-operative Society Ltd.

Tan, J. (2016). NTUC FairPrice volunteer programme to open to members of the public. *Channel News Asia*. From <http://www.channelnewsasia.com/news/singapore/ntuc-fairprice-volunteer-programme-to-open-to-members-of-the-pub-8187438> Accessed 5.11.17.

The Registry of Co-Operative Societies Ministry of Culture, Community and Youth. (2016). *Annual report on the co-operative societies in Singapore 2016*. Singapore: Ministry of Culture, Community and Youth.

Ting, L. (2015). FairPrice online: A frustrating experience. *The Straits Times*, October 7, 2015. From <http://www.straitstimes.com/tech/fairprice-online-a-frustrating-experience> Accessed 27.10.17.

Toh, E. M. (2017). NTUC FairPrice offering discounts on healthier rice products. *Today*, August 20, 2017. From <http://www.todayonline.com/singapore/fairprice-cuts-prices-encourage-switch-white-rice> Accessed 27.10.17.

Voinea, A. (2016). Should co-ops call themselves social enterprises? *COOP News*, September 13, 2016. Co-operative Press Ltd.

Yeo, D. (2013). *Best practices in supply chain management in the retail industry*. Presented at Singapore Healthcare Management, August 20, 2013, Singapore.

Yong, C. (2015). *NTUC FairPrice a role model for social enterprises: PM. The Straits Times*, September 17, 2015. From <http://www.straitstimes.com/singapore/ntuc-fairprice-a-role-model-for-social-enterprises-pm> Accessed 27.10.17.

Further reading

Bloomberg, L. P. (2017). *Company Overview of NTUC Fairprice Co-operative Limited*. Bloomberg L.P.

Malaysian National Co-operative Movement. (2015). *ASEAN co-operative organization*. Petailing Jaya: Malaysian National Co-operative Movement.

The International Co-operative Alliance. (n.d.). *Co-operative facts & figures*. Brussels: The International Co-operative Alliance.

Tulus, R., & Iye, B. (2015). *Co-operatives and the ASEAN economic blueprint: Call for greater co-op engagement and visibility*. The International Co-operative Alliance. From <http://ica.coop/media/news/co-operatives-and-asean-economic-blueprint-call-greater-co-op-engagement-and-visibility> Accessed 17.08.17.

Korea's consumer cooperatives and civil society: the cases of iCOOP and Hansalim*

Sunhwa Kim[1], Yena Lee[1], Hyojin Shin[1] and Seungkwon Jang[2]

[1]Department of Management of Co-operatives, Graduate School, Sungkonghoe University, Seoul, Korea [2]Division of Business Administration, and Department of Management of Co-operatives, Sungkonghoe University, Seoul, Korea

20.1 Introduction

Since the 1960s, Korea has achieved a rapid industrialization under an authoritarian regime. However, the aspiration for democracy has also gradually increased. With the growing social movements of farmer, labor, gender, and the environment, Korea's consumer cooperatives have been actively engaging in social issues.

The aims of this chapter are to analyze the historical context, current status, social and legal issues of Korea's consumer cooperatives. For these purposes, we are conducting a literature review. The multifactor theoretical model (Jensen, 2013) can illustrate the macro and micro dimensions of cooperatives. For the macro perspective, we investigate the relationship between the market and consumer cooperatives, highlighting the roles of the civil society movement in the emergence and development of consumer cooperatives. For the microlevel analysis, the organizational structure and practice of Korea's consumer cooperatives are examined.

We describe, first, a brief history and the current status of Korea's consumer cooperatives. Second, we discuss Korean consumer cooperatives that have played roles in Korean society as a whole and their contributions to forming an organic and domestic agri-foods market. Third, we focus on the institutionalization and legal situation in close relation to the characteristics, organizational structure, and practice of Korea's consumer cooperatives. This chapter is based on the case studies of iCOOP and Hansalim, the two largest consumer cooperatives in Korea.

---

* An earlier version of the chapter was presented at the 10th ICA Asia Pacific Regional Research Conference held at VAMNICOM, Pune, India, November 5–6, 2015.

Waking the Asian Pacific Cooperative Potential
DOI: https://doi.org/10.1016/B978-0-12-816666-6.00020-3

20.2 A brief history and the current status

20.2.1 Evolution of Korea's consumer cooperatives

20.2.1.1 The foundation stage: 1986–1998

Following the model of lifecycle in member-owned business (Birchall, 2011), the foundation stage of Korea's consumer cooperatives lasted from the late 1980s to the late 1990s. Rapid industrialization and urbanization caused a downturn in the agricultural sector and the debasement of the social fabric of rural communities.

After democratization in June 1987, civil society grew in varied fields. With the economic growth, the middle-class was formed and their consumptions were diversified. In the late 1980s, consumer cooperatives in Korea introduced a "direct sales" business model in which producers in rural communities and consumers in urban areas organized a cooperative and directly traded agri-foods through collective purchase. This was based on critical thinking as to the pressure of the open market policy and conventional farming. It performed as a voluntary solidarity movement of producer and consumer that aimed to protect domestic organic agriculture and provide consumers with healthy foods. This business model could develop consistently through the growth of the middle-class and the trend of having a lifestyle of well-being.

20.2.1.2 The growth stage: 1998–the present

Consumer cooperatives advanced in scale and business, and the legal framework for them began to form. Consumer cooperatives made federations through their own distribution channels to enhance their business effectiveness. After the Consumer Co-operative Act was enacted in 1999, which gave consumer cooperatives legal status as nonprofit organizations, the federations started to open retail stores and the number of members increased.

However, they could only sell organic agri-foods. This restriction was removed in the revised Consumer Co-operative Act of 2010, which also approved the establishment of consumer cooperative federations and their legal status. From the late 2000s, their businesses started to expanded in scale. Moreover, they enhanced their capacity of distribution and systemized the certification of products.

20.3 Categories and structures of Korea's consumer cooperatives

There are four major consumer cooperative federations rooted in different social movements in Korea. This chapter focuses on the cases of iCOOP and Hansalim, the two largest consumer cooperatives in Korea (Table 20.1).

Hansalim was founded in 1986 by activists of social and farmer movements in rural areas. It adopted a cooperative model in 1987 and was renamed "Hansalim Consumer Co-operative" in 1993. Finally, it changed its name to "Hansalim Union." The word "Hansalim" means "save all life and Earth," which demonstrates the philosophy and orientation of the organization. Hansalim tried to connect farmers and consumers through the direct trade of organic food and various activities to understand each other. This cooperative consists of 23 cooperatives, 643,677 members, 114 producer communities, and 2150 households of producer members. It is currently running 215 stores and made US$385 million in sales in 2017.

iCOOP was developed from a "21st-century Consumer Co-operative Federation" in 1997, performing as a coordinating organization for local consumer cooperatives. In 2000, the federation decided to include a producer's association as part of the board of directors, which was originally consumer-oriented. The history of iCOOP can be traced from the grassroots movement including labor, student, and political movements. The activists of these

TABLE 20.1   Characteristics and current status of iCOOP and Hansalim (December, 2018).

Name of cooperative	Hansalim	iCOOP
Year of foundation	1986	1997
Social movement	Farmer movement	Labor movement
	Hansalim movement (save all life and the Earth)	
The core values	Saving dining table (food)	Ethical consumption
	Saving agriculture	
	Saving life	
The revenue (million US$)	391	519
The number of members	661,143	282,720
The number of member cooperatives	23	98
The number of stores	2221	231

Source: Data from: Jeong, E. M. (2006). The characteristics of consumer co-operatives in Korea (in Korean). Rural Economy, 29(3), 1–18; Lee, D. Y., & Hwang, M. J. (2013). Study on spreading ethical consumption through consumer co-operatives (in Korean). Seoul: Korea Consumer Agency. Annual Reports, and the Reports for Annual General Meeting, and the homepages.

movements started consumer cooperative business for advocating civil society movement. In addition, with the slogan of "ethical consumption," iCOOP emphasizes its identity as a consumer cooperative and practices the values. It is shown that iCOOP had 95 cooperatives and managed 219 retail stores in 2017, and its sales accounted for US$503 million.

20.4 The characteristics and the roles of Korea's consumer cooperatives

20.4.1 Civil society

Korea's consumer cooperatives are mediators between consumers and producers (Lee & Hwang, 2013). Through various rural–urban exchange activities, they contribute to rebuilding the disconnected relationship between producers and consumers (Kim, 2004). Cooperatives have provided clear information about production and distribution processes for the consumer so as to build trust in relations between consumers

and producers. Consequently, Korea's consumer cooperatives, by selling organic agri-foods, contribute to the growth of organic food production in Korea. Producers obtain a stable income from cooperatives because the cooperatives have a long-term contract with farmers. Additionally, consumer members pay in advance for financing producer members' work (Jeong, Kim, & Kim, 2011). This also makes it possible to maintain stable prices for consumers. These systems, that is, prepayment and stable prices, are beneficial to both producers and consumers.

Korea's consumer cooperatives regard boosting domestic organic agriculture and supplying consumers with reliable and safe foods as core values. Thus producers are regarded as important partners and members of consumer cooperatives, not just food providers. Reflecting on this feature, consumer cooperatives pursue diverse policies to help ensure a stable income for producers who otherwise would have to endure fluctuating prices. These policies are carried out with the involvement of consumer members.

Consumer cooperatives form producer members' associations. In the case of Hansalim, 100 households of producer members launched "Hansalim Producer Association" in 1988. There are 114 "producer communities" who have a monthly meeting to exchange information and discuss production planning and crop management (Hansalim White Paper, 2016).

Similarly, the iCOOP Association of Producer Group was formed, which changed its name to Farmer's COOP in 2018. Being a partner of iCOOP, it maintains a more professional and independent status for producers.

Korea's consumer cooperatives have been considering agricultural issues seriously. This is attributable to three factors. First, Korean agriculture was affected by a number of financial crises and economic downturns as well as inadequate government policies. Since the late 1980s, farmers with small holdings have faced challenges due to the opening of the Korea's agri-food market. A flood of cheap imported products has been threatening Korean farmers' right to live. Meanwhile, the overall rate of food self-sufficiency in Korea has been consistently downturned. It is expected that food prices will soar. Second, there have been some food safety problems. The public wanted to ban the import of beef from the United States due to mad cow disease in 2008. A melamine-tainted milk powder crisis also happened in the same year. It has resulted in public concerns over food safety. The public became conscious of the direct connections between food safety and their whole lives. As food safety issues such as foot-and-mouth disease and avian flu have continued, the number of consumers interested in organic and domestic agri-foods is growing gradually.

Korea's consumer cooperatives are conducting various campaigns such as GMO (genetically modified organism) labeling and anti-gene-manipulation (Kim & Huh, 2014). For example, members of cooperatives aim not only to provide reliable and safe foods for students, but also to support agriculture, the environment, and the economies of local communities. This is just one example of the many social activities undertaken by consumer cooperatives. These activities contribute to enhancing the number of members in cooperatives.

Most members are middle-aged, middle-class housewives. They participate in activities such as cooking classes, volunteering for child daycare, and group study on social issues related to, for instance, food safety and the identity of cooperatives (Baek, 2012). Consumer cooperatives provide various programs and help their members become active members. Cooperatives organize various committees, thus, improving members' management skills and enhancing members' cooperation. This also encourages members to take part in community and societal issues and to be aware of politics and membership.

Cooperatives are actively engaging in campaigns for the protection of the environment (Huh, 2008). In 2014, members of cooperatives tried to create a safe society with regards to the privatization of healthcare, gas, and water. These activities can empower members to change their communities, to gain self-confidence, and also to influence members who don't engage actively to become more active members.

Consumer cooperatives are part of a whole community working closely with NGOs, social enterprises, and social welfare institutes. Cooperative movements have a strong presence in provincial towns such as Wonju and Hongsung (Jung, 2008). Moreover, consumer cooperatives remain active in fostering healthcare delivery in local communities.

The Korean cooperative movement achieved remarkable growth in a short period of time. Consumer cooperatives, a first-runner of social economy, support building communities for social economy, establishing new cooperatives and helping social economic organizations. They also try to provide education and consultation to new cooperatives.

20.4.2 Market

The early development of consumer cooperatives was closely related to globalization around Korea's agriculture and agricultural market. The Korean government was under pressure to open the agricultural market from the mid-1980s. Some countries, especially the United States, continuously urged Korea to open the market from 1986. Threats of the open market policy mainly affected small and medium-sized enterprises and the agricultural sector. The situation of Korean agriculture worsened. The debt of Korean farming households increased more than 6-times from $339 in 1980 to $2192 in 1986, while the rural population in Korea decreased from 32.4% in 1980 to 17.1% in 1990. Furthermore, the amount of agri-foods imports increased from $1.8 billion in 1986 to $3.7 billion in 1990.

Korea's consumer cooperatives have tried to reach the organic agri-foods market since 1986. They have contributed to bringing an environment-friendly lifestyle into the mainstream and the stabilization of food prices as well as solving problems of the sustainable food chain to enhance their credibility.

Hansalim and iCOOP have both raised public awareness of issues relating to food safety and organic farming and tried to suggest food safety criteria. The criteria are reflected in the list of products with which consumer cooperatives deal, their principles, and their own peculiar certification system.

Korea's consumer cooperatives mostly deal with fresh environment-friendly agri-foods. However, processed goods made from environment-friendly agri-foods account for an increasing part of the products. The criteria for selecting agricultural and processed products differ between cooperatives.

The criteria for selecting goods that Hansalim has adopted closely correspond with the organization's value orientation such as "save agriculture" and "save all life and Earth." By adding as few artificial elements as possible, it aims to thereby create goods for a sustainable ecosystem and agriculture. Although consumer members participate in the process of selecting new products, consumers' demands are not easily accepted if the product is assumed to be incompatible with the purpose of the Hansalim movement.

In contrast, iCOOP tends to reflect members' demands positively. iCOOP members participate in the processes of selecting, developing, and improving new products. For instance, demanding highly for products such as sugar and coffee, iCOOP decided to supply those products through fair trade.

Korea's consumer cooperatives have made efforts to establish their own schemes to obtain consumers' trust in safe foods. In the early 2000s, the Environment-Friendly Agriculture Certification Mark System became obligatory legally so consumer cooperatives must state the social reliability of the agri-goods they sell via certification from the government or independent certification bodies. However, each consumer cooperative has created their own unique certification system along with the National Certification of Environment-friendly Agri-food.

In addition to the national certification system of environment-friendly food in Korea (i.e., a third-party audit system), Hansalim's own quality management of products, called "self-certification system" (i.e., a second-party audit system between producers and consumers), has been employed. It is based on trust and relationship between producers and consumers and their honesty. For this system to be managed properly, all producers of Hansalim are obliged to submit an inspection chart that shows detailed procedures, data, and facts of the production process (Hansalim Introductory Book, 2017). This self-inspection is run by a voluntary group of members. The self-certification system gives its own certification mark to products such as fruits with low pesticides.

In iCOOP, a quality management system inspects the distribution process as well as the production process. The iCOOP Certification Centre has established a third-party audit system, called "iCOOP certification," so as to secure the credibility of the products provided. Specifically, agri-food, livestock, and processed products are inspected three times.

Also, iCOOP constructed production clusters to supply safer and trustworthy environment-friendly goods by integrating the processes of producing environment-friendly agri-foods and processed foods. By disclosing this process to members and nonmembers, the clusters perform the function of securing the reliability of iCOOP products and the transparency of the production system. Whenever a problem is discovered during the certification process, both iCOOP and Hansalim usually ban the shipment of the relevant product.

Korea's consumer cooperatives have played a crucial role in the price-reduction of environment-friendly agri-foods (Jang & Lee, 2008). There are large fluctuations in prices of agricultural products depending on the climate and the season. Consumer cooperatives have helped to ease the fluctuation in market prices by introducing a stable price scheme. The scheme contributes to protecting domestic agriculture and a continuous supply of safe foods, ensuring a stable income for producers. Besides, they lower the price by delayering the distribution channels. For instance, the price of environment-friendly agri-foods supplied by iCOOP was cheaper than the mainstream retailers' foods (Lee, 2013).

20.4.3 The state

The Korean government put great efforts into economic development and intervened in the economic system to lead this development. With financial incentives and tax benefits to particular strategic industries, large companies supported by the government have grown into chaebols. These economic and industrial policies developed an antagonistic sentiment against conglomerates or chaebols in Korea.

The consumer cooperative movement was born out of civil society activism against the government and big corporations. Since the political democratization in the 1980s, political and social structures have shifted rapidly toward liberal democracy. But Koreans have also faced fierce competition in the globalized market economy. To overcome this challenge, the government is moving toward deregulation and privatization.

The Korean government legislated special laws on eight different cooperative sectors, namely agricultural, fishery, forestry, tobacco growers, small and medium enterprises, credit unions, community credit cooperatives, and consumer cooperatives. Each cooperative sector is regulated and monitored by special laws and the relevant ministries. Most cooperative laws were established under government initiative. However, the enactment of Consumer Co-operative Law, initiated by consumer cooperatives independently and being civil society—based, was finally legislated in 1999.

Before 1999, consumer cooperatives were actually run as nonprofit organizations or private companies, neither controlled nor protected by legal systems. Although consumer cooperatives leading new civil society movements along with consumer movement showed possibilities of autonomous lifestyle and grassroots movement, they had many limitations in their business activities due to the absence of the law and policies regulating the establishment and management of consumer cooperatives.After the enactment of the Consumer Co-operatives Act, 1999, consumer cooperatives were able to obtain public confidence and start building the framework of their management.

In 1998, iCOOP formed its framework within the Consumer Co-operative Act. In order to obtain contributions of a certain amount of money regulated by the Act, iCOOP developed the cooperative movement. In 2010, a comprehensive amendment bill of the Consumer Co-operatives Act has expanded the business scope of consumer cooperatives by allowing consumer cooperatives to sell general consumer goods (Park, 2010).

The previous Act restricted the range of goods of consumer cooperatives to agri-foods. The amended Act allows consumer cooperatives to establish federations/national federations to implement mutual aid businesses, and to be supported by the central and local governments.

20.4.4 Organizational structure

Hansalim consists of the Hansalim Federation established by a cooperative association that has 23 nationally distributed cooperatives and a producer's association that producer members joined. Each member cooperative of Hansalim is composed of a headquarter−branch−district organizational structure. For instance, Hansalim Seoul, the largest in the member cooperatives in Seoul, Incheon, and a few districts of Gyeonggi-do, has 270,000 members.

iCOOP is composed of 98 nationally distributed member cooperatives based on the Consumer Co-operatives Act, and iCOOP producers' association based on the Framework Act on Co-operatives. iCOOP strengthens the solidarity between consumers and the organization and supports the establishment of cooperatives.

Korea's consumer cooperatives have collective ownership structures. Members are not eligible to trade membership. The dividends of Korea's consumer cooperatives are decided in accordance with their own constitution and conventions.

Hansalim allocates 73% of total values to producers, and the rest (27%) is used for the distribution process including labor costs, physical distribution, promotion, education,

member activities, financial support to the socially deprived, etc. For rice only, 84.6% of the total value goes to producers, which leaves no margins. Those who want to be a member of Hansalim only need to contribute an initial equity payment. The amount of the payment is slightly different according to the member cooperative. The amount of the contribution is automatically added up whenever they purchase products from Hansalim through either off-line stores or home delivery. When there are surpluses depending on business performance, they are sometimes allocated to members according to a resolution of the general meeting.

iCOOP have had two types of members since 1997; one type who pays monthly membership dues in addition to their contribution and the other who pays only contributions when joining the cooperative. Furthermore, there is a system called the "responsible contribution," where about one million Korean Won per member can be invested as a contribution to a certain purpose needing funds in business. Members who have paid this are provided with different financial benefits.

20.5 Conclusion

As Korea's consumer cooperatives developed in the 1990s, it was required that they be institutionalized by the legal system. The Korean government wanted to foster organic farming and so the Environment-Friendly Agriculture Promotion Act of 1997 was legislated. Similarly, in 1998, the Consumer Co-operatives Act went into effect, by which consumer cooperatives were only able to provide environment-friendly agri-foods to their members. Later, the Act was revised to allow them to operate other businesses. Nevertheless, consumer cooperatives have still played a key role in Korea's organic food market.

The legislation process of the Consumer Co-operatives Act was different from other acts concerning cooperatives. Mostly government legislation initiatives came first, followed by cooperatives. For consumer cooperatives, however, the Act and policy were formed after the growth of consumer cooperatives and civil society. Therefore the background of the legislation, enactment, and amendment of the Consumer Co-operatives Act demonstrates the autonomous characteristics and identity of consumer cooperatives.

The governance of Korea's consumer cooperatives is designed for working together with producers and consumers. The stakeholders of consumer cooperatives with common interests make decisions collectively. This governance seems to reflect the distinctive character of consumer cooperatives in Korea.

Moreover, member directors engage in their cooperative management with autonomy and transparency. Thus there are unlikely to be nonmember professional directors. Korea's consumer cooperatives emphasize democratic participation more than management professionalism. In addition, most members of consumer cooperatives are women, especially housewives. Female members have voluntarily established cooperatives as democratic organizations, taking part in various social activities as well as purchasing processes.

Korea's consumer cooperatives have emerged from the civil society movement. They have developed mainly the retail business of organic agri-foods. These aspects have enacted and implemented the legal foundation, interacting with the roles of the state. It is also related to the decision-making process with producers.

References

Baek, E. M. (2012). The meaning of housekeeping work for women, who participate in consumer co-operatives: Focused on the activities of *iCOOP* in Busan (in Korean). *Journal of Women's Studies, 22*(2), 71–107.

Birchall, J. (2011). *People-centred businesses: Co-operatives, mutuals and the idea of membership.* UK: Palgrave Macmillan.

Hansalim. (2016). White Paper, *Hansalim.*

Hansalim. (2017). Introductory book, *Hansalim.*

Huh, M. Y. (2008). Alternative consumption culture and implication of coops – Focused on the Minwoo coop (in Korean). *The Journal of Rural Society, 18*, 7–36.

Jang, W. S., & Lee, J. E. (2008). Achievements and challenges of Korea's consumer co-operatives (in Korean). *Korea Co-operative Research, 27*(1), 179–201.

Jensen, A. (2013). The labor managed firm – A theoretical model explaining emergence and behavior. *Sharing Ownership, Profits, and Decision-making in the 21st Century Advances in the Economic Analysis of Participatory & Labor-Managed Firms, 14*, 295–327.

Jeong, E. M. (2006). The characteristics of consumer co-operatives in Korea (in Korean). *Rural Economy, 29*(3), 1–18.

Jeong, E. M. (2012). Various branches and the flow of Korea's consumer co-op movement since the 1980s, the origin and evolution of Korea's consumer co-operative movement (in Korean). *Green Tree Press,* 304–340.

Jeong, E. M., Kim, D. H., & Kim, M. M. (2011). The economic fruits and policy tasks of consumer co-operatives in Korea (in Korean). *Korea Rural Economic Institute.*

Jung, G. H. (2008). The role and implications of local community movement in an era of ecological crisis (in Korean). *Economy and Society, 78*, 57–82.

Kim, H. (2004). Principles and directions for urban-rural living community movement (in Korean). *Korean Journal of Organic Agriculture, 12*(1), 67–80.

Kim, S. H., & Huh, C. D. (2014). A study of co-op in Korea: Reviewing the history through social movement frame (in Korean). *Environmental Philosophy, 17*, 5–33.

Lee, D. Y., & Hwang, M. J. (2013). *Study on spreading ethical consumption through consumer co-operatives.* Seoul: Korea Consumer Agency. (in Korean).

Lee, G. N. (2013). Analysis of the economic role of Korea's consumer co-operatives, focusing on the price level and volatility of environment-friendly agricultural products (in Korean). *Consumer Issues Research, 44*(1), 179–196.

Park, S. Y. (2010). *Amendment contents of the consumer co-operatives act and extended suggestions.* Seoul: Korea Consumer Agency. (in Korean).

Webpages

DureCoop Homepage: <http://www.dure-coop.or.kr>.
HappyCoop Homepage: <http://www.happycoop.or.kr>.
Hansalim Homepage: <http://www.Hansalim.or.kr>.
iCOOP KOREA Homepage: <http://www.iCOOP.or.kr>.

Further reading

Cho, W. H. (2010). *The progress and challenges for promotion of environment-friendly organic farming by co-operatives in Korea (in Korean). 2010 the first half year conference* (pp. 85–102). Seoul: Korean Association of Organic Agriculture.

Hansalim. (2015). *One step closer in harmony- Hansalim 2014 Hansalim Annual Report* (in Korean). <http://www.Hansalim.or.kr/wp-content/uploads/2015/06/2014-annual_report_korea.pdf>.

Happycoop. (2015). *2015 Report for an annual general meeting of representatives* (in Korean).

iCOOP Korea. (2012). *Ethical consumerism: A most beautiful practice – iCOOP KOREA 2012 annual report* (in Korean). <http://m.blog.naver.com/iCOOPkorea/20192361290>.

iCOOP Korea. (2015). *Ethical consumerism: A most beautiful practice – iCOOP KOREA 2014 annual report* (in Korean). <http://lemonhee.cafe24.com/ebook/ebook2/2014_Kor.pdf>.

Jang, J. (2012). The role and challenges of Korean co-operative sector in the era of framework act on co-operatives (in Korean). *Journal of Korean Social Trend and Perspective, 86*, 289–320.

Kim, C. G., Jung, H. G., & Moon, D. H. (2012). Production status and market prospect of internal and external environment-friendly agricultural products (in Korean). *Rural Economy*, 14.

Kim, C. G., Kim, J. Y., & Kim, S. S. (2012). Alternative food movement and Korea consumer co-operatives, mainly *Hansalim* (in Korean). *Regional Sociology, 14*(1), 117–143.

Kim, H. (2013). What is community movements: Focusing on Koreas' consumer co-operatives movement (in Korean). *Hwanghae Review*, 16–39, 2013 Autumn.

Lee, D. Y., & Ham, Y. S. (2010). A study on the third sector to discover value and strategy for promotion program: Focusing on consumer co-operatives (in Korean). *Journal of Governmental Studies, 16*(1), 181–214.

Lee, M. Y. (2012). The history of establishment and development of consumer co-operative with sales shop (in Korean). *The origin and development of consumer co-operative movement in Korea.*

2. Case studies of Asian co-ops, including cross-country comparison

Consumer cooperatives' model in Japan

Akira Kurimoto

Hosei University, Tokyo, Japan

21.1 Introduction

Japanese consumer cooperatives have evolved into the world's largest consumer cooperative organizations in terms of membership and turnover and they have exhibited strong features of member participation. They developed a unique model characterized by the predominant membership of housewives, home delivery as a major business model, and a strong social movement dimension. Key research questions to address is why and how this successful model has emerged and evolved.

Japanese-style consumer co-ops have been commended as a model of member participation since the 1980s. They are an example of a successful consumer cooperative movement formed by the initiatives of civil society. The joint workshop held by the International Cooperative's Alliance (ICA) Consumer Committee and Women's Committee held in Tokyo in 1986 appreciated the active member participation of Japanese co-ops, which was echoed in President Marcus' keynote speech on the basic values of cooperatives presented at the ICA Congress in 1988. The ensuing ICA Congresses in 1992 and 1995 resolved the issue of cooperative values and principles, often referring to the Japanese model as one of the best practices.

However, Japanese co-ops have faced intensified competition under the lingering recession and consumers' changing lifestyles accompanied by growing individualism. The turnovers of these co-ops have been stagnating since the mid-1990s, despite still increasing their membership. As a result, the per capita monthly purchase has been decreasing from JP¥19,000 in 1991 to JP¥10,600 in 2014. Store retailing has been most seriously affected by competition and could not return to profitability. However, nonstore retailing is sustaining turnover, while joint buying through the *Han* groups has been replaced/supplemented by individual home delivery.

This chapter starts with the description of a brief history and the structure of consumer cooperatives in Japan. Then, it explains the Japanese consumer cooperative model's characteristics. It identifies the macro and micro factors contributing to the Japanese model's success. It analyzes the impact given by consumer co-ops as a champion of food safety and reliability. In conclusion, it discusses the sustainability of the Japanese model.

Waking the Asian Pacific Cooperative Potential
DOI: https://doi.org/10.1016/B978-0-12-816666-6.00021-5

21.2 Overview of Japanese consumer cooperatives

Japanese consumer co-ops can trace their history to the late 19th century. The first cooperative shops, which modeled the Rochdale Equitable Pioneer's Society, were set up in Tokyo, Osaka, and Kobe in 1879, just 12 years after the Meiji Restoration. After years of trial and error in the course of industrialization, three types of co-ops emerged, namely co-ops attached to companies/factories for their employees, worker-oriented co-ops associated with a radical labor movement, and citizen co-ops organized by middle-class people. At the end of the Second World War, they were mostly destroyed; the left-wing co-ops were liquidated by the militaristic government, while the neutral ones were deprived of trading licenses and finally destroyed by air raids. The consumer movement had to start from scratch, although the legacy of the movement was inherited and kept alive through cooperative leaders.

The history of consumer co-ops in the postwar era can be divided into four epochs; the mushrooming of buying clubs seeking scarce food in the 1940s; the emergence of worker-oriented co-ops sponsored by trade unions in the 1950s, the flourishing of consumerism-based citizen co-ops during the 1960s through to the early 1990s; and then stagnating growth since the mid-1990s onward (Kurimoto, 2017).

Just after the Japanese surrender in 1945, the entire economy fell into chaos due to the massive destruction of production and distribution facilities. Faced with this, the US occupation introduced drastic reforms to democratize the economy such as the agrarian reform, legitimization of unions, and the antimonopoly legislation. The rationing system for staple food as a part of a wartime supply mechanism could not function effectively to support the daily life of consumers. Most of the urban population faced a serious shortage of food and daily necessities as well as being subject to rampant inflation. They had to rely on black markets, visit farmers to barter their valuables for food or starve to death. Under such circumstances, numerous buying clubs were formed by residents in the districts or by workers in the factories/offices. Their mission was to procure food for members from farms/factories and so were often called "buying associations." They had mushroomed at an incredible speed; more than 6500 co-ops were operating in 1947. However, most of them lacked effective management and support systems. They largely collapsed soon after the rationing system began functioning. The number of co-ops had swiftly shrunk to roughly 1000 by 1948, when the Consumer Cooperative Act was enacted. As such the first boom of consumer co-ops came to a quick end. The Japanese Consumer Co-operative Union (JCCU) was set up as a national body in 1951 to help the revival of consumer co-ops under the new legislation.

In the 1950s, trade unionism entered an expanding phase and started supporting "worker's welfare businesses" to supplement its main function of collective bargaining. In this process, worker-oriented co-ops were created to undertake economic activities to meet workers' various needs under the sponsorship of trade unions. The local trade union councils assisted to set up "worker-led community consumer co-ops" in the 1950s, enabling these co-ops to operate relatively large stores in comparison and competition to small retailers. These trade union-based co-ops provided a variety of food and consumer goods in local cities prior to the advent of supermarkets and achieved quick success by automatically enrolling unionists as co-op members and attracting a wider range of consumers. This triggered the reaction of retailers, leading to intense anti-cooperative campaigns. However, their success was short-lived due to the lack of management skills or member education; they failed to compete with supermarkets introduced by progressive retailers in the late 1950s. Some of them disappeared, while others transformed into citizen co-ops in the 1960s. On the other hand, trade unions and consumer co-ops worked together to set up worker-oriented co-ops such as labor banks, insurance co-ops, and housing co-ops. Today labor banks and insurance co-ops established themselves as "workers' welfare enterprises" in which trade unions retain a strong influence.

The rapid economic expansion in Japan since the late 1950s drastically enhanced the standard of living, while it brought a massive migration of people to large cities. This process was synchronized with revolutionary changes in consumption and distribution patterns. Manufacturers established the mass production and wider distribution of packaged groceries using chemicals as food additives, which often caused serious health problems. Fresh food was now processed in more industrialized ways, making massive use of pesticides and antibiotics. Consumers were concerned with these chemicals as well as the high inflation, misleading labeling, and air/water pollution. Such circumstances gave momentum to the consumer movement seeking safer foods and a healthier environment. One of the responses that emerged was "citizen co-ops" backed by housewives in the 1960s and 1970s. Some co-ops invented the "joint buying" or home delivery to *Han* groups[1] that made collective orders and received products on a weekly basis. Citizen co-ops were set up in all seats of prefectural government until 1980, attracting a wide range of consumers; the membership of the consumer cooperative movement expanded from 2 million to 14 million, while the turnover has grown 10 times between 1970 and 1990. Thus the Japanese

model of consumer cooperatives was created with housewives as a driving force.

The consolidation of the buying functions, however, was slow in comparison with their European counterparts as primary co-op societies continued to buy from local suppliers and develop their own CO-OP brand products. In 1958 however, major co-ops established a wholesale federation to pool their buying power at the national level. This federation then integrated local buying functions and finally merged with the JCCU in 1962, aiming at strengthening the central buying and national coordination. During the 1980s, "core" primary co-ops were established through merging smaller societies in many prefectures under the JCCU's guidance. In the 1990s, co-ops formed regional consortiums, beyond prefectural borders, which now cater for nearly 90% of the overall turnover of co-ops.

Since the mid-1990s, however, the turnover of consumer co-ops has stagnated because of the lingering recession and stiffer competition seeking to get a larger market share. The number of independent retailers continued to decline, but even some of the larger department stores and supermarket chains also failed. As a result, the concentration was intensified; the Aeon Group and Seven & I Holding became the biggest retailers through a number of mergers and acquisitions. To meet the challenges of more women working outside the home and with a more individualized lifestyle, co-ops introduced individual home delivery, partly supplementing and partly replacing joint buying. They also made efforts to strengthen their buying power through regional consortiums. They succeeded in maintaining their overall turnover in the past decade, while the declining store sales has been offset by the growing home delivery sales.

---

[1] *Han* means a small organizational unit. *Han* groups consist of several members in the neighborhood.

Consumer co-ops are regulated by the Consumer Co-operative Act (1948), which classifies co-ops into categories according to the type of business (retailing, healthcare, insurance, housing, and so on) and areas of operation (communities or workplaces). Retail co-ops provide members with food, nonfood products, and various services. The typical retail co-ops operating in communities are called *citizen co-ops*, which account for 70% of the total co-op membership. *Workplace co-ops* operate in companies and government offices to serve employees working in these institutions. *Extended workplace co-ops* are hybrids of these types and have incorporated local consumers living in the communities adjacent to the institutions. *University co-ops* and *schoolteachers' co-ops* cater to the specific needs of the constituencies within these institutions including students, faculty members, and schoolteachers. *Medical* or *health co-ops* provide health and social care services at hospitals and clinics. *Insurance co-ops* or *kyosai* provide consumers with life and general insurance policies. *Housing co-ops* sell or rent mainly collective houses and provide maintenance and/or repair services. Other than these, there are also co-ops that specialize in *elderly/child care provision, environmental conservation*, and so on.

Japanese consumer co-ops have a three-tiered structure stretching from primary co-ops to prefectural/national unions/federations. According to the Consumer Co-operative Act, 300 or more consumers may establish a primary co-op, while federations can be set up at the secondary and tertiary levels. The prefectural unions and inter-prefectural consortiums are formed by primary co-ops. National federations composed of insurance, housing, and university co-ops also exist. The JCCU with several categories of affiliated members has the dual functions of being a national center for all types of co-ops as well as a national consortium for retail co-ops.

21.3 Japanese consumer cooperative model: Its characteristics

Japanese consumer cooperatives exhibit unique features of a successful model in both economic and social terms. The most distinctive feature has been the membership predominantly consisting of women, particularly housewives. They constitute the majority of members and of board members. The characteristics of the Japanese model can be summarized as (1) active female member participation, (2) home delivery as a business model, and (3) a strong social movement dimension (Kurimoto, 2010). Women started buying clubs to buy unadulterated pure milk from reliable producers in the 1960s. These groups evolved into *Han* groups of consumer co-ops. *Han* groups are small units where several members in the neighborhood join to channel their voices to the co-op. They were invented by the Tsuruoka Co-op, which was established under the initiative of local trade unions in 1955. Originally the cooperative asked members to gather together at a given member's home where co-op staff instructed them on how to practice self-service, instead of them visiting individual houses. *Han* groups proved to be an effective way of facilitating communication between members and management. This experience was highly appreciated and has been disseminated throughout the country since the 1960s. In pursuit of member democracy and participation as the essence of cooperation, S. Å. Böök praised *Han* groups as "an interesting example of a combination of very local autonomy with the responsibility for, and identity with, the whole."[2] As a matter

---

[2] Böök, S. Å., 'Co-operative Values in a Changing World', *ICA Studies and Reports Vol.19*, 1992, pp. 113–114.

of fact, they are a reflection of the Asian collectivist culture. In addition, various channels and ways of member participation have been developed such as district committees, consumer panels, and study groups. Mr. Lars Marcus highly appreciated such experiences of member participation in his keynote speech, "Basic Values of Co-operatives" at the ICA Stockholm Congress in 1988.

The second key feature is the unique business operation of home delivery. Joint buying was invented partly as a response to the institutional impediment to operating stores and partly as an innovation grasping opportunities based on members' needs. This system of home delivery is unique to *Han* groups, in which members regularly place orders to co-op delivery staff who distribute food and daily necessities in the next week. The system was invented to serve consumers who were concerned and wanted to buy safer food that was free of hazardous additives, chemical residues, and so forth. It also fits the needs of the population in the newly developed out-of-town areas, where they lacked shopping facilities. It presupposed the collaboration of members for ordering, receiving, and sorting products among them. Such voluntary works contributed to the low-cost operation, while members were compensated by the convenience. In addition, it's easy for members to raise complaints or requests to the management through delivery personnel, who in turn responds to their voices to improve products and the operation. Such feedback has worked and strengthened member loyalty to the co-ops. Thus the joint buying system could combine economic efficiency with member participation. Institutionally speaking, co-ops did not have to bother about the resistance from retailers; there was no regulation pertaining to home delivery. However, the joint buying model has faced various challenges caused by the changing environment in the 1990s, and has been replaced or supplemented by individual home delivery.

The third feature is the strong social movement dimensions reflecting on the associational aspect of cooperation. As previously mentioned, co-ops had sprung from ethical consumerism and ecological campaigns that sought to find alternative solutions to a raft of problems associated with the rapid industrialization and rampant corporate power in the 1960s and 1970s. These co-ops have been a driving force of the consumer movement both in terms of resource mobilization and playing the role of a focal point in the National Liaison Committee of Consumer Organizations (Shodanren) since 1956 and the Consumers Organization of Japan (COJ) since 2005. Co-ops also took an active part in pacifist campaigns when the threat of nuclear war was widely felt in the 1980s. They were involved in the wider concerns pertaining to environment conservation and social welfare in communities. They undertook campaigns for establishing consumer rights through learning, collecting signatures, and petitioning to governments, resulting in the enactment of pro-consumer legislations in the 1990s—2000s. As such they have been oriented toward ethical consumer culture from inception, which is quite different from the workers' culture that had dominated consumer co-ops in many European countries.

21.4 Macro factors affecting consumer cooperatives' development

The emergence and evolution of the Japanese consumer co-op model has been the result of a number of key macro factors. The overall socioeconomic background since the 1950s can be summarized as rapid industrialization and economic growth, the energy shift from coal to oil and nuclear power, the revolution in production and distribution patterns, the consumer revolution and consumerism, the degrading environment and ecologist campaigns, the urbanization synchronized with depopulating rural areas, weakening community ties, and the shift from extended families to nuclear families in which housewives take care of household chores.

21.4.1 Protectionist industrial policy

The most important macro factor that directly affected the evolution of consumer cooperatives was the structure of distributive trade and commercial legislation for protecting small retailers introduced by a corporatist state. The Japanese distribution system had been characterized by low productivity associated with numerous small retailers and a complicated structure. In fact, the number of retail shops continued to increase until peaking at 1.7 million in 1982. The retail industry has functioned as a safety valve for unemployment, while small retailers were always pressed to curb competition by forming cartels or lobbying against modernized large-scale retailers. They had raised their strong political voice to the ruling party as they had votes and money to push their protectionist stance in formulating commercial policies. Thus the Department Store Act was enacted to regulate the permission for store opening and operating dates and hours in 1956. The advent of supermarkets in the late 1950s brought revolutionary changes in the grocery distribution system with the introduction of chain-stores and a self-service system. Hence the Department Store Act was replaced by the Large-scale Retail Store Act in 1974 to include newcomers such as general merchandise stores and supermarkets in the regulatory framework, which required developers to undergo an examination by the Commissions for Adjusting Retail Activities before filing notice to open new stores with a selling floor exceeding 1500 square meters (3000 square meters in megalopolis). It also required large store operators to conform to various restrictions on operating

hours and a minimum number of closing days. Cooperatives were also obliged to similar regulations published by the competent ministries, but they prioritized the home delivery that has been out of the scope of restrictions. These regulations delayed modernization in retailing, but could not reverse the declining trend of independent retailers despite government subsidies and low-interest loans. However, since 1990, deregulation was introduced due to domestic and foreign pressure and finally this Act was replaced by the Large-scale Retail Store Site Act in 1998, which aimed to regulate the environmental impacts of retail operations (traffic jams, noise, and garbage) rather than the adjustment of interests among retailers.

21.4.2 Legal impediments to consumer cooperatives

This institutional framework has delivered a persistent impact on the evolution of consumer cooperatives. The Consumer Co-operative Act had contained several impediments to success, namely cooperatives were not allowed to trade with nonmembers, trade in other prefectures, or undertake credit businesses. The prohibition of nonmember trade, especially, had a long-standing effect on the evolution of co-ops. Cooperatives had been threatened from time to time by anti-cooperative campaigns organized by retailers' associations who insisted on stricter enforcement of the prohibition of nonmember trade. The campaign in 1954—59 was a reaction to the successful stores established by worker-led local consumer cooperatives, in which retailers requested a strengthening of the regulations on nonmember trade, and confining cooperative membership to consumers under the poverty line. Cooperatives resisted such moves by mobilizing members to patronize cooperative shops, raise share capital, and recruit new members. Under such circumstances, the JCCU called for a nationwide campaign to strengthen co-ops, while its efforts to form an alliance with women's associations, etc., resulted in the foundation of the National Liaison Committee of Consumer Organizations (*Shodanren*) in 1956. Finally, this anti-cooperative campaign generated two outcomes; first, the Special Retail Measures Law of 1959 added further restrictions to nonmember trade prohibition, introducing the element of coordination of interests with small retailers; second, more progressive retailers turned to opening supermarkets. Thereafter cooperatives had to fight retailers' persistent campaigns until 1986, when the stance of public commercial policy was reversed to favor competition.

21.5 Micro factors for success

21.5.1 Role of women cooperators and university cooperatives

Under such a socioeconomic and institutional framework, women cooperators emerged as a major driving force in civil society, championing the consumer cooperative movement. The bulk of women had played the traditional gender role of housewives and taken major responsibility for housekeeping such as shopping, cooking, and child/elderly care. Although they had accomplished increasingly higher education, they were expected to stay home as housewives by social convention and institutional arrangements. In this sense, they were generally deprived of opportunities to express their concerns on food safety, unfair trade practices, and environmental degradation and to take part in collective action. These housewives found consumer co-ops to be a vehicle to make their voices heard in the interest of ethical consumers. Since they had time to spare and energy to act, they took part in co-op activities to solve consumer problems.

They extensively learned about consumer issues, conducted various activities, and became lay leaders of co-ops. It is estimated that more than 100,000 women members are in leadership roles at the neighborhood, school district, municipal, and prefectural levels. Some of them became leaders of nonprofits, social enterprises, community organizations, or even politicians. As Professor Kawaguchi put it, "Japanese consumer co-ops occupy the position of godmothers comparable with faith organization's role in promoting non-profits in the US."[3]

In addition, to such consumer leadership, managers and employees of university co-ops also played an important role in developing consumer co-ops. They perceived the limitations of expanding membership and business since the operation of university co-ops has been confined to campuses and students are turned over every few years. They found a new frontier of expansion in the communities outside the campus by helping local housewives to set up consumer co-ops since the mid-1960s, while consumer co-ops sought to obtain management expertise that university co-op leaders and employees accumulated from the business operations. Hokkaido University Co-op opened a branch for faculty staff adjacent to the campus that became Sapporo Citizen Co-op (today's Co-op Sapporo) in 1965. Some university co-ops in Tokyo and Saitama prefecture helped to launch Tokorozawa Co-op (today's Co-op Mirai), while Doshisha University Co-op assisted to set up Rakuhoku Co-op (today's Kyoto Co-op) in 1964—65. Then consumer co-ops were set up in most prefectural capital cities until 1980 and many of the leaders of university co-ops became the founders or top leaders of these consumer co-ops. University co-ops have brought new ideas such as CO-OP brand products and regional consortiums to consumer co-ops as well.

---

[3] Kawaguchi, K. (2006), "Social economy and consumer co-ops," in *Gendai Seikyo Ron no Tankyu*, CCIJ.

21.5.2 Role of consumer cooperatives' leadership

Consumer co-ops turned disadvantages into advantages. They have developed a unique business model of home delivery that overcame the key obstacle of accessing capital. Joint buying was invented to facilitate a low-cost retail operation. It could be started with relatively little capital; co-ops didn't have to make a heavy investment in store sites, buildings, and furniture, all they needed were computers, warehouses, and delivery vans. It didn't require sophisticated techniques of store operation, which could have only been obtained by hiring expensive managers or taken years of training. In the 1980s, technological innovations were made; computer-read order sheets replaced the cumbersome tallying of individual order sheets in *Han* groups; withdrawals from members' bank accounts liberated members from the chore of handling cash; and semiautomatic sorting machines facilitated efficient picking of products in warehouses. These innovations were soon shared among co-ops, accelerating the expansion of co-ops. In the 1990s, individual home delivery was introduced as another innovation.

To cope with the institutional impediment prohibiting nonmember trade, consumer co-ops adopted the strategy of persuading all customers to become co-op members and have conducted membership drives every year since 1960. They have also raised share capital by asking members to invest more since they lacked other financial instruments.[4] They have involved members in governance in various ways through *Han* groups, district committees, and consumer panels in addition to the legally required organs such as annual general meetings (AGMs) and the board. Thus they have developed strong member participation based on the identity principle of membership as owners and users. Such adherence to membership has resulted in independent organizations. It might be said co-ops have succeeded in translating the disadvantage of nonmember trade prohibition into an advantage.

21.6 Impact of Japanese model on members and wider society

Consumer co-ops have played a key role in establishing food safety and the emergence of a sustainable society. The total membership of consumer co-ops surpassed 28 million or 49.5% of total households, that means that one in two families belong to them. It is much bigger than agricultural co-ops (roughly 10 million) and trade unions (nearly 10 million). The percentage of households holding membership in citizen co-ops is highest in Miyagi prefecture (75.1%), followed by Niigata prefecture (61.6%), and then Hokkaido (60.4%).

The total retail turnover of consumer co-ops amounted to JP¥3.1 trillion or 2.67% of the market, making them the third largest retailer in 2015 after the Aeon Group and Seven & I Group. Several large cooperatives are ranked in the ICA's Global 300,[5] but their size is more clearly demonstrated by the fact that the aggregated membership of consumer cooperatives affiliated with JCCU is close to 70% of its European counterpart affiliated with Euro Coop, while their total turnover accounts for about 27% of the latter's in 2011. As far as the quality is concerned, Hasselmann already noted in 1989 that, "[t]he Japanese consumer co-operative movement is the only national

---

[4]   As a result, share investment per capita amounts to US$300, much higher than the US$1.3 in the United Kingdom.

[5]   The ICA's Global 300 for 2015 ranked Co-op Mirai as 146th, JCCU as 147th, Co-op Sapporo as 191st, Co-op Kobe as 208th, and U Co-op as 258th in the retail sector; and Zenrosai as 98th, FJCC as 101st, and JCIF as 270th in the insurance sector.

organization of consumer co-operatives outside Europe which has succeeded in achieving power and influence," while Birchall suggested that, "[t]he Japanese movement has much to teach not only Asian but also western European and north American consumer co-operatives about how to run a successful consumer co-operative movement."[6] Since food retailing accounts for 82% of co-ops' turnover, they have put special emphasis on food and had great impacts on food retailers and manufacturers through consumer campaigns and the development of alternative products. Although such initiatives were soon copied by competitors, co-ops have played a leading role in enhancing food safety standards while they exercised price leadership in some limited commodities such as kerosene oil for heating.

Consumer co-ops are widely recognized as the strongest consumer organization that conducts consumer campaigns and develops alternative products and distribution systems. They developed CO-OP label products from 1960 onwards and succeeded in creating a brand image of being "safe and reliable," reflecting consumers' viewpoints and eliminating hazardous ingredients and excessive packaging, while spreading adequate information on contents and usage, and breaking the control over prices. They also initiated direct transaction with producers (*Sanchoku*) to reflect consumer viewpoints in the production of raw food. These practices are now widely mimicked by competitors. Co-op members took part in the development process of CO-OP products and *Sanchoku* by sampling and feedback. They also undertook consumer education on unit pricing, the value of a balanced diet, financial life planning, and an environment-friendly lifestyle. Such activities fit in with rethinking the wider patterns of consumption for healthy eating and environmental protection. The "My bag"

campaign initiated by co-ops to replace plastic bags succeeded in changing consumer behavior and contributed to a reform of the Container/Packaging Recycling Act in 2006.

Consumer co-ops have played a pivotal role in promoting corporate social responsibility campaigns against food additives and hazardous products, cartels and controlled prices, and environmental degradation through the backing of *Shodanren* in terms of consumer mobilization and finance. In the 1990s, *Shodanren* was the focal point of campaigns to enact a series of pro-consumer legislations including the Product Liability Act of 1994; Consumer Contract Act of 2000; Food Safety Basic Act of 2003; Consumer Basic Act of 2004; and the Whistleblower Protection Act of 2004. For this, it won recognition as the key entity representing consumers' voices in Japan. Consumers' collective action was introduced in the revised Consumer Contract Act of 2006, with strong consumer backup, enabling qualified consumer organizations to file lawsuits against the unlawful conduct of service providers on behalf of affected consumers. The COJ, set up as a nonprofit organization, was recognized as a qualified consumer organization by the Cabinet Office in 2007, which have the authority to initiate lawsuits for the suspension of the inappropriate provisions and practices of service providers. As of March 2018, there are 17 qualified consumer organizations, most of which were set up and supported by consumer co-ops.

21.7 Conclusion

Despite the adversarial environment characterized by protectionist industrial policy and legal impediments, an ethically focused civil society enabled the emergence of the world's

---

[6] Hasselman, "Japan's Consumer Movement: The World's Largest Consumer Co-op Organization" p. 9; Birchall, *The International Co-operative Movement*, p. 180.

largest unique consumer cooperative movement. They have managed to maintain their social mission as well as their participatory culture in the face of increasing competition and globalization.

Consumer cooperatives are facing multiple challenges derived from a changing environment, an aging population and low birth rate, bipolarization of income, tougher competition with supermarkets and convenience stores, and the growing impacts of information technology and globalization removing economic barriers. To continue to lead the way, these challenges need to be addressed by strengthening internal governance and leadership, and ensuring professional management to enhance competitiveness. With the growing size of consumer cooperatives, it is imperative to increase member participation, invest in member education and staff training, and ensure smooth succession of leaders and managers. In addition, they need to give tangible impact to securing food safety and integrity in the extended supply chain, protecting the consumer's rights and contribute to a more sustainable society. As the largest consumer associations and enterprises in the world, Japanese consumer co-ops are expected to continue to lead in building "democratic alternatives to state-led capitalism" (Kurimoto, 2005).

References

Kurimoto, A. (2005). *The institutional change and consumer co-operation: Japanese vs European models. Consumerism versus Capitalism?* Gent: Amsab-Institute of Social History.

Kurimoto, A. (2010). *Evolution and characteristics of Japanese-style consumer co-ops. Toward contemporary co-operative studies: Perspectives from Japan's consumer co-ops.* Tokyo: Consumer Co-operative Institute of Japan.

Kurimoto, A. (2017). *Building consumer democracy: The trajectory of consumer co-operation in Japan, 1950—2010. Global history of consumer co-operation since 1850.* Brill.

Further reading

Grubel, R. (1999). The consumer co-op in Japan: Building democratic alternatives to state-led capitalism. In E. Furlough, & C. Strikwerda (Eds.), *Consumers against capitalism?* Maryland: Rowman & Littlefield Publishers, Inc.

Kawaguchi, K. (1992). A development model of the co-operative movement: Japan type. *What are the viable development models and contributions for the future?*, Tokyo.

Kurimoto, A. (2001). Innovating a joint buying system through IT. *Review of International Co-operation, 94*(1), International Co-operative Alliance, Geneva.

Kurimoto, A. (2008). *Structure and governance of networks: Cases of Franchising and co-operative chains. Strategy and governance of networks.* Springer.

Kurimoto, A. (2013). *Chapter 23: Japan. International handbook of cooperative law.* Springer.

Vacek, G. (1989). Japan. In J. Brazda, & R. Schediwy (Eds.), *Consumer co-operatives in a changing world* (Volume 2). Geneva: International Co-operative Alliance.

Consumer cooperatives summary

Akira Kurimoto

Hosei University, Tokyo, Japan

22.1 Introduction

The Asian region has undergone drastic changes since 1965, particularly in the post-Vietnam War era. It has been transformed from battlefields to markets, bringing in the rapid economic development described as the "East Asia Miracle" by the World Bank. Ronald Dore attributed these processes to "late development effect" that was realized by catching up with the industrialized economies of the West, while Chang Kyung-Sup characterized them as "compressed modernity" that generated unexpected social problems. Rapid industrialization and urbanization have drastically changed consumer behavior from cooking raw materials to buying processed/cooked food, while the traditional wet markets and "mom-and-pop shops" have been largely replaced by modern store formats such as supermarkets, hypermarkets, and convenience stores. Such a retail revolution started attracting, and largely being driven by, world-class retailers that sought to penetrate this most populous region with growing potential to become enormous consumer markets. Foreign mega retailers such as Carrefour, Metro, Tesco, and Walmart came to the region, but Asian retailers such as Japanese Jusco (Aeon) and Seven Eleven, and Hong Kong's Dairy Farm also entered into these markets. These foreign businesses established themselves as leading retailers obtaining high market shares, although some had already withdrawn due to various reasons. The level of consolidation of the industry is growing, but remains smaller in comparison with European countries.[1] Under such circumstances, food retailing has undergone unprecedented changes that made the difference between winning and losing in these decades. Successful consumer cooperatives emerged in Asia, but they have taken diverse trajectories in different political and socioeconomic contexts. Here the cases of the most successful consumer cooperatives in four countries are examined, namely NTUC FairPrice in Singapore, Saigon Co.op in Vietnam, Hansalim and iCOOP in South Korea, and citizen cooperatives in Japan.

---

[1] Elizabeth Howard, ed. *The Changing Face of Retailing in Asia Pacific*, Routledge, 2010, pp. 1–11.

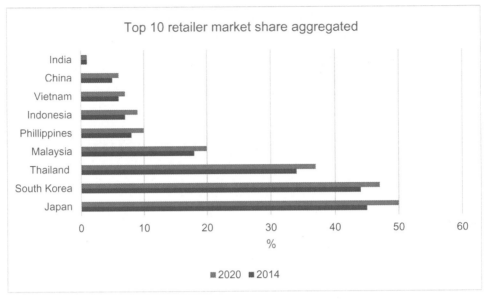

Source: *IGD: Understanding Asia's Rapidly Evolving Retail Markets, 2015.*

22.2 Consumer cooperatives in the Asian context

When Asian nations got independence in the late 1940s, most of them were characterized by agrarian societies in which agriculture was the dominant industry with farmers constituting the bulk of the population. So, it was natural that the new independent governments gave concentrated efforts to the promotion of agricultural cooperatives to enhance food production, while they showed much lower interest in consumer cooperatives. However, rapid industrialization and massive migration from rural areas started forming working-class and middle-class sectors who often lived in apartments on the outskirts of large cities. At the same time, such a development caused various consumer/environmental problems such as inflation, hazardous products, disguised labeling, and air/water pollution, while changing patterns of consumer behavior and growing concerns regarding the safety and quality of food have been increasingly recognized. Under such circumstances, consumer cooperatives have emerged in cities to cater to local residents and in workplaces to serve consumers in local communities and employees in public institutions, companies, and universities. The International Co-operative Alliance Asia-Pacific Consumer Committee was set up in 1988 to exchange experiences and provide technical assistance. Some successful co-ops emerged in Japan, South Korea, Singapore, and Vietnam, while other co-ops have faded in the capital cities of Thailand, Malaysia, and the Philippines. There are many factors affecting the success and failure of consumer co-ops, but here we examine state policy, relationship with social movements, and retail expertise.

22.3 Legal framework and state policy

The legal framework and state policy have been strong macro factors affecting to the evolution of consumer co-ops. We can observe the stark contrast between favorable treatments and impeding ones. The Co-operative Societies Act in Vietnam offers many privileges to co-ops (support of staff training, market enlargement, new technology application, capital access, and low leasing fees on land in addition to tax exemption), but also leaves them subject to strong state supervision and control by people's committees (governments). The Co-operative Societies Act in Singapore follows the common law tradition in which the Registry of Co-operative Societies and the Singapore National Co-operative Federation have jointly issued the Code of Governance for Co-operatives. Co-ops don't pay tax while they have to contribute to the Central Co-operative Fund to develop new co-ops in Singapore. In contrast, the sector-specific Consumer Co-operative Act in Japan has some impediments including completely prohibiting nonmember trade, limiting trading area in prefectures, and excluding credit business. The Consumer Co-operative Act in South Korea followed this pattern and confined business activities to the trade of environment-friendly produce and processed food. This law was amended to enable co-ops to deal with general consumer products and form federations in 2010.

Accordingly, state policy on consumer co-ops varies significantly. A wide range of state support and promotion measures in Vietnam enabled Saigon Co.op, as a state-driven entity, to achieve exceptional success in rapidly developing modern retail formats in a short period and to become the largest retailer in the country, however, the cooperative identity still needs to be established since its ownership and membership is still ambiguous. As such, consumer co-op has been created by top-down efforts. In Singapore, NTUC FairPrice enjoyed the best locations of supermarkets in the housing & development board flats that accommodate 80% of Singaporeans or nearby the mass rapid transit stations that provide public transportation. Such

favorable treatments seem to be attributable to tripartism (see section 22.4). On the other hand, some governments have been indifferent to consumer co-ops, even giving impediments such as the prohibition of nonmember trade under the pressure of small retailers such as in Japan and South Korea. In these cases, consumer co-ops had no choice other than creating member-based organizations with consumer investment, patronage, and governance from the bottom up. That resulted in the coexistence of separate national organizations reflecting different missions and strategies. Japanese co-ops enjoy a small tax concession that is diminishing, while the Korean co-op has no tax relief.

22.4 Relationship with social movements

The relationship with social movements is also an important factor in the evolution of consumer co-ops. Singapore has a strong tradition of social corporatism in which employer organizations, trade unions, and the government pursue a cooperative relationship (tripartism). The National Trade Union Congress (NTUC) is a dominant national center of unions with 230,000 members that has a close relationship with the ruling People's Action Party. It has a wing of "social enterprises" operating a wide range of businesses including retailing, food business, insurance, healthcare, eldercare, childcare, leisure, and so on with a social mission to moderate the cost of living. NTUC FairPrice with 56% of the retail market and NTUC Income as a top composite insurer are flagships. Only members of trade unions affiliated with the NTUC are eligible for co-op membership. Saigon Co.op also has a mission to stabilize price, but its relationship with social movement is still in the beginning phases, reflecting the weak representation of consumers' interests.

South Korean consumer cooperatives have different origins, but most of them were started by labor and civil movements in the 1980s, and many of their leaders have such backgrounds. Even now, cooperatives maintain close relationships with labor unions and civil organizations. They involve farmers as members or tie up with farmers' groups to maintain equal partnership with producers. They strongly promote environment-friendly agriculture and campaign to buy locally grown produce.

Consumer co-ops in Japan have mixed experiences. In the 1950s, trade union–based cooperatives had been established in the insurance and banking sectors (today's Rosai and Rokin), while housewives set up buying clubs to buy unadulterated food as a part of the consumer movement in the late 1960s, that evolved into today's citizen co-ops as a mainstream of consumer co-ops. Citizen co-ops have been involved in consumer/ecological campaigns and are often seen as a stronghold of the consumer movement, while their relationship with trade unions remains weak, except for the network organization known as the National Council of Workers' Welfare (Rofukukyo).

22.5 Micro factors contributing to success

There are some micro factors contributing to the success of consumer co-ops. All the cases described demonstrate that these co-ops had the right business strategies under the various circumstances. NTUC FairPrice and Saigon Co. op have succeeded in deploying a variety of modern retail formats in the best locations to enjoy an early advantage before competitors built up the retail networks in their respective countries. It should be noted that the former has shared technical know-how of advanced store operations with the latter, and they have set up a joint venture to develop hypermarkets in Vietnam, while the latter also benefited from

technical know-how given by Swedish and Japanese consumer co-ops. NTUC FairPrice developed a supply chain linking suppliers and distribution centers for dry groceries and fresh food with a wide range of private brands, while Saigon Co.op expanded the capacity of warehouses to support rapidly proliferating stores and started developing their own brands.

The Japanese and Korean consumer co-ops took deferent trajectories. They were late comers in food retailing since most of the best locations had already been occupied by major supermarket chains. They suffered from the prohibition of nonmember trade on top of the regulations of the Large-Scale Retail Store Acts. Under such circumstances, they developed home delivery to consumer groups, and later to individual consumers, as an alternative. They found advantages of non-store retailing that required little capital for operations compared with opening/running stores and fitted lifestyle of consumers who wished to buy safer products with low pesticide and food additives. Today, home delivery accounts for 70% of co-ops' turnover in Japan, while store sales exceed home delivery in iCOOP. In Japan, co-ops developed supermarkets and convenience stores, but have not tried to compete with mega stores except for some large co-ops, while iCOOP concentrated on opening mini stores called Natural Dream stores. In Japan, they built distribution centers and food laboratories to secure the quality and safety of food, while the iCOOP Group developed organic food clusters consisting of warehouses and processing plants. Both movements also developed private brands for processed food with low food additives and promoted direct transaction with farmers for sourcing environment-friendly produce. In these processes, they have encouraged members to participate in governance and product development through monitoring products and voicing their opinions.

22.6 Challenges facing consumer cooperatives

The Asian region faces challenges of demographic transition in different ways. The shrinking population associated with low birth rates and the rapidly aging population creates multiple problems in maintaining the workforce and social security system in East Asia and Singapore, while the growing young population necessitates the securing of employment and building of infrastructure in other Asian countries. The retail industry will have to adjust to this mega trend to respond to the changing needs of the population.

No doubt globalization and the information and communication technology revolution will bring stiffer competition in food retailing. International and Asian giant retailers seek expansion in this growing market and lead further concentration. The fully automated stores where purchases are recorded linked with use of smart phones are being introduced after pilot projects while Amazon is threatening home delivery business of grocery items. How Artificial Intelligence will unfold and transform our society and economy is unknown, but it will have great impacts on the future of consumer co-ops.

22.7 Conclusion

Asian consumer co-ops have taken varied trajectories reflecting the different socioeconomic and political contexts in which they operate. They have created unique models by either a top-down or a bottom-up approach, both of which are different from co-ops in Europe. Co-ops in Singapore and Vietnam achieved rapid deployment of modern retail formats before competitors built them and became large retailers, while co-ops in Japan and South Korea have developed home delivery businesses to groups or individuals relying on member participation for financing and patronaging. Facing the challenges of demographic transition and stiffer competition, Asian consumer co-ops need to enhance competitiveness through consolidation and investment in modern technology, while they have to maintain their cooperative identity with strong member participation. In this chapter we could not cover other good examples such as some consumer co-ops operating as member-driven organizations in India or Foodstuffs as the largest supermarket chain in New Zealand totally owned by Kiwi retailers. We shall continue looking for and analyzing best practices in the Asian and Pacific region.

Further reading

Howard, E. (Ed.), (2010). *The changing face of retailing in the Asia Pacific*. Routledge.

ICA Committee on Consumer Co-operation for Asia and the Pacific. (2012). *The present status of consumer co-operatives for Asia and the Pacific: 2012, ICA Asia and Pacific*, New Delhi.

Larke, R. (2006). Trends in retailing in East Asia. In M. Krafft, & K. M. Mantrala (Eds.), *Retailing in the 21st century*. Springer.

Nick, M. (2015). *Understanding Asia's rapidly evolving retail markets*, IGD.

Credit Co-ops

Teachers Mutual Bank case study

Peter Mason

Cufa Ltd, Sydney, Australia

23.1 Introduction

People-centered cooperation around personal finances has existed in Australia since 1905 through credit cooperatives (Butterfield, 2016; Lewis, 1996); however, the more formal structures of Australian credit unions came into existence in 1946 (Cutcher & Kerr, 2006; Lewis, 1996), mostly at a community level and predominately through parishes and industry associations (Cutcher & Kerr, 2006). The emergence of credit unions was also driven by market realities, "during WW2 the personal credit market was dominated by loan sharks and hire-purchase finance companies, who often charged interest rates in excess of 80 per cent" (Cutcher & Mason, 2013, p. 256). This resulted in the New South Wales (NSW) government acting to regulate the market with the 1941 NSW Small Loans Facility Act (Lewis, 1996, p. 9).

This chapter examines a teachers' credit union that began in a northern suburb of Sydney, Australia. By keeping faithful to its original mission to look after the banking needs of teachers, it has grown into one of the biggest mutuals in the financial cooperative sector in Australia. This chapter will highlight the journey of the credit union as it developed into what became a tightly

regulated and competitive market, all the while staying committed and relevant to its membership.

23.2 Credit unions and their origin in Australia

The credit union model, it has been argued (Cutcher & Kerr, 2006, p. 35; Cutcher & Mason, 2013, p. 256; Lewis, 1996, p. 14), was bought to Australia by Kevin Yates after his return from WW2 duty when he was stationed in Canada, hence, Australia's credit union federated structure has been modeled on the North American credit union system. As the credit union financial model became more well known, industry-specific credit unions began to emerge. The subsequent growth of credit unions was partially driven by a government-imposed credit restraint that limited the access of average Australians' to loans, with 1961 seeing Australia go into a short-lived recession (Lewis, 1996).

Globally, financial cooperatives in their various guises have a long history of people coming together to informally save and borrow from each other (Moody & Fite, 1984). They are an expression of people understanding that together they can improve their individual

Waking the Asian Pacific Cooperative Potential
DOI: https://doi.org/10.1016/B978-0-12-816666-6.00023-9
253

circumstances (Evans, Grell, & Klaehn, 2006). While credit unions are spread across the globe in 103 countries (WOCCU, 2013),[1] the effectiveness and utility of credit unions are often contested.

Credit unions are formed on a set of principles and a philosophy that is based on "liberal and Christian ideals" (Cutcher & Kerr, 2006, p. 34). Such a philosophy sees people unite and create shared norms, a sense of shared values, and a common identity. The operating principles of credit unions are categorized into three main areas. The first area is *democratic structure*, where the principles speak to (1) open and voluntary membership, (2) democratic control, and (3) nondiscrimination. The second area is *service to members*, which covers (1) distribution to members to ensure members are provided with fair rates of interest and dividends on shares in the institution, (2) building financial stability, and (3) service to members, which ensures that the financial cooperative improves the economic and social wellbeing of all members. The last area is *social goals*, which actively promote (1) on-going education, (2) cooperation among cooperatives, and (3) social responsibility.

The lived experience of the early founders of the credit union in this case study speaks to their agency within their community. The role of everyday life (de Certeau, 1984; de Certeau, Giard, & Mayol, 1998; Lefebvre, 2003) and the "reflexive re-enactment of a proscribed series of roles and expectations ... provides spaces for minor occurrences of subversion" (Bennett, 2005, p. 3). Subversion manifests itself in financially unskilled, untrained people creating a financial institution. The social identity and the performances (Goffman, 1973) within both the community and the individuals play a role in the credit union's operations and its potential to adapt and meet the needs of the community. Also, the diversity of the context of each individual's role in the development of their credit union and the mobilization of the membership of each credit union materializes differently depending upon the socioeconomic, political, and geographical environment in which the people find themselves.

Credit unions that emerge through the efforts of a local group of people can be in response to a number of external and societal factors including exclusion from the formal economy, that is, through the exclusion from access to the various commercial forms of financial services. Sometimes the desire to develop a credit union is in response to the local financial institutions not meeting the needs of the community due not only to access, but also the types of financial products these institutions offer, perceived unaffordability of interest rates, or financial products that do not meet social needs. Other causes of the development of credit unions is that of a sense of control, a desire to put in the hands of the community their financial destiny, and for control of the financial resources that a community generates.

Often there are outside influences that have sought to convince a local community of the need to develop their own institution. Sometimes the main factor influencing community action is a government that seeks to address a market failure. Often geographical, demographic, and socioeconomic factors influence the commercial banking sector to perceive a group of people as not commercially viable. The emergence of collective action to address this deficit through a group coalescing together has numerous motivating factors that are not always necessarily driven by external forces. Bonds of membership are often driven by the desire to strengthen existing bonds of relationship and leverage community similarities. The commonality of identity in terms of being a teacher is reinforced in spheres of everyday

---

[1] The WOCCU official statistics only account for those organizations/countries that provide data. Unofficially there are financial cooperative movements in numerous other countries.

activity such as the financial institution where one banks. This both leverages and enhances a sense of solidarity among members and provides a space of reciprocity to occur.

23.3 Hornsby Teachers Credit Union

In the early 1960s, Rob Dobson and John Ryan, the secretaries of the Hornsby Teachers Association (a branch of the teacher's union), commenced discussions about starting a credit union for the teachers in Hornsby, a middle-class northern suburb of Sydney, Australia. At that time, there was a nation-wide credit squeeze where the banks were wary of lending to teachers even though they had steady incomes.

The initial mobilization of participation in a credit union is heavily dependent on a number of factors, these include the quality of leadership and the inclusive or exclusionary nature of the community within which the credit union is situated. In the case of NSW Teachers Credit Union, there were two well-respected people that were able to instill the requisite confidence and trust along with the ability to provide good quality leadership in the early stages of development. Maak states that leadership, "is a relational and inherently moral phenomenon that cannot be captured in traditional dyadic leader-follower relationships" (Maak, 2007, p. 329). While this case study has noted the role of the early founders, there were other actors that played leadership roles that also impacted on the emergence of the credit union who were in positions of power and could influence and mobilize members.

The first steps in the formalization of the Teachers Credit Union came in 1966, when Bob Dobson spoke to Stan Arneil, who was at the time the League Development Officer with the Australian Federation of Credit Union Leagues, along with the General Manager of the Federation, Les Robinson. At this stage, they were assisted to register their credit union

under the NSW Cooperation, Community Settlement and Credit Act of 1924. It was at the Golden Horse Shoe Café in Hornsby on September 27, 1966, that the first meeting of the Hornsby Teachers Credit Union occurred. The principle of their credit union was that they would treat everyone fairly…to give members…an attractive savings scheme, a way of obtaining personal loans…and an opportunity to solve personal financial problems through cooperation' (Butterfield, 2016, p. 14). The core philosophy was of "teachers helping teachers" (Butterfield, 2016, p. 15).

The membership of each credit union materializes differently depending upon the socio-economic, political, and geographical environment in which the people find themselves. Often the institutions arise through the endeavors of individuals within a community as was the case with the Hornsby Teachers Credit Union. Credit unions also emerge through the efforts of a local group of people, which can be in response to a number of external and societal factors including exclusion from access to loans; it is recognized through these local leaders that their economic exclusion "could be solved only by strengthening the networks of solidarity among their citizens" (Putnam, 2002, p. 4).

The initial operations of the credit union saw the organizers facing enormous difficulties and challenges in the day to day functioning of their credit union. While they were able to have regular meetings, they struggled to develop the business due to existing work commitments as they were all teaching and working on a fulltime basis. In order to grow their credit union, they often used lunchbreaks and the time after school to reach out to other teachers to join the credit union and to take deposits. "It was hard work those very early days…We'd go around to other schools at lunchtime to try and drum up business but we couldn't get very far because we only had an hour, so we relied on word of mouth"

(Butterfield, 2016, p. 15). The geographical spread of teachers also created a challenge along with the problem that the demand for loans was greater than the deposits they had collected. At this stage, it was identified that there was a need for payroll deductions rather than the physical and time-consuming act of cash collection.

23.4 NSW Teachers Credit Union

The Department of Education finally agreed to do payroll deductions, but only if they covered all NSW teachers as they didn't want to have to set these deductions up for multiple teachers' credit unions. On September 20, 1967, the Hornsby Teachers Credit Union changed its name to NSW Teachers Credit Union at its first annual general meeting. At this stage, the credit union had 29 members and AUD$644 in assets. By 1969, the volunteers were struggling to keep up with the increased workload (Butterfield, 2016, p. 17). In order to address the needs of the credit union's lending portfolio, the League lent the credit union funds so they could generate a surplus and, therefore, begin to employ staff and secure an office facility.

It was then that Ken Miller, when appointed as the general manager of the NSW Teachers Credit Union, introduced payroll deductions. The negotiations to introduce payroll deductions took a significant amount of time as the process was manual and took some time to process variations by the Department of Education. It was Ken Miller who proposed that rather than waiting six weeks for the variations of the payroll to be calculated and then paid, that the credit union would receive the payroll cheque. If there were any overpayments, the credit union would pay back the department immediately, therefore, moving the risk away from the Department of Education to the credit union. This, however, also meant that the credit union enjoyed good cashflow and was able to manage this risk effectively as they were close to their membership. This not only meant that the credit union was able to conduct their business in a timelier manner, but it also meant that the teachers were paid quickly. Payroll deduction had a huge impact on the credit union and by 1976, it had 12,934 members and AUD$9.6 million in assets with 16 employees (Butterfield, 2016, p. 6). It was at this stage, 10 years after the credit union commenced, that cash withdrawals were introduced.

The 1960s and 1970s saw many credit unions emerge in Australia. At the peak of credit union formation, there were 833 credit unions nationwide (Benson, 2007, p. 105; Davis, 2007, p. 6). Credit unions were thriving and they were often at the leading edge of providing innovative services to their members. In 1979, the NSW Teachers Credit Union computerized and by 1982, they were a part of the Redi-Access Network, which allowed members of credit unions to withdraw from other credit unions. In 1983, the NSW Teachers Credit Union introduced automated telling machines (ATMs). The Australian credit union movement had some notable firsts; the Teachers Cooperative Credit Union in Queensland had the first ATMs operating 24-hours a day in Australia (Lewis, 1996, p. 152).

The 1970s and 1980s witnessed a high level of growth in both members and in assets, by 1991, NSW Teachers Credit Union had 65,448 members and had surpassed AUD$1 billion in loans to members (Butterfield, 2016, p. 7). At this time, the NSW Teachers Credit Union was the largest credit union in Australia. In an ongoing commitment to the needs of their members, in 1992, they established a call center where members could call to pay bills via the telephone. It was at this time that they sought to open up their membership bond and they allowed the grandparents and grandchildren of the teachers to become members.

NSW Teachers Credit Union was technologically proactive within the nascent development of the World Wide Web, launching a website in 1997. In a continual drive to adapt to the changing patterns of consumer behavior and needs, in 2000, 24-hour home banking services were introduced.

NSW Teachers Credit Union throughout its over 50-year history had a nonbranching strategy in providing services to its members. The credit union never sought to have multiple branches for their members to visit; deposits, loan applications, and repayments were all processed at teachers' workplaces. The teachers' staffroom was regularly visited for any business transactions that needed to occur. During the 2010s, transactional banking moved from visiting branches and onto what was first a computer and then a smart phone. The credit union had not been hampered by an expensive branch network when the members moved from physical to virtual interaction.

During the 2008 financial crisis, there was a world-wide central bank propensity to implement deposit insurance schemes to calm the markets. On October 12, 2008, Australia joined many other countries in providing a guarantee on deposits, not only for the customers of the banks, but also for the members of credit unions. Initially, Australia put in place a 3-year guarantee of deposits with a limit of AUD $1,000,000 (Abacus, 2009, p. 53) in an effort to provide confidence in the Australian banking sector. This changed to a guarantee of deposits of up to AUD$250,000 on a permanent basis on February 1, 2012.

23.5 Teachers Mutual Bank

The banking crisis shook the confidence of the Australian public in the banking sector, mostly due to the news and images they were seeing about the financial collapse in some southern European countries and the actions being taken by the US Federal Reserve to prop up the US economy. Credit unions were seen as less safe than banks even though they were regulated and monitored in exactly the same way as banks. During this time, regulations were changed, which opened up the possibility, subject to sufficient capitalization, for credit unions to move away from this moniker and be called a bank. In 2011, credit unions with at least AUD$50 million in capitalization were allowed to use the term bank without having to demutualize.

The NSW Teachers Credit Union changed its name to the Teachers Mutual Bank in 2012. It was during this time that there was a shift in language in the credit union sector, a larger discussion around mutuality, and the meaning of this to credit unions. Mutualism has been defined as "self-help through cooperation" (Mathews, 2008, p. 45). "Rational mutuality can provide purpose and meaning in people's lives, while lack of mutuality can adversely affect self-esteem." (Jordan, 1985, p. 1). However the meaning of the term mutuality can shift over time "to bring stability and cohesion …[in] a changing economic and social environment" (Cutcher & Kerr, 2006, p. 42). The concept of membership was moving to that of "customer-owned" rather than what was seen in the sector as a dated concept of "member."

The regulatory changes that occurred during the mid-1990s to enable credit unions to compete saw increased compliance pressures placed on credit unions, many of which struggled to keep up with the new reporting and compliance obligations. This created a rapid upswing in the amalgamations of credit unions as the bigger credit unions absorbed the smaller credit unions, a phenomenon that is still continuing today. Many credit unions merged with other credit unions that had a completely different bond of membership. Today, there are credit unions and mutual banks that are an amalgamation of teachers, nurses, public service, blue collar and white collar, and geographically bonded credit unions. This has led to the opening of bonds where there is no commonality of membership. Often the amalgamations have led to credit unions and mutual banks that have had to reinvent their identity to appeal to the broadest market. This has resulted in these financial institutions framing their identity around products and services rather than the central platform of a membership bond.

As Cutcher (2008) has argued, "Credit unions...have drawn on a different 'historically established meanings' of service in responding to the needs of communities in the present." (Cutcher, 2008, p. 331). The amalgamations and mainstreaming of credit union bonds into simple geographic bonds, for example, the amalgamation of an airline credit union with a scientists' credit union have seen credit unions reinterpret their membership bond to simply covering a geographic location. This has led to the members of the credit union having no commonality with each other nor a sense of solidarity or a place for reciprocity to thrive. The consequence of this is the degeneration of the credit union into just a financial institution where the only reason for utilizing the services has become contingent on the rate of interest on loans or savings and the kind of service being offered. The social mission disappears and so too does the sense of belonging and ownership within the original membership.

The founders, board, and management of what was then, Hornsby Credit Union, and subsequently, NSW Teachers Credit Union, and ultimately, Teachers Mutual Bank, were, on the one hand, keenly focused on the needs of their membership, but conversely, understood that their credit union was a business that needed to compete with other financial institutions. Their focus was to not only give their members good financial products, but they also understood that their business had a social responsibility within the wider

community in which teachers played a significant role. In 2017, the Teachers Mutual Bank was at the forefront of the Australian Banking sector in producing a sustainability report in which they demonstrated their social responsibility in expending 5.39% (TMB, 2017, p. 13) of their pretax profits on community initiatives such as education scholarships for their members along with assisting over 1800 disadvantaged children (TMB, 2017, p. 14).

Teachers Mutual Bank merged with the smaller Western Australian credit union, Unicredit in 2015. Understanding the importance of "alliance" (James, 2018), the credit union brand was enhanced rather than the membership mainstreamed into the exiting Teachers Mutual Bank brand through rebranding as UniBank. When the Fire Brigades Credit Union was merged into Teachers Mutual Bank, it followed a similar pathway in 2016 by being called Firefighters Mutual Bank.

As of March 2018, Teachers Mutual Bank had nearly AUD$7 billion in assets (TMB, 2018) and more than 191,000 members (TMB, 2017, p. 6). Rather than discarding the original bond of the credit union, Teachers Mutual Bank worked hard to not only maintain, but to enhance and develop, the teachers' identities within their brand and within the values of the institution, thus, preventing the degeneration of the credit union. Similarly, they have endeavored to develop the bond of firefighters' identities within that separate brand.

23.6 Conclusion

The early journey of Teachers Mutual Bank (NSW Teachers Credit Union) was not dissimilar to that of many other Australian credit unions that emerged in the 1960s and 1970s. They faced the same challenge of running a financial institution with volunteers with limited resources with the dual challenge of meeting members expectations and needs all the while positioned within an industry that is, on the one hand, highly competitive and, on the other hand, highly regulated. The development and success of the Teachers Mutual Bank (NSW Teachers Credit Union and the preceding Hornsby Credit Union) was due to homogeneity, and trusted leadership. The closeness of the members to the credit union due to a tightly defined bond has, from the earliest days, focused the institution on the needs of the members and situated its relationship closely around their vocational identity in not only the products that they provide, but also in the location in which they provide these services. At the core of a credit union's existence is trust, which in turn enables participation and eventually solidarity. Trust has a number of forms according to Arneil (2006), that of thick trust and that of thin trust. Thin trust is a form of trust that is placed on the generalized other (Putnam, 2000) or what Arneil calls "civic trust" (Arneil, 2006, p. 125), while thick trust is positioned with people that one has had interaction with previously. Thick trust and reciprocity developed from the very beginning between the initial volunteers and the members, created a sense of solidarity that lasted until today.

Even though the institution faced challenges with regulation, it focused on members' needs and innovated for the benefit of the members, all the while ensuring that it stayed true to their membership bond. The homogeneity of Teachers Mutual Bank along with their other individually branded mutual banks, reinforces the narrative that homogeneity within a group engenders a greater sense of civic commitment and higher levels of community ownership and one which is less financially stratified (Morenoff, Sampson, & Raudenbush, 2011; Portney & Berry, 1999).

It could be argued that credit unions and other community-owned financial institutions provide cover for the neoliberal agenda and present an acceptable face for collective action,

solidarity, and communal elements contained within a cooperative structure. This case study demonstrates that the reverse could be true, that cooperative structures are primarily founded on desired social benefits in the first instance with the tools of free enterprise deployed in a manner that will benefit the social mission of an institution and its members.

References

Abacus. (2009). *Market Scan 2009*. Retrieved from Sydney.

Arneil, B. (2006). *Diverse communities: The problem with social capital*. Cambridge: Cambridge University Press.

Bennett, A. (2005). *Culture and everyday life*. London: Sage Publications.

Benson, M. (2007). *Market Scan 2007*. Retrieved from Sydney.

Butterfield, C. (2016). *Teachers Mutual Bank: 50 years putting you first*. Preston: Bounce Books.

Cutcher. (2008). Strong bonds: Maintaining a commitment to mutuality in a deregulated environment – The case of Australian credit unions. *Journal of Co-operative Studies, 41*(1), 22–30.

Cutcher., & Kerr, M. L. (2006). The shifting meaning of mutuality and co-operativeness in the credit union movement from 1959 to 1989. *Labour history* (91), 31–46.

Cutcher, L., & Mason, P. (2013). Credit unions. In M. Parker, G. Cheney, V. Fournier, & C. Land (Eds.), *The Routledge companion to alternative organisation*. Abingdon: Routledge.

Davis, K. (2007). *Australian credit unions and the demutualization agenda*. Melbourne Centre for Financial Studies.

de Certeau, M. (1984). *The practice of everyday life*. Berkeley: University of California Press.

de Certeau, M., Giard, L., & Mayol, P. (Eds.), (1998). *The practice of everyday life* (Vol. 2). Minneapolis: University of Minnesota Press.

Evans, A., Grell, S., & Klaehn, J. (2006). A technical guide to increasing citizen participation. In W. C. o. C. Unions (Ed.), *World council of credit unions*. Madison: WOCCU.

Goffman, E. (1973). *The presentation of self in everyday life*. New York: The Overlook Press.

James, S. (2018). *Informal discussion/interviewer: P. Mason*.

Jordan, J.V. (1985). *The meaning of mutuality*. Paper presented at the Stone Center Colloquium.

Lefebvre, H., & Norbert, G. (2003). Mystification: Notes for a critique of everyday life. In S. Elden, L. Elizabeth, & E. Kofman (Eds.), *Henri Lefebvre: Key writings* (pp. 71–83). New York: Continuum.

Lewis, G. (1996). *People before profit: The credit union movement in Australia*. Sydney: Wakefield Press.

Maak, T. (2007). Responsible leadership, stakeholder engagement, and the emergence of social capital. *Journal of Business Ethics*, 74(4), 329–343.

Mathews, R. (2008). Things worth fighting for: Facing down the demutualisers. *Journal of Co-operative Studies*, 41(1), 45–50.

Moody, J. C., & Fite, G. C. (1984). *The credit union movement: Origins and development 1850 to 1980*. Dubuque: Kendall/Hunt Publishing Company.

Morenoff, J. D., Sampson, R. J., & Raudenbush, S. W. (2011). *Neighborhood inequality, collective efficacy, and the spatial dynamics of urban violence*. Retrieved from Ann Arbor.

Portney, K. E., & Berry, J. M. (1999). Neighborhoods and social capital. In V. Hodgkinson (Ed.), *Civil society in the United States*. Ford Foundation.

Putnam, R. D. (2000). *Bowling alone: The collapse and revival of American community*. New York: Simon & Schuster Paperbacks.

Putnam, R. D. (2002). *Democracies in flux: The evolution of social capital in contemporary society*. Oxford: Oxford University Press.

TMB. (2017). *Teachers Mutual Bank Limited annual report and sustainability update 2016–2017*. Retrieved from Sydney.

TMB. (2018, March). *Public disclosure of prudential information*. Retrieved from Homebush.

WOCCU. (2013). Membership Services. Retrieved from <http://www.woccu.org/memberserv/membership>.

24

From resilience to unlimited opportunities: the First Community Credit Cooperative's (FICCO) experience

Bienvenido P. Nito[1], Isagani B. Daba[2] and Ernest Marc V. Castillo[3]

[1]Senior Fellow of the Center for Research and Communication of the University of Asia and the Pacific, Philippines [2]Former Chairman of First Community Credit Cooperative, Philippines [3]Research Associate for the School of Economics, University of Asia and the Pacific, Philippines

24.1 Growth of credit cooperatives in the philippines

Credit cooperatives are mostly community-based and grassroots financial institutions operating in rural and urban areas. In some regions, they are the principal financial institutions serving the savings and credit needs of thousands of small savers and borrowers.

Relampagos, Lamberte, and Graham (1990) believed credit cooperatives in the Philippines were generally the most successful financial institutions operating outside the Central Bank's control. Similar to banking institutions, credit cooperatives perform a financial intermediation function. However, they have greater flexibility in carrying out savings mobilization and lending functions since they are not covered by Central Bank regulations. They are considered informal financial intermediaries.

24.1.1 Early years

The positive developments of credit cooperatives in the 1990s have improved tremendously the image of cooperatives since the Marcos regime in the 1970 s, which sponsored many cooperatives that consequently failed due to its dole-out strategy. This strategy turned people to become dependent on dole-outs.

Geron and Casuga (2012) described the direct government interventions in the 1960 s and 170 s when the government used credit as a major instrument for agricultural development in the Philippines. The government established several institutional structures that served as channels of credit in ensuring that credit was provided to the agriculture sector.

Dating back to 1952, the Rural Bank Law was enacted allowing the establishment of family-owned rural banks in many municipalities.

Several incentives were given to encourage this. These incentives included 50% government equity, access to preferential rediscount rates, tax exemption, and technical assistance. In the same year, the Agriculture Credit Cooperative and Farmers' Association (ACCFA) was established to develop small farmers' cooperatives. The cooperatives were used as channels of small production credit and marketing loans to farmers. After a decade of operations, ACCFA was plagued by serious default problems. Its operations were then limited to the provision of unsecured loans to land reform beneficiaries.

Additionally, the government implemented a massive rice production program popularly known as *Masagana99*. This was due to the rice production setback in 1973 when a series of natural calamities hit the country. *Masagana99* provided farmers a technology package that included technical assistance, high-yielding variety seeds, fertilizer, and credit subsidy to achieve the program's goal of increased rice production. The credit scheme offered noncollateral loans and extension services by rural banks and other channels of credit that included small farmers' cooperatives.

The rice production program of *Masagana99* was followed by other commodity-based credit programs. Credit subsidies were implemented to bring about higher production of corn and other farm products, fish, and so forth. Funds for these programs were provided at subsidized interest rates through the Central Banks' rediscounting facility.

Several assessments on the effectiveness of the various subsidized government credit programs were conducted toward the end of the decade. Most of the credit programs suffered from very low repayment rates resulting in the weak financial performance of most of the financial institutions, rural banks in particular, that were used as conduits of cheap government funds. The flow of credit from most of the credit programs implemented during the period declined over time due mostly to high levels of default, disqualification of many borrowers and rural banks from program participation (due to massive default problems), termination of major foreign backed on-lending projects, and rediscounting restraints.[1]

Esguerra (1981) saw that *Masagana99* not only offered low-cost loans to farmers but also "conveniently provided the sponsoring government the means of political and ideological support by publicizing its concern for the rural poor without necessarily altering the prevailing structures of asset ownership which is the main source of inequality." He cited the government's assessment as to why the program failed considerably and the nonrepayment of loans:

1. Low production due to factors like inadequate assistance and supervision from production technicians; insufficient employment of the recommended package of technology; natural and human-made disasters.
2. Attitude of farmer-borrowers who viewed credit as a dole-out from the government and guarantee coverage as a condonation of non-payment.
3. Misuse of credit proceeds.
4. The increasing financial burden of farmer-borrowers due to village savings fund, village guarantee fund, land amortizations, irrigation fees, taxes, and so forth, that limited their repayment capacity.

Learning from these mistakes, credit cooperatives have gone through many reforms. Relampagos et al. (1990) attributed the errors as partly due to lack of coordination among primary cooperatives. To avoid these, some credit cooperatives have sought to strengthen intercooperative linkages to promote sharing of technical expertise and even surplus financial resources among themselves. Thus there now exists a number of secondary and tertiary associations or

[1] Ibid.

federations of credit cooperatives that oversee wider coordination among primary cooperatives.

24.1.2 Positive developments in credit cooperatives

Llanto (1994) made a distinction among cooperatives established in the Philippines. He distinguished two types:

1. Credit cooperatives that were organized from the voluntary and collective effort of individuals who united under a common bond to service the financial needs of members.
2. The "instant" cooperatives that were organized by self-interested external parties and motivated by the immediate and instant access to government credit programs.

Llanto believed that the first type of credit cooperative was more stable and could survive a financial crisis given the discipline and support of its officers and members. The first type of credit cooperative, the focus of his study, had the "potential to become financially stable and strong financial institutions because of the maturation and consolidation process that it and its members have undergone throughout the years. For any decline in financial performance, they have the capability to bounce back and emerge as strong institutions."

On the contrary, the second type of cooperative, while able to provide instant access to credit to its "members" would, over time, face financial difficulties due to loan delinquency problems and diminishing support by "instant members." Clearly these were the characteristics of the farmer credit cooperatives established in the time of the *Masagana99* program during the Marcos regime.

Following the decades of decline in the credit cooperative subsector, positive developments were seen in the succeeding decades. The emergence of credit cooperatives particularly in the countryside was generally credited to the initiatives of a handful of founding members who pooled their small resources to address financial problems. Relampagos et al. (1990) attributed the development of credit cooperatives to the "nurturing of collective efforts of the members and demonstrating capability to serve the common interests of their members." This enabled credit cooperatives to expand their sphere of influence in communities and institutions. As a result, membership grew and inspired other people from different income groups to join.

Llanto (1994) further described credit cooperatives as helpful organizations in building up people's savings and accessing low-cost credit that was not available from traditional lending institutions such as banks. Over the years they demonstrated self-reliance, depending strongly on members' savings with little external funding. Growth of the majority of these credit cooperatives was not fueled by the infusion of external funds. They depended on internally generated capital to sustain operations and enhance viability as financial intermediaries.

The physical assets and capital of credit cooperatives also expanded. Some diversified their business activities to respond to the changing demands of their members. Llanto in his 1992 survey revealed that 60% of the total income of credit cooperatives came from lending activities. Some credit cooperatives derived income from investments and other activities. He cited that the "other income" component of total income signified the credit cooperatives' proportionally large involvement in, and exposure to, nonfinancial activities. Llanto described the profile of members as small farmers, businesspersons engaged in microenterprises, and rank-and-file to middle-level employees.

24.2 The start of FICCO

In 1954, 17 faculty members and nonteaching staff of Ateneo de Cagayan decided to form the Ateneo Credit Union or ACU with the encouragement and guidance of Fr. William Masterson, S.J., founder of the School of Agriculture of Ateneo de Cagayan. With only 27.30 pesos as total initial deposits, ACU strived to fulfill the credit needs of its members. In 1961, ACU formally registered with the Cooperative Administration Office as Ateneo Cooperative Credit Union (ACCU).

The leaders of ACCU saw that being a closed-type cooperative was a challenge for attracting members and increasing its resources. Their products and services were limited to the perceived needs of their school-based members. Consequently, leaders of ACCU went to public and private offices, village chapels, and community groups to conduct cooperative orientations and premembership seminars. They also focused on market vendors as prospective members.

From a school credit union confined within the campus, ACCU opened itself to the community of Cagayan de Oro City in 1970. That year marked the beginning of the 8-hour, full-time service given to members. ACCU further planned construction of its own building in the next three years. Its members grew to around 200 and assets amounted to a little over 180,000 pesos.

24.2.1 Macro factors

As stated earlier, the decade of the 1970s until the early 1980s saw the emergence of state-sponsored cooperatives and other credit providers such as rural banks. The direct government intervention was to establish several institutional structures that served as channels of credit in ensuring that subsidized credit was provided to the agriculture sector. This program intervention became problematic to ACCU and to other organic cooperatives fitting the characteristics Llanto offered in his description of the first type of credit cooperative: "organized from the voluntary and collective efforts of individuals who united under a

common bond to service the financial needs of members."

The dole-out strategy of the government in organizing cooperatives eroded self-reliance as it turned people to become dependent on such dole-outs. Membership was scarce to "organic" cooperatives such as ACCU due to perception toward cooperatives as conduits of government credit subsidies and the attitude of farmer-borrowers viewing credit as a dole-out from the government.

As a response to this challenge, ACCU created an Education Committee (EdCom) made up of volunteers (initially of only 3 members), including Isagani Daba, that campaigned for membership while educating the communities on the nature and principles of cooperativism. The EdCom recruited people and made sure they were provided with appropriate educational inputs regarding the cooperative, especially in terms of values, its operation anchored on mutuality, the responsive products and services that it offered, and the sharing of benefits. The credit union leaders also made certain that the ACCU was operated efficiently, resulting in greater returns to members.

In its bid to reach new members, ACCU decentralized its operations in 1972, making credit more tailored to its varied membership by creating chapters in several small villages, districts, and other homogeneous groups within its membership. A full-time professional manager was employed. A resolution was approved by its members in 1974s general assembly to consider acquiring a plot and putting up a building on it.

In 1975 the members voted to change the credit union's name to First Community Credit Cooperative, Inc (FICCCO). Its members approved restructuring its bylaws to conform to the regulations decreed by the then Bureau of Cooperatives.

In the succeeding years, FICCCO was recognized as the Most Outstanding Community Cooperative in the Region consecutively from

Number of Members

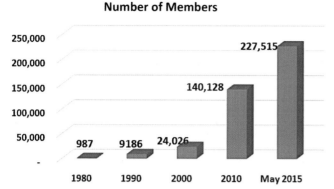

FIGURE 24.1 FICCO's growth of membership from 1980 to 2015. Source: *FICCO*.

Tota Assets (in mil.)

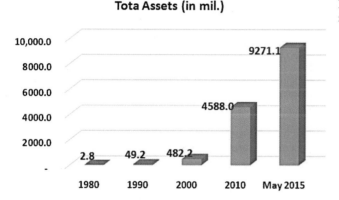

FIGURE 24.2 FICCO's growth of total assets from 1980 to 2015. Source: *FICCO*.

1977 to 1979 by the Ministry of Local Government and Community Development. The efforts of its leaders paid off as FICCCO's membership increased from 200 in 1970 to 987 in 1980, with an average growth of seven new members each month. Resources also increased to P 2.8 million. FICCCO's building was completed and EdCom launched its monthly regular premembership seminar. FICCCO formally developed its manual of policies for perusal of members and nonmembers. By 1990, membership reached over 9000 and resources grew to Php 49.2 million. Figs. 24.1 and 24.2 present the growth of membership and assets of FICCCO.

In 1993, FICCCO changed its name to First Community Cooperative (FICCO) as it became a multipurpose cooperative. In responding to the growing needs of its members, FICCO diversified its products and services, therefore not limited to only providing credit. Currently it offers 43 types of loan products, insurance protection—life, property, health, mortuary—and a number of fee-based services, such as mobile cash transfers, cable TV, water refilling stations, and gift certificates. This shows that FICCO has adapted to the needs and challenges of the ever-evolving socioeconomic environment.

The Cooperative Development Authority's national and regional offices recognized FICCO's contributions to national cooperative development and the upliftment of the quality of lives of its members through awards such as "Most Diversified in Business," a "Trail Blazer" among cooperatives, "Top Grosser" awards, and "Most Outstanding Cooperative in the Region" repeatedly in 1997 and 1998.

24.2.2 Micro factors (growth strategies)

It was during the decade of 2000–10 when FICCO grew exponentially. Members grew from 24,026 to 140,126 and assets jumped from 482 million pesos to 4.5 billion in 2010. One of FICCO's strategies was product development. It developed viable products, with five types of savings deposits, 43 types of loans, and mutual aids meant to help the poor and the middle class and free them from the clutches of loan sharks.

Market development was also key to its growth. FICCO identified those most dependent on informal sources of credit. These were market vendors, microentrepreneurs, farmers, fisherfolk, and employees of private and government agencies. EdCom focused its vigor in convincing these market segments to join. The visionary leaders went to offices, villages, remote areas, and public markets in Cagayan de Oro City to promote FICCO.

As membership grew, the need to open more offices to bring its services closer to resource-scarce member-owners became imperative. While its general assembly approved the opening of branches as early as 1986, the first branch was opened only in 1992.

As more branches were opened, membership grew. However, this was not attributed to a formal marketing plan and a well-funded advertisement or recruitment scheme. FICCO relied mainly on word-of-mouth of satisfied members. Members convinced relatives, friends, neighbors, coworkers, fellow vendors, drivers, farmers, and others to join FICCO.

The opening of branches was cautious. In 2000 FICCO had only eight branches. Having mastered documentary requirements and the processes of opening branches, it went full-steam in the following decade. Forty-five more offices were opened, raising the number of members to more than six times by the end of 2010. Today, FICCO has 80 offices and 314,984 members.

FICCO do not open branches haphazardly. Certain indicators are monitored and considered earnestly. These are the number of existing and potential members in the area, total loans, capital and deposits of those members in nearby FICCO offices, growth prospects, ideal location, security, and other opportunities. After the decision is made to open a branch, a trainers' training for EdCom volunteers is conducted. Volunteers are expected to spearhead member recruitment efforts of the branch. Members of credit, audit, and inventory committees are also trained to provide management and support for credit evaluation and internal control.

FICCO has ventured into new businesses aligned with the developing technologies of the 21st century and considering the needs of its members. The following programs have recently been put in place:

- Mobile banking and money transfer. FICCO now provides mobile banking, money transfer and ATM services to its members with its network of 80 offices and 19 more slated to come. FICCO is also planning to upgrade its member service by allowing loan applications, loan releases, and payments online.
- Risk protection, both life and nonlife. Cooperative Insurance System of the Philippines or CISP, which had a little over P 200 million in assets when FICCO became majority shareholder in mid-2013, now has P 1.55 billion in resources. In late 2016, FICCO acquired a nonlife insurance company, the R&B Insurance Corporation, for P 250 million. The latter is now in the process of being merged with CISP.
- Integrated Co-op Financial System (ICFS). FICCO, whose business is 90% credit, invested in five capital deficient (or losing) cooperative banks and turned them around.

FICCO's acquisitions of and investment in cooperative banks, insurance, and asset management are part of a grand plan to integrate cooperative financial services. The objective is for the sector to have just one cooperative bank (versus today's 26 weak banks), one cooperative insurance (two at present), one cooperative asset management (two at present), and one cooperative investment company (none at present). Integrating financial services to benefit cooperatives and their members will serve as a unified platform for the 207 cooperative federations all over the country.

In addition, FICCO is pursuing the formation of cooperative federations that will provide health care and quality water at lower costs to members, and forming a corporation that will go into mass housing and real estate development.

24.3 The FICCO culture

Strengthening organizational culture is part of FICCO's overall strategy. As FICCO adapts itself to the needs and challenges of the ever-evolving socioeconomic and technological environments, it never wavers in upholding its culture. The following are FICCO's declarations and manifestations.[2]

24.3.1 Total member care

- Quality service takes form in different types of services delivered efficiently and at low cost.
- Transparency and accessibility of services.
- Service with personal touch as an offshoot of the close ties between staff and members.
- Active participation of members as a natural consequence of closer ties.

24.3.2 Good governance

- Stewardship and ownership.
- Transparency and democracy.
- Accountability.
- Common good.
- Self-reliance as moving spirit of FICCO, not from donations and grants.
- Recognition of rights and responsibilities by members, leaders and staff make it easier to govern FICCO. No special treatment, no vested interest.

24.3.3 Defining values

- Sacrifice; as FICCO stakeholders are willing to go the extra mile if doing so will redound to the good of the organization.
- Discipline translated by following policies and procedures consistently.
- Volunteerism not opportunism.
- Lean organization means FICCO hires only when absolutely needed. No hiring of relatives within third degree of consanguinity or affinity.
- Controlled costs and expenses.
- High return to members. Among cooperatives, FICCO charges the lowest loan interest, in view of volunteerism, lean organization, and controlled cost.
- Aggressive yet sure-footed moves to open branches, take-over cooperative banks and insurance organizations.

24.3.4 Challenges faced by cooperatives

The history of Philippine cooperative development is volatile. It is characterized by scenarios of growth and decline. Government enthusiasm and attempts to use cooperatives as a platform for development did not contribute to sustained growth and stability of the

---

[2] Daba (2018, May). Credit Co-ops and Sustainable Development: Case of FICCO Evolving Challenges and Limitless Opportunities.

cooperative movement. In fact, when the new Cooperative Code (R.A. 9520) was signed into law in 2009, all cooperatives were required to reregister with the CDA. After a year, the CDA reported only 18,000 cooperatives had reregistered out of the total of 90,000. Looking back on the development of cooperatives in the Philippines, its history is littered with abandoned or nonfunctioning cooperatives.

The following challenges are faced not only by FICCO but also by many, if not all, cooperatives in this country as observed over half a century of cooperative development.

- *Low confidence by the general public in cooperatives.* The many cooperative failures that people saw in their communities is the chief reason many people distrust cooperatives. Many have invested money in cooperatives. A national cooperative federation attributed mismanagement as the top cause of failure, particularly integrity issues on the part of the leaders and top management. This situation remains persistent today.
- *Government programs created a culture of dependence.* Most socialized credit programs promoted by the government were dismal failures. People viewed this kind of funding as a dole-out which encouraged them not to pay loans. When Masagana99 and *Maisagan*a were implemented, some provinces had past due rates as high as 96%.
- *Failure to live by the core values of Cooperativism and institutionalizing them.*
- *Slow organizational development.* Organized by the grassroots members (e.g., farmers, teachers, vendors, workers), the exposure of cooperative people to training is very limited. While training on organization development is available, the cost is beyond reach of struggling cooperatives. This results in the shortage of qualified officers and staff.

24.4 Further challenges among cooperatives in the philippines

Cooperatives that hurdled the early challenges and managed to succeed are confronting new challenges. Medium to large cooperatives now face:

- *Over liquidity.* Cooperatives with over liquidity will have to look for safe investment opportunities or find ways to expand services to members. Failure to do so will put pressure on return on assets and could result in lower returns to members. It could lead to members' dissatisfaction and lowering of confidence.
- *Lack of trained manpower to support expansion, new ventures. Hiring from outside could pose problems on culture alignment.* Relying from within, on the other hand, could slow down expansion as it takes time for those in the lower rungs (newly hired) to align with the culture of the organization.
- Integrated Co-op financial system (ICFS).
- Government Financial Institutions' conflicting role with Credit Cooperatives.
- *Leadership succession.* A common problem of most Cooperatives is its aging leadership. Most of the blame should be laid on the present leadership. Many of them stick to their positions even if they are already in their 70s or 80s. Prospective young leaders find it hard to be part of the leadership, thus, they go elsewhere.
- Slow adaption by the grassroots to new technology that could help facilitate transactions.
- Cooperative taxation.

24.5 Conclusion

FICCO has contributed to the realization of the United Nation's Sustainable Development

Goals (SDG). These are: eradication of poverty and hunger, improved health and wellbeing, quality education, gender equality, decent work and economic growth, clean water and sanitation, industry, innovation and infrastructure, sustainable life on land, reduced inequalities, peace, justice and strong institutions, and partnership for goals, among others.

FICCO's business activities have provided its members and its immediate communities access to the following services that fulfill and improve the quality of lives of various stakeholders:

- Value chain, mass housing, health care and water supply initiatives are part of the priority concerns.
- Accessible and affordable credit (benefits the users even more when they share in the income), affordable health care, ICFS and utilities owned by the grassroots contribute not only to poverty reduction, wealth redistribution, countryside development and nation building, but more importantly, to empowerment.

Many struggle to relate cooperatives with anything other than loans or credit. Indeed, the most enduring image of cooperatives in the country has something to do with borrowing money. This prevalent understanding of the nature of cooperatives, however, is a misconception. Cooperatives around the world have been uplifting lives, promoting social cohesion, raising productivity, reducing inequalities, and advancing economic growth and economic development in many ways. Aside from extending loans for various purposes, cooperatives have empowered many to enrich their lives through entrepreneurial activities, informal education, and practical training. They serve to anchor collective efforts of people in the conduct of business, production, trade, marketing, service provision, and so forth.

References

Daba, I. B. (2018, May). Credit co-ops and sustainable development: Case of FICCO evolving challenges and limitless opportunities. Case presentation during the Cooperative Research Conference on Mobilizing Co-ops in the Pursuit of Sustainable Development Goals. University of Asia and the Pacific, Pasig City, Philippines.

Esguerra, E. F. (1981). Some notes on the Masagana 99 program and small farmer access to credit. *Philippine Sociological Review* (29), 35–43.

Geron, M. P., & Casuga M. S. (2012). Credit subsidy in Philippine agriculture. Discussion paper series no. 2012–28. Philippine Institute for Development Studies. Makati City, Philippines.

Llanto, G. M. (1994). The financial structure and performance of Philippine credit cooperatives. Discussion paper series no. 1994–04. Philippine Institute for Development Studies. Makati City, Philippines.

Relampagos, J. P., Lamberte, M. B., & Graham, D. H. (1990). A study of the operations and credit performance of selected credit cooperatives in the Philippines. Working paper series no. 1990–23. Philippine Institute for Development Studies. Makati City, Philippines.

Further reading

Castillo, E. T. (2018, May). Opportunities and challenges to cooperatives in attaining Sustainable Development Goals. Keynote presentation during the Cooperative Research Conference on Mobilizing Co-ops in the Pursuit of Sustainable Development Goals. University of Asia and the Pacific, Pasig City, Philippines.

Daba, I. B. (2017, November 7). Business case presentation on FICCO: Quick survey questions [E-mail to the author].

FICCO — First Community Cooperative. (n.d.). Retrieved July 15, 2018, from http://www.ficco.org/.

Terosa, C. L. (2016). Co-operatives and Sustainable Development Goals. MASS-SPECC Co-op Development Center Journal. MASS-SPECC Cooperative Development Center, Cagayan De Oro City, Philippines.

Existential challenges of cooperatives and credit unions in Indonesia
Credit union trajectory in trying times, and the successful case of Keling Kumang Credit Union

Robby Tulus[1] and Munaldus Nerang[2]

[1]Regional Director (Emeritus) for Asia Pacific, International Co-operative Alliance (ICA). Founder and Chief Advisor, Federation of People-based Co-operative Enterprises (INKUR Federation), Indonesia, and Credit Union Central Organization (CUCO), Indonesia [2]Federation of People-Centered Co-operative Enterprises (INKUR), Indonesia

25.1 Cooperatives in Indonesia: a historical view

Indonesia, the fourth largest country in the world with a population of over 260 million, was colonized by many European imperial powers from the 16th century up until its independence in 1945. The colonizers were the Netherlands, England, Portugal, and Japan. The Dutch came in the 16th Century primarily to enhance trade and overthrow the Portuguese, and to some extent the Spaniards, as its main competitors. However, it was the Portuguese traders who brought Christianity into Indonesia, which propelled infighting with autonomous kingdoms under the influence of Islam. The Dutch established VOC (East Indies Conglomerates) in 1602, which was considered to be the first multinational company in the world.

Within the cooperative sphere, the influence of past colonizers could not be discounted. The cooperative idea was first introduced by a regent in central Java by the name of R. Aria Wiraatmadja in 1896, who studied the credit cooperative system in Germany and then established a bank for civil servants called the "Hulp en Spaarbank" (HS), an abbreviated version of the original name *"De Poerwokertosche Hulp en Spaarbank der Inlandsche Hoofden."* His motivation to set up HS was driven by concern when he saw that ranking civil servants were victimized by unscrupulous moneylenders charging high rates of interest. While the idea of Wiraatmadja to set up HS was arguably driven by the urban-based concept of Schultze Delitsch in West Germany, his vice-regent De Wolff van Westerrode tried to convince the regent that it would have been more appropriate to establish credit cooperatives based on the concept of Wilhelm Friedrich Raiffeisen.

Westerrode argued that the latter would be more inclusive and owned by members themselves including poor people in rural areas. However, the conversion from the Hulp en Spaarbank into credit cooperatives based on the Raiffeisen model did not happen. In its place Wiraatmadja expanded the clientele of HS by incorporating other disadvantaged people in the area. This concept of Wiaraatmadja was laudable as it was aimed at helping the poor. However, HS became a precursor of the current state bank of Indonesia, the Bank Rakyat Indonesia, or popularly known as BRI, one of the largest Indonesian state banks that is also actively involved in the microfinance sector. The outcome would have been far different should Wiraatmadja have converted HS into people-based and people-driven credit cooperatives as suggested by De Wolff van Westerrode. The colonial government still dominated the sociopolitical forces during this pre-independence period. Cooperatives were formed and largely exploited as a tool for increasing community welfare, and at the same time, to bolster loan disbursements using government funds. Self-help efforts as championed by the Raiffeisen model were totally overpowered by the sociopolitical agendas of the government.

The debt-based concept of a bank as introduced by Wiraatmadja lingered well into Indonesian independence on August 17, 1945, at which point the 1945 Constitution was enacted based on the *Pancasila ideology*, the five key principles devised by Sukarno, the President of Indonesia, as the embodiment of the basic principles of an independent Indonesian state. Dr. Mohammad Hatta, the cofounder of Indonesian independence, became the vice-president of Indonesia. It was Hatta who promoted the concept of economic democracy, and he was the most prominent figure to ensure economic democracy was to be incorporated in the 1945 Constitution as a principal conduit for driving

the Indonesian economy. His concept of economic democracy was duly enshrined in the 1945 Constitution, namely in article 33, which stated, "The Economy will be organized as a mutual endeavor based on the spirit of companionship/brotherhood." The annotation of this article stated clearly that the enterprise that befits article 33 is a "Co-operative."

25.2 Cooperatives in the postindependence years

The prevalent thoughts of Hatta in creating an economic system that is based on mutuality and cooperation was immediately captured by community leaders following the independence of the Republic. There was a sudden surge to form single purpose cooperatives such as producer cooperatives and consumer cooperatives as well as savings and loan cooperatives all over the country. The formation was, nonetheless, imbued by a sense of political triumph or the "revolutionary zeal" that still resonated from the independence movement; so cooperatives were hastily formed from the top down by political frontrunners for mere political ends.

On July 5, 1959, President Sukarno issued Presidential Decree no. 5/1959, due to the inability of the Constitutional Assembly of Indonesia to achieve the two-thirds majority to reimpose the 1945 Constitution. The Decree, read by Sukarno, ushered in the period known as the "Guided Democracy" (1959–66). The system of "Guided Democracy and Economy" encompassed a number of big agendas that gave the government overriding powers to become regulators and actors of development. The government refused any further support from the World Bank and the International Monetary Fund, and cooperatives once again became handmaidens of the government. Political parties were even allowed to engage actively in cooperative development. Decree no. 5/1959 was followed by Government Regulation no.

60/1959, instructing all cooperatives to adhere to Law 79/1958 within the context of guided democracy and guided economy. This new regulation, in effect, abolished the autonomy of cooperatives, allowing the government to take all initiatives by way of a top-down mechanism. Under such a regulatory environment cooperatives were literally handcuffed and used only as political tools of the government. There were around 45,000 cooperatives officially registered in the late 1950s, most of which were essentially subordinated to the whims of the government's political agendas.

The "New Order" era came about in 1965, after the abortive coup of the communist party and which marked the fall of Sukarno's guided democracy. The "New Order," established in 1966 by President Suharto, was characterized by the strong political role of the military, the bureaucratization and corporatization of political and societal organizations, and selective, but effective, repression of opponents. Strident anticommunism remained a hallmark of the regime for its subsequent 32 years. During those years, the government was intent to make cooperatives a vehicle for strengthening civil society based on professionalism. Cooperative Laws no. 12/1967 and no. 25/1992, which replaced no. 12/1967, were enacted to ensure that cooperatives played a significant part in economic growth. Up until the fall of Suharto in 1998, these cooperatives were run by way of patron–client relations between the powerful and big conglomerates. The target for rice self-sufficiency was being pursued by integrating cooperatives into the existing economic policy by providing lots of incentives to the Village Unit Co-operatives, popularly known as the KUDs.

President Abdurachman Wahid (popularly known as "Gus Dur"), with his rich experience in NGO communities and the cooperative movement in earlier years, fittingly declared his more progressive views on cooperatives. His democratic political agenda set in motion new policies that prompted government officials to recognize the autonomy and independence of cooperatives. The role of the Ministry Co-operatives and Small & Medium Enterprises was confined to regulatory and supervisory roles alone, and the Ministry was effectively downgraded from a fully-fledge Ministry to that of a State Ministry.

The sensible and progressive policies enacted by Gus Dur were unfortunately short-lived. Subsequent governments reversed his policies by repositioning the Ministry of Co-operatives and SME, once more, as a mere technical executor of the government's development agenda. The reinstatement of the "top-down" role of the government recreated the old pattern of collusion with cooperative leaders, resuming the dependency syndrome of the cooperative movement on government support. Coupled with the rise of globalization and free markets, the cooperative ideals gradually eroded and the movement became more attuned to the government's neoliberal policies. Many government-supported cooperatives became almost identical to private sector corporations, as they were controlled by a small number of board members instead of member-owners.

A new Co-operative Law, no. 17/2012, was enacted by the government coinciding with the International Year of Co-operatives in 2012, which was more akin to embodying the characteristics of a private enterprise. A group of genuine cooperative leaders challenged and countered this new law because it digressed from the Indonesian Constitution of 1945, article 33, as well as the universal Co-operative Identity Statement of 1995. And under the guidance of a young cooperative leader, Suroto, a judicial review was staged at the Constitutional Court, upon which the Co-operative Law was deemed unconstitutional and ultimately canceled altogether; in turn, the earlier law, no. 25/1992, was reinstated. The cancellation of Law no. 17/2012 by the Constitutional Court revealed the fact that the Law was not only defective in its epistemological sense, but also brought to light the dominant approach of the government to once again use cooperatives as tools for its own policies and development agenda.

Of late, the government of President Joko Wdodo has instilled more favorable policies since 2014 by deregistering and eradicating no less than 60,000 fraudulent and fake cooperatives. Unaffected cooperatives, which are still operating with weak governance and capital mobilization, are being rehabilitated with some technical assistance and financial support. There are obvious signs of progress in the rehabilitation and development processes of these cooperatives, yet their sustainability remains to be seen. What is at stake seems to be the more recent incompatible policies of the government by the introduction of cheap loans to economically weak communities through the so-called "KUR," channeled through state banks. The latter seem to be in direct competition with well-established cooperatives that are offering loans based on market rates.

The fluctuating environments under which cooperatives have been operating in Indonesia over the past century since the colonial period until now, have given rise to a multitude of successes and failures among those cooperatives that are more or less dependent on government support either technically and/or financially.

All in all, however, any successful cooperative one could observe during this postindependence period are primarily indebted to the most distinguished thoughts of Dr. Mohammad Hatta (1902–80).

25.3 The emergence and growth of credit unions in Indonesia

The hallmark of cooperative development during Suharto's New Order Regime was the unbridled growth of the Village Unit Cooperatives (KUDs). Prior to the surge of KUDs,

the government passed Co-operative Law no. 12/1967, which was a progressive legislation in comparison with previous ones imposed under the guided democracy period. Under this new Law, no less than 46,000 pseudo cooperatives were abolished and deregistered, leaving only 18,000 that remained registered as functioning cooperatives.

This figure was further reduced to 8000 that were considered genuine cooperatives. It was during this rehabilitation period, in the late 1960s, that the credit union idea was introduced by CUNA International to Indonesia. The Director General of Co-operatives, under the Ministry of Transmigration and Co-operatives of Indonesia, Mr. Ibnoe Soedjono, comprehended the credit union concept as introduced by CUNA International, a system that will be built from the ground up based on intensive training and education. Ibnoe Soedjono then challenged Rev. Karl Albrecht SJ, the founder of the credit union movement of Indonesia who studied credit unions from the SELA (Socio-Economic Life of Asia) network, to show the relevance and potential of credit unions in the Indonesian context. Together with Robby Tulus as cofounder, Rev. Albrecht accepted the challenge by first setting up the Credit Union Counselling Office of Indonesia (CUCO-Indonesia) in 1970, then by offering credit union education at the grassroots level by way of an andragogy approach, and eventually by motivating low-income members to form credit unions themselves as their own initiatives. An incubation period of 5 years was offered by Director General Soedjono to see if credit unions were indeed relevant and prospective. By every measure, credit unions within the incubation period were viable and deemed prospective as they grew from 9 primaries in 1970 with 733 members to 197 primaries in 1975 with 14,834 members. In 1972 CUCO's leadership had already gained the confidence of the Asian Confederation of Credit Unions (ACCU) to host the first Asia-wide

Credit Union Leaders Seminar in Indonesia, which offered fresh ideas to build effective credit unions from the ground up by means of intensive education.

Although formed as legitimate member-based cooperatives, and abiding by Co-operative Law no. 12/1967, credit unions were not given official registration by the government at that time. Law no. 12/1967 was superseded by a Presidential Instruction under the New Order regime of President Suharto. Presidential Instruction no. 2 in 1978 was a top-down directive from the government to form BUUDs (Village Unit Agencies), which subsequently transformed into KUDs, to promote and cultivate so-called "economic order" in rural areas. One KUD had to be established in each subdistrict, and any other cooperative existing in a village under a given subdistrict had to be merged into the KUD. Incipient credit unions were also forced to join the KUDs in the districts where they subsisted. Despite several incentives offered by the government, credit union members were nonetheless wary of joining the KUDs, and more so of being integrated and subordinated as a subunit under the KUD structure.

Credit union growth has been more discernable outside the Island of Java. Although they were started in Java, and to some extent in North Sumatra, credit unions did not take off as rapidly in Java inasmuch as commercial and state banks were mostly concentrated in this most populated Island of the country during the early 1970s. Credit union seeds planted in provinces of North Sumtara, East Nusa Tenggara, and West Kalimantan shot up fast and vastly, with more moderate ones sprouting in Bali and Lampung, all of which are relatively more extensive compared to those in Java.

The sense of belonging among various ethnic groups in North Sumatra (the Batak tribe), West Kalimantan (the Dayak tribe), and East Nusa Tenggara (Timorese and Florenese tribes) may have contributed to the building of strong common bonds in these credit unions, and further emboldened by the spiritual credence emanating from the Catholic church, which has considerable followings in those provinces. Nonetheless, credit unions are open to all religious communities as can be witnessed from the demographics nationwide.

Fast forward, the total membership nationwide has now reached 859 credit unions with 2,933,221 individual members, shares of 6.8 trillion rupiah, deposits of 17.8 trillion, loans outstanding of 21.2 trillion, and assets of 28.7 trillion rupiah (Aprox. US$2.2 billion— Statistical Report of 2017). Growth and development did not come easy. During the 25th anniversary of CUCO-Indonesia in 1996, a respected scholar from Germany predicted that the credit union movement in Indonesia would die a slow death due to its slow growth compounded by legal obstruction from the government. The flip side of this argument is that any growth, albeit slow, requires a momentum where it will propel vigorously once the economic scope and scale emerge. There were 1497 credit unions with 255,673 members worth 108 billion rupiah in 1996. The momentum emerged only in the year 2000, when the number total credit union members remained about the same (356,327), but primary credit unions consolidated themselves well by merging with others or dissolving naturally. There was a total of only 1090 primaries in 2000, yet they had doubled their assets to 242 billion rupiah. The movement consolidated further, and only 859 credit unions remained at the end of 2017, but with assets of 28.7 trillion rupiah. The obervant German scholar would have recanted his earlier forecast and statement in view of the exponential growth and development of credit unions since 1996.

Credit unions in West Kalimantan constitute the largest number of members and total assets because of their specific methodology in mobilizing membership savings.

Their innovative method of combining a microfinance debt-based mechanism and a credit union savings-based formula resulted in an accelerated mobilization of savings, bringing about a solid institution that is maintained by the continuous education of its members. The case study of Keling Kumang given here illustrates one of the fastest and most innovative credit union development practices in Indonesia.

25.4 Keling Kumang case study

The birth of credit unions in Kalimantan (or "Borneo" as it is more popularly known) was a response to the dire socioeconomic conditions of people at the grassroots level. The economic conditions of the inland communities in West Kalimantan were so bad and precarious since their main commodity, that is, rubber, was generating only a meagre income, far from their expectations. Development is concentrated in Jakarta, the capital city of Indonesia on the Island of Java. Outlying provinces outside Java, in particular Kalimantan, supplied an immense amount of cash to Jakarta from the exploitation of the rich natural resources existing on this island. Infrastructure, especially roads and bridges, in Kalimantan were neglected.

Grassroots communities in West Kalimantan decided to empower themselves to raise their self-esteem by way of self-help and solidarity in the spirit of "Gotong Royong," this being an Indonesian cultural attribute of "working together and helping each other." The failure of top-down development approaches during the Suharto era as described in Section 25.2 created the impetus among community leaders in West Kalimantan, notably Mercer, Munaldus, and Florus, not to repeat the failures of the KUDs. Lessons from credit union growth in other parts of Indonesia were learned, incipient credit unions were also forced to join the KUDs

in the districts where they subsisted. Despite several incentives offered by the government, credit union members were nonetheless wary of joining the KUDs, and more so of being integrated and subordinated as a subunit under the KUD structure.

The community spirit among the Dayak people remains strong, and these values augur well for cooperative development, especially for credit unions. Hence the credit union model was chosen as the most suitable vehicle for self-empowerment among the low-income communities in West Kalimantan.

Credit unions grew and developed on fertile grounds in West Kalimantan. People are hardworking and industrious, and the Catholic Church added great value to the social and spiritual aspects of credit union development. Priests in many parishes continued to raise the spiritual life force of leaders and communities to join and support the credit union activities, although these clerics never got involved in the credit union structure themselves. Their fundamental role has been to give moral support and, in effect, became a moral compass to ensure that the ethical values of credit unions are maintained and sustained. The groundwork and foundation of strong moral values is nonetheless insufficient if not supported by good governance and gainful business practices.

The Keling Kumang Credit Union (KKCU) started 26 years ago and is rooted in the mentioned philosophy. It started in the small villages of Tapang Sambas and Tapang Kemayau, in the hinterland of West Kalimantan with 87 families on March 25, 1993. The credit union has grown quite rapidly and currently possesses close to 170,000 members with assets of 1.3 trillion rupiah covering the entire province of West Kalimantan. It ranked second in Indonesia in terms of membership (Financial Report of KKCU—April 30, 2018).

The KKCU mission is "To serve members from different backgrounds, primarily peasant-farmers, micro & small enterprises, employees, and young people in West Kalimantan, offering responsible and sustainable financial services to reduce poverty and raise members' living standard." In its effort to intensify market penetration by providing responsible and sustainable financial services, KKCU adopts the PEARLS Standard of the World Council of Credit Unions in a consistent manner. However, KKCU's commitment to reducing poverty and raising members' living standard was exacerbated by its lack of experience and expertise in this respect. To overcome this shortfall, KKCU took steps to strengthen its scant human resource capacities by partnering with well-known NGOs, namely Good Return from Australia, Solidaridad from the Netherlands, and Microsave. Partnership with these able bodies ultimately closed the capacity gap in terms of human resources.

In the year 2012, when the membership of KKCU continued to grow and expand, members voiced their aspirations that they were not only in need of financial services, but also of other services such as production, marketing, and consumption. KKCU undertook a spinoff mechanism by facilitating the creation of other services through the establishment of member-driven single-purpose cooperatives, namely agriculture, retail, and service cooperatives. All these cooperative entities were then grouped together under one holding umbrella called the Keling Kumang Group (KKG). A foundation was also set up under KKG to manage the Keling Kumang Vocational School, an embryo for future higher education (college or university) that focuses on teaching specialized skills to support the growing needs of communities in both rural and urban areas. Under its service cooperative flagship, KKG also built a hotel in the township of Sintang to cater to visitors and members coming from all parts of Kalimantan (formerly known as Borneo).

25.4.1 KKCU: a successful cooperative model

Although credit unions were ridiculed and forced to join the KUDs during the New Order era of President Suharto, the situation has reversed completely since the end of the 1990s. KUDs began to collapse and diminish with the withdrawal of external funding from the government. In contrast, credit unions continued to grow and surge after the downfall of the New Order of President Suharto. The main reason why KKCU and other credit unions in Indonesia became successful was due to the fact that all credit unions, since the onset of the movement in the early 1970s, consistently and faithfully adhered to three main pillars as their standard operating formula, that is, education, self-help, and solidarity. The faithful adherence to these pillars is a far cry from the way KUDs were organized from the top down by the government in the past. Credit unions all over the country including KKCU were developed from the ground up by way of intensive training and education based on their own strengths (i.e., self-help without any funding from outside), and vertical integration in order to maintain solidarity at all levels. The impact of faithful adherence to these three pillars has been significant in terms of members' loyalty and sense of ownership. The ICA Co-operative Identity Statement (Definition, Values, and Principles) also became a crucial guide that has been adhered to faithfully.

There are other macro factors that contributed to the growth of KKCU. With the downfall of the Suharto regime in 1999, credit unions in Indonesia were finally recognized as genuine cooperatives by the new reform government so that they were not forced to join the KUDs, but were registered as single-purpose cooperatives instead. The newly installed Minister of Co-operatives, in 1999, was a former NGO leader, and the NGO he was leading happened to work closely with the Credit Union Counselling Office in the 1980s within the civil society network. This legal recognition became a compelling motivation for community members to join the credit union because they felt safe keeping their money in the credit union instead of in commercial banks. KKCU, thus, benefited from this enabling regulatory environment as well. Concurrent with this legal recognition, however, KKCU was also active in promoting the concept of prudential management, which it gained from the Asian Confederation of Credit Unions through its vigorous engagement at the Asia region. Prior to October 2000, KKCU was progressing fairly well in terms of its membership growth on account of its adherence to the three pillars and the ICA Identity Statement. But philosophical strength alone was not considered enough. Commercial banks and other financial institutions have active branches all over west Kalimantan, and this posed a great challenge to KKCU in attracting savings and deposits from communities in urban as well as rural areas of the province. Such a challenge could not be left to chance alone. KKCU was essentially rural based with its head office located in a village, and it could not let commercial institutions mobilize savings from rural communities, inasmuch as funds mobilized would more likely be spent in the capital city of Jakarta to benefit the rich. KKCU, thus, instilled a sense of crisis to motivate their members in rural areas to save in their credit union, and concurrently ensure that governance and prudential management be immediately put in place. KKCU came to the realization that financial transactions can no longer rely on manual hand posting, and must, therefore, be computerized. It had to enhance strategic planning processes, which was done rather casually, so that clear performance-based measurements were developed and executed.

In an effort to become more competitive, KKCU participated in a special training organized by the Asian Confederation of Credit Unions in 2000, during which the concept of strategic planning and the PEARLS prudential standards were inculcated. The rigorous application of these concepts has had a profound and positive impact on KKCU.

The prototype introduced by the World Council of Credit Unions (see below) became the guiding feature to promote the image of KKCU in the marketplace. This prototype emphasized the safety and soundness of the credit union for which quality products and services must be created, coupled with effective recruitment of trustworthy and capable people on the board of directors, supervisory committee, and in management. The KKCU must also consistently build and maintain its strong leadership, rich culture, and effective system of governance.

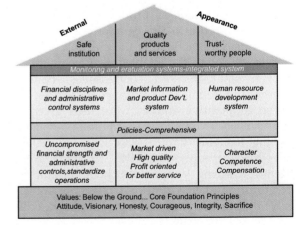

Subsequent to the proper execution of the training and education of members/leaders/staff as well as the inculcation of professional management and prudential standards, the growth of KKCU was quite remarkable as can be witnessed in these tables:

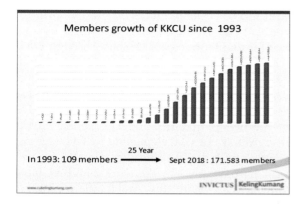

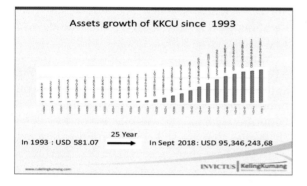

Notwithstanding, this impressive growth would not have been possible if KKCU did not persevere and engage a professional consultant to undertake a thorough assessment of KKCU. As a first attempt, a consultant from a firm called "Business Therapy" in Jakarta was selected and hired to guide KKCU with strategic planning based on a balanced scorecard (BSC) including the development of a remuneration system that modified the previous Rajin Malas Sama Saja system into a key performance indicators (kpi) system. From 2010 to 2013, KKCU carried out its strategic planning activities based on the BSC. Although the strategic plan facilitated by the Business Therapy institute in Jakarta managed to increase both the membership and assets of KKCU, the big issue of loan delinquency has not been

mitigated. For that reason, KKCU identified another partner in Australia called "Good Return," a well-known NGO with a good track record in conducting microfinance services. In partnership with Good Return, KKCU enhanced the quality of its loan portfolio. A social performance management concept was employed in conjunction with a renewed KKCU mission statement, "To provide responsible and sustainable financial services to members in West Kalimantan in an effort to reduce poverty and increase the quality of life."

This renewed mission provided the needed impetus to improve and rectify the credit union system of governance, so the focus has shifted from mere quantitative growth to better quality performance in both the economic and social spheres. It was further enhanced by pledging to the attainment of a triple bottom line so that clear measures are in place to support environmental programs that will ensure KKCU's sustainability. When the partnership contract with Good Return came to an end, KKCU went into a new partnership with Microsave, who introduced the concept of a probability poverty index (PPI, a more advanced concept from the previous "progress out of poverty index"). The PPI provides the tools to reduce poverty and, thus, enhances the pursuit of KKCU's social performance.

Microsave facilitated the innovation of a new formula for KKCU to implement its social performance, namely "measure, uplift, stride, and spinoff." "Measure" pertains to defining the level of poor members using the PPI tool; "uplift" pertains to poor members with low income whose mindset needs to change through intensive training in financial literacy, financial capability, and field schooling in order to become more enterprising; "stride" pertains to generating family income by organizing self-help groups that will be funded through credit union loans with continued guidance by the KKCU entrepreneurship team (there are currently 116 self-help groups); "spin-off" pertains to setting up cooperatives other than credit unions whose products and services are needed by the community such as consumer co-ops, producers co-ops, service co-ops, and so forth, organized in rural areas where such products and services are scarce or costly.

The results of the spinoffs of KKCU have been promising. Members of KKCU are now able to meet their agricultural needs readily from their new nonfinancial co-ops at low costs, hence, alleviating their poor conditions and ensuring that they stay out of poverty. Cooperatives that emerged following the spin-off strategy are grouped under the KKG and comprise 10 different cooperative entities.

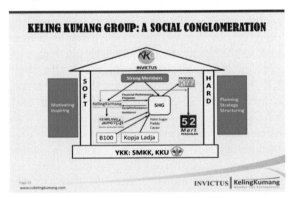

The KKG is an indigenous innovation and presumably the first model in Indonesia that could well be emulated by other credit unions. Credit unions in Bali, Lampung (South Sumatra), and Southeast Moluccas have already experimented with spinoffs to establish other nonfinancial cooperative sectors. The concept of diversification, which led to spinoff strategies, was first introduced by Robby Tulus and colleagues from the Association of Socio-Economic Cadres in Indonesia. It is patterned after similar models such as SANASA in Sri Lanka and Mondragon in Spain.

In summarizing the factors that guided the KKCU into becoming a successful credit union, the answer points to the newly added pillar of "innovation" to the previous three pillars of

education, self-help, and solidarity because the credit union would be slow-moving if no new breakthroughs were discernible. Through effective governance and good leadership, KKCU has proven itself to be capable of jumping out of its comfort zone when assets and membership boomed as it entered the new millennium. The recruitment of qualified and trustworthy human resources was a vital element to KKCU's success coupled with the identification of strategic overseas partners that could work hand in hand with KKCU. With the proliferation of other cooperative sectors under the KKG, a new partner from Holland called Solidaridad has been identified and is now actively collaborating with KKCU as well as KKG.

Munaldus Nerang, as the founding father of KKCU, plus the current regenerated leadership, anticipate that growth and development will continue at pace if all the key factors mentioned are faithfully adhered to, despite major existential challenges that are still coming from within and without. These challenges will be described here.

25.4.2 Overcoming existential challenges of KKCU

From within, KKCU needs to improve its institutional capital ratio and also manage its relatively high delinquency ratio. To overcome these issues, KKCU has carefully screened and recruited sufficient professional and capable staff with university degrees. In order to do so, KKCU has adopted an intensive strategic planning process using the KOGMA approach introduced by Microsave. (KOGMA stands for KO = Key Objectives, G = Goal, M = Measures and A = Activities.) This KOGMA approach is cherished because it is founded on two footings. The first is *Institution*, as introduced by the World Council of Credit Unions by way of PEARLS (Protection, Effective financial structure, Asset quality, Rates of return and cost, Liquidity, and Signs of growth) to be used as a management tool, a standardized evaluation ratio/formula, a comparative ranking, and to facilitate supervisory control. PEARLS is important as a prudential management tool in order to build a safe and sound credit union institution, thereby also checking and supervising institutional capital as well as delinquency. However, one foot is still missing and that is social performance management, focusing on *Members* as the second footing. Members' survey and education are, thus, crucial in checking and supervising the conditions of members' livelihood, quality of life, and their wellbeing. The effort of KKCU to reduce loan delinquency and capital adequacy is to have a balanced focus on both the institution and the members as two key footings.

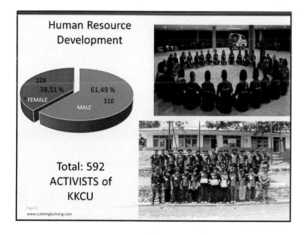

From without, competition from commercial banks and government lending programs must also be managed. Of late, the government has launched a formal financial service for local communities all over the country. It is called KUR (Kredit Usaha Rakyat) or Credit for Peoples' Enterprises. This credit facility offered by the government is actually well-intentioned as it aims to support the productive efforts of local communities all over the country. However, this massive credit scheme, channeled through commercial banks, poses a clear dilemma in the financial services sector on account of its competitive (low) rate of interest, making it difficult for financial institutions

including credit unions to compete in a fair and healthy manner. Furthermore, the current surge of information technology makes it increasingly difficult for financial cooperatives and microfinance operators to compete with commercial banks, which are now appointing agents in all parts of the country to do away with their branch operations, hence, becoming more cost-effective when combined with the use of information technology. The common practice of commercial banks of imposing the 5 Cs (character, capacity, capital, condition, and collateral) standard for extending loans is obviously far too intricate for poor people to understand. KKCU has, thus, used a two-pronged approach by way of KOGMA, that is, the strengthening of its institution by way of prudential management, and providing easy-to-understand services to its members by way of social performance management to beat the competition. The latter is extremely crucial and, thus, easy-to-understand services have to be preceded by intensive membership education.

25.4.3 Education: a key element

The experience of KKCU has shown thus far that mobilizing savings from members has been fairly swift and easy after the adoption of intensive *financial literacy training*. The more difficult task is to achieve KKCU's social mission of trying to reduce poverty and raise the living standard of economically weak members. It requires a change in mindset. Consumerism is on the rise because members are continuously bombarded with commercial advertising on local television to keep spending more and more for instant gratification. Improving KKCU's educational programs is a challenge because *field education* must become more transformative with focus on building the habit of thrifting and changing the consumeristic mindset, so as to transform members' mindsets. Appropriate education, once again, has been programed to ensure that (1) the credit union must remain safe and sound, (2) the credit union board and management must have the capability to implement social performance management of high quality, and (3) financial capital and social capital must be balanced.

KKCU Head Office in the Village of Tapang Sambas, West Kalimantan.
www.cukelingkumang.com

Further reading

Baswir, R. (2010). *Peoples economy versus neo-liberlism. Ekonomi Kerakyatan versus Neoliberalisme.* Jakarta: Delokomotif. In the Indonesian language.

Burger, D. H. (1957). *Economic sociological history of Indonesia—Sedjarah Ekonomis Sosiologis Indonesia.* Djakarta: JB Wolter. Indonesian language.

Boeke, J. H. (1954). *Reason and purpose: Regulation of the Bumi Putera co-operative association. Alasan Dan Maksud: Aturan tentang Perkumpulan Koperasi Bumi Putera.* Jakarta: Djawatan Koperasi. Indonesian language.

Macpherson, Ian (1995). *Co-operation, conflict and consensus.* Vancouver: B.C. Central Credit Union.

Tulus, R., Suroto. (2015). *History of Co-operatives in Indonesia.* Paper presented at the Asia Pacific Co-operative Research Partnership Seminar, Bangkok, January 2015.

Tulus, R., Munaldus, Karlena, Y. (2002). *BUNG HATTA, Bapak Kedaulatan Rakyat, "Remembering a Century of Bung Hatta"*, Sri-Edi Swasono (Ed.). Indonesian language.

Tulus, R., Munaldus, Karlena, Y. (2007). *IBNOE SOEDJONO. Building independent co-operatives in the corridor of the co-operative identity*, Djabaruddin Djohan (Ed.). Indonesian language.

Tulus, R., Munaldus, Karlena, Y. (2014). *QUO VADIS. The Indonesian credit union movement.* Tonnio Irnawan (Ed.). Indonesian language.

Tulus, R., Munaldus, Karlena, Y. (2016). *CO-OPERATIVES: How to grow and sustain.* Jakarta: Kompas Gramedia Publication. Indonesian and English languages.

In conclusion, it is worth repeating what Munaldus Nerang, as the founding father of KKCU, and the current regenerated leadership anticipated, that is, that the growth and development of KKCU within the framework of the KKG will continue at pace if all the mentioned tangible activities are faithfully adhered to.

The SANASA movement—Sri Lanka
The pursuit of social order through cooperative leadership, vision, and innovation

Robby Tulus

Regional Director (Emeritus) for Asia Pacific, International Co-operative Alliance (ICA). Founder and Chief Advisor, Federation of People-based Co-operative Enterprises (INKUR Federation), Indonesia, and Credit Union Central Organization (CUCO), Indonesia

26.1 Historical background of SANASA

The SANASA movement was started in 1978 as an embryo of the credit union movement in Asia under the auspices of the Asian Confederation of Credit Unions (ACCU)[1]. At that point, the credit union movement in Asia was by and large promoted and developed by leaders who were imbued by socioeconomic thoughts spearheaded by the Socio-Economic Life of Asia (SELA). SELA is a network originated by the Jesuits in Asia. In 1963, Walter Hogan SJ, a Jesuit priest, led a committee for the development of socioeconomic life in Asia, and conducted a seminar on credit unions and community development in Bangkok, Thailand. Following this seminar, a number of Jesuits from many other Asian countries began

promoting the idea of credit unions as an instrument for socioeconomic development. Before the SELA seminar, credit unions had already started in Korea in 1961 under the pioneering leadership of a Maryknoll sister, that is, Sr. Maria Gabriella. It was following the SELA seminar that the Jesuits and other participating Catholic clergies began the promotion of credit unions in many other countries in Asia, namely in Hong Kong, Taiwan, Japan, Indonesia, Thailand, and Malaysia. The ACCU was established in 1971 in Korea, and founded by representatives of all seven mentioned countries.

The ACCU organized an Asia-wide leadership seminar in Bangkok in 1977 and brought together a group of community leaders from the South and Southeast Asia regions. Sri Lanka was then represented by three distinct institutions,

---

[1] The Asian Confederation of Credit Unions, ACCU for short, was formed on April 28, 1971, by delegates from 9 Asian countries, namely Japan, Hong Kong, Korea, Malaysia, the Philippines, Indonesia, Taiwan, Thailand, and South Vietnam convened in Seoul, Korea. A board was elected, and an office opened in Seoul, and it began its mission to help member credit union organizations to promote and expand credit unions for the socioeconomic development of people in Asia.

namely representatives from The Lady Lochore Loan Fund (LLLF), the Archdiocese of Sri Lanka, and the Thrift and Credit Societies of Sri Lanka. The latter was popularly known as SANASA. The LLLF was under the preview of the Ministry of Finance of Sri Lanka, one of the few profit-making government institutions with no grant or budgetary allocation from the government. The Archdiocese of Sri Lanka assigned a representative from a primary credit union in one of its parishes. SANASA was then represented by *P.A. Kiriwandeniya*, who was then active as leader of the national heritage movement and the Sarvodaya Foundation. However, Kiriwandeniya had a vision to revive the Thrift and Credit Societies of Sri Lanka, which had remained dormant since 1964.

Credit unions in other parts of Asia were by and large spearheaded by the philosophical underpinning of the SELA, a Jesuit inspirational pursuit. The logical choice of ACCU at that time was to work with a credit union that was started by a parish in Colombo as its initial laboratory. Neither LLLF nor SANASA were given the preferential option. What was overlooked was the fact that P.A. Kiriwandeniya had a vision to establish a viable cooperative movement following his comparative study at the "Pondok Pesantren" (Muslim School) cooperative system in Indonesia, and saw a parallel approach undertaken by the credit union system being promoted by the Credit Union Counselling Office in Indonesia. His research study on cooperatives assigned by the International Co-operative Alliance (ICA) in 1976, followed by his grasp of the credit union concept during the leadership seminar in Bangkok in 1977, catapulted a fresh energy on the part of P.A. Kiriwandeniya to revive the dormant thrift and credit co-op societies based on the credit union philosophy and operating principles.

The leadership of ACCU visited the Walgama Society in Kegalle district where P.A. Kiriwandeniya resided, and they saw his vision and commitment to establishing a "new

social order" in Sri Lanka by reviving the dormant Thrift and Credit Co-operative Societies (TCCS). P.A. Kiriwandeniya's vision was to first reform the old TCCS's that were established from the top down during British colonial rule, and which were patterned after the Credit Society Act of India in 1904, by way of empowering them from the ground up. Once these TCCS's were reformed, transformed, and empowered, a solid movement at the grassroots would be enabled to create a new social order in Sri Lanka by way of the TCCS or popularly known as the SANASA Movement. ACCU's choice was to have SANASA as its primary member from Sri Lanka. The latter was a departure from the more coherent approach of credit union development, which started from the social and economic thrust of the SELA network in the Asia region.

26.2 Early challenges of SANASA

The struggle to revive the TCCS came at a time when Sri Lanka embarked on an "open economic policy" in the late 1970s to follow the lead of the so-called NICs (newly industrialized countries) in Asia. The idea for such revival was to try and help the underprivileged in most rural areas to promote self-help as they would likely be left behind with the opening up of the economy, and the privatization program that followed. However, upward mobility among workers was mostly concentrated in the industrial sites, particularly within the free trade zone, whereas people in rural areas were still deprived and left behind.

P.A. Kiriwandeniya projected that the gap between the rich and poor would widen with foreign investments pouring into the country. He, thus, envisioned that cooperative development must be pursued from the ground up by the rural folks themselves so they can master their own destinies. Past socialist mishaps could be remedied by having self-reliant cooperatives that also created local entrepreneurship among the rural poor.

Through the revival efforts since 1978, which is just over a 40-year period, the SANASA movement succeeded in establishing 8,424 primary TCCSs, creating 13 business entities with 16,000 employees, encompassing 3,7 million individual members and users, with total assets of LKR150 billion (Approx. US$857 million), where the Federation of Thrift and Credit Co-operative Societies plays a key role in ensuring that participatory democracy by TCCS members remains strong.

This attainment in 2019 was not without challenges during the early stages of SANASA's development. The revival process started from the ground up with intensive training and education of young leaders who saw that 4000 dormant TCCSs since 1964 could be fired up again to become an institutional base for identifying and solving problems afflicting the rural poor. P.A. Kiriwandeniya empowered these young people to resuscitate and transform the existing TCCSs into a social and economic force in rural areas. Monthly meetings were organized to allow members to participate actively in building and supervising the operations of the TCCSs themselves. The primary TCCS was not intended to become a big entity with thousands of members, but to remain cohesively strong in terms of quality and not quantity. The cooperative thrust was derived from the Buddhist teaching, particularly Theravadan Buddhism, that promoted self-help, mutual approaches, and practical solutions to problems. Monthly interactions among members attracted rural households to come together and discern their common socioeconomic concerns to find the right solutions by themselves. It was envisioned by P.A. Kiriwandeniya that if thousands of local primary TCCSs could solve local problems themselves, then a "new social order" could emerge in rural areas to countervail the trends of privatization and industrialization that were happening at a fast pace in Sri Lanka. This long-term vision of Kiriwandeniya, with the "think-big and start-small" approach, seemed reminiscent of the teaching of Fritz Schumacher "small is beautiful," as well as Buddhist economics, whose message is to honor the small, the local, the democratic, the ethical, and the right livelihood of people left behind.

This genuine effort, however, was met with harsh resistance from the institution of the Co-operative Registrar. Efforts of self-help, self-governance, and self-responsibility of the TCCSs promoted by SANASA undermined the role of the Registrar who ought to have been the one to initiate, educate, organize, and supervise the cooperative organization. Under the Co-operative Society Law that was enacted in 1972, which was still in force in the late 1970s, Chapter VI stated that *"interpretation of the by-laws is done by the Registrar, and it will be final and cannot be questioned in a court."*

Chapter IX stated that *"Amended section 48 authorizes the Registrar as a result of an enquiry/inspection and after giving a notice of the Society to: a) Remove the offending committee member or members and fill the resulting vacancy in accordance with the by-laws, and b) Dissolve the committee and elect a new committee or appoint a suitable person or body of persons to manage the affairs of the society."* Thus, the autonomy and independence of TCCS to solve internal problems during monthly membership meetings (MGMs), contradicted the common practice of a cooperative under the Co-operative Society Law of Sri Lanka, that it must engage the Registrar in all aspects of its operations. The dominant role of the Registrar was already enshrined in the first Co-operative Law of Sri Lanka of 1911, patterned after the Credit Co-operative Act of India in 1904, and specifically formulated for credit cooperatives, known as the TCCS. This law was amended in 1921 to cover all other types of cooperatives.

Despite resistance from the government, SANASA's TCCSs grew by leaps and bounds, to such an extent that the National Assembly of SANASA in Galle in 1979 was attended by no less than 150,000 members, transported by around 4000 buses from all over Sri Lanka. Each succeeding year participants at the National Assembly increased exponentially until such time that mass meetings of this nature were no longer allowed by the president of Sri Lanka in the late 1990s for political reasons. However, SANASA and its leadership remained completely apolitical. SANASA remained fiercely independent yet its relationship with the government continued to be pursued in a respectful manner. The emphasis on transparency and accountability made the SANASA movement well-respected by the government, and also by a host of partner agencies from all over the world.

The early partners and supporters of SANASA were the Community Aid Abroad of Australia in the late 1970s, followed by the Co-operative Development Foundation of the Co-operative Union of Canada in the early 1980s. The Co-operative Union of Canada then morphed into becoming the Canadian Co-operative Association (CCA) in 1987.

CCA became the major sponsor of SANASA through its bilateral program with Canadian International Development Agency (CIDA) called the Sri Lanka Credit Union Development Assistance Program (SRICUDAP) in the late 1980s, focusing on education and training that led to the development and construction of the SANASA Campus. Then came HIVOS and RABO Bank from the Netherlands, United States Agency for International Development (USAID) from the United States, and Swiss Inter-Cooperation.

During the post-Tsunami reconstruction period from 2005 onwards, new sponsorship came from the World Council of Credit Unions (WOCCU) and Developpement International Desjardins (DID). Ever since the start of building its partnership with sponsoring agencies, SANASA established the so-called "donor consortium," allowing all sponsors to interact openly to guide and give advice to SANASA, but always within the context

of SANASA's Agenda and not those of the external partners. This shows the strength of SANASA in ensuring that its development agenda will not be dictated from the outside, but guidance and advice were welcomed to strengthen governance and maintain SANASA's transparency and accountability. Although some donors tried to enforce their own development agendas, SANASA resisted such attempts by ensuring that all donors put their agendas forward at the donor consortium and either adapt and conform their schemes to the SANASA's development objectives or be disengaged from the consortium.

One of the key concerns of donors pertain to the vast amount of funding SANASA received from donors, and how it affected the independency of the TCCSs. However, it was finally understood by the donor consortium that all external funds were earmarked and utilized for infrastructure and educational purposes only, while the funds for lending were entirely mobilized from within by the TCCS themselves. This self-help and self-reliant mindset became the cornerstone of SANASA's sustainability, and the unavoidable occurrences of loan delinquencies were well contained.

26.3 SANASA's growth and development amid continuing challenges

P.A. Kiriwandeniya, who received a Doctoral Honoris Causa degree, had a vision to create a "new social order" in Sri Lanka that went beyond just creating a thrift and credit cooperative movement, but a sustainable social and economic advancement of society. The *vision* of SANASA is *"New Social Order Based on Cooperative Principles and Values."* Its *mission* is *"To organize community by conducting activities to achieve the intended vision of SANASA."*

The achievement in the early 1980s was attributable to SANASA's focus on strengthening primary TCCSs at ground level based on self-help, an approach which was clearly distinct from the proliferation of multipurpose cooperative societies in Sri Lanka promoted and sponsored by the government during that period. This progress of SANASA was once again met with another challenge. During the presidential elections of December 1988, Prime Minister Premadasa (as he then was) of Sri Lanka, unveiled a program called "Janasaviya."

This national program of poverty alleviation, and ultimately poverty elimination, was well-intentioned as 1.9 million families (or half of Sri Lanka's 16 million people at that time) were living below the poverty line of LKR700 per month. In the process, foreign aid and foreign investments were pursued to finance the Janasaviya Programme. This being a government program, the Ministry of Food, Agriculture, and Co-operatives was assigned the first tier to implement the program. Within the context of Janasaviya, SANASA was invited to participate in the so-called "Million Housing Program" (MHP) for the poor, which was administered by the National Housing Development Authority. A loan fund from USAID to the amount of US$40 million was earmarked to build low-income houses. However, the implementation was poor and loan recovery was only 60%. USAID recommended to the government that it would be best if SANASA were to become the channel for these funds. Albeit reluctant to accept such external funds, SANASA leadership was forced to accept this recommendation due to the political situation at that time. The result was devastating. Many new primary societies were formed just to take advantage of these MPH funds. SANASA eventually opted out of this program due to the fact that a debt-based program from external sources did not work

amidst the bottom-up and internally generated savings-based approach that had been the hallmark of SANASA all along. However, the residual effects of the MHP lingered for quite some time, prompting the leadership of SANASA to instill extra education and training programs to establish the needed discipline among these primary societies.

Another challenge emerged during the period 1988–89 when the JVP insurrection, also known as the 1989 Revolt, erupted. The JVP (Janatha Vimukthi Peramuna) as a Marxist movement began to terrorize both the state machinery and those sections of civil society opposed to its thinking. The country almost came to a standstill with offices closed and daily lives interrupted. However, SANASA remained consistent in upholding its neutrality from politics, so much so that the development process of the TCCSs remained unharmed.

It was also during this turbulent period that SANASA leadership sought both technical and financial assistance from the Co-operative Development Foundation of Canada (subsequently called the CCA) in the mid to late 1980s, generating the bilateral SRICUDAP program as previously mentioned. Intensive capacity building continued during the first 5 years of the 1990s through technical assistance from the WOCCU. The WOCCU and CCA worked together to intensify the capacity building of primary societies by grading these societies, and further monitoring their activities by way of WOCCU's PEARLS[2] system.

In 1996, when the Federation of TCCS (FTCCS) was sufficiently consolidated, the SANASA leadership initiated a major structural reform by diversifying the thrift and credit system into other sectors in order to

---

[2] WOCCU PEARLS is a financial performance monitoring system designed to offer management guidance for credit unions and other savings institutions. It is designed by WOCCU as a set of financial ratios employed to assess the financial stability of credit unions. The ratios are grouped under six crucial areas of performance, which are: Protection; Effective financial structure; Asset quality; Rates of return and costs; Liquidity; Signs of growth.

achieve its vision of a new social order. To achieve this vision, SANASA's founding father, Dr. P.A. Kiriwandeniya, envisaged that this important milepost opened an ideal avenue for the creation of new sectors that are needed, owned, and controlled by SANASA members themselves. The new sectors, however, would be regulated under a legislative framework that is different from the cooperative legislation, so there are stand-alone entities that are officially and legally differentiated.

These stand-alone entities are apportioned into four different "SANASA Pillars" as:

Pillar 1: Banking and Finance—which consists of the TCCS system and a development bank
Pillar 2: Insurance and Risk Management— which consists of the SANASA Insurance Company Ltd

Pillar 3: Marketing and Consumer Affairs, Construction—which consist of SANASA Producer Consumer Alliance (SANEEPA), SANASA Engineering and Development Company (SEDCO), SANASA Travels Ltd, SANASA Printers and Publishers Ltd, SANASA Security Services Ltd, and SANASA Media Networks.
Pillar 4: Education and Capacity Building— SANASA Campus Ltd.

As seen in Diagram 26.1, these four pillars combined are currently called the *SANASA Group*. The innovation of a "group structure" by SANASA's leadership derived from a conviction that a diversification of services by members of the SANASA Movement is an important goal to protect members from being usurped by private companies that are

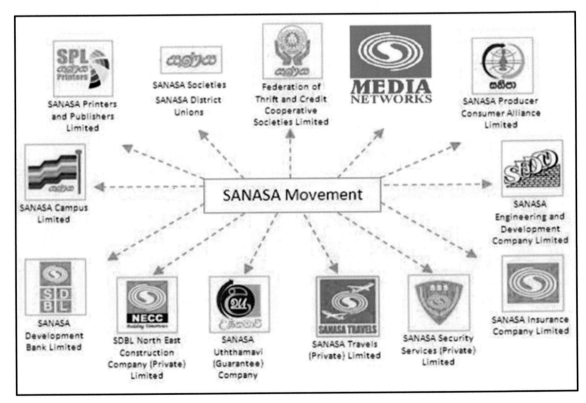

DIAGRAM 26.1   SANASA group.

rendering diverse yet competing services as well as a protection against possible interference by government bureaucracy.

The successful diversification efforts of SANASA, which culminated in this group structure, must be attributed to the effective interplay between vision, innovation, and leadership.

26.4 Growth and development of SANASA's four pillars

The SANASA movement expanded exponentially following the diversification process,

and with the four pillars' approach SANASA is hopeful that it can move more amenably to greater heights.

26.4.1 The first pillar: banking and finance

SANASA rested on the fundamental premise that the TCCS, from the primary to the federation levels, must continue to generate sufficient internal financial resources to sustain the SANASA Movement. However, there would be occasional needs on the part of the TCCS

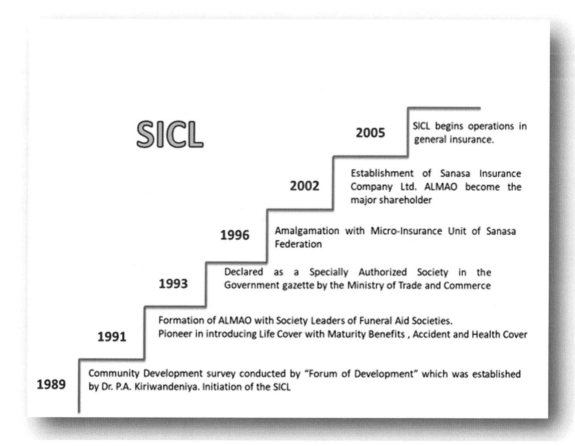

SICL

2005   SICL begins operations in general insurance.

2002   Establishment of Sanasa Insurance Company Ltd. ALMAO become the major shareholder

1996   Amalgamation with Micro-Insurance Unit of Sanasa Federation

1993   Declared as a Specially Authorized Society in the Government gazette by the Ministry of Trade and Commerce

1991   Formation of ALMAO with Society Leaders of Funeral Aid Societies. Pioneer in introducing Life Cover with Maturity Benefits , Accident and Health Cover

1989   Community Development survey conducted by "Forum of Development" which was established by Dr. P.A. Kiriwandeniya. Initiation of the SICL

DIAGRAM 26.2 Incremental growth of SANASA insurance.

2. Case studies of asian co-ops, including cross-country comparison

system to obtain additional funds during times when their liquidity became low. Rather than relying on outside commercial financial institutions to obtain additional funds, SANASA's leadership decided to set up their own bank called the SANASA Development Bank Limited (SDBL). Unlike the TCCSs that are registered under the Co-operative Society Law, the SDBL is incorporated as an investors-oriented firm (IOF) with registration as a specialized bank under the Central Bank Act. As such, SDBL is under the supervision of the Central Bank. At the outset, the majority of shares of SDBL derived from the primary, secondary (district), and national federation of TCCS. However, in view of SDBL being an IOF or business corporation, other external agencies and investors could buy shares as well. SDBL's vision and mission, however, remained solidly grounded in support of primary societies and their (poor) members in order that it remains a cooperatively-owned bank and not to be demutualized as was the case with the Peoples' Bank of Sri Lanka. The vision of SDBL is to raise the income levels of the poor through cooperative and development-oriented services, whereas the mission is to establish a development bank equipped with the capacity to provide a range of financial and complimentary services as well as to strengthen the SANASA Movement. The existence of SDBL prompted a major shift in the financial services originally offered by the FTCCS. Prior to the establishment of SDBL, the FTCCS took on the main role as lender to the district unions. With this role taken over by SDBL, the FTCCS had to focus more on providing capacity building and financial management as well as auditing the district unions. The majority of board members of SDBL consisted of representatives of the SANASA Movement, but due to the fact that shares

are also owned by investors outside the SANASA Movement, a new dynamic was inevitable. SDBL must be responsive to all its constituents yet the movement must remain its preferential option.

This is a crucial challenge that needs to be managed carefully by representatives of the SANASA Movement. Leaders of SANASA are by nature more socially-inclined as compared to the external board members of SDBL as well as professional managers who are more business-oriented. The leadership of Dr. P.A. Kiriwandeniya and Ms. Samadani Kiriwandeniya, has been key in creating a balanced approach to maintaining the stability of SDBL.

26.4.2 The second pillar: insurance and risk management

The Sri Lanka Insurance Company Ltd (SCIL) has been a tremendous success due to its innovative products and outreach to the poor. SCIL was registered in 2002 under Insurance Law, namely the Regulation of Insurance Industry Act No. 43 of 2000 with Amendments in the form of Act No. 3 in 2011. It began operations in 2005 as a specialized insurance provider following a gradual and well-planned development process starting in 1989.

The embryo of SICL was an organization called the "All Lanka Mutual Assurance Organization" (ALMAO), an insurance arm of SANASA prior to its incorporation under Insurance Law. Diagram 26.2 describes the evolutionary growth of SICL from 1989 onwards.

SICL offers both life and general insurance products for low-income groups in rural areas of Sri Lanka. As an insurance company under the National SANASA Federation, the vision of SICL is the creation of a *"A new society based on Co-operative principles,"* and its mission is *"To strengthen*

the society through adequate Risk coverage and
developing the community Through
comprehensive risk cover."
SICL focuses on micro insurance that can be
patronized by low-income households and
poor people in rural areas since SICL
products are simple and affordable. The
insurance products are designed in such a
manner to make it less expensive and,
hence, accessible to low-income households,
yet able to build capital reserves that ensure
solvency and sustainability. Best practices
are being documented by SICL to evolve a
micro insurance model that can be shared
with other countries.

One product, in particular, that is highly
innovative and not often found in the
normal life and general insurance business
is the "Weather Index Based Crop
Insurance" policy of SICL, a micro insurance
policy that provides financial support to the
insured farmer who encounters a possible
decrease in their agricultural crop due to the
occurrence of extreme weather conditions.
Financial support is given through payouts,
triggered by a prespecified pattern of
indices related to weather risks. For the time
being, this weather index insurance (WII) in
Sri Lanka is confined to the risk of excess or
deficit of rainfall.

Despite the fact that SICL has been quite
successful as an insurance business that caters
to low-income households and farmers, there
remain many challenges that SICL is trying to
overcome. The main challenge is to try and
change the mindsets of farmers and rural
folks toward insurance owing to several
factors, namely (a) a lack of knowledge and
trust about insurance; (b) the belief of farmers
that they can bear the losses by themselves;
(c) the belief of farmers that insurance
(including micro insurance) is a luxury
product; and (d) the fact that farmers still
maintain their fatalistic mindset that God will
protect their crop and cultivation.

Major challenges facing the weather index
insurance policy have to do with (a) a lack
of customer confidence in the reliability of
rainfall data; (b) a lack of awareness of WII;
(c) the fact that farmers still have a negative
attitude toward insurance; (d) the inability
of farmers to pay premium upfront;
(e) inadequate experience of WII among
office and field staff; (f) difficulty in
obtaining daily rainfall on a weekly basis;
and (g) difficulty in arranging reinsurance
support during the initial period.

Despite all these challenges, SICL has been
progressing well. It has received a National
Achievement Award as a result of introducing
"Devijaya" (life insurance policy) in the Sri
Lanka market. SICL ranked 5th in terms of the
number of policies issued among all Sri Lanka
insurance companies in 2013, 2014, and 2015.

26.4.3 The third pillar: marketing, consumer affairs, and construction

SANASA established its own marketing and
production company in 1995 called
SANEEPA. SANEEPA built business
development centers (BDCs) to act as a
national information hub.

The BDCs served to link producers and
consumers, and to coordinate four
complementary activities via its computer
system. The four activities are, namely
(a) technology transfer for production
enhancement, (b) marketing, (c) business
consulting services, and (d) information
sharing.

These activities are interlinked because
high-quality production requires first and
foremost ready markets, whereas business
consulting services will ensure solid
business plans are in place, and a sound
database and information system must be
set in place. The BDCs maintained a
comprehensive database, which can be

accessed by members as well as nonmembers. Nonmembers using the services of the BDCs are be encouraged to become SANASA members and will be charged a fee. Members are charged a lower fee, and production groups among members pay a collective fee. In August 1999, SANASA set up SANASA Engineering and Development Company Limited (SEDCO) in which 46 SANASA societies invested an initial share capital of SLR210 million. SEDCO build housing projects for the community, and also provide engineering consultancy and technical assistance. SEDCO developed not just row houses and apartment buildings as living quarters, but also a shopping mall in the heart of the Gampaha district. They provide modern architectural and structural drawings for builders, and also plan to build the Nuwara Eliya Holiday Resort Project. SEDCO has shown its capacity to build modern real estate hubs with lucrative earnings during the early stages of its development. The challenge is for SEDCO to be able to carefully predict the real estate market, which often fluctuates. SEDCO's mandate is such that it must be able to manage the risk to ensure that the high-cost of constructing such a large infrastructure will not disturb the liquidity of the SANASA Movement including the SDBL. The stakes are high, hence, professional real estate developers at SEDCO must also be highly motivated and equipped with social entrepreneurship skills to safeguard the SANASA Movement through good or bad times.

26.4.4 The fourth pillar: education and capacity building

Education and training has been SANASA's strength from the very beginning. P.A. Kiriwandeniya as founder of the movement believes that a new social order can be attained by empowering people through continuous education and training. It is not enough to gain economic success if people are not socially-motivated to sustain the wellbeing of their families and communities. Since the outset, primary societies and district unions have been conditioned to undertake membership education. Monthly membership meetings are conducted to encourage members to interact and understand the fundamentals of credit unions, discuss practical issues in a democratic manner, and open up opportunities for skills development such as animal husbandry, financial literacy, financial management, and any other skill that will generate more income for families. These initial education and training sessions at the grassroots level led to the idea of building a SANASA Education Campus in Kegalle, following the acquisition of land filled with rubber trees in that district. A close and effective partnership was then created with the CCA in the early 1980s with a special focus on education and training for members of the SANASA Movement. Through a bilateral agreement with CIDA in 1988, CCA built the nucleus for constructing a more comprehensive education campus for SANASA.

FIRST BUILDING OF THE SANASA EDUCATION CAMPUS

සණස අධ්‍යාපන මණ්ඩපයේ පළමු ගොඩනැගිල්ල

First building of the SANASA education campus

Dr Kiriwandeniya envisioned a campus that will not just offer pure academic teachings like other higher educational campuses, but also a place where students and SANASA members could learn practical skills. Around the physical structure of the incipient campus, a number of skill-based development centers were established such as fruit gardens, animal husbandry facilities, and even a kindergarten school. The progression of the education campus transpired systematically to the extent that leaders and officers of the TCCSs could avail themselves of a full range of practical subjects on financial management, accounting, human resource development, marketing, as well as IT.

The campus also created a banking and insurance facility to train employees of the SDBL and ALMAO. An international center was duly constructed in 2003 to allow visiting scholars and foreign partners to stay with full board and lodging facilities.

CURRENT MAIN BUILDING OF SCL.

Current main building of SANASA Campus Ltd

In 2003, the SANASA education centre was made a limited liability company with the name, SANASA Campus Ltd (SCL). Its exponential growth and development led to the SCL earning degree awarding status in January 2014 from the higher education authorities (Extraordinary Gazette Notification of January 24, 2014). Currently the SCL is composed of two distinct faculties. The first being the SANASA Institute of Business and Development Studies (SIBDS), offering a 4 year Bachelor of Science degree program in three authorised subject areas—Regional Science and Planning, Banking and Finance, and Insurance and Risk Management and certain diploma and certificate courses. The second is the Centre for Cooperative and Community Studies (CCCS), offering educational and training programs of SCL, for members of SANASA and other cooperative societies, as well as other civic and community organizations.

26.5 Future sustainability of SANASA

The four pillar approach introduced by the founder and dynamic leader of SANASA, Dr. P.A. Kiriwandeniya, has stood the test of time, which bodes well for SANASA's future sustainability. The focus on education and training supported by the well-established grassroots TCCSs as well as business entities of SANASA, show all the signs of a movement that is built to create a sustainable future.

The commitment of SANASA's leaders and members to help communities was evident following the disastrous Tsunami at the end of December, 2004. When the Tsunami struck on December 26, 2004, the first concern was for those TCCS members living in the affected coastal areas of Sri Lanka. On December 28, 2004, SANASA leaders and staff visited the impacted areas, and with their own funds, distributed more than 200 lorries of dry rations, clothes, medicine, and other emergency supplies across the affected areas. SANASA took care of the funerals and burials of 650 of the deceased in the Southern Province, and establsihed 5 "work camps" with 100 volunteers to coordinate the rehabilitation and renovation activities. Affected children were given social support and school equipment. As the emergency relief efforts started to subside, SANASA turned its attention to long-term rehabilitation efforts. SANASA conducted a rapid survey to map out the disaster-affected areas by recruiting 90 field officers. The survey results showed the extent of the damage to the TCCSs as well as their immediate communities. The scale of the disaster was overwhelming, with 37,362 people dead or missing, 16,832 injured, 551,894 displaced, and 192,920 families impacted. 89,800 houses were completely destroyed, and 41,780 were partially destroyed. A sustainable rehabilitiaion plan was promptly developed and SANASA successfully rebuilt its sustainable, self-reliant communities in all affected areas.

In addition to the disaster relief program, SANASA has also shown its commitment to achieving its triple bottomline by launching a program called "SANASA Lassana Lanka Program" (SLLP). SLLP is an environmental policy that was drawn up back in 2006, prior to the declaration of the ICA Blueprint of 2020. This program aims to safeguard the environment by having SANASA members engaged in various environmental activities within their primary TCCSs such as tree planting and water conservation. From 2016, SLLP combined their activities with the Sri Lanka Next—A Blue Green Era, the government environmental policy initiated by the president to develop 10,000 sustainable smart villages with support from SANASA. The first phase of 100 villages have been developed by SANASA with the help of TCCS leaders and members. SANASA has also pledged to support the achievement of the relevant United Nations Sustainable Development Goals (SDGs) 2030 through the SLLP. Two distinct projects were initiated with the Ministry of Environment to safeguard endangered plant species and to prevent coastal erosion as well as a tsunami prevention program by

conserving a mangrove ecosystem along the coastal areas where the TCCSs subsists. SANASA also continues to educate members on the SDGs in order to achieve the relevant goals. To do so, the FTCCS has conducted various community engagement programs.

The diversification approach of SANASA means that SANASA has not restricted its operations solely to providing financial services to members, although such diversification stemmed from the needs of the members of the TCCSs as financial cooperatives. The multitude of business spheres outside of the cooperative legal framework is nonetheless aimed at strengthening the capital ownership base of members.

The challenges and uphill battles that SANASA managed to overcome throughout its growth and development processes bear evidence to the unfailing leadership of Dr. P.A. Kiriwandeniya, who managed to combine vision and innovation toward the creation of a vibrant people-based movement. It has been a longstanding desire on the part of Dr. Kiriwandeniya to create a new surge of leadership within the SANASA Movement by encouraging and educating the younger generation to come forward with leadership skills that could meet the current changing demands and development needs. The strong charisma, courage, vision, perceptiveness, dedication, commitment, and flexibility that are legendary in the person and leader, Dr. Kiriwandeniya. seem awfully hard to emulate. Notwithstanding, the collective leadership that exists within the SANASA Movement and the growing leadership of Ms. Samadani Kiriwandeniya, may prove able to create a new generation of capable leadership under the watchful eye of Dr. P.A. Kiriwandeniya. Sustaining the democratic structure of SANASA while at the same time protecting the movement against external interferences will be the most obvious test of SANASA's sustainability in the future.

The SANASA model of safeguarding its credit union system by developing other entities is worthy of further in-depth study in the future. SANASA has been lauded by a throng of credit union and cooperative organizations and leaders due to its unique approach that is distinct from other conventional credit union movements under the umbrella of the Asian Confederation of Credit Unions. In the end analysis, this uniqueness is an admirable result attributed to the chemistry of leadership, vision, and innovation.

Further readings

Fisher, I., Hardy, L., Ish, D., & MacPherson, I. (1999). The SANASA model, *co-operative development through micro finance, center for the studies of co-operatives*. University of Saskatchewan.

Kiriwandeniya, P.A. (2006). Cooperatives and the rebuilding of Sri Lanka after Tsunami. Retrieved and reviewed from www.peace.coop/main/wp-content/uploads/2006/08/P-%20A-_Kiriwandeniya.pdf

Kiriwandeniya, P.A. (2017). Socio-economic conglomeration of the SANASA group. *Presentation at the Credit Union Central of Kathulistiwa, Pontianak, West Kalimantan, Indonesia.*

Liyanaarachchi, N. (2016). *Cooperative financial services & rural development*, Status Report of SANASA, Sri Lanka. *Presentation at ICA/ACFSMC seminar, Dali, China.*

Schumacher, E. F. (1973). Small is beautiful, *a study of economics — As if people mattered*. Blond & Briggs.

SELA, Socio Economic Life in Asia. Retrieved and reviewed from www.sjapc.net/2015/05/it-all-began-sela/.

WIKIPEDIA (1987–1989). *JVP insurrection*. Retrieved from https://en.wikipedia.org/wiki/1987-1989_JVP_insurrection.

WOCCU (June 2019). *PEARLS technical guide*. Retrieved from www.woccu.org/documents/.

Summary: credit union case studies
Credit Unions in Asia and Australasia: carving their own identity

Romulo M. Villamin

Institute of Cooperative Studies, MASS SPECC Cooperative Development Center, Tiano-Yacapin St., Cagayan de Oro, Philippines

The five credit unions featured in this chapter are success stories in their own right. From humble beginnings, they parlayed people's common desire to help themselves through collective action into ever-growing membership and financial resources. They overcame adverse political and market conditions to create a space in their countries' own financial system for people who could otherwise have been "excluded" had they not pooled their resources and endeavored to institutionalize cooperation.

Their collective stories are a product of ordinary people's search for alternative means of providing for their financial needs, strengthened by the vision of improving their lives. This search was either led by a visionary leader or aided by co-op promoting development institutions that brought in the experience of successful cooperatives in the West. Their individual stories, however, are a reflection of the historical, cultural, and socioeconomic circumstances in which they took root and prospered.

First, the government created different environments for the credit unions to operate in—in some cases restrictive, in others supportive. But the cooperatives in all cases persisted. In Indonesia and the Philippines where cooperatives are written in the constitution, the government promoted their own cooperative program and tried to force credit unions to be subordinated to government-sponsored cooperatives. But the credit unions survived the pressure and the threat. Thrift and credit societies faced the same threat from the government in Sri Lanka but also persisted. In Australia, credit unions faced tight government regulations in a very competitive market environment and prospered. Only in Nepal was the government deemed to be supportive and it facilitated the development of credit unions.

Second, culture and tradition played a part in the resiliency of the credit unions at the face of external pressures. Mutual aid and cooperation are inherent in the culture of most Asian societies, referred to as *Gotong Royong* in Indonesia, *Bayanihan* in the Philippines, and

Guthi, Parma, Dhikuti, and *Dharmabhakari* in Nepal. In Sri Lanka credit unions derived cultural inspiration from *Theravadan* Buddhism that promote self-help and mutual approaches to solving problems.

Third, development institutions, mostly with a religious orientation, played an enabling role in supporting credit unions especially in their formation stage and subsequent development. They did so by reinforcing self-help initiatives at the community level in those countries. In Australia this role was played by parishes and industry associations.

It can be said, perhaps, that the cultural underpinnings of traditional cooperation and the enabling support provided by development institutions strengthened the resolve of the credit unions to overcome the challenges that accompanied their formation and the initial stages of their organizational development and growth. Such resolve certainly drew inspiration from the experience of credit unions that were already established institutions in North America and Europe.

These credit unions have become established institutions themselves, strong enough to withstand existential threats from changing governments and political climate. Their preoccupation is now focused on expanding market presence in national economies that are all aiming at higher economic growth. Here, these credit unions have followed different paths in their individual stories of growth and expansion—stories that could very well reflect the prospects as well as the challenges that credit unions as a whole in their respective countries will face in the future.

The Teachers Mutual Bank in Australia, for instance, has taken the classic path of sticking to financial services and deepening these services to strengthen member support and market presence, following the example of successful credit unions in the West. It has resisted the temptation of demutualizing and losing its cooperative identity by preserving a common bond of membership. The Vijaya Youth Club Credit Union Saving and Credit Cooperative Limited in Nepal has also endeavored to deepen its financial services to members while expanding its social services (social security, maternity programs, education opportunities for the poor) in its effort to contribute to poverty alleviation in the country.

Keling Kumang Credit Union (KKCU) in Indonesia has expanded to nonfinancial services in response to members' desire for support in production, marketing, and procurement of consumer goods. But in order to maintain its focus on financial services, it opted to form separate cooperatives engaged in agriculture, retail and services, and a foundation to run a vocational school. All these enterprises now operate under the umbrella of Keling Kumang Group. The First Community Cooperative (FICCO) in the Philippines has taken the same route except that it chose to become a multipurpose cooperative, venturing into insurance, cable TV, water refilling stations, and so forth. FICCO has also invested in cooperative banks, asset management, funeral services, and plans to go into health services, mass housing, and real estate development.

SANASA, which sprang from revitalized thrift and credit cooperative societies in Sri Lanka, has also diversified into development banking, insurance and risk management, marketing, consumer goods, construction, and formal education. Like KKCU, it established these enterprises as separate entities under the SANASA group. But unlike FICCO and KKCU, these diversified enterprises serve all the thrift and credit cooperative societies that make up what is now known as the SANASA movement.

Diversification from purely financial services to nonfinancial services pursued by the four Asian credit unions may be the same strategy of most credit unions in their respective countries. This can best be understood as an attempt by credit unions in particular and cooperatives in general to address market failure in these countries and the inability of their governments to respond to the challenge. In less-developed economies, this challenge is huge and will continue to be so. Against this reality, no individual credit union or cooperative can adequately address the challenge, however big and successful it may be. The individual approach will always be limited and the economic and social impact of cooperatives in these countries will continue to be circumscribed as it is now. What is needed is a systemic approach whereby cooperatives work together to effectively meet the challenge of national development—and serve as a counterweight to mainstream neoliberal ideology that persists to this day.

Worker Co-ops

The sociopolitical environment of worker cooperatives in the Philippines: basis for addressing the worker contractualization issue

Leo G. Parma[1], Maria Antonette D. Pasquin[2] and Bienvenido P. Nito[3]

[1]Chairman, Kagawani Foundation, Inc., Founder and Former CEO and Chief Business Builder of Asiapro Multi-Purpose Cooperative, Social Entrepreneur and Advocate of Worker Cooperatives, Pasig, Philippines [2]Instructor, School of Law and Governance, University of Asia and the Pacific, Pasig, Philippines [3]Research Fellow, Center for Research and Communication, University of Asia and the Pacific, Pasig, Philippines

Worker cooperatives have been the center of debate concerning their role in the social and economic transformation of society. On one hand, they are identified by relevant literature as a form of business and conduits of change insofar as they are mechanisms for job creation and income generation (International Labour Organization and International Co-operative Alliance, n.d.). On the other hand, they are described by some literature as the "most oppositional" form of cooperative to capitalism given its rejection of the traditional employer—employee relationship as manifested in a conventional firm. This is because in the case of worker cooperatives, "labor hires capital rather than capital hires labor" given that the workers of the business enterprise are at the same time its owners (Wright, 2010). However, this is seen by left-wing writers as an ambiguous class position and they accordingly reject their transforming potential.

While much has already been said about the role of worker cooperatives internationally across many countries, there continues to be a dearth in the literature on this type of cooperative's role in addressing the plight of precarious workers, especially in the Philippines. What has been claimed so far regarding worker cooperatives in the Philippines is that they came into existence to primarily address issues surrounding the country's labor market like unemployment and precarious working conditions, especially of contractual workers (Cataluña, 2000). Such experience has worldwide ramifications.

Nowadays, with the resurgence of the debates about the highly contested issue of contractualization[1] after the incumbent President Rodrigo Duterte vowed to end it, there is a need to further investigate this organizational model in the Philippines. It is through the exploration of the history and evolution of the phenomenally successful first worker cooperative, Alpha Co-operative, that an understanding of such a type of worker cooperative in the Philippines has been achieved and policy and legal issues have been clarified. Alpha Co-operative, now with a membership of 80,000 workers, has demonstrated how the vision and understanding of human resource management by one man who saw an unjust reality can lead to a solution, a new just reality, a new model with international implications.

The study uses primary data obtained through interviews with key informants— mainly with the founder of Alpha Co-operative—and secondary data from Parma, Pasquin, and Nito (2017)[2] and Parma, Ramirez, and Domingo (2014)[3]. Moreover, the study employs the theoretical explanation of the development of worker cooperatives of Jensen (2013). Such a framework allows the study to identify and analyze the macro and micro factors that presently challenge and hold back the worker cooperative movement in the Philippines, and to ultimately provide concrete recommendations or appropriate solutions to overcome such challenges as Alpha Co-operative has done.

28.1 History of worker cooperatives in the Philippines: a case of alpha co-operative[4]

28.1.1 Historical context

The history and conceptualization of the worker cooperative model in the Philippines can be traced from the beginnings of the first officially identified and currently largest worker cooperative in the country—the Alpha Co-operative. It was mainly born as a response to the pervasive issue of "endo"[5] or growing number of contractual workers[6] with unstable jobs, indecent wages, and poor benefits.

[1] Contractualization is most commonly used in the Philippines to refer to a nonpermanent employment arrangement entered by an employer and employee either directly or through a third-party agency (manpower service provider). The concept is also closely associated with another popularized concept called ENDO or end-of-contract practice, which has been claimed by most labor groups to be against the rights and welfare of workers (see Paqueo & Orbeta, 2016 for further details of the issue in the Philippines).

[2] Parma et al. (2017) interviewed key informants who occupy managerial positions in different worker cooperatives and surveyed a total 80 respondents from four worker cooperatives (20 deployed worker-members each)—all of which operate nationwide and have been established or in existence for at least 10 years. Except for Worker Co-operative A, which also produces its own products, specifically fiberglass boats, all worker cooperatives focus on providing labor services to companies in various industries (mostly in the processing and service industries) through contractual employment.

[3] Parma et al. (2014) collected various primary and secondary data through interviews and document analyses for the case study of Alpha Co-operative from its birth until 2012.

[4] This account has been largely based on an interview with the founder of Alpha Co-operative (Parma, 2017) as well as secondary sources of the historical economic and social conditions of the Philippines.

[5] See footnote 1.

[6] In fact, based on the Philippine Statistics Authority (2016), there continues to be a growing number of nonregular workers in the Philippines.

A decade after the implementation of the export-oriented strategies of the Marcos regime, unemployment and underemployment trends created instability in the national economy (Pasquin, 2018). The heightened competition among industry players has led to the closing down of certain companies, which, at the initial implementation of free trade in the middle part of the 1980s, can no longer keep up with the competition.[7] Meanwhile, those who stayed in the business despite the economic changes coped by implementing adjustment measures in their business operations such as (a) the utilization of more efficient technology and (b) the use of a flexible labor force (Macaraya, 1999; Alonzo, 1991 as cited in Cainglet, Vega, & Zapata, 2012)." From then on, contractualization has become an industry-wide practice and claimed to have been institutionalized in the Philippines with the establishment of the Herrera law,[8] albeit not without abuses as the unintended consequences. For instance, reports about companies not remitting the right wages and benefits to their workers, which consequently leads to street protests—among the most recent ones reported involved a manufacturing company in Bulacan, Philippines (Rey & Bautista, 2018).

Foreseeing no workable solutions offered by government, labor, or business sectors, the worker cooperative movement in the country took flight beginning from KEW Co-op in 1996 (no longer operating) and Alpha Co-operative in 1999. Alpha Co-operative, comprised then of only the founder with several contractual workers from various activities such as factory operations, administrative functions, retail, and socially-conscious entrepreneurs and professionals, envisioned itself as an organization providing a safety net to these marginalized workers by organizing them into a worker cooperative, which in return, could provide the socioeconomic benefits lacking in their previous work arrangement as contractual employees.

28.1.2 The main challenge: lack of understanding of the worker cooperative model

The concept of a "worker cooperative" has undergone, and perhaps arguably still undergoes, a series of conceptual evolutions as shared by the founder of Alpha Co-operative. Prior to the establishment of Republic Act (RA) No. 9520, otherwise known as the Philippine Co-operative Code of 2008 and in the early years of this first worker cooperative, the concept of a "worker cooperative" was absent from any of the national legal frameworks of the country—hence lacking the legal basis for their operations.[9] The founder of Alpha

---

[7] "The 1980s showed a rather uneven performance of the economy as GDP growth ranged from −7% in 1984 and 1985 to 6% in 1988. During the first five years of the 1980s, there was a chronic deterioration in economic performance as 1984 and 1985 posted negative growth. The second half of the 1980s showed increases in growth until 1990. Per capita GDP for 1980−1982 averaged $848. From 1983 to 1990, however, per capita GDP tapered off to $587 mainly due to the combined effects of the deterioration in the exchange rate as well as slow growth in output production (Solon & Floro, 1993)."

[8] Attributed to the late senator and labor leader (a pillar of the Trade Union Congress of the Philippines) Ernesto "Boy" Herrera for paving the way for labor contracting with the amendments he introduced in 1989 to the Labor Code. By including a bill mandating [the] regularization of employees who have rendered six months of continuous service, others claim that companies were given an opportunity to not regularize employees and simply rehire them after laying off for five months (Fernandez, 2016).

[9] It is only by virtue of RA No. 9520 in 2008 that formal recognition was given to worker cooperatives defined in Article 23 (t) as "one organized by workers, including the self-employed, who are at the same time the members and owners of the enterprise. Its principal purpose is to provide employment and business opportunities to its members and manage it in accordance with co-operative principles."

Co-operative mentioned that other challenges during the initial phase involved resistance from some local government leaders and agencies that found the worker cooperative to be a new or unfamiliar type of cooperative. Because of this, the founder of Alpha Co-operative had to think of ways to communicate the nature of such a model in such a way that it could be grasped by government, the prospective members, and client companies.

The cooperative has been a poorly understood business model according to Mazzarol, Mamouni-Limnios, and Reboud (2011), which resulted in its loss of favor in the 1990s and its disappearance from academic textbooks. This was also related to the emergence of the neoliberal competitor. The definition of the worker cooperative model was an international academic endeavor in the 1980s and 1990s by English academics following the "discovery" of Mondragon by Robert Oakeshott (1973). This effort to understand and clarify the worker cooperative was also an endeavor in the Philippines. The worker cooperative was defined as a hybrid bundle of individual and collective rights as well as economic and personal rights (Mygind, 1992). In this regard, the worker cooperative owner must wear four "hats," those of owner, shareholder, investor, and employee. It is the way the roles are balanced, and the tensions associated with this that leads to success or degeneration.

The founder recalls that he first encountered the idea of a worker cooperative through Mr. Bernardo Cataluña, one of the first writers of a book on worker cooperatives in the Philippines. Inspired by the worker cooperative model of the Mondragon Co-operative Corporation (MCC), the founder then sought to operationalize the concepts he learned as deemed fitting to the needs of Filipino workers. Two underlying concepts from this idea of a worker cooperative are emphasized by the founder, namely work and ownership or entrepreneurship. This dual aspect of work gives the identity of a "worker" while the aspect of entrepreneurship bestows the identity of a "co-owner" to any member of such an organization. Merging these two identities into one concept of a "worker–owner" member of a worker cooperative thereby affords the Filipino translation of *"ka-gawa"* (co-worker) and *"ka-ani"* (co-harvester). Putting together these two roles results in *"kagawani"* or *"gawanihan,"*[10] which the founder further explains as the act of working and harvesting the fruit of such work together as a collective. In a way, this only echoes the basis of cooperatives—the old idea of "cooperation."[11] From these two concepts, the founder identified the essence of the worker cooperative model in the Philippines—that which marries both the entrepreneurial (or capitalist) best practices and the cooperative principles.[12] It was clear to the founder that the model entailed a paradigm shift from the traditional employer–employee employment arrangement to the *"co-opreneur"* (from the perspective of the members) or *"co-opitalist"* approach, which underscores the very essence of cooperation among involved stakeholders.

In fact, Alpha Co-operative started out as a spinoff multipurpose cooperative from the initial manpower agency of the founder. Later on, the cooperative registered as a multipurpose

---

[10]   According to the Alpha Co-operative's founder, this term is also inspired from the "Filipino indigenous trait" called *"bayanihan,"* which more specifically refers to the act of helping one another to achieve a common goal. Other Filipino terms such as *tulungan* or *damayan* are also commonly interchanged with *bayanihan* (Ang, 1979).

[11]   Cooperation is defined as the social process by which individuals work together to realize a common objective or goal; cooperatives have grown and continuously make a niche in society (International Labour Organization, 2007).

[12]   In Spain, the government initiated a new form of organization, Sociedades Laborales (worker corporations) designed to enable workers to engage in entrepreneurial activities to preserve their jobs.

cooperative given the wide array of services it offers to client companies and members in particular. Since then, Alpha Co-operative has engaged in providing job contracting services to client companies in various industries. Indeed, such historical account affirms other studies that identify a common factor behind the formation of worker cooperatives, that is, having emerged as a response to domestic labor issues.[13]

28.2 Overcoming challenges during the initial phase

Rather than giving in to the birth pains of starting the first cooperative for precarious workers, the founder of Alpha Co-operative led the enterprise to grow as quickly as possible to achieve economies of scale. Rapid growth became possible because the stakeholders themselves, both the business and labor, were made to recognize and realize that the cooperative model catered to their respective interests. On the part of business, having the cooperative as the service provider addressed the vicious cycle of low productivity among those businesses confronted with seasonality such as in the agricultural industry. Such businesses are faced with the problem of low productivity given that they incur additional costs due to the constant retooling of their workers at the start of every peak season only then to be dismiss them toward the start of the lean season. At the same time, for the workers, such seasonality also entails intermittent flow of income.

The worker cooperative model, through Alpha Co-operative, then became a solution by augmenting such gaps—specifically through the provision of skilled workers for the business during peak season and engaging the workers in trainings or other means of livelihood during the lean season so as to ensure

financial stability for the workers. Because of these value-added benefits for both the business and labor, Alpha Co-operative eventually was able to attract a market—more client companies and members without much marketing and despite difficulties of other institutions still grasping the overall concept or organization model of a worker cooperative. Driven by the demands of both businesses for sustainable productivity and of labor for job security, Alpha Co-operative continued to grow at a phenomenal rate and expanded its operations to different areas of the country (Parma et al., 2014). See Fig. 28.1.

The initial 60 members exponentially grew in number as well as client partners. In 2002, Alpha Co-operative had a total of 9,734 member-workers. However, in 2017, it already has a total record of 70,790 member-owners with client partners mostly in the construction industry (58.96%) and then followed by the manufacturing industry (33.65%), while the rest fall in other industries. Meanwhile, in terms of membership by industry, the 2012 record of Alpha Co-operative reveals that the worker cooperative had the most members in the Agribusiness (63.49%) followed by those engaged in merchandising, sales, and promotion (Retail-MSP) (21.17%) and lastly by auxiliary, property management or industrial-manufacturing, quick service (API-MQS) (15.34%). See Fig. 28.2.

Accompanying this growth were also the benefits provided for the member-workers. Data from Parma et al. (2014) cited various packages of assistance (hospitalization and death benefits, livelihood loans, multipurpose loans, emergency loans, appliance loans, educational loans, group loans, and *Kinabukasan* or provident funds) and financial benefits (interest on share capital or dividends, cash convertible leaves, and patronage refund or productivity incentives), which Alpha Co-

[13] See Albanese & Jensen (2015) and Borzaga, Depedri, & Galera (2015) for the cases of Australia and Italy.

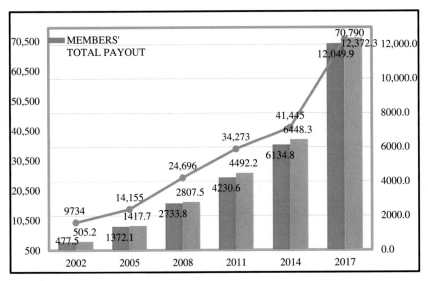

FIGURE 28.1 Growth in membership and members' total payout (in PHP thousands) of alpha co-operative 2002–2017.[14]

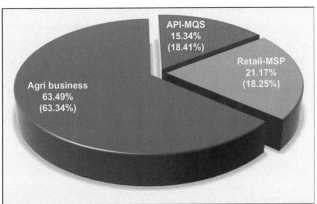

FIGURE 28.2 Membership by industry of Alpha Co-operative in 2011 (percentage count in parentheses) and 2012.[15]

operative offered to their members from the onset. As found in the narratives of worker-members of Alpha Co-operative, belonging to such a worker cooperative made them better off because it addressed their problems of the lack of benefits and indecent wages from their previous ailing contractual conditions. By joining the worker cooperative, the member-workers are ensured of, at the very least, the minimum wage and mandated benefits that guarantee them access to basic necessities for survival (Parma et al., 2014).

In more recently gathered data, Alpha Co-operative reported a total of PHP1.2 billion or about $23 million[16] remitted premium contributions to mandated benefits (Social Security System, Pag-Ibig/Housing, PhilHealth, among others). Alpha Co-operative continues to

[14] Alpha Co-op. (May 22–23, 2017).

[15] Alpha Co-op. (May 22–23, 2017).

[16] 23, 058, 600.00 dollars as of June 14, 2019 peso–dollar foreign exchange rate.

supplement these mandated benefits with self-administered and funded benefits such as hospitalization and death benefit subsidies, a members' financial program, and retirement benefits, which otherwise would be absent when one is employed in a conventional manpower agency (Alpha Co-op, May 22–23, 2017).

28.3 Macro challenges in the growth phase: the state's underdeveloped role and weak legal structure

From 2000 to early 2010, the increasing size of Alpha Co-operative in terms of members and client companies has attracted others to also form themselves into similar worker cooperatives. In fact, the four worker cooperatives in the study of Parma et al. (2017) are few of those that followed almost the same worker cooperative model as that of the Alpha Co-operative. However, the danger of not having the appropriate legal framework resulted also in the rise of those worker cooperatives that only claim cooperative status in name, but maintain their respective operations the same as that of a conventional manpower agency. Such phenomenon was candidly described by the founder of Alpha Co-operative as the *"lechon manok syndrome."*[17] The growth of these worker cooperatives without a great deal of knowledge nor proper education on how a worker cooperative must operate, has eventually led to many cases of abuse such as not consistently providing government-mandated benefits[18] and cooperative benefits like productivity

incentives and interest on share capital derived as being co-owners of the cooperative. It is speculated by the founder that such organizations only claimed cooperative status to avail themselves of tax exemptions and other benefits endowed by the government on cooperatives.

These types of worker cooperatives were not immediately called to attention by regulatory bodies because even the authorities still had a limited understanding of the concept of worker cooperatives, which were then already rampant in other countries. By 2010, the founder of Alpha Co-operatives recalls that many labor groups, which noticed their numbers being diminished by the birth of these cooperatives and manpower agencies, also began raising oppositions against the worker cooperative movement in general. From then on, regulations on cooperatives engaged in providing services to companies started to become more constraining or counter-developing for worker cooperatives like Alpha Co-operative.

Since 2010, the issues surrounding these cooperatives engaged in providing labor and job contracting services persisted. The first legal document to have lumped the cooperatives in the issue of contractualization was the Department Order (DO) 18-A of the Department of Labor and Employment (DOLE).[19] Because of this, those cooperatives engaged in providing services to client companies at that time became subjected to DOLE in the same way as conventional manpower agencies. This then further created confusions as to the nature or identity of such cooperatives. Hence, in 2012, the

---

[17] Nearest direct translation of this is "roasted chicken syndrome." This means that just like the roasted chicken business is, at first glance, easily replicated and so one can observe how there are so many such businesses, the initial worker cooperative concept as first embodied by Alpha Co-operative was soon enough replicated by others, albeit not following the whole model or even being faithful to the universal cooperative principles.

[18] This includes allocating for the members' social and health insurances and home development mutual funds (also known as the Social Security System, PhilHealth, and Pag-Ibig benefits respectively).

[19] In MC 2012-12, a Contractor was defined as "refers to any person or entity, including a cooperative, engaged in a legitimate contracting and subcontracting arrangement providing either services, skilled workers, temporary workers or a combination of services to a principal under a Service Agreement" (Cooperative Development Authority, 2012).

Co-operative Development Authority (CDA), the regulatory agency of all cooperatives in the Philippines, attempted to address these issues by disseminating Memorandum Circular (MC) No. 2012-12.

This MC attempted to clarify the definitions of a labor service cooperative and a worker cooperative (see Appendix A Table 28.A1), and for some worker cooperatives, this made a dent on the legal framework of cooperatives. Based on the results of the interviews from Parma et al. (2017) as well as the founder of Alpha Co-operative, this policy, which recognizes a "labor service co-operative," only legitimized the creation of a type of cooperative that is only limited to the engagement of contracting and subcontracting activities. Because of this, misconceptions about the nature of worker cooperatives aggravated not only related government agencies (SSS, PhilHealth, BIR, etc.,), but also even the business partners and the worker-members themselves in terms of adherence to laws and regulations.

The key informants argue that the fact that such legislation recognizes a type of cooperative, which has the traditional employer−employee relationship, runs contrary to the democratic nature of a cooperative[20]. They explain that tagging members as employees would essentially mean a different set of responsibilities, benefits, etc., as compared to a genuine member-owner. In fact, others claim that adhering to this employer−employee relationship may end up giving birth to another hierarchical labor structure that is different to the worker cooperative model. Worker cooperatives, with members seen as employees, only then defeat their purpose of addressing the employer−employee issues as

presented in Ellerman (1992) regarding the master−servant worker relationship. Until now, the definitions of a labor service cooperative and a worker cooperative found in this MC 12-12 are being adopted in the Revised Implementing Rules and Regulations (IRR) of the CDA promulgated on March 18, 2015 (Cooperative Development Authority, 2015).

Aside from these, the issuance of DO 174 of the DOLE is a cause of confusion. DO 174 imposes more regulations on various organizations (manpower agencies and cooperatives alike) and private companies engaged in contractual employment. As shared also by a key informant,[21] their own cooperative had to let go of almost three-fourths of their worker-members operating in various parts of the country in 2016 just to avoid any further complications due to the heated issue of contractualization. Another issue raised by key informants about the political environment toward worker cooperatives is with regard to the role of regulators. This is captured in the narration of one of the key informants:

> "The worker co-operative as a business model is now highly regularized by a government agency − the Department of Labor and Employment (DOLE) that is supposed to equally protect its workers who are also classified technically as laborers. DOLE has become biased [against] to the worker co-operative movement. Sadly, the main agency of the government, the Co-operative Development Authority (CDA) seems to be weak and hopeless in protecting and standing up for the co-ops...[22]"

The CDA is mandated by virtue of the 1987 Constitution Sec. 1 and Sec. 6 of Art. XII and the RA 6939 to promote cooperatives as "instruments of equity, social justice and economic

---

[20]   This democratic nature of a cooperative is explicitly identified in ILO's definition of a cooperative, that is, an "autonomous association of people united voluntarily to meet their common economic, social and cultural needs and aspirations through jointly-owned and democratically-controlled enterprises" (Sterling, 2014).

[21]   Personal Communication, General Manager, Worker Co-operative A, 2017 (lifted from Parma *et al.*, 2017).

[22]   Personal Communication, Operations Manager, Worker Co-operative D, 2017 (lifted from Parma *et al.*, 2017).

development" (Philippine 1987 Constitution; Congress of the Philippines: 8th Session, Republic Act 6939, 1990). This is remarkably like Italy, which has the support for cooperatives written into the Italian constitution as vehicles for the promotion of nonspeculative economic activity. This has been supported by the state's powerful institutional elites—the Italian Republican Party, the Communist Party, the Catholic Church, and LEGACOOP. This has resulted in the crafting of legislation leading to the building of a "co-operative state within a state" (Jensen, 2011, *unpublished)*. However, in the Philippines, there is more of a predatory state as defined by Rothchild-Whitt (1979). The gathered data shows that worker cooperatives in the Philippines are having difficulties in terms of getting their perspectives or interests accounted for by regulators, especially CDA, in legislation.

Indeed, the political environment in the Philippines is the most cited source of external challenges for the development of genuine worker cooperatives in the country. Precisely because there are still a lot of misunderstandings about the nature of worker cooperatives on the part of the government, most of the policies it formulates tend to restrict the capacity of worker cooperatives to expand their operations in various industries and eventually provide more benefits to their worker-members.

28.4 Micro challenges in the growth phase: the overriding capitalist mentality among worker cooperatives

On top of the aforementioned external pressures, worker cooperatives included in this study also identified internal challenges that contribute to the further delimiting of the capacities of worker cooperatives in the Philippines. The lack of understanding of worker cooperatives, both among cooperative leaders and other member-workers, constitute

the most cited internal challenge among worker cooperatives (Parma et al., 2017). Because of this, many worker-members continue to view themselves as "employees" of the cooperative rather than as co-owners. Meanwhile, some cooperative leaders may view themselves as the sole owners of the worker cooperative.

For the founder of Alpha Co-operatives, the challenges experienced with leadership successions by some worker cooperatives come about precisely because of the existing lack of democratic governance and participation among some worker cooperatives, which are in competition with the instincts to continue to operate a capitalist firm. If a democratic element was present, that is, the worker cooperative is then not managed like a family business, the transition to the next generation of cooperative leaders would not have been an issue. This can then also explain why, based on the results of Parma et al. (2017), indicators of participation within the cooperative resulted in a nearly neutral value (equal to or less than 3.5) compared to other social factors, which means minimal participation in cooperative governance among the surveyed deployed worker-members, consequently preventing them from acting in a transformational capacity. See Appendix A (Table 28. A2). In this regard, it can be further claimed that the overriding capitalist mentality of a firm continues to also pose a challenge among worker cooperatives, especially in terms of cooperative governance or management.

28.5 Theoretical interpretation

The historical account of the evolution of worker cooperatives in the Philippines, as seen primarily through the experiences of Alpha Co-operative, highlights the major role of the state, through the involved regulatory agencies (DOLE and CDA) in shaping the growth and development of worker cooperatives. The data gathered reveal that the state's role is perceived by worker cooperatives as constraining rather than enabling for the worker cooperative movement. For instance, during the initial years of Alpha Co-operative, the first worker cooperative, the new identity assumed by the worker-owners allowed them to maximize their benefits as derived from being co-owners, members, and workers of the cooperative. However, this identity has now slowly been changed to the traditional employee or worker identity due to the policies that were later enforced in the country. Because of this, some worker cooperatives end up stuck as small-sized worker cooperatives due to regulatory difficulties in scaling up, unlike Alpha Co-operative, which managed to do so in the past. The existing political environment coupled with a strong capitalist mentality, lacking a true understanding of the principles of cooperativism among the worker cooperatives that came after Alpha Co-operative and their respective client companies, then result in the abasement of the concept of worker cooperatives in consonance with the universal cooperative principles.

Given this, the claim that with an inappropriate legal structure, worker cooperatives could degenerate into a more conventional capitalist firm as presented by Jensen (2016) is especially manifested in the history of Alpha Co-operative in the Philippines. In fact, the micro challenges identified in this study already show signs of the struggle between having a capitalist or a more democratic governance system among worker cooperatives. Because of this, much effort is required to create an appropriate legal framework for the worker cooperatives in the Philippines. As the International Co-operative Alliance's Blueprint for a Co-operative Decade has already pointed out, "This [legal] framework plays a critical role for the viability and existence of co-operatives" (Mills & Davies, 2013). Without this structure, many worker cooperatives may be established in the country, but would eventually be degenerate either because of heightened market competition or state regulation.

While the macro factors mostly appear to destabilize the worker cooperative movement in the Philippines nowadays, the data gathered still provide insights into the role of the micro factors in the success of worker cooperatives in the Philippines such as the presence of key leadership and socioeconomic benefits to member-workers (Table 28.A3). Both play a huge part in the sustainability of the organization and stem from a firm commitment to the cooperative identity—with its core values and principles of cooperation. This was precisely the case of Alpha Co-operative as observed from its initial phase to its growth phase. The leadership of the founder with a clear concept of a worker cooperative fueled the expansion of Alpha Co-operative despite having no direct support or clear legal framework from the government. This is because this key leadership, faithful to the concept of a worker cooperative, also translated and facilitated actual socioeconomic benefits for the members as attested in the experience of Alpha Co-operative.

28.6 Conclusion

From the mentioned findings of this case study, it can be argued that despite the various macro- and microlevel challenges encountered by worker cooperatives, the model continues to empirically show, as in the case of Alpha Co-operative, how it can viably address precarious work in contractualization. In the areas of human and economic security, worker cooperatives such as Alpha Co-operative can be a safety net for marginalized workers struggling against unemployment and poverty. Worker cooperatives, then, do not operate on the often-conceived notion of contractualization or temporary employment. Such cooperatives secure continuous work for worker-members, which may not necessarily mean having the member-workers in the same type of work in the same client-company. Rather, member-workers are given the opportunity to have a more stable source of income and better benefits through the service agreement between worker cooperatives and their client companies in a per project or contract basis.

While the study only mentions the legal framework as a clearly problematic aspect in the development of worker cooperatives in the Philippines, in no way does it, however, claim that this is the only constraining factor, nor that there aren't other enabling elements that currently facilitate their development. In fact, this study also shows that worker cooperatives involved in the study must still further improve in facilitating other thematic areas in the Blueprint Strategy, especially in participation among worker-members, identity, and legal framework. In other words, the model has significant international implications in the transformation of capitalism by addressing the lack of legitimacy in the conventional employment contract. Besides, this study is only one among the many related literature citing the worker cooperative model's contribution to transforming the world of work today.

Based on these findings, there is, then, a need for those involved in tripartite governance—private sector, government, and civil society—to openly have a dialogue on the potentials of such a model, and support and conduct further studies on worker cooperatives in the country to confirm their effects on both labor and business before forwarding policies. Otherwise, these legislations may restrict more than strengthen worker cooperatives.

References

Albanese, M., & Jensen, A. (2015). Worker co-operatives in Australia and Italy. In A. Jensen, G. Patmore, & E. Tortia (Eds.), *Co-operatives in Australia and Italy: Comparative analysis and theoretical insights*. Firenze University Press, Italy.

Alpha Co-op. (May 22–23, 2017). Mobilizing co-operatives in pursuit of sustainable development goals. *2017 Research Conference on Co-operatives. Pasig City, Philippines* (unpublished).

Ang, G. R. (1979). The Bayanihan spirit: Dead or alive? *Philippine Quarterly of Culture and Society*, 7. Retrieved from https://www.jstor.org/stable/29791626.

Borzaga, C., Depedri, S., & Galera, G. (2015). Emergence, evolution, and institutionalization of social co-operatives in Australia and Italy. In A. Jensen, G. Patmore, & E. Tortia (Eds.), *Co-operatives in Australia and Italy: Comparative analysis and theoretical insights*. Italy: Firenze University Press.

Cataluña, B. M. (2000). *Entrepreneur worker co-operative*. Manila, Philippines: Manila Victor Prints.

Congress of the Philippines 8th Session. (1990 March 10). Republic Act 6939: *An Act Creating the Cooperative Development Authority to Promote the Viability and Growth of Cooperatives as Instruments of Equity, Social Justice and Economic Development, Defining its Powers, Functions, and Responsibilities, Rationalizing Government Policies and Agencies with Cooperative Functions, Supporting Cooperative Development, Transferring the Registration and Regulation Functions of Existing Government Agencies on Cooperatives as such and Consolidating the Same with the Authority, AppropriatingFunds Therefor, and for Other Purposes*. Retrieved from http://www.chanrobles.com/republicacts/republicactno6939.html#.W_-KB2gzbIU.

Cooperative Development Authority. (2012, July 18). *Memorandum circular order no. 12- 2012: Revised guidelines in the registration of labor service and worker cooperatives*. Retrieved from http://www.cda.gov.ph/images/Issuances/MCs/MC2012-12-Revised-Guidelines-Reg-Labor-Service-Workers-Coops.pdf.

Cooperative Development Authority. (2015). *Revised rules and regulations implementing certain and special provisions of The Philippine cooperative code of 2008*. Cooperative Development Authority. Retrieved from Office of the President: http://www.cda.gov.ph/resources/issuances/implementing-rules-and-regulations/revised-rules-and-regulations-implementing-certain-and-special-provisions-of-the-philippine-cooperative-code-of-2008.

Ellerman, D. (1992). *Property and contract in economics: The case for economic democracy*. Blackwell.

Fernandez, B. (2016). *How contractualization became the norm among Philippine businesses*. Business Mirror. Retrieved from https://businessmirror.com.ph/how-contractualization-became-the-norm-among-philippine-businesses/.

International Labour Organization. (2007). *Handbook on cooperatives for use by workers' organizations*. International Labour Organization. Retrieved from: http://www.ilo.org/wcmsp5/groups/public/---ed_emp/---emp_ent/documents/publication/wcms_094046.pdf.

International Labour Organization and International Co-operative Alliance. (n.d.). Cooperatives and the sustainable development goals a contribution to the post-2015 development debate. Retrieved from https://sustainabledevelopment.un.org/content/documents/1247ilo.pdf.

Jensen, A. (2011). Insolvency, employee rights and employee buyouts — A strategy for restructuring. Unpublished Doctoral Thesis.

Jensen, A. (2013). The labor managed firm — A theoretical model explaining emergence and behaviour. In: D. Kruse (Ed.), Sharing ownership, profits, and decision-making in the 21st century (Advances in the economic analysis of participatory and labor managed firms), 14: 295—325. https://doi.org/10.1108/S0885-3339(2013)0000014020

Jensen, A. (2016). The 1980s worker cooperative buyout experience in Australia. Learning from Praxis. *Journal of Entrepreneurial and Organizational Diversity*, 5(1), 54—78.

Mazzarol, T., Mamouni-Limnios, E., & Reboud, S. (2011) Co-operative enterprise: A unique business model? Paper submitted for the Australia and New Zealand Academy of Management (ANZAM) Annual Conference, Wellington 7—9 December.

Mills, C., & Davies, W. (2013). *Blueprint for a co-operative decade*. Coop International Co-operative Alliance. Retrieved from: http://ica.coop/sites/default/files/publication-files/blueprint-for-a-co-operative-decade-english-1707281677.blueprint-for-a-co-operative-decade-english.

Mygind, N. (1992). The choice of ownership structure. *Economic and Industrial Democracy*, 13(3), 359—399. Available from https://doi.org/10.1177/0143831X92133004.

Oakeshott, R. (1973). Mondragon: Spain's oasis of democracy. In J. Vanek (Ed.), *Self-management, economic liberation of man*. London: Penguin.

Paqueo, V.B., & Orbeta Jr., A.C. (2016, December). Beware of the "end contractualization!" battle cry. *Discussion paper series*.

Parma, L.G. (2017, July 7). Interview on the genuine worker co-op model. (M. A. Pasquin, Interviewer).

Parma, L. G., Ramirez, L. F. A., & Domingo, A. B. (2014). In V. Ramirez (Ed.), *Social enterprise: Work that uplifts human life 4*. Pasig, Philippines: University of Asia and the Pacific.

Parma, Pasquin, & Nito. (2017). *The social economy of worker co-operatives: A case study on worker co-operatives as a solution to the issue of contractualization in the Philippines.* A conference paper. 12th ICA-AP Regional Cooperative Research Conference, Seoul, South Korea. Retrieved from http://www.ica-ap.coop/sites/ica-ap.coop/files/ICA-AP2017_Maria%20Antonette_Pasquin_Paper_S14.pdf

Pasquin, M.A. (2018, June). *An inquiry to the socio-economic practices of worker co-operative membership in providing sustainable livelihood to contractual workers in the banana plantation: A case study of ATC worker co-operative in Davao, Philippines.* A Master's Thesis. University of Asia and the Pacific, School of Law and Governance.

Philippine 1987 Constitution. Article XII, Sections 5 and 6. Retrieved from http://www.chanrobles.com/article12.htm#.W_-IS2gzbIU

Philippine Statistics Authority. (2016). *2014 survey of employment: Statistics on non-regular workers*. Quezon City: Philippine Statistics Authority.

Rey & Bautista. (2018). *LOOK: Why NutriAsia workers are on strike*. Rappler News. Retrieved from https://www.rappler.com/nation/205166-reason-nutriasia-workers-on-strike.

Rothchild-Whitt, J. (1979). The collectivist organization: An alternative to rational bureaucratic models. *American Sociological Review*, 44, 509—527. Available from https://doi.org/10.2307/2094585.

Solon O., & Floro, M. (1993). *The Philippines in the 1980s: A review of the national and urban level economic reforms*. Working Paper. Urban Development Division, Transportation, Water and Urban Development Department, Environmentally Sustainable Development, the World Bank.

Sterling, S. (2014). *Promotion cooperatives: A guide to ILO recommendation no. 193 C*. Geneva: International Labor Organization.

Wright, C. (2010). Worker cooperatives and revolution: History and possibilities in the United States. *Graduate Masters Theses* (Paper 19).

Further Reading

Nito, B.P. (2017, July 12). Interview on labor service and worker co-operatives. (M. A. Pasquin, Interviewer).

Appendix A

TABLE 28.A1   Labor service co-operative versus workers co-operative in the Philippines.

	Labor service co-operative	Workers co-operative
As to nature of activities	Engaged in contracting and subcontracting arrangements as defined by law	May engage in labor and production including contracting and subcontracting arrangements in support of its main activity as defined by law
As to the existence of an employer–employee relationship	The existence of an employer–employee relationship is at all times observed in contracting and subcontracting arrangements during the deployment of the member. A trilateral relationship exists between and among the principal, contractor, and the member employees	The self-employed individual is allowed by the cooperative in regard to its enterprise

Cooperative Development Authority. (2015, June 29). Revised rules and regulations implementing certain and special provisions of The Philippine cooperative code of 2008. Cooperative Development Authority: Retrieved from Office of the President: http://www.cda.gov.ph/resources/ issuances/implementing-rules-and-regulations/revised-rules-and-regulations-implementing-certain-and-special-provisions-of-the-philippine-cooperative-code-of-2008.

TABLE 28.A2   Benefits of worker co-operative members.

Benefits	Worker co-op A (%)	Worker co-op B (%)	Worker co-op C (%)	Worker co-op D (%)	Total average (%)
Mandatory benefits (from labor code)					
SSS	100	100	100	100	**100**
PhilHealth	100	100	100	100	**100**
Pag-ibig/Home Development Mutual Fund (HDMF)	100	100	100	100	**100**
13th month	100	100	100	100	**100**
Total average (%)	100	100	100	100	
Cooperative benefits					
Interest on share capital/dividend	50	67	71	100	**72**
Patronage/productivity funds	5.0	74	50	85	**53**
Skills training	10	15	50	30	**26**
Hospitalization insurance	45	74	43	95	**64**
Provident funds/loans	50	33	7.0	25	**29**
Total average	**32**	**53**	**44**	**67**	

*Values rounded up to the nearest tens place.

TABLE 28.A3   Perception of worker co-operative members on their socioeconomic conditions.

Socioeconomic conditions	Worker co-op A	Worker co-op B	Worker co-op C	Worker co-op D	Total average/ indicator
Human conditions					
Medical benefits	4.15	4.26	3.21	4.5	4.03 (Agree)
Skills development	3.95	4.19	3.79	4.65	4.15 (Agree)
The sense of worker cooperative ownership	4.15	4.19	3.50	4.7	4.14 (Agree)
Total average/worker cooperative	**4.08 (Agree)**	**4.21 (Agree)**	**3.50 (Neutral)**	**4.62 (Strongly Agree)**	
Economic conditions					
Salary	3.30	3.63	3.21	3.85	3.50 (Neutral)
Other sources of income	3.25	3.63	3.79	4.00	3.67 (Agree)
Job security	3.85	4.11	3.50	4.35	3.95 (Agree)
Total average/worker cooperative	**3.47 (Neutral)**	**3.79 (Agree)**	**3.5 (Neutral)**	**4.07 (Agree)**	
Social conditions					
Voting rights	3.70	3.93	3.64	4.55	3.96 (Agree)
Expression of ideas/opinions	3.85	3.93	3.93	4.35	4.01 (Agree)
Transparency of worker cooperative documents	3.65	3.70	3.07	4.30	3.68 (Agree)
Opportunities to represent worker cooperative outside	3.6	3.78	3.50	3.75	3.66 (Agree)
Support from colleagues	4.1	4.19	4.21	4.60	4.23 (Agree)
Job ladder	3.5	3.78	3.79	3.60	3.67 (Agree)
Total average/worker cooperative	**3.73 (Agree)**	**3.89 (Agree)**	**3.69 (Agree)**	**4.19 (Agree)**	

Parma, Pasquin, & Nito. (2017). The social economy of worker co-operatives: A case study on worker co-operatives as a solution to the issue of contractualization in the Philippines. *A conference paper. 12th ICA-AP Regional Cooperative Research Conference, Seoul, South Korea. Retrieved from http://www.ica-ap.coop/sites/ica-ap.coop/files/ICA-AP2017_Maria%20Antonette_Pasquin_Paper_S14.pdf.*

Collectivism as a strategy for success in Indian worker cooperatives: case study of Koppa Transport Cooperative Society

Sureshramana Mayya[1] and Yashavantha Dongre[2]

[1]Poornaprajna Institute of Management, Udupi, India [2]University of Mysore, Mysore, India

As governments throughout the world decided to cut services and withdraw from regulating markets, cooperatives are being seen as useful mechanisms to manage risks (Bello, 2010). But this may not prove to be good in countries like India where deregulation is seen to be a process of encouraging and patronizing the private sector. Not that cooperatives are not important in India. With over 0.6 million cooperatives, India probably has the world's largest cooperative sector. Cooperatives occupy an important place in the Indian economy and are considered an essential pillar of the economy along with the public and private sectors. The cooperative movement in India is largely state-directed, and since independence in 1947, the national government as well as state governments have supported and interfered with the cooperative movement. While agricultural cooperatives, dairy cooperatives, marketing cooperatives, and cooperative banks constitute a major chunk of cooperatives in the country, there are not many worker

cooperatives. Cooperatives are based on the idea that collectively people can achieve goals that none of them could achieve alone and this seems to be apt in the case of some of the successful worker cooperatives in the country.

29.1 Workers cooperatives in India

Worker cooperatives, though not large in number, are among the most significant subsections of cooperative endeavours in India. Like many other countries, Indian worker cooperatives are also owned and controlled by those who work in them and are run for the mutual benefit of members. Based on the nature of the enterprise, the formation of workers' cooperatives is classified into three categories, namely (1) industrial cooperatives, (2) workers takeovers, and (3) labor cooperatives.

It is held that with the ongoing global economic crises and the whole world witnessing the collapse of the capitalist free market, and on the other hand, the failure of the socialist-based command economy, the viable third alternative is democratically-owned and managed cooperatives (Restakis, 2010). Viewed in this context, a worker cooperative with a combination of two components, namely democratic organisation and an economic enterprise, where both must be healthy for the cooperative to thrive (Audebrand, 2017), has a lot of relevance. Edward S. Greenberg (1986) has demonstrated that democratic workplaces foster a cooperative and egalitarian relationship inside and outside the workplace. Worker cooperatives have the objective of creating and maintaining jobs, they generate wealth, improve the quality of life of the members, provide dignity, allow democratic management, and promote community and local development (CICOPA, 2005). This is well illustrated by workers' cooperatives in India as well. Still, following the global trend, the number of worker-controlled firms is much less than the number of investor-controlled ones. According to Dow (2003), the reasons for the lower number of worker-owned enterprises are limited personal wealth and the nonavailability of external financing. Here again, the experience of many worker cooperatives in India shows that procuring adequate capital is central to their formation and success.

Even though cooperatives in India were started before independence and the first cooperative enactment came back in 1904, worker cooperatives did not find a place on the national scene until as late as the 1960s. Beginning from the 1970s, partly driven by the need for workers in the unorganized sector to unite and protect their jobs and partly because of the congenial environment and state support, worker-owned enterprises started to be established. Based on the national census of 2011, the National Worker Cooperative Federation of India had estimated that there were about 38,880 worker cooperatives with an estimated 2575 million members. It is of interest to note that some of the earliest and largest worker cooperatives like Uralungal Labour Contract Cooperative Society Limited (ULCCS Ltd), the Kerala Dinesh Beedi Workers' Cooperative Society (KDB), and the Indian Coffee House (ICH) were all started in the state of Kerala, which was governed by the state government led by the Communist Party.

29.2 Transport cooperative society, Koppa

The TCS, in Koppa, located in the southern state of Karnataka in India, was started as a breakaway enterprise from the erstwhile Shankar Transport Company (private) Limited. The Shankar Transport Company was considered to be one of the most efficient bus services in Shimoga, Chikkamagalur, and some parts of the South Kanara districts, comprising nearly 85 routes. This company employed around 350 workers. However, this private company paid relatively low wages, and the working conditions were not satisfactory.

Low wages, a rising cost of living, and workplace harassment, on the one hand, and the emergence of the local unit of the trade union, the Transport and General Mazdoor Union (R), on the other hand, brought about an awakening among the workers and accordingly, they resorted to striking in July 1987. The management dealt with the strike harshly by dismissing 27 workers who were at the forefront of the agitation. It also suspended certain workers and initiated various other tactics to crush the resistance. The strike did not produce the desired result, the reason being a lack of effective leadership. As usual, the Shankar Transport Company continued to pay less than the minimum wage fixed by the government.

The agreement made regarding salary and other terms and conditions between the workers and management during 1987 ended on June 30, 1990. Hence, on July 1, 1990, the workers union submitted a charter of demands to the management. The major demands included an average increase in salary to the extent of Rs. 225 per month, the granting of a medical allowance of 8% of their salary, the payment of a shift allowance, an increase in the daily batta, a dearness allowance as per cost of living index, the granting of an accommodation rental allowance of Rs. 100 per month, leave facilities, and free passes to the family members of the workers.

In spite of repeated requests and negotiations, the management of Shankar Transport Company failed to respond positively to the workers' demands. Finally, the workers led by Sri. Chikke Gowda, supported by the All India Trade Union Congress (AITUC) and contemporary trade union leaders like Sri B.K. Sunderesh and Sri. Renukaradhya, started encroaching on the sacred territory of management prerogative. However, nothing positive came out of the "Demand Week" or "Hunger Strike" and many rounds of discussions were held between workers and management. Even the conciliation efforts conducted by the Labour Commissioner, Bangalore, and Assistant Labour Commissioner, in Chikkamagalore district under Section 12(1) of Industrial Disputes Act of 1947 failed to settle the dispute between the management and workers.

Lastly, the majority of workers affiliated to Chikkamagalur District Transport and General Mazdoor Sangha (R), supported by the AITUC and other leftist organizations started a total strike on December 15, 1990. This strike paralyzed the whole bus transport in and around Malnadu region affecting bus services of nearly 80 routes of Koppa, Kalasa, Balehonnur, Sringeri, and N R Pura Talukas.

The strike lasted 53 days. On February 6, 1991, the whole Malanadu region observed protests and bundhs in support of the workers movement. Support organizations like AITUC, the Student Federation of India (SFI), and the

All India Youth Federation, (AIYF) supported the cause of Shankar Transport Employees Union. Sri Chikke Gowda, leader of Shankar Transport Employees Union and General Secretary of Chikkamagalur District Transport and General Mazdoor Sangha emerged as an effective leader channelizing the movement of workers. However, the management remained firm in its stand and did not agree to pay salaries equal to that of other transport companies. Instead, the management declared a lockout on February 7, 1991, and retrenched all the workers. Within a few days, the management of Shankar Transport Company surrendered 67 permits of 80 routes to the government. This amounted to the closure of the unit. On hearing the shocking news of the lockout, the transport union convened a general body meeting and decided to withdraw the strike. Accordingly, on February 8, 1991, the Workers Union submitted a strike withdrawal notice to the management. But the management wanted to get rid of all striking workers.

Now, it had become imperative on the part of the workers to strive hard to save their jobs. Sri. B.K. Sunderesh, the local communist leader was mainly responsible for promoting the ideals of cooperation—specifically of common ownership—among the unemployed employees of Shankar Transport Company. He motivated them to make an attempt to protect their jobs in the closed unit. Initially, the workers explored all possible avenues to get the transport unit run by the management. It was only when they failed in their efforts to find a solution that the workers volunteered to run some buses and control their destiny.

A fraction of employees decided to mobilize their compensation funds and sought permission to run buses on a cooperative basis. Accordingly, in a meeting of the Regional Transport Authority held on February 11, 1991, under the chairmanship of Dr. S. Subramanya, the employees union of Shankar Transport Company got six permits and permission to run seven buses on a cooperative basis. All 273 workers got their compensation funds from Shankar Transport Company, out of which 130 workers agreed to invest their compensation amount of Rs 4.85 lakhs as basic capital and, thus, the TCS was formed.

On the other side, the Shankar Transport Company, in a bid to escape from its problems, resorted to downsizing by splitting into four small companies, namely Ravishankar Transport, Shambushankara Transport, Udayashankara Transport, and Navashankara Transport. All these four units agreed to employ 100 loyal employees.

Thus the TCS started its operations in the selected routes of Malanadu region from March 8, 1991. The union leader, a former mechanic of Shankar Transport Company, Sri Chikke Gowda, was the chief promoter along with 10 other workers as copromoters. Later, on May 16, 1991, the TCS got formally incorporated and started its operations.

It may be observed that the Shankar Transport Company was a highly successful company until 1987, but its success was also dependent on its exploitative nature in handling its employees. A sense of insecurity and also a kind of deprivation were prevalent among the employees for a long period of time. But they were, somehow, not able to come together and succeed in resisting it. However, during 1987, all of them joined together and they did go for some kind of protest. But as a result of the lack of effective leadership among themselves, their protest met with failure. After this failure, they went back to work and they found that they were subjected to more exploitation. This insecurity and exploitation and also a feeling of the humiliation of the failure of their earlier attempt was fresh in their minds and they were waiting for proper leadership. So when it came, they were able to organize themselves and start their own enterprise.

As a first step, the workers pooled their compensation funds of Rs 4.85 lakhs and invested it during 1991. The fund increased to Rs 5 lakhs by March 31, 1992. During 1992, there were only 126 members. In addition to the share capital, society borrowed a sum of Rs 6.34 lakhs from banks and other financial institutions toward operating expenses during 1991–92. The TCS adopted, more or less, the management structure of the old firm. The study revealed that, although founder members were able to help define managerial responsibilities and to influence key decisions in setting up the cooperative, during the formative stage, they remained quite heavily dependent on Chikke Gowda, the president of the cooperative society.

Between 1995 and 2015 many developments took place. Chikke Gowda, the founder president, was involved in a financial scandal and he was forced to leave the cooperative. Severe competition was posed by the private transport unit, which was now operating under different names. Political forces and bureaucratic hurdles pulled the cooperative down. At the same time, the cooperative and its members showed tremendous resilience and maturity. They stood firm. Their spirit of collectivism did not diminish. They found new leaders and they improved their service quality. They found new routes to operate and made the local population feel that the cooperative cared for them much more than the private transport units did. All this has made TCS grow and shape up into a success story. Eventually, TCS became a household name and the private transport company could not compete with the collective might of the workers and was closed down.

29.3 Challenges and strategies

29.3.1 Raising capital

Raising much-required financial resources was the immediate problem faced by TCS. The cooperative had secured permits to operate buses along six routes and had also put in an application for another 30 routes. It had in its possession only five buses and those were used ones. The worker-members had contributed all their compensation funds toward their initial capital. But it was not sufficient. The first board of directors with support from outside leadership came up with a good plan to overcome this challenge. The first initiative came from the worker-members, who agreed to work for lower wages until the cooperative started making a profit. Financial contributions, in the form of loans, came from both members and local people all of whom were willing to accept lesser interest rates than the prevailing market rates and, most importantly, bus manufacturers were convinced to supply new buses and spare parts on a deferred payment basis. This gave the much-needed impetus and by its second year running the cooperative made operating profits and there was no looking back after that.

29.3.2 Leadership

Leadership is the most crucial aspect of the growth and sustainability of any cooperative. The workers of Shankar Transport Company had not succeeded in their efforts of getting better amenities in the past, mainly due to a lack of proper leadership. Chikke Gowda filled this void and provided the initial leadership by taking everybody along and also by effectively articulating the issues at hand. However, the more important issue is that the next line of leadership got ready quite quickly. About a decade after its formation, there came a big leadership crisis with the incumbent president, who was also their leader and the founder president, being accused of misappropriation of funds, and eventually, he was sent out of the organization and his primary membership was terminated. But the next line stood its ground. In a way, things worked out more

positively since the aura of the big leader was not there putting others on the second fiddle and there emerged a more democratic, participative, and collective leadership. It is at this stage that the cooperative became a stable organization.

29.3.3 State patronage

The role of the state government has been an important challenge to be overcome over the years. In fact, it remains a critical challenge even at present. In the initial years, there were problems related to the incorporation of the TCS as a worker cooperative since, according to the prevailing legislation, workers could not be members of the same cooperative where they were earning their wages. At this juncture, state government officials responded positively. They felt the needs of the workers as well as the prevailing public sympathy to their cause and helped the cooperative to register as a service cooperative. Luckily for TCS, the legislations eventually changed and it could become a full-fledged worker cooperative. However, the state has neither supported TCS financially nor given any concessions or exemptions over the years. On the other hand, notices were served to the cooperative for tax compliance, payment of higher route fees, and also uncalled for inspections and inquiries were initiated a number of times. Many of these negative steps were either the handiwork of the private transport houses or that of corrupt bureaucrats, but the sad thing is that the state machinery did not create any special space for this special cooperative. The present board members say that this is one challenge they are trying to overcome, but so far in vain. The love—hate relationship continues. The cooperative recieved the best cooperative award from the state government and the next month, the same government came out with a penalty on the cooperative on some or other pretext. TCS has resisted state intervention successfully so far. They are not in harmony with the state, but the overall image of the cooperative is too good for any official to go for extreme steps such as superseding the board or penalizing them in any other manner.

29.3.4 Lack of innovation and diversification

This is an area where TCS is found to be highly wanting. Except for the computerization of office work and the introduction of ticket issuing machines, no other innovation has been reported in the past two decades. It has not diversified its business. Literature throws light on 94-year old ULCCS, a celebrated case of a labor contract society from the Indian state of Kerala, which diversified into new ventures like an industrial park, a total solution provider, plumbing, electrification, interior decoration, IT software, and tourist services (Sharma, 2018). After 23 years running, TCS does not have a website and has not adopted any professional marketing strategies. Out of 70 buses, they have been running only 50 buses as permitted by routes, the services of spare buses are not utilized properly. The leadership and members seem to be highly risk-averse and are not willing to diversify into any other business, not even that closely related to the transport sector. In a way, this is the result of another related challenge, that of expansion of membership, which TCS has not taken up

29.3.5 The monopoly of initial members

One of the features of the TCS is a declining tenured number of employees and declining employee members between 1991 and 2019. We have observed from records of TCS that all their employees were members during 1991–92. During the past 23 years, the membership has

declined from 244 to about 160. The board of management seems to be hesitant to admit new workers as members. The rationale explained by the president is that new workers are not familiar with the sufferings of the pioneers and, therefore, may not be as responsible as initial members. The cooperative is resorting to appointing contract workers and since they are not tenured employees, they will not be eligible to become members as per the bylaws. This might pose a danger of turning the enterprise into a monopoly of the initial members. It was rightly observed elsewhere that "a danger worth mentioning is that a successful transport society may itself after some years become monopolistic, with the original members owning all the capital and employing nonmembers as drivers." (ILO Office, 1963, p. 134). This situation, if occuring in future could be a black spot on the otherwise vibrant workers' cooperative.

29.3.6 Present position

More than 23 years have gone by since the workers started managing their society to keep their employment intact. Like other successful innovations, TCS influenced the status of ordinary working people and remained efficient and competitive. The success of the cooperative society is the result of the hardships and dedicated efforts of the employees/members in the past. It preserved their jobs, but favorable state policies and support would only help them to make special contributions to economic life; otherwise, they will fade away. For the past 23 years, it successfully negotiated its growth without compromising its democratic principles. The cooperative society celebrated its silver jubilee on January 3, 2017. TCS remains a cooperative of repute and has in fact indirectly contributed to similar cooperatives emerging in other regions as well. However, the present situation is not all that rosy.

Due to competition from private and government-owned buses, profits are falling. The management of TCS has been anticipating government support. According to Godwin Jayaprakash, Managing Director of TCS, a constant increase in insurance charges, the cost of buses, high tax rates, ever-increasing fuel costs, etc., have exerted pressure on their financial performance and they have not increased the salary of their staff for the past three years. The cooperative pays a huge income tax of around INR 150 million every year and this is a big burden. TCS is hoping that the state and the central governments would be supportive and ensure that the cooperative will not fall into a debt trap.

Conclusion

The TCS story is all about the collective might of the workers. It is a case of rather poorly educated, rural, but skilled workers realizing that they can survive only when they join together and share the good and the bad among all. The result of this collectivism resulted in a clear victory over an exploitative private service provider. No one believed that TCS would succeed, not only because its founders were poorly educated and had no money, but also because they belonged to different castes and religions. But the workers' collective strength made it a landmark. It inspired many other worker groups to join together and initiate cooperative endeavors. TCS also proves that a worker takeover is a possibility, and if it can succeed in a service sector enterprise, there is every reason for policymakers to believe that such success can be replicated. In this sense, the story of TCS may be more important than the much older and bigger worker cooperatives of the country. The greatest contribution of TCS is that at both the state and the national levels, policymakers are now willing to provide space for cooperatives in the process of state withdrawal from specific sectors.

TCS is at a crossroads again. The old founder members are all retiring, and soon their number will be just a handful. But the old guard is not inclined to admit new members. The result is that the "owner–employee" (full members–contract workers) relationship is reemerging. If this persists, TCS is likely to go the way the erstwhile private company did. When TCS became successful, it was all due to the commitment and collective efforts of workers and all credits were to them. If they cannot negotiate the current problem and succumb, again, it would require the workers to be blamed. The state has not been considerate and the private sector around is hostile, but then, that is how the market would be expected to be. TCS has succeeded earlier under a similar environment and so there is no reason to believe that it cannot do so now, if the real strength, that of collectivism, is understood and put to its best use.

References

Audebrand, L. K. (2017). Expanding the scope of paradox scholarship on social enterprise: The case for (re)introducing worker cooperatives. *M@n@gement*, *20*(4), 368–393. Retrieved June 27, 2019, from https://www.management-aims.com/fichiers/publications/en_1513684480.pdf.

Bello, D. A. (2010). *The role of cooperative societies in economic development*. Retrieved September 26, 2018, from https://mpra.ub.uni-muenchen.de/23161.

CICOPA. (2005). *World declaration of worker cooperatives*. Retrieved from http://cicopa.coop/wp-content/uploads/2018/02/world_declaration_on_worker_coops_en.pdf.

Dow, G. K. (2003). *Governing the firm: Workers control in the theory and practice*. New York: Cambridge University Press.

Greenberg, E. S. (1986). *Workplace democracy: The political effects of participation*. Ithaca: Cornell University Press.

ILO Office (1963). *Cooperative management and administration*. Geneva

Restakis, J. (2010). *Humanizing the economy: Co-operatives in the age of capital*. Canada: New Society Publishers.

Sharma, S. K. (2018). *ULCCS-The saga continues*. New Delhi: ICS Domus Trust.

Further Reading

Campbell, J. (1990). *Property rights and the organization of economic activity by the state.* Retrieved from https://www.researchgate.net/publication/259975661_Campbell_John_L_and_Leon_Lindberg_1990_Property_Rights_and_the_Organization_of_Economic_Activity_by_the_State_American_Sociological_Review_555634-47?enrichId = rgreq-0b01d85900eda6741957833cd6640ce6-XXX&enr.

Chris Cornforth, A. T. (1988). *Developing successful worker cooperatives.* London: Sage Publications.

List of cooperatives. (2018). Retrieved from Wikipedia: https://en.wikipedia.org/wiki/List_of_cooperatives#India.

Mayya, S. (2003). Workers cooperatives in India: Its social, economic and potential contributions. Retrieved July 30, 2019, from https://shodhganga.inflibnet.ac.in/handle/10603/131273.

Nadeau, L. N. (2018). *The cooperative history: The next stage of human history.* Madison. Retrieved October 24, 2018, from https://www.cases.pt/wp-content/uploads/2011/02/The-Cooperative-Society.pdf.

National Cooperative Union. (2016). Indian cooperative movement: *A statistical* profile. New Delhi: National Cooperative Union. Retrieved from http://ncui.coop/wp-content/uploads/2018/06/A-STATISTICAL-PROFILE-2016.pdf.

Olsen, E. (2013). *The relative survival of worker cooperatives and barriers to their creation.* Foundation for Enterprise Development. Retrieved June 28, 2019, from https://institute.coop/sites/default/files/resources/070%202013_Olsen_The%20Relative%20Survival%20of%20Worker%20Cooperatives%20and%20Barriers%20to%20Their%20Creation.pdf.

Rahman, S. U. (1983). *Cooperative sector in India after independence.* New Delhi: S. Chand and Company Limited.

Rajendran Edathumkara, Jineesh, P.S., & Soman, T.K. (2013). Munnettam: Uralungal labour contract cooperative society. In *Vijayagadha* (p. 133).

Sapovadia, V. (2007). *Evaluating effectiveness among cooperatives vis-a-vis other social institutes — A case study of NABARD's rural innovation fund & other schemes.* Ahmedabad: Co-operative Innovation: Influencing the Social economy, CANADA CONGRESS 2007. Retrieved from http://ssrn.com/abstract = 985884.

Soni, A. K., & Saluja, H. P. S. (2013). A study of committees on the development of cooperative movement. *Golden Research Thoughts, 2*(7), 2−3.

Thomas Isaac, M. W. (2017). *Building alternatives-the story of India's oldest construction workers' cooperative.* New Delhi: Left Word Books.

ULCCS. (1928). *The bylaws of the ULCCS.* Kerala, India: Vadagara.

Reforms, H. L. (n.d.). *A hundred small steps — Planning commission.* Planning Commission, Government of India. Retrieved September 26, 2018, from http://www.planningcommission.nic.in/reports/genrep/rep_fr/cfsr_all.pdf.

Successful cooperatives across Asia: ULCCS—the icon of successful cooperatives in India

T.P. Sethumadhavan

Uralungal Labour Contract Cooperative Society, Madappallly, Kerala

30.1 Introduction

Uralungal Labour Contract Co-operative Society (ULCCS), based at Kozhikode, Kerala, India, is one of the largest labor contract worker cooperative societies in Asia and has based its competitive advantage on quality, sincerity, and honesty. ULCCS was started in 1925 by 14 members with an investment of 37 Paisa (US$0.042). It has grown to be at the forefront of construction and infrastructure development in Kerala, India, ever since. From humble beginnings with these 14 members working in construction, ULCCS has diversified into different areas "creating new types of jobs for the highly skilled generation coming to the fore" (Thomas Isaac & Williams, 2017: p. 17). ULCCS has evolved into a "diversified complex co-operative system" with 8000 employees and members in areas such as information technology (IT), IT-enabled services (ITeS), tourism, social welfare, education, and skills development. UL Cyber Park is the only special economic zone in India set up by a labor contract cooperative society and is in the forefront of IT services through its fast-growing IT services company, UL Technology Solutions. In the area of caring for the community through various activities, ULCCS Foundation focuses on the underprivileged sections of society such as disabled or mentally challenged children and senior citizens. ULCCS launched Cambridge English Centre of my excellence at Kozhikode during 2020 to give more thrust to Communication skill of students. As the Co-operative society involved in social upliftment, ULCCS identified Technical, Domain and Communication skills as the major pillars for augmenting employability of educated youth in India.

ULCCS's vision is to create a skill-based cooperative through skills development programs and has identified a huge skill gap in the required and available skills in the cooperative. ULCCS launched UL Education where the major focus is on improving employability skills among students and unemployed youths. In addition, ULCCS identified education and

325

skills development as strategic areas and launched the Indian Institute of Infrastructure and Construction and the UL Skill Academy and DDU-GKY Centre in Kerala. These institutions envisage providing customized courses, skilling programs, and appropriate placements for augmenting employability through an industry interface. UL Education envisages promoting education at the school, secondary school, and undergraduate and graduate levels. ULCCS is the only primary cooperative society in the country with permanent membership in the ICA.

30.2 Genesis of Uralungal Labour Contract Co-operative Society

The many transformations that have taken place over the years in Indian society and the cooperative sector that gave birth to the unique ULCCS experience are described by Thomas Isaac and Williams (2017: p. 80), "The Uralungal Labour Co-operative Society in north Malabar is the only one of its kind in Kerala: here the poor labourers through their mutual cooperation take up public works and share the profits amongst themselves." The emergence of this culture, the incubator of ULCCS, is distinct from western societies.

This emergence and the context through which ULCCS evolved as one of the leading cooperative societies in Asia is based on certain success factors, namely workers welfare, discipline, responsibility, modernization, diversification, quality, social commitment, and time management. Currently, ULCCS has many subsidiary organizations in different forms with a cooperative nature under the ULCCS group of institutions, namely ULCCS Ltd.

All these activities, in addition, are based on a deeper vision of a democratic socialist state, which will have repercussions in influencing its capacity to remain true to its mission encapsulated by what Thomas Isaac and Williams (2017; p. 42) state, "From its beginning, ULCCS envisaged a democratic and egalitarian social world in which the Co-operative plays a key role."

30.3 Background to the formation of Uralungal Labour Contract Co-operative Society

During the pre-independence era in India, ULCCS faced many challenges both at the macro and micro levels. Most of these challenges were during its inception period. These challenges were overcome through appropriate measures in a culturally specific way, which then facilitated the success of the organization.

Indian culture toward the end of the 19th century was in a state of transition out of which ULCCS was born. The Co-operative Credit Societies Act was established in 1904 in India during British rule, following the recommendations of the Edwards Committee, which lead to the formation of three types of cooperatives. In 1912 there was the emergence of consumer cooperatives and primary agricultural cooperatives. Moreover, during this period, economic recession occurred as a result of the First World War and the prices of cash crops were reduced substantially. This lead to a study on credit cooperative societies in 1914 by the MC Lagan Committee resulting in the Government of India Act on cooperative law being enacted in 1919 and this facilitated the amendment of the cooperative law by regional governments based on a need analysis leading to the Travancore Central Co-operative Bank being formed in 1915 based on the mutually helping society act formed during 1914. Cooperative societies in the Malabar region of the state were established based on Madras Co-operative Law up until 1969. Cooperative societies played a key role in socioeconomic growth in Kerala, especially in the Malabar region, which was under British colonial rule and it was here that Vasco de Gama first entered India. This region is populated by more than 94% Malayalam (local vernacular language) speaking people of Hindu and Muslim religions.

During the 19th century, a lot of social injustices and inequalities based on the caste and creed system were prevalent in the region as well as the exploitation of the poor by landlords during colonial rule. Only landlords received full ownership of the land, whereas those belonging to other castes like Thiyya were given half ownership, and agricultural laborers were considered as tenants. Landlords used to show cruelty toward tenants, resulting in widespread poverty—fertile ground for new ideologies, religions, and philosophies.

In 1839 German missionary Herman Gundert started implementing missionary activities in the Malabar region. This included societal upliftment, English education, and the establishment of educational institutions including religious conversions to Christianity. During the 19th century, in the renaissance period, a lot of social reformists started working in the region to uplift the people. A learned Indian scholar and social reformer, Vayaleri Kunhikkannnan Gurukkal, emerged as *Vagbadanandha* and started promoting a renaissance movement in the region. He is credited with being the founder of the *Atmavidhya sangham* movement (a group of intellectuals and professionals who sought change) during 1917, which paved the way for ULCCS.

As a result of the Soviet revolution in 1918 awareness programs on world movements, social upliftment, and socioeconomic development started in the Malabar region. People started reading Lenin's views, and during the modern colonial phase, Christian missionaries worked for political coordination among the different regions and showed interest in promoting English education. Progressive movements slowly emerged in the region, especially in the coastal village of Karakkad and the Urungal region, which was the focal center for the emergence of the communist party and ULCCS under the leadership of social

reformists like Karappayil Kanaran master and Chappayil Kunheru gurukkal. The name Uralungal came into existence through agricultural development created by the *Brahmins* and upper castes in the region including land ownership laws and social structure. Karakkad had lot of fishermen, weavers, etc., involved in traditional sectors. Growing poverty among laborers including issues related to caste, creed disparity, and changes in the modern world after the First World War forced them to form cooperatives.

During the 1920s, four cooperative institutions were established in the Malabar region. The Uralungal Aikyananaya Sangham was formed during February 1922, and then around 11 laborers tried to form a labor cooperative under the banner Uralungal Co-operative Society. However, it was on February 13, 1925, that 11 workers, 1 farmer, 1 laborer, and 1 merchant (altogether 14 persons) registered the Uralungal Labour Contract Society, which was involved in road construction and maintenance works. Initially they started working on small road or building maintenance jobs and earned a small income out of this.

Over the years many transformations have taken place in ULCCS: "The emergence and the context through which ULCCS evolved as one of the leading co-operative societies in Asia is based on workers welfare, discipline, responsibility, modernisation, diversification, quality, social commitment and time management" (Thomas Isaac & Williams, 2017: p. 80).

ULCCS has been in construction and infrastructure for more than nine decades. It has a highly skilled technical team with more than 1000 engineers. ULCCS is used to recruit appropriate talents from premier institutions. The team includes many highly experienced professionals. ULCCS has provided millions of man-hours of employment in all phases of infrastructure construction, roads, bridges, airports, and buildings—right from feasibility studies, estimation, and design to project management and execution. It has trained thousands of employees from rural backgrounds and groomed them to become highly-skilled technicians, supervisors, and engineers. It has become a highly sought-after workplace for young engineers, mostly from civil, electrical, and mechanical engineering streams. Through hundreds of large-scale projects, ULCCS has amassed a wealth of knowledge and experience that can be utilized to impart skills education in the country.

Diversification has boosted the society's skill base significantly. Through UL Cyber Park and UL Technology Solutions, ULCCS has gained expertise in facility management, software project management, geographic information systems (GIS), systems integration, and software application and development.

ULCCS has access to a wide network of academic and industry partners across the globe. ULCCS is working with institutions of repute across the country and abroad for technical collaborations including institutions from the United Kingdom, the Netherlands, Germany, and Singapore in the areas of construction, infrastructure, tourism, hospitality, services, IT, ITeS, agribusiness, dairy business, entrepreneurship, education, skills development, and student placements.

ULCCS also leads in disaster relief, fulfilling its social mission. Devastating floods totally affected the state of Kerala with an economic loss of more than Rs40,000 crores. ULCCS was involved in working in community rehabilitation and formed a cooperative alliance to rebuild Kerala named CARe with the support from the Co-operative Department, Government of Kerala, and a consortium of cooperatives. Taking into account the advancements in construction and infrastructure technology, ULCCS is promoting prefab technologies including cost-effective housing. ULCCS is working with government toward rehabilitation and is planning to build an environment-friendly and climate-friendly construction and infrastructure ecosystem in the state.

30.3.1 Challenges

1. Internal:

During the initial phase, ULCCS faced many internal and external challenges that initially affected their work, namely the limited capacity/productivity of members including limited experience and capability in site experience in managing road and construction projects. Moreover, paperwork and the tendering process was onerous and required a lot of procedural and office work. In addition, during 1944—45, there was an unrealistic increase in wages. There were also the problems of finding working capital, conducting membership drives, and retaining values, while addressing gender inequality, as examples of some of the major internal challenges faced by the society.

2. External:

The resistance on the part of private contractors and their monopoly and corruption affected work allocation and progress. Moreover, a lack of support from authorities substantially demotivated the activities of the society. As a result, cooperatives were barely surviving and were less sustainable during their initial two to three decades.

30.3.2 Overcoming the challenges

In order to overcome these challenges, ULCCS adopted certain strategies including price undercutting to get jobs and experience. Moreover, ULCCS grew in reputation through efficient and quality work. They collected share capital through instalments/informal sources and sundry creditors. "Together these three sources of capital were crucial to the cooperatives survival during its first twenty years" (Thomas Isaac & Williams, 2017: p. 92) and "Despite the expansion in membership the values underpinning the co-operative were maintained and even strengthened" (Thomas Isaac & Williams, 2017: p. 93).

30.4 Macro factors as a key to emergence and success

1. State:

    During the past five decades, the communist government is regularly elected in Kerala. The state government became involved in the role of cooperative facilitator and became used to providing an appropriate environment and assistance for sustainable growth. All cooperatives are under the control of the Ministry of Co-operatives with the Secretary and Registrar of Co-operatives as the administrative heads at the state level. At the administrative level there are registrars at the district level, and assistant registrars to supervise the cooperatives at the field level. ULCCS receives help from the Co-operative Department, which includes government equity under B-class shares, funding assistance, facilitating measures to acquire loans, auditing assistance, and conducting elections on time. Officials from the Co-operative Department stationed at the headquarters of ULCCS are regularly auditing the accounts of the society so as to publish timely annual audited account statements.

2. Civil Society:

    "ULCCS origins are linked to the social renaissance and nationalist struggles of the early twentieth century" and "when powerful workers movements sprang up in Malabar, Nationalist movements took a radical turn and the Communist party emerged as a hegemonic force in Malabar," and "the radicalisation of Malabar in the 1930s and 1940s influenced the formative

years of the co-operatives" (Thomas Isaac & Williams, 2017: p. 82)

    All political parties, trade unions, and political leadership appreciate the efforts of ULCCS in construction, infrastructure, IT, ITeS, tourism, services, education, skills development, career, and technology-based activities for the state. All these activities are in tune with tradition, technology, and talent. In a state like Kerala, where all political parties struggle for existence, it is notable that ULCCS could exhibit a quantum leap in size and influence in the state over the years without any political barriers. ULCCS is handling projects worth more than Rs2700 crores (1 crore rupees is equivalent to US$137,902.5) per annum with an annual turnover of Rs900. Moreover, no trade union system exists in the organization. Not even a single day was lost up to today due to a strike or workers unrest or protest. All political parties support the developmental activities of ULCCS.

3. Market Structure:

    The success of ULCCS lies in its effective networking and diversification in tune with stakeholder needs. This is in tune with advancements in technology, moving their competitive advantage from laboring to IT. Most of the programs were oriented toward the welfare of workers and their families. Across the country, the services sector supersedes primary agriculture and secondary industry sectors. Moreover, the services sector creates more than 68% of the employment opportunities in the country. As a sequel to globalization, the global village concept is acquiring momentum across the globe in education, skills, career, and services. ULCCS is effectively addressing the challenges faced as a sequel to demand—supply mismatch through related diversification processes.

30.5 Micro factors as a key to emergence and success

30.5.1 Legal structure

"At the time ULCCS was formed in 1924 there were no official by laws governing a labour contract society. The co-operative had to create its own by laws" (Thomas Isaac & Williams, 2017: p. 81). This left room to "create a labour society in their own image." They defined the objective of the society to promote the economic interests of the labourers of the society and to find suitable and profitable employment for them" (Thomas Isaac & Williams, 2017: p. 81).

ULCCS now has five classes of members, which include A-, B-, C-, D-, and E-class members. All the members holding A-, C-, and D-class shares are working in the organization. A-class members are permanent members having voting rights. B-class membership related to government share, which forms 90.59% of the share capital, don't vote. C-class members do not have voting powers. But over the years they can become A-class members. Those who've recently joined the organization constitute D-class members. All the members will receive an employee provident fund, insurance, gratuity, shares, welfare fund, mediclaim scheme, and interest-free loans. There is no retirement age in the organization; they can work as much they can and the employee provident fund benefits will be available till 60 years of age.

The term of the governing body is for a period of five years. Directors are elected democratically by A-class members. The board of directors convenes daily under the leadership of the chairman and reviews the work progress. All worker members are given a bonus at a rate of 20% twice per year. As of June 2019, ULCCS had approximately 577 A-class shareholders (they have voting rights, of which 478 are working A-class members); 2246 C-class shareholders

(C-class members do not have voting rights and 2044 C-class members are working); 14,946 D-class members with no voting rights; 6830 nonmembers; and 40 E-class members (E-class members are shareholders and will get incentives, but have no voting rights).

Currently ULCCS has 807 engineers of which 36 are of A-class and 251 are of C-class members. The technical staff of 550 come under the nonmember category. Workers come under A, C, and nonmember categories. It is the oldest labor contract cooperative in Kerala and the biggest in India. As of 2019, it had 9185 workers, among which 2885 were worker-members (31.4%).

30.5.2 Governance structure

ULCCS has a governing body comprising of an elected board of 13 directors with 3 women members. Among the elected board of directors, one representative is from scheduled caste/scheduled tribe. The governing body is headed by a chairman and vice chairman. Members used to elect the directors continuously for several terms based on their performance and track record. The current chairman has been leading the organization for more than two decades.

The organizational structure of ULCCS extends from the workers to the chairman. Only A-class members have voting powers. But all members will get a bonus and other benefits. It is a worker-owned cooperative institution. All decisions are taken by the elected board on behalf of the members. Annual general body meetings are held as per the Co-operative Act. As long as a member is working in the organization, the shares of the member are kept with the society until the member leaves the organization. The governance structure of ULCCS facilitates its workers to work sincerely with commitment with maximum work efficiency.

30.5.3 Cultural systems

ULCCS workers excel in leadership skills and team spirit so as to contribute toward an increased work efficiency and productivity. There are structured communication and leadership pathways in the working environment. This work culture facilitates them to work with the utmost sincerity and commitment. Each project is headed by a director with team leaders.

All workers are provided with employee benefits including free food. In addition, they are provided with casual, annual, and sick leave as per the norms of the organization. This ensures that the degree of participation in delivering a higher productivity is paramount among workers, demonstrating the features of a high-performance work system and the competitive advantage of applying the seven cooperative principles.

30.6 Conclusion

ULCCS has survived, grown, scaled up, and diversified in tune with the demands and advances in technology. Being embedded in a socialist culture based on equality and democracy it has not degenerated democratically or departed from its cooperative values (Greenberg, 1988). It has demonstrated how a bottom-up government assistance program is far superior to a top-down policy in promoting cooperative development (Thomas Isaac & Williams, 2017)

ULCCS was established in 1925 with the objective of alleviating poverty among workers. Over the years, ULCCS had grown, which necessitated the governing body to diversify into different potential sectors based on need analyses. Addressing the lack of education (Witt and Redding, 2014) as the key obstacle to cooperative emergence and success, ULCCS is setting out to address the demand for better education, talent, and career in tune with the growth in the services sector. This motivated ULCCS to diversify into different sectors like tourism, IT, ITeS, education, skills development, social welfare, education for challenged groups, and daycare homes for senior citizens.

ULCCS has an unblemished track record of relentless commitment to quality. It is one of the most preferred organizations for the development of roads, bridges, and allied infrastructure. Considering the meritorious service performance of the society, the Government of Kerala appointed ULCCS as an accredited agency in departments such as Finance, Local Self Government Department, Tourism, Labour and Cooperation for execution of projects without tender procedure.

The establishment of Sargaalaya, Cyber Park and the Indian Institute of Infrastructure and Construction are three examples of how ULCCS has acted on the government's behalf and successfully conceptualized, constructed, and operated large institutions that would ordinarily have been operated by the government.

UL Cyber Park is the first IT special economic zone park in the Malabar region and it is also the first of its kind to be developed by a labor contract cooperative society in the world. Ms. Nikken Sekkei, Japan, one of the world's leading architects, prepared the master plan for the campus with a total built-up area of 2.7 million square feet. ULCCS established ULTS, an IT company to promote IT and to generate employment. Currently, ULCCS have many subsidiary organizations in different forms with a cooperative nature as under the ULCCS group of institutions, namely ULCCS Ltd.

ULCCS had received several national and international awards and recognitions for its pioneering works and is associated with the United Nations, UNDP, ILO and the ICA in the areas of development and extension programs.

Appendix

Excerpts from an interview with Rameshan Paleri, Chairman of ULCCS about the success of ULCCS

1. *What have been the main obstacles to success at ULCCS?*

    The main obstacles to success was the existing system prevailing in the State during early nineties. The monopoly of contractors affected the work of ULCCS including the work allocation process in the initial phases. The limited capacity/productivity of members including limited experience and capability of in site experience in managing road and building construction projects affected the work progress. Moreover paperwork and tendering process was hectic which required a lot of procedural and office work. Unrealistic increase in wages and the problem of working capital. Membership drive and retaining values and Gender inequality were some of major challenges faced by the Society. Moreover lack of support from authorities substantially demotivated the activities of the society.

2. *How were these obstacles overcome at ULCCS?*

    During the initial phase of three to four decades major focus was to attract funds for sustenance. Members worked hard to get funds from landlords, local people and available resources to mobilise funds as working capital. In order to overcome the challenges ULCCS adopted certain strategies including price undercutting voluntarily to get the job and work experience. Moreover gained reputation through efficient and quality work. Collected share capital through instalments/informal sources and sundry creditors. Unique work culture coupled with commitment, timeliness, sincerity and transparency in work facilitated to overcome the obstacles. Consortium of co-operatives facilitated ULCCS to acquire funds for infrastructure projects.

3. *What factors contributed to the success of ULCCS?*

    The success of ULCCS is through sincerity, vision, commitment, innovativeness, quality consciousness and passion to take projects and to complete it within the scheduled period. Unique work culture and interpersonal relations paved way for success of ULCCS. Moreover ULCCS could successfully diversify in to potential sectors based on stakeholders demand in tune with sustainable development goals envisaged by United Nations the technology and future of work.

4. *How and why did ULCCS make the transition to IT?*

    In tune with the socioeconomic changes prevailing during late 20th Century a lot of transformations emerged in the country. Globalisation, transition from joint family system to nuclear family system, growth of services sectors, National IT policy paved way for ULCCS to look for new initiatives. Services sector started superseding both agriculture and industrial sectors which created more than 50% employment opportunities during these period. Moreover Kerala could achieve total literacy during this period. Total literacy, increasing unemployment among educated youth coupled with students acquiring professional degrees in technical education compelled the parents to look for lucrative employment opportunities in new gen areas. Future of work is also changing. According to the National Policy for Skill Development and Entrepreneurship, India is one of the youngest nations in the world with more than 62% of its population in the working age group (15—59 years), and more than 54% of its total population below 25 years of age. It is further estimated that the average age of the population in India by 2020 will be 29 years. To reap this demographic dividend which is expected to last for next 25 years, India needs to equip its workforce with employable skills and knowledge so that they can contribute substantively to the economic growth of the country. Our country presently faces a dual challenge of paucity of highly trained workforce, as well as non-employability of large sections of the conventionally educated youth, who possess little or no job skills. Therefore there is an urgent need to improve the quantity and quality of skill development initiatives in the country.

This paved way for ULCCS to diversify in to IT parks and technology verticals. ULCCS is the only primary Co-operative in Asia which effectively diversified in to IT, ITeS Special economic zone, Technology solutions, skill development institutions, education, tourism, agribusiness and food processing ventures. Taking in to account the need for increasing employability ULCCS diversified in to education and skill development.

Reference

Thomas Isaac, T. M., & Williams, M. (2017). *Building alternatives* (Book review). Left World Books, New Delhi.

Further reading

150 years of the co-op (Special Supplement). (1994). *New Statesman & Society, 7*(June 17), i–xiv.

1960s: Trend toward fewer, larger farms means major changes for co-ops. (1999). *Rural Cooperatives, 66*(1), 28–37.

1980s: Mergers, consolidations change look of U.S cooperatives. (1999). *Rural Cooperatives, 66*(1), 48–55.

Abalkin, L. (1988). Reviving the cooperative movement. *World Marxist Review, 31*(June), 53–59.

Attwood, D. (1989). Does competition help co-operation? *The Journal of Development Studies, 26*(October), 5–27.

Baumgardner, J. (1988). The division of labor, local markets, and worker organization. *Journal of Political Economy, 96*(June), 509–527.

Ben-Ner, A. (1984). On the stability of the cooperative type of organization. *Journal of Comparative Economics, 8*(3), 247–260.

Carter, N. [Reviewer]. (1989). Worker cooperatives in theory and practice [Book Review]. Open University Press, 1988. *Political quarterly, 60*(April/June): 247–250.

Co-operate and prosper (Mondragon). (1991). *Economist, 311*(April 1): 61.

Ellerman, D. (1984). Theory of legal structure: Worker cooperatives. *Journal of Economic Issues, 18*(September), 861–891.

Governance in next generation cooperatives requires best efforts of board, management. (1991). *Farmer Cooperatives, 57*(January), 10–11.

Harris, A., Stefansson, B., & Fulton, M. (1996). New generation cooperatives and cooperative theory. *Journal of Cooperatives, 11*, 13–28.

Henry, S. (1985). Community justice, capitalist society, and human agency: The dialectics of collective law in the cooperative. *Law & Society Review, 19*(2), 303–327.

Lerman, Z., & Sedik, D. (2009). *and individual land tenure: Lessons from Central Asia*. FAO/REU Policy Studies in Rural Transition No. 2009-3, FAO Regional Office for Europe and Central Asia, Rome-Budapest. http://www.fao.org/fileadmin/user_upload/Europe/documents/Publications/Policy_Stdies/AgDevelopment CA_en.pdf

Let's "Do-It-Ourselves": Building a Participatory Economy in South Asia. (2013, May 6–8). *Think pieces for the UNRISD conference "Potential and Limits of Social and Solidarity Economy"*.

Merrett, C. D., & Walzer, N. (2003). *Cooperatives and local development: Theory and applications for the 21st century*. Armonk, NY: M. E. Sharpe, ISBN 0-7656-1123.

Russell, R., & Hanneman, R. (1992). Cooperatives and the business cycle: The Israeli case. *Journal of Comparative Economics, 16*(December), 701–715.

Santosh Kumar S. (2018). ULCCS-The Saga continues, Published by International Co-operative Alliance-.

Sazama, G. W. (2000). Lessons from the history of affordable housing cooperatives in the United States: A case study in American affordable housing policy. *The American Journal of Economics and Sociology, 59*(4), 573–608.

U.S. Department of Agriculture (USDA). (1997). *Strengthening ethics within agricultural cooperatives*. Washington, DC: USDA, Rural Business-Cooperative Service.

Whyte, W., & Whyte, K. (1991). *Making Mondragon: The growth and dynamics of the worker cooperative complex* (2nd ed.). Ithaca, NY: ILR Press.

Worker cooperatives as a model for family business succession? The case of C-Mac Industries Co-operative Ltd in Australia

Dr. Anthony Jensen[1] and Frank Webb[2]

[1]University of Newcastle, New South Wales, Australia [2]Business Clarity, New South Wales, Australia

31.1 Introduction

Worker cooperatives and worker-owned firms occur in sometimes iconic fashion, for instance, the Mondragon Co-operatives in Spain and the "Workers without Managers" factories in Argentina. They carry the aspirations of many who want to transform capitalism into a democratic society based on values of equality, participation, and solidarity (Owen, 1972; Oakeshott, 1978). However, worker cooperatives are still not present in large numbers worldwide. Why this scarcity occurs has been a topic of debate articulated by Pérotin (1999) as to whether there is a problem of "entry or exit." In between these extremities sits the "degeneration thesis," which proposes that worker cooperatives are subject to an internal determinism to decline and degenerate (Webb & Webb, 1920). It is argued that this is due to the capture of cooperatives by managerial elite and the exclusion of new members as

a cooperative goes through a three-stage life cycle process (Lichtenstein, 1986). In this regard, there has been a recurring interest as to how the number of new worker cooperatives can be increased and their demise decreased.

A new opportunity has emerged in the area of family-owned business succession with a generation of "baby boomers" who want to retire, but lack a suitable successor or exit plan. The 2019 transition of the Richer Sounds business in the United Kingdom to its 521 employees, using an employee-owned trust, is testament to an innovative succession plan and a fairer way to run a business. In the process, the business transformation addressed concerns such as job insecurity, low wages, and escalating inequality.

The worker cooperative, it is argued, also provides another solution. A win—win solution for an owner to exit extracting their capital while workers retain their jobs and, thus prevent an often destructive trade sale. To date, this has been a poorly documented process from owners' and workers' perspectives.

This chapter uses the case study of C-Mac Industries Co-operative Ltd in Western Sydney, Australia to study how cooperatives deal with startup challenges and degeneration. Using a participation action research (PAR) method this study first identifies the barriers C-Mac experienced in getting started and its subsequent success; second, how these barriers could be overcome; and third, it identifies the factors involved in contributing to success. Finally, we examine whether this unique business model is one of innovation or one that is, replicable in the Australian context.

31.2 C-Mac Industries Co-operative Limited

C-Mac Co-operative is a small-sized manufacturing firm in greater Western Sydney, one of the heartlands of manufacturing in Australia. The company C-Mac Industries Ltd was formed 52 years ago in 1967 in the garage of Cliff McMaster with the support of his wife Margaret. As a "jobbing shop" the company produces a range of innovative solutions in metal—custom designed industrial acoustics, nursery horticultural equipment, and detailed sheet metal (most notably used to make the transporter in the Mad Max Fury Road) and gear cutting.

The company established an excellent reputation for quality and the ability to manufacture most items to a customer's specification. The company expanded to 40 employees and a $3 million–$4 million turnover within the then tariff-protected Australian manufacturing sector. It expanded by acquiring a number of smaller companies and was noteworthy for being seen as a good place to work and not a sweat shop.

TABLE 31.1 Profit and Loss.

Year	2013/14	2014/15	2015/16	2016/17	2017/18
Sales	3679	3673	3972	3937	4610
Profit Before Tax (PBT)	(90)	103	159	(47)	68

With the exposure of the manufacturing sector to international competition in the 1980s, compounded by the global financial crisis in 2008, C-Mac's profitability fluctuated from profit to loss (Table 31.1).

Succession became a key issue for this family firm after ownership and management passed on to the second generation. Cliff's son Robert took control, but had no successor.

Inspired by his Christian ethics of justice and dignity for working people, Robert sought a different option, a win–win, that would both favor his staff and preserve the family legacy. Inspired by the Australian Employee Buyout Centre (AEBC), a pilot project set up by the Australian Federal Government to assist firms adjust during the global financial crisis through an employee buyout to save jobs, Robert began a nine-year journey to find the best method and legal structure to transfer his marginally profitable business to the staff in Australia.

Democracy and participation were embedded in C-Mac Co-operative from the start. A staff buyout committee was elected from blue- and white-collar workers. A shadow network governance model was introduced that consisted firstly of direct democracy in the (1) general meeting and (2) tool box fortnightly meetings and secondly indirect democracy in the (3) elected board of directors and the (4) elected staff council, which represented all nonmanagerial staff.

The transition of the business to the staff was achieved on July 1, 2017, on a walk-in, walk-out basis. This brought 35 diverse individuals together with contradicting views, which eventually resulted in a series of debates around cost control versus staff development leading to a Tuckman's (1965) group formation process of forming—storming—norming—preforming, a rite of passage for the cooperative to evolve and face challenges. The cooperative traded profitably in its first financial year incurring a loss in the second year with a change in the business model. Rob McMaster remains as the Director of Marketing one day per week.

31.3 Overcoming legal obstacles and agreeing on the value of the business

After the initial meetings, the first task was to agree on a value for the business, which was impacted on by the legal structure. Over a seven-year period, Robert was presented with three "deals" as a way to value and sell the business to the staff.

The first legal structure recommendation was an ESOP (employee share ownership trust) recommended by the AEBC. An external company accountant valued the business and the ESOP was considered to be a vehicle by which there could be tax advantages to enable the transfer of the business to the staff with the owner's capital to be paid to the family out of company super profits. There were no super profits to make this work. It failed.

The second method relied on a standard methodology using EBIT (earnings before interest and tax) to value the business. An accountant valued the business from zero as the business was then unprofitable. The staff declined the offer and recommended the business be sold on the market.

The third method was to put the company on the market and let the market determine the value. After 14 months, the best offer was a walk-out, walk-in offer, that is, the business is exchanged at a zero value and no finance changes hands. The owners agreed that they would rather offer the same deal to the employees to ensure jobs were saved and the family legacy preserved rather than go to a trade sale and be broken up. The staff had many objections and reservations regarding the sale price and restrictions on the members selling the business and there was an attempt to capture the difference between a willing buyer and a willing seller in a memorandum of understanding (MOU).

Robert had appointed two advisors, the authors of this chapter, to work with the staff to resolve these objections and issues and manage the buyout representing staff in negotiations with the owner/manager. He was prepared to pay for the consultancy, accounting, and legal fees associated with a 10-step process. The legal structure of the ESOP was rejected as being unsuitable first because there were no super profits and second because a worker cooperative suited the culture of solidarity, equality, and unity. As one worker stated "I don't want to be an investor. I want to be a good welder" and the General Manager agreed, "The cooperative is perfect for us."

However, the worker cooperative was not a well-known structure and C-Mac was the first to use this following the National Cooperative Law being introduced in 2012. Each state manages and implements the Australian Cooperative Law (ACL) and the New South Wales Fair Trading Department, the body that manages the local cooperatives and associations, was not familiar with its application to worker cooperatives. International advice was sought to resolve these issues.

The cost to C-Mac to facilitate the transition and demonstrate proof of concept was in the region of $160,000. This produced a proof-of-concept template for others to follow at what would be a much-reduced cost. In many European countries and the United States, such services are provided at no charge by state-funded cooperative development agencies because of the social benefits to stabilizing communities and spreading workplace democracy and wealth.

31.4 Methodology: participatory action research at C-Mac

The methodology of the C-Mac project used the democratic process of PAR, whereby the authors engaged by C-Mac facilitated a debate and discussion every Wednesday for 18 months with the elected Staff Buyout Committee. This involved identifying obstacles, making suggestions, and debating how to overcome them, then working through a 10-step process to achieve the transfer of ownership. This was an exercise in building social capital and skills for the next stage of ownership.

This coaching process was seen as being far more powerful than orthodox consultancy; a "uniquely powerful way to cogenerate useful knowledge about organizations" (Greenwood & Santos, 1991). C-Mac Co-operative is an ongoing experiment in democracy and is subject to a series of discourses associated with the three life cycle stages of a worker cooperative necessary for longevity (Lichtenstein, 1986).

The 10-step process occurred in both a linear fashion and also concurrently. The 10 steps were:

1. Initial meeting with owner
2. Elect Staff Buyout Committee
3. Business plan development
4. Valuation of business
5. Structuring the deal
6. Registration of the cooperative
7. Finance raising
8. Legal structure
9. Member training
10. Exit of owners' funds

In this forum, the brief to the advisers was to facilitate the transfer of the business to reluctant workers. The barriers and obstacles to the workers taking over the business reflected the classic debates and tensions outlined in Greenwood and Santos's (1991) work at the Mondragon Fagor Co-operative. The PAR process facilitated debates arising out of the tensions between its financial success and its participative, educative, and social dimensions; the number of board meetings; cost control and democracy; tolerance of mistakes and actions to address carelessness; staying with open membership or restricting membership; of dealing with worker—management tension; and of distributing profit.

In addition, a structured questionnaire was administered to the workers eight months after the buyout to assess whether perceptions had changed post buyout.

The experience of common owned companies formed in the 1980s in Australia, later disappearing in contrast to the rest of the world, was a definitive example of degeneration and the subject of learning from praxis (Jensen, 2017) passed onto C-Mac to ensure that the new owners of C-Mac were aware of the challenges.

31.5 Key obstacles to the emergence of the C-Mac cooperative

The worker buyout phenomenon in the 1980s prompted a great deal of academic research in Italy, Spain, France, the United Kingdom, and the United States. Ben Ner (1988) argued that workers were disadvantaged in the startup phase compared to the investor firm as workers had specific obstacles that needed to be overcome—workers are risk averse, workers lack access to startup and working capital, and workers lack professional managerial/accounting skills. This resonated with Paton's (1989) book The Reluctant Entrepreneurs, "This is a book about men and women who became entrepreneurs not by choice but out of necessity."

There were also issues such as selecting and piloting a new legal structure and training staff in cooperative values and participatory decision making, which were foreign to them. The workers were also faced with negotiating the value of the business with their boss. How workers at C-Mac dealt with these challenges will be discussed here.

31.6 Overcoming the financial obstacles

Throughout the process, the Staff Buyout Committee were adamant that there was no point in encouraging the owners to think they would purchase the business until the issue of finance was resolved; they were not prepared to invest their own funds and inject cash into the company. This was the essential criterion that guided discussions.

The main objection was the unprofitable state of the business. A marketing seminar set in motion a web-based marketing strategy and a Future Search Workshop endeavored to tap all the workers' and owners' ideas and merge them into a strategic plan. However, the business was returned to profitability by a general improvement in the economy and the factory manager who had been given the opportunity to run the business some years before due to the ill health of the owner. By a stringent attention to costs supplemented by the reluctant downsizing of 10 staff members by the owner, the business began to perform better financially than it had for many years. This then opened the way to discuss raising the necessary finance for the worker buyout.

The business coach/accountant was able to unpack the complexity of the balance sheet, typical of family companies, and explain to the workers that fundamentally the business was sound and presented a good opportunity. It was made clear that the profitability of the C-Mac business model was drawn from its hybrid of manufacturing "all things metal," backed up by a research and development grant

TABLE 31.2 Demographic Details of Membership.

Age	<20	20−29	30−39	40−49	50−59	60−69
Number	1	8	2	4	6	7

subsidized by the Australian Tax Office. This grant rewards C-Mac for innovation in metalworking processes. As an example, C-Mac had invented a wet sand bagging machine—it remains the only one on the market.

The staff wanted to raise capital without providing personal guarantees. This problem was solved by C-Mac's owner and the bank. C-Mac had proposed that it would guarantee each worker a $5000 loan to invest in the company to pay out debts owing to the owners including the previous year's unpaid factory rent of $264,000 due to the founder's widow Margaret McMaster.

This offer was rejected as being too risky. The workers limited their financial exposure by negotiating a $100 limit per worker to their investment securing agreement that the deal could proceed on the basis that membership would be $100 a share. That was the limit of each member's exposure. The demographics of the membership spread from a group of young workers unlikely to have savings and a group of older workers who were nearing exiting the business.

See Table 31.2.

The alternative of vendor finance was also raised. Margaret McMaster agreed to the principal of patient capital; she was prepared to leave the $264,000 in the company interest free and have it repaid at $5000 per month. The owner also guaranteed the overdraft until the bank came up with a solution. The Buyout Committee was adamant that it would not discuss the matter further until an overdraft was agreed, potentially the Commonwealth Bank of Australia—the company's bank for 50 years. This facility was finally established after 18 months of negotiation by Frank Webb. In an unprecedented and unique situation in

Australia, the Commonwealth Bank of Australia agreed to an unsecured overdraft of $250,000 based on a strong business plan, strong trading results, and strong management and staff.

At the time, C-Mac's General Manager stated, "the bank has become a key competitive advantage."

31.7 Overcoming risk aversion

As discussed, the offer of a $5000 personal loan for each member from C-Mac to buy the business was rejected as it involved risk. The workers also stated that they did not want to risk losing their homes as directors of the business if it failed. These decisions potentially scuppered the deal as the registration of the cooperative required that there were five directors with three internal directors. In many ways, the reluctance reflected the demographic of the firm with many young workers without capital and a number of older workers nearing retirement and not interested in lengthy commitments. Two external directors, the chairman, and secretary were recruited and Rob McMaster became a director. A member of the Staff Buyout Committee agreed to be a director.

31.8 Overcoming access to financial skills and cooperative expertise

Over time as each step unfolded a panel of experts on employee buyouts and cooperatives was assembled. Rob McMaster contracted the authors of this chapter as advisors to manage the process with the aim of overcoming all the identified obstacles. Frank Webb, a business coach and accountant specializing in small businesses, was able to bring a high degree of understanding to the family firm. Anthony Jensen, from his research on worker

cooperatives around the globe, was able to interpret and advise on the direction of the discussions through the 10-step process. The Employee Buyout Manual produced by Price Waterhouse in 1986 provided invaluable direction. International experts were consulted.

A solicitor, Dale Chapman, from Addisons Lawyers, a legal firm specializing in cooperatives was engaged by Rob MacMaster to represent the workers in the final negotiations with the owners over the details of the sale and provide advice on cooperatives. It was his use of appropriate words and new perspectives that overcame the standoff in negotiations on the MOU. This brought comfort to the workers and lowered their risk perception. As this proposed legal structure contained issues that the Registry of Co-operatives in New South Wales (NSW) had not experienced, the advisory team had to be innovative. For instance, the Mondragon Co-operatives in Spain have internal capital accounts for each worker's annual profit share. This was not possible under NSW cooperative legislation. However, a solution was recommended by the cooperatives solicitor who suggested this feature could be written into the employment contract.

31.9 Success of C-Mac cooperative

Was this transition to employee ownership a success? This is difficult to discern after only two years in operation. However, we choose to interpret success in relation to the stage in the cooperative's life cycle that the business has reached and the ability to counter degenerative forces.

Lichtenstein (1986) outlines the three life cycle stages:

- Stage1: start up consisting of a honeymoon period of high participation and optimism.
- Stage 2: featuring the contraction of democracy and crucial conflict and debate.

- Stage 3: reaching a resolution and the return of robust democracy and a new optimal point of efficiency between democracy and the market (Westenholtz, 1986).

Financially C-Mac navigated Stage 1 with a successful transfer of ownership to the staff who did not have capital to purchase the business. It is still trading profitably. C-Mac is seen as a moderate financial success as after the first year of trading it delivered $100,000 net profit on a turnover of $4.5 million. However, this is well below the 10% net profit that the firm should make and pointed to inefficiencies around the work process, which are being addressed.

C-Mac has a viable balance sheet based on acquiring a net gain of assets in the purchase transaction. It demonstrates the success of the buyout concept and how workers can acquire substantial assets in a win—win scenario and begin the process of transforming a marginally profitable manufacturing business in a declining market.

Socially C-Mac is seen as a success from the perspective of work and operating democratically, but caution must be used in interpreting the results. In particular, the survey found that work was not an alienating experience in the employee-owned C-Mac. However, this is most likely due to the fact that work is varied (a jobbing shop) rather than because it became a worker cooperative. Nevertheless, it is an empowering experience as good jobs had been preserved in the ownership/governance transfer where the staff survey (9 months after becoming a coop) demonstrated members believed they had sufficient control in their jobs (83%), which they also found interesting (87%). Just as important was the finding that work had high levels of intrinsic satisfaction— work gives a sense of purpose (90%); it is an opportunity to use my skills (96%); and work gives me a career (83%). Extrinsic satisfaction was not as high—work enables me to earn money for my family (62%); and work gives

me freedom by earning money (76%). Importantly from a work—life balance it demonstrated a healthy perspective when only a minority (14%) stated that work was the most important thing in their lives. This may explain the reluctance to do overtime by some.

To put this in perspective, C-Mac needed to be viewed within the context of the cooperative life cycle. The survey showed C-Mac started Stage 1 with both optimism by half the staff as well as a wait and see position by the other half. Positives and negatives emerge. The business evolved into Stage 2 (conflict), a dialectical process whereby relations between management and the board became conflictual. In addition, collective action from the shop floor put forward questions and issues to the board.

C—Mac demonstrated it is an evolving experiment in industrial democracy, and not a one-off innovation, but subject to an evolutionary process as members work out, through discussion and debate, the optimum point of efficiency where the tension between the market effect on costs and revenue meet with democratic aspirations (Westenholtz, 1986).

31.10 Factors contributing to the success of buyouts

Three factors that explained the success of the worker buyout phenomenon of the 1980s in Europe were strong management, cohesive culture, and ongoing advice (Paton, 1989). These were present in the process of the C-Mac buyout.

First, strong leadership and management. In this regard there were two key people involved in C-Mac's success that had strong beliefs about the future of employee ownership. In the first instance, success can be attributed to Robert McMaster the son of the founders. He is a visionary and was incredibly persistent, patient, and flexible over a period of nine years trying to find a pathway to pass on the business to the staff. He was prepared to invest significant finances to make this happen and demonstrate proof of concept and provide a pathway for others to follow.

Success must also be attributed to the factory manager, Steve Grlyak, who was the right person to take the business into employee ownership. He supplied strong management, leadership, and judgment on what the deal should look like and one he "could sell to the staff." Having worked for C Mac for 24 years, he worked his way up from the shop floor from the position of toolmaker to factory manager. He was able to articulate the obstacles and was insistent that there was no deal until the obstacles were overcome. He then led the staff to make the "leap of faith" that it was safe to take on the business.

The Staff Buyout Committee consisting of Sabrina Tawil, Craig Zawody, and Ivan and Luke Rigg demonstrated collective leadership, common sense, and financial prudence in thrashing out solutions and communicating with the rest of the workforce and in doing so, emulated the Rochdale cooperative pioneers.

Second, the advisory team continued after the buyout. John Cooke, a specialist in manufacturing, became chairman and organized strategic planning sessions confirming C-Mac would proceed by acquisition with the invitation supplied by the General Manager, "Join Us" and "Unity." Frank Webb became a director then chairman. Steve Grlyak, the general Manager. Anthony Jensen was appointed advisor to the board supplying cooperative expertise. The business accountant was able to provide an understanding of a complex family company. Legal advice was given by a solicitor who specialized in cooperatives. International discussions were held with academic experts at Mondragon Cooperative Corporation and the UK Employee Ownership Association.

Third, the issue of a cohesive culture is a work in progress. For half the staff, work was transformed. The change in ownership and introduction of participatory network governance

transformed the business in this direction as seen by the staff survey: around 50% stated that they were more engaged; work was more meaningful (50%); they had more influence (44%); they were more productive (39%); more participative (48%); C-Mac was a better place to work (58%); but more stressful (16%). Importantly, however, around 50% were undecided. It is clear that more work needs to be done to find out why half the firm don't feel work has been transformed.

Historically, it must be restated that the specter of failure and degeneration does hang over C-Mac (Jensen, 2017) from the 1980s experience. Aware of this, C-Mac's vision is to form a cluster of worker cooperatives by merger and acquisition and transform other factories one business at a time.

31.11 Conclusion

A unique set of circumstances, combining strong individual belief and commitment to the workforce, enabled C-Mac Cooperative and its members to overcome the challenges of transforming a family company to a worker-owned co-operative and providing a potential succession solution. The strength of the case study was in the ability to overcome the obstacles confronted in Stage 1. Referring to Jensen's theoretical model (2017) there was the Macro presence and support of the state (Federal Government in the Australian Employee Buyout Centre), civil society in the Christian drive of Robert McMaster and the labour vision of Manager Steve Grlyak. There was initially a market for C-Mac's manufacturing expertise and the co-operative thrived. Lansbury and Wailes (2003) describe this alignment as a "favourable conjuncture.".

However this alignment began to crumble as firstly the jobbing manufacturing market contracted as it always does in election years and the co-operative began the slide to insolvency. This then was accompanied by inner conflict, where the case demonstrated that a dialectical process of debate had difficulty co-existing with the managing of the business. Achieving a cohesive culture, moving from old school to new school, takes time and needs thorough training in Human Relations and Participative Management This was put off in preference to keeping members working and the price was paid for lack of training.of a lack of training was paid. In a surprise ending at the last hour a "white night" appeared and bought C-Mac, absorbed it into his company and relaunched the business employing some of the C-Mac members. The journey from a family owned firm to a worker co-operative and finally being absorbed into another family business was a fitting ending with implications for business succession.

The case study of C-Mac Co-operative demonstrated that genuine participatory democracy can be introduced into industry in Australia, where there is very truly little experience of this, and it does not necessarily need to succumb to the forces of degeneration. In the end democracy triumphed and got stronger but the business just ran of time and money before the market turned with work flowing in from Australian firms withdrawing their manufacturing from China due to the Corona 19 virus.

The C Mac experience has been one of the most important experiments in worker democracy and participation in Australia. It was important because it was so closely observed as it proceed through definite stages that were so predictable from previous research around the globe. We saw at first hand the polarised debates between social values and economic priorities and how these played out in practice and were grounded in the democratic structure. The importance of team education in participative management, The democratic governance model worked but the world economy beat C-Mac. Timing is important in any process and in this case the times were against us C-Mac.

References

Ben Ner, A. (1988). *The life cycle of worker-owned firms in market economies, Journal of Economic Behaviour and Organisation* (10, pp. 287–313). North Holland: Elsevier Science Publishers.

Greenwood, D., & Santos, J. (1991). *Industrial democracy as a process: Participatory action research in the Fagor Co-operative Group of Mondragon.* Stockholm: The Swedish Centre of Working Life.

Jensen, A. (2013). *Insolvency, employee rights and employee buyouts — A strategy for restructuring.* Unpublished Doctoral Thesis, University of Sydney, Australia.

Jensen, A. (2017). Learning from Praxis -The worker co-operative experience in New South Wales in the 1980s. *Journal of Enterprise and Organisational Diversity, 8, 1.*

Lansbury, R. D., & Wailes, N. (2003). The meaning of industrial democracy in an era of neo- liberalism. In P. Gollan, & G. Patmore (Eds.), *Labor essays. Partnership at work: The challenge of employee democracy.* Annandale: Pluto Press.

Lichtenstein, P. M. (1986). The concept of the firm in the economic theory of "alternative" organizations: Appraisal and reformulation. In S. Jansson, & A.-B. Hellmark (Eds.), *Labor- owned firms and workers' cooperatives* (pp. 51–72). UK: Gower Publishing Company Limited.

Oakeshott, R. (1978). *The case for workers' coops.* London: Routledge & Kegan Paul.

Owen, R. A. (1972). *New view of society.* London: MacMillan.

Paton, R. (1989). *Reluctant entrepreneurs.* Milton Keynes: Open University Press.

Pérotin, V. (1999). *Why there are not more labor-managed firms. Paper presented at the Yaraslov Vanek Memorial Conference.* New York, NY: Columbia University.

Tuckman, B. (1965). *Developmental sequence in small groups, Psychological bulletin* (63, pp. 384–399). USA: American Psychological Association.

Webb, S., & Webb, B. (1920). *Industrial democracy.* London: Longmans Green and Co.

Westenholtz, A. (1986). Democratic management and efficiency. In S. Jansson & A.-B. Hellmark (Eds.), *Labor-owned firms and workers' cooperatives* (pp. 140–154), England: Gower Publishing Company.

Further reading

Jensen, A. (1988). *Irrational materialism: The worker co-operative alternative in New South Wales.* Unpublished Master's Thesis. University of Sydney.

Sarti, D. (2006). *Managing dualities in cooperatives: Some evidences from the Italian retail sector.* International Association for Employee Financial Participation Conference, Mondragon.

2. Case studies of Asian co-ops, including cross-country comparison

Korea's worker cooperative and organizational transformation: the case of Happy Bridge Co-operative*

Jongho Won[1] and Seungkwon Jang[2]

[1]Department of Management of Co-operatives, Graduate School, Sungkonghoe University, Seoul, Korea [2]Division of Business Administration and Department of Management of Co-operatives, Graduate School, Sungkonghoe University, Seoul, Korea

32.1 Introduction

Among the various types of cooperatives in Korea, worker cooperatives are the newest and smallest in scale and scope. Nevertheless, worker cooperatives as the newest form of cooperative are growing steadily. There were 514 worker cooperatives[1] as of July 10, 2018. It seems to be a considerable number, but it is less dramatic compared to 13,583 cooperatives,[2] which is the total number of cooperatives formed by the Framework Act on Cooperatives[3] since 2012.

The aim of this chapter is two-fold; one is to describe a brief history over 30 years since the 1980s, and the other is to discuss challenges and success factors through the case study of Happy Bridge Co-operative (HBC),[4] which is one of the largest worker cooperatives in Korea.

---

* An earlier version of the paper was presented at the APCRP held at Sungkonghoe University, Seoul, Korea, November 2017. This case study is based on the authors' own inquiry, so the data and stories are all derived from our own observations and interviews.

[1] According to Korea's legal system and official statistics by the government, there is no formal notion of worker cooperative. Instead of worker cooperative, the term, *employee co-operative*, is used in the Act.

[2] *Korea Social Enterprise Promotion Agency.* Homepage. www.coop.go.kr/COOP/ (accessed July 14, 2018). This number doesn't include the number of co-operatives formed by the special acts such as agricultural cooperatives, consumer cooperatives, credit unions, etc.

[3] http://elaw.klri.re.kr/kor_service/lawView.do?hseq = 44518&lang = ENG (accessed July 14, 2018).

[4] www.happybridgecoop.com/ (accessed July 14, 2018).

The history of Korea's worker cooperatives can be traced back to the early 20th century. When Japanese colonialists occupied the Korean peninsula from 1910 until 1945, the first stage of Korea's worker cooperatives emerged as a "revolutionary liberation strategy" to organize Korean workers resisting Japanese rule (Ji, 2018, p. 417). After the liberation from Japanese colonial rule, the second stage of the worker cooperative movement was seen in between the 1960s and 1990s when the radical Korean cooperatives were characterized by "worker self-management and community democratization." The third stage of worker cooperatives has been characterized as a job development strategy since 1997 (Ji, 2018).

The current movement of worker cooperatives in Korea had been led by social movements, noticeably, the antipoverty and labor movements in the 1980s. And worker cooperatives' operation was guided by the cooperative identity and principles even if they didn't have the legal and institutional foundation (Kim, 2016). But the experimental effort by the social movements has kept moving forward building worker cooperatives without institutional and physical resources.

The history and the case study of worker cooperatives can provide answers to the following research questions on worker cooperatives. Why are worker cooperative numbers so small in Korea? What challenges did worker cooperatives face? How do they overcome these challenges? What are the success factors of worker cooperatives?

32.2 Development of Korea's worker cooperatives

The current Korean worker cooperatives have been closely related to the producer cooperative movement of the 1990s. The anti-poverty movement in Korea began working with the worker cooperative union in order to eradicate the economic disadvantages of deprived communities and to establish alternative democratic communities (Kim, 2016). However, the worker cooperative movement was concentrated in certain industries such as apparel and construction, and was unable to survive due to a lack of professional and technical expertise. As a result, it has started to enter mainly labor-intensive service industries.

Since then, efforts to use scarce social resources have led to the establishment of five self-sufficiency centers nationwide so the producer cooperative movement has gained momentum (Kim, 2012). Nevertheless, poor people, whose competitiveness is weak, continue to suffer from hardships due to certain limitations such as marketing, financing, management ability, and skills.

After the financial crisis of 1997, civil society organizations have tried to create decent jobs. Further, as the National Basic Living Security Act[5] was enacted in 1999, the self-sufficiency policy was institutionalized and gradually changed as a self-sufficiency community business movement supported by the Korean government.

In 2000 leaders of producer cooperatives had formed the Federation of Workers Cooperatives and started to pursue independent worker cooperatives. And producer cooperatives in the recycling and building industries as well as start-up companies seeking alternative values, came together to establish the Alliance of Alternative Firms in 2007.

As the Social Enterprise Promotion Act[6] was enacted in 2007, some companies started to receive social enterprise certification from the government. In spite of seeking to avoid

[5] http://elaw.klri.re.kr/kor_service/lawView.do?hseq = 45557&lang = ENG (accessed July 14, 2018).
[6] http://elaw.klri.re.kr/kor_service/lawView.do?hseq = 24346&lang = ENG (accessed July 14, 2018).

government subsidies, member companies of the Alliance of Alternative Firms, like the self-sufficiency communities, need social enterprise certification in order to receive government financial subsidies such as labor costs and workspaces.

Worker cooperatives in legal terms have begun to be created since the Framework Act on Co-operatives came into effect in 2012. Happy Bridge (HB), then a joint-stock company, was converted into be a worker cooperative in 2013. It became one of Korea's biggest worker cooperatives in terms of worker members and revenue (Won and Jang, 2017).

In 2014 the Korea Worker Co-operatives Federation was re-launched and new worker cooperative members started to operate, but it changed its name to the Korea Federation of Worker Co-operatives (KFWC)[7] in 2016. As the various types of organizations, for instance, Woojin Bus, Dounuri, iCOOP Co-operative Support Center, and In's Care have joined the KFWC, the worker cooperative movement has gradually expanded.

32.3 Becoming a worker cooperative

As of February, 2018, HBC has 121 employees, 84 members, 12 associate members, and 25 nonmembers. During the initial conversion process, founding members of HB sold part of their shares to employees at face value (5000 won). And then employees paid 10 million won as an investment and joined as members. Since the founders had all their remaining shares turned into an investment, HB was able to build enough assets without additional borrowing from the bank. Nowadays to become a member, one has to work for 3 years or more, and each person has to pay 10 million won.

After converting to a cooperative, HBC had continuously grown all of the supply chain from production to sales. The total sales of HBC continued to grow from KRW31.5 billion (operating income KRW1.5 billion) in 2013 to KRW64 billion (operating income KRW0.9 billion) in 2017. HBC pays an incentive through the General Assembly for the distribution of profit. In addition, it gives a difference in the form of prize money by selecting the most excellent team and the most excellent employee, but this selection is also rotated to each team. In addition, a dividend is paid, but the amount is allocated as an investment. So, members cannot get cash until they leave the cooperative. HBC promotes additional contribution through a contribution dividend (7%) and compensates the contribution (Table 32.1).

Following the Framework Act on Cooperatives, the HB's becoming a worker cooperative gave a fresh turning point to the worker cooperative movement. HBC is the first successful worker cooperative so as for some to follow the worker cooperative movement. The worker cooperative is a business not just for poor people anymore. HBC shows the possibilty of worker cooperative as a self-managed business organization.

HBC was also involved in activities related to sharing experience and knowledge in order to learn the experience of Mondragon Co-operative and to share it with other Korean business organizations. In 2013 it has made an agreement with the University of Mondragon for the education of its members and has been working on cooperative training by establishing the Happy Bridge Mondragon Co-operative management research institute (HBM).[8] A lecturer of the University of Mondragon was sent to introduce Mondragon Co-operative's management practices as well as values and

[7] www.kfwc.or.kr/ (accessed July 14, 2018).

[8] http://happybridge.tistory.com/ (accessed July 14, 2018).

TABLE 32.1 Happy Bridge Cooperative's Financial Status.

Year	Sales	Operating income	Operating income to sales (%)	Asset	Debt	Capital	Debt ratio (%)
2012	31.51	1.5	4.8	7.53	4.07	3.45	54.1
2013	34.85	1.46	4.2	9.99	5.58	4.41	55.9
2014	36.14	0.86	2.4	9.93	5.28	4.65	53.2
2015	39.54	1.14	2.9	10.82	5.62	5.2	51.9
2016	42.5	1.41	3.3	11.5	6.0	5.5	52.2
2017	64.0	0.93	1.5	10.6	6.4	4.3	60.4

HB General Assembly Report 2018, unit: Billion Korean WON, 1 US dollar = 1130 Korean Won (February 15, 2019).

principles to HBC members and other Koreans. In addition, the Mondragon Team Academy (MTA), an entrepreneurial education program at Mondragon School of Management, is being introduced to cooperative entrepreneurial culture in Korea. The MTA is currently developing a change-maker training program that will not only teach how to make a start-up in the form of a cooperative, but also learn how to find self-identity and live together as a team.

32.3.1 The state

The state's impact on cooperatives is mainly related to the policy level, specifically to regulatory legislation. Since 1987, the labor environment has been greatly improved, which led to the amendment of the labor law due to the result of workers' protests and the democratization movement. The Labor Standards Act set the norm and many workers were guaranteed basic working conditions and wages. At that time, HB's founding members were mostly college students so they were involved in the civil rights movement in the form of labor and student movements.

Through Korea's financial crisis of 1997, much of the labor law was altered to provide employers with flexibility in employment. It eventually became troublesome in Korean society in the sense that new legal environments allowed for the restructuring of labor relations and to hire part-time and temporary workers. Because of the unrest of labor relations and the rising unemployment rate, workers took to the streets. Likewise, HB's founding members also started their own businesses in order to survive. Though they have not been competitive as small business organizations, they have shared their experiences with each other, and gradually developing a medium-sized business structure as they have been moving forward.

In 2000 the government enacted the National Basic Living Security Act and began to search for the ways of reducing the unemployment rate through businesses and self-employment, etc. Civil society organizations and worker cooperatives for improving the conditions of employment have been progressing so little. Nonetheless, they were actively participating in self-help enterprise projects, which were supported by the government.

Since the Social Enterprise Promotion Act (2007) was enacted, worker cooperatives are certified as social enterprises because they can receive government support while emphasizing their identity as a company that can create social value. HB was also strongly connected with those who participated in self-help enterprises or social enterprises, but it was judged that the characteristics of the business and organization did not fit well with self-help enterprises or social enterprises.

When the Framework Act on Cooperatives was enacted in 2011, HB had decided to become a worker cooperative. HB's management judged that a worker cooperative could take advantage of their philosophy and business. And they thought that it was a good opportunity to strategically create social value.

32.3.2 Market

The 1997 Asian financial crisis brought great change to the social and economic structure of Korean society. Under an urgent bailout by the International Monetary Fund, the Korean government was unavoidably exposed to neoliberal economic policies and opened its doors to international capital and corporations to invest and operate. Many people became unemployed through intensive restructuring, and high-interest rates caused many self-employed people to become bankrupt. On the other hand, as the global IT boom emerged, the service and the IT industry suddenly became the center of Korean industry. At that time, the franchise industry was spreading in the food-service industry and a lot of unemployed people entered the franchise business.

The founding members of HB were also trying various forms of self-employment to find their own way to live. They started a distribution business of food materials in a central region in Korea first, and then members from Seoul joined later. HB's founders gradually started to look at the franchise industry. As the first case of mad cow disease broke out, the sales of meat-based food distribution businesses declined sharply, and all of the major businesses were put on the brink of bankruptcy.

They had been trying various types of franchises for different sales offices, but repeatedly failed. They introduced the concept of "Cold Noodle in Big Basin," and made a brand called *Hwapyeong-dong king's cold noodle*, which sold meats and noodles together and persuaded restaurant owners to join their franchise. They guaranteed that the franchisees would have autonomy as much as possible. Owing to the success of *Hwapyeong-dong king's noodle* they have overcome the crises with the franchises.

Afterward, they founded a subsidiary, *the Food Core*, which integrated manufacturing and distribution networks. And they launched the second franchise brand, *Noodle Tree*, but the response in the market was not positive. Thus *the Food Core* was once again in crisis because of the global financial crisis and the second wave of mad cow disease. Many employees left the company and the business had to be restructured and the second brand, *noodle tree*, was abandoned. Some people left *the Food Core* to establish a new company to operate the franchise, *noodle tree*.

The *noodle tree*, which changed its brand strategy to "good quality for the price," attracted female customers in their 1930s and 1940s. The scattered members were reunited under the name Happy Bridge. Since the business had continued to grow and the size of the organization had grown, it is no longer possible to operate the organization. So new organizational structures and visions were needed for the organization, which lead to Happy Bridge Co-operative. HBC began to draw media attention by the decision to convert to a worker cooperative. As social demands for the cooperative franchise model increased, numbers of mass media outlets shed light on HBC's business model and stories.

32.3.3 Social movements and worker cooperative movement

The HB's founding members participated in social movements in different areas in the

1980s. When democratization including that of the labor movement emerged in 1987, Korean society as a whole faced a great turning point. However, the worker cooperative movement had been separated from the labor movement. Although the producer cooperative movement began in the 1990s, it had been only a minor movement. Together with the emerging workers' self-management enterprise since 1997, the producer cooperative movement continued its campaign as a self-help community movement. The Korean Workers Co-operatives Federation was initially formed in 2003 (it has been later re-launched in 2014), whose members, however, have not increased as much as its leaders had expected. Later it expanded to the Korea Association of Alternative Firms. After the enactment of the Framework Act on Cooperatives in 2012, HBC and other worker cooperatives have been developing a cooperative union of working people in which HBC has been the president of the organization.

Table 32.2 summarizes the macro factors of HB's transformation processes into HBC. The three factors, that is, the state, market, and social movement are illustrated by obstacles and actions.

32.3.4 Organization

Although the Korean worker cooperative movement was developed in the 1990s, there has not been someone who has managerial experience in a business of considerable scale or a small to medium sized enterprise as a worker cooperative. Even the founding members of HB had no experience of managing a worker cooperative. They had been running a company, and their employees were regarded as family. But HB couldn't build a powerful business system and the shared cooperative vision.

However, concerning the lack of understanding of worker cooperatives, HB has organized training sessions for employees, visited foreign worker cooperatives, invited experts, and held in-house seminars and forums. After a year of preparation, HB held the inaugural general meeting to convert it to a worker cooperative, HBC, in February 2013.

32.3.5 Governance

Since no one had experience in managing a worker cooperative, they suffered a great deal of frustration. Members were also required to participate in decision making led by the founding members who used to have a hierarchical relationship with their fellow members, formerly their subordinates. There was no model for worker cooperatives, so they made a mix of the governance of Mondragon and the participatory decision-making structure of the Korean cooperative. But it did not work as expected.

Although Mondragon's board of directors took advantage of the electoral method, there was also an atmosphere of over-politicization, and a confrontation between the board and the management was formed. HBC invited a lecturer from Mondragon University[9] to educate all members and to introduce the MTA[10] in order to allow the members to "unlearn" their old habitual work practices in new ways. In addition, HBC is trying to create a governance structure that might fit the characteristics of HBC by interacting with not only worker cooperative practitioners, but also professional business researchers. Over the past five years, HBC has experienced a lot of trial and error. And it has come to realize that not only structural problems, but also members' perceptions should be adjusted and relearned at the same time.

---

[9]   www.mondragon.edu/en/home (accessed July 14, 2018).

[10]   mondragonteamacademy.com/ (accessed July 14, 2018).

TABLE 32.2 The Macro Factors of HB's Transformation Process.

Factors		Obstacles	Actions
MACRO	State	• Labor Law amendment by civil rights movement (1987)	• HB members also participate in the social movement as university students
		• Labor Law amendment after the financial crisis (1997)	• Start a business for a living
		• National Basic Living Security Act (2000)	
		• Social Enterprise Promotion Act enacted (2007)	• HB consider converting, but do not (not mature and not fit)
		• **The Framework Act on Co-operative enacted (2011)**	• HB decides to convert (as a chance)
		• The new government takes friendly policy for social economy (2017)	• Cooperative franchise suggests as an alternative business model
	Market	Asian financial crisis (1997)**Neoliberal economics was spread in Korea**	• Collaborative work through a human network • Delivery service to partner restaurants
		• First BSE (bovine spongiform encephalopathy) • Partner restaurants were closed (2004)	• Start the franchise business (Korean cold noodle) • Persuade bankrupt partner restaurants to join the franchise • Build a cooperative franchise system (cobrand and autonomy)
		• Second BSE • Global financial crisis (2007)	• Many members leave and separate organization for surviving • Start up a new venture outside the company
		• Economy depression (2009)	• Brand concept change (Good quality and cheap) • After second brand success, former members come back to HB
		• CSR and fair franchise model (2017)	• Angel campaign as CSR activity and focus on social value
	Social Movements and Worker Cooperative Movement	• Labor movement (1987)	• Founding members participated in democratization movement
		• Producer cooperative movement (the 1990s)	• HB existed just as a human network
		• Employee own company movement (1997)	
		• Self-support community movement (2000)	
		• Korea Workers Co-operative Federation (2003)	
		• Korea Alternative Company Federation (2007)	• Consider joining, but do not join
		• Korea Federation of Worker Co-operatives	• Join and become the leader

32.3.6 Human resource management

Many of the problems HBC has faced as a worker cooperative were based on emotional aspects that have been accumulated over previous experiences. When HB was still a corporation, there were a lot of unresolved issues in organizational behavior including motivation, leadership, and so on. But after becoming a "democratically controlled" cooperative, complaints and hidden agendas of organizational behavior poured out at once. In the transition process, a change in management was not properly implemented. They hurt each other emotionally so that there were increasingly complicated issues that were difficult to resolve simply by "talking." The Korean educational system and organizational culture made things worse. Since childhood, Koreans are taught collectivistic ways so they may not usually be aware of the significance of individual differences and cultural diversity. The misunderstandings and prejudices toward each other were further hardened, and their behaviors and attitudes were not changed.

There was also a tendency to interpret the members' roles and responsibilities in different ways. In order to overcome these problems, HB has reorganized its business organization by reflecting the opinions of the members and has been boldly challenging new business. They have introduced various training programs in order to become an organization that learns and promotes continuous dialogue and mutual understanding. In addition, a project has been developing a new performance appraisal method in order to tackle the issue of controversial evaluation indicators.

The micro factors of organization, governance, and human resource management are summarized in Table 32.3, concerning HB's transformation into a worker cooperative.

32.4 Conclusion

From the six factors discussed, we can explain how HBC is doing business, good or bad, and how HBC becomes an exemplar of worker cooperatives in Korea. First, the institutionalization of worker cooperatives by state legislation has been essential in that HBC could become a cooperative. Owing to the enactment of the Framework Act on Co-operatives, it became possible for HB to take action to convert to a cooperative. In Korea, the state became a key player in legislation and institution building.

Second, HBC is doing businesses as a food service franchise under fierce competition. This business environment drives HBC to be more innovative and creative than other worker cooperatives whose businesses are related to a stable and mature environment such as public service, social service, and transportation industries. Because the environment and competitors of the food service industry are volatile and unpredictable, the organizational culture of HBC derived from HB and its founders is said to be risk-taking rather than risk-averting. HBC's business model and business environment play a key role in making it possible to be innovative.

Third, Korea's social movements including the worker cooperative movement have laid the foundation of HBC by supplying workers and managers with a socially responsible mind. The founders and some members of HBC used to be student movement activists and engaged in progressive social movement as well. This background and experience are enabling HBC to become a leader of the worker cooperative movement. HBC is performing a key role in the collaboration of worker cooperatives so far.

Fourth, the organizational structure of HBC is that of a worker cooperative, while other facets of an organization such as strategy,

TABLE 32.3   The Micro Factors of HB's Transformation Process.

Factors		Obstacles	Actions
MICRO	**Organization**	• Convert to worker Cooperative • **Not enough understanding about cooperatives** • **Nobody has experience in a worker cooperative**	• Visiting worker cooperatives (Canada, France, and Spain) • Seminars of workers cooperatives • Invite professionals
		• No dominant thought	• Vision workshop and make a vision statement
		• No congruent strategy	• Open forum for members to congruent strategy
	Governance	• Hierarchy between members	• Unlearning training through MTA methodology
		• **Benchmarking Mondragon** • But trouble between the management team and governing bodies	• Make a special committee for governance • Open forum for members to talk to each other • Network with professionals (management professors)
		• The election for directors is overheated and becomes a popular vote (one person four votes in first voting)	• Clarify governing body qualifications and raise basic standards
		• Not working for the standing council and members find it hard to communicate to governing bodies formally	• Will abolish standing council • Members council reorganize for communication
	HRM	• Emotional trouble between members	• Will divide into independent organizations
		• Don't consider difference and diversity	• Interview personally and make a career development plan
		• Misunderstanding and prejudice about members' roles and responsibilities	• Education and continuous dialogue
		• Lack of unlearning (attitude and behavior)	• Training through MTA methodology
		• No proper performance assessment indicators	• Action learning with a professional group

leadership, processes, and other organizational routines still have far to go. HBC is a converted cooperative and, therefore has to change all organizational behaviors, which takes time to adjust members' behaviors. In this sense, organizational development practices, especially learning from Mondragon and MTA, are crucial efforts.

2. Case studies of asian co-ops, including cross-country comparison

Fifth, one of the main differences between a cooperative and a corporation is the governance structures and practices. From the establishment of HBC, the governing bodies, that is, the board of directors and members council have been considered as key institutions and so HBC has tried to design them in their own way. But governance practices are perceived differently by the members. Since their conversion in 2013, HBC is still experimenting with its governance structural design and practices, which is critical for the future success of HBC.

Sixth, human resources of HBC are closely related to other aspects of organization and governance. The cores of changes in management, organizational development, and democratically controlled governance practices are all based on highly motivated, cooperative minded, and socially responsible workforces. It is a really huge challenge for HBC to be the leader of Korea's worker cooperatives.

What, then, can the case of HBC do for Korean society? HBC has suffered many confusions and difficulties throughout their organizational transformation process. The founding members, having pursued democratic decision-making since the early days of establishment, judged that the cooperative change was a good way to maintain the spirit.

Due to insufficient experience and incompetence in cooperative operation, the conversion to a worker cooperative led to a lot of confusion in making decisions and operations. There was a variety of dynamics that were different from the prior understanding of a cooperative, and the unexpected happenings and perceptions of the values. The founding members themselves, who led the cooperative transformation, also manifested diverse conflicts because they did not have the leadership to overcome the turmoil and the experience needed in managing a cooperative.

Unlike in Italy and Spain, there are no worker cooperatives with noticeable sales volumes and full-time workers in Korea. HBC will be a new way of venturing. This spirit of challenge was able to create a new milestone in Korea. HBC was able to find new directions by networking with external experts. In addition, as Korea's most successful worker cooperative, HBC collaborates with various cooperatives, creates new businesses, and transmits the voices of the cooperative sector. Considering Korea's worker cooperatives in their early stages, the impact of HBC is tremendous. The conversion of a worker cooperative has shown new possibilities. The success of HBC will become an illustrative experiment of worker cooperatives in Korea.

References

Ji, M. (2018). The worker cooperative movement in South Korea: From radical autonomy to state-sanctioned accommodation. *Labor History*, 59(4), 415–436.

Kim, J.-W. (2016). Study on the establishment and operating characteristics of the early worker co-operatives in South Korea (in Korean). *Economy and Society (Critical Sociological Association of Korea)*, Summer, 110, 82–121.

Kim, S.-O. (2012). *Mondragon's Miracle (in Korean)*. Gyeonggi-do, Korea: Critical Review of History.

Won, J.-H., & Jang, S. (2017). Becoming a co-operative with self-organizing process: The case of Happy Bridge Co-operative (in Korean). *Korea Business Review (Korean Academic Society of Business Administration)*, 21(1), 261–282.

33

Workers' cooperatives as a solution to social exclusion in Japan

Yurie Kubo

School of Commerce, Meiji University, Tokyo, Japan

33.1 Introduction

Japan achieved economic growth through rapid industrialization from the mid-1950s to 1970s causing the economic gaps among people in terms of income and living standards to become relatively small. Behind this stood the Japanese-style welfare state, which provided life security through employment in the public and market sectors. Companies paid wages and other benefits sufficient to cover the cost of living of not only the employees but also their families.

However, the intensification of global competition in the 1980s and the collapse of the bubble economy in the 1990s revealed the vulnerability of this system. Poverty, homelessness, and many other issues related to social exclusion became widely seen in this country. The basic problem was that the social security system developed in a time of industrialization, and economic growth guaranteed life security only for "regular," mostly male, workers.

Research on European cooperatives, the third sector, and social enterprises tends to insist on two features, namely resilience in times of crisis and the impact of job creation (e.g., Birchall & Ketilson, 2009; Borzaga & Defourny, 2001). Less well known is the positive impact of Japanese cooperatives on problems associated with social exclusion in an era of low growth and economic crisis.

This chapter aims to understand how Japanese workers cooperatives emerged in the late 20th century, overcoming obstacles to starting up, and to identify the factors that have enabled them to develop successfully until today. There are two main streams in the workers cooperative movement. One was born as a spinoff from the trade union movement and the other was developed from the consumer cooperative movement. They created alternative workplaces for people who had been excluded from the regular labor market such as unemployed workers, women, and people with disabilities.[1]

---

[1] The term "workers cooperative" is an internationally recognized generic term. In this chapter, it includes both workers cooperatives (Rokyo) affiliated with the JWCU and workers collectives (W.Cos) federated in the WNJ.

33.2 Contexts of social exclusion

33.2.1 Poverty and social exclusion

According to the Ministry of Health, Labour and Welfare, the relative poverty rate in 2017 was 15.7% and that of children was 13.9% above the average of organization for economic co-operation and development countries. Moreover, not only an income gap, but also absolute poverty is widely seen. The poverty line, which represents half of the median disposable income of the total population, is decreasing, from ¥1.5 million in 1997 to ¥1.2 million in 2017. Although Japan is regarded as one of the economic powerhouses of the world, some people die of hunger because of a lack of access to food. People living in poverty are often excluded from social relations and access to public support. Not only people living alone, but single parents who live with their children—sometimes due to intellectual or mental disabilities—face this kind of problem.

Several economists have demonstrated that the key factor in social exclusion is past unfavorable events that cause multiple difficulties (Abe, 2010; Kume et al., 2010). For example, the experience of unexpected lay-off due to industrial accidents, mental diseases, and company reorganizations cause poverty and create difficulties of outplacement, leading to a lack of confidence and alienation from family and friends. The experience of divorce also causes the same kind of negative spiral. So in Japan, people are under huge pressure not to fail or be derailed from their predetermined lane in which people may enjoy public, private, and community-based forms of support for wellbeing.

33.2.2 Deteriorating employment security

The key characteristic of the Japanese welfare state is that it has provided life security through the market sector. During the period of economic growth from the mid-1950s to the early 1970s, Japan nearly achieved full employment.[2] In addition, to generous seniority-based wages, companies provided various benefit packages such as a housing allowance and a sustenance allowance for male workers' wives and children. Also, they paid part of individual workers' social insurance premium for the national health and pension insurance.

However, only regular employees, almost entirely men, received the benefits offered by this system. Since the bursting of the economic bubble in the early 1990s, companies reduced the employment offers for new graduates. Many young people could not get stable jobs; the period was referred to as an "employment ice age." One of the most urgent social issues is that the youth who didn't get regular jobs at the time, are still engaged in unstable jobs or unemployed.[3] In the worst cases, people in their 30s and 40s are staying at home without any social relations except for their parents (the so-called Hikikomori, social recluses).

---

[2] The companies employ new graduates and provide them with vocational training. To develop and retain skilled human resources, the companies provided long-term employment till the retirement age and the wage system was structured based on the length of service.

[3] The people who did not engage in any regular employment, called *Free-ters*, were regarded as having started a new work culture where people could "freely" choose not to engage in regular employment in companies. Also because of a fast-aging population, the Japanese government and the Federation of Economic Organisations treated employment problems for the elderly as the more urgent issue. Therefore public policy addressing unstable employment or unemployment of youths was postponed (Hamaguchi, 2013).

At the same time, the deregulation of the Worker Dispatching Act was implemented, making it easy for companies to employ nonregular workers. When the world economic crisis broke out in 2008, many "disposable" workers were "thrown away" by companies; some workers, including young people, were ousted from the company dormitories where they lived and were forced to live on the street.

This symbolized the fact that the social safety net failed and nonregular workers were forced to "slide down" into extreme poverty when they were fired by these companies. The overall unemployment rate was 2.1% in 1991, but it rose to 4%−5% in the later 1990s and early 2000s. The rate of nonregular employment (part-time employees, *arbeit* workers, dispatched workers, etc.,) was about 15% of the total workforce in the mid-1980s, growing to 20% in the mid-1990s and 37% today (half of all female workers are employed in nonregular jobs).[4]

The solutions to the problem of the failure of the safety net are either to correct the disparity between regular and nonregular workers or to create alternative workplaces where people are equally included. Cooperatives' key function in society is in providing a solution to economic and social problems. Japanese workers cooperatives have engaged in the latter, creating workplaces for unemployed people and for people who have some difficulties in working in the regular labor market.

33.3 Two streams of workers cooperatives

In addressing the failure of the safety net, two streams of workers cooperatives emerged. The first grew out of the trade union movement and the second out of the consumer cooperative movement. These organizations provided infrastructure support for the establishment of workers cooperative businesses, overcoming obstacles like risk, access to capital, and skills.

33.3.1 Japan Workers' Co-operative Union

Japan Workers' Co-operative Union (JWCU) is a 50,000-member organization with an annual turnover exceeding ¥30 billion (Kubo, 2017: p. 56). In the 1980s and 1990s, workers cooperatives mainly engaged in building maintenance and sanitation work. They gradually shifted to develop more sustainable jobs to meet the needs of the times. JWCU's current main businesses are elderly care ($9 million), childcare ($7.2 million), and support for youth and the poor ($1.8 million).

JWCU emerged during the 1970s from a trade union of middle-aged and older workers temporarily employed by a national unemployment relief project created in the post-WWII period. This public project provided daily employment for unemployed people. The main jobs were in civil engineering and public sanitation works. The government ended this project as Japan's economy was revived. The trade union had tried to secure their jobs commissioned by the national government through extreme actions including strikes, but they finally failed. Leadership was provided by Mr. Goshu Nakanishi, chairman of the union, who proposed a policy of "democratic reformation." To secure jobs for union members, union officers created self-organized business units called *Jigyodan* across Japan to seek business opportunities from the public and private sectors. They encouraged workers to participate in management and to improve the quality of their work.

---

[4] Ministry of Health, Labour and Welfare, Labour Force Survey 2018.

These democratic small business units became the workers cooperatives that form the current JWCU. Later, inspired by the 1985 statement of the International Co-operative Alliance (ICA),[5] they identified their *Jigyodan* units as workers cooperatives. They founded a national council for *Jigyodan* units independent from the union in 1979 and renamed it JWCU in 1987.

As the workers cooperatives of JWCU were originally set up by union activists and precarious workers, one characteristic of this group is to look for opportunities to work with people with difficulties such as unemployment, psychiatric and intellectual disabilities, alcohol and drug dependency, etc. A business unit in Tokyo named Workers Net Rings provides public and domestic cleaning services. The unit leader himself had suffered from these problems and currently focuses on creating an inclusive workplace for those people.

33.3.2 Workers' Collective Network Japan

Workers' Collective Network Japan (WNJ) is a 10,000-member organization with an annual turnover of $13.6 million (Kubo, 2017: p. 56). Each of its 400 member organizations—called Workers Collectives (W.Cos)—is independent and maintains a membership of several to 100 members. In their early stages, W.Cos were operating stores and delivering goods for the consumer cooperative Seikatsu Club.[6] Later they created businesses such as catering, community cafés, and elderly care.

These W.Cos were formed in the 1980s by members of Seikatsu Club, which was created primarily by housewives to make joint purchases of safe food including privately branded

products produced under strict safety criteria. Seikatsu Club's key policy is that members should actively participate in every stage of the product cycle, namely cultivation, production, distribution, consumption, and disposal or recycling.

Inspired by the workers collective movement in the United States, W.Cos were established to operate consumer cooperative stores and provide home delivery. They intended to accelerate the shift in the economic model, making consumers aware that they were responsible for production and distribution as well.

Also, to counter society's dominant "male breadwinner" model, they showed that women could create jobs and make a positive impact on "society at large." W.Cos tend to involve not only women, but young people with difficulties. For instance, according to a survey by Fujii et al., in 12 W.Cos in the Kanagawa prefecture, 64 workers out of 751 have handicaps of some kind. In addition, senior members accompany younger members to help them find solutions and support them as coworkers. A W.Cos named Carry, engaging in household services in the Kanagawa prefecture, is a typical case where senior workers and young people with difficulties are working together.

33.4 Considerations on the development of workers cooperatives

33.4.1 Factors facilitating and impeding success

Workers cooperatives emerge successfully when a number of enabling macro factors are

---

[5]   At the annual ICA conference in 1985, Dr. A. F. Laidlaw, a Canadian cooperative activist, declared the importance of creating jobs through workers cooperatives in the 21st century.

[6]   *"Seikatsu"* means livelihood, life, or wellbeing. They use the terms *"Seikatsu-sha,"* which literally means "living people" instead of "labor" or "consumer." This concept is also applied to their political movement. They organize a local political group named Seikatsu-sha Network that turned out dozens of city council members from the cooperative.

present. These macro factors include the role of the state, the role of civil society, and the presence of a favorable market (Jensen, 2013).

Both JWCU and WNJ have developed based on their principles. There are some differences in organizational structures and governance, but the democratic and cooperative principles of organizational management gave their existence in Japanese society a particular significance—they have been proposing totally different meanings of working and living.

Several social welfare policies were conducive to the significant development of workers cooperatives. Especially since the 1980s, it has become apparent that the country's demographic dynamics would change rapidly due to aging and depopulation. Therefore the government was forced to change the conventional model of elderly care based on women's shadow work. Enacted in 1997, the Long-term Care Insurance (LTCI) Act allowed the private sector to provide elderly care through a quasi-market.[7] In 2013 the Act for Independence Support for Poor and Needy was enacted, and the government began to offer support to homeless people, people with disabilities, and people with other difficulties. These elderly care services and consultation and training programs for the needy opened the door to civil-sector organizations and created a huge opportunity for workers cooperatives to gain a stable and constant financial base.

However, most of the business areas in which workers cooperatives engage are generally unprofitable. Most are engaged in the public sector or quasi markets[8]—they would lose their financial base if these social policies were abolished. There are some practices that are totally independent from public policies such as creating community cafés or selling products, although those businesses tend to be conducted in the red.

Central Jigyodan, JWCU's biggest worker cooperative, overcomes this problem. It is a 7000-member organization with an annual turnover of $16.3 million and 350 business units and activities throughout Japan. Its rational financial and human resource management ensure its sustainability. They recruit and train unit directors at their central office and share business and organizational know-how, which allow them to disperse successful business models to units across Japan. Successful units share their profits with the central office for use in covering deficits or founding new units. This cross-subsidization system supports the financial stability of the entire group.

There are no infrastructure organizations that represent and integrate various cooperatives and voluntary organizations in Japan. Japan's cooperative legislation is divided by sector such as agriculture, fishery, forestry, and consumption. Furthermore, there is no system that legally supports worker cooperatives. But in April 2018, the Japan Co-operative Alliance (JCA) was founded to promote collaboration among various cooperatives. In this context, it is expected that the practice of the worker cooperatives, which have a special energy as emerging organizations, can encourage the rejuvenation of traditional cooperatives.

---

[7] Not only workers cooperatives, but other cooperatives such as consumer, agricultural, and health cooperatives engage in elderly care services under the LTCI system. Some case studies are shown in Kurimoto and Kumakura (2016).

[8] For example, the annual turnover of JWCU's biggest elderly persons' cooperative is ¥1.4 billion, about 60% of which comes through LTCI. The employment training program is another important financial base. For instance, a business unit of Central *Jigyodan* in the Saitama prefecture named Sylvan Tofu Maker has seven workers and nine people who are accepted as trainees through the independence support system for people with disabilities. Their monthly turnover is approximately ¥200,000 and the funds from the public system amount to ¥600,000 covering personnel costs (Kubo, 2017: p. 57).

33.4.2 Characteristics of workers cooperatives

The two workers cooperative organizations, JWCU and WNJ, have been successful for some time, an accomplishment that can be related to micro factors associated with their democratic business models (Jensen, 2013). These factors include organizational structure, governance, and human relations management.

33.4.2.1 *Organizational structures*

The organizational structures of JWCU and WNJ are complex as shown in Fig. 33.1. The "primary co-operatives" shown in the figure basically mean the cooperative bodies that conduct the business of the worker cooperatives.

JWCU has multiple member organizations. For example, in the mid-1980s Central Jigyodan was initially set up and directly managed by

the head officer of JWCU to replicate the successful model of Jigyodans. Since then, JWCU has deployed branches and units nationwide. Other individual member organizations engage in various businesses and activities from agriculture to research and development.

WNJ consists of nine prefectural unions that were organized in a bottom-up style. Individual W.Cos were created before of the prefectural unions, which were established to support the sustainable development of the W.Cos. The individual W.Cos are organized according to business and geographic areas and the size of each organization is small.

33.4.2.2 *Governance*

At the field level, where activities are carried out, JWCU and WNJ maintain the principles underlying workers cooperatives. All workers have equal voting rights and participate in

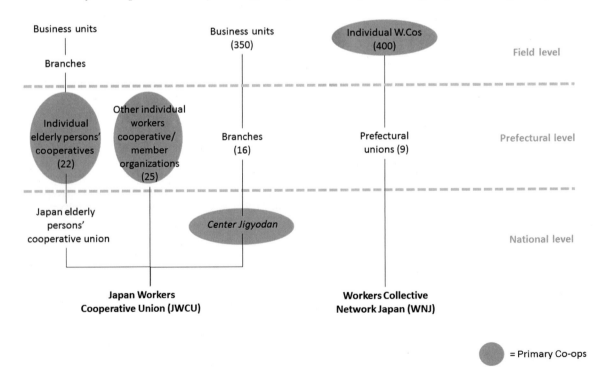

FIGURE 33.1   Organizational Structures of JWCU and WNJ

business and organizational management. In the case of JWCU, the central office plays a leading role in making decisions on the strategies and annual policies put in place. But workplace democracy is guaranteed for the business units through various kinds of workers meetings. WNJ puts more priority on direct democracy. Most W.Cos are small and encourage the rotation of board members.

Since the birth of the movements until the 1990s, workers cooperatives were purely governed by workers. However, as they went into social care services, both JWCU and WNJ contrived ways to reflect the voice of local residents, for instance, through organizing voluntary community meetings open to community members. In a sense, workers cooperatives have gained the orientation to be multistakeholder cooperatives or community cooperatives.

33.4.2.3 Composition of members

Regarding its composition of members, in the early stages of their movement, most members of JWCU were low-wage workers, who were middle-aged and older, but now they have a diverse range of worker-members. In the case of Central Jigyodan, for example, about 60% are women of various ages; 20s (10%), 30s (11%), 40s (15%), 50s (25%), 60s (25%) and 70s (5%) (Fujii, Harada, & Ohtaka, 2013: p. 234). In contrast, because most members of WNJ continue to be women who joined in the early stages of the movement, their membership is aging.

33.4.2.4 Human relations mobilization

JWCU generally recruits members through a public job-placement office. In contrast, WNJ enrolls members mainly from consumer cooperative members and by word of mouth. The former way of recruiting enables JWCU to bring diverse kinds of people into the cooperative movement; it is relatively difficult to recruit people who are highly motivated and enthusiastic about the cooperative movement.[9] The WNJ approach addresses this problem, but has a problem in that the cooperative membership remains homogeneous.

Both JWCU and WNJ pay attention to the seventh principle of the ICA, namely concern for community. When they set up new business units or cooperatives, they actively encourage local residents to join their activities by showing documentary films or through conversations on their daily businesses. This kind of publicity has enabled them to involve diverse people in their activities.

33.5 Impacts and challenges

The impacts of workers cooperatives can be seen in their contributions to job creation and the provision of social services in the late 20th century. This means that they are comparable to the social enterprises that emerged in Europe (Borzaga & Defourny, 2001). The workers cooperatives in Japan were dedicated to creating workplaces for unemployed people and people who could not find jobs in the ordinary labor market. Both JWCU and WNJ involved young people with intellectual or psychiatric disabilities and with social relationship problems like *Hikikomori*.

A common challenge for JWCU and WNJ is to foster young leaders. Both of them provide opportunities for all members to learn business and organizational management through meetings, but training young leaders remains their

---

[9] About this problem, Central Jigyodan has been applying a solution; it recruits "nationwide directors" at the central office and dispatches them to their business units. Directors are responsible for disseminating policy and philosophy, but also share their business know-how. For instance, supporting unit leaders to facilitate meetings in a democratic way, offering tips for applying for public services, etc. (Kumakura, 2016).

biggest challenge. A special unit of Central Jigyodan organizes visits to other business units for directors who have served 6 months. New directors learn organizational management from the practices of other units. However, there is so far no formal curriculum for the management of workers cooperatives— for example, how leaders can improve member participation in governance and management.

WNJ's member organizations have been led by executives who joined early in the movement and now are over the age of 60. Although the number of younger members is increasing following the acceptance of people with disabilities, they generally are followers of the older members. The challenge is to train such members to be active and independent. This effort was taken in a public employment and social welfare program, which is described as an "intermediate" workplace for employment training for the poor and needy. In essence, workers cooperatives dedicated themselves to creating inclusive workplaces for young people with difficulties before youth employment problems were recognized as social problems.

Conclusion

As a trade union of unemployed people, JWCU tried to provide socially useful services performed by its members. WNJ attempted to create jobs for people excluded from the labor market, so-called "full-time housewives," seeking to liberate women from conventional male-dominated society. Given that Japan's working population exceeds 65 million people, the 50,000 belonging to JWCU and WNJ seem few in number. However, their impact is substantial. One significant factor of social exclusion is the government's failure to adapt its social security systems to the age of economic stagnation. Workers' cooperatives have dedicated themselves to job creation and service

provision, but have also played an advocacy role for creating a better working society.

As mentioned previously, the cooperative movement in Japan has begun to develop inter-cooperation, overcoming long-standing separation. The campaign demanding a legal framework for workers cooperatives started discussion among activists and an all-party parliamentary group was organized in 2008. This campaign is led not only by leaders of workers cooperatives, but also by key figures of other types of cooperatives. Cooperation with nonprofit sector organizations and the strengthening influence on politics with the common goal of creating a better society will be an important line of development.

References

Abe, A. (2010). Social exclusion and earlier disadvantages: An empirical study of poverty and social exclusion in Japan. *Social Science Japan Journal*, Institute of Social Science, University of Tokyo.

Birchall, J., & Ketilson, L. H. (2009). *Resilience of the cooperative business model in times of crisis*. International Labour Office, Sustainable Enterprise Programme.

Borzaga, C., & Defourny, J. (Eds.), (2001). *The emergence of social enterprise*. Routlege.

Fujii, A., Harada, K., & Ohtaka, K. (Eds.), (2013). *Social enterprise tackling social exclusion*. Keiso Shobo. (Japanese).

Hamaguchi, K. (2013). *Young people and work: Untangle the "joining company" system*. Chuko Shinsyo La Clef. (Japanes).

Jensen, A. (2013). The labour managed firm – A theoretical model explaining emergence and behaviour. In D. Kruse (Ed.), *Advances in the economic analysis of participatory and labor managed firms* (14, pp. 293–327). United kingdom: Emerald.

Kubo, Y. (2017). Current situation of workers co-operatives' store operation. *Co-operative Research Journal: Niji*, No. 658, JC General Research Institute (Japanese).

Kumakura, Y. (2016). Organisational structure and infrastructure functions of work integrated social enterprise: A case of centre Jigyodan of JWCU. In A. Fujii (Ed.), *Development and challenges of Japanese work integration social enterprise: Focused on infrastructure organisation*. Zenrosai Kyokai. (Japanese).

Kume, K., et al. (2010). The picture and the factor of social exclusion among non-regular workers. *RIETI Discussion Paper Series*, 10-J-025 (in Japanese).

Kurimoto, A., & Kumakura, Y. (2016). Emergence and evolution of co-operatives for elderly care in Japan. *International Review of Sociology*, 26(1), Routledge.

Further reading

Campbell, J. C. (1992). *How policies change: The Japanese government and the aging society*. Princeton University Press.

Defourny, J., et al. (Eds.), (2014). *Social enterprise and the third sector*. Routledge.

Fujii, A. (2013). Social inclusion in Japanese workers' collectives: Actual situations and conditions. *EMES-SOCENT Conference Selected Papers*, No. LG13-04, EMES European Research Network.

Gilchrist, A., & Taylor, M. (2016). *The short guide to community development* (2nd edition). Policy Press.

Poole, M. (1986). *Towards new industrial democracy—Workers participation in Industry*. Routledge and Kegan Paul.

Nakanishi, G. (1986). *Trade union's spirit of adventure*. Roudou-Jyunpousha. (Japanese).

Ridley-Duff, R., & Bull, M. (2011). *Understanding social enterprise: Theory & practice*. Sage Publications Ltd.

Witt, M. A., & Redding, G. (2013). Asian business systems: Institutional comparison, cluster, and implications for varieties of capitalism and business systems theory. *Socio-Economic Review*, 11(2), Oxford University Press.

34

Summary
Worker co-operatives: creating the future we want

Anthony Jensen

University of Newcastle, Callaghan, Australia

The ILO's "Future of Work We Want" project calls us to empower workers in jobs they prefer that are engaging, interesting, and inclusive. This challenges the inevitability of the scenario of the "precariat," a new class of casualized individualized worker, a citizen in a society experiencing dramatic and rapid change. This deterioration provoked the ILO to ask "What will the enterprise look like tomorrow, what are the decent jobs of tomorrow; what does work mean to us in terms of earning a living and giving life meaning and direction?" The ILO concluded that the future is not decided, "the future we want is there for us to create."

The study of worker cooperatives in this part illustrates six different cases across five countries (India, the Philippines, South Korea, Japan, and Australia) with different political economies that can be used to promote discussion and offer solutions to the problem of securing good jobs. In such a study seeking to understand cooperative viability, context is everything when there is a need to clarify how obstacles to worker cooperative formation are overcome and the factors crucial to success are quantified. Witt and Redding (2013) defined different Asian business systems, which help us understand the nature of the worker cooperative in Asia. They advanced new forms of capitalism in a spectrum of political economies:

- Socialist system—India (the state of Kerala)
- Post socialist system—India, China, Vietnam and Laos
- Advanced city state system—Singapore and Hong Kong
- Emerging Southeast Asian system—the Philippines, Indonesia, Thailand and Malaysia
- Advanced Northeast system—Korea and Taiwan
- Liberal corporate system—Japan
- Mediated liberal market economy system—Australia

The six case studies demonstrated the range of problems that worker cooperatives are able to solve in different political economies and presented road-maps for overcoming obstacles and identifying factors enabling success.

34.1 Socialist system—solidarity in job creation

ULCCS (Uralungal Labour Contract Co-operative Society) founded in 1924, with 14 members including an inspiring chairman, is based on the values of democracy and equality and was embedded from the start in the emerging communist culture of Southern India addressing the inequality and class and caste discrimination of the region. ULCCS demonstrated a refusal to degenerate through solidarity with the rising number of contract workers by creating a special nonvoting membership for untenured employees. Their commitment to equality and democracy was strengthened over their 90 years as the membership rose to 7000 through the influence of the communist culture and support of the state post-independence. ULCCS demonstrated its collective dynamism by diversifying into information communication technology (ICT) enabled services, tourism, social welfare, and education.

34.2 Post socialist system—a collective response

The Transport Co-operative Society (TCS), in the predatory (meaning high level of corruption) state of India, was formed in 1991, through the collective action of 130 workers of a bus company over pay and conditions brought about by a local trade unionist advocating for strike action. Eventually a local communist union leader suggested a cooperative to save their jobs. Collectively the uneducated workers overcame obstacles and invested their compensation, worked for lower wages, overcame state opposition, and inspired other cooperatives to emerge. Lacking an external culture of solidarity, currently TCS are experiencing a decline in membership from 244 to 160 members and appear to be at a crossroad due to the original members not being inclined to admit new members. They have inspired the formation of other cooperatives.

34.3 Emerging Southeast Asian system—individual triumph

Alpha Co-operative is situated in the predatory state of the Philippines. It was formed in 1999 by a social entrepreneur and human resource manager and several contractual workers to address the plight of precarious contractual workers in the Philippines. In the true sense of the word the founder was a social entrepreneur in a predominately Catholic society (with a commitment to social justice) addressing an unjust reality with a new just reality. The precarious worker movement in the Philippines was brought about due to the ability of companies to downsize workers at the end of 6 months right before they were required to become permanent workers. Alpha Co-operative replaced this practice with the supply to companies of skilled workers on a continuous contract. This model was received with such acclaim for solving the problem that it expanded rapidly to 80,000 members.

34.4 Advanced Northeast system—civil society activists for democratizing workplaces

Happy Bridge Co-operative (HBC) in South Korea converted from a joint stock company to a worker cooperative in 2013 with 84 members among 121 employees who as activists had participated in social movements. Worker cooperatives had originally emerged in Korea as a revolutionary liberation struggle against Japanese occupation, evolving into worker self-management and finally job development and the antipoverty movement. HBC demonstrates the precarious nature of a transition to worker ownership where "through conflict and debate a new organisational form was born."

34.5 Liberal corporatist system—the catalyst of civil society movements

Japan Workers Co-operative Union (JWCU) is a 50,000-member organization formed in 1987 and was inspired by the chairman of the trade union to form worker cooperatives to secure work for its members in the area of building maintenance sand sanitation works. These worker cooperatives were formed by union activists and precarious workers and embraced people with difficulties and disabilities. The Workers Collective Network Japan (WNJ) has 10,000 members in 400 workers collectives formed by the consumer cooperative Seikatsu. Both were formed by civil society movements to address social exclusion in Japan.

34.6 Liberal market economy system— worker buyout of a family business

C−Mac Industries, a manufacturing firm in Australia, was formed in 2017 in a worker buyout of a 50-year old family company by its 30 members. It represents a solution to the problem of family business succession when there is no one to take over. The vision is to preserve skills and jobs in manufacturing. It is seen as a win−win where the family preserve their legacy and the workers preserve their jobs. The catalyst was the Christian son of the owner who saw social justice in looking after the workers who had been loyal over the years.

34.7 Proof of concept

These six different cases demonstrate the power and rewards of collective action in overcoming the difficulties of raising finance, addressing risk, acquiring skills, and providing working capital. The result was to preserve and create good jobs, to solve economic and social problems, and to address market failure while overcoming the disconnected nature of capitalism.

34.8 Scaling up

Building on the work of Greenberg (1983), four strategies as a method of facilitating a worker cooperative sector can be identified:

- Brick by brick whereby sectors of society are converted one business at a time by business succession and worker buyouts—C-mac, HBC, and TCS
- Replication and inspiration for others to follow—Alpha Pro offering a hybrid model with a cooperative supplying labor and a corporation supplying capital that has vast potential
- Revolution and job creation following social breakdown or environmental catastrophe—ULCCS
- Rising consciousness of civil society demanding value-based organizations to address exclusion—JWCU and WNJ emerging from trade unions and consumer cooperatives

These case studies provide a window to view the range and potential of worker cooperatives to advance sustainable growth and economic democracy through systems of democratic planning and worker self-management. Planning the awakening of Asia Pacific cooperatives as a third pillar of the economy is the next step to realizing this potential.

References

Greenberg, E. S. (1983). *Context and cooperation: Systematic variation in the political effects of workplace democracy, . Economic and Industrial Democracy* (Vol. 4, pp. 191−223). London: Sage.
Witt, M. A., & Redding, G. (2013). Asian business systems: Institutional comparison, cluster, and implications for varieties of capitalism and business systems theory. *Socio-Economic Review, 11*(2), Oxford University Press.

PART 3

Toward an Asian Scholarship on Co-ops

Deconstructing cooperative success in the Asia Pacific region

Yashavantha Dongre[1], Akira Kurimoto[2], Seungkwon Jang[3], Robby Tulus[4], Morris Altman[5] and Anthony Jensen[6]

[1]University of Mysore, Mysuru, Karnataka, India [2]Hosei University, Chiyoda City, Tokyo, Japan [3]Sungkonghoe University, Seoul, Republic of Korea [4]Regional Director (Emeritus) for Asia Pacific, International Co-operative Alliance (ICA). Founder and Chief Advisor, Federation of People-based Co-operative Enterprises (INKUR Federation), Indonesia, and Credit Union Central Organization (CUCO), Indonesia [5]Dean & Chair Professor of Behavioural and Institutional Economics & Co-Operatives School of Business, University of Dundee, Dundee, United Kingdom [6]University of Newcastle, New South Wales, Australia

Arriving at any opinion/judgement about Asia Pacific cooperatives through an Asia Pacific perspective should probably begin with the question as to whether there exists anything called regional values and regional culture that creates a regional model. Barring two important countries in the Pacific—Australia and New Zealand—the rest of the region, in particular the Asian region, has thousands of years of human history and culture. The core of the culture of this region, if any, lies in its heterogeneity and the core value is at best tolerance. It is now effectively argued that the entire debate of the 1990s on the so-called Asian values as differentiated from that of Western values was primarily political and there is not much substance in it. In fact, studies have demonstrated that it is difficult to establish a common set of values for the Asia Pacific region that is different from the rest of the world. It has also been established that the Asia Pacific region is probably more heterogeneous than other regions of the world.

There are more than 50 countries in the Asia Pacific region. Cooperatives exist in almost all of these countries, but only 33 countries are members of the International Co-operative Alliance. The region houses the world's largest share of cooperatives in terms of numbers, but their average size is small with only 34 cooperatives appearing on the list of the top 300 cooperatives in the world based on turnover in US dollars (World Cooperative Monitor, 2018). Agricultural cooperatives (including allied sectors such as animal husbandry), credit cooperatives, consumer cooperatives, and worker

Waking the Asian Pacific Cooperative Potential
DOI: https://doi.org/10.1016/B978-0-12-816666-6.00035-5

cooperatives constitute the bulk of cooperatives all over the world and this trend is similar in the Asia Pacific region as well. Therefore the case studies used in this volume have been drawn from these sectors. The case studies come from 11 countries that are under different economic and political statuses. This has given us an opportunity to compare cooperatives across sociopolitical and economic systems as well as across important subsectors of the cooperative sector. The process of analyzing how these cooperatives faced challenges and what strategies they adopted to overcome them, how do they sustain and survive, do they follow any distinct/unique methods, etc., needs to begin with an understanding of the socioeconomic and political climate of these countries.

35.1 The state and civil society

A dominant state (strong government) with state-directed development policy, weak civil society with loose community organizations, and hierarchical social relationships with gender inequality are the most visible features of most Asia Pacific countries. There might be exceptions, but such exceptions are for one or another attribute among those mentioned and only in a small number of cases. The political systems in the countries from where the case studies have come from vary from liberal democracy to single party rule. The economic systems vary from market economy, directed economy, and centrally planned economy to mixed economy. On the social side there are varied religions, innumerable ethnic groups, hundreds of languages, and varieties of value systems in the region. Given this, the task of identifying a set of common factors is an unenviable task.

Historically, the majority of the countries in the Asia Pacific region had foreign influences, and in most cases foreign occupation. It looks as though the long-standing foreign rule or a foreign power dictating terms to the local

people has had a tremendous impact. After independence almost all of these countries elected governments that are highly dominant and almost omnipresent. Individual charismatic leaders have outshined the institutional structures and be it state, private, or the civil society, a lot of positive changes have been induced due to the impact of individual leaders. Cooperatives have not escaped this trend, though they are pronounced as value-based, principle-driven, democratic organizations. Wherever the cooperative leaders were strong and charismatic, they withstood state interference and even used state machinery to support cooperatives. Where cooperatives did not have such leaders, state dominated the cooperatives and dictated terms.

35.2 Findings through case studies

The case studies used in this volume show that cooperatives in the Asia Pacific region have some common challenges and have also followed some common strategies to overcome such challenges both across countries and across subsectors of cooperatives.

35.3 Macro factors

One predominant factor common to all countries is the strong presence of state. Barring the exception of Australia, where in fact cooperatives do not have a significant presence in the economy, in all the other countries state machinery is closely associated with the cooperative sector. State seems to be keen to keep a close watch or even to control agricultural cooperatives. The states' role looks moderate in the case of credit cooperatives and worker cooperatives and it is lowest in the case of consumer cooperatives. Governments, both national and regional within a country, have facilitated, patronaged, and even financed cooperatives in almost all Asian countries. The state has also intervened, directed, and controlled cooperatives. In almost none of our case studies show the presence of a level playing field for cooperatives with that of the state sector and private sector. Cooperatives have compromised in such situations, persuaded the state machinery and secured better leverage, and learnt to operate within the given space. In a way this situation has not come in the way of the success of cooperatives, but it has certainly made cooperatives hold back and be cautious in terms of expansion and diversification of activities.

The second common feature is the impact of globalization and the consequent increase in competition from the private sector. Irrespective of which subsector a cooperative belongs to, almost all of them have faced this challenge. Here again, irrespective of the subsector, cooperatives across Asia and the Pacific have experienced the tensions of a new economy dominated by private service providers. The successful cooperatives were found to be innovative and tried to keep themselves afloat through strategies specific to their territories. The adoption of technology and cost reduction, gaining the trust of members and customers through quality and price balancing, seizing market opportunities whenever a new opportunity comes up, and of course impressing upon stakeholders the social focus of cooperative enterprises, have all contributed to the success of successful cooperatives.

35.4 Micro factors

The most important micro factor affecting cooperatives in the Asia Pacific region seems to be leadership. Cooperatives that have not done well have had problems with leadership with issues of one-person domination or disinterested, less competent leaders. In the case of the successful cooperatives, leaders, either the founder/chairman/CEO or the board

members, have exhibited utmost commitment and vision in molding their cooperatives. There were leaders who were with their cooperatives for a long period and they have also ensured a good succession plan for the next generation of leaders to take over. It is important to note that in the majority of these cooperatives not only do we see a healthy succession plan, but also a smooth transition. A typically Asian feature could be that of a hierarchical relationship with members generally following a leader when such a leader is found to be working for the betterment of the cooperative.

The second critical issue at the micro level is the response of a cooperative to the needs of its members. Whether it is in the case of consumer cooperatives in Japan and Singapore, agricultural cooperatives in Australia and India, or worker cooperatives in the Philippines and India, we find that the successful cooperatives have all made efforts to cater to the needs of the member customers. Cooperatives whose revenues depend on nonmember customers have faced difficulties as customers shift loyalty when they think a private service provider offers a better deal either on price or quality parameters. But when members needs are converted into business activities, members flock around the cooperatives and in fact are found to attach themselves more and more when the cooperative is under a competitive disadvantage.

The case studies do point at some common features for cooperatives in the region and many of these features are quite different from those of Western countries. However, we may not be able to say whether they are unique to the Asia Pacific region, for similar features are reported from cooperatives in Africa and Latin American countries as well. However, based on these facts, if we conclude that the so-called common features of cooperatives are in fact associated not with a specific region, but with the economic or political status of the countries in the region, we are likely to go wrong. In the

Asia Pacific region itself, we have economically advanced countries like Japan and Singapore where the cooperatives function in a completely different setting compared to advanced Western economies. At the same time, in the very same region we have pronounced liberal democracies (India) where the state intervenes too much in the cooperatives as well as economies in transition (Vietnam) where the state provides a more conducive atmosphere for cooperatives to operate.

35.5 The Asia Pacific model

There are varieties of capitalism within the Asia Pacific region and for that matter there are varieties of capitalism within some of the Asian countries like India. However, by itself the "varieties of capitalism" model cannot be fitted into the cooperatives in the region. For that matter, any typology that has been put forth so far seems to be inadequate to explain the success of Asia Pacific cooperatives. The political economy perspective seems to be useful in so far as explaining the love—hate relationship existing between states and cooperatives (in particular politicians and cooperators), but it cannot effectively argue out successful cooperative models. This is because Asia is too diverse to fall easily into typologies drawn by and based on Western experiences and perspectives. The case studies show that the Asia Pacific region is undergoing changes in terms of values, knowledge base, and professionalism. This is well illustrated in the cooperative sector as well. States are slowly, but definitely allowing greater space for cooperatives. This may not be because they want to do that, but because the market structures are forcing the state to change. With the lesser role of the state in the market, the role of constructive competitors is increasingly played by cooperatives. Successful cooperatives in the

region are able to perform despite state intervention and despite the overwhelming presence of the private sector. The best way to understand cooperatives in the region is not to try and fit them into a single basket. Such categorization is not possible even within one country of the region.

One thing that emerges by closely looking at the case studies of successful cooperatives is that they are driven more by micro factors than macro factors. Macro factors may or may not be favorable to the cooperatives, but where the micro factors are favorable, cooperatives have succeeded in resisting, adapting, and even manipulating the macro factors. In this sense, it is the leadership and membership that are the base on which the success of successful cooperatives in the region is built. So it seems that the best way to explain cooperatives in the Asia Pacific region is to develop models based on the factors internal to the organization. Macro factors are changing anyway and for the good in most countries, driven more by markets than by state. It is the micro factors that decide the long-term sustainability and overall health of cooperatives in the region.

We have outlined in this book the first stage of a research project to define and illuminate an Asia Pacific Scholarship on cooperatives, grounded in values and cultures distinct from Europe and North America. The cases outlined in the book demonstrate the potential for this Asia Pacific Scholarship to inform policy through a process of praxis and, therefore, bring about an enabling environment to awaken the potential of the Asia Pacific cooperative movement.

Reference

World Cooperative Monitor, 2018. Exploring the Cooperative Economy, Report 2018. Brussels: Eurocise/International Co-operative Alliance. <https://www.ica.coop/sites/default/files/publication-files/wcm2018-web-1542524747.pdf> [accessed 16.02.2020].

Epilogue

Anthony Jensen

University of Newcastle, NSW, Australia

This remarkable book on Asian Pacific cooperatives is the result of 5 years of collaborative work by a group of academic revisionists who decided to challenge the prevailing wisdom that cooperatives were not applicable as a business model and could not deliver sustainable social and economic transformation. In doing so they demonstrated that another world was possible in the context of the Asian Century and a time of an emerging western existential crisis. This is summed up by Otto Sharmer of MIT (U Lab):

> We live in an age of profound disruption, where something is ending and dying, and something else is wanting to be born. What's ending and dying is a civilization that's built on the mindset of maximum me or [the] bigger the better and of special interest group decision making that has led us into a state of organised irresponsibility.

> What's being born is less clear. It's a future that requires us to connect with a deeper level of our humanity—to discover who we really are and who we want to be as a society.

> How can we build the capacity to sense and actualize a future that we feel is possible, we know is possible, but isn't quite there yet?

This book demonstrates through the 21 case studies of Asian Pacific Cooperatives in 11 countries that there is indeed the possibility of a different sustainable future built by ordinary people and that it has already taken shape in successful Asian Pacific Co-operatives.

Bali Conference 2014

This book had its genesis at the ICA Research Conference in Bali in 2014 when the idea was floated that a cross-cultural comparative study of cooperatives in different countries would enrich our understanding of why the nature of cooperatives varied so dramatically across the region creating a conundrum for policy makers. This became the Asia Pacific Co-operative Research Partnership (APCRP) a loose grouping that was open to all who were interested in advancing comparative research. It became formalized as a body, the APCRP, linked by a Memorandum of Understanding with the University of Newcastle.

This thought was definitely in the zeitgeist as Yashavantha Dongre, Akira Kurimoto, Morris Altman and, the next day, Robby Tulus agreed to support the idea and an editorial board was formed. It realized the aspirations that had taken shape in conversations earlier with Bien Nito of the University of Asia Pacific in the Philippines. Seungkwon Jang joined the board 2 years later. The group agreed on three core findings:

- The greater contribution of cooperatives across the Asia Pacific is hampered by a lack of research and data into their contribution to society and the solving of social and economic problems.
- Cooperatives are not visible in the Asian political, academic, and business scenes as governments lack statistics and case studies of successful cooperatives relating to their contribution to national economies.
- There is a need to explore the prospects for a uniquely Asian scholarship separate from the hegemony of Western influence.

Akira Kurimoto outlined five key research objectives to build visible and viable cooperatives in the Asian region. These were adopted by the APCRP:

- Solid basis of research and development activities at national and regional levels to overcome a lack of statistics and cultural barriers.
- Map and showcase best practice in region—notwithstanding that although there are failures, there are also many positive examples.
- Strengthen the liaison between institutions and subsectors at national and regional levels.
- Contribute to enabling policy and legislative development.
- To develop an Asian scholarship separated from the hegemony of Western scholars.

Practical outcomes were defined *as identifying and researching best practice cooperative case studies in each country, understand their formation and growth in different political and economic contexts, and develop strategies for their replication and scaling up across the region.* In addition, it would demonstrate how cooperatives solve local problems.

Bangkok Conference 2015

The APCRP next met in Bangkok where participants agreed to the comparative research of successful cooperatives across four cooperative sectors and began to identify the countries in which research could be conducted and access obtained:

- Agricultural cooperatives
- Consumer cooperatives
- Finance cooperatives
- Worker cooperatives

The APCRP also defined its objectives:

Practical outcomes: *To identify and research best practice cooperative case studies in each country, understand their formation and growth in different political and economic contexts, and develop strategies for their replication across the region. Demonstrate how cooperatives solve local problems.*

Policy development: *To build the capacity of the partner institutions across Asia through the production of developmental tools: policy making, communicating the benefits of cooperatives, the ability to analyze economic benefits, and the production of case study material on cooperatives.*

Philosophical reflection: *To reflect on our economic and social models as vehicles for integral human development and sustainable and inclusive economic growth exploring the possibilities of a new form of civil society.*

Theoretical development: *To understand and promote cooperatives as a robust development model by contributing to the development of theoretical models for understanding the emergence, evolution, and behavior of cooperatives within the varieties of Asian business systems.*

Comparative research project: *What makes for successful consumer, agricultural, finance, or worker cooperatives? Are there alternative ways of succeeding? What makes for failure? What are the*

*institutional factors that enable cooperatives?
What are the disablers of cooperative development?*

APCRP chose a methodology that uses a theoretical explanatory model consisting of macro and micro factors that explain cooperative emergence and evolution, and success or failure, in different socioeconomic and political contexts.

Pune Conference 2015

The third meeting was in Pune, India, where the APCRP members decided to align their work with the International Cooperative Alliance Asia Pacific (ICA AP) Research Committee and coordinate their meetings. It was also decided that its first project would be the production of a book of successful cooperative case studies. A template was developed to guide the structure of chapters to enable a cross-national case study comparison.

The process began by attracting and consolidating 21 case studies across 11 countries and the 4 cooperative sectors. This included 34 academics working on the project. The extraordinary cooperative case studies across the Asia Pacific outlined in this book could prompt us to reach for the superlatives expressed by Aneurin Bevan, of the UK Labour Party, and Race Mathews from the Australian Labour Movement when they exclaimed "I have seen the future and it works" on their visit to the Soviet Union and the Mondragon co-operatives respectively.

But we are now armed with the lessons from history that proves that cooperatives succeed, fail, regenerate, and make compromises. This was reflected by the APCRP defining the themes of the book to be the obstacles cooperatives faced, how they overcame those obstacles, and what were the factors related to success.

Seoul Conference 2017

Approximately 30 members of the APCRP project met in Seoul including a number Skyping in. The proposed book now came to 40 chapters and had taken shape to the extent that a publishing contract had been awarded by Elsevier for a book entitled "Waking the Asian Pacific Co-operative Potential".

It was at the Seoul Conference that the theoretical approach developed by Witt and Redding (2013) was put forward proposing that Asian capitalism had a number of varieties distinct from Western capitalism and could not be understood by using Western business models. This enabled the 11 countries to be categorised into 5 types of Asian capitalism leading to a deeper understanding of the different types of cooperative formation in Asia.

In addition, the editorial board met in Delhi, Seoul, Mysore, and Newcastle (NSW) to decide on methodologies and review submitted chapter manuscripts.

Historical praxis

The Asian cooperative movement has grown in awareness though "praxis" whereby practical interventions and advances to start cooperatives are followed by periods of retreat and reflection in the face of the model failing in some countries, before starting the cycle again. In this context, cooperatives can be seen as instruments to radically transform society or offer an alternative model within the capitalist system. It is this tension that we now explore through the five waves of cooperative praxis.

First wave: visionaries to pragmatists 1844–1900

These dilemmas and tensions have plagued the cooperative movement since its inception in Rochdale in 1844. Holyoake (1891) commented on the Rochdale Pioneers' economic success as their cooperative model swept the United Kingdom, ending up in 1900 as the largest business in Europe and by 1930 having captured 30% of the UK grocery market. Starting from their first shop in Toad Lane "their inspiration was communistic. They had no idea of founding a race of grocers but a race of men" Holyoake (1891) living in villages of cooperation eschewing individual pursuits of wealth and aiming to transform industrial liberal market capitalism. Dropping this viewpoint and focusing on the business model resulted in a mission draft described by Thornley (1981:10) as a "right turn at Toad Lane."

Second wave: interventionists 1900—44

With cooperatives and credit unions having such spectacular success in addressing poverty in the United Kingdom and Europe, the colonial powers transplanted the cooperative model into Asia introducing cooperative legislation as a pragmatic, but paternalistic, solution to addressing the poverty of their colonial subjects. This occurred first in India. Rita Rhodes describes this strategy in *Empire and Co-operation—How the British Empire used cooperatives in its development strategies 1900—70*. Rita Rhodes (2012) discusses the tension between the aspirations of the nascent cooperative movement and the economic reality and exploitation of the colonial period. She describes cooperation as follows:

> It was an ideology greatly different to the pervading imperialism, which sought foreign domination, the exploitation of local populations and natural resources, and imposed government at odds with national forms. Co-operation as it grew in Britain from the ideas of Owen and others, encouraged self-management and economic and social democracy.

With top-down state support, large cooperative sectors emerged across Asia. At the core of our research and cross-country comparisons is the issue of whether cooperatives will simply be another business model that will incorporate members into a market society or will they be a force transforming capitalism into an economic democracy, as Rhodes described, where major decisions are made by the majority. Mazzarol, Reboud, Limnios, and Clarke (2014:11) wrote that:

> During the first half of the 20th century co-operatives were seen as providing a valuable mechanism for the enhancement of social and economic outcomes for society. Early economists such as Alfred Marshall could see the benefits offered by co-operatives to resolving many of the economic and social imbalances of society without the need to resort to the extremes of Marxism.

Third wave: developmentalists 1944—90

Essential to the preindependence struggles and postindependence nationhood across Asia has been the promotion of cooperatives as a transforming force and model for a just society. Cooperative sectors were state-dominated or state-directed such as in Vietnam, Indonesia, Sri Lanka, and, to some extent, in Singapore. Jawaharlal Nehru the socialist Prime Minister of India, had strong faith in the cooperative movement. While opening an international seminar on cooperative leadership in South East Asia in 1958 he said (Kumar Singh, 2016):

> But my outlook at present is not the outlook of spreading the cooperative movement gradually, progressively, as it has done. My outlook is to convulse India with the Cooperative Movement or rather with cooperation to make it, broadly speaking, the basic activity of India, in every village as well as elsewhere; and finally, indeed, to make the cooperative approach the common thinking of India. Therefore, the whole future of India really depends on the success of this approach of ours to these vast numbers, hundreds of millions of people.

Fourth wave: rationalists 1990—2007

With the liberalization of the global economy in the 1980s market forces were unleashed and competition became the dominant driving force coupled with the deregulation, privatization, and demutualization of cooperatives. The advancing tide of cooperation was rolled back. In addition, Mason (2017) comments that cooperatives as a developmental tool were too slow and inefficient and lost favor with government policy makers. The decline in the fortunes of cooperatives postindependence was summed up succinctly by Mazzarol et al., (2014:11) drawing on the research of Kalmi (2007):

> [T]he declining interest in co-operatives in the field of economics was a signal that there has been a quiet rejection of collaborative or collective approaches to economic organisation, Further, economics had sought to apply top down rather than bottom up grassroots solutions to solving economic problems.

The former colonizers returned as investors prizing open national economies and opening the way for a new wave of economic exploitation, sweat shops, and environmental degradation through the penetration of multinational corporations. Cooperatives suffered mission drift. When economic success overpowered their social mission, instead of being a vehicle for transforming capitalism they become a vehicle to incorporate cooperatives into the market system of flexible accumulation.

Fifth wave: revisionists 2007 to present day

However, in the contemporary period post the 2007 global financial crisis "the intellectual and moral failure of the neo liberal extreme capitalist western model" Bratton and Gold (2012) has been laid bare for the world to see. The theory of ineffectiveness of cooperatives has been challenged by substantial cooperative success stories across the Asia Pacific region— 21 of which are in this book. This is now accompanied by an emerging Asian theory on cooperatives that enables an understanding of how cooperatives in Asia identified and

overcame obstacles, and in so doing defined the factors of superior competitive advantage, Altman (2020). Proof of concept has been achieved. A new system is being outlined.

Conclusion

Asian business systems are different to Western business systems, and thanks to Witt and Redding (2013) we have a way of understanding how cooperatives form within different cultural and political contexts. A fascinating insight of Witt and Redding (2013) is the concept of multiplexity whereby different economic systems coexist in one economy.

In the successful case study cooperatives in this book, we see them coexisting as Rajarmabapu in India, SANASA (Federation of Thrift and Credit Co-operative Societies) in Sri Lanka, or the Japanese consumer cooperative sector as bottom-up innovators. We also see how the state can act proactively as in Vietnam to act as a catalyst for the emergence of Saigon Co-op and its joint venture with Fair Price Co-op in Singapore. The case of a farmer specialized cooperative in China informs the potential evolution of the cooperative sector.

The worker cooperatives selected in this book demonstrate that a democratic production system can be built business by business. Redding (2005) offers an insight into how capitalism can be reformed by redesigning the four key factors of a business system to deliver greater access to wealth and opportunity through cooperatism : the sourcing of capital, the stabilising of labour markets, the norms of ownership and the stabilising of production systems.

The aim of this book is to bring an understanding of how these inspiring examples succeeded so we can awaken the potential of the Asian Pacific cooperative movement and offer the prospect of cooperative solutions as an alternative to the unsatisfactory liberal market or state-commanding models. In our search for a more balanced approach to distributing wealth and opportunity as we proceed into the Asian century, cooperatives offer a practical system for creating the future we want.

References

Bratton, J., Gold, J. (2012). Human Resource Management. Theory and Practice. Palgrave Macmillan: Hampshire.

Holyoake, G. J. (1891). *The cooperative movement today.* London: Methuen.

Kalmi, P. (2007). The disappearance of co-operatives from economic text books,. *Cambridge Journal of Economics, 31* (4), 625–647.

Kumar Singh, S. (2016). Future of the cooperative movement in India and abroad. Redshine International Press. Lunawada India.

Mason, P. (2017). Personal communication.

Mazzarol, T., Reboud, S., Limnios, E., & Clarke, D. (2014). *Research handbook on sustainable co-operative enterprise.* Cheltenham.: Edward Elgar.

Redding, G. (2005). The thick description and comparison of societal systems of capitalism. *Journal of International Business Studies, 36,* 123–155.

Rhodes, R. (2012). *Empire and co-operation: How the British Empire used cooperatives in its development strategies, 1900–1970.* Edinburgh: John Donald.

Thornley, J. (1981). *Jobs and dreams.* London: Heinman.

U Lab : Changing Business, Society, and Self https//www.youtube.com/watch?v = gF8wV9OIUHc.

Witt, M., & Redding, G. (2013). Asian business systems: Institutional comparison, clusters and implications for varieties of capitalism and business systems theory. *Socio Economic Review, 11,* 265–300.

Index

Printed in the United States
By Bookmasters